W9-ABU-943

The Complete Book of
NEEDLECRAFT

The Complete Book of
NEEDLECRAFT

Janet Kirkwood • Ilse Gray • Lindsay Vernon • Elizabeth Ashurst • Margaret Maino

Exeter Books
NEW YORK

First published in the USA 1983
by Exeter Books
Distributed by Bookthrift
Exeter is a trademark of Simon & Schuster
Bookthrift is a registered trademark of
Simon & Schuster
New York, New York

ISBN 0-671-06062-7

Printed in Hong Kong

Art Editor
Bridget Heal

Sewing Editor
Lindsay Vernon

Knitting and Crochet Editor
Penny David

Embroidery Editor
Ruth Farnsworth

Assistant Editor
Dorothea Hall

Editorial Assistants
Janet Mundy
Virginia Roundell

Designers
Linda Cole
Heather Garioch
Anne Lloyd
Jane Willis

Picture Editor
Zilda Tandy

Picture Assistant
Lesley Robins

Production
Brenda Glover
Mike Emery

Contributors
Dressmaking
Janet Kirkwood

Sheila Brull
Eleanor Hobbs
Beryl Miller
Lindsay Vernon

Toys
Ilse Gray

Home sewing
Lindsay Vernon

Eleanor Hobbs
Jane Iles

Embroidery
Elizabeth Ashurst

Deborah Barclay
Philippa Bergson
Carolyn Cannon
Heather Clark
Valerie Davies
Marcia Greenberg
Dorothea Hall
Eleanor Hobbs
Margaret Humphrey
Caroline Hurry
Jane Iles
Eileen Lowcock
Bonny Phipps
Margaret Rivers

Knitting
Margaret Maino

Mary Ann Barnett
Sandy Black
Jean Litchfield
Susan Read

Crochet
Margaret Maino

Jean Litchfield
Edy Lyngaas
Susan Read
Celia Thompson

Contents

Note
Measurements in this book are given in yards, feet and inches, with the metric equivalent in brackets afterward. To facilitate working, conversions are not always precise, so choose one system or the other and follow it consistently throughout. See note on metric conversion on p352.

Dressmaking

Making clothes for yourself and for other people provides an endless source of satisfaction as well as a great saving in cost. By learning just a few techniques you can easily make attractive and unique garments and, as your knowledge and skill increase, you can make clothes for the whole family based on the master-sheet patterns in this book.

For the beginner all the necessary techniques build up gradually into a complete sewing course. The practical information is interspersed with projects; some of the garments are so simple that they can be made from measurement to all sizes – including dolls' clothes. For the more ambitious dressmaker this chapter is a useful reference work as well as an instructional guide for combining and adapting all the major pattern pieces and offering suggestions for varying detail in, for example, necklines or sleeves.

Whatever line is currently in fashion, basic pattern shapes remain the same; here you will find not only all the pattern pieces (given in a variety of sizes on the pull-out master sheet) but also suggestions for adapting them to give all the different styles you may want to make.

Basic tools and equipment

For pattern cutting :
Paper scissors
Dressmaker's graph paper and large sheets of tracing paper (greaseproof paper, obtainable in rolls, will do)
Transparent adhesive tape
Pencil, eraser
Yardstick
Tape measure (preferably plastic-coated so that it does not stretch)
Triangle or T-square for drawing and adjusting patterns, straightening grain of fabric
Flexible curve (a drawing aid obtainable from art suppliers)
Cutting out :
Dressmaking shears — they must be good quality and very sharp
Tailor's chalk — white and colored
Dressmaker's pencil or **carbon paper** for marking fabric
Pins — fine stainless steel
Magnet — for picking up spilled pins

For hand sewing :
Needles in a variety of sizes. Choose a size which is fine enough to pass easily through fabrics, yet thick enough not to bend or break. The eye should be large enough to take the thread comfortably
Special-purpose needles — crewel for embroidery; darning and upholstery needles; leather or fur needles; bodkin for threading elastic
Thread appropriate to the fabric; choose a matching shade or one shade darker. Use mercerized cotton for general purposes; pure silk for silks; synthetic thread for knitted, bonded, man-made or heavy-duty fabrics: medium-weight thread for decorative stitching and hand-worked buttonholes
Basting thread in contrasting color to fabric
Thimble (preferably metal) to fit middle finger of your sewing hand
Pin cushion — a wrist pin cushion is useful
Small sharp scissors for finishing or trimming seams and cutting notches
Pinking shears (optional)
Good working light — an adjustable desk lamp is useful
Storage for your equipment (a box or rack helps you select threads easily)

For fitting and pressing :
Full-length mirror
Hem gauge for marking hem height — choose one which is fully adjustable and easy to operate by yourself
Iron (dry or steam) with adjustable temperature range
Pressing cloths — a 24in (60cm) square of cotton is most useful; moisten with water when pressing woolens and some synthetics. If you use fine lawn or muslin details will show through
Ironing board with smooth-fitting cover
Sleeve board (for pressing sleeve seams (you can substitute a tightly rolled towel)
Tailor's ham — a firmly stuffed cushion used for pressing curved seams and collars; you can make one by stuffing a shaped cotton pillow with sawdust (or substitute a small rolled up towel)
Velvet pressboard for velvet — this has a fine, needle-like surface so that velvet remains uncrushed

For machine sewing :
All dressmaking can be done by hand sewing but a sewing machine is undoubtedly time- and labor-saving. If you are buying a machine, examine as many brands as possible, read all the literature and ask for demonstrations. Decide whether you are likely to use all the applications offered and choose accordingly. Whichever type of machine you choose, make sure that you have a comprehensive instruction book. Read it carefully and familiarize yourself with the threading techniques before you start to sew. Always try out the different stitches, stitch lengths and tensions on a spare piece of fabric before beginning a project
Straight-stitch machines (most old treadle or hand-operated machines are in this category) will sew only with straight stitches but can be splendidly reliable. They are the most limited of all machines in techniques although it may be possible to buy some attachments, such as one for working buttonholes
Swing-needle machines These can do zigzag stitching as well as straight sewing. They are electrically operated, usually by a foot pedal, which leaves both hands free for manipulating fabric. This category is probably the most useful for home dressmakers
Automatic machines These sophisticated and expensive models are for skilled dressmakers. In addition to straight and zigzag stitching, they will overlock edges and work a selection of embroidery patterns and stitches
Machine accessories Most machines include some accessories. The most useful are: extra bobbins, spare and special-purpose machine needles, piping foot and seam ripper

Choosing fabric

The choice of fabrics available to the home dressmaker is enormous; different selections of fibers, weaves, weights, colors and patterns are introduced at least twice a year. The fibers from which fabrics are made fall into two main categories: natural and man-made. Natural fibers are spun from animal and vegetable products (silk, cotton and linen) or from animal fleece (wool). Man-made fibers are those made industrially from minerals and chemicals (such as nylon and polyester).

The introduction of new man-made fibers, developed for their low cost and easy-care quality, has contributed greatly to the variety of fabrics available today.

Except for knitted jersey fabrics, most man-made fibers imitate natural-fiber fabrics: for example, taffeta, which was once made in silk, is now made in rayon, polyester or nylon. Man-made fabrics are sometimes blended with natural fibers to obtain a combination of the best characteristics of each. However, it is unlikely that man-made fibers will supersede natural ones, certainly for the time being, because it is not yet possible to make a man-made fiber as warm as wool or as cool and absorbent as cotton.

Fabrics should always be labeled with their composition; note this when buying so that you have a guide to washing, pressing, the type of thread to use in finishing and general after care. Always ask your shopkeeper if the information is not given on the fabric.

Fabrics are often sold by generic names, such as chiffon or denim. Such names denote the type of weave, weight or finish of the fabric and these are described in more detail, right, and with some suggestions on how to use them. Special handling points shown by symbols are also explained above right. When choosing fabric for a specific garment, keep a mental check list of its requirements. Is the garment for winter, summer or mid-season? For evening or day? Formal or informal? Does the style demand certain qualities such as softness or stretchiness? Do you want to match an existing garment to it?

It may help to examine similar garments in a shop before you choose and, if possible, try them on so that you can see the effect of a color or design.

It usually helps to ask the shopkeeper to show you suitable fabrics for garments with special requirements. In a large store the buyer can be very helpful if you shop at a quiet time.

If you are new to dressmaking, choose fabrics which are easy to handle – this includes most cottons and many woolens (but not worsteds which may pucker at the seams and need careful pressing).

Examine patterned fabrics to see whether they have a one-way design (such as flowers which would be upside down if you reversed the fabric), a napped pile (which must lie in the same direction on each section of the garment – see p94), or features such as plaids which must be matched carefully at seams. In some cases you will need to allow more fabric if you choose any of these (see p16).

Consider the construction of the garment and the positioning of the pattern on it. As a general guide, large motifs should be made into simple designs with few seams so that the motif can be centered on a main panel. Garments with intricate seams and panels usually look best in plain fabrics.

Two or more fabrics can be combined in one garment; use one for a yoke, border, collar or cuffs and the other for the main pieces. Many fabrics are made to coordinate; a plain fabric may match a dominant color in a pattern; a striped fabric can be teamed with a plaid one in identical colors; a small print can go with a large version of the same pattern. When planning your own coordination, try to match the fibers and weights of the fabrics so that they will need the same handling and cleaning.

Make a note of zipper sizes, buttons, interfacing, lining requirements and thread, and buy these with the fabric so that you can match colors and weights.

Fabric glossary

 Use thread appropriate to fabric

 Special care necessary when ironing

 Pins mark fabric; place within seam allowance

 Use special seams

 Take extra care when cutting out

 Fabric liable to fray; overcast edges

The fabrics listed below which are identified by their trade names may be known more commonly by a descriptive term such as 'a wool-cotton mixture'. The list is intended not only to help you choose fabrics for dressmaking but also to assist in altering ready-made items.

Acetate Lustrous man-made cellulose fiber which can be woven to produce a satin, taffeta, brocade or raw silk effect; also used for jersey fabrics and linings

Acrilan (trade name) An acrylic fiber

Acrylic A fiber derived from oil with a wool-like appearance. Soft and bulky, it is used for knitted, woven, permanently pleated or pile fabrics

Barathea Fine cloth with a broken rib weave in wool, silk or blends with man-made fibers

Batiste Fine light-weight fabric in plain weave cotton or man-made fibers; heavier when made in wool

Brocade Heavy fabric with rich complex Jacquard weave in silk or man-made fibers. Different weights for evening wear and soft furnishings

Broderie anglaise Open embroidery produced on linen and cotton fabrics. Design consists of holes outlined in embroidery

Buckram A cotton or linen fabric heavily stiffened with paste or glue for interfacings and lampshades

Burlap (hessian) Coarse openly woven fabric made from jute yarns. For upholstery and wall coverings

Calico Plain weave cotton fabric, usually with all-over printed design in various weights and widths

Cambric Plain weave fabric of medium-weight cotton or linen fiber. Now used for summer dresses

Canvas (duck) Heavy plain weave fabric, closely woven. Cotton or man-made fibers in various weights, it is used for interlinings, upholstery and accessories
Celanese (trade name) A nylon or rayon fiber
Cheesecloth Loose plain weave cotton fabric; the texture is uneven due to highly twisted yarns
Chenille Tufted fabric knitted or woven usually from cotton or viscose fiber.
Chiffon Sheer, delicate, plain weave fabric from silk or man-made fiber; can feel rough; drapes well. For evening dresses, scarves and blouses
Chintz Closely woven cotton with multi-colored, often floral, print; sometimes glazed. For soft furnishings
Clydella (trade name) Light-weight woven cloth, 80% cotton/20% wool
Corduroy Hard-wearing fabric with lengthwise cords of pile in various widths and weights. Cotton or man-made fibers. For coats, dresses and trousers
Cotton Fabric made from cotton-plant fiber; woven or knitted. Listed here under generic names
Courtelle (trade name) Acrylic fiber
Crash Loose plain weave coarse cotton or linen fabric for soft furnishings
Crêpe Slightly crinkled puckered surface made from highly twisted natural yarn or man-made fibers. Various weights; hangs and drapes well; for blouses, dresses and evening wear
Crêpe de Chine Traditionally a sheer soft silk fabric; now often in man-made fibers
Cretonne Cotton fabric similar to unglazed chintz
Crimplene (trade name) Textured polyester fiber; fabric is bulky, soft and repels stains

Dacron (trade name) Polyester fiber
Damask Jacquard weave fabric for soft furnishings, similar to brocade but flatter and reversible; usually linen, or viscose rayon fiber
Denim Tough cotton fabric with twill weave giving color and white effect; can be brushed
Dicel (trade name) Cellulose acetate fiber fabric
Dralon (trade name) Acrylic fiber used widely for soft furnishings
Drill Hard-wearing twill weave fabric in cotton, linen or man-made fibers
Duette (trade name) Double jersey in blend of Courtelle and Lirelle
Dynel (trade name) Modacrylic flame-retardant fiber

Enkalon (trade name) Nylon fiber

Faille Soft silk or man-made fiber fabric with narrow horizontal ribs. For evening wear
Felt Dense fabric of wool or hair fibers compressed with heat and moisture. For toys, accessories and appliqué
Flannel Plain or twill weave fabric with soft napped surface in wool
Flannelette Cotton or man-made fiber fabric with brushed surface for warm shirts and nightwear
Fortrel (trade name) Polyester fiber

Gabardine Closely woven twill weave fabric in wool, cotton or blends. Used for rainwear, skirts, suits
Gauze Sheer openly woven fabric; made in many fibers
Georgette Like chiffon with a more pronounced crêpe appearance. Fine but crisp in wool, silk or man-made fibers
Gingham A firm woven fabric of cotton, blended or man-made fibers with vertical and horizontal colored yarns forming checks and stripes
Grosgain A plain weave fabric with a pronounced horizontal rib in silk or rayon for suits, ribbons and trimming

Hopsack Double plain weave forming a loosely structured fabric in wool or linen
Huckaback Fabric with a woven raised pattern, using linen, cotton or man-made fibers. Absorbent; used for towels and glass cloths

Jacquard Type of loom producing complex woven structures. Jacquard knitted fabrics have complex color patterns
Jersey Any weft or warp knitted fabric in various weights and fibers which drapes well, stretches and is crease resistant. Double jersey is more stable than single

Lace Decorative open structure. Traditionally hand-made, now woven or knitted using cotton yarn or man-made fibers. For evening and wedding dresses, soft furnishings and trimmings
Lamé Woven or knitted fabric with metallic threads; covered with acetate or polyester film
Lawn Light weight sheer plain weave fabric in cotton, cotton/man-made fiber blends or linen. For blouses, summer clothes and interfacings in fine fabrics
Linen From stem of flax plant in various weights, often with a rough slub texture. Tough, absorbent, cool; crease resistant when blended with man-made fibers
Lirelle (trade name) Polyester fiber: gives but does not stretch or shrink

Madras Fine hand-woven Indian cotton with stripes and plaid patterns
Marquisette Open, loose fabric woven from cotton, silk or man-made fibers. Can have spot designs from extra yarns
Milium (trade name) Lining fabric with heat-retaining finish obtained by application of aluminum
Modacrylic Modified acrylic fibers with flame-retardant properties
Mohair Hair fiber from the Angora goat, often blended with other fibers in knitted and woven fabrics
Moiré A watermark pattern usually applied to silk, acetate/viscose, rayon or grosgrain. Used for evening wear
Muslin Fine, loosely woven cotton fabric. For baby clothes, light-weight interfacings and patterns

Needlecord Corduroy woven with fine vertical cords of pile
Neospun Staple acrylic yarns used mainly for double jersey fabrics

Plain weave

Hopsack

Twill

Houndstooth

Satin

Net Fairly crisp woven mesh fabric with geometric holes. For dresses, curtains, trimmings or interfacings. Cotton net is highly inflammable so try to buy flame-retardant brands
Ninon Sheer soft light-weight fabric in silk or synthetic yarns
Nun's veiling Fine soft plain weave fabric in wool or synthetic fibers
Nylon (polyamide) Man-made petro-chemical fiber; fine, strong and elastic. Knitted and woven nylon fabrics shed creases and dry quickly; non-absorbency is difficult in hot weather and gives problems with static electricity

Organdy Sheer plain weave fabric in cotton or synthetic fibers. Can be treated to retain crispness for dresses, children's clothes and interfacings
Organza (silk organdy) Plain openly woven fabric in silk or man-made fibers
Orlon (trade name) An acrylic fiber
Ottoman Similar to faille but with wider ribs, in wool, silk or synthetics

Peau de soie Heavy, satin weave fabric with a lustrous sheen, in silk, rayon or synthetics. For formal wear
Piqué Firm cotton fabric with raised, dotted, ribbed or honeycomb surface
Plissé Puckered texture on cotton or man-made fiber fabrics
Polyester Versatile man-made fiber, petroleum-derived. Woven or knitted into many textures and finishes
Poplin Crisp durable plain weave fabric with a soft sheen and fine ribs; cotton or cotton/man-made fiber blends

Rayon Man-made fiber (viscose rayon) derived from cellulose. Fabrics can resemble silk, cotton, linen or wool

Sailcloth Plain weave strong canvas-type fabric in cotton or man-made fibers
Satin Weave which gives a smooth, shiny surface in silk, cotton or man-made fibers. Types include crêpe-backed, double-faced, slipper (light, tightly woven) and duchesse (heaviest)
Seersucker Texture of puckered stripes on cotton and cotton blends
Serge Durable twill weave fabric in wool or man-made fibers. For uniforms, tailored suits and coats
Shantung Plain weave in raw silk or man-made fibers, spun for slub effect
Silk Natural continuous filament produced by the silk worm. Types include China and Japan (linings), Honan or pongee (slight slub), shantung, surah, Thai (heavy, slubbed, vivid colors) and tussore (raw silk with uneven texture, natural color)

Taffeta Crisp, plain weave fabric in silk or rayon. Types include faille taffeta, shot (iridescent), moiré and paper (light-weight)
Terylene (trade name) Polyester fiber
Ticking Strong cotton with woven vertical stripes; with waxed surface for covering mattresses and making pillows and cushions
Terrycloth Woven in cotton or cotton blends with uncut loops on one or both sides. Can also be knitted to make stretchy fabric. Hard-wearing and absorbent
Trevira (trade name) A polyester fiber often blended with natural fibers to make woven or knitted fabrics such as silky jersey or gabardine
Triacetate Modification of acetate. Man-made cellulose-based fiber with a crisp, silk-like handle
Tricel (trade name) Triacetate fiber
Tulle Fine net in silk or nylon
Tweed Rough-textured woven (sometimes knitted) wool or wool blend often with multicolored yarns, identified by place names or patterns, e.g. Harris or Houndstooth

Velour Knitted or woven fabric with thick short pile. Use wool velour for coats, terry velour for bath towels
Velvet Woven warp pile fabric from silk, cotton or man-made fiber yarns. Types include façonné (cut), Lyons (for furnishings) and panne (pronounced one-way silky pile). Pile can be uneven to give textured effects
Velveteen Woven weft pile fabric, usually cotton; less dense than velvet
Vincel A modified rayon fiber, generic name modal, often blended with cotton or polyester. Strong and dull in appearance, like cotton
Vinyl (polyvinyl chloride) Non-porous synthetic coating for woven or knitted fabrics of various weights. For raincoats and upholstery
Viyella (trade name) Light-weight woven fabric, 55% wool/45% cotton
Voile Light-weight sheer openly woven cotton or cotton blends, wool or silk

Whipcord Like gabardine but heavier, with a pronounced cord in cotton, wool, man-made fibers or blends. For uniforms and riding gear
Wincey Type of flannelette; brushed woven cotton fabric
Wool Fiber from the fleece of sheep. Fabrics may be woven or knitted and are warm and absorbent; often blended with man-made fibers to make them less expensive and easier to wash
Worsted Finest quality wool fiber, with smooth hard yarns. Can be woven or knitted; hard-wearing with a smooth non-fibrous surface

Zibeline Heavily napped woven coating fabric in wool, combined with camel or mohair fiber

Herringbone

Types of velvet weave

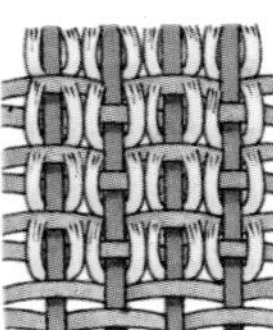

Weft knit

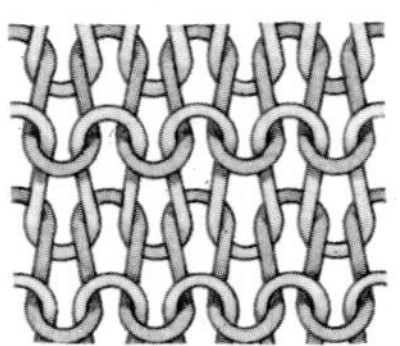

Warp knit

Measuring figures

Children							
	chest	22	24	26	28	30	32
	waist	20	22	24	25	26	26
	hips	22	24	27	30	32	34
	neck to waist	$8\frac{1}{2}$	9	$9\frac{1}{2}$	12	13	14

Paper patterns for garments are cut to fit a range of figure sizes with average proportions for each size. The sizes given for commercial patterns and for the master pattern sheet in this book (see table above) refer to body measurements, not garment measurements. The necessary amounts of ease – extra room for comfort when moving, stretching and sitting – are all incorporated so if you actually measure the pattern pieces in most cases they will be larger than the stated body size.

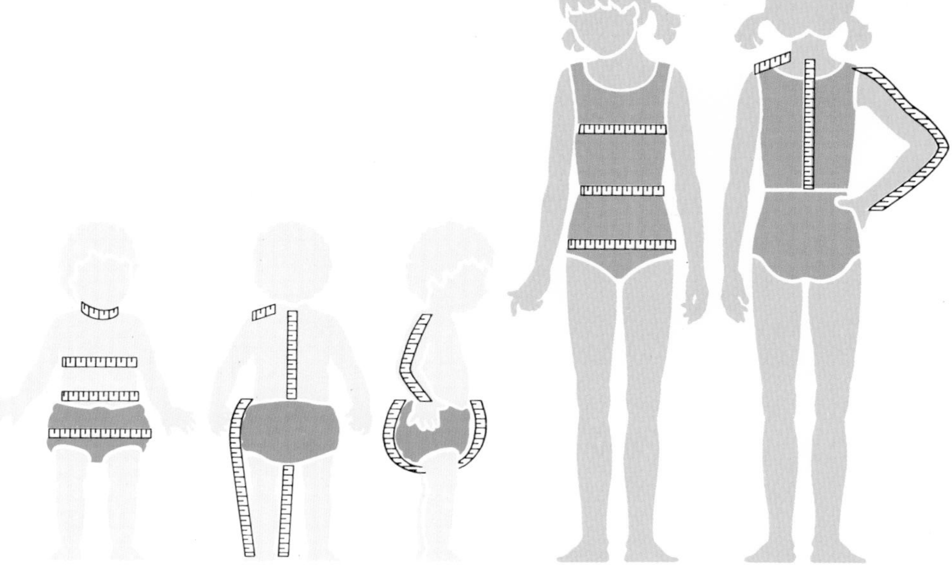

To decide which pattern size to use, measure the bust/chest, waist and hips, and compare them with the list of sizes. If you are making a garment for yourself, ask someone else to measure you. For blouses and shirts, choose the size nearest or slightly larger than your bust/chest measurement.
For slacks and skirts, choose by hip size, rather than waist measurement which can easily be adjusted. If you are making a dress you can use the bodice of one size group with the skirt from another if this is appropriate; adjust the waist to fit accordingly.
If the measurements you want fall exactly between the sizes given, you can draw the pattern to the right size by drawing the outlines exactly halfway between those of the two sizes. More instructions about this are given on p16.
When you have chosen your pattern size, trace off the outlines so that you can check all the remaining measurements. Add the amount for ease where needed to your own measurements (see below) and compare the total with the dimensions of the pattern. (Where the pattern is in two or more parts, as on a blouse or slacks, divide your measurements appropriately.)
In all cases where your measurements differ from those on the pattern, you should alter the pattern to fit – see p72.

Children
Measure children in their underwear (including diapers when worn) and without shoes.
Chest: measure around the widest part of chest, under shoulder blades. Add 2in (5cm) for ease.
Waist: if there is a natural indentation, measure around this. On a plump child, measure around the position shown. Add $\frac{3}{4}$in (2cm) for ease.
Hips: measure around fullest part of buttocks. Add 2in (5cm) for ease.
Back of neck to waist: measure from nape of neck to waist down center of back.
Shoulder width: measure from side of neck to point of shoulder.
Neck: measure around base of neck. Add $\frac{1}{2}$in (12mm) for ease.
Length of arm: measure from point of shoulder over bent elbow to wrist.

Dress length: measure from nape of neck to finished length.
Skirt length: measure from waist to finished length.
Slacks, pants: measure from back waist under crotch to front waist. Add 1in (2·5cm) for ease. Measure outside leg from waist to ankle; inside leg from crotch to ankle with shoes on.

Men	chest	36	40	44
	waist	30	34	38
	hips	38	42	46
	neck	15	15½	16

Women	bust	34	38	42
	waist	26	28	32
	hips	36	40	44
	neck to waist	16¼	16½	16¾

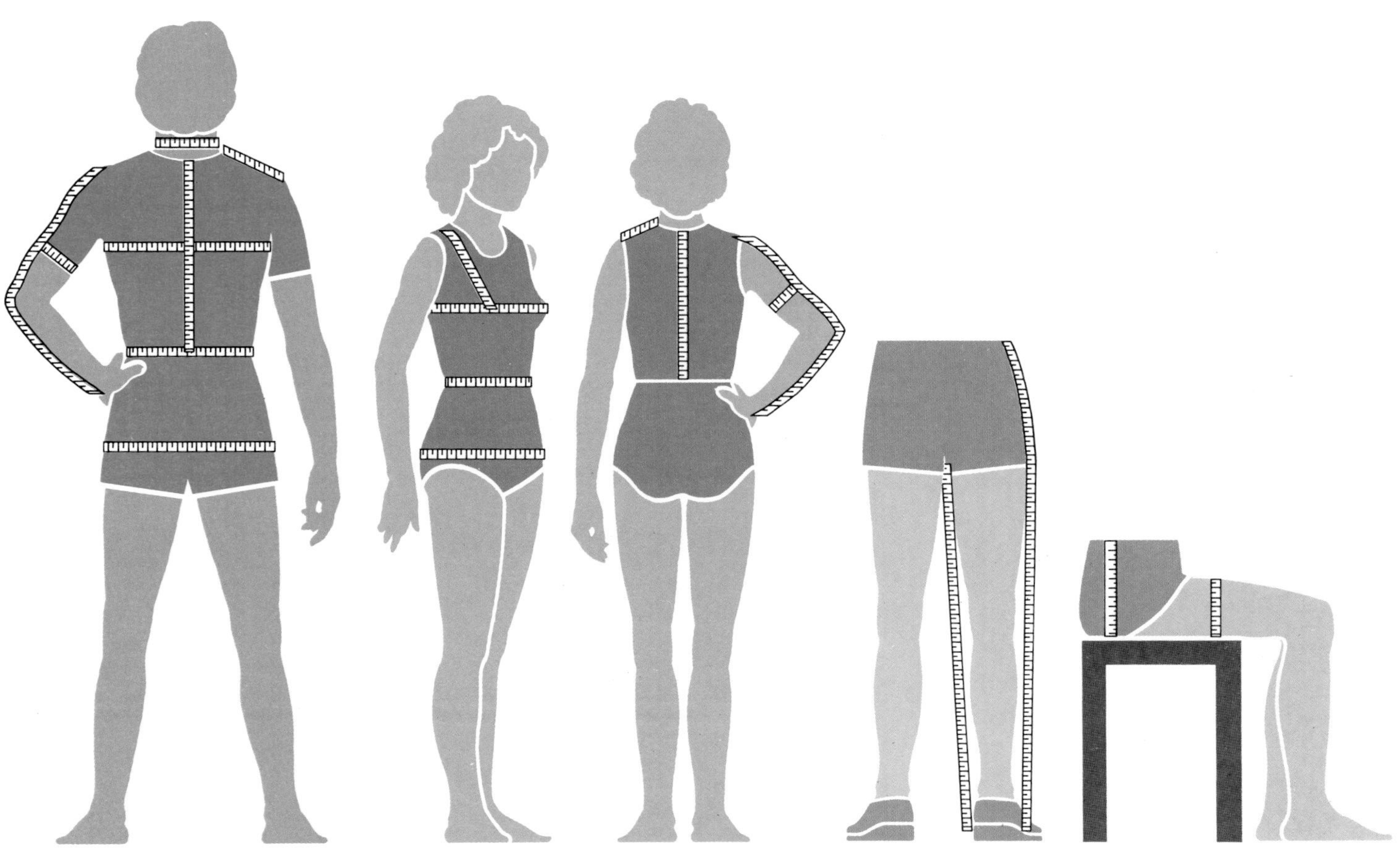

Men
Take measurements over a T-shirt and shorts or light-weight slacks.
Chest: measure around the fullest part. Add 2in (5cm) for ease.
Waist: measure around the point where the waistband of slacks normally lies in a comfortable wearing position. Add ¾in (2cm) for ease.
Hips: measure around the fullest part. Add 2in (5cm) for ease.
Back of neck to waist: measure from nape of neck to waist down center back.
Shoulder width: measure from side of neck to point of shoulder.
Neck: measure around the neck at the Adam's apple. Add ½in (12mm) for ease.
Length of arm: measure from point of shoulder over bent elbow to wrist.
Wrist: measure for cuffs around arms 3in (7·5cm) above wrist bones. Add ½in (12mm) for ease.
Upper arms: measure around widest part when arm is bent. Add 2in (5cm) for ease.
Shirt length: measure from nape of neck to finished length.

Women
Take measurements over underclothes.
Bust: measure around the widest part of the back, under arms and over bust point. Add 2in (5cm) for ease. Measure depth from center of shoulder down to bust point.
Waist: measure around natural curve of waist while breathing naturally. Add ¾in (2cm) for ease.
Hips: measure around widest part, usually 6½–9in (17–23cm) below waist. Add 2in (5cm) for ease.
Back of neck to waist: measure from nape of neck to waist down center back.
Shoulder width: measure from side of neck to point of shoulder.
Neck: measure around base of neck. Add ½in (12mm) for ease.
Length of arm: measure from point of shoulder over bent elbow to wrist.
Wrist: measure around arm about 3in (7·5cm) above wrist bone. Add ½in (12mm) for ease.
Upper arm: measure around widest part when arm is bent. Add 2in (5cm) for ease.
Dress or blouse length: measure from nape of neck to finished length.
Skirt length: measure from waist down center back to finished length.

Slacks
Take measurements while wearing the shoes you will want to wear with the slacks. Men and women are measured in the same way.
Waist and hips: as for other garments.
Outside length: measure from waist straight down outside leg to required length.
Inside leg: measure from crotch, straight down inside leg to required length.
Crotch: take measurement when sitting down from side waist to the seat of chair. Take a second measurement from back waist, through crotch to front waist. Add 1in (2·5cm) for ease.
Stomach: measure across the stomach at its fullest point between normal side seam position (i.e. outer edges of the hipbones). Note distance of measurement from waistline and measure pattern at corresponding point.
Seat: measure across seat at hipline between normal side seam position.
Thigh: measure the widest part and add 2in (5cm) for ease.

Using patterns and cutting out

The individual pieces of a garment are cut from a paper pattern giving their shape and size, unless they are so simple they can be cut from measurements. Most pattern pieces show half a garment section; they are cut on double fabric so that when the pieces are opened out the right and left sides are identical. This necessitates careful preparation and accurate folding of the fabric so that the weave is correctly positioned on all sections of the garment. To help you achieve this, pattern pieces always show a line which must be placed parallel with the straight grain of fabric, i.e. the warp threads which run lengthwise (weft threads run across from selvedge to selvedge).

You may sometimes wish to turn a pattern piece so that the grain line is at 90° or even 45° to the warp in order to use the fabric in a specific way, such as placing stripes horizontally or squares diagonally on a section of a garment, but for the beginner it is generally advisable to follow the instructions on the pattern.

Using commercial patterns
These are sold in packs containing all the separate pieces you need to make a garment in one size. The pieces usually have instructions printed on them and the pack includes a detailed instruction sheet.

Using the master-sheet patterns
The patterns for the basic wardrobe in this book are given in a variety of sizes on the master sheet.
Refer to the key on the sheet to find the appropriate outlines (specified with the cutting instructions) in the required size.
Lay the master sheet flat on a firm surface and secure the top corners with masking tape. Lay a sheet of tracing paper over one of the outlines you want and trace over it. Trace the others onto separate sheets. Make sure that you have traced all the pieces you need to complete the pattern.

Seams, hems and construction points
All seam allowances and hems are included on commercial paper patterns but should be added to patterns from the master sheet. To do this, draw a line $\frac{3}{4}$in (2cm) outside the traced outline for all seam allowances and 2in (5cm) for hem allowances. Mark any other construction points, such as darts and straight grain.
The inside line on the pattern (i.e. the traced line from the master sheet) is the fitting line or line along which the seam should be stitched.

Pattern alterations
Compare the pattern measurements with your own and make any necessary alterations. If you are adapting the design, draw the new outlines on the pattern. Double-check the fabric requirements specified on the basic design if you have made any alterations at all or if you are planning to use a fabric of different width or with a one-way design or nap. Where you are substituting complete pattern pieces, make your own cutting layout to calculate fabric quantities.

Calculating cutting layouts
If you have some spare fabric of the width you intend to buy, the simplest way of calculating how much you need is to lay out the pattern pieces in the most economical way and then measure how much you have used. Otherwise, use sheets of paper cut to the right width and laid out in a long piece. Make sure you allow for pattern pieces to be placed against folds where necessary and position all grain lines accurately.
Make a miniature drawing of the layout to keep as a reminder.

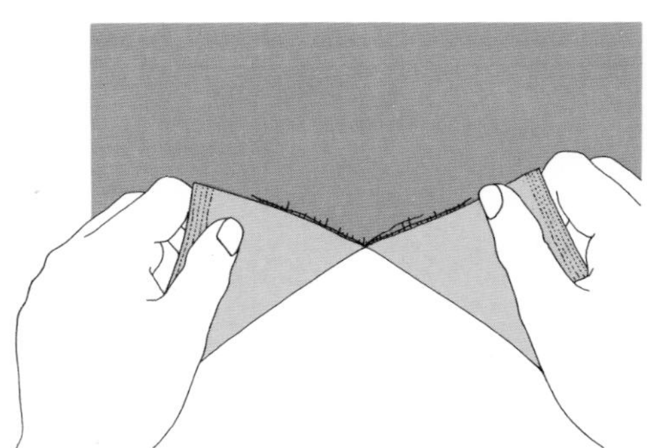

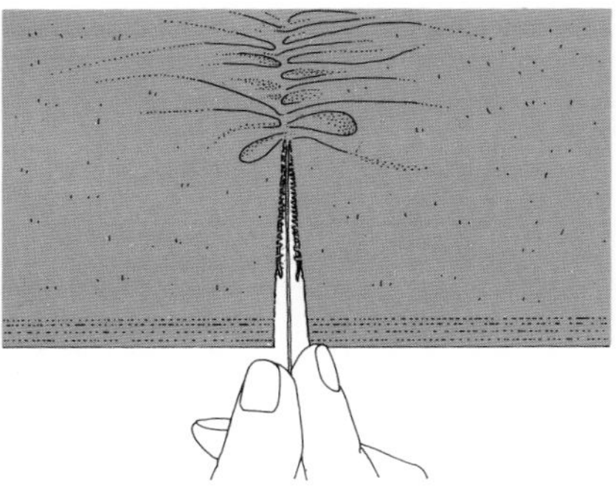

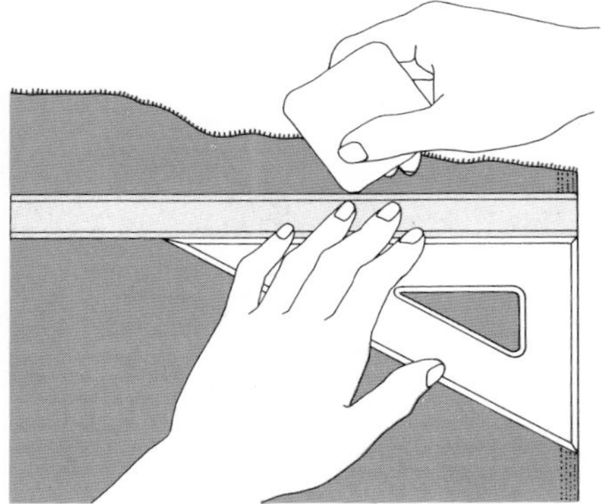

Preparing the fabric
Start by straightening the weft grain.
Plain weave cottons and cotton blends
Snip into the selvedge 1in (2·5cm) from one end of the fabric. Tear across the fabric from the snip to the opposite selvedge. Repeat at the opposite end of the fabric.

Plain weave wools and linens Snip into the selvedge for 1in (2·5cm), find a loose weft thread along the snip and pull it firmly across to the opposite selvedge. Snip the thread there and withdraw it completely. This will leave a distinct line along which you can cut.

Other weaves and jersey Use a T-square and align it along the selvedge with the long section across the fabric. Butt a longer rule against its edge and draw along one side of this with chalk; cut along the line.

The following abbreviations are used for all dressmaking instructions in this book:

RS - right side RH - right hand CF - center front
WS - wrong side LH - left hand CB - center back

Basic tools and equipment 10
Measuring the figure 14
Fitting and altering patterns 72
Fitting and altering slacks 98

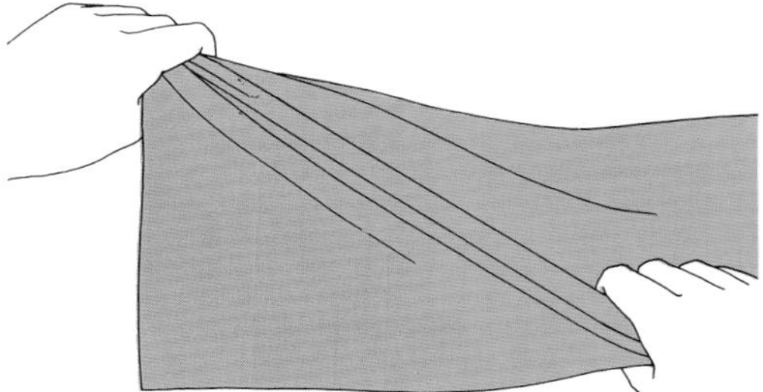

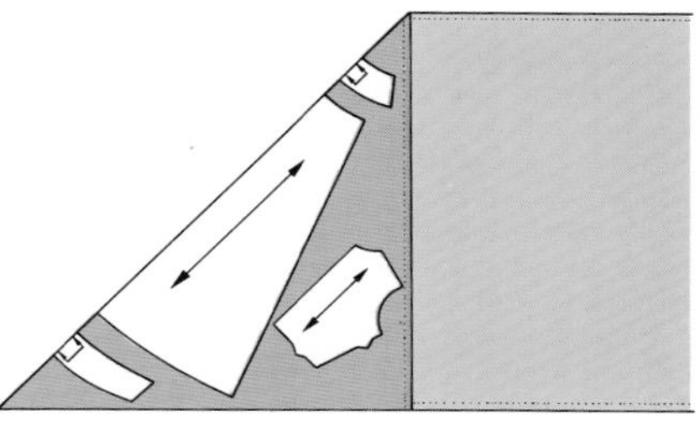

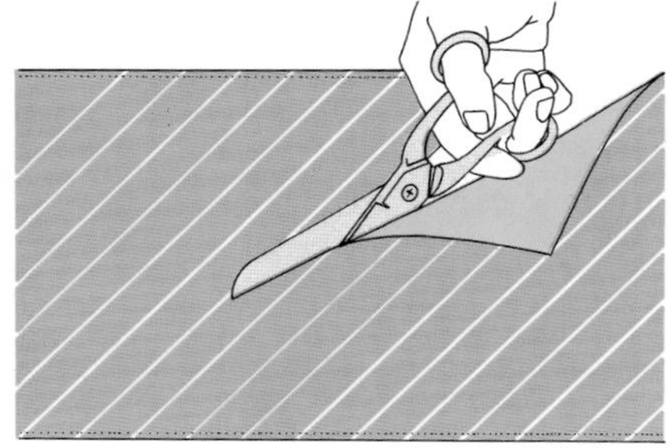

Checking the grain Fold the fabric in half lengthwise with all edges even. If this is not possible without some distortion of the fold, straighten the grain by pulling the fabric diagonally from corner to corner.
Press the fabric lightly to remove any creases.

Using the bias grain
The bias grain runs diagonally across the warp and weft threads; fabric pulled on this line is stretchy. For this reason bindings are often cut on the bias grain so they will fit around curves smoothly, and garments are sometimes cut with the bias grain running vertically because of the extra ease and drape or design interest that this gives.
To find the true bias, fold the fabric diagonally so that the selvedge lies exactly along the weft edge. Press the fold lightly with your fingers, being careful not to stretch it.
Bias garments Leave the fabric folded and place the pattern on the fold just as if the fold were on a warp thread.
Bias strips Open out the fabric and mark strips of the required width from the crease line.

Patterned fabrics
Part of the craft of good dressmaking is in skillful cutting and placing of patterned fabrics.
Before cutting out, study the fabric to see whether it has a particular motif which should be centered on a section of the garment or whether the design has an obvious direction so that the tops of all the pattern pieces should point the same way, instead of dovetailing as shown on many layouts.
To make the most of the pattern you may have to ignore the suggested cutting layout and devise your own to suit the fabric.
Centering designs It may help to cut the pattern through single fabric. On pattern pieces placed on folds draw a complete shape of the pattern piece, rather than the usual half, so that you can place it on the fabric accurately. To cut the full pattern shape, use a sheet of tracing paper twice the size of the shape. Fold it in half and place the fold on the fold line of the pattern. Trace the shape onto the paper in the usual way, then cut around the tracing through both thicknesses of paper.
On asymmetric complete shapes, such as sleeves, reverse the pattern from left to right when cutting the second piece.
Stripes and plaids To cut stripes and plaids to match at seams, draw a straight line in each direction across the center of the pattern on each section to be matched. Place the lines on one pattern piece to dominant lines on the fabric and place the second piece so that its lines match the corresponding lines on a pattern repeat. Double-check all positions before cutting out and be sure that the pattern on the under layer of the fabric is aligned with that on top.

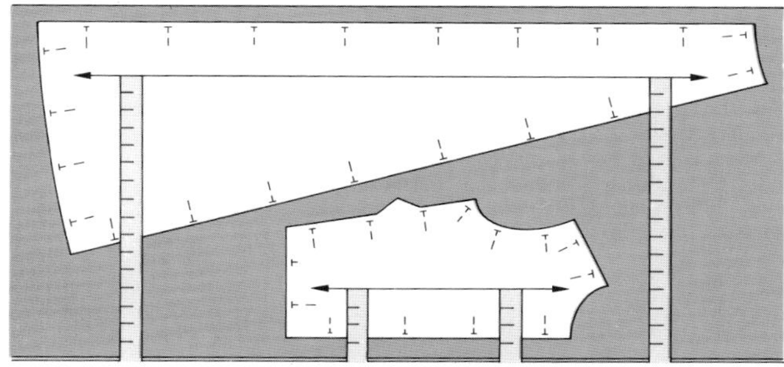

Cutting out
Fold fabrics as shown on the cutting layout. Place main pattern pieces first, with grain lines parallel to selvedges and specified pieces on the fold. Pin pattern to both thicknesses of fabric, placing pins with points inward at about 4in (10cm) intervals on straight edges, closer on curves.
Using sharp shears, cut around edge of pattern through both thicknesses of fabric (don't cut along edges placed on folds). Cut any notches outward.
Mark construction points with tailor's tacks (see p18) before unpinning and removing pattern.

Basic stitches

You must choose the most suitable stitch for each dressmaking process for both ease and speed of sewing and the best finished appearance. Instructions for the stitches are given for a right-handed person; reverse them if you are left-handed. Start and finish all rows of hand stitching with a double back stitch (see right), hidden on an inside fold where appropriate.
Start and finish machine stitching by reverse stitching or by pulling the upper thread through to the WS and tieing securely to the under thread.

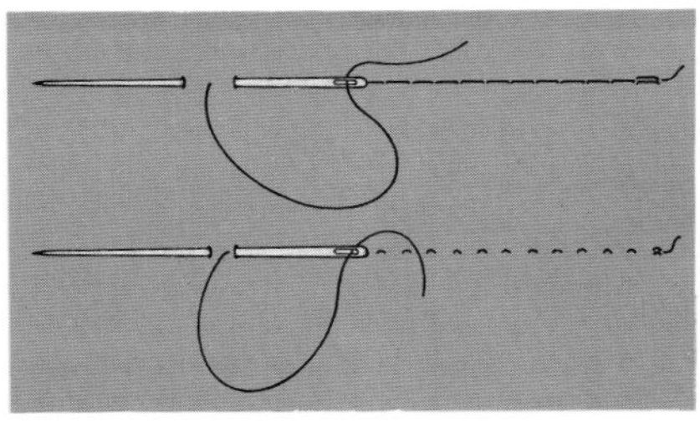

Back stitch and blind stitch
Use back stitch for making seams by hand and for beginning and ending lengths of thread. Use blind stitch for inserting zippers by hand.
Working from the RS for prick-stitched zippers and with RS together for back-stitched seams, insert the needle and bring through fabric $\frac{1}{8}$in (2–3mm) farther along stitching line. Take a stitch back to the starting point for back stitch, or over only 1–2 threads for blind stitch, and bring out the needle $\frac{1}{8}$in (2–3mm) farther along.
Continue in this way, always inserting the needle behind and bringing it out in front. The stitches will thus overlap underneath but appear continuous on top with back stitch and as dots with blind stitch.

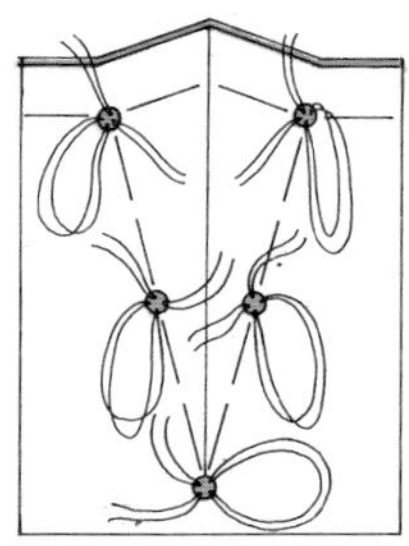

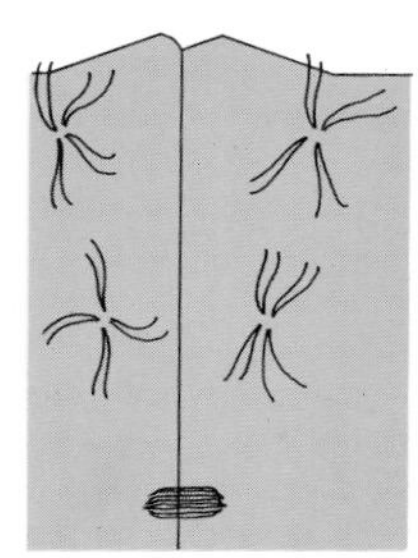

Tailor's tacks
Use for marking construction points on fabric after cutting out and before unpinning pattern. Use doubled basting thread in contrasting color to fabric. Take 2 small stitches through all layers, forming a large loop between stitches. Cut thread, leaving long ends. Unpin pattern and cut threads between fabric layers.

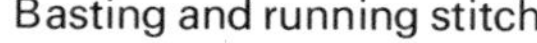

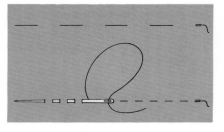

Basting and running stitch
Use basting for holding fabric together temporarily for fitting and stitching. Use running stitch for gathering, fine sewing and decoration. Secure thread with a back stitch and weave needle in and out of fabric, taking evenly spaced stitches $\frac{1}{8}$in (2–3mm) apart for running stitch and $\frac{3}{8}$in (10mm) long for basting. Finish with a back stitch.

Diagonal basting
Use to hold facings after turning and before pressing. Secure thread with a back stitch and take stitches through fabric at right angles to the edge, spacing evenly. The stitches will be diagonal on one side and straight on the other.

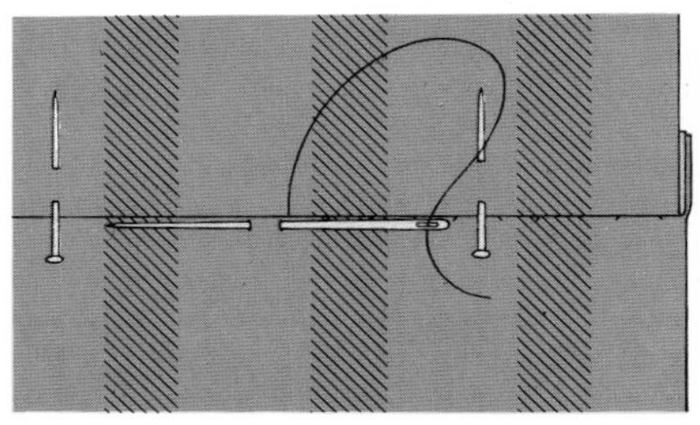

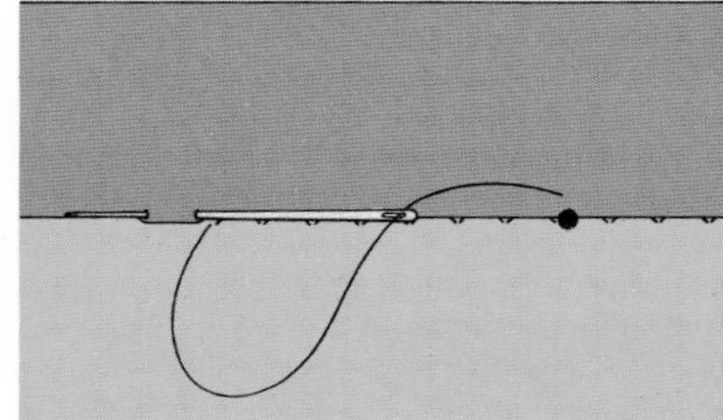

Slip basting and hemming
Use slip basting instead of regular basting when matching patterns such as plaids and stripes. Use slip hemming for hems and for joining 2 folded edges invisibly.
Working on the RS, fold under the seam allowance of one of the pieces. Position and pin the fold onto the other piece so that the pattern matches. Secure thread with a back stitch, slip needle through upper fold and then through corresponding piece of fabric opposite, taking a tiny stitch when slip hemming. Working evenly, take stitches through each piece of fabric alternately.

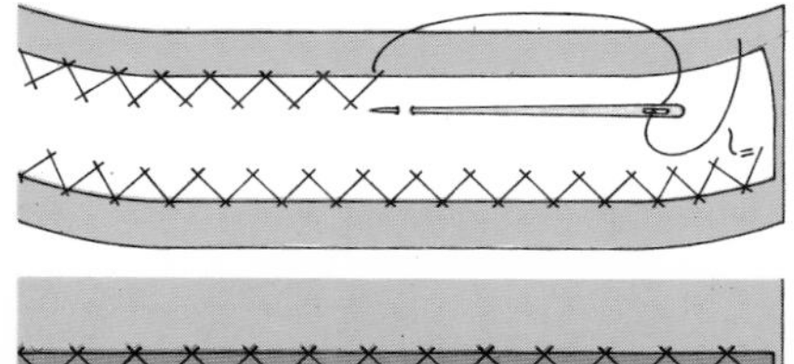

Catch stitch (herringbone stitch)
Use for hand-stitching interfacing to fabric or for securing single hems for a flat finish.
Work from left to right, taking a small horizontal stitch in the upper layer and then a small horizontal stitch in the lower layer diagonally as shown. Do not pull stitches tight.

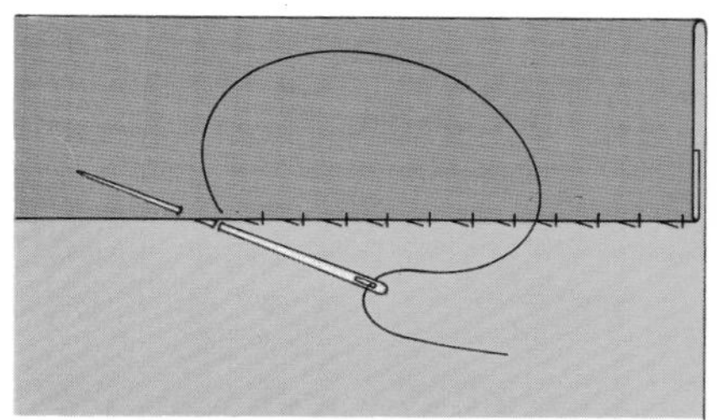

Hemming

Use for turning raw edges and where a stronger stitch than slip hemming is needed.
Working from right to left, work 2 back stitches through the edge. Take a small straight stitch into the single fabric below the edge, then insert the needle diagonally upward through fold in hem ¼in (5–6mm) farther on.

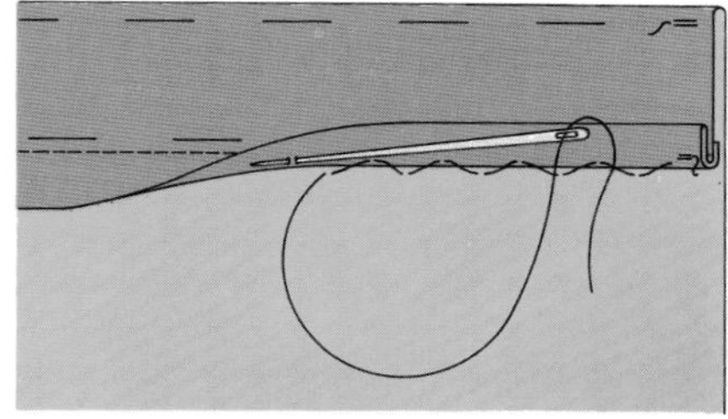

Blind hemming

Use for hems where the raw edge is finished but not necessarily turned under. Baste hem about ¼in (5mm) from finished edge and turn back edge along the basted line. Take a small stitch through hem edge and then pick up 1–2 threads from fabric below. Continue along edge working stitches loosely.

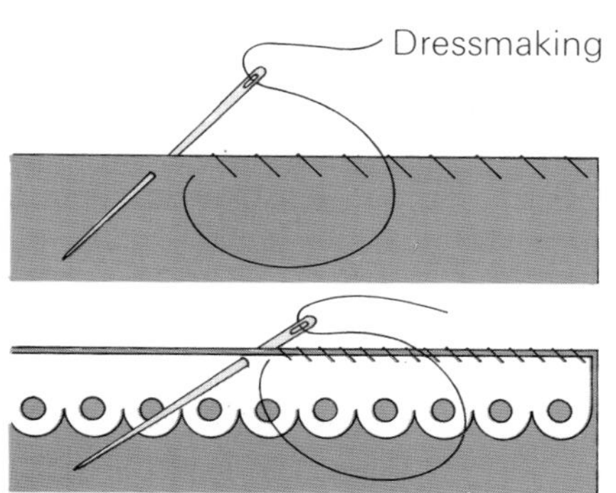

Overcasting and whip stitch

Use for finishing raw edges and for joining edges and attaching trimmings by hand. Work from right to left taking tiny diagonal stitches over the edge, keeping them evenly spaced and sized.

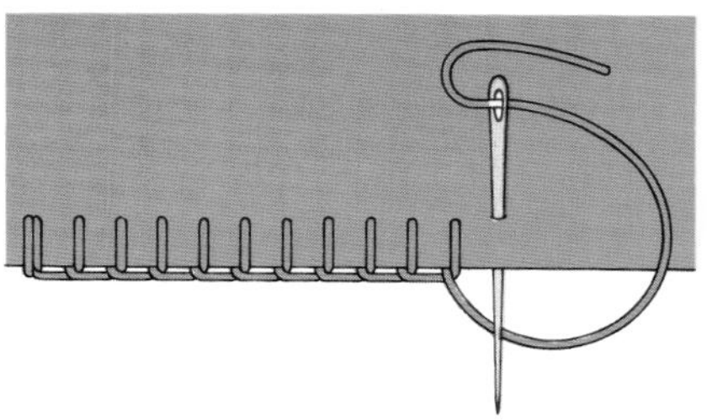

Blanket stitch

Use as a decorative edge finish.
Working from left to right with the edge toward you, insert needle through fabric ¼in (5–6mm) from edge. Bring around under edge and insert in the same place. Bring around and insert ¼in (5–6mm) farther along. Keeping loop of thread below needle, pull through so that loop lies on edge.

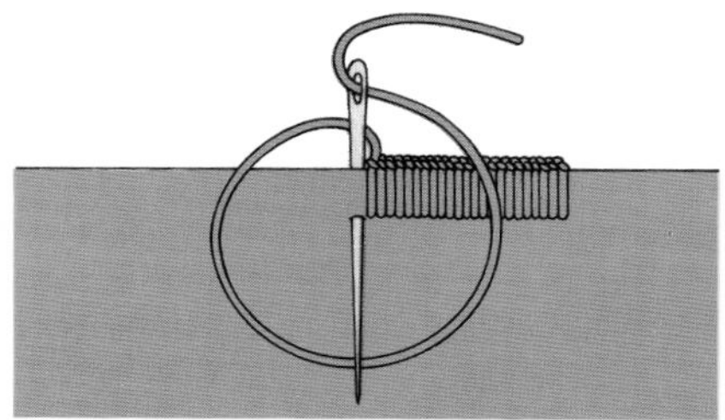

Buttonhole stitch

Use for hand-stitched buttonholes. Work closely and firmly as shown, with the edge away from you. Work from right to left forming a tiny loop at the top of each stitch. Do not pull stitches too tightly or the edge will pucker.

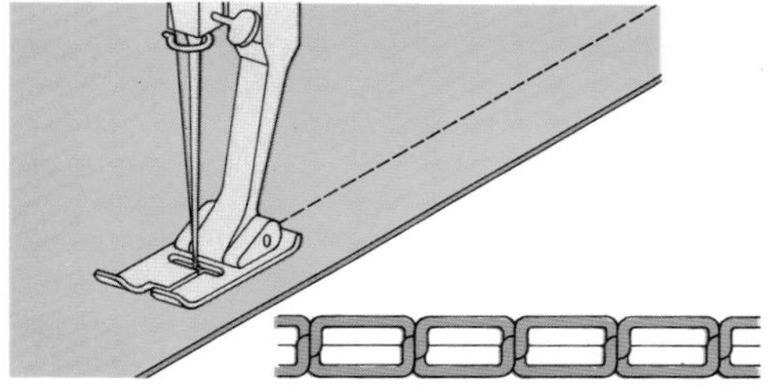

Lock stitch

This is the regular machine stitch used for most seams. Follow your machine manufacturer's instructions for correct stitch length and tension and always test these on a spare piece of fabric before beginning a project.
If you are not used to machine-stitching, practice on drawn straight and curved lines on scraps of fabric.

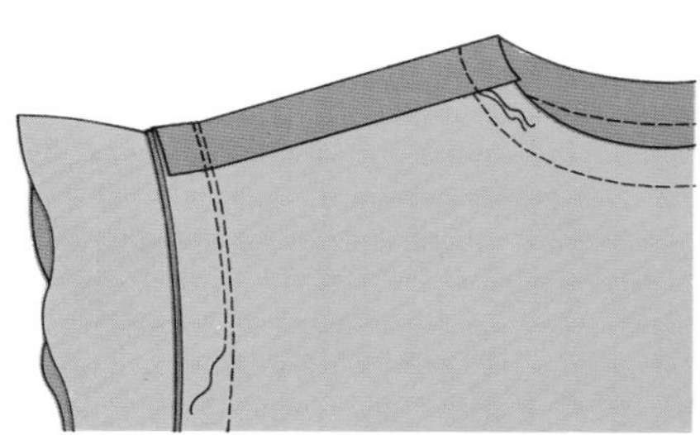

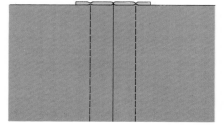

Stay stitching and under stitching

Use stay stitching to prevent edges, particularly curves, from stretching before seaming by machine-stitching just outside fitting line in direction of grain.
Use under stitching to hold down facings by machine-stitching turnings to facing ⅛in (3mm) from seamline before facing is turned to WS.

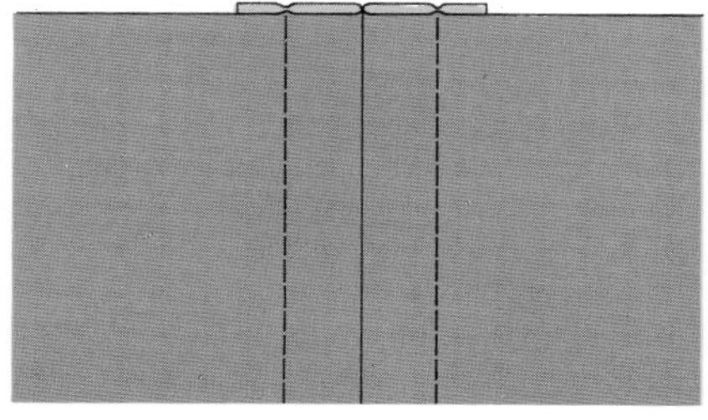

Top stitching

Use as decoration by stitching in buttonhole twist on both sides of seamline or along an edge to emphasize a shape. The stitching can be worked either by hand (when it is also known as saddle stitching) or by machine.

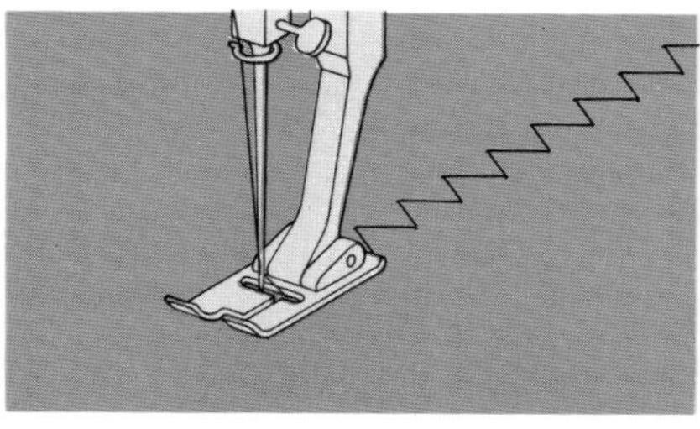

Zigzag stitch

This is a mechanical stitch worked on machines with a zigzag attachment and used for finishing raw edges or as decoration. Test length and width of stitch on a spare piece of fabric. Keep the stitching straight when finishing edges by positioning the edge of the fabric in the center of the foot.

Seams and edge finishes

Seams are used to join pieces of fabric and are usually machine-stitched, although hand stitching can be just as strong and is more flexible. Plain seams, correctly made, give the line of a garment through shaping but they should be almost invisible. Decorative seams can emphasize lines of a design and become a main feature of a garment. The seam you choose should be suitable for the type of garment you are making and for the fabric you are using, but it is often a matter of personal taste whether you use, for example, a welt seam or a channel seam.

Always follow the seam allowances – the fabric left between the seamline and the edge – unless you have made fitting alterations.

To prevent fraying, the edges of seam allowances are self-finished in some seams. In other seams a separate finishing method should be used.

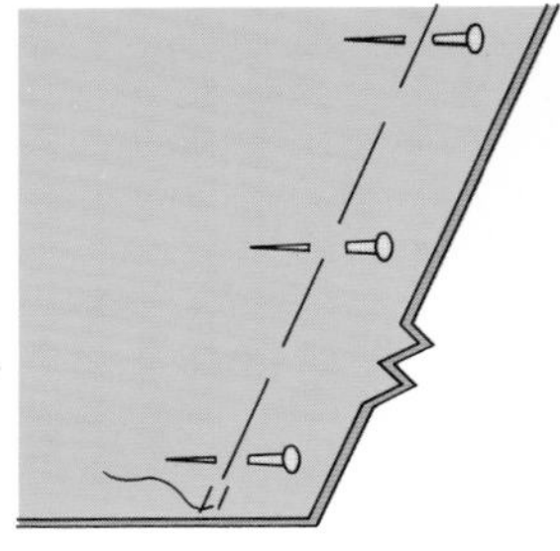

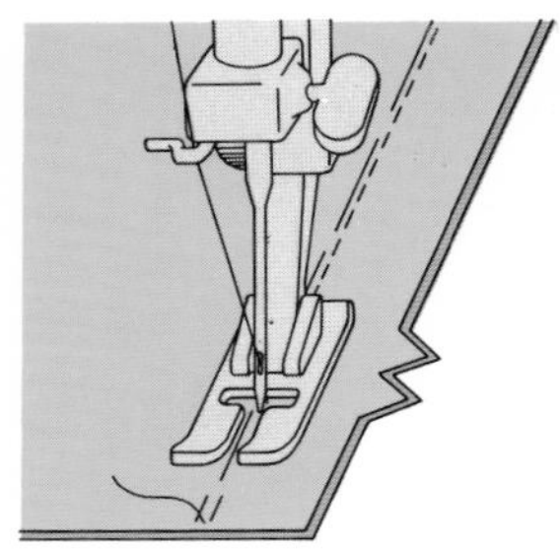

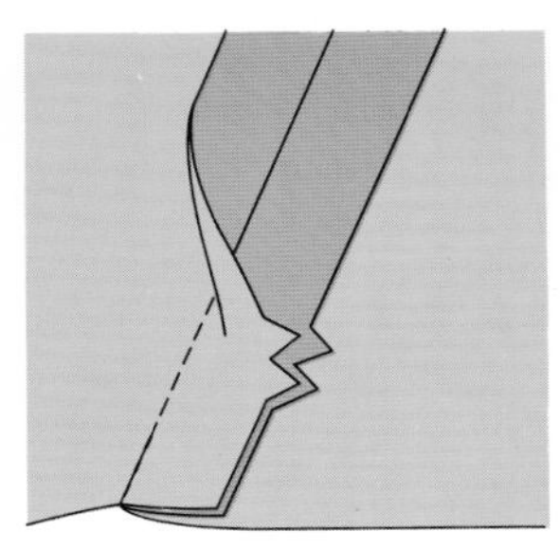

Plain seams

Plain seams are most frequently used in all forms of sewing and are sometimes known as open seams.

1 Place the pieces of fabric to be joined with RS together (unless otherwise directed) and with edges even. Pin at the ends, at any notches, at the center and then at about 2in (5cm) intervals in between. Place the pins at 90° to the edge so that stitching can be worked over them.

2 Hand-baste along the seamline. On easy-to-handle fabrics – and as you gain confidence and experience – this step can be omitted.

3 Place the fabric under the presser foot with the edges to the right. Position the needle on the stitching line about $\frac{5}{8}$in (15mm) from the back edge. Lower the presser foot and reverse-stitch to the back edge for reinforcement. Stitch forward to the end of the seam, close to one side of the basting. Reverse-stitch for $\frac{5}{8}$in (15mm) to finish off. Remove the basting.

4 Press the seam as stitched to embed the stitching into the fabric, then open the seam so that it lies flat and press again.

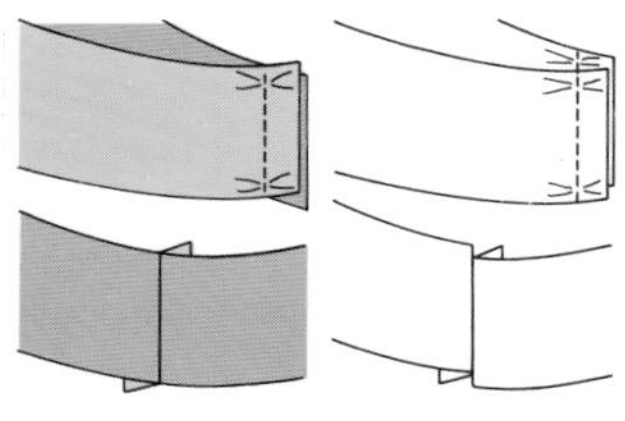

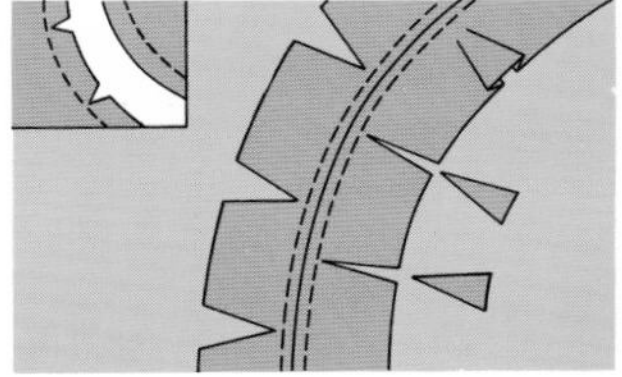

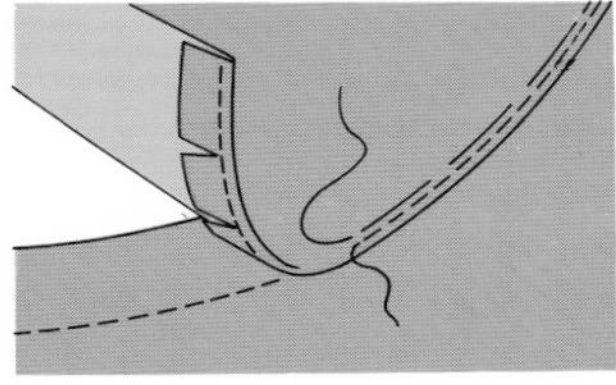

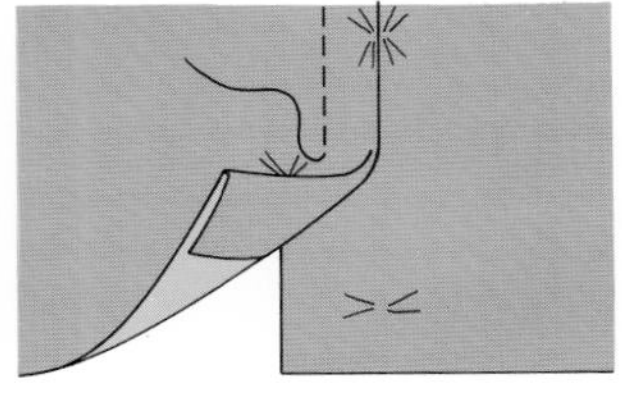

Straight seams and curves

When seaming straight edges adjoining curves, as on shoulder seams of neck facings, place the pieces together so that the curved edges meet on the seamline. This may mean that the corners of the seam allowances are uneven. When the seam is pressed open, however, the curved edge will be continuous and the projecting corners of the seam allowances can be trimmed even with the curve.

Plain curved seams

Use this method to join convex and concave edges.

1 Stay-stitch just outside the seamlines on both edges to prevent stretching.

2 Clip the seam allowance up to the stay stitching on the concave edge at even intervals to relieve strain.

3 With RS together, pin and baste the edges with the concave edge uppermost – the clips will open out as you do. Machine-stitch exactly on the seamline so that none of the stay stitching shows on the RS.

4 Finger-press the seam open and cut notches from the convex edge to reduce fullness.

5 Close the seam, press seam as stitched and then open, using tip of iron only.

Curved top-stitched seam

Use top stitching as a decorative alternative to a plain seam for joining convex and concave edges.

1 Stay-stitch just outside seamline on both edges.

2 Fold under the seam allowance of the convex edge, baste near the fold and press carefully. Cut off half the original seam allowance to reduce bulk. Cut notches in the edge.

3 Lay the convex edge over the concave edge so that the fold lies exactly on the seamline. Pin and baste.

4 Top stitch through all thicknesses on RS close to the folded edge.

5 Press from the RS using the tip of the iron only.

Tucked seam

Use for a decorative tucked effect.

1 Fold under the seam allowance of one edge. Pin and baste.

2 Working with the RS of both pieces uppermost, lay the folded edge onto the seamline of the second edge so that the raw edges are even on the underside.

3 Pin, baste and then machine-stitch $\frac{1}{4}$–$\frac{3}{8}$in (5–10mm) from the fold through all thicknesses.

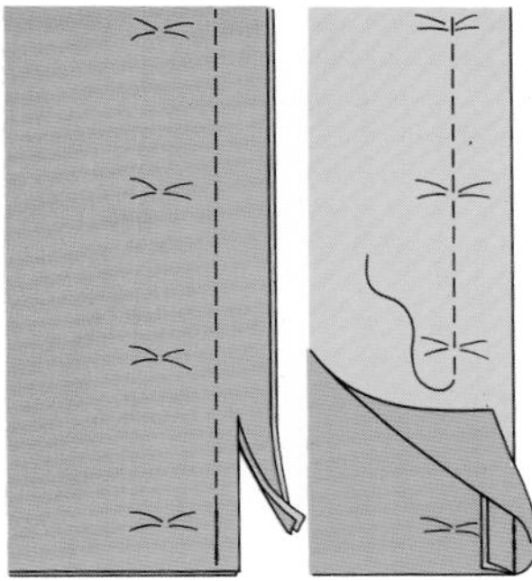

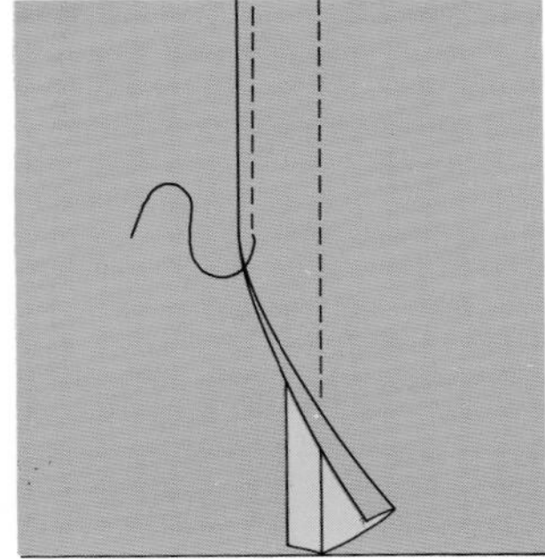

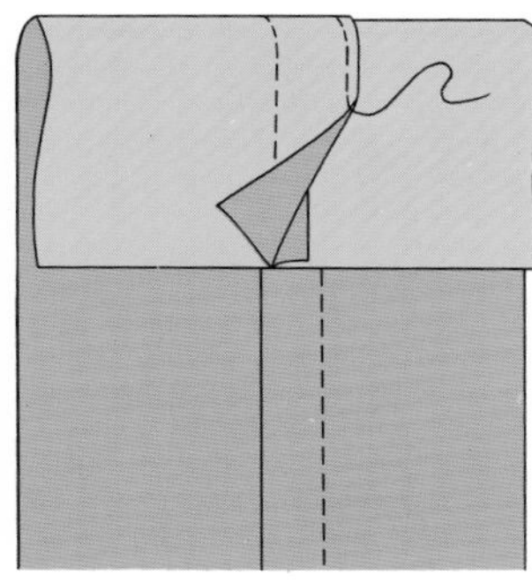

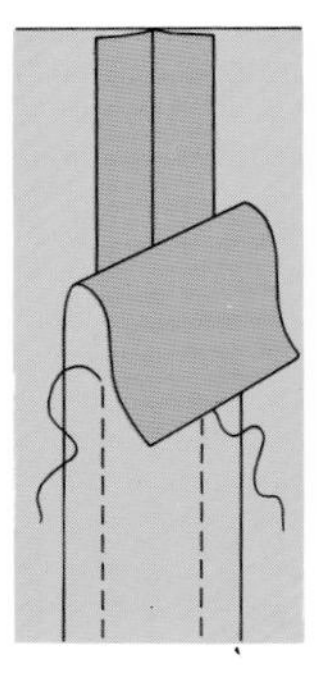

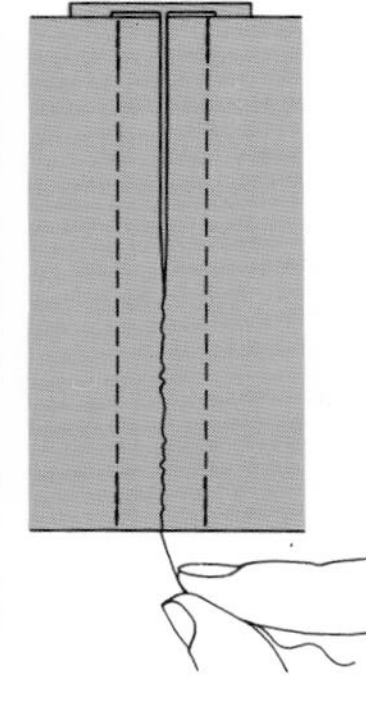

French seam
Use this neat, self-finishing seam for thin fabrics which fray easily, for sheer fabrics on which edges show through to the RS and for clothes which need frequent washing such as blouses and nightwear.
1 With WS facing, pin, baste and machine-stitch the edges together about $\frac{1}{4}$in (5–6mm) from the seamline. Press as stitched.
2 Trim the seam allowances to $\frac{1}{8}$in (3mm) in from the stitching and press the seam open.
3 Turn the RS of the fabric together, fold on the stitched line and press.
4 Baste, then machine-stitch along the seamline.
Press as stitched.

Flat felled seam
Use as a strong flat self-finishing seam on shirts, jeans, most sports clothes and reversible fabrics. Either side of the finished seam may be used as the RS.
1 Start by forming a plain seam.
2 Press the seam open and trim one of the allowances to half the original width.
3 Press the other allowance over the trimmed one and fold under the edge $\frac{1}{8}$in (3mm). On curved seams clip into the raw edge just short of the fold at even intervals.
4 Pin, baste and then machine-stitch near the fold through all thicknesses.

Welt seam
Use as a decorative seam for slacks and heavy-weight fabrics where a flat finish is required.
1 Stitch a plain seam. Press as stitched.
2 Trim the underseam allowance to within $\frac{1}{8}$in (3mm) of the stitching.
3 From the RS top-stitch $\frac{1}{4}$in (5-6mm) from the seamline, catching the untrimmed seam allowance on the WS.

Channel or slot seam
Use as a decorative seam on medium-weight fabrics.
1 Pin and baste a plain seam. Press open.
2 Cut a matching or contrasting strip to length of seam and $\frac{1}{4}$in (5–6mm) wider than the total turnings.
3 Working from the WS, center the strip on the seam and pin in position. Baste from the RS.
4 Working on the RS, machine-stitch through all thicknesses at an equal distance from both sides of the seamline.
5 Remove all basting so that the strip shows through on the RS.

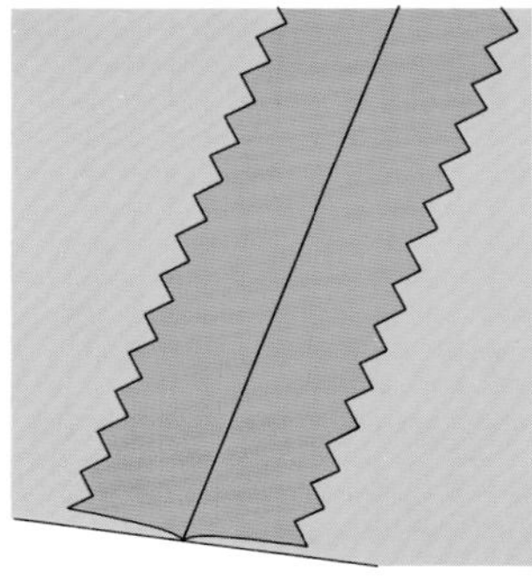

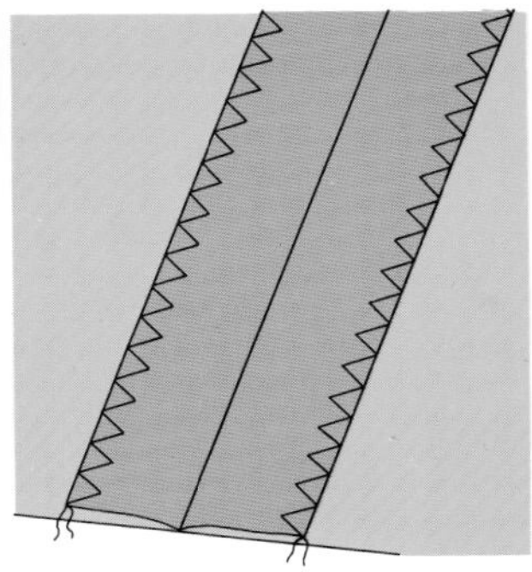

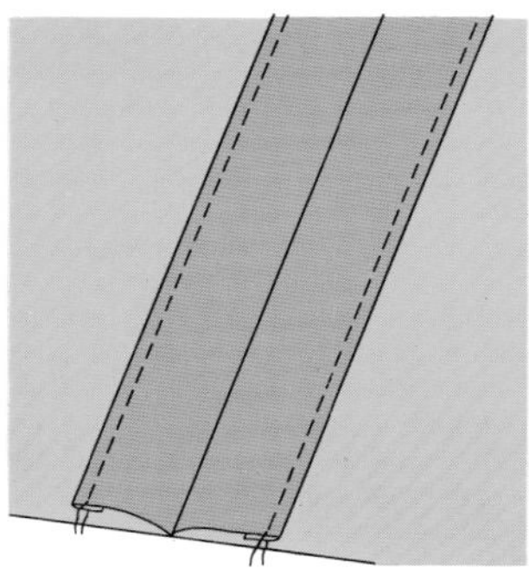

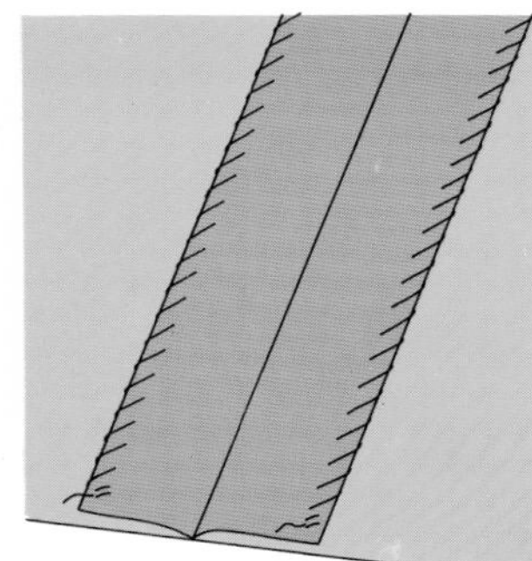

Pinking
Use to finish edges on closely woven, non-fraying fabrics such as fine wool, cotton, felt or vinyl. Simply trim off about $\frac{1}{8}$in (3mm) from the seam allowances with pinking shears.

Zigzagging
Use to finish edges which tend to fray. Adjust width of stitch according to fabric, using a narrow stitch on fine fabrics and a wider stitch for heavier ones. Edges pressed in the same direction may be zigzagged together.

Turning and stitching
Use only for fine fabrics. Turn under the seam allowance for about $\frac{1}{8}$in (3mm) and machine-stitch close to the fold.

Overcasting
Use on fraying fabrics if your machine does not do zigzag stitch. Trim edge of seam allowance neatly and work even overcasting along it.

Simple poncho, tabard and kaftan

This is a versatile pattern, involving a minimum of sewing and fitting. It is suitable for all bust sizes from 32in (80cm) to 42in (105cm). Make the poncho in wool, wool mixtures or a light-weight waterproof fabric (the hood is optional), and the tabard and kaftan in light-weight wool, jersey, cotton and cotton mixtures. The edges of all the garments may be finished with bias binding (either bought or cut from fabric into 1in/2·5cm strips). Flexible straight braid could be used for the poncho. Choose the binding in an appropriate weight and fiber for the fabric being used.

You will need

fabric and binding in the following quantities for each garment:
kaftan: $3\frac{1}{2}$yd (3·1m) fabric, 45in (115cm) wide; $13\frac{1}{2}$yd (12m) binding
poncho: $2\frac{1}{2}$yd (2·2m) fabric, 54in (140cm) wide; 8yd (7·4m) binding
tabard: 2yd (1·8m) fabric, 36in (90cm) wide; 10yd (9m) binding
matching sewing thread

Cutting out

Draw pattern for required garment to scale to sizes shown on measurement pattern (1 square = $\frac{3}{8}$in/1cm). If you are making the tabard, compare the shoulder width with your own and adjust if necessary.
Cut out the fabric as shown on the layout charts. Note that the shoulders of all garments are placed to folds.

Using patterns and cutting out 16
Basic stitches 18
Seams 20
Binding 25

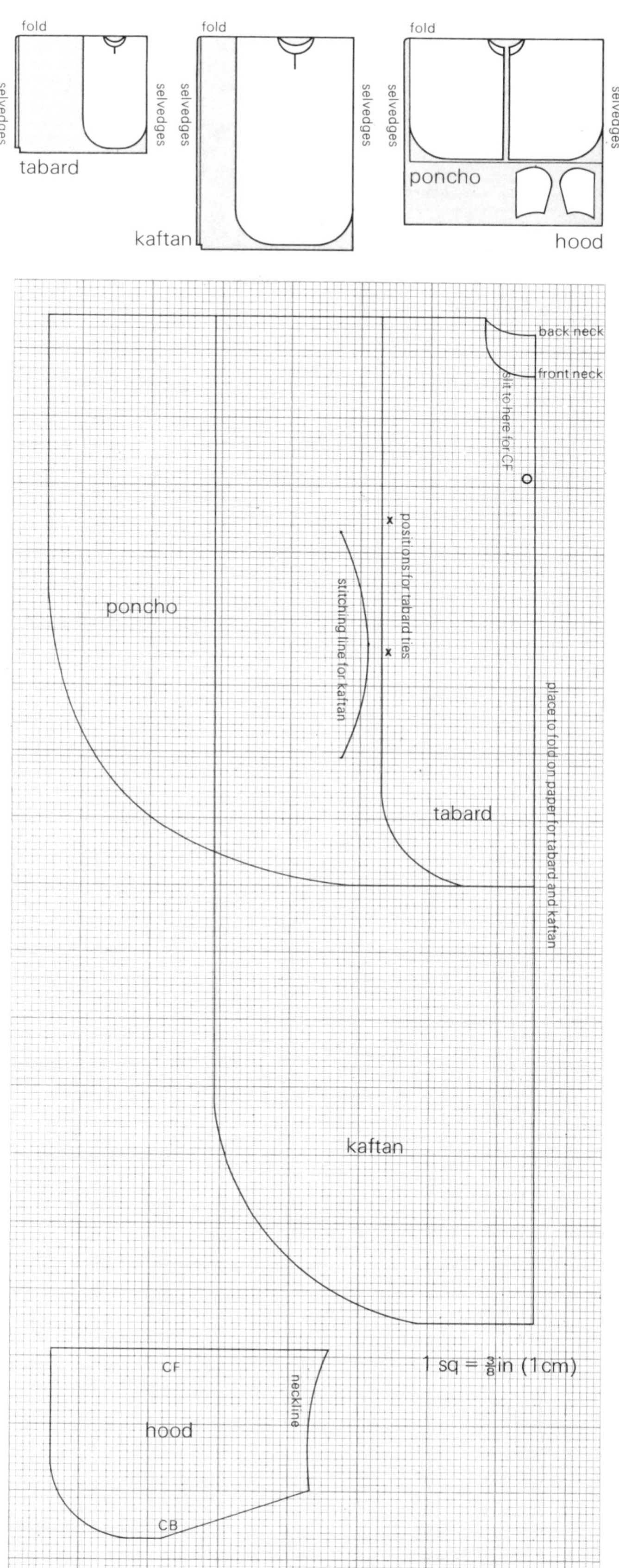

Using patterns and cutting out 16
Basic stitches 18
Seams and edge finishes 20

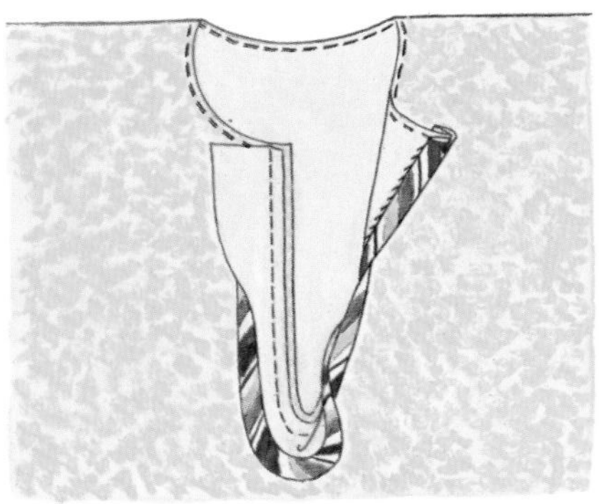

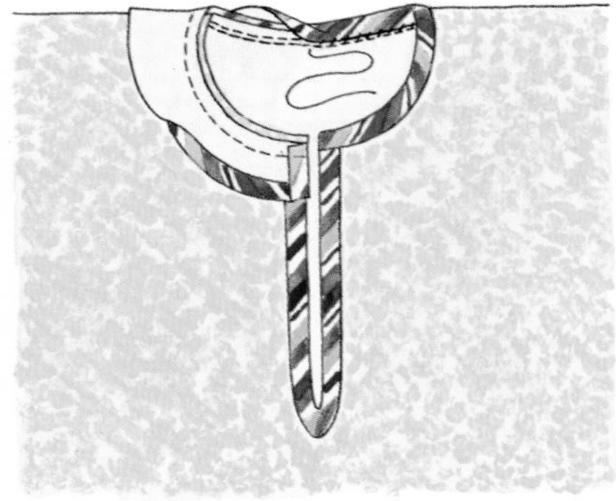

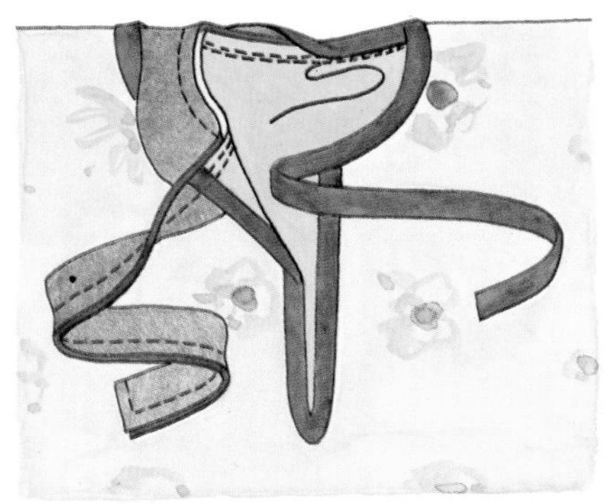

Making the tabard and kaftan

1 For front opening cut down center neck to circle. Cut a strip of binding to twice the length of opening; bind the edges (see opposite).

2 For a neck finish without ties, cut binding to circumference of neck plus $\frac{3}{8}$in (10mm) for hems. Fold under $\frac{1}{4}$in (5mm) at each end of binding and bind neck edge.

For a neck finish with ties, cut binding to fit neck plus 22in (56cm). Fold binding in half lengthwise, RS together, stitch across short ends and, from both ends, for 11in (28cm) toward center making $\frac{1}{4}$in (5mm) seams. Fit neck edge into remaining part of binding, turn ties RS out and finish off neck.

3 For ties at side of tabard, cut 8 × 18in (46cm) pieces of binding and fold in half lengthwise with RS together. Stitch across one end and down length along foldline on bought bias binding or making $\frac{1}{4}$in (5mm) seams on cut bias. Turn RS out. Baste ties to front and back side edges in positions shown on pattern.

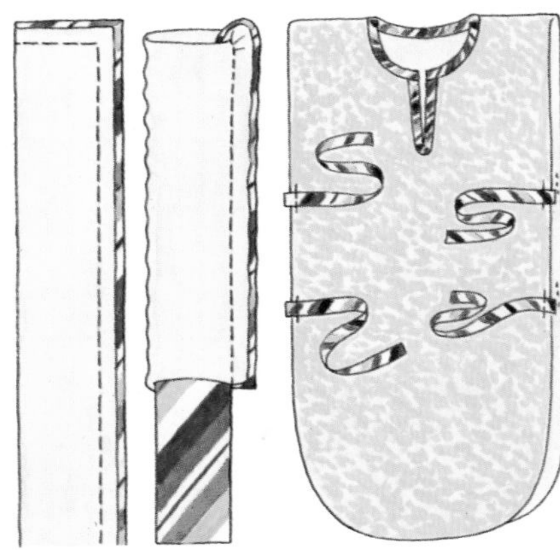

4 Try on garment and adjust width and length if necessary. On kaftan only, baste front to back along stitching line indicated on pattern. Adjust to fit by moving line farther in or out if necessary. Apply binding all around outer edges of both kaftan and tabard.

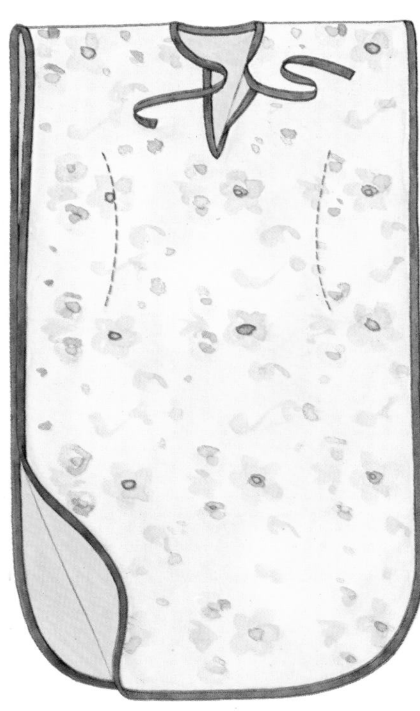

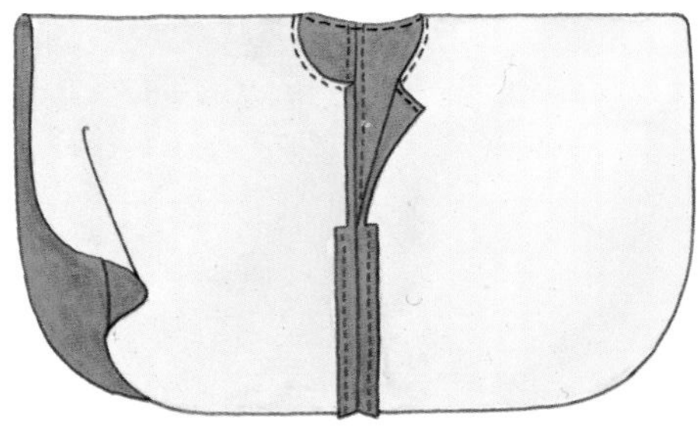

Making the poncho

1 With RS together baste and stitch CB seam and CF seam to circle. Press seams open and trim CF turnings at opening to within $\frac{1}{4}$in (6mm) of stitching. Top-stitch $\frac{3}{8}$in (1cm) away from seamline down CB seam and on CF seam below opening.

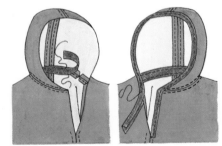

2 With RS together, baste and stitch CB seam of hood. Press seam open and top-stitch on each side of seamline. With RS together baste and stitch hood to neck edge. Trim seams to $\frac{1}{4}$in (6mm) of stitching, clip curves, press seams open.

3 Cut a length of binding to fit neck edge. Place binding flat over seam turnings. Baste and stitch in position along each edge.

4 Cut a piece of binding to fit edge of opening and hood. Turn under ends for $\frac{1}{4}$in (5mm), fold binding in half lengthwise, RS facing out, and press. Slip binding over CF edges and outer edge of hood.

Baste and stitch along edge of binding through all thicknesses.

Bind outer edge of poncho in the same way.

Binding

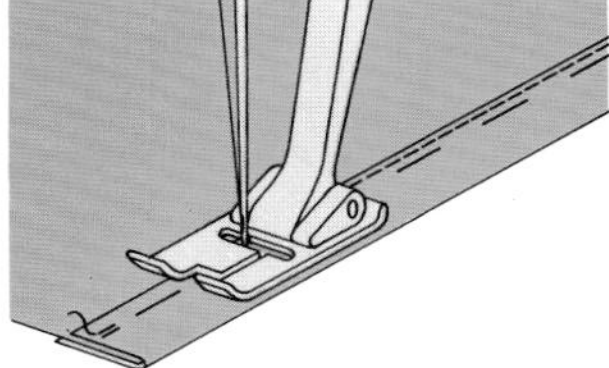

Straight seam binding
Use manufactured binding or decorative braid to finish straight edges and thick fabrics. Trim seam allowance from pattern and fold binding over edge with slightly more on the WS. Baste, then machine-stitch along edge through all thicknesses.

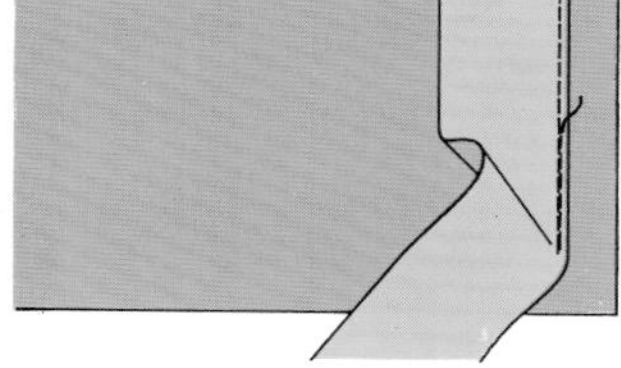

Binding corners
1 Trim seam allowances from pattern. With RS together, place binding edge $\frac{1}{8}$in (3mm) less than half binding width from edge. Baste, then machine-stitch $\frac{1}{8}$in (3mm) from edge to corner; back-stitch by machine for 1–2 stitches.

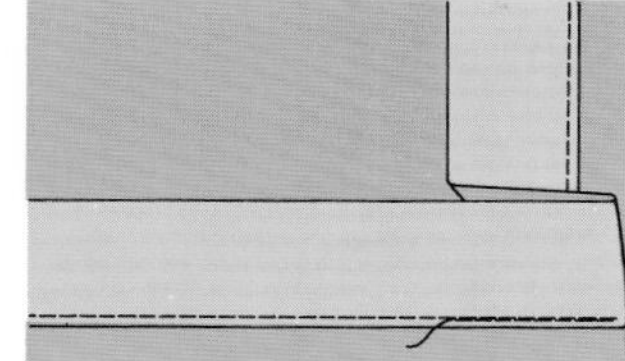

2 Fold binding diagonally at corner so that it continues at 90° to the first edge. Baste edge then machine-stitch.

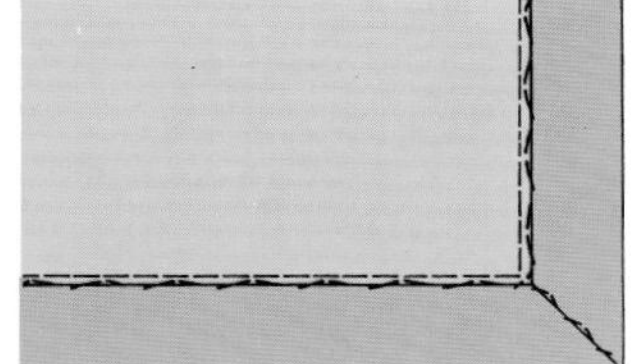

3 Fold binding to WS, forming a miter at the corner. Place edge outside stitched line and hem in position.

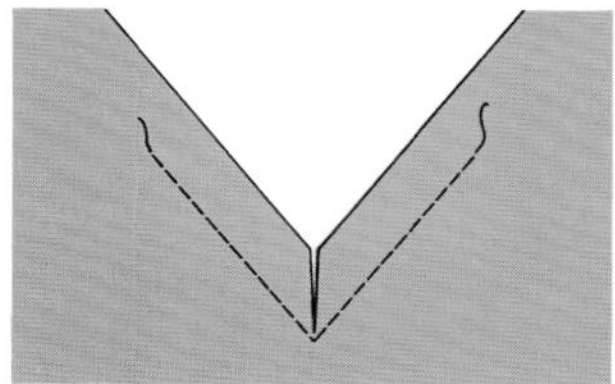

V-shapes and slit openings
1 On V-shapes stay-stitch for 1in (2·5cm) on each side of point on a line $\frac{1}{8}$in (3mm) less than half binding width from edge. On slit openings start stay stitching $\frac{1}{4}$in (5mm) in from the slit at the top, tapering to a point at the bottom.

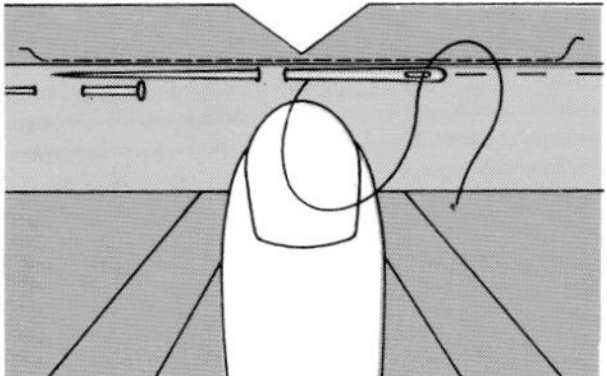

2 Clip into the point to within 1 thread of the stitching. Open out the V-shape or slit to form a straight line. With RS together, baste binding to stay-stitched line. Machine-stitch $\frac{1}{8}$in (3mm) from edge with fabric facing up to avoid catching a fold at the point.

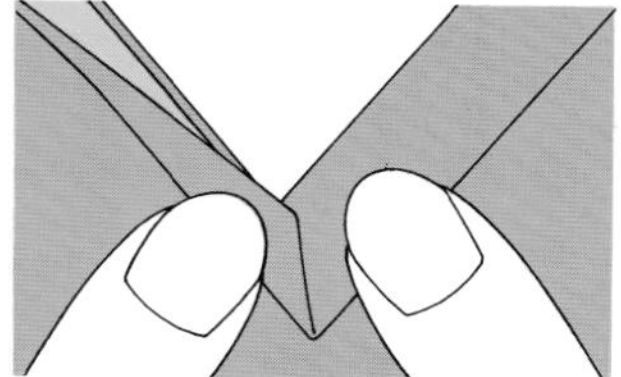

3 Working from the RS, push binding at the point through the clip and form a miter on the RS.

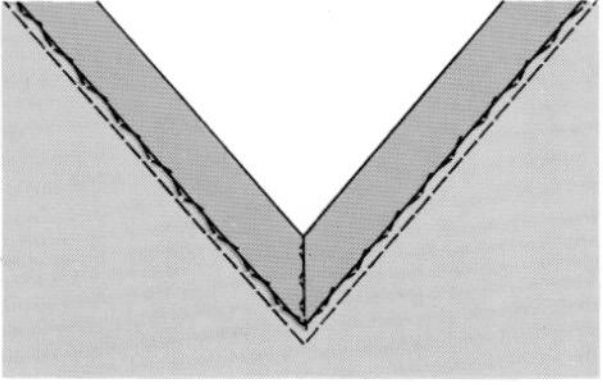

4 Turn rest of binding onto WS and form a miter at the point. Place remaining edge of binding outside stitched line and hem in position.

Bias binding
Use for curved edges. Manufactured bias binding is made in two widths, $\frac{1}{2}$in (1·2cm) and 1in (2·5cm), with ready-pressed seam allowances of $\frac{1}{4}$in (6mm) on both edges. If you are cutting your own strips, decide finished width and cut strips to four times this width (fitting lines are a quarter of this width from each edge).

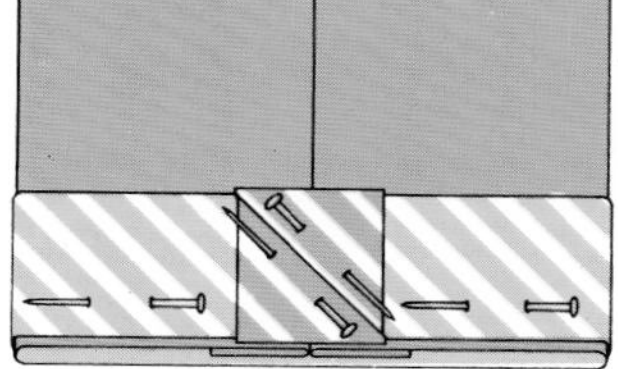

Joining strips Cut ends of bias strips on straight grain, slanting in the same direction. With RS together, place the ends as shown and machine-stitch making $\frac{1}{4}$in (5mm) seams. Press open and trim off protruding corners.
Continuous strips Pin binding around edge to determine length, fold back ends and butt together diagonally. Crease the folds, open out and stitch together along the crease line.

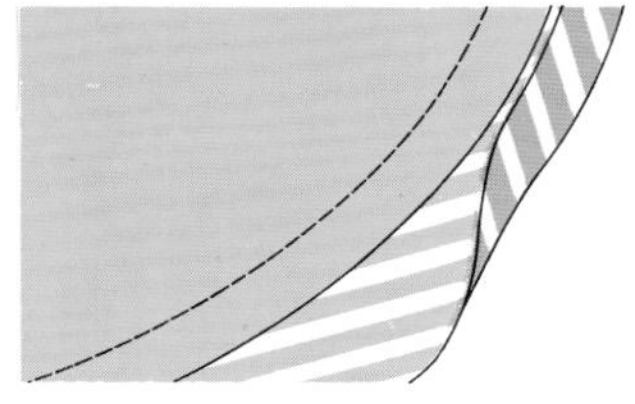

Attaching bias strips
1 Trim edge to be bound to fitting line. With RS together and edges even pin and baste binding to fabric along seamline of binding.
2 On cut strips, fold under seam allowance of the second edge and press it, being careful to avoid stretching.

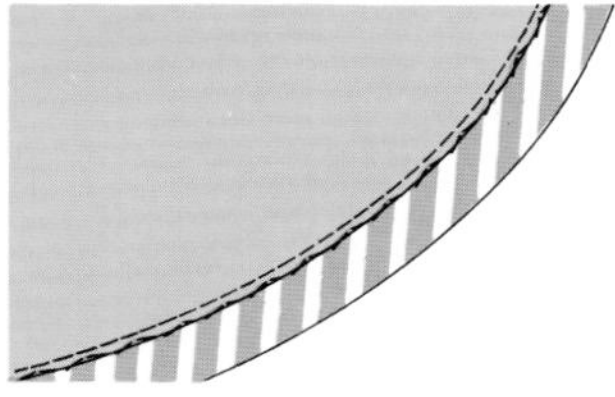

3 Turn folded edge to WS and place it just outside stitching line. Baste and hem in position.

Zippers

Zippers are a neat and strong device for fastening openings in seams. They are usually meant to be inconspicuous, as shown in the methods here, although they may also be applied decoratively (see p57).
There are two main types of zipper: the conventional type which is closed at one end and is used for openings in dresses, skirts and slacks, and open-ended zippers which separate at the bottom and are used for jackets and cardigans.
Choose a zipper with a tape in a color to match your garment and in a weight to suit the fabric.
Generally nylon zippers are more suitable for dresses and skirts in medium- and light-weight fabrics, and metal zippers are better for slacks and heavy-weight fabrics.
Measure the length of openings from the seamline, not the edge of fabric.
Where no length of zipper is specified, use an 8in (20cm) zipper for adult slacks and skirts where the opening is from waist level, and a 6in (15cm) zipper for children's garments.
For dresses with a CB opening, measure the length of the seam between the seamlines at the neck and waist and add 8in (20cm) for it to extend into the skirt. Both methods of inserting zippers shown here are for overlapped openings. If you would prefer the opening to lap the opposite way, simply reverse the directions. Plain lapped zippers may be stitched by hand, using blind stitch, or by machine.
Zippers in fly fastenings should always be stitched by machine for strength. Use a piping foot on the machine so that the stitching may be worked close to the edge of the zipper teeth.

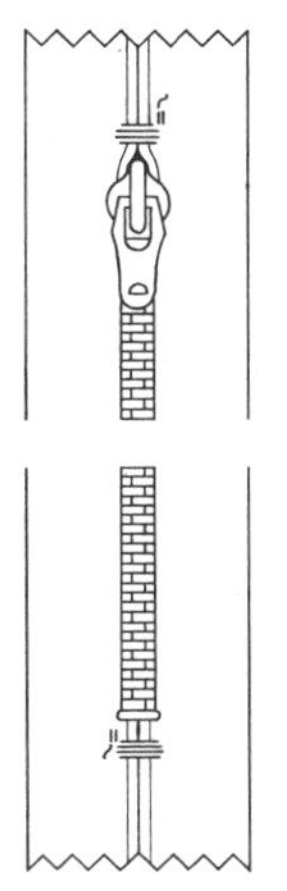

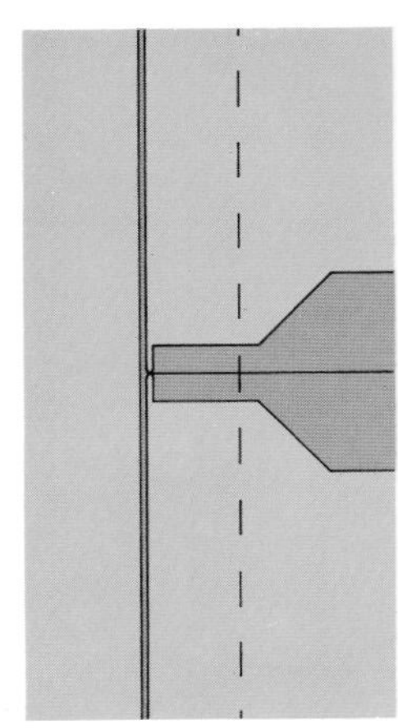

Preparing the opening
Stitch any seams that cross or enter the opening and trim the hems to $\frac{1}{4}$in (5mm) of the stitching for slightly more than the seam allowance of the opening.
For overlapped openings mark the position of the zipper and stitch and finish the seam to the beginning of the opening.
If both ends of the opening are enclosed, overcast the ends of the zipper tape together at the top.

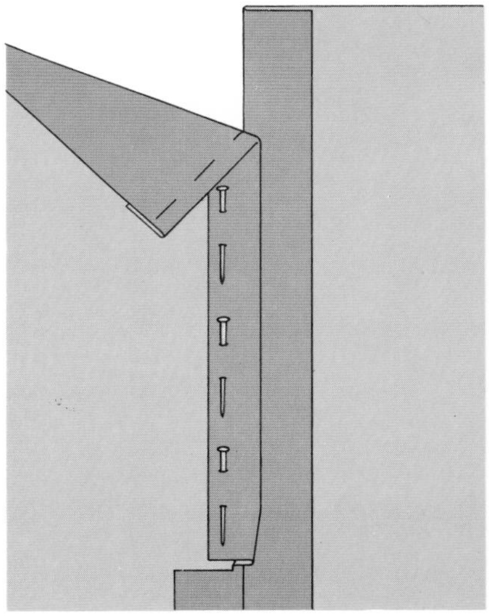

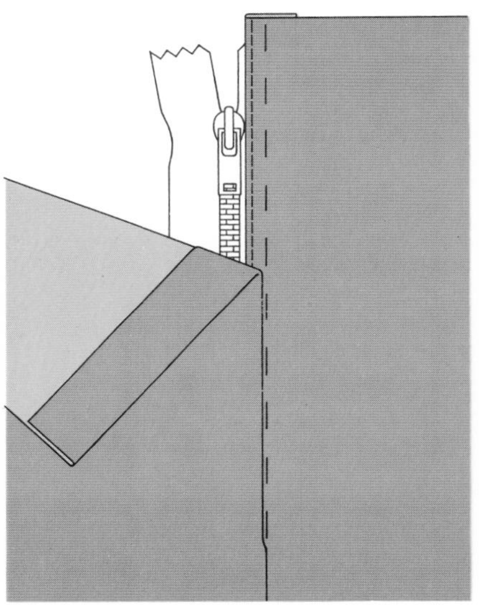

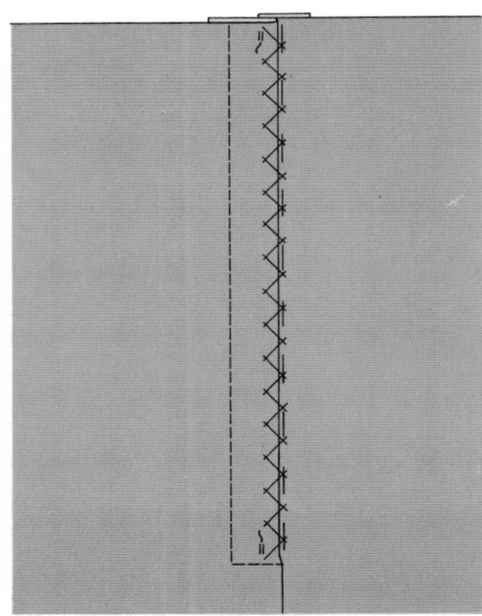

Plain overlapped opening
This is a general method of inserting a zipper which may be used in any position on a garment.
1 Baste along the seamlines of opening Snip seam allowance of LH side (RH if looking from RS) $\frac{5}{8}$in (15mm) below lower end of opening to within $\frac{1}{8}$in (3mm) of the stitching. Fold and pin the hem on this side to project $\frac{1}{8}$in (3mm) beyond seamline.

2 With both zipper and garment RS up, position the extended fold close to the RH edge of the zipper teeth.
Baste close to the teeth, then check that there is enough room for the zipper to close smoothly. Stitch just outside the basting.

3 Overlap the LH side of opening to RH side so that the seamlines correspond. Catch-stitch to hold in place.
Working from the WS, baste the other half of zipper to garment close to edge of zipper teeth. Working from RS from top, top-stitch along basting, pivot fabric and stitch at 90° or 135° to previous stitching as far as seamline. Remove catch stitching and basting.

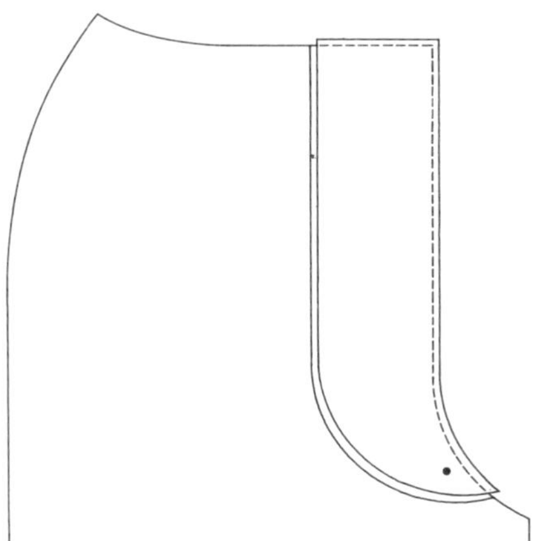

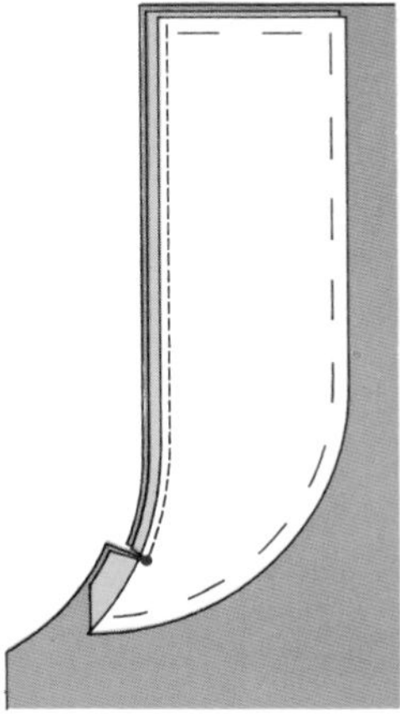

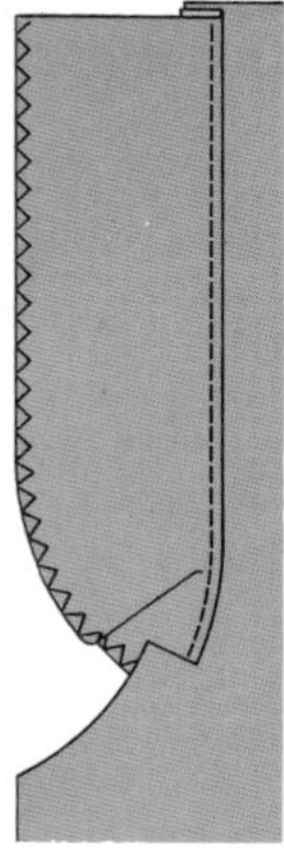

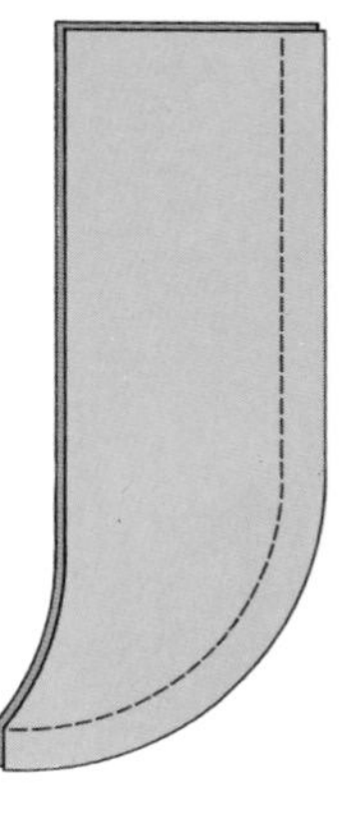

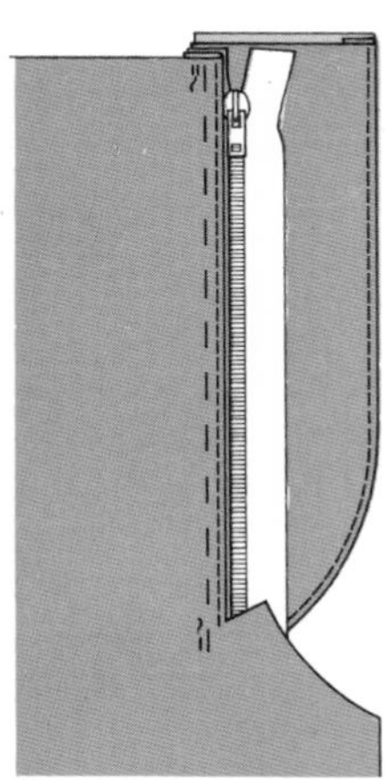

Zipper in fly fastening

This is a fully concealed zipper with an interior flap for slacks.

To make a pattern for fly facing and flap, if these pieces are not supplied, place zipper onto CF of paper pattern with top $\frac{1}{2}$in (12mm) below waistline. Mark a dot on pattern at base of zipper teeth. Place tracing paper over pattern and trace dot. Draw a line parallel to and 2in (5cm) from CF to 2in (5cm) above dot, then continue in a curve to 1in (2·5cm) below dot. Add $\frac{3}{4}$in (2cm) seam allowance along CF edge. Using this pattern, cut out 2 pieces in slack fabric, 1 piece in interfacing and 1 piece in lining fabric.

1 Baste interfacing to WS of 1 piece cut in slack fabric for fly facing. With RS together, place facing onto left slack front and stitch from waistline to dot. Trim seams and clip to dot. Press seam toward facing and under-stitch. Finish free edge of facing, turn facing to WS, baste and press.

Make a line of basting 2in (5cm) in from CF to 2in (5cm) above dot, then continue in a curve to dot.

2 To make flap, with RS together, pin, baste and stitch remaining shaped fabric piece to lining piece along curved edge. Trim, turn to RS, top-stitch curved edge and finish raw edges together. Baste along CF on RH front and clip into the seam allowance level with dot. Fold under seam allowance $\frac{1}{4}$in (6mm) outside CF line from dot to waistline. Placing base of zipper level with dot, baste fold to zipper close to zipper teeth. Position flap under zipper tape, matching waistline edges and inner edge of flap with tape. Baste and stitch to dot, working close to zipper teeth.

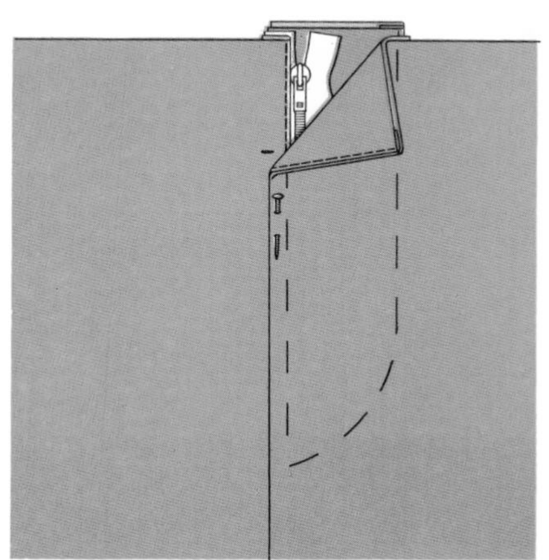

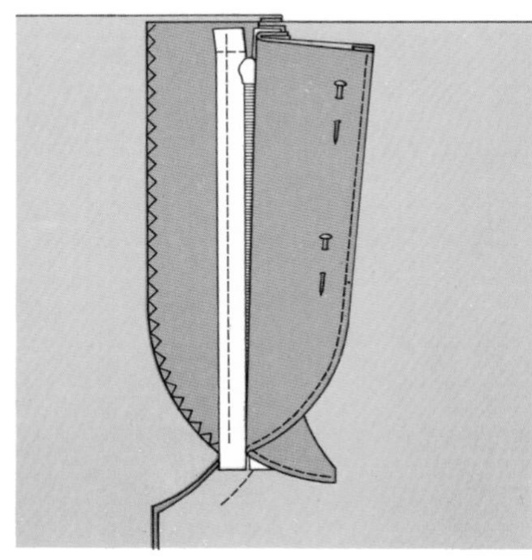

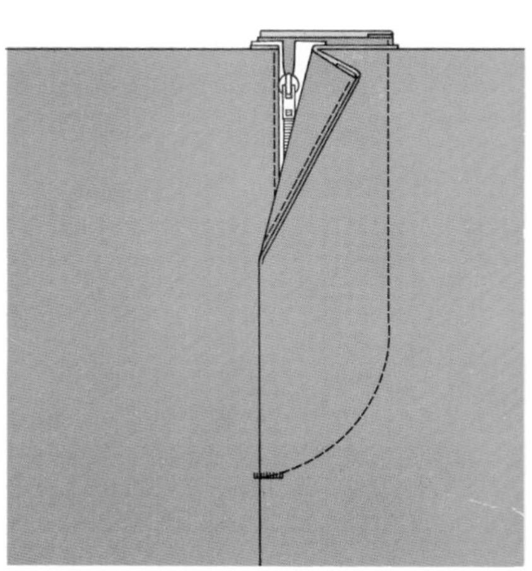

3 With RS together and matching CF lines, pin, baste and stitch CF seam of slacks for 1in (2·5cm) below dot Press seam open and finish. Pin both halves of zipper opening together on RS so that CF lines correspond.

4 Turn to WS, fold flap back and pin out of the way. Fold back the left slack front. Stitch remaining half of zipper tape to facing only, working from the lower end upward and stitching about $\frac{1}{4}$in (6mm) from edge of tape. Open zipper and secure top ends of tape by stitching across on waistline.

5 Baste facing to left front following first basted line. Turn to RS and top-stitch along basted line. Buttonhole-stitch a small safety bar across bottom of zipper opening.

Hems

Using patterns and cutting out 16
Basic stitches 18

A hem, formed by turning up an unfinished edge, is usually the last step in making a garment; occasionally it may be done earlier.
Hems should be of different depths according to their position on the garment and the fabric you are using. An average hem allowance is 2in (5cm) for the bottom edges of slacks and skirts and 1in (2·5cm) on the bottom of sleeves and shirts or blouses. However, it is better to reduce this to about $\frac{5}{8}$in (15mm) on flared and circular hems because of the fullness. On sheer fabrics you should either increase it to 4in (10cm) in order to make a double hem or reduce it to $\frac{1}{8}$in (3mm) for a rolled hem, particularly on circular skirts or scarves. You will probably want to have a deeper hem on children's clothes so that they can be let down as the child grows. You must mark the hemline of slacks and skirts while they are being tried on. It is not safe simply to turn up a hem along the line marked on the pattern because it should be an even distance from the floor; this can be affected by the contours of the body, by the shoes you wear and by the fabric itself which may have dropped where it is on the bias grain. Leave bias and circular skirts to hang for a few days before you turn up their hems.
Hems are usually hand-stitched although you can machine-stitch for decorative effect, as on denim, or where the hem will not show, as on the bottom of a blouse.

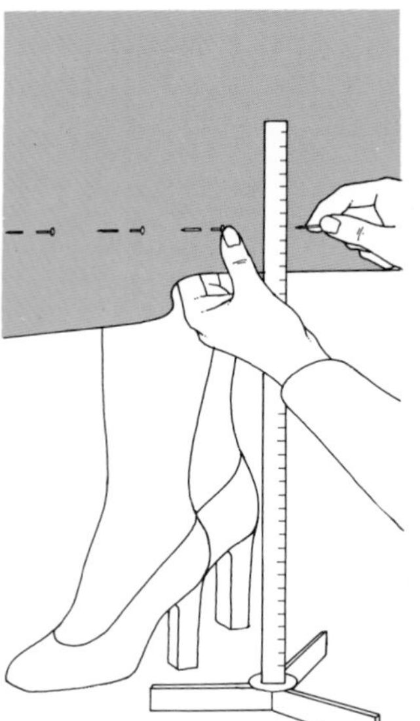

Marking the length
When making a garment for yourself, ask someone else to mark the hem for you so that you can stand straight; wear the shoes you plan to wear with the garment and if there is a belt fasten it.
Mark the required finished length from the floor using a yardstick or hem marker and pins or tailor's chalk. Work a row of basting along marked line.

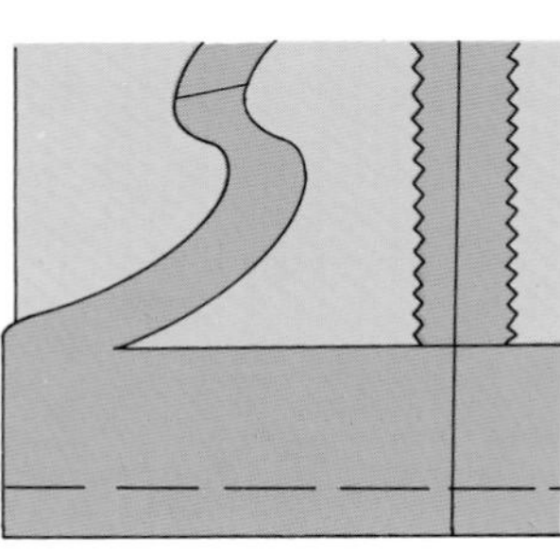

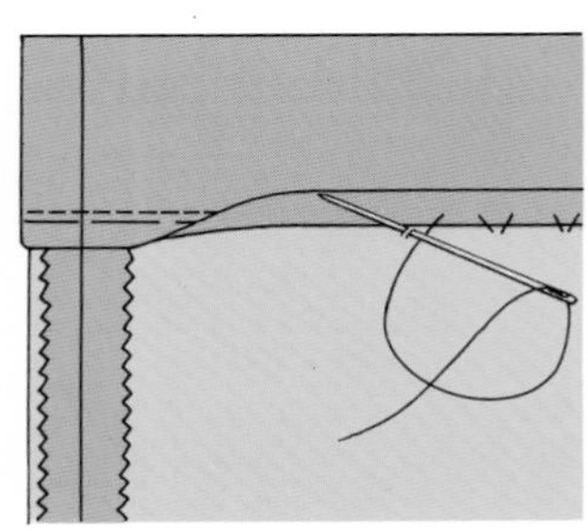

Straight hem
Fold hem to WS along basted line and work a second row of basting through folded edge. Lay garment on a table and mark required hem depth from fold with chalk. Trim off any surplus fabric.
Light- and medium-weight fabrics Turn the edge under $\frac{1}{4}$in (5mm) or half the hem depth for a double hem. Machine-stitch along the fold. Secure the hem by either blind hemming or slip stitch.
Thick fabrics and jersey
Finish the edge by zigzag stitching, overcasting or straight binding. Secure hem by blind hemming.

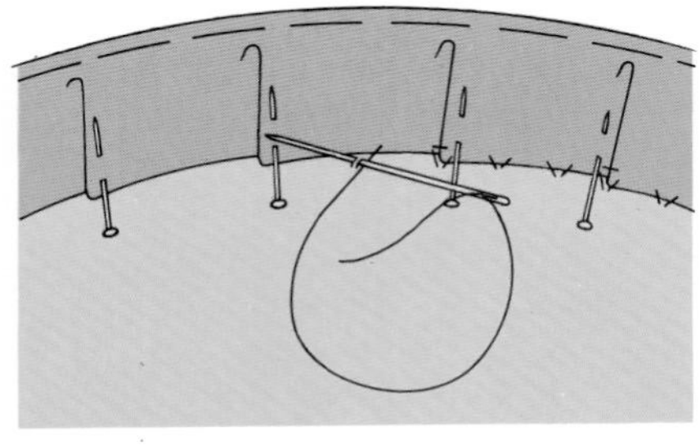

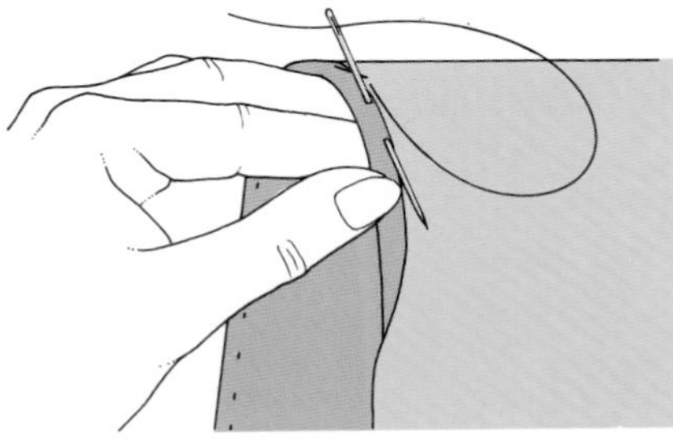

Flared hem
Pin up as for a straight hem. You will find that small folds appear where the upper edge of the hem is fuller than the fabric below. Finish hem edge by zigzagging, overcasting or with bias binding after reducing the fullness by one of the methods below.
Wools If the fabric can be shrunk, work a row of gathering stitches $\frac{1}{4}$in (5mm) from the upper edge. Pull up the thread until the edge lies flat. Place cloth or paper between fabric and hem, and press gently with the tip of the iron and a damp cloth to shrink away the fullness. Leave to dry, then finish edges; blind-hem in position.
Other fabrics Pin the fullness into tiny pleats. Slip-stitch hem, securing pleats with back stitches.

Rolled hem
This is a very narrow hem which should not be pressed. Use for pure silk or sheer fabrics such as chiffon where a wider flat hem would not be right.
Hold the edge of the fabric between your index finger and thumb. Roll the fabric as you stitch, turning under not more than $\frac{1}{8}$in (3mm). Make the tiniest possible slip stitches.

Shirring and gathering

Gathering is a decorative way of reducing fullness so that a wide piece of fabric fits into a smaller space. It is done by making 2 rows of running stitches, then pulling one end of the threads tightly and pushing the fabric evenly along them to the opposite end until it measures the required width. The running stitches may be sewn by hand or by using a long machine stitch (pull bobbin thread to make gathering).

Shirring consists of several rows of gathering worked in a panel so that the fabric flutes out above and below to its full width. Today shirring is usually made of rows of machine stitching using ordinary thread on top and an elastic thread (sewing thread with a central core of elastic) in the bobbin. This gives the shirring a snug but strong and stretchy finish.

Both gathering and shirring can be used for cuffs, yokes, waistbands, ruffles or for an entire bodice. Most fabrics may be gathered to reduce a fabric of $1\frac{1}{2}$–2 times the required width. Some light-weight fabrics can be reduced from 2–3 times the required width for a really full effect. It is advisable to work a test piece on a 12in (30cm) square of your fabric so that you can judge the effect.

Ruffles are made by gathering a strip of fabric to fit a narrower edge. They can be made in various depths and be used for trimming necks, sleeves and hems. Light- or medium-weight fabrics are suitable for ruffles as well as lace or eyelet embroidery edgings which have the advantage of ready finished hems. If you are adding a ruffle to a pattern, decide on its depth and subtract this amount from the pattern piece. Add $\frac{3}{4}$in (2cm) seam allowance to both pieces, plus a hem allowance on the ruffle.

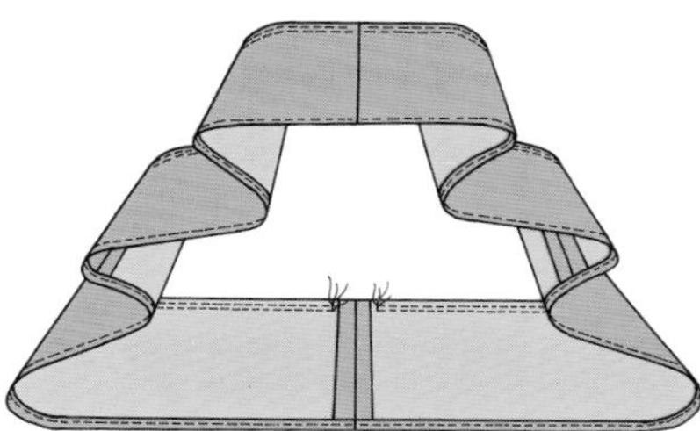

Preparing gathering
Calculate the amount of fabric to give required fullness; cut out and seam any joinings necessary.
Make a row of running stitches $\frac{1}{8}$in (3mm) inside seamline of edge to be gathered and then a parallel row $\frac{1}{8}$in (3mm) outside seamline.

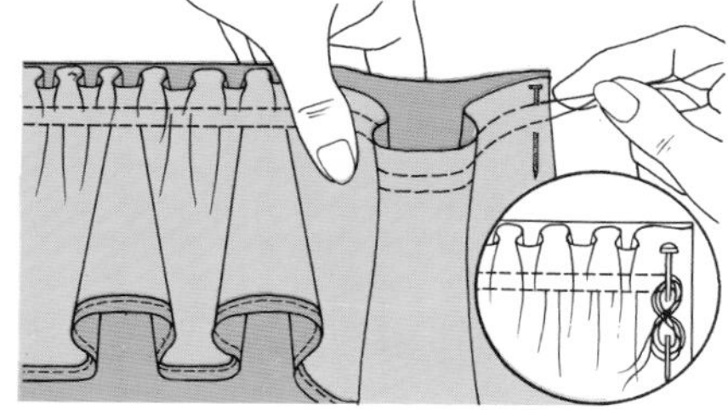

Attaching gathering
Divide gathered edge and the edge to which it is to be attached equally.
With RS together, pin edges at corresponding points, placing pins at right angles to edge. Pull up threads until longer edge fits shorter one. Wind thread ends around a pin. Distribute gathers evenly, pin and baste along seamline.

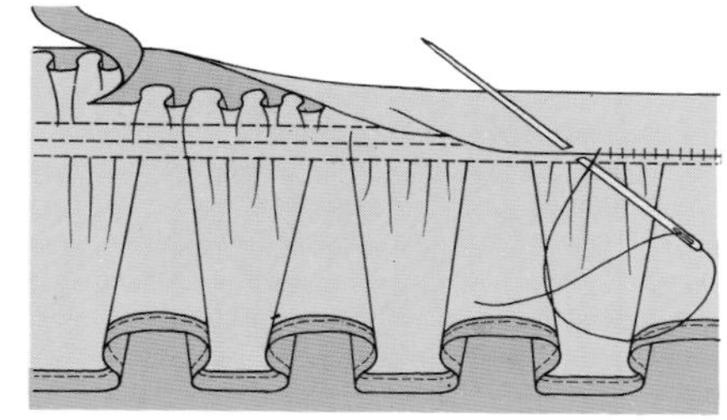

Finishing gathering
Machine-stitch along seamline with gathered side facing up to avoid flattening. Remove gathering threads. Press seam allowances away from gathers using point of iron up to seamline only. Trim seam allowance of gathered edge to $\frac{1}{8}$in (3mm) of stitching. Fold under straight edge for $\frac{1}{8}$in (3mm) and stitch fold to seamline.

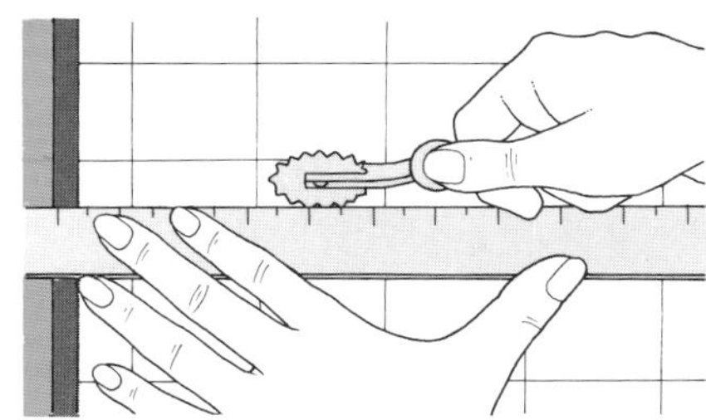

Preparing shirring
Wind elastic thread onto bobbin by hand without stretching it. Set tension to normal with 7–8 stitches to 1in (2·5cm), or with longer stitches for tighter shirring. Press fabric and mark out lines for shirring, spacing them $\frac{3}{8}$–1in (1–2·5cm) apart. Alternatively, shirring may be stitched along lines of fabric design (e.g. plaids).

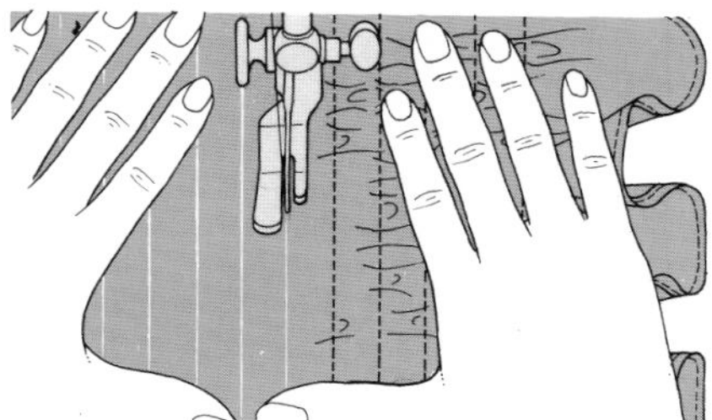

Stitching shirring
If shirring starts just below an edge, such as a cuff or sun top, stitch a narrow hem before doing the shirring. With RS of fabric facing up, stitch along each marked row. Cut the ends leaving 3in (7.5cm). For the second and subsequent rows hold the fabric flat by stretching the previously stitched rows.

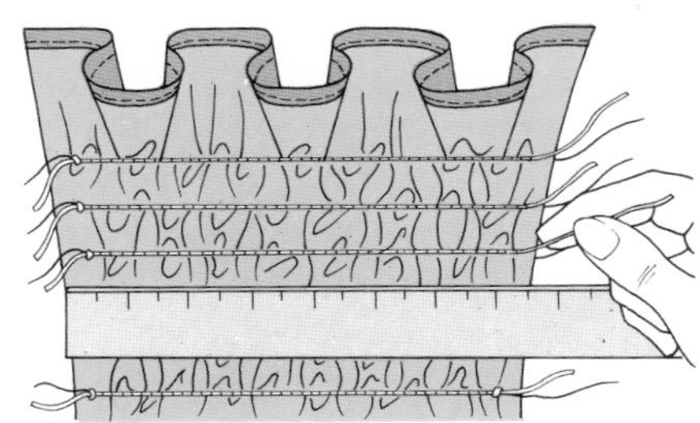

Finishing shirring
Check the width of the shirred panel and if necessary pull up the elastic threads to make the required size. Bring thread ends to WS of fabric and knot with the elastic ends.

Shirred dress and dirndl skirt

The sun top, dress and skirts photographed here are all made from wide strips of fabric, seamed to form a continuous piece and shirred or gathered to size. The strips are rectangles cut to measurement so you don't need a paper pattern. Make the garments as described below or as the variations shown.
You can use any soft fabric; the amount depends on the finished effect you want and the design of the fabric. An average skirt fullness is $1\frac{1}{2}$–2 times the hip measurement although up to $2\frac{1}{2}$–3 times may be allowed on fine fabrics. Double fullness on the bust is generally flattering.
You can add a ruffle of any depth to the skirts or dress. Allow a fullness of $1\frac{1}{2}$–2 times the hem width.

You will need
calculated amount of fabric (see below)
sewing thread to match fabric
shirred garments: shirring elastic
dirndl skirt: 8in (20cm) zipper; interfacing for waistband

Calculating measurements
Sun top or dress Measure from armpit over bust to 2in (5cm) below waist for sun top or to required length for dress. Add 3in (7·5cm) for hems.
Skirt Measure from waist to required length. Add 3in (7·5cm) for turnings and hems.
Ruffle Decide depth of ruffle (e.g. 6–10in/15–25cm) and subtract from basic length. Add 2in (5cm) for a hem.

Fabric amounts for each garment
If your chosen fabric can be used with the warp threads running from side to side and the required length of the garment is less than the fabric width, buy a length equal to the required fullness, plus 4in (10cm) for shoulder straps or waistband.
If the fabric cannot be turned sideways divide its width into the required fullness, rounding up to give a complete multiple. Multiply this figure by the required length and add 6in (15cm) for hems, shoulder straps or a waistband.

Cutting out
If using the warp threads horizontally, trim the fabric width to the required garment length including seams.
If using the warp threads vertically, cut across the fabric width to make pieces of the required garment length including seams. Join the pieces along one edge with $\frac{5}{8}$in (15mm) plain seams and trim the total width to give the required fullness plus $\frac{5}{8}$in (15mm) for seams. From the excess cut a strip of fabric for the waistband of the dirndl skirt or 4 strips 2in (5cm) by twice the length from shoulder to underarm for tie-on shoulder straps.

Making shirred garments
1 Turn under 1in (2·5cm) on all top edges and 2in (5cm) on bottom edge of sun top.
2 Work shirring for complete depth of bodice for sun top and dress and for 3–6in (7·5–15cm) on a separate skirt or on skirt of dress. Adjust shirring to width, then stitch remaining side edges together.
3 For shoulder straps, fold each strip in half lengthwise, with RS together. Machine-stitch down long sides making $\frac{1}{4}$in (5mm) seams. Pull through to RS, turn in raw ends and slip-stitch.
4 Try on bodice, pin straps in a comfortable position. Overcast firmly in place on inside of bodice.
5 Finish by turning up hem or attaching ruffle.

Zippers 26
Hems 28
Shirring and gathering 29
Waistbands 38

Making the dirndl skirt

1 Work rows of gathering stitches $\frac{5}{8}$in (15mm) and $\frac{1}{4}$in (5mm) from the top edge of the fabric.

2 Join the side edges with RS together, leaving a $8\frac{3}{4}$in (22cm) opening at the top of the seam. Insert the zipper.

3 Finish the waistband and divide the outside lower edge into equal sections. Divide the top edge of the skirt into the same number of sections.

4 With RS together, pin skirt to waistband, matching corresponding sections. Pull up the gathers evenly to fit the waistband, pin, baste and then machine-stitch.

5 Press the seams onto the waistband and trim them. Finish the waistband and turn up the hem or attach a ruffle.

Fastenings

Using patterns and cutting out 16
Basic stitches 18

Buttons and buttonholes, snaps and hooks and eyes are all means of fastening overlapping openings. Usually the design of the garment suggests which fastening to use although they are sometimes interchangeable.
Hooks and eyes are made in various styles suitable for fastenings on areas which take more strain than snap fasteners, such as necklines and waistbands. Eyes are made as either loops or bars.
Use snaps for neck and shoulder fastenings, for openings on sheer fabrics or where buttonholes are impractical. There are two types of snap: those which are sewn on (see right) and those which can be applied with a special tool (follow manufacturer's instructions).
There are two main types of buttonhole – slit and loop. The edges of slit buttonholes may be finished by close buttonhole or zigzag stitch on light- and medium-weight fabrics, or with binding in matching or contrasting fabric on medium- and heavy-weight fabrics. Loop buttonholes may be made by stitching or from strips of fabric. Always make a trial buttonhole on a scrap of garment fabric to check that you have chosen the right method and that the button will pass through it easily. Calculate this for slit buttonholes by adding together the diameter and thickness of the button. For loop buttonholes double the diameter of the button.

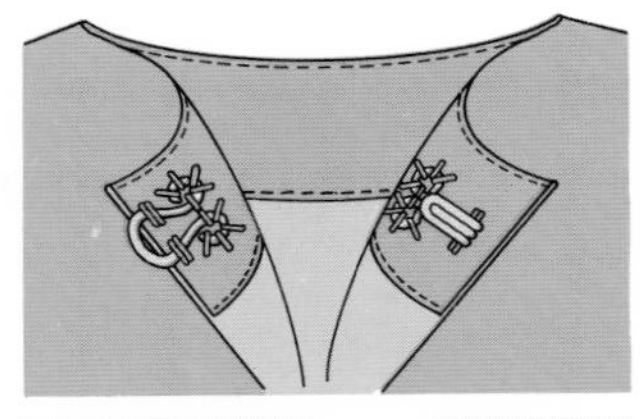

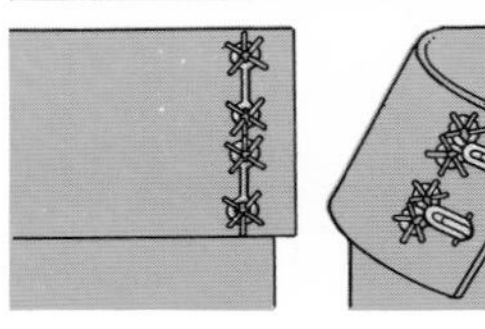

Hooks and eyes
If edges of garment just meet (e.g. necklines) position loop of eye to protrude by $\frac{1}{8}$in (3mm). Place hook $\frac{1}{8}$in (3mm) in from opposite edge to allow for garment's pull.
If edges of garment overlap, position hook on upper half well away from edge. Place eye on underlap to align with it. Attach by oversewing through holes with extra stitches over shank of hook.

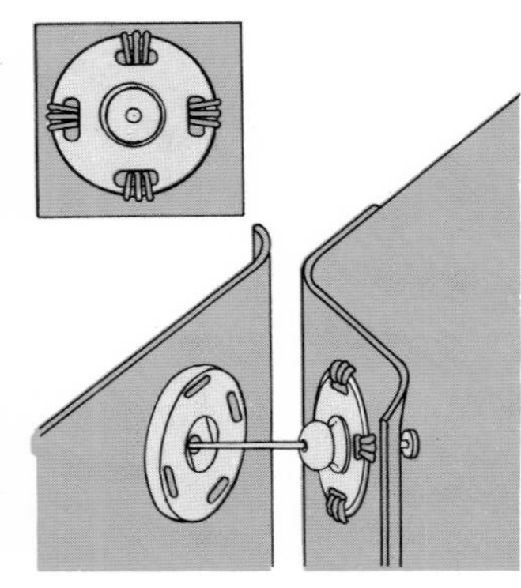

Snaps
Attach the ball half flat side down to WS of overlap with 2–3 overcasting stitches in each hole. Place socket half to RS of underside and position exactly by inserting pin through center of both halves. Overcast socket in the same way.

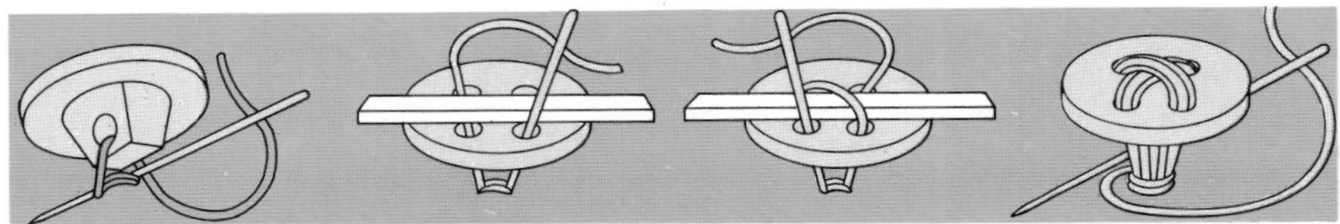

Buttonhole positions
Buttonholes should be made horizontally for maximum strength on most garments but they may be vertical on shirt fronts or tabs with small buttons. Their exact position is determined by the position of the buttons.
On single-breasted front openings on shirts, blouses and dresses, the buttons should lie on the CF line, beginning not less than half button width from the neckline and finishing not less than 3in (7·5cm) from the hem. Spacing in between should be regular and about 3in (7·5cm) so that the garment does not gape. In other positions buttons should not be less than three-quarters of their width from the overlap edge.
Begin by marking the button position on the paper pattern with a dot. Draw a straight line inward from the dot to the required buttonhole length. Mark vertical buttonholes equally above and below mark. Transfer the markings to the fabric using tailor's tacks in one color for the button and in another for the buttonhole. When the pattern is removed from the fabric, draw in the buttonhole with a dressmaker's pencil.

Buttons
Buttons should always have a shank between them and the fabric to allow for the thickness of the overlap. This shank may be part of the button or you can form one as you sew it on.
Shank buttons Attach with button thread in a color to match fabric. Position shank parallel to buttonhole. Secure thread with 2–3 back stitches, then stitch through shank as shown.
Sew-through buttons Attach with button thread in a color to match button. Secure thread in button position with 2–3 back stitches.
Bring up needle through hole in button, lay a wooden matchstick across button and take stitch over stick to second hole and through fabric. Repeat on second pair of holes if button has 4 holes. Work alternately between the pairs, taking several stitches over the button and through the fabric: alternatively complete one pair before starting on the next. Remove stick, hold button away from fabric and make a shank by winding thread around stitches. Work 2–3 back stitches through shank to finish off.

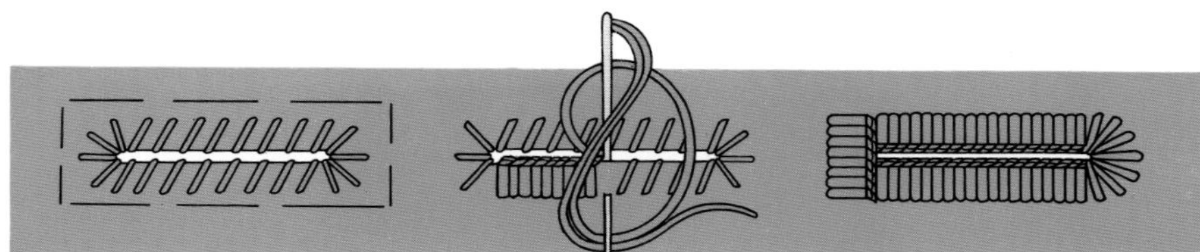

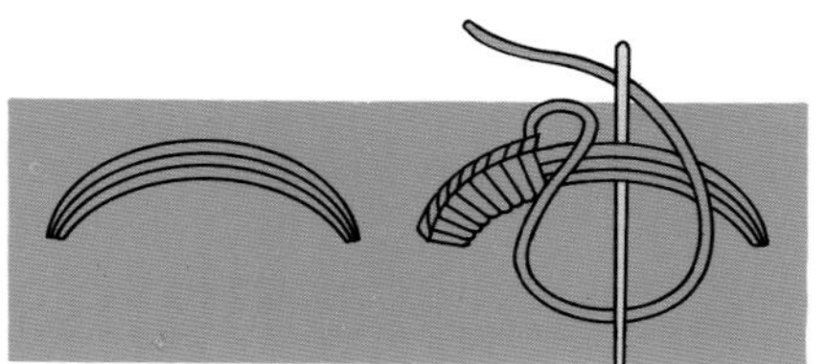

Stitched buttonholes
Work these through top and facing layers of the garment and stitch by hand as shown here, or by machine according to the manufacturer's instructions.
Baste around buttonhole position and cut along the buttonhole slit through all layers of fabric, using fine sharp scissors. Finish the raw edge by overcasting.
Horizontal buttonholes: using button thread or fine matching thread, begin at the inside end of the slit and work around closely and evenly in buttonhole stitch. At the outside end, work straight stitches in a fan shape, then continue in buttonhole stitch along the opposite edge. Work a bar across the inside end as shown.
Vertical buttonholes: work as for horizontal but with a bar at both ends.

Button loops
Use as buttonholes, with metal hooks where metal loops are clumsy or as belt loops. Make the loops in button thread or sewing thread.
1 Secure thread on WS at end of loop position, bring through to RS and take a tiny stitch at opposite end, leaving a loop of required length. Return to starting point, leaving a loop of the same size. Repeat for extra strength.
2 Buttonhole-stitch over the loops.

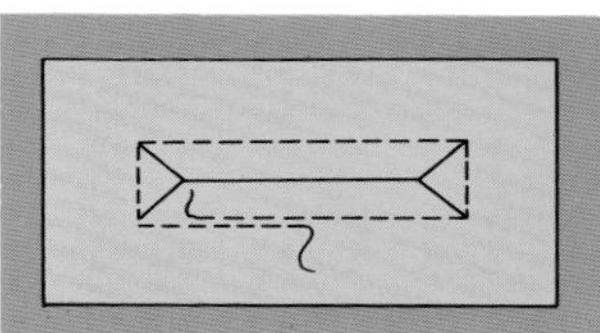

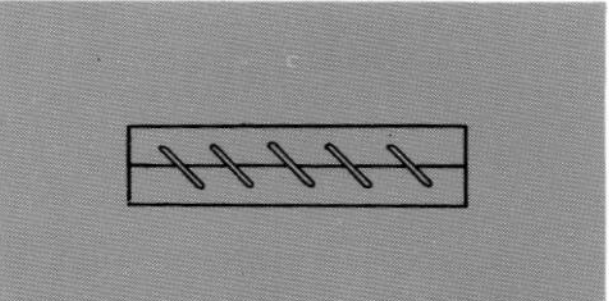

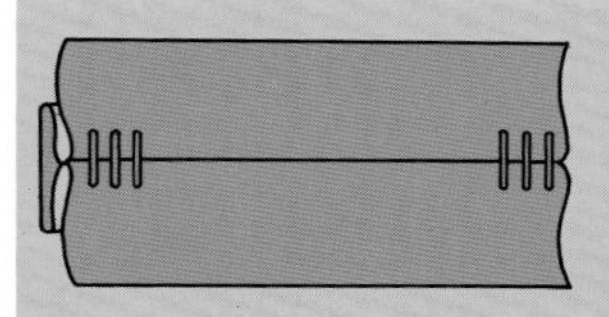

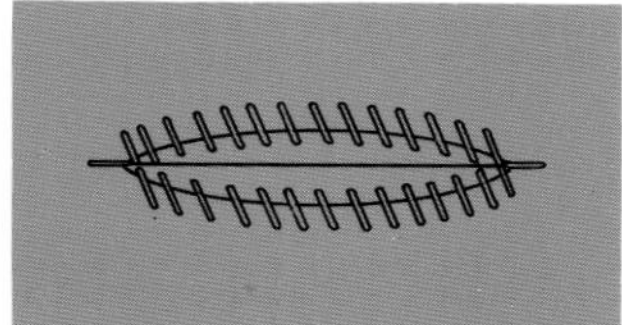

Bound buttonholes
Start these on the top layer of the garment and finish after attaching facing.
1 For each buttonhole cut bias fabric 2 × 1½in (5 × 4cm) longer than buttonhole.
2 Center bias fabric over buttonhole position with RS together. Machine-stitch a rectangle to finished size of buttonhole, running last stitches over the first to secure.
3 Cut into rectangle as shown, taking care not to cut stitches at corner.
4 Pull fabric through buttonhole slit so that it forms a binding on RS. Roll binding to meet in center of slit and overcast lightly together.
5 Turn to WS and gently pull fabric at each end of buttonhole into inverted pleats. Overcast together.
6 Attach facing and baste in finished position. Slit the facing under each buttonhole, turn under the edges of the slit and hem to the back of the buttonhole.

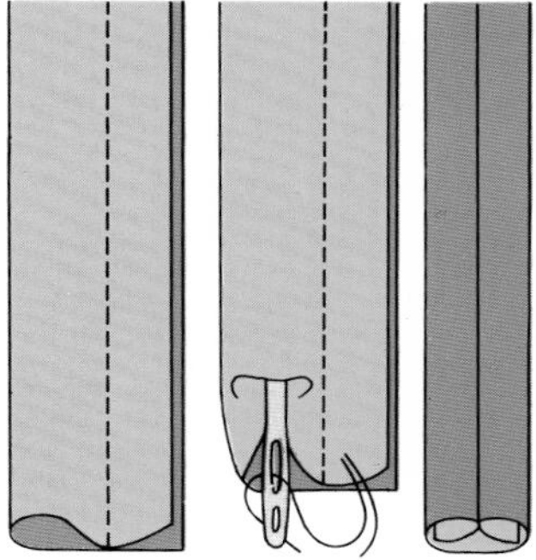

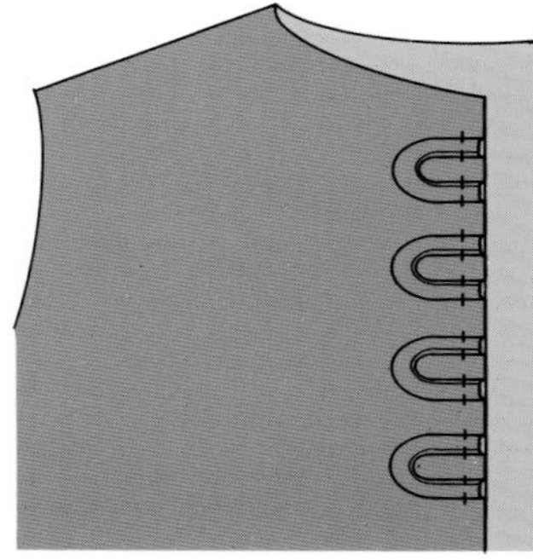

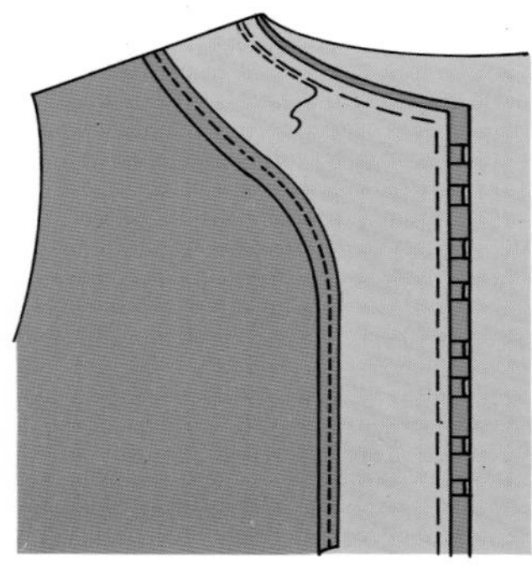

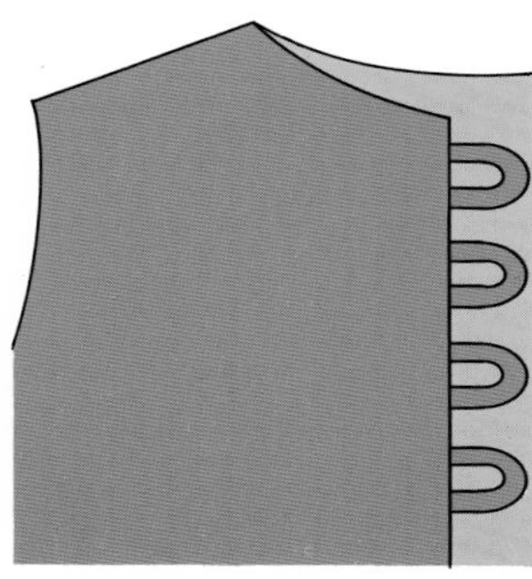

Rouleau loops
These are a decorative alternative to slit buttonholes, particularly for neck and sleeve openings with domed or rectangular buttons or on openings where there is no overlap. Attach them before the facing.
1 Cut bias strips 1⅛in (3cm) by twice diameter of button plus 1½in (4cm). If making several buttonholes cut a long strip 1⅛in (3cm) wide and trim to length after step **3**.
2 With RS together, fold strip in half lengthwise and stitch ¼in (6mm) from fold.
3 Attach a blunt-end needle to one end of rouleau and insert into opening to pull strip RS out.
4 Place the rouleau in position on the garment with the seam facing inward and the ends of the strip toward the opening. Secure with a few back stitches on the seamline.
5 Attach the facing and turn to WS to expose loops.

Simple smock and dirndl blouse

Measuring the figure 14
Basic stitches 18
Seams 20

The smock shown opposite can be made as a maternity dress, as it is here, a sundress or a nightdress, and you can cut a simple paper pattern to any size and length from your own measurements. You don't need a pattern at all to make the loose-fitting multi-size dirndl blouse because each section is made from a rectangle of fabric.
Use soft fabrics such as cotton lawn or fine jersey for both garments so that the gathers hang smoothly.

Dirndl blouse
You will need
fabric, 36in (90cm) wide: $2\frac{3}{4}$yd (2·50m)
binding, $\frac{1}{2}$in (12mm) wide: $1\frac{1}{2}$yd (1·20m)
matching sewing thread
rolled elastic: 20in (0·50m)
narrow cord for drawstring: $1\frac{3}{4}$yd (1·50m)
contrasting stranded embroidery floss

Cutting out the blouse
Cut out the pieces to the sizes shown on the cutting chart ($\frac{3}{4}$in/2cm seam allowances are included throughout).

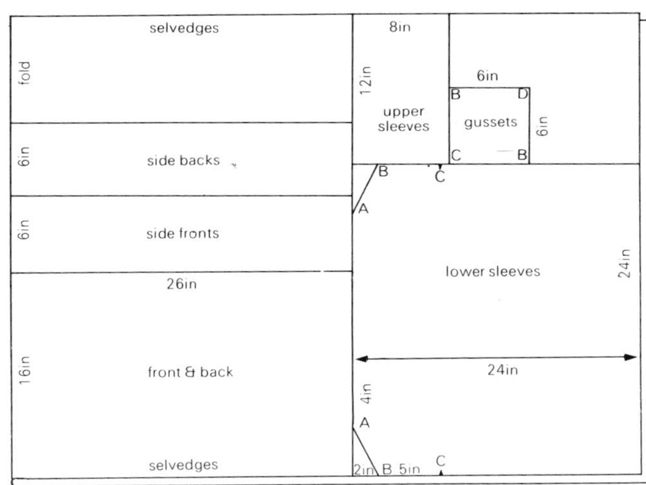

Making the blouse
1 Make a gathering line between points A along the fitting line at the top of each lower sleeve. Draw up evenly to fit the lower edge of the upper sleeve and stitch.
2 Stitch each lower sleeve seam to point C. Insert the gusset to the remaining section, matching points B and C.
3 Seam the sleeves and gussets between the side fronts and back, stitching from the top edge to base point of gusset (D). Then stitch the side seams from point D to the bottom.
4 Join the side fronts to the front and the side backs to the back. Work feather stitch (see p170) over the seamlines. Slit the CF for 6in (15cm), roll a narrow hem tapering from $\frac{1}{4}$in (5mm) to almost nothing at the bottom and blanket-stitch, taking care that the bottom is securely stitched.
5 Roll a $\frac{1}{4}$in (5mm) hem around the neck of the blouse and blanket-stitch, leaving an opening on each side of the front slit.

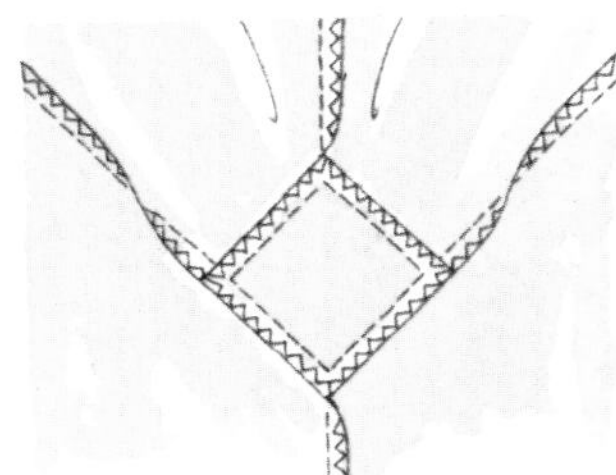

6 Roll hems at the bottom of each sleeve and blanket-stitch. Make casings 3in (8cm) above the hems by stitching binding flat on the WS. Insert elastic and draw up to fit. Join the ends and trim off the excess.
7 Turn up a narrow hem along the bottom of the blouse and slip-stitch.
8 Insert the cord through the neck hem to form a drawstring.

Binding 25
Hems 28
Fastenings 32
Pockets 92

Smock

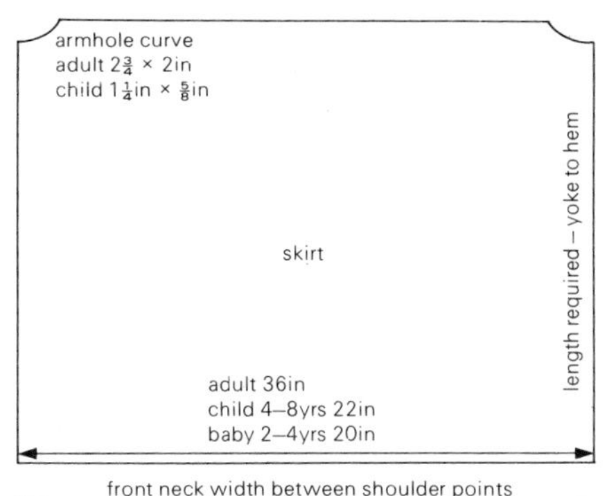

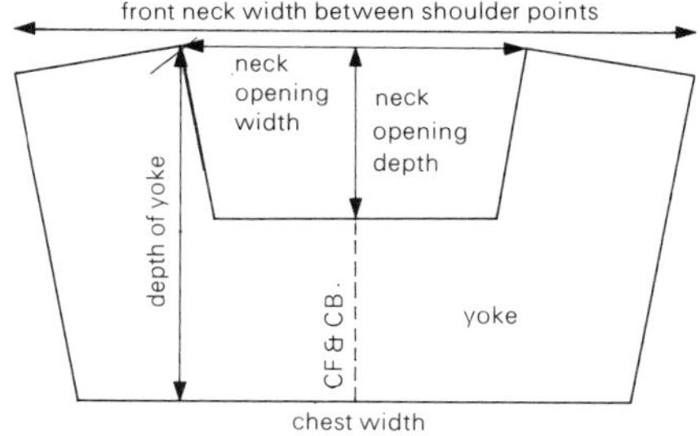

You will need

fabric, 36in (90cm) wide: twice required length from shoulder plus 8in (20cm)
matching sewing thread
buttons (optional)

Making the smock pattern

Draw the pattern pieces to the sizes shown on the diagram. Note that the side neck edge is parallel to the side yoke edge. Add $\frac{3}{4}$in (2cm) seam allowances all around the yoke and at the top of the skirt. Add a 2in (5cm) hem to the skirt.

Cutting out the smock

Skirt Cut 2 pieces from the pattern (front and back are the same).
Yoke Cut 2 pieces from the pattern plus 2 pieces for lining the yoke. From spare fabric cut facings or 1in (2·5cm) bias strips for finishing lower armhole curves. (Alternatively cut bias strips to bind neck and armholes completely.)
Pockets Cut patch pockets.

Making the smock

1 With RS together place yoke onto yoke lining. Stitch around neck edges and arm edges (unless binding these completely). Trim seams and turn RS out. Join and press open shoulder seams on yokes and yoke linings. (Alternatively, join shoulders and place yokes and lining with WS together and baste around neck and arm edges.)

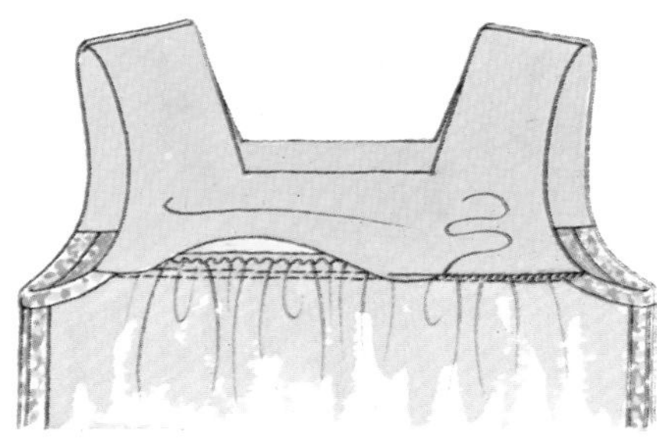

2 Join and press open side edges of skirt. Finish lower armhole curves with facing or binding (unless you are binding the armholes completely).
3 Gather top edges of skirt to fit bottom edges of yoke and stitch with RS together. Turn under and press seam allowances at bottom of yoke lining. Slip-stitch folds to seamlines.
4 If you wish to make an opening, cut down the CB to 2in (5cm) below yoke edge. Cut a bias strip from excess fabric and bind. Fasten with buttons and loops. (Bind armholes and neck if necessary.)
5 Turn up and stitch hem.

Interfacings, underlinings and interlinings

Interfacings
Few garments are made without an interfacing. This is a backing fabric applied to the main fabric before finishing to give extra strength and crispness to certain areas of a garment such as facings, collars and cuffs (see shaded areas in diagram). Interfacing materials are made in many different fibers, weights and degrees of crispness. Besides woven fabrics which are suitable for interfacings, there is a wide range of non-woven types made especially for the job. These can be used for most dressmaking purposes and are economical in that they can be cut in any direction, as there is no grain line to consider.

Choosing an interfacing
The interfacing must support the fabric without dominating it. Test it by holding the top fabric over the edge of a piece of interfacing. The fabric should roll gently over it. The care requirements of the top fabric and interfacing must be the same—non-wovens can usually be washed or dry-cleaned. Non-woven interfacing is made in 2 forms: one is sewn to the fabric and the other is attached by ironing. Usually it is a matter of personal choice, although iron-on interfacings tend to stiffen as well as support the fabric.

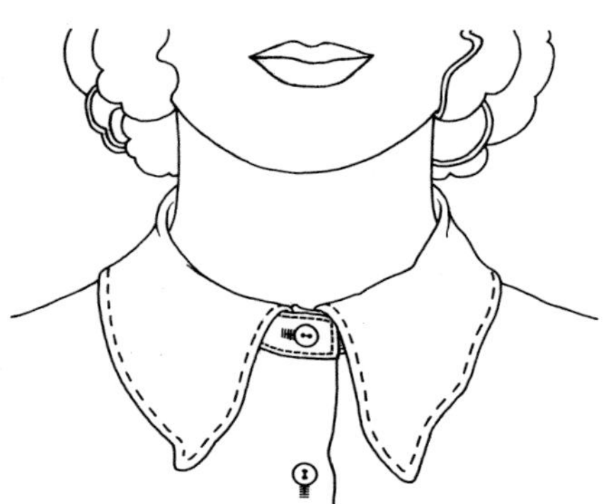

Collar with too soft an interfacing is floppy and will not hold its shape after washing.

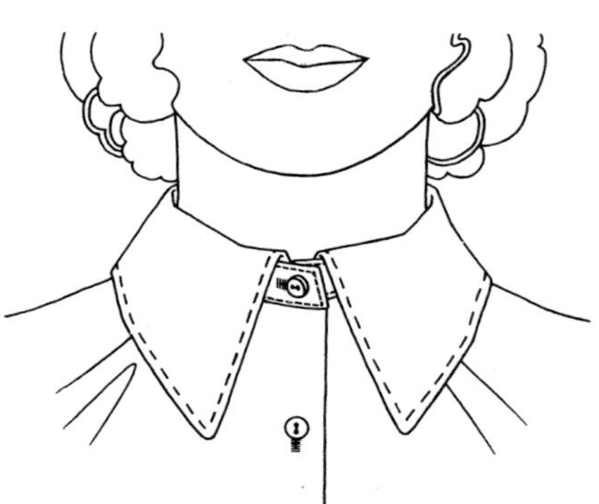

Collar with too firm an interfacing is uncomfortable to wear and will not mold around neck.

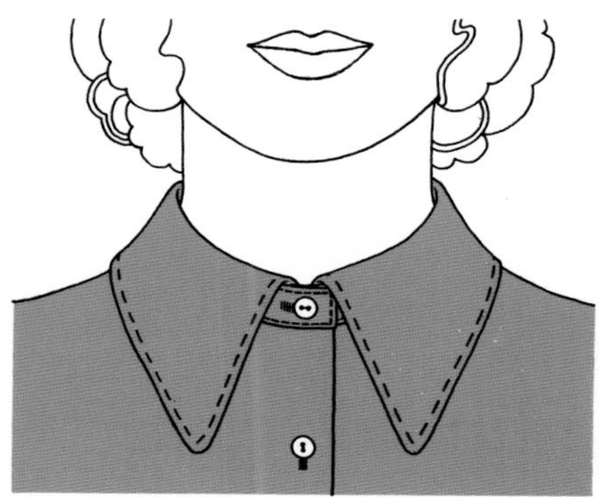

Collar with correct interfacing for fabric is comfortable to wear, molds to shape of neck and retains crispness.

Fabrics for interfacing

Main fabric	**Interfacing**
Dress-weight cotton, linen, wool	Pre-shrunk lawn, iron-on, non-woven
Suit-weight cotton, linen, wool	Cotton, iron-on, non-woven
Man-made fabrics	Non-woven
Pure silk	Lawn, pure silk organza
Sheers	Soft organdy, pure silk organza, transparent iron-on
Stretch fabric	Bias-cut woven interfacing of proportionate weight; special non-woven

Applying interfacing
Cut out the interfacing from the same pattern piece used for the section being interfaced. Usually it may be applied to main fabric or to the facing.
Heavy-weights Trim off the seam allowances all around the interfacing. With WS together, align the edges of the interfacing with the seamline of the fabric and baste in position. Secure by ironing (using a firm pressing motion so that it adheres smoothly) or by catch-stitching, according to type.

Light- and medium-weights
Baste interfacing to WS of garment sections just outside seamlines and iron on if necessary.
Treat interfacing and top fabric as one when stitching seams. Trim interfacing edges close to stitching before finishing seams.

Underlinings

An underlining is an additional layer of fabric mounted onto the back of certain top fabrics before assembling to give extra support, shape or opacity.
Underlining is essential on loosely woven fabrics to prevent sagging and stretching and it is also useful for concealing construction details such as seam allowances and hems on sheer fabrics.
Garments may be completely underlined or some areas may be left in top fabric only where a soft sheer effect is required, as on the sleeves of a blouse for example.
Interfacing should also be used on those areas which require it; apply it after the underlining.

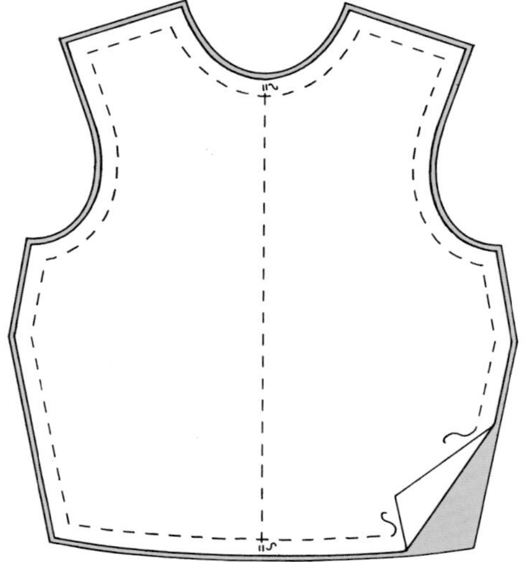

Choosing an underlining

Underlining fabrics should have both the same care requirements and the same amount of give or elasticity as the top fabric. Decide the effect you require in the area of the garment – on a dress, for example, you might choose a softer underlining for the bodice than for the skirt.
Choose the underlining in a color to enhance the top fabric and hold the two together against the light to judge whether the top fabric is adversely affected by the underlining.

Fabrics for underlining

Main fabric	Underlining
Silk, rayon, fine wool, linen	Pure silk organza, Japanese silk
Cotton	Taffeta, satin, chiffon
Lace	Lawn, muslin
Chiffon, sheers	Marquisette
Knitted fabrics	Light-weight tricot

Applying underlinings

Calculate the amount of underlining required by making a cutting layout.
Cut out the entire garment in top fabric and then cut out the pieces to be underlined in underlining fabric. With WS together, place each underlining section onto the appropriate garment section. Baste together down the center and all around the edge, just inside the seamlines. Transfer all pattern markings and work as if the 2 pieces were single fabric.

Before turning up hems, blind-hem underlining to top fabric just below the hemline.
Stitch the hem and facings to the underlining only.
Alternatively on very thick fabrics you may find it easier to treat the underlining separately from the top fabric for marking darts, tucks and pleats, then put the two layers together and treat them singly for seams and hems.

Interlinings

An interlining is a fabric applied to the inside of a garment after the underlining and interfacing, if any, to provide extra warmth.
Interlining fabrics should be light-weight and not bulky. Suitable fabrics are lamb's wool, polyester batting or fleece, felt, blanket fabric and cotton flannel. The care requirements should be the same as for the top fabric.

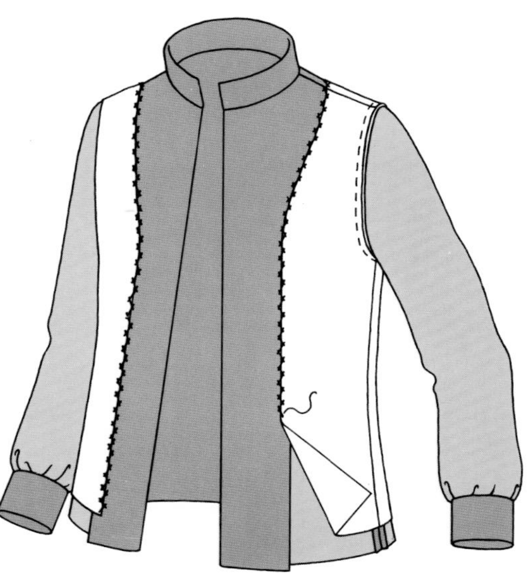

Applying interlinings

Check that your pattern has enough ease to allow for the added thickness. Sleeves are not usually interlined because it makes them too bulky.
Cut out and make up the interlining as for a lining, catch-stitch to the inner edges of the facings and baste to seam allowances around armholes.
Alternatively, treat the interlining as an underlining of the lining by mounting it to the WS of the lining, stitching the seams and then applying the 2 fabrics to the top fabric as if 1 layer.

Waistbands and cuffs

Basic stitches 18
Fastenings 32
Interfacings 36

Waistbands are used to conceal raw edges and to give a firm finish along the waistline at the top of skirt and slack openings. They can also be a decorative feature when made in unusual shapes or with the fabric cut at 90° to the garment or in a contrasting fabric, perhaps matched to cuffs, pockets or collars. Cuffs have a similar function at the lower edges of sleeves. They may be made with an opening or as a continuous band and are usually attached to extend the sleeve, although they can also be attached to turn back onto it.
Straight bands for cuffs or waists are usually made up from one piece of fabric which is folded in half lengthwise to form an outside and a facing section. These sections are cut in 2 pieces on shaped bands (i.e. where one edge is larger than the other) and stitched together around the edges. This method may also be used for straight waistbands; to reduce bulk on thick fabrics cut the facing section from lining fabric. Finish waistbands and most cuffs with a fastening.

Cuff patterns
If no cuff pattern is supplied, or you would like a different style, it is quite easy to make your own pattern.
Straight cuffs On all cuffs without an opening, the cuff must be wide enough for your hand to pass through comfortably. On ungathered and short sleeves, measure the lower edge and use this as the width of the cuff.
On gathered sleeves measure the width around your hand and add 1 in (2·5cm) ease. Draw a rectangle to the required width by twice the required depth and add seam allowances all around. Place this pattern on double fabric to cut out a pair of cuffs.

Cuffs with an opening Add an extra 2in (5cm) for an overlap.
Decide the depth of the cuff (e.g. 2in/5cm) and double it. Draw a rectangle to the calculated width by required depth and add seam allowances all around. Use this pattern to cut out each cuff through single thickness.
Mark the beginning of the overlap and the center of the long sides, excluding seam allowances and overlap.

Waistband patterns
Draw a rectangle to required waistband depth (e.g. 1–2in/2·5–5cm) by the waist measurement plus 1 in (2·5cm) ease plus $1\frac{1}{4}$in (3cm) for an overlap.
2-piece bands Add seam allowances all around the rectangle and use this pattern to cut 1 piece of fabric for band and 1 piece of fabric or lining for the facing.
Self-faced bands Double the depth of the band. Add seam allowances all around. Use this pattern to cut 1 piece of fabric for the waistband.
Shaped waistbands Draw required shape and add seam allowances all around.
Cut out and make as a 2-piece band.

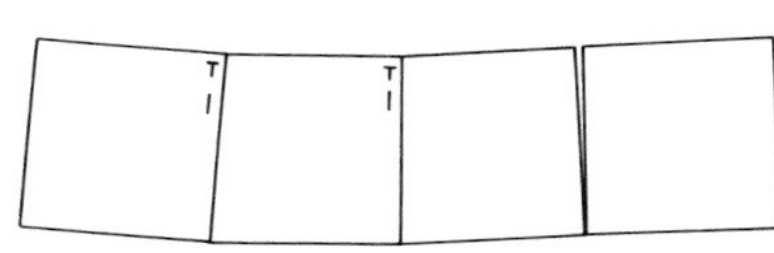

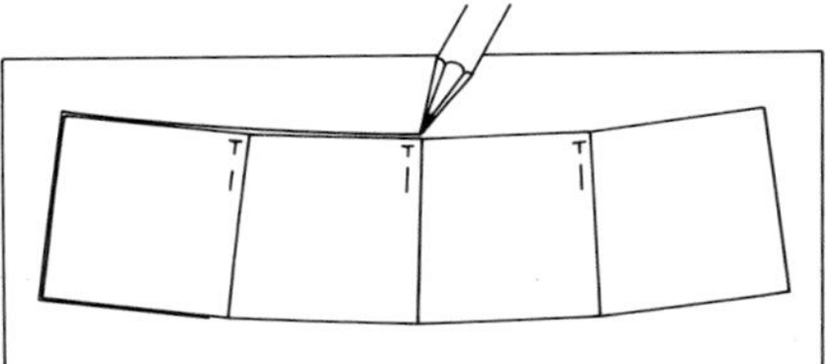

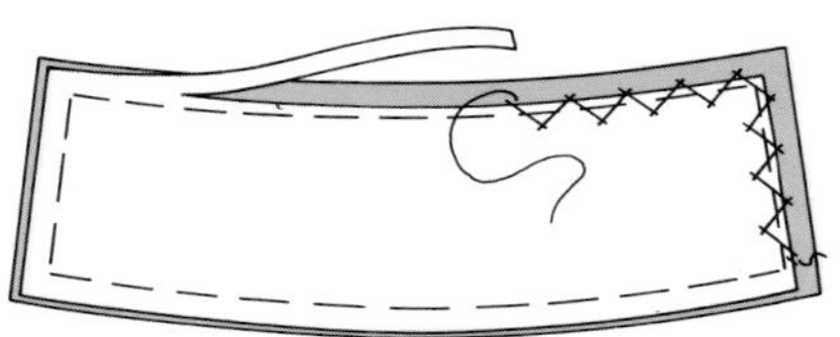

Shaped cuffs Measure your wrist loosely, then measure arm (or sleeve edge if ungathered) at required cuff depth above wrist. Draw a rectangle to required depth by upper width measurement and cut out. Divide the long edge of the rectangle into 4 equal sections and cut along lines to within $\frac{1}{8}$in (3mm) of opposite edge.
Close each slit to one-third of difference between upper and lower cuff measurements.

Place pattern on a new piece of paper and draw around shape. Add seam allowances all around. Fold pattern in half widthwise and crease the fold lightly. Open out and use the crease mark as a straight-grain line. Cut 2 sections of fabric for each cuff.

Interfacing
Both waistbands and cuffs should always be interfaced to retain their shape. Choose a suitable interfacing for your fabric or use grosgrain or boned stiffening for really firm waistbands. Make the interfacing the same size as the finished cuff or waistband (including seam allowances). Apply the interfacing to the section of fabric which will form the outside of the band before finishing and attaching to the garment.

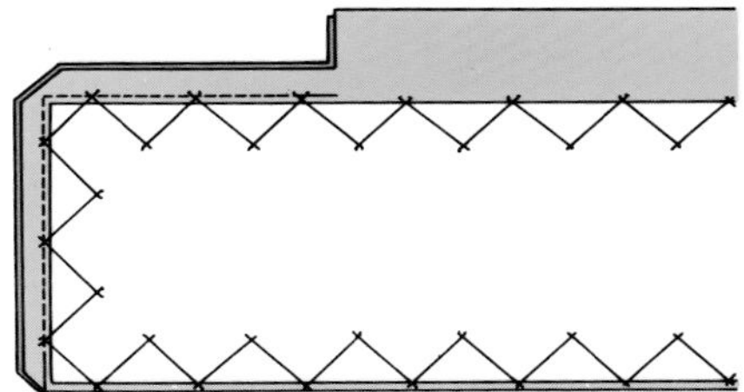

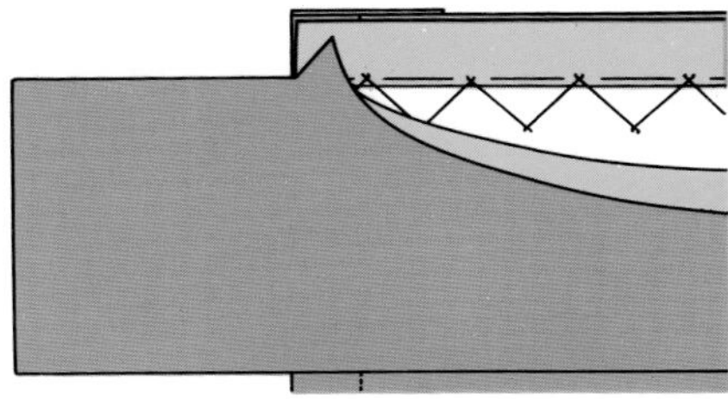

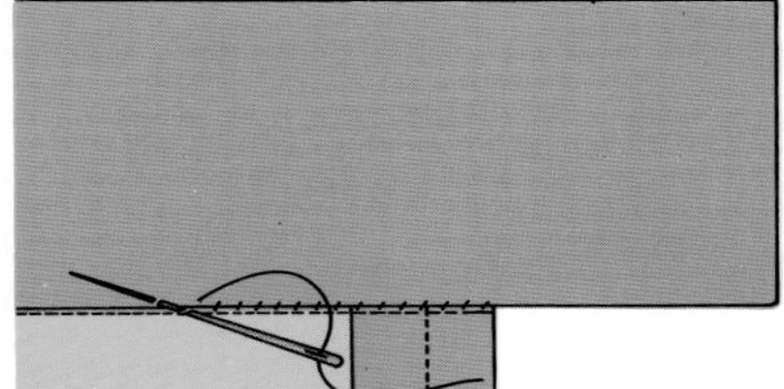

Making the band
1 Self-faced bands: fold the fabric in half lengthwise with RS together. Two-piece bands: place sections with RS together and stitch along seamline of top edge.
2 Stitch down short ends of band and along the long side to the end of the overlap. Trim the corners and the seam allowances. Turn RS out.

Attaching the band
Pin and baste interfaced edge of band to garment with RS together, raw edges even and center points matching. Check that the overlap lies in the correct position (on side openings this should be toward the back).

Machine-stitch band into position, trim seam and press upward into band. Turn under the seam allowance on the facing, place just above the seamline and hem. You may like to finish by top-stitching all around the edge of the band.

Turn-back cuffs
Cut out like shaped cuffs, making the narrow edge fit the bottom of the sleeve and the wide edge fit it at the required cuff depth from the bottom.
1 With RS together, stitch the 2 pieces together along the short ends and the longer edge. Trim the seam allowances and cut across the corners diagonally to within $\frac{1}{8}$in (3mm) of the stitching. Turn RS out and press.

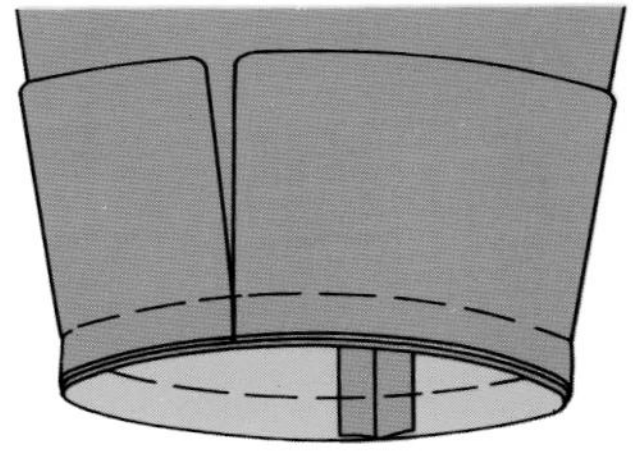

2 Pin and baste cuff to sleeve with RS together and raw edges even.

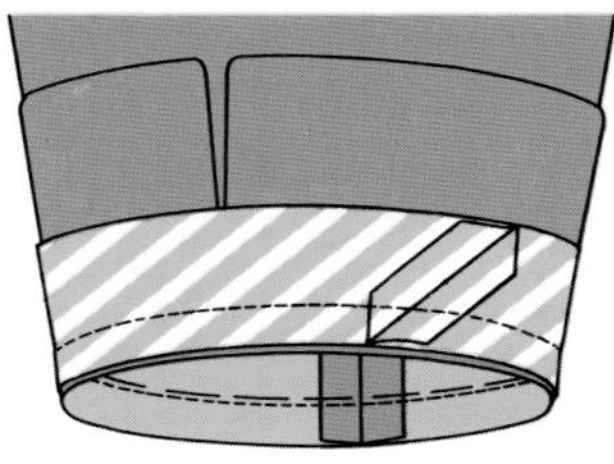

3 Cut and join a bias strip, 1 in (2·5cm) wide, to fit edge. With RS together and raw edges even, pin, baste and stitch along seamline. Turn cuff downward and press seam up toward sleeve.

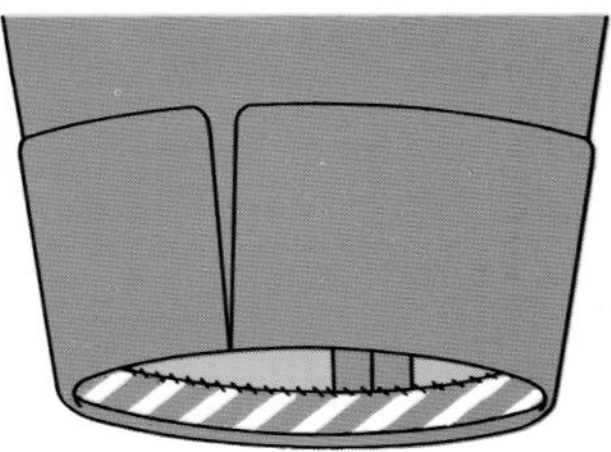

4 Turn bias strip completely to inside of sleeve and press along seamline. Turn under the raw edge and slip-stitch to the inside of sleeve. Turn up cuff so that fold lies about $\frac{1}{8}$in (3mm) below strip.

Double turn-back cuffs
Straight cuffs Cut pattern as for single straight cuffs but to fit sleeve edge. Cut out the fabric with the top edge of the pattern placed to a fold.
Shaped cuffs Draw a rectangle 4 times the finished depth of the cuff by the width of the upper edge. Fold the pattern in 4 horizontally. Draw a line on each side, tapering to the required width of the cuff (i.e. to fit sleeve).
Cut along these lines. Open out the pattern and cut each cuff through single thickness.

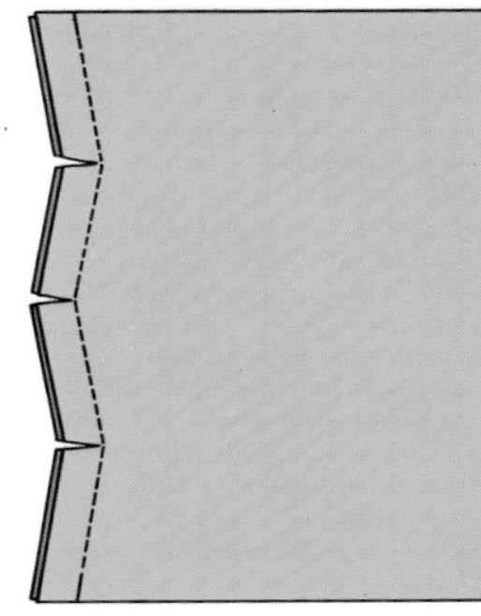

Finishing shaped cuffs
1 With RS together and zigzag-shaped sides aligned, stitch short ends of cuff together. Snip curves and press the seam open.

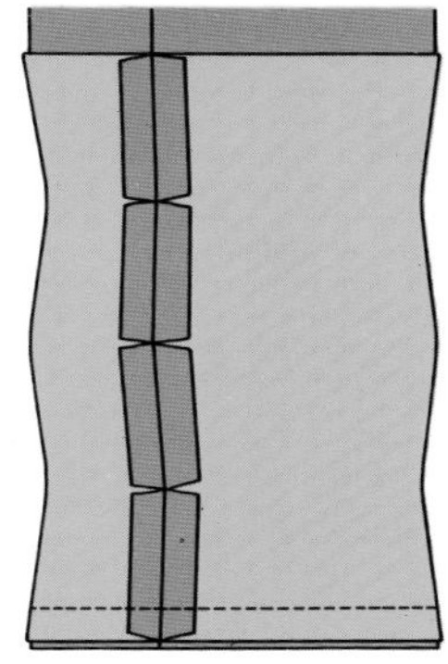

2 Slip the cuff onto the sleeve, with RS together, seams aligning and raw edges even. Pin, baste and stitch into position. Press seam allowances toward the cuff.

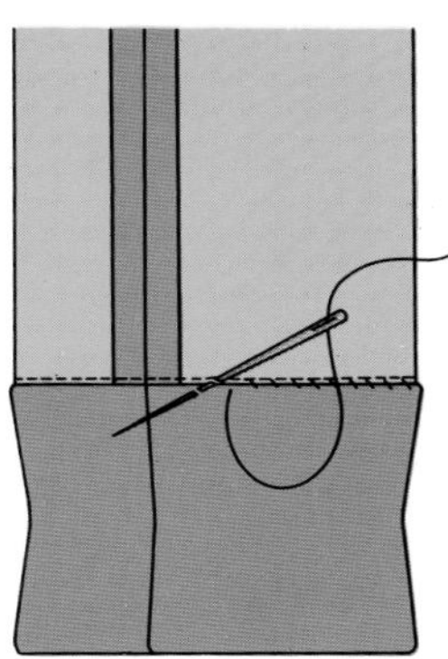

3 Turn sleeve inside out. Turn under seam allowance on remaining raw edge of cuff and press. Place the fold to the seamline and slip-stitch in position. Turn the sleeve RS out and fold up the cuff so that the seamline is just covered.

Pleating

Basic stitches 18
Hems 28

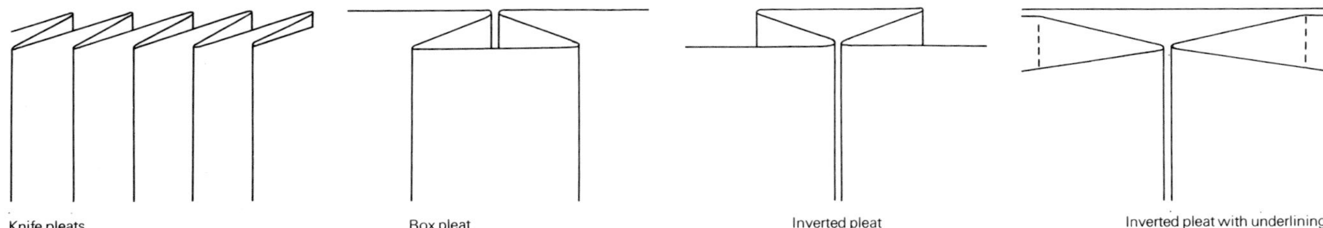

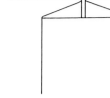

Knife pleats | Box pleat | Inverted pleat | Inverted pleat with underlining

Different types of pleats may be made by folding fabric in different ways. Knife pleats are a series of folds going one way; box and inverted pleats are knife pleats facing each other on either the inside or outside of the garment. Single inverted pleats may also be made in seam openings (e.g. in CB seams above the hem – see method opposite).
It is not difficult to plan your own pleating design. Series of pleats are easiest to form on the straight grain of fabric, particularly when you can use patterns such as stripes or plaids, and you can make a fully pleated skirt from a strip of fabric by this method (see page 43).
Single pleats may also be added to plain skirt patterns, in which case they can be formed on the bias to give a better line on flared skirts.
The depths of pleats may vary from about $\frac{3}{4}$–3in (2–8cm). Consider the fabric you are using and the effect you want to achieve. Generally, the heavier the fabric the deeper the pleats should be. Shallow pleats tend to open out and are best made in groups so they can give a fan effect.
To make a firm pleat, choose crisp fabrics able to form a sharp crease under pressure or steam, such as worsted woolens, linen and firm cottons. Polyesters and acrylics can also be used but you should test them first. Finish washable fabrics with edge stitching so that the pleat lines remain even.
Extra bulk on pleated skirts from waist to hips may be minimized by top-stitching the pleats through all thicknesses and releasing them from the hipline. You can then trim the excess fabric from the underside and finish the area with a separate underlining to support the tops of the pleats.

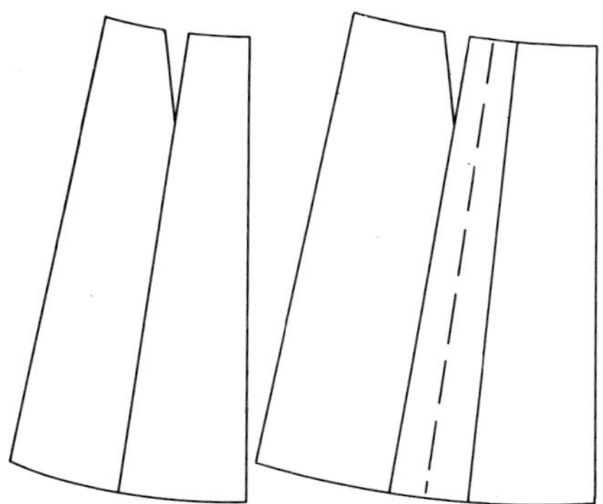

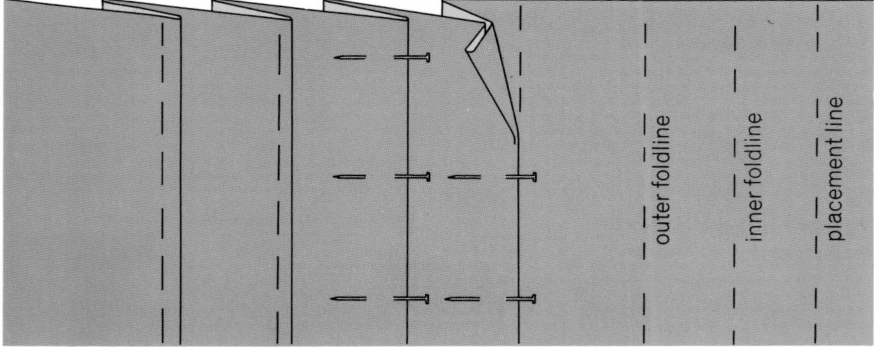

Adding pleats to patterns
To add single knife pleats to plain patterns, mark position of pleat with a straight line down length of pattern. (The diagram shows the line drawn as an extension of the inner dart line.) Slit pattern along line and open out to twice required pleat depth. Insert a strip of paper to fit and draw a line down its center to mark inner foldline. The outer foldline and placement line lie along the edges of the strip.

Marking foldlines
Paper patterns should show 3 lines for each pleat: outer foldline, inner foldline and placement line.
The arrangement of the lines varies according to the type of pleat, but in each case the pleat depth is always the distance from the outer foldline to the inner foldline.
Transfer the markings from pattern to fabric with tailor's tacks worked at regular intervals down the lines, using a contrasting thread for outer foldlines and different colors for inner foldlines and for placement lines.

Pinning and basting pleats
Remove pattern. Working from left to right on the RS, fold the first pleat along the outer foldline and place fold on placement line. Pin fold through all thicknesses. Repeat for remaining pleats, removing tailor's tacks as each pleat is pinned. Baste pleats through all thicknesses, using silk thread to avoid marking.

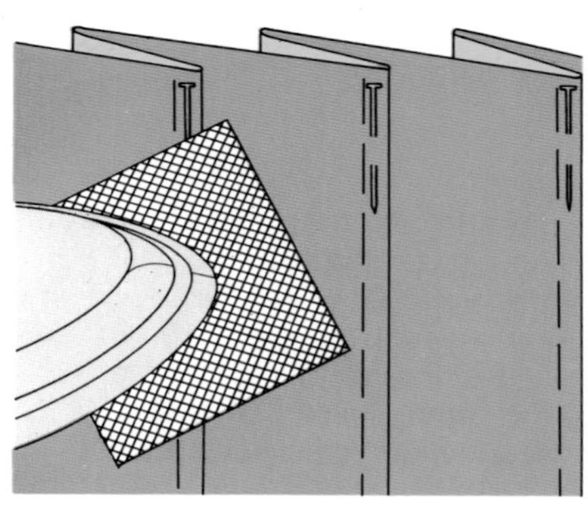

Pressing pleats
1 Place pleats RS up on ironing board, supporting the rest of the fabric on a chair or table to prevent pleats being distorted. Press folds, using a pressing cloth. If sharp pleats are required, dampen the cloth and let pleats dry before moving them.

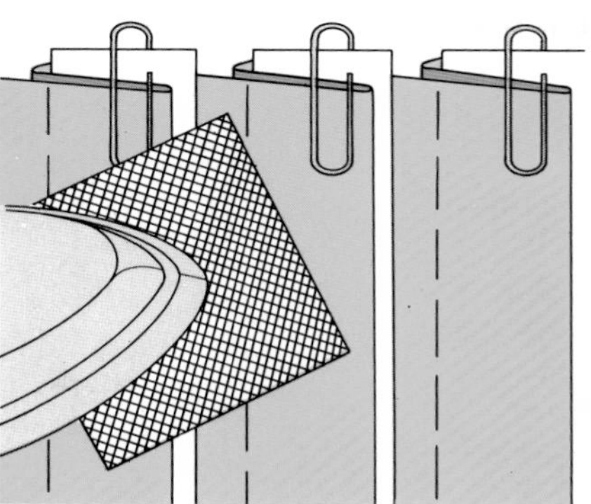

2 Place pleats WS up on ironing board and press again. If ridges are formed by the under folds, gently press beneath each fold and then insert a strip of thin cardboard under each pleat and press again.

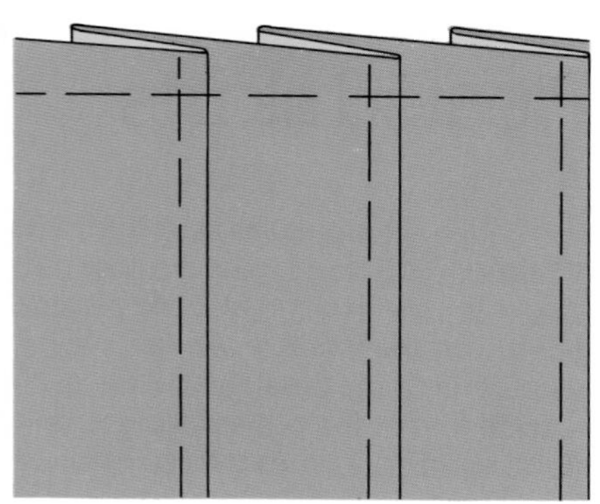

Securing upper edge
Hand-baste through all layers along seamline of upper edge to hold pleats firmly in place.

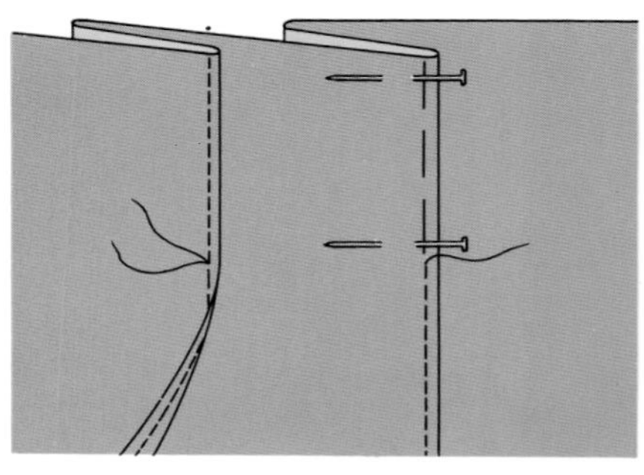

Top stitching and edge stitching
If you are combining top and edge stitching do both after turning up the hem but before attaching the waistband. Do edge stitching first from hem to the top of the pleat. Cut off the threads, leaving long ends. Continue top stitching through all thicknesses from hips to waist. The lines of stitching should meet exactly. Tie ends on WS.

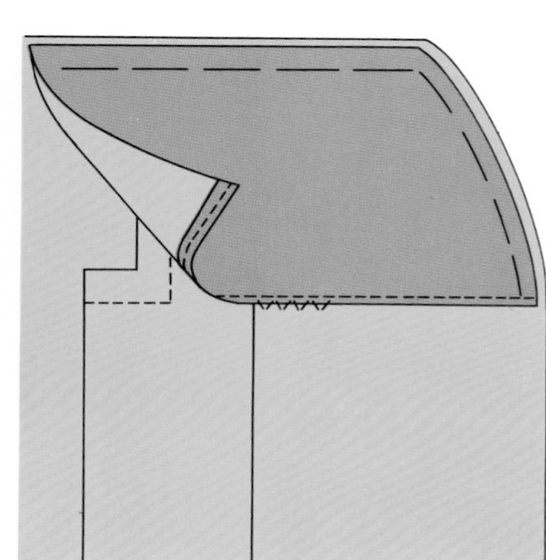

Stitched pleats with underlining
Top-stitch each pleat in usual way then turn to WS and stitch across inside pleat at bottom of top stitching to inner pleat fold. Trim undersides of pleats to within $\frac{5}{8}$in (1·5cm) of stitching. Cut an underlining from lining fabric to width of garment section and to depth of pleating, plus seam allowances. Finish lower edge and baste underlining in place along top and side edges with WS together. Slip-stitch lower edge to tops of pleats.

Inverted pleats, separate underlining
1 Decide the depth and length of pleat and add depth measurement to seam allowances for required length plus $\frac{5}{8}$in (1·5cm).
2 Stitch seam to top of pleat and press open seams including pleat. Fold back raw edges and turn up hem. Baste pleat foldlines together for length of pleat and open seam again.
3 Cut matching underlining to pleat length, plus $\frac{5}{8}$in (1·5cm) seam allowance at the top and hem allowance at the bottom, by full pleat depth plus seam allowances.
4 Turn up hem on underlining to correspond with garment. With RS together and raw edges even, position underlining on pleat seam allowance. Baste and machine-stitch in position along sides and across top through underlining and turnings only.

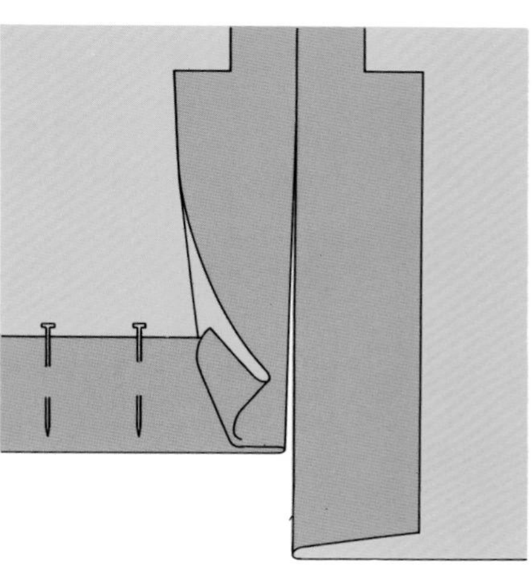

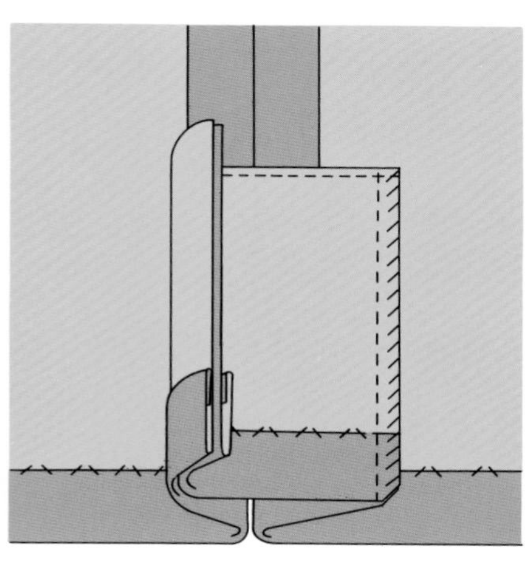

Pleated skirts

Measuring the figure 14
Hems 28
Waistbands 38
Pleating 40

You can make a pleated skirt from a long straight strip of fabric—you don't need a paper pattern because there is no intricate shaping and the pleats can be marked directly on the fabric. For close pleating, where the inside fold of the pleat lies on the same line as the outside fold of the previous pleat, you need a strip of fabric equal to 3 times the hip measurement (including ease); seam the fabric to make up the width if necessary. For adult sizes this usually requires a great deal of fabric but it is possible to make a more economical version from one width of 54 or 66in (137 or 168cm) fabric or two widths of 36in (90cm) fabric by spacing the pleats farther apart. The charts show how to calculate the amount of fabric required and the pleat depths.

If you are planning to base the pleat depth on the fabric design (e.g. stripes and plaids) you need not mark the foldlines with tailor's tacks, providing you keep the depth even throughout. You should experiment first by pleating a small area so that you can see the effect on the pattern. With regular designs you can change the effect substantially by the depth of pleats and the lines you choose for the outer and inner folds (see opposite). Remember that this might make it difficult to match the pattern formed to the basic pattern if you are attaching the pleats to that fabric on a bodice, for example.

Making the skirt

1 Measure and mark the skirt length across the fabric, adding hem and waist seam allowances. On patterns to be matched at seams, check the length of the repeat and round up the skirt length to a multiple of it. Cut each width to this length and then trim off the excess amount.

2 Mark the pleat fold and placement lines, starting and ending with a seam allowance next to a single pleat depth on each width so that seams always fall on an inside fold of a pleat. Trim off any excess fabric.

3 Turn up single hems on each width and blind-hem. Join sections of the skirt, matching pattern where necessary, leaving an opening for the zipper in a side seam. Press all seams flat as stitched, trim seams diagonally across corners of lower edge and overcast together.

4 Pleat fabric, basting from hipline to hem but leaving upper part pinned only on each pleat. The skirt should now fit at the hips but must be adjusted at the waist.

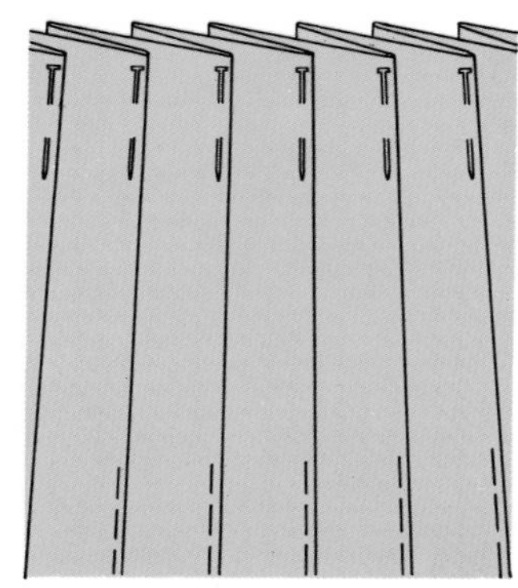

Fitting the waistline

Use the chart as a guide to calculate how much to adjust each pleat. Turn under the extra amount on each pleat at the waist, tapering down to original pleat depth at the hips.

Pin, baste and check fit before inserting zipper and attaching waistband. The example on the chart is for a 26in (65cm) waist and 36in (90cm) hips.

Fitting pleats at waistline

	For example:
1 Add 2in (5cm) ease to waist.	26in + 2in = 28in
2 Find the difference between this figure and the hip measurement plus 2in (5cm) ease.	38in − 28in = 10in
3 Divide the amount by the number of pleats, e.g. 40 pleats.	10in ÷ 40 = ¼in for tapering each pleat

Calculating close pleating

Distance between pleats is equal to pleat depth.

	For example:
1 Measure hips; add 2in (5cm) ease.	34in + 2in = 36in
2 Decide depth of pleat and divide into total hip measurement to give number of knife pleats (box or inverted pleats will be half this).	36in ÷ 1in = 36 pleats
3 Multiply pleat depth by 3 to give distance between pleat lines.	1in × 3 = 3in
4 Multiply total hip measurement by 3 to give total width of fabric.	36in × 3 = 108in
Add 1½in (4cm) for seam allowances.	108in + 1½in = 109½in
5 Divide total by your fabric width; round up for required number of widths (cut waistband from excess).	109½in ÷ 36in = 4 (rounded up)
6 Multiply number of widths by skirt length (round up to multiple of pattern repeat) to give total amount.	4 × 28in = 112in

Pleating for a given width of fabric

Distance between pleats is usually more than depth of pleat.

	For example:
1 Measure hips; add 2in (5cm) ease.	34in + 2in = 36in
2 Subtract 1½in (4cm) seam allowances from width of fabric.	54in − 1½in = 52½in
3 Subtract hip measurement to give amount of pleating fabric.	52½in − 36in = 16½in
4 Decide depth of pleat (e.g. 1in/2·5cm) and multiply by 2. Divide total into amount of pleating fabric to give number of pleats.	16½in ÷ 2 = 8 + ¼ (add this ¼in to seam allowances)
5 Divide hip measurement by number of pleats to give space between placement line and next pleat line.	36in ÷ 8 = 4½in

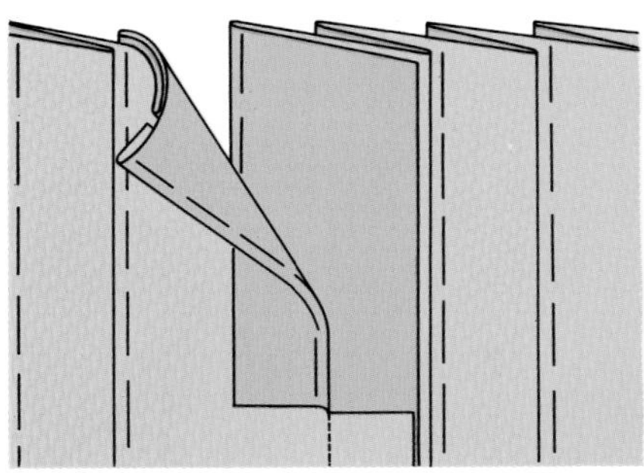

Zippers in pleated skirts
1 Stitch seam to lower end of zipper opening. On WS clip into LH seam allowance, turn back and baste.

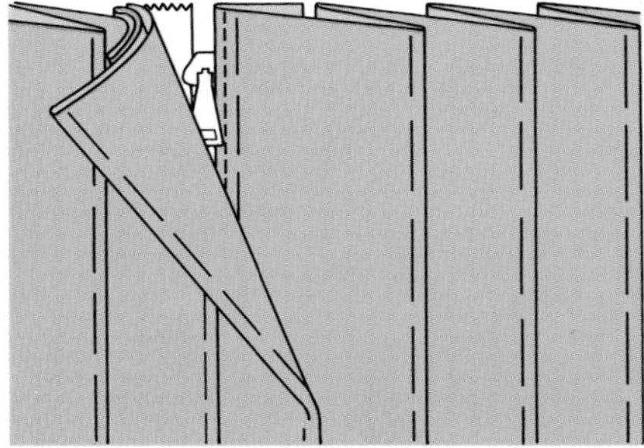

2 Working on RS with lower end of zipper even with end of opening, baste folded edge close to zipper teeth on RH side, then machine-stitch as close to teeth as possible. On WS baste and then machine-stitch LH side of zipper tape to seam allowance only. The zipper will thus be hidden inside the pleat.

Darts and tucks

Basic stitches 18

Darts are stitched tapered folds made on the wrong side of fabric to shape and mold it to the contours of the body. They are formed in bodices to give fullness to the bust; in skirts and slacks to taper the fabric from hips to waist; at the shoulders to give ease over the back; and in tight sleeves to give ease at the elbows. It is essential to check their position against your body before cutting out (after adjusting the pattern for overall size) so that you can achieve a smooth fit.

Tucks are stitched folds made on the straight grain on the right side of fabric as decoration or to give shaping. They may be formed in a close series as blind tucks or they may be spaced out. They can vary in width from $\frac{3}{4}$in (2cm) to tiny pin size of about $\frac{1}{8}$in (3mm) for use on small areas. They may be made to the full length of a garment section or they could be stitched part of the way down to give fullness below. When made like this on the wrong side they are known as dart tucks.

Pin tucks can be made on most fabrics but wider tucks should be made only on fabrics which can take a sharp crease. You can add tucks to any pattern by forming them in the fabric before cutting out.

Checking bust darts
Cut out half the bodice pattern in spare plain cotton. Mark dart positions but do not form them. Wearing your usual bra and a closely fitting sweater, pin the fabric in position on the sweater. Place a pin in the fabric at the point of your bust and check whether the dart points directly to it. If it doesn't, re-draw the angle of the dart when you remove the pattern.

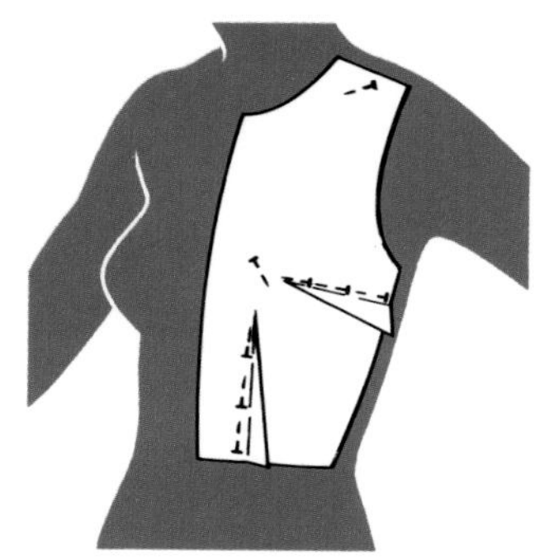

Enlarging bust darts If you have a full bust, increase the side and waist darts and add the same amount to the side and waist edges. If your bust is rounded, make the darts shorter and stitch them in a slight curve.

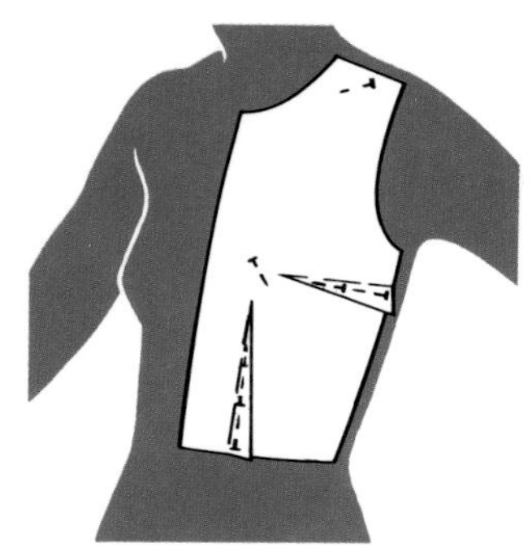

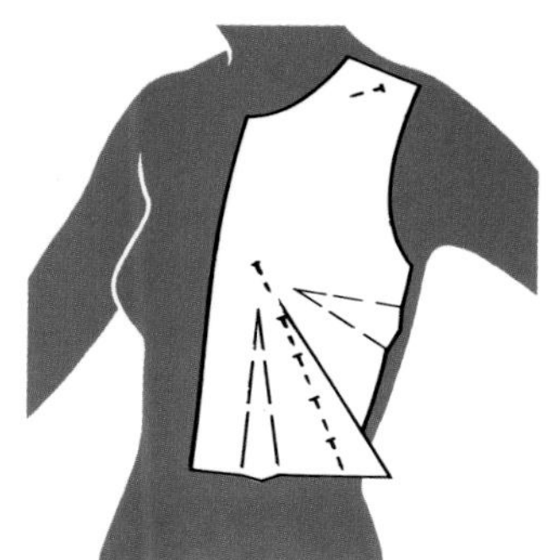

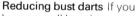

Reducing bust darts If you have a small bust in proportion to your back, reduce the darts by stroking away the fullness so that the fabric lies closely against the body and pin the dart to the required reduced amount. Take in the side and waist seamline by the same amount. Alternatively you can combine the waist and side darts in a diagonal dart from the corner of the bodice.

Checking hip darts
Cut out half the pattern in spare plain cotton and mark the darts but do not form them. Wear a smooth-fitting skirt and pin the sample to it. You will need help in fitting the skirt at the back.

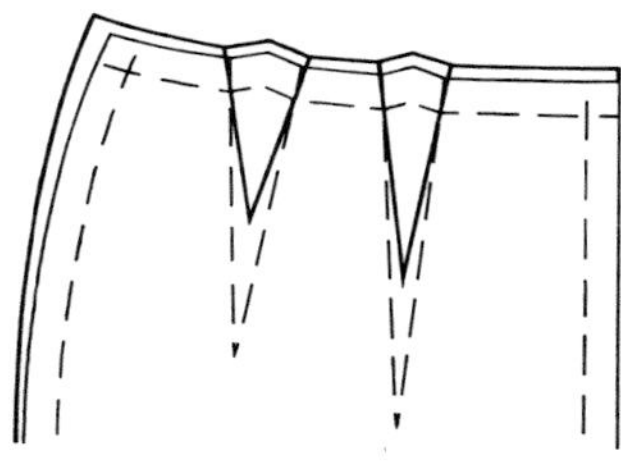

Protruding seat To add fullness over the seat shorten the darts, raise the waistline and add width as shown. Curve darts very slightly inward when stitching.

Protruding hip bones If this causes pulling across the front of the garment, move darts farther toward side seams. If you have to increase the size of the dart, add the same amount to the side edges.

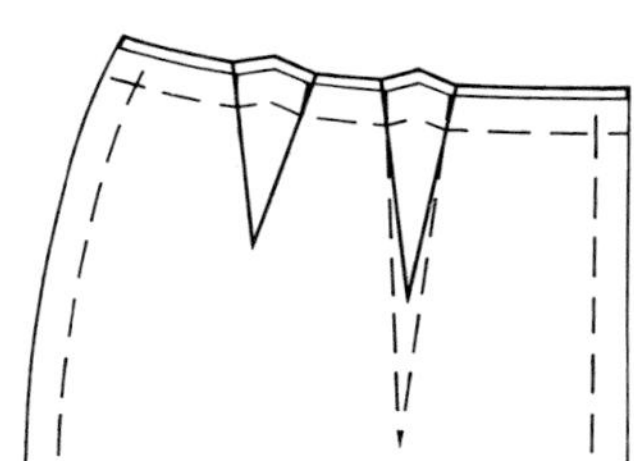

Reducing waist size If your waist is small in proportion to your hips, take in the amount to be reduced equally on the front and back at the side seams. Alternatively reduce the amount taken in and make extra darts.

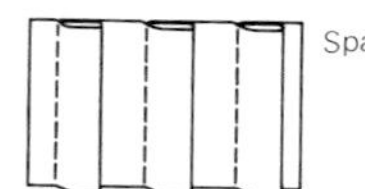

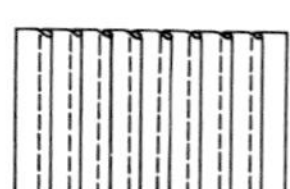

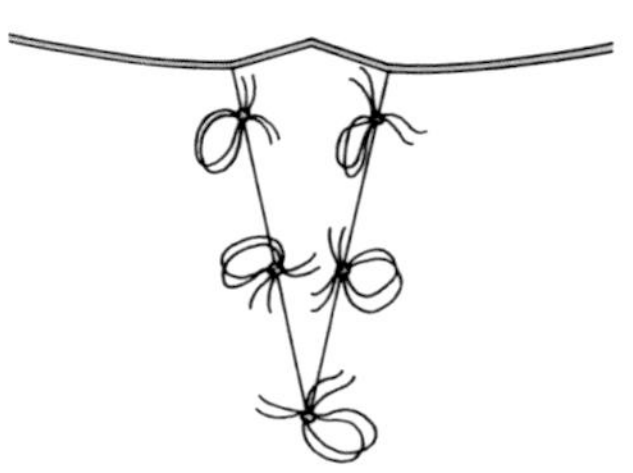

Making darts
Darts are shown on patterns as thin triangles or diamonds. If your pattern is on thick paper, use a hole punch to make perforations at the point, base and center of the dart. Mark the darts with tailor's tacks.

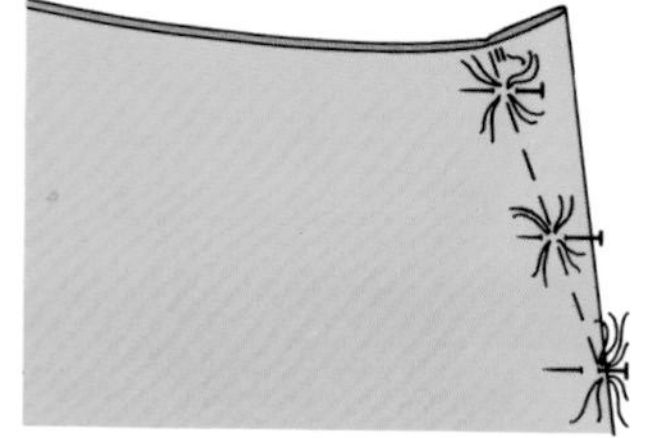

Basting darts
Working on the WS, fold dart in half lengthwise with RS together, matching tailor's tacks. Pin and baste along stitching line between tacks. Remove tacks.

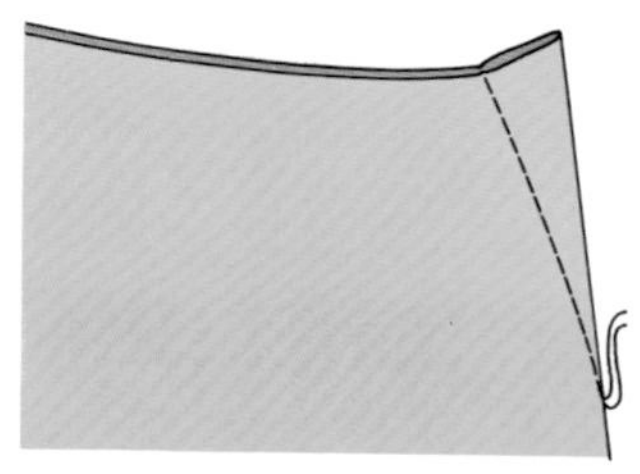

Stitching darts
To prevent the dart from bulging, stitch from its base toward the point in a subtle curve. Don't pull fabric while stitching. Cut off threads, leaving 4in (10cm) ends.

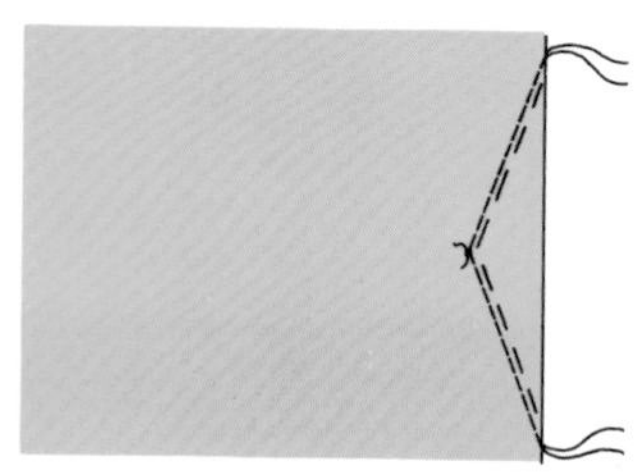

Contour darts
Stitch in 2 steps starting from the widest part and working to the point.

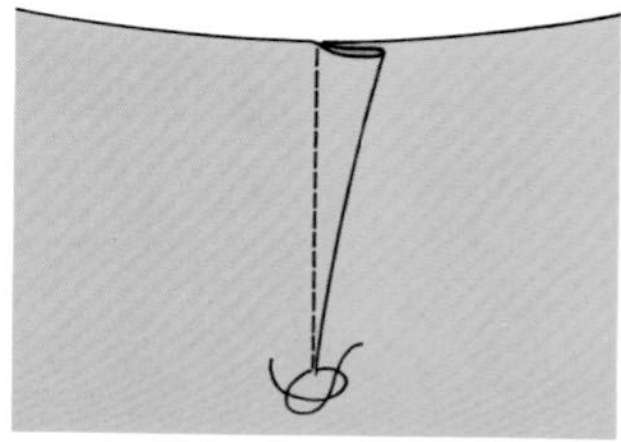

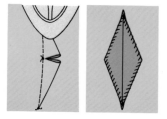

Finishing darts
Knot ends of threads together exactly at point of dart.

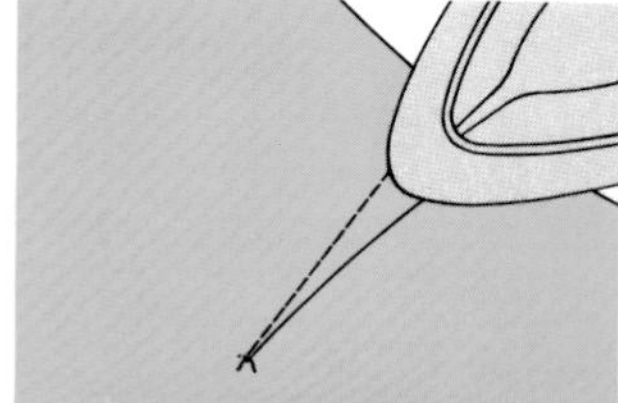

Pressing darts
Press before main garment seams are stitched. Lay garment over rounded end of ironing board or over a tailor's form to mold dart. Press toward point with fold of dart to center of garment.

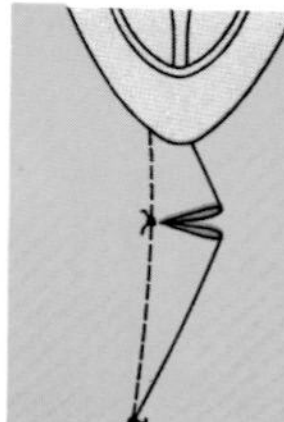

Contour darts Clip at widest part and press toward center.
Thick fabrics Cut open down center fold and press dart flat. Finish raw edges with overcasting or zigzag stitch.

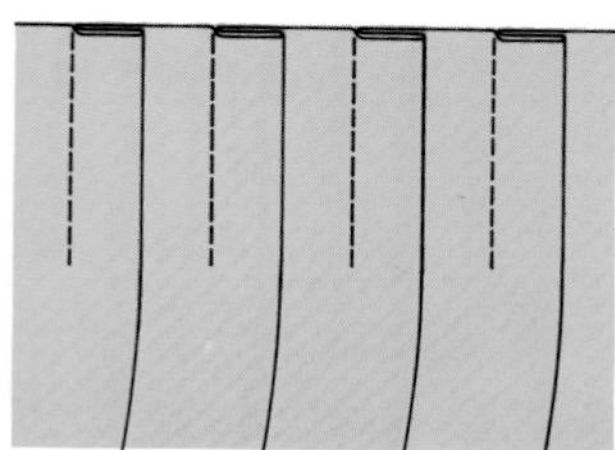

Dart tucks
Working on the WS, bring tuck markings with RS together, baste and machine-stitch. Tie off thread ends on WS. Press stitching only to avoid creasing the folds.

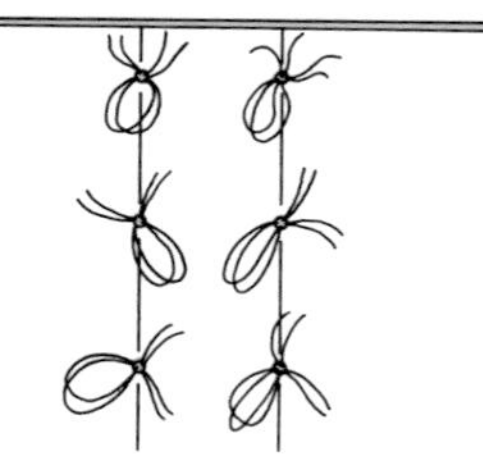

Making tucks
Patterns If tucks are marked on the paper pattern, make tailor's tacks at regular intervals down the stitching lines. Remove pattern, fold tuck in half lengthwise with WS together and matching tailor's tacks. Baste and stitch along stitching line.

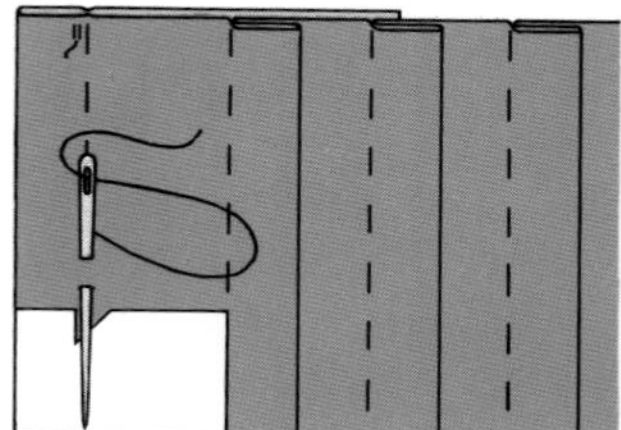

Gauges Use a gauge to mark fabric where tucks are not shown on a pattern. Cut a cardboard strip to width of tuck plus space required between them. Cut a notch the tuck width away from LH edge. Starting at RH edge, form the first tuck and baste it. Place RH edge of gauge to basting, fold under fabric level with LH edge of gauge, baste and stitch in line with notch.

Pressing tucks
Press each tuck as stitched, using a pressing cloth. Then press all tucks in final direction. Work a line of stay stitching along the fitting line at the top of the tucks to hold them in place during remaining part of garment construction.

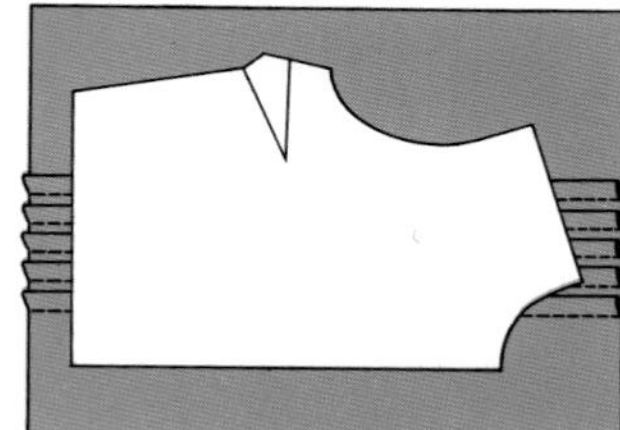

Adding tucks to patterns
Decide where you would like tucks (e.g. in bands on each side of the CF) and check that they do not cross any darts. Mark the tucks in a suitable position on the fabric with a gauge, stitch and press them. Lay the paper pattern over them and cut out in the usual way.

Circles

To make a skirt, cape, blouse or ruffle from a full or semi-circle you don't need a paper pattern. They can be cut out from fabric by drawing concentric circles for the waist or neck opening and for the hem. The finished length is determined by the size of the opening, the width of fabric and the way it is folded. It is possible to increase the length by seaming a strip of fabric to the selvedge before cutting out but this may leave you with a seam in an unattractive position on the garment. Don't add length by joining onto the circular edge of the cut fabric because it is very difficult to obtain a smooth effect when seaming bias edges in this way. Choose fabrics which are soft and drape well on the bias grain. Avoid stripes and plaids because they will run in different directions at seams.
Finish the outer edges of circular garments with binding or with a shallow or rolled hem.

Drawing circles
For full-circle garments draw a semi-circle to be cut through double fabric, which will give you the full circle when opened out. For semi- and quarter-circles draw a quarter circle.
1 Find the center of the circle (see detailed instructions opposite) and place the end of a yard-stick at that point. Mark off the length of the required radius (see opposite/below) at the edge of the fabric in chalk.
2 Turn the stick, keeping the end at the center, marking the length of the circle at 1in (2·5cm) intervals until you reach the opposite edge. Join the marks with a chalk line.

Quarter-circles
You can make a hip-hugging skirt from a quarter-circle. It is cut in 1 piece and made with a CB seam, so that the bias grain falls at the front and the straight grain at the back. Draw the quarter-circle on single fabric, using a radius of two-thirds of your waist measurement.

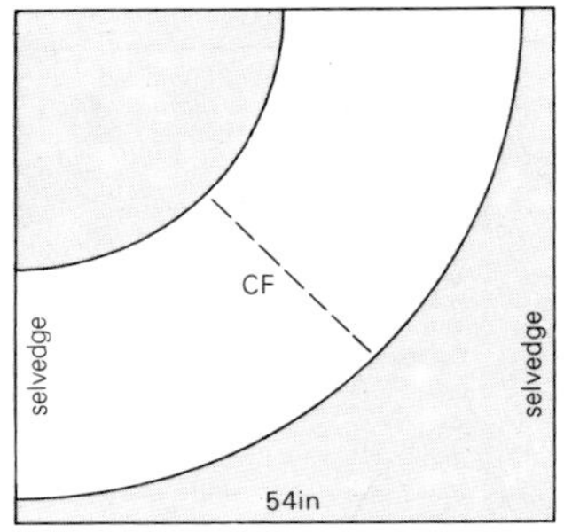

slit
fold
selvedges
54in

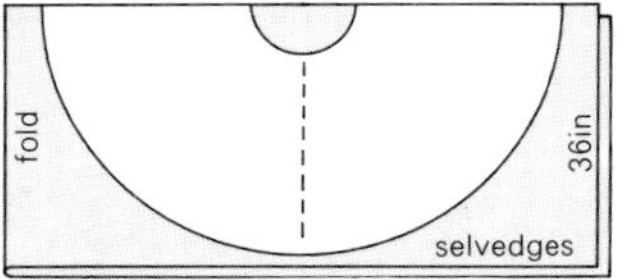

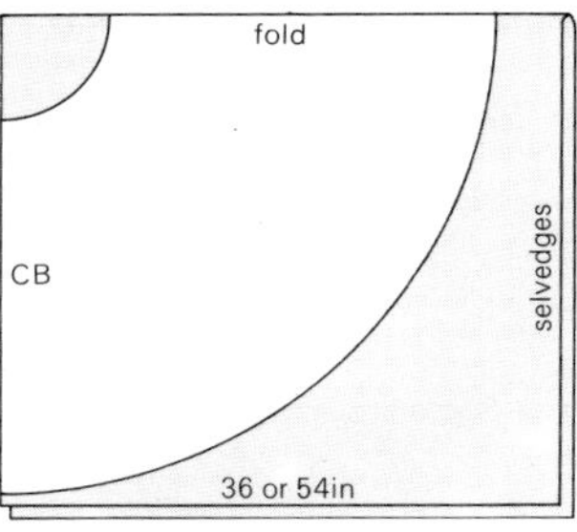

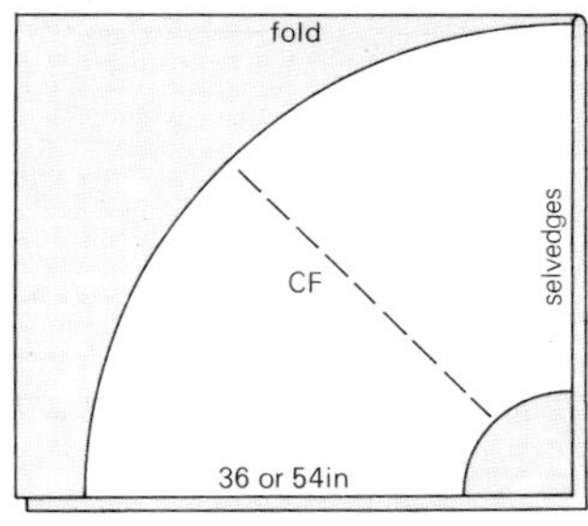

Full circles
In wide fabric a short skirt or blouse can be cut in 1 piece. To make an opening slit the fold and form a CB seam. For a 24in (60cm) waist, maximum length is $22\frac{3}{4}$in (58cm) in 54in (136cm) fabric or 26in (65cm) in 59–60in (150cm) fabric.
In 36in (90cm) fabric you can make a mid-calf-length skirt by folding the fabric in half widthwise, cutting 2 semi-circles and seaming them together at the sides. For a 24in (60cm) waist maximum length is 32in (80cm).
1 Fold fabric as shown for appropriate width. For the length of the radius to draw the waist or neck opening, calculate one-sixth of their circumference and draw a semi-circle from edge to edge.
2 Determine the maximum finished length by measuring from the curve to the edge of fabric. Add your required length (including hem allowance) within this maximum to the radius of the waist or neck curve and draw a second curve to this length, keeping the end of the yardstick at the center.
3 Allow $\frac{5}{8}$in (15mm) for seams at waist or neck and cut out.

Semi-circles
These can be cut in 1 or 2 pieces, depending on whether you want the straight or bias grain to fall at the CF or CB. If cutting in 2 pieces the seams will fall at the sides; with 1 piece the seam will come at the CB. In 54in (136cm) fabric with a 24in (60cm) waist, maximum length is $45\frac{1}{2}$in (116cm). In 36in (90cm) fabric maximum length is 32in (80cm).
1 Fold the fabric widthwise as shown above. To draw waist or neck opening calculate the radius as one-sixth of their circumference. Place the end of the ruler at the appropriate corner of the fabric and draw a quarter-circle from edge to edge.
2 Calculate the finished length as a full circle and draw a second quarter-circle.
3 Cut out as for a full circle.

Seams 20
Binding 25
Zippers 26

Hems 28
Waistbands 38
Darts 44

Ruffles
Use circles for cuffs or around a neckline. For longer edges you will need a lot of fabric to cut several circles of same circumference, slit each to the center and join them to make the required length. To save fabric you can cut ruffles from semi-circles.

1 For a ruffle to fit exactly around a cuff or neck, measure the edge to which the ruffle will be attached. Draw a circle with a radius of one-sixth this length for the inner edge of the ruffle. Draw a 2nd circle for the outer edge to give the depth of the ruffle plus ⅝in (15mm) seam allowance. Cut out allowing ⅝in (15mm) for seams along inner edge.

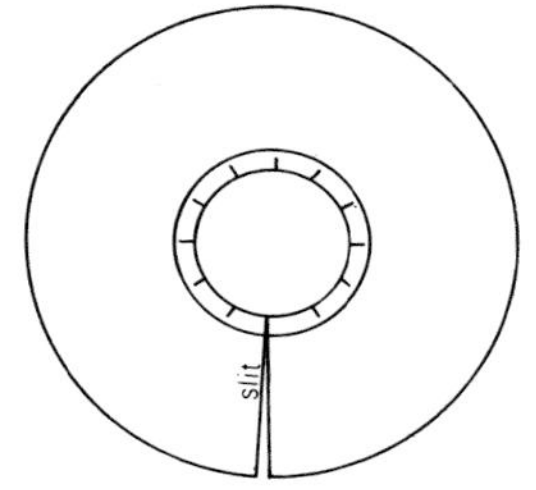

2 Stay-stitch ⅝in (15mm) from the inner edge and clip into edge up to stitching. Pin and stitch inner edge in position. Turn under hem.

3 To make longer ruffle, clip each circle to center, seam straight edges with RS together.

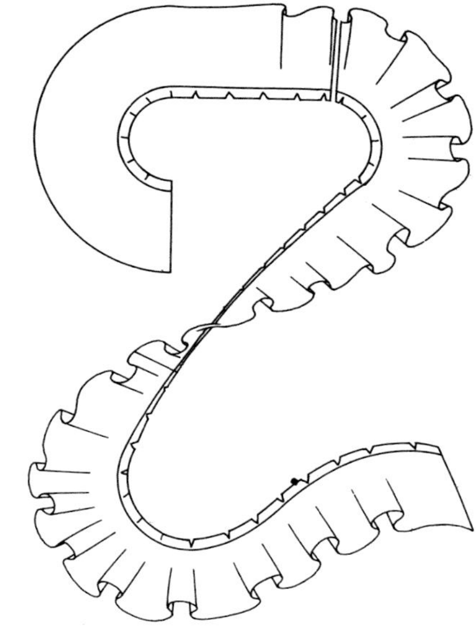

Calculating fabric amounts
Add together the measurement of the radius and required length to give the basic garment length

Full circles Double the basic garment length and, if this is less than fabric width, buy twice this length

If your basic garment length is more than the fabric width, buy four times this length.

Semi- and quarter-circles
Check that the basic length is less than fabric width. Buy the basic length for quarter-circles or twice basic length for semi-circles. You will be able to cut binding from spare fabric but may have to allow extra for a waistband.

Neck openings
Calculate the circumference of the neck opening, allowing enough room for the head to pass through if this is the only opening. For a good fit adjust the neckline, making it higher at the back than the front, and draw in darts at the center of the curve to fit the opening at the shoulders.

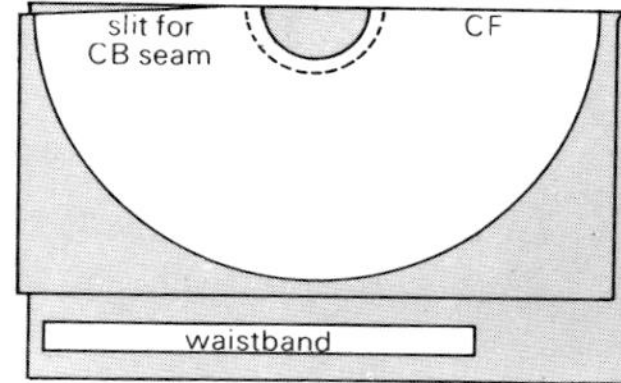

Circular skirts
You will need
fabric in calculated amount (see left)
matching sewing thread
8in (20cm) zipper
stiffening and fastenings for waistband

Making skirts
Stay-stitch the waistline and stitch side seams or CB seam, leaving an opening for a zipper. Insert the zipper and attach a waistband. Leave the skirt to hang for several days before turning up the hem.

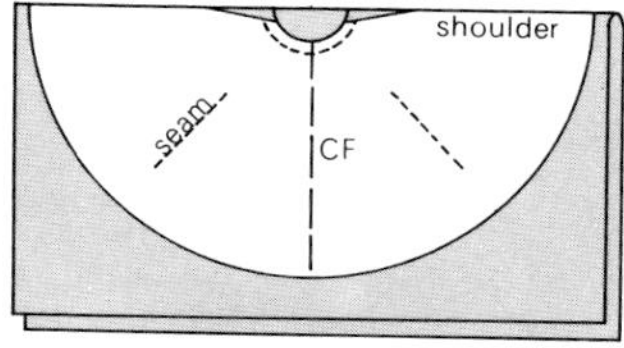

Circular blouses
You will need
fabric in calculated amount (see left)
matching sewing thread
bought or cut bias binding to fit circumference of neck and hem plus enough to tie a bow at neck (optional)

Making blouses
Stay-stitch the neck curve and stitch the darts and any seams. Try on the blouse and make any adjustments to the shoulders to give a good fit. Pin the front to the back from underarm to waist to give a comfortable fit. Machine-stitch along the pinned line. Bind the neck edge and hem.

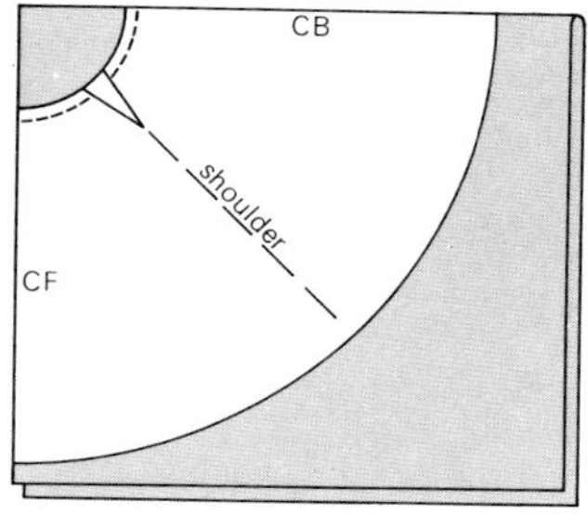

Circular capes
You will need
fabric in calculated amount (see left)
matching sewing thread
bought or cut bias binding to fit front edges and circumference of neck and hem
fastenings

Making capes
Stay-stitch the neck curve and make the darts. Bind the neck, front edges and hems in one continuous length. Attach fastenings.

Evening dress

Master pattern sheet
Using patterns and cutting out 16
Seams and finishes 20
Zippers 26
Hems 28
Darts 44
Facings 58
Linings 88

This is a basic pattern for a halter-neck bodice which can be teamed with a dirndl skirt (see p30) to make a sundress or with a circular skirt (see p46) to make an evening dress as shown here.
Alternatively, you could extend the bodice straight from the side bust darts to hip level to make a sun top. The halter ties may be converted to shoulder straps (see p90) which fasten at the back.

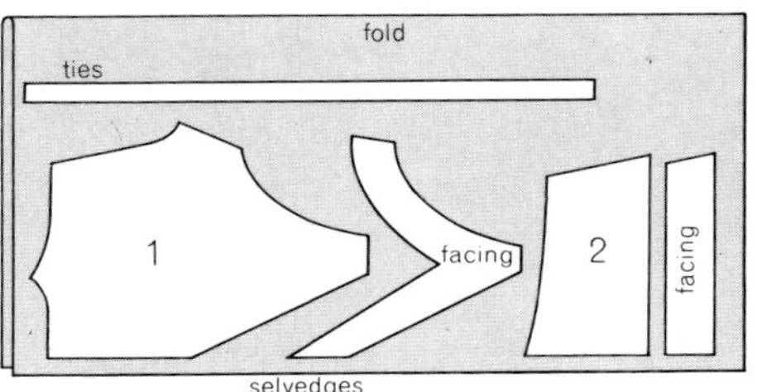

You will need
main fabric/lining 36in (90cm) wide: $\frac{3}{4}$yd (0·80m) for bodice plus required amount for skirt
matching sewing thread
12in (30cm) zipper

Cutting out
Trace appropriate pattern pieces from the master sheet in the required size and add seam allowances all around. If not lining the dress, make a facing pattern for the front bodice neck and armhole (pattern piece 1) and the back bodice (pattern piece 2). Place the pattern on the main fabric as shown and cut out. Cut out the skirt. (If lining the dress, cut out lining in the same way.) From the remaining main fabric cut 2 strips each 23 × 1$\frac{1}{2}$in (60 × 4cm) for neck ties.

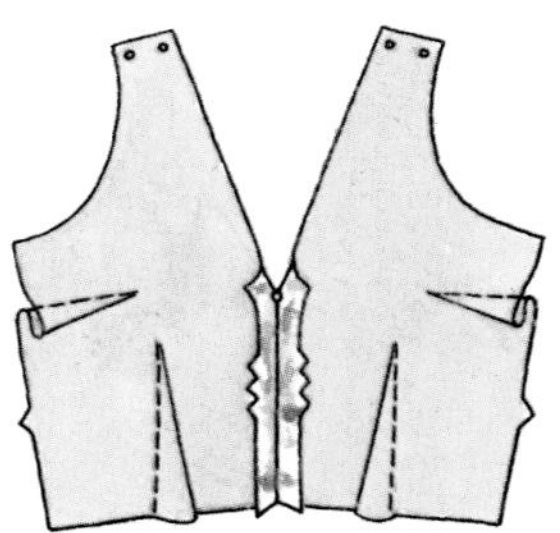

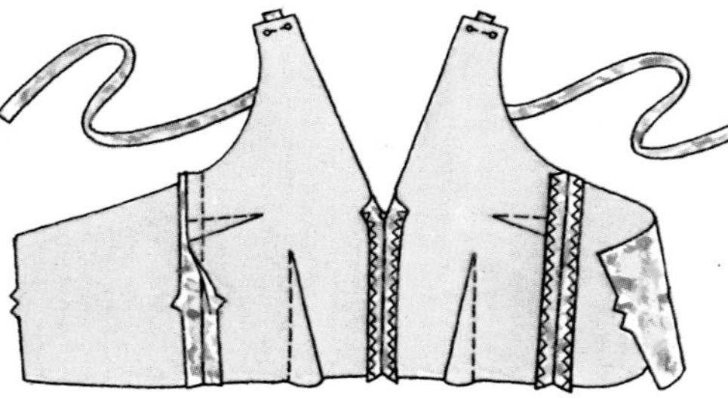

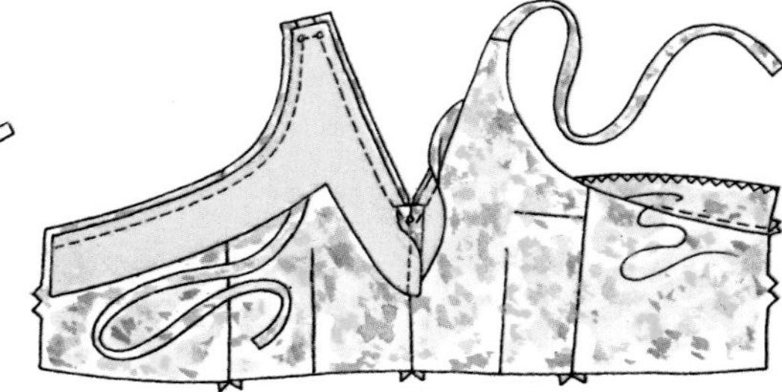

Making the dress
1 Stay-stitch seamline of front neck and armhole edges of front bodice. Fold, baste and machine-stitch darts on front and back. Press darts down and into center. With RS together and matching notches, baste and machine-stitch the CF seam as far as circle. Finish and press seam open.

2 With RS together fold the neck ties in half lengthwise and machine-stitch $\frac{1}{4}$in (5mm) in from the raw edges, leaving one end open. Cut across corners and turn ties RS out. Press. Baste the ties to RS of front bodice between circles at top edge. With RS together matching notches baste and machine-stitch front to back bodice at sides. Finish and press seams open.

3 With RS together join front and back facings; with RS together attach facings to bodice. (Alternatively, make lining bodice as dress bodice and with RS together stitch at neck and back.)

4 With RS together baste and machine-stitch CB seam of skirt, leaving 6$\frac{1}{2}$in (16·5cm) open below waistline for zipper.
With RS together matching CFs and CBs, baste and machine-stitch skirt (and lining) to bodice. (Slip-stitch bodice lining to seamline.)
Press seam upward and finish edges together.
Insert zipper into CB opening. Turn up hem.

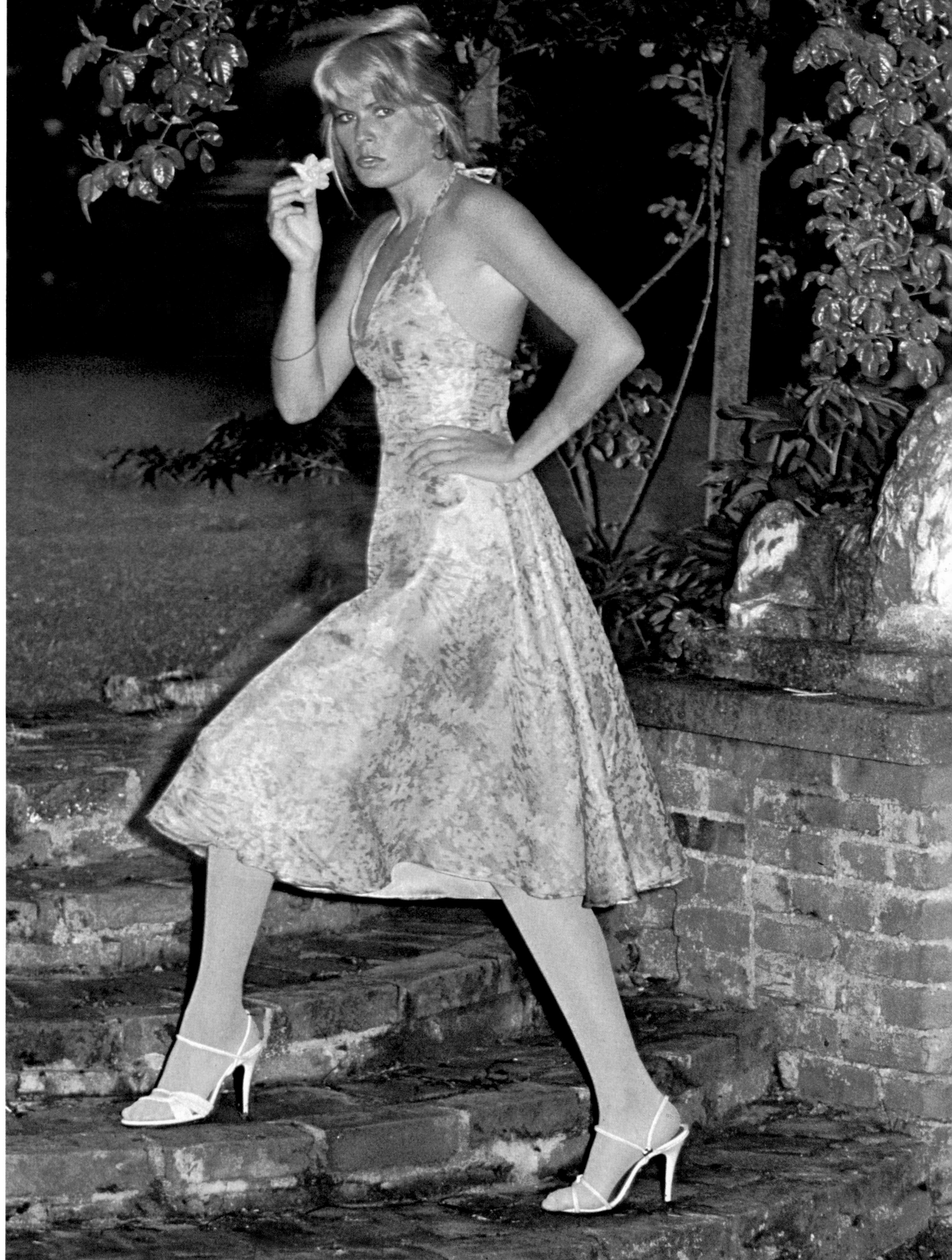

Bikini and T-shirt

This simple bikini is made from two pattern pieces, the top being an adaptation of the evening dress bodice shown on p48.
The T-shirt is cut from a pattern based on a rectangle drawn to body measurements and the shorts are an adaptation of the slacks shown on p100. For all garments use stretchy fabric such as terry cloth or cotton jersey.

You will need
fabric, 36in (90cm) wide
bikini: $\frac{7}{8}$yd (0·80m) main fabric and lining or contrasting fabric
T-shirt: twice required length from shoulder plus $1\frac{1}{2}$in (4cm)
matching sewing thread
elastic $\frac{1}{4}$in (5mm) and $\frac{5}{8}$in (15mm) (bikini only)

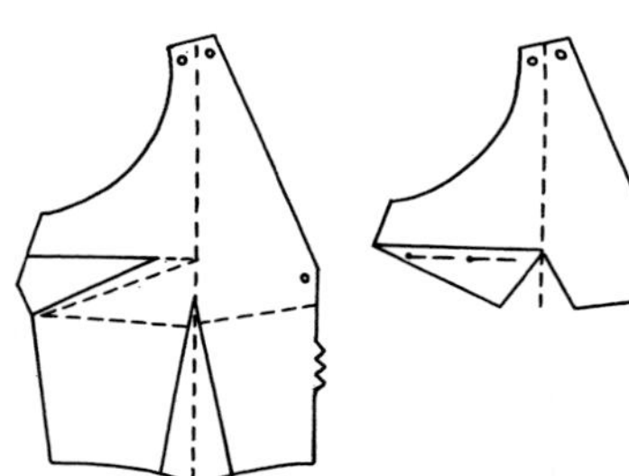

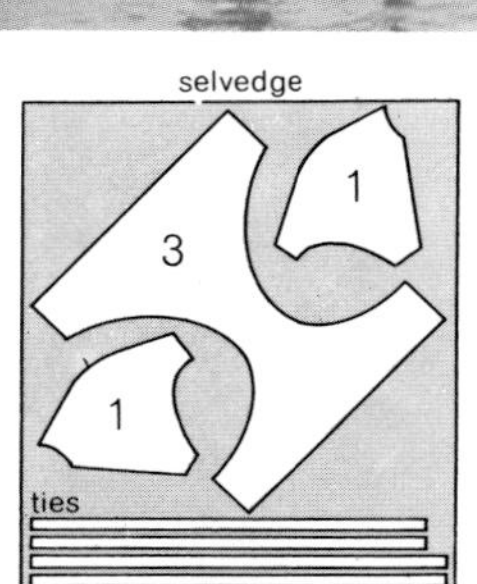

Cutting out the bikini
Trace pattern piece 3 in the appropriate size from the master sheet, placing the CF and CB to a fold on double paper. Adjust the side-seam length if you want the pants to be briefer or deeper. Add seam allowances all around. Open out the pattern.
Lay the pattern pieces on the fabric as shown and cut out. Cut 2 strips for neck ties each $23\frac{1}{2}$in × $1\frac{1}{2}$in (60 × 4cm) and 2 strips for bottom band and ties each $23\frac{1}{2}$ × $2\frac{1}{4}$in (60 × 6cm). Cut out the lining fabric in the same way, omitting the ties. Mark the bust darts with tailor's tacks.

Adapting the pattern
For bikini top, trace pattern piece 1 from the master sheet in the appropriate size. Draw a line through the center of the waist dart to the center of the top edge. Measure down $6\frac{3}{4}$in (17cm) on the line and mark.
Measure down the CF $\frac{1}{4}$in (5mm) from the circle and, using a flexible curve, draw a line from this point to mark at waist dart and up to the bottom line of side bust dart. Cut along this line. Continue both the lines of side bust dart to the vertical line.
Slash center line of waist dart to new point of side dart. Close side dart to open pattern at bottom edge to form bust dart. Insert and tape paper between slash. Add seam allowances all around.

Making the bikini
1 Stay-stitch front and side edges of bikini top, stitch CF seam of main fabric and lining to circle. Fold and stitch all darts. Make neck ties as for evening dress and baste in position.
2 With RS together matching CFs and outer edges, baste and stitch lining to main fabric along front neck and sides. Trim seams, clip curves and cut across

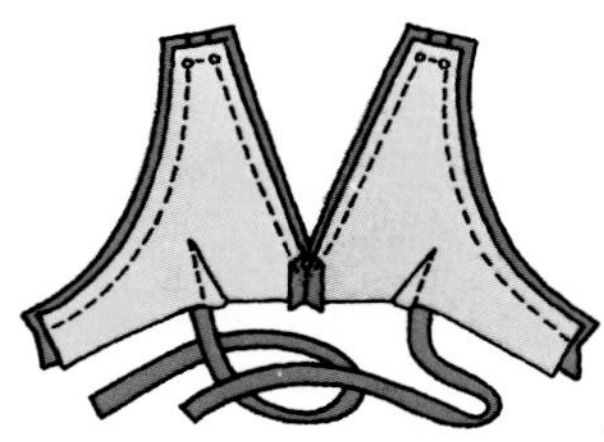

corners. Turn RS out and press. Baste lower edges together.
3 Join pieces for band on one short edge. With RS together, matching seamline of band to CF, baste upper edge of band to lower edge of top. Fold remaining length of band in half, RS together and machine-stitch $\frac{1}{4}$in (5mm) from raw edges across ends and long edge to side of top. Trim corners diagonally and turn RS out. Fold under raw edge for $\frac{1}{4}$in (5mm) and hem to seamline on WS leaving $\frac{3}{8}$in (10mm) open at each end.

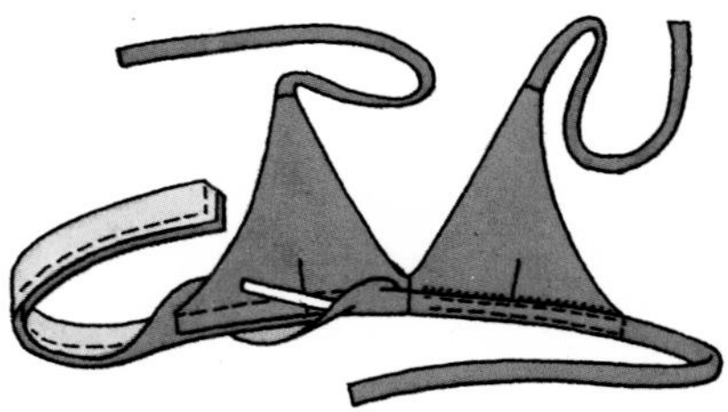

4 Cut $\frac{5}{8}$in (15mm) width elastic 2in (5cm) shorter than lower edge and thread through band, securing at each end. Hem openings.

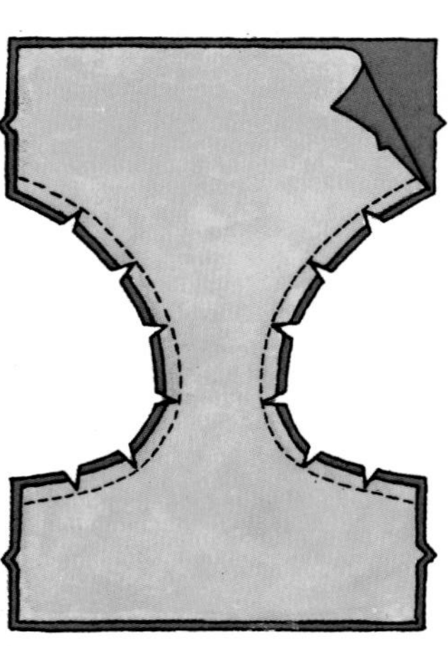

5 With RS together baste and machine-stitch the main fabric to the lining of the pants around leg edges. Trim raw edges, clip curves, turn RS out and press.
6 Open out both sections at side edges, join front to back with RS together, leaving $\frac{5}{8}$in (15mm) open at leg edges. Press seams open.
7 Baste lining to main fabric $\frac{5}{8}$in (15mm) from top edge with WS together. Trim top edge of lining just above basting. Fold under $\frac{1}{4}$in (5mm) and then a further $\frac{3}{8}$in

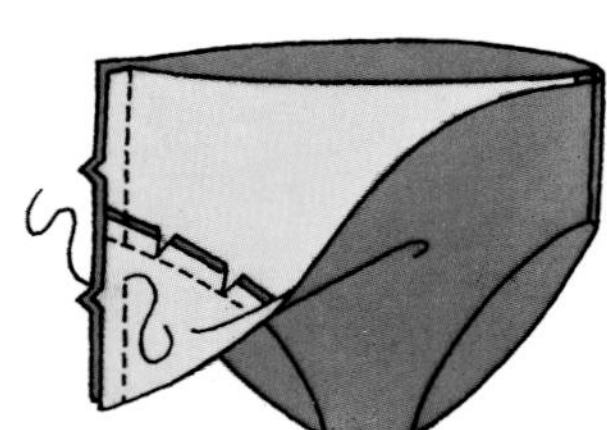

(10mm) on main fabric, machine-stitch through all thicknesses, leaving an opening of $\frac{3}{8}$in (10mm). Machine-stitch along the fold. Insert $\frac{1}{4}$in (5mm) elastic through casing, adjust to size and stitch. Close opening.

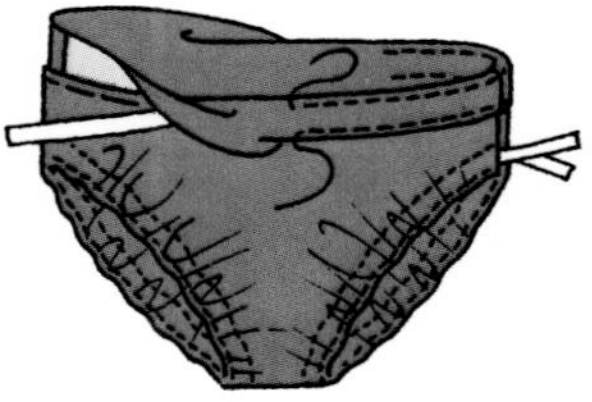

8 Machine-stitch close to leg edges and $\frac{3}{8}$in (10mm) in from first stitching line. Insert elastic through casing, adjust to size and stitch. Close opening.

Master pattern sheet
Basic stitches 18
Seams 20
Darts 44
Difficult fabrics 94

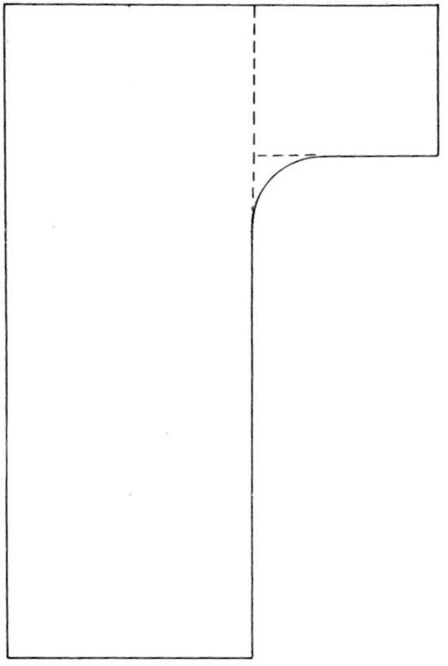

T-shirt

Making the pattern

Draw a rectangle to a quarter of hip or bust/chest measurement (whichever is larger) by required length from shoulders. Extend top (shoulder) line to RH side for required sleeve length. For width of sleeves, add 2in (5cm) to upper arm measurement for an adult, $1\frac{1}{2}$in (4cm) for a child and 1in (2·5cm) for a baby. Draw a line half this measurement below shoulder line. Draw lines at 90° from underarms to shoulders; draw underarm curve as shown. Mark neck opening at least a quarter of head circumference from LH line. Add $\frac{3}{8}$in (10mm) all around, except center fold, for seam allowances and hems.

Cutting out

Use pattern to cut out 2 pieces (front and back are identical). Cut each piece on double fabric, placing straight edge to a fold.

Making the T-shirt

Join front to back along shoulders as far as neck opening. Join side edges and underarms in a continuous seam, trim the raw edges to $\frac{1}{4}$in (5mm) and press open. Turn under remaining seam allowance on neck edges, baste and herringbone-stitch. Turn under and herringbone-stitch hems at bottom and sleeve edges.

Basic skirts

Master pattern sheet
Using patterns and cutting out 16
Seams and edge finishes 20
Hems 28
Gathering 29
Fastenings 32
Waistbands 38
Darts 44
Facings 58

This wraparound skirt is easy to fit and sew. The pattern pieces can be adapted to other basic skirt styles as shown overleaf.

You will need (for either skirt)
fabric 36in (90cm) wide:

waist size	26	28	32in
	(65	70	80cm)
28in length	$2\frac{1}{4}$	$2\frac{1}{4}$	3yd
(70cm length)	(2	2·30	2·70m)
41in length	$3\frac{7}{8}$	$4\frac{1}{4}$	$4\frac{3}{8}$yd
(105cm length)	(3·50	3·80	3·90m)

matching sewing thread
waistband interfacing
4 buttons (tailored skirt only)

Cutting out
Trace the appropriate pattern pieces in the required size from the master sheet. For the tailored version, omit the front facing and straighten the side edges from the hipline. Increase the pieces to required length, plus hem on gathered skirt, by extending side edges and drawing hemline parallel to bottom edge. Add seam allowances to top and both sides. Add seam allowance to hemline of tailored skirt.
Lay the pieces on the fabric as shown right and cut out. On the gathered skirt mark the large Os, CFs and self-facing foldlines with tailor's tacks. On tailored skirt mark CFs and darts. After step **1** of making the skirt, cut the waistband from remaining fabric to the length of the top edge by $2\frac{3}{4}$in (7cm) for the gathered skirt or by 4in (10cm) for the tailored skirt, plus seam allowances all around. Cut ties for the gathered version to the same width as the waistband by 36in (90cm) (LH tie) and 27in (70cm) (RH tie). For the tailored skirt cut facings 3in (7·5cm) wide to the length and shape of the front edges and hem. These facings may be cut from contrasting fabric if you wish.

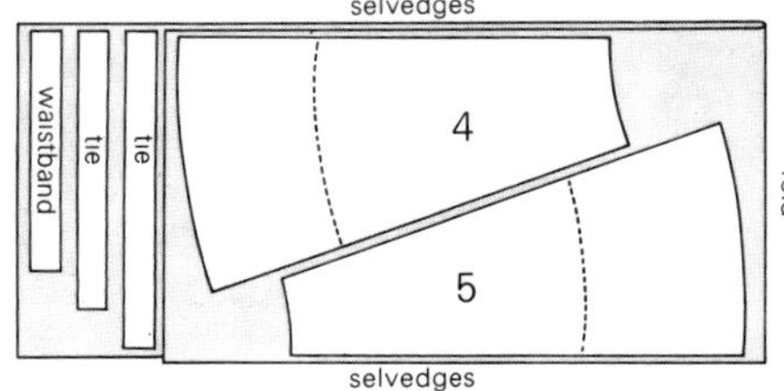

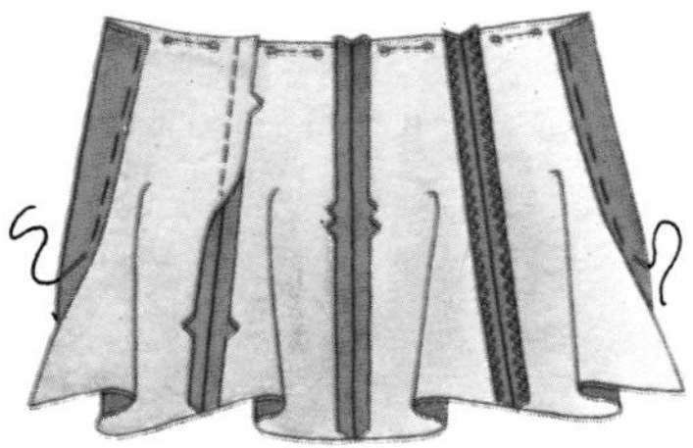

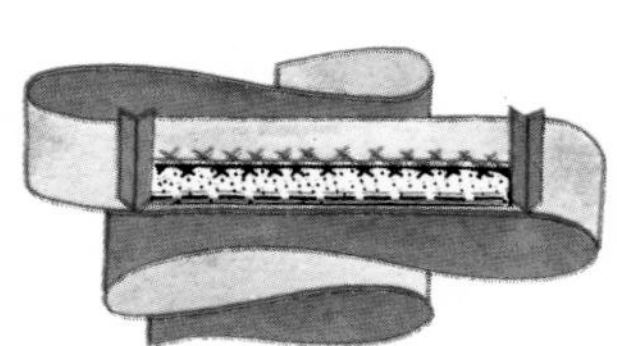

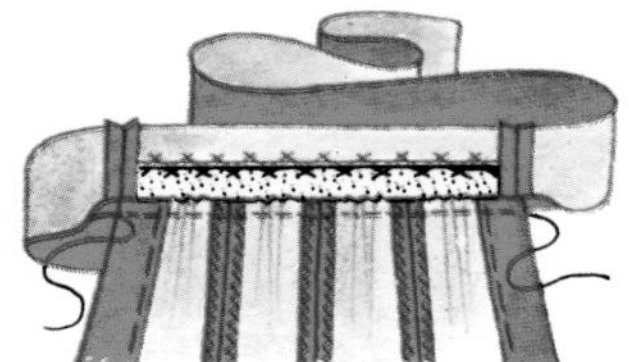

Making the gathered skirt
1 With RS together and notches matching, join skirt backs (pattern piece 5) at the CB and then join fronts (pattern piece 4) to the back at the sides. Gather between large Os to make waist fit from CF to CF. Fold and press self facing to inside along foldline. Baste to within 6in (15cm) of the bottom edge.

2 Fold waistband in half lengthwise with WS together, finger-press fold and open out. Repeat, folding band widthwise. Baste interfacing to one long edge of band on WS and catch-stitch to lengthwise foldline. With RS together join ties to each end of band, placing long tie on left as shown.

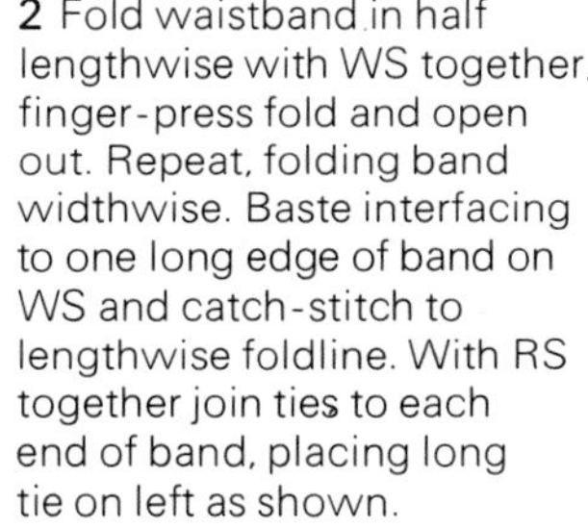

3 With RS together, pin interfaced edge of band to skirt, matching widthwise foldline to CB seam and seamlines of band to skirt folds. Adjust gathers evenly. Baste and machine-stitch. Press seam toward band.

4 With RS together fold ties in half lengthwise. Baste and machine-stitch across short ends and along open edges to band. Trim seams, cut across corners diagonally and turn ties RS out. Press so that seamline is exactly on the edge.

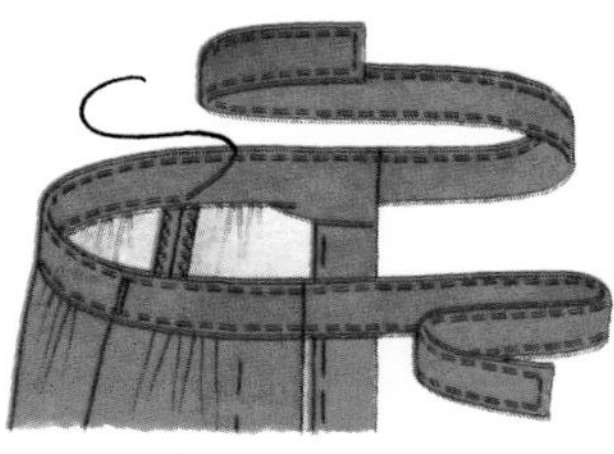

5 Turn under the free edge of the band along stitching line and place to seamline. Baste, enclosing all thicknesses. Top-stitch $\frac{1}{16}$in (2mm) in from edge on each side along length of band and ties. Work a $1\frac{1}{8}$in (30mm) buttonhole on band at RH seam.

6 Open out facings at lower edge. Turn up and stitch hem. Fold down facings again and slip-stitch to hem at lower edge. Blind-hem remaining length of facings to skirt to hold in place.

Making the tailored skirt
1 Stitch darts on fronts and back, join fronts to back at sides and join CB seam. With RS of facing to WS of skirt, stitch facings to skirt fronts and hemline. Pin and stitch ends of facings together diagonally to make mitered corners as shown. Grade seam, press toward skirt and under-stitch. Turn facings to RS; turn under seam allowance along free edge. Top-stitch to skirt.
2 Attach waistband and make 4 horizontal buttonholes, placing the first on the RH front in the center of the band and the others below in the center of the facing $2\frac{1}{2}$in (6·5cm) apart.
Attach buttons to LH front.

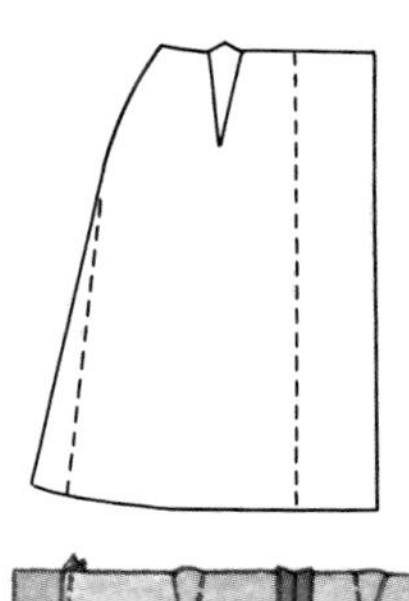

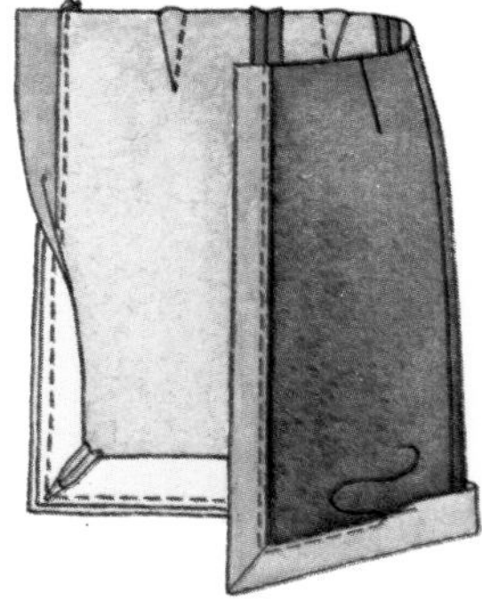

Zippers 26
Pleating 40
Fitting and altering skirts 72
Pockets 92

You will need (all sizes)
fabric, 45in (115cm) wide
flared skirt: 1½yd (1·30m)
skirt with pleated front: 2yd (1·80m)
skirt with gathered front: 2yd (1·80m)
gored skirt: 2yd (1·80m)
matching sewing thread
8in (20cm) zipper
stiffening and fastenings for waistband

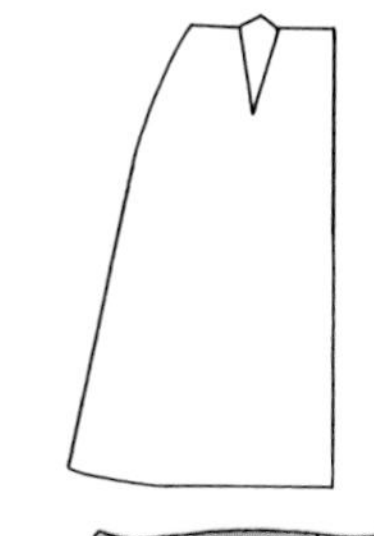

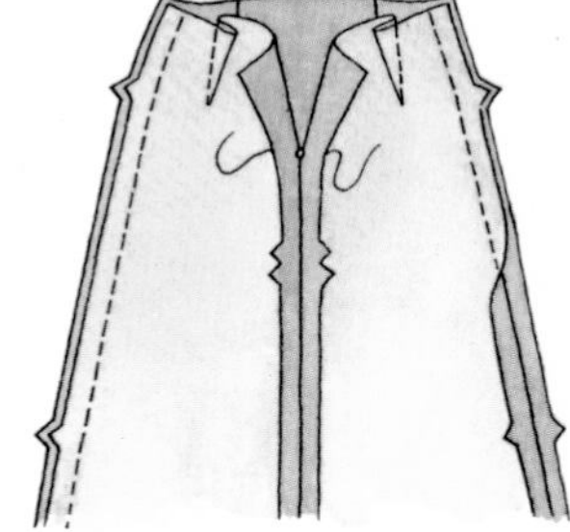

Flared skirt
A flared skirt pattern is a basis for a wide variety of skirts. All the skirts illustrated here are variations of the basic method – you can even cut off the pattern at hip level and add a gathered, circular or pleated skirt to it.
Quantities are given for 45in (115cm) fabric, the most economical width for all styles. You can, of course, plan your own layout for other widths (see p16).
Adapting the pattern Trace pattern pieces 4 and 5 to required length, omitting front wrap and facing. Add seam allowances to waist, side and CB edges; add a hem allowance at the bottom. Place the pieces on double fabric with CF to fold. Cut out and mark CF, CB and darts with tailor's tacks. Cut out the waistband.

Making the skirt Form and baste all the darts. Join the front to the back skirt at the sides with a plain seam and baste only; baste the CB seam leaving an opening from waistline of 8in (20cm) for the zipper. Try on the skirt and adjust for fit if necessary. Machine-stitch darts and seams. To finish the skirt, insert the zipper, attach the waistband and turn up the hem.

Skirt with pleated front
Adapting flared skirt pattern Draw a line through the front inner dart line to hem. Slash along line and spread pattern for 6in (15cm); insert and tape paper between slash and draw a line along center for inner pleat fold. Cut on double fabric, with CF on fold.
Making the skirt Mark pleat lines as shown with tailor's tacks. Stitch darts on both front and back. Form pleats and top-stitch for 8in (20cm) from waist. Join front to back at sides, join CB seam. Finish like flared skirt.

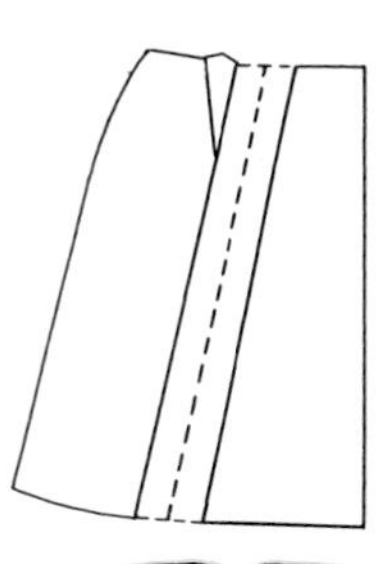

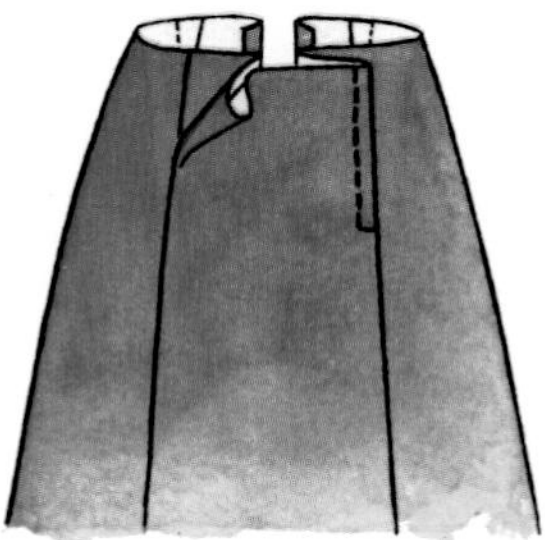

Skirt with gathered front
Adapting flared skirt pattern Mark pocket shape on front pattern piece. Add $2\frac{3}{4}$in (7cm) to CF edge and cut on double fabric, placing new CF edge to a fold. Cut waistband and pocket pieces.
Making the skirt Make pockets and run 2 rows of gathering threads on waistline between pocket curves. Make darts in skirt back, join front to back at sides. Join CB seam and draw up gathers evenly so that skirt fits waist. Finish like flared skirt.

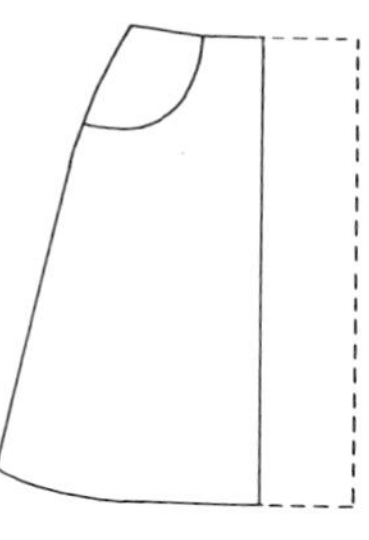

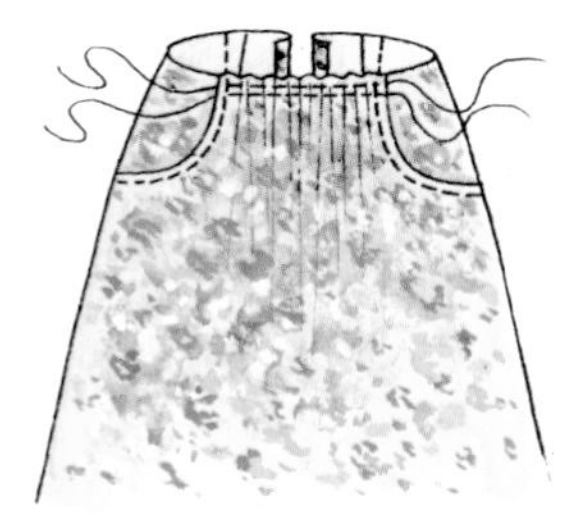

Gored skirt
Adapting flared skirt pattern Draw a line through center of darts to hem on front and back. Slash along line to point of dart, close dart to open pattern. Insert and tape paper between slash. Join center of hemline and waistline and cut pattern on this line. Add seam allowances to each new edge and to CF. Mark grainline through center and cut on double fabric.
Making the skirt Join sections with plain seams. Finish like flared skirt.

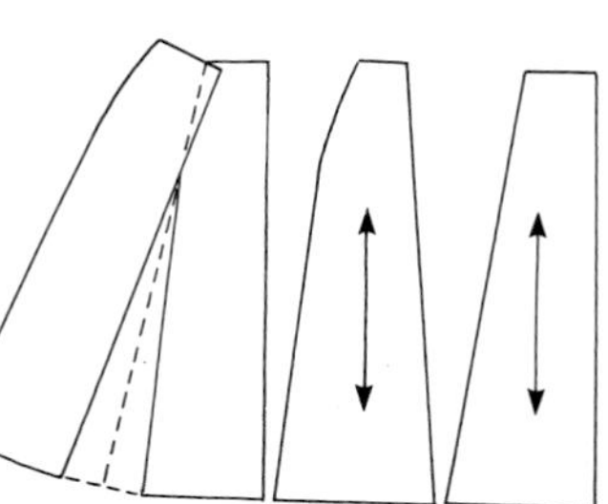

Necklines and yokes

Basic stitches 18
Facings 58

The plain high neckline shown on the dress bodice on p68 forms the basis for a wide variety of necklines. You can re-shape it completely (re-shape the facing to match) or incorporate a yoke, an opening or some form of decorative finish.
Alternatively, you could add a collar (see pp78, 80).

To insure success with any of these variations, it is advisable to make a sample first in an inexpensive fabric. Cut out the bodice with the plain high neckline and baste darts, shoulders and side seams. Add the variations to this so that you can see the exact position and effect before you start on the garment.

Designing new necklines
Always decide on the front neckline first. You can then cut the back to the same shape or leave it at the original height, simply adjusting it to correspond to any new shoulder-seam length at the front.
Using cotton tape pinned to the sample around your neck, create the new size and shape of neckline you want. To transfer the new neckline to your pattern, fold the sample in half down the CF and lay the pattern over it so the CFs correspond. Trace the shape of the tape, using a flexible curve to draw a smooth line. Add seam allowances (unless finishing with binding) and cut out.

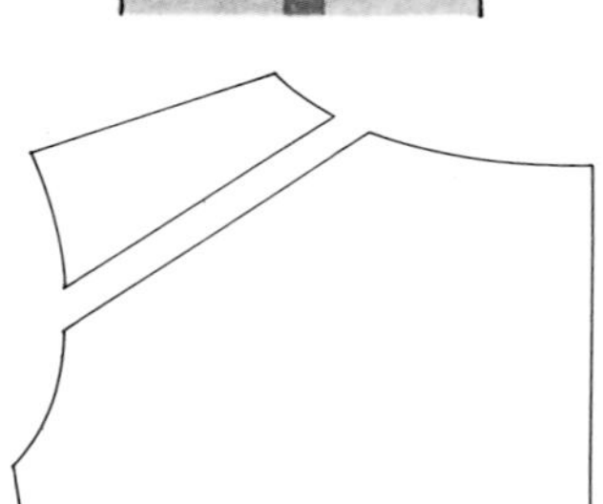

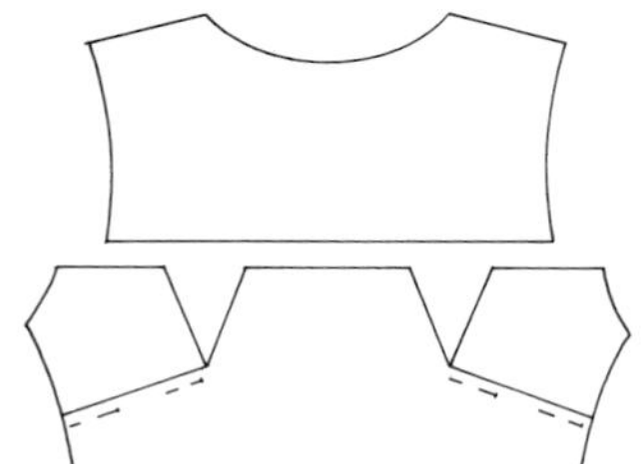

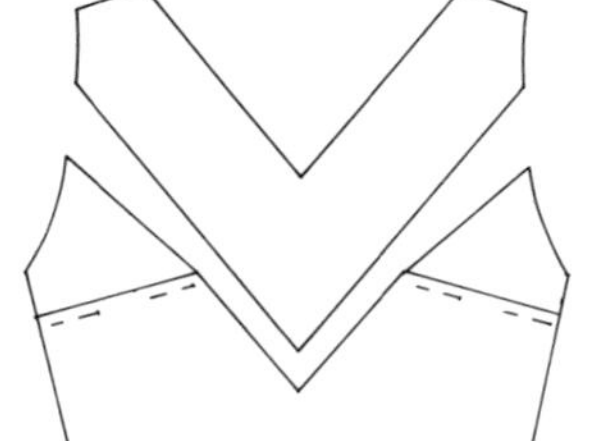

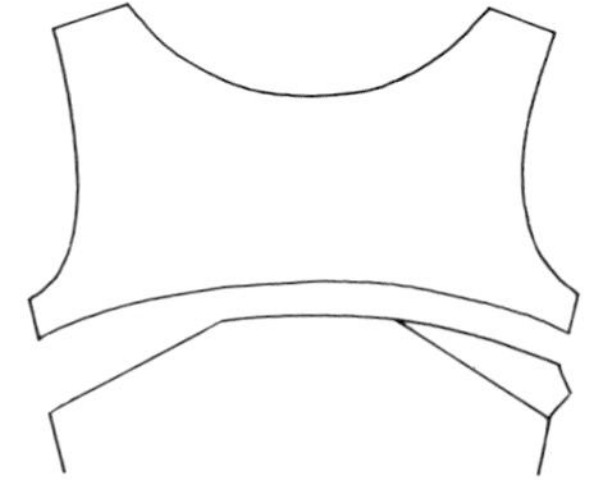

Designing yokes
To determine yoke lines use the same method as necklines, deciding the neck shape first and then the position of the yoke, which need not necessarily follow the same shape as the neck. Transfer the yoke line to your pattern and cut along it. Add seam allowances to both edges.

Shaping with yokes
You can add shaping to garments at the yoke line in several ways.
Gathers If the bodice has no side bust darts, simply add the extra amount for gathers to the CF before placing pattern to fabric fold. If there are side darts, cut the yoke line and then slash down from it to the dart point. Slash the center line of the dart and overlap the edges to close it. Open the yoke line by the same amount and do the gathering on this section.
Darts A V-shaped yoke can be used to give similar shaping to darts without the added thickness of darts. Slash the yoke line, close the dart to open the pattern at the armhole.

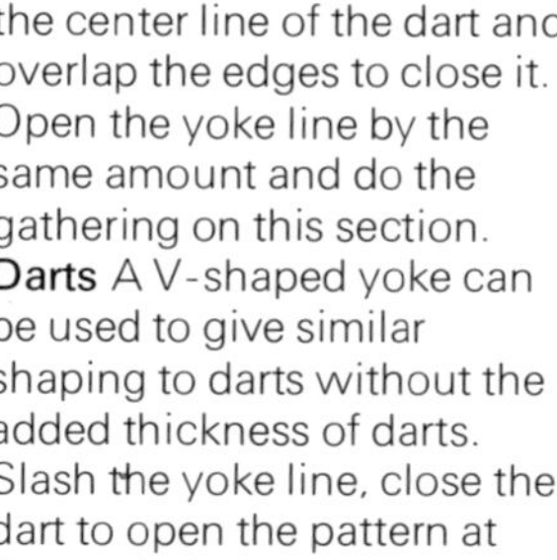

If a straight yoke line falls on the top or bottom line of side bust dart, cut away the dart to shape the bodice.

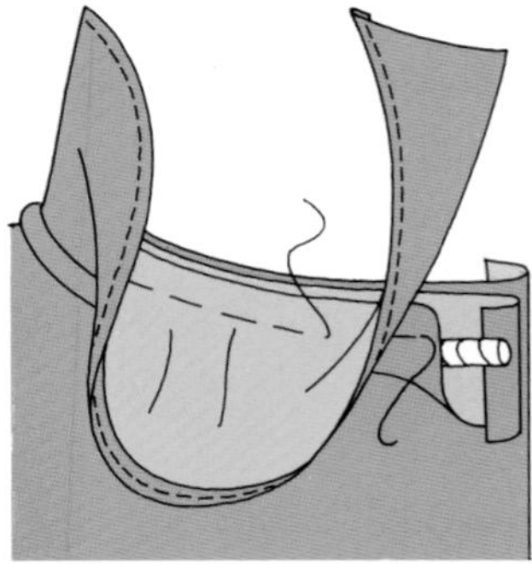

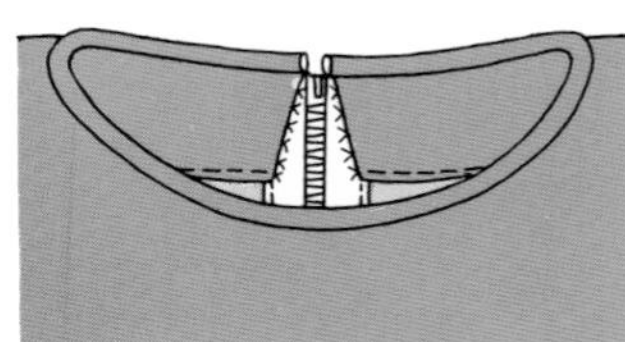

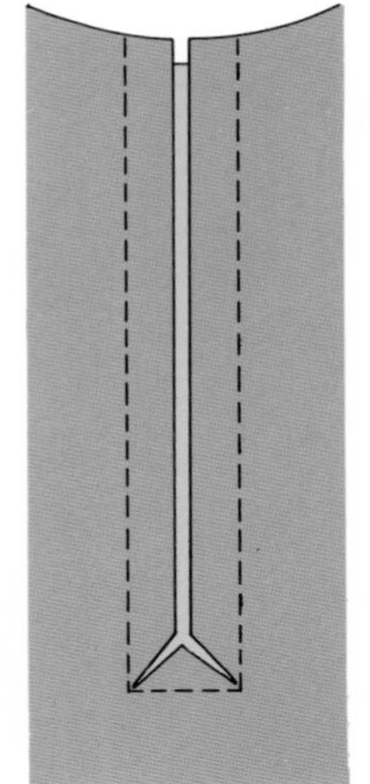

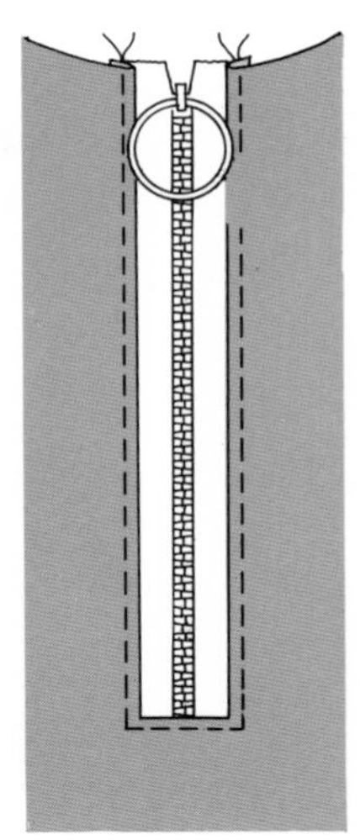

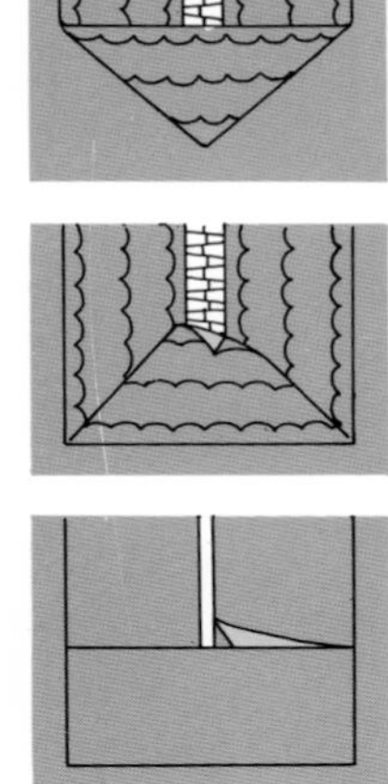

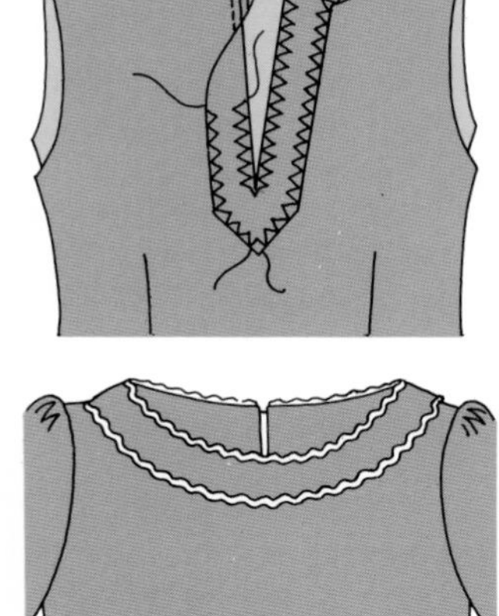

Corded neckline
Cut a bias strip to twice the seam allowance plus circumference of cord by circumference of neckline plus seam allowances. With RS together baste one edge of bias strip to neck edge. Lay cord along WS of strip and place free edge of strip to neck edge. Baste close to cord through all thicknesses. Apply the facing on top, using a cording foot to stitch as close as possible to the edge of the cord.

Decorative zipper opening
Mark the length of the opening on the CF. Work stay stitching to $\frac{1}{4}$in (5mm) on each side and below the mark and cut along the mark and out to the corners. Fold under the fabric along the stay-stitched line and press. Pin, baste and machine-stitch folds to the zipper.
Applying braid Place one edge of the braid to the edge of the zipper, mitering the corners at the bottom in one of the ways shown.
Baste and machine stitch along both edges of the braid. This method may also be used to apply braid to a plain slit opening as shown.

Reverse facing
This may be applied to any shape of neckline and you can cut the facing in self or contrasting fabric.
Apply the RS of the facing to the WS of the garment. Trim the edges but do not under-stitch. Turn to RS. Finish the outside edge of the facing with decorative stitching or with braid.

Decorative variations
Rouleau loops Apply to each side of opening (see p33) and attach the facing. Fasten the loops by lacing with cord.
Band opening Finish opening (see p60) and fasten with buttons and buttonholes (see p32).
Scalloped edge – see p102.
Keyhole opening – see p60. Add to CF neck and finish neck with binding and ties (see p22).
Bound neck Use bias-cut strips of self or contrasting fabric, mitering at the point on V-shapes or at the corners on square necklines (see p25).
Metal eyelets Add to a plain slit opening and lace with cord.

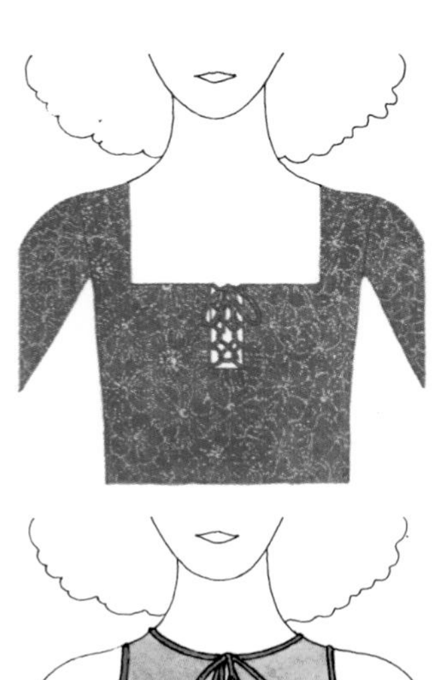

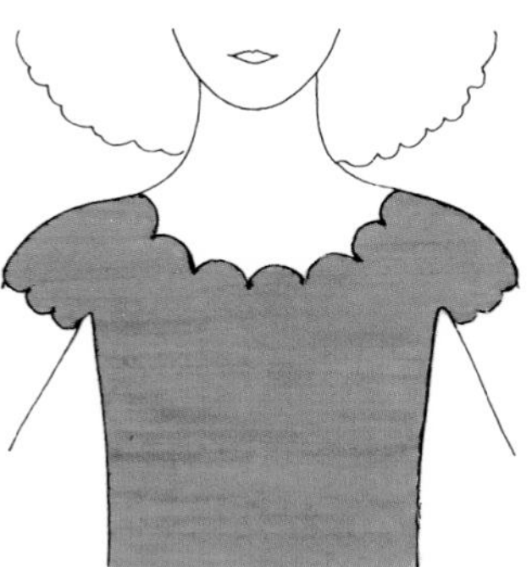

Facings

Facings are bands of fabric cut to the same shape as an edge (e.g. neck or armhole), stitched to it and turned over to give a neat, flat finish. They usually consist of pieces which correspond to those of the garment and are seamed together before they are joined to it. Neck and armhole facings can be combined by cutting them together for garments with narrow shoulders where separate facings would overlap.

Both types of facing can be made in thinner fabric than the main fabric in order to reduce bulk. Extended facings are cut with the garment, then folded back along a front or back opening to eliminate unnecessary seams.

Patterns for facings are always included in commercial paper patterns but you can easily draw your own if you have altered the shape of the edge to be faced or if you are using the master-sheet patterns from this book.

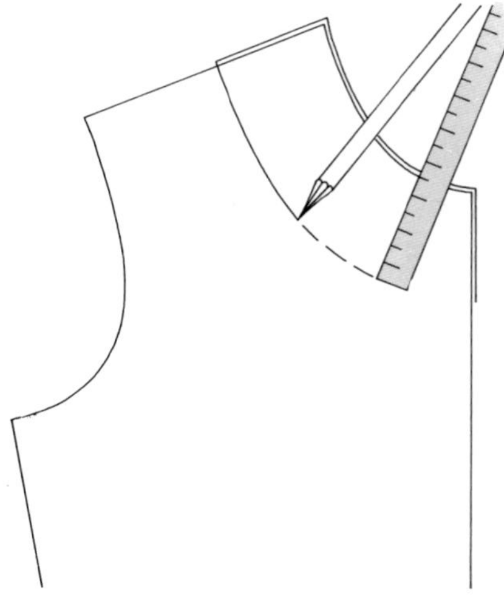

Cutting shaped facing patterns

Fold out any darts on edges to be faced. Cover the pattern piece with tracing paper and trace the edge. Trace along and mark 3in (7·5cm) down adjoining side edges, then draw a line from the marks parallel to the first line. Cut out fabric from this pattern, placing it on the same grain as for the main pattern piece.

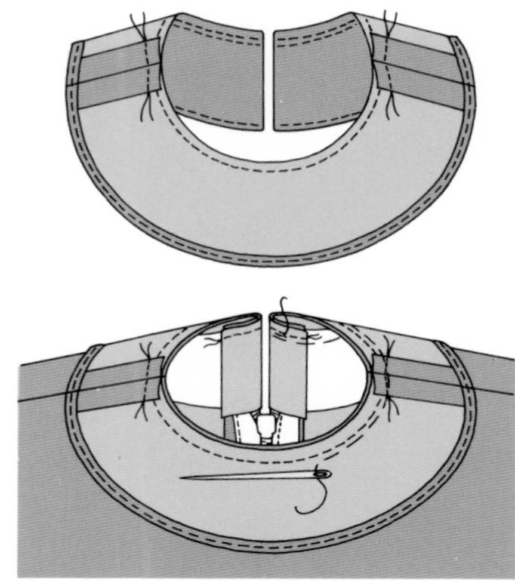

Attaching shaped facings

1 Stay-stitch edges of both garment and facing. Apply interfacing.
Stitch seams of both garment and facing and press open. Stitch any darts on edge to be faced and insert zipper if used. Finish outer edge of facing.

2 With RS together, matching seams, pin and baste facing to garment. Open zipper and wrap ends of facing around it.

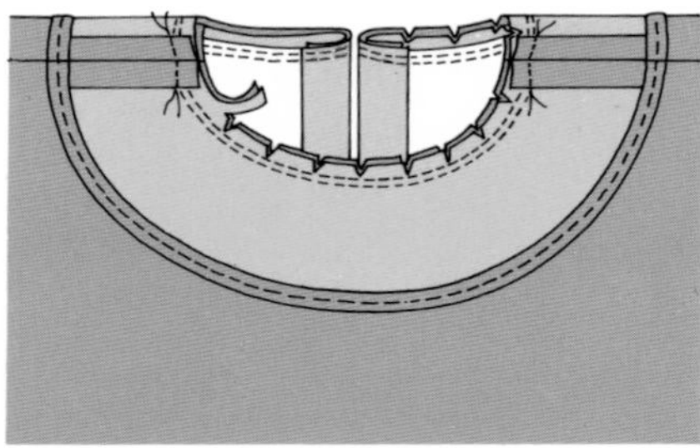

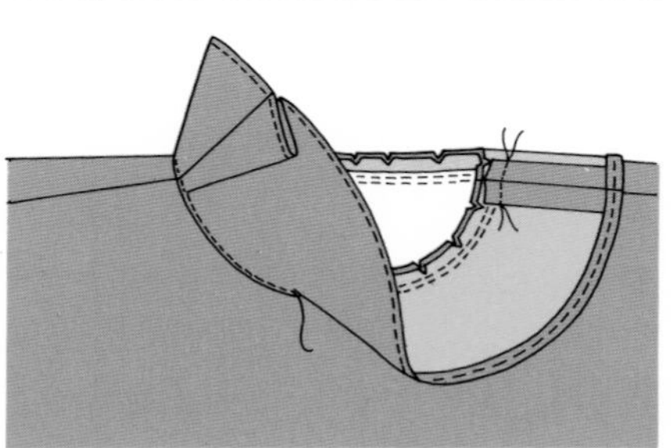

3 Stitch facing to garment just inside line of stay stitching. Grade seams, clipping into curves. Under-stitch facing to prevent it from rolling to the outside of garment. To do this, turn facing away from garment and stitch through facing and seam allowance, close to stitching line.

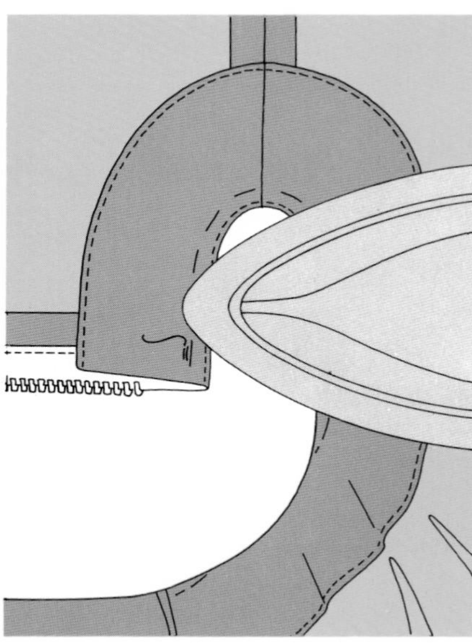

4 Turn facing to inside of garment, so that seamline just rolls inside.
Baste around inner edge of facing to hold in position. Press.

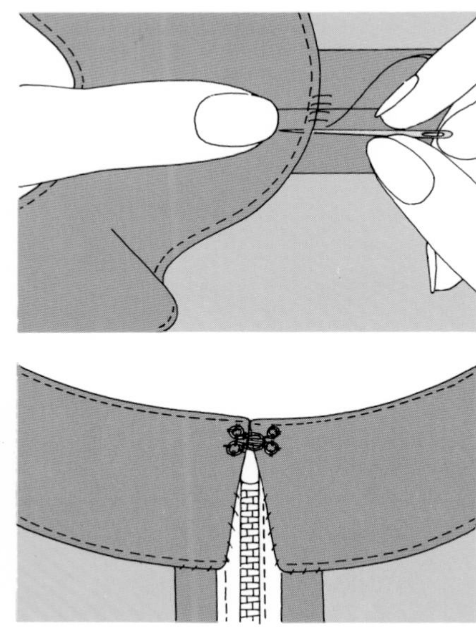

5 To secure facing to garment, catch to seam allowances of garment. Turn in ends of facing and hem to zipper tape. Sew on hook and eye.

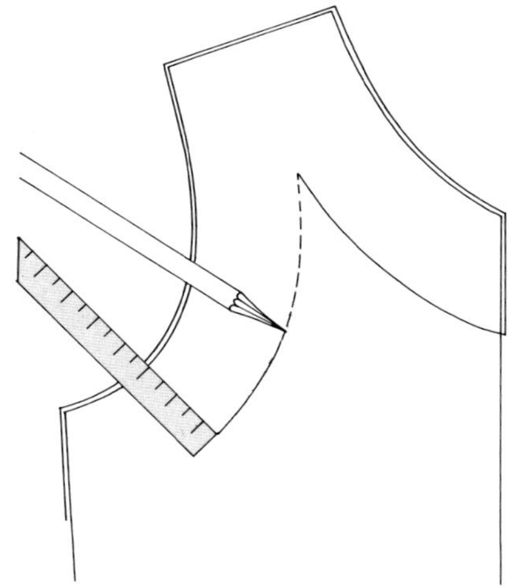

Cutting combined facings
Cover the pattern pieces with tracing paper and trace the edges to be faced. Trace along and make a mark 3in (7·5cm) down the adjoining side edges, then draw lines from the marks parallel to the curved edges. Stop when the lines intersect. Cut out fabric from pattern, placing it as for main pattern piece.

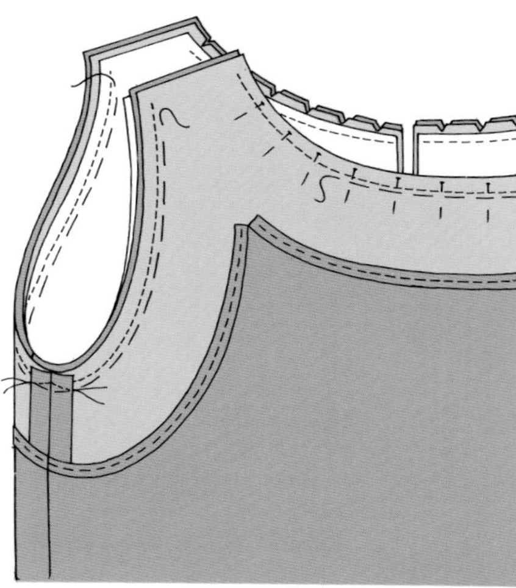

Attaching combined facings
1 Prepare edges and interfacing as shaped facings. Stitch and press side seams of both garment and facings, but leave shoulders unstitched. Finish outer edges of facing. With RS together, matching seams, join facing to garment, ending stitching at shoulder seamlines. Trim and clip seams; under-stitch as far as possible.

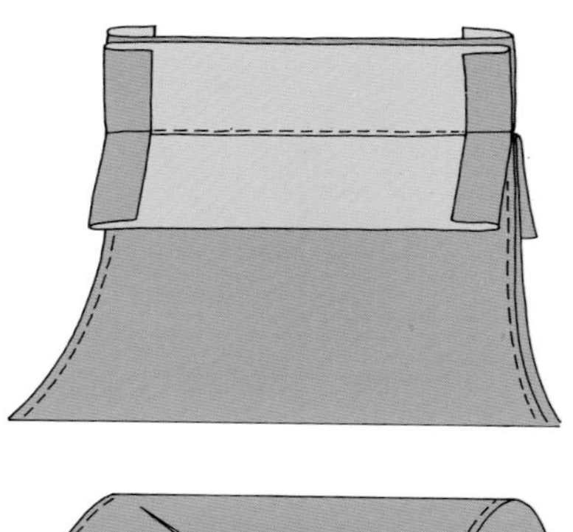

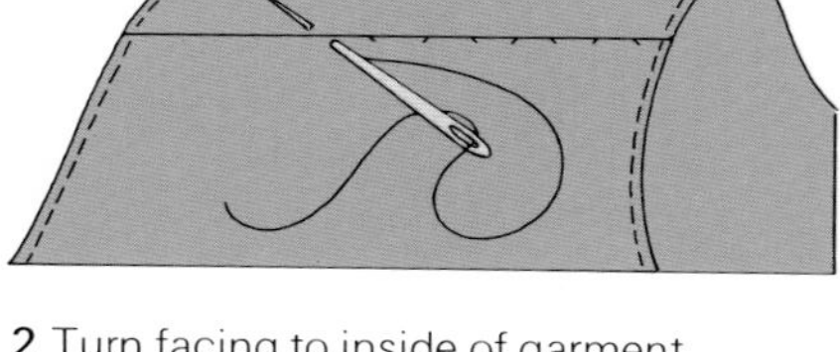

2 Turn facing to inside of garment. Baste and stitch shoulder seams, working on garment only, turning facing edges aside as shown. Trim shoulder seams and press open with point of iron. Turn in shoulder seams of facing and slip-stitch together as shown.

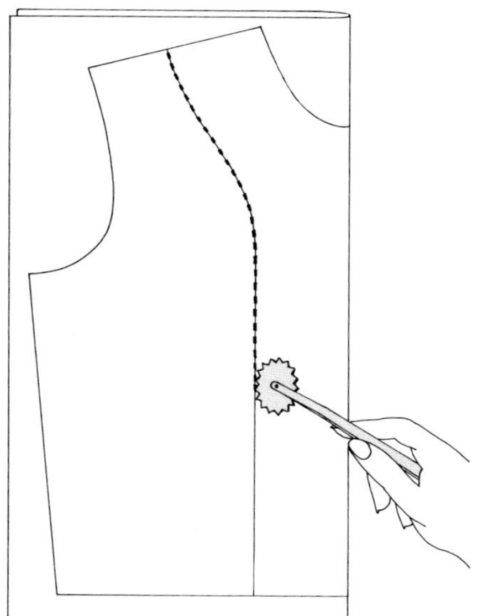

Cutting extended facing patterns
Place seamline of edge to be faced to a fold on paper as shown. Draw around complete pattern piece on one half of paper. Turn paper over and trace a line 3in (7·5cm) inside neckline and edge. Trace neckline and 3in (7·5cm) of shoulder. Open out paper and use pattern to cut facings with bodice pieces. Cut back neck facing separately.

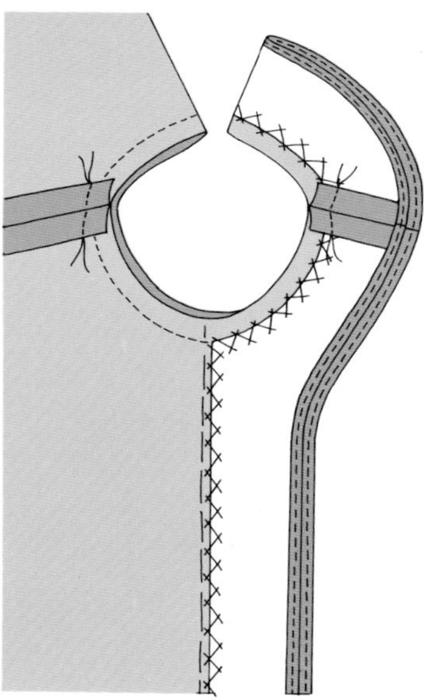

Attaching extended facings
1 Stay-stitch curved edges. If garment has a buttoned fastening, make sure that CF lines are marked with basting. Attach interfacing to WS of facings and catch-stitch along the inner edge which will form the foldline. Stitch and press open shoulder seams. Finish facing edges.

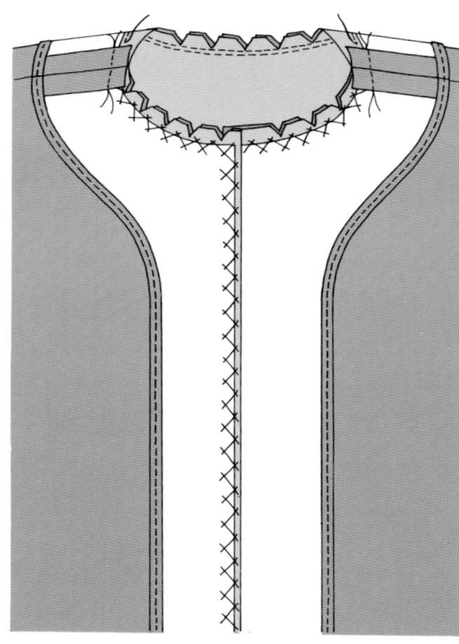

2 With RS together, turn front facings back over garment along foldlines. Matching shoulder seams, pin, baste and stitch facing to garment. Trim and grade seams, under-stitch. Press and turn facing to inside of garment.

Openings

Any of the openings shown here may be used in sleeves or as a CF neck opening in bodices – simply increase the length of the slit from a minimum of 3in (7·5cm) in sleeves to 6in (15cm) in bodice so that you can pull it over your head easily. Make sleeve openings before stitching the underarm seam, and neck openings (with the exception of faced slit openings) before attaching the front to the back, so that you are working on a flat fabric. Slit openings in seams may be made anywhere on a garment, e.g. at the back or sides of a skirt or blouse.

Slit openings in seams
Mark opening position on pattern. Increase seam allowance to 1in (2·5cm) on sleeves or 2in (5cm) on neck openings from $\frac{5}{8}$in (15mm) below base of opening to top on each side. Stitch seam to base of opening and finish edges, including those of opening. Press seams open. Press under edges of opening along seamline.

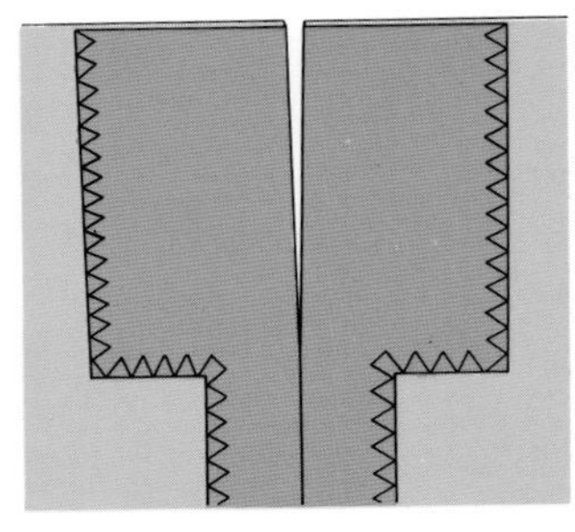

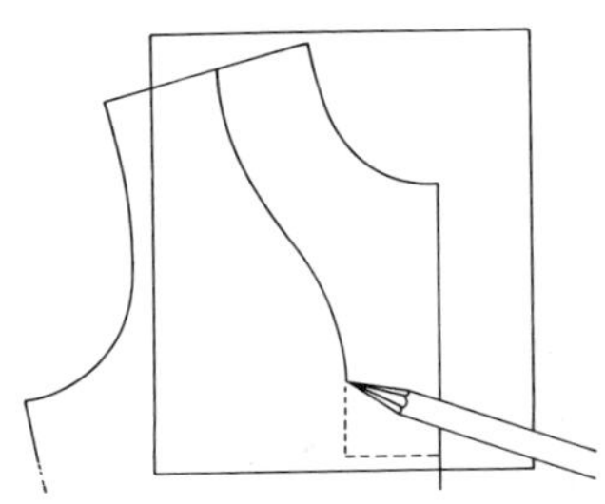

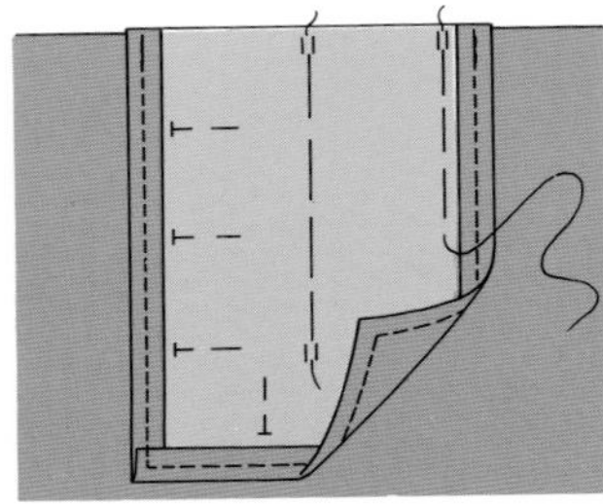

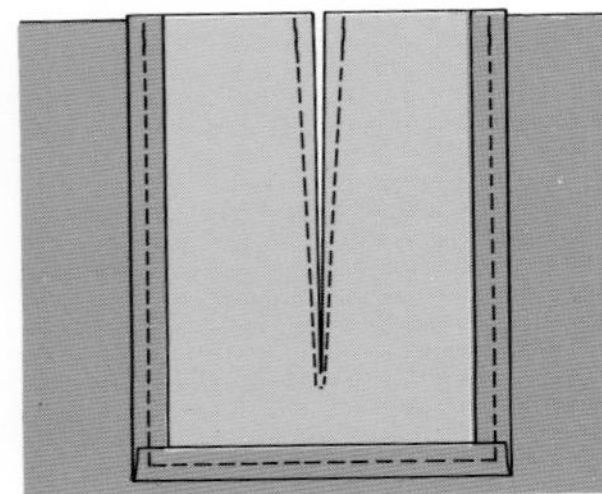

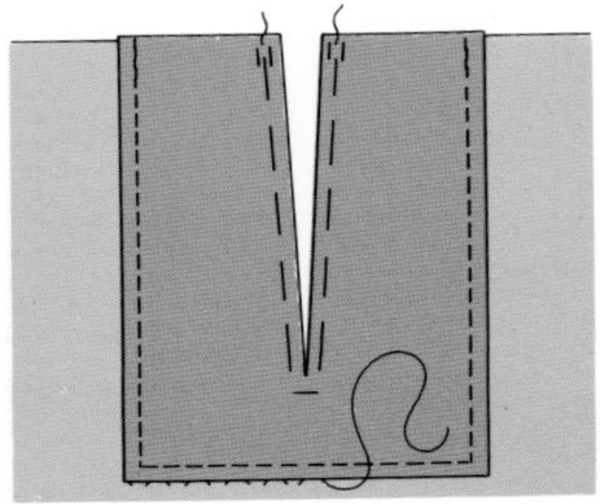

Faced slit openings
Cut the facings for sleeve openings from self fabric $2\frac{1}{2}$in (6·5cm) wide × $4\frac{3}{4}$in (12cm) long. Turn under the side and upper edges and stitch. Cut the facing for a neck opening to the same width by $7\frac{1}{2}$in (19cm) long, combining it with the neck facing as shown.
1 With RS together and matching center of facing to slash line, baste facing to garment along slash line and edges. Machine-stitch $\frac{1}{4}$in (5mm) in from either side of slash line, tapering to a point at the end. Stitch the remaining portion of the neck facing. Cut along slash line to within 1–2 threads of the point.
2 Turn facing to WS and baste close to stitched edge. Press. Slip-stitch lower edge to garment.

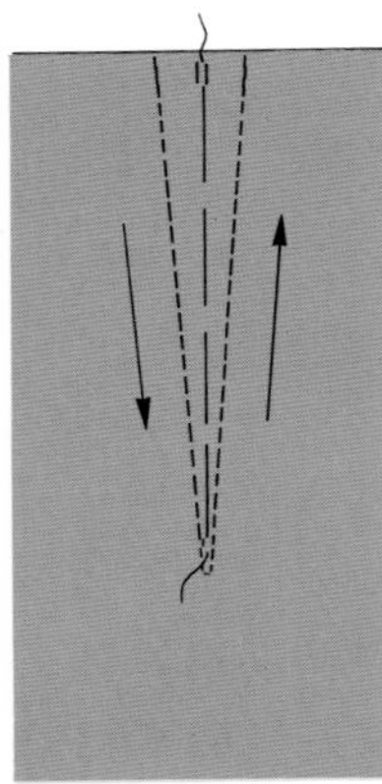

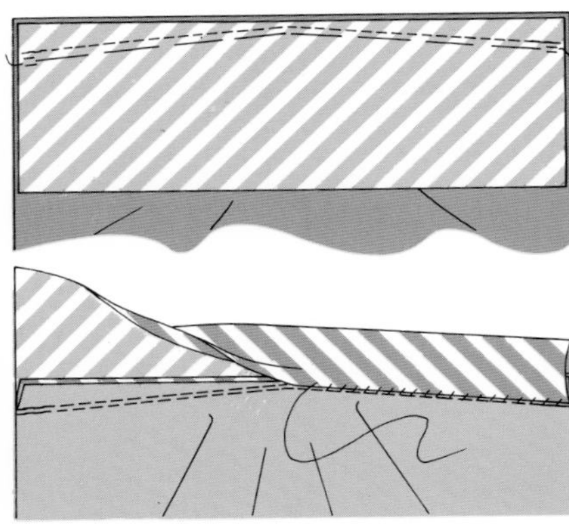

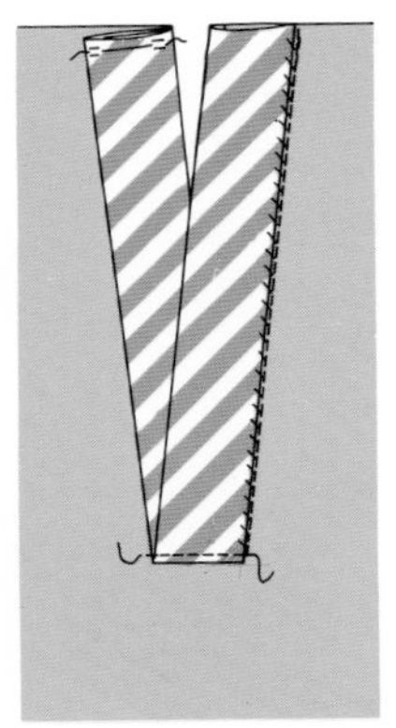

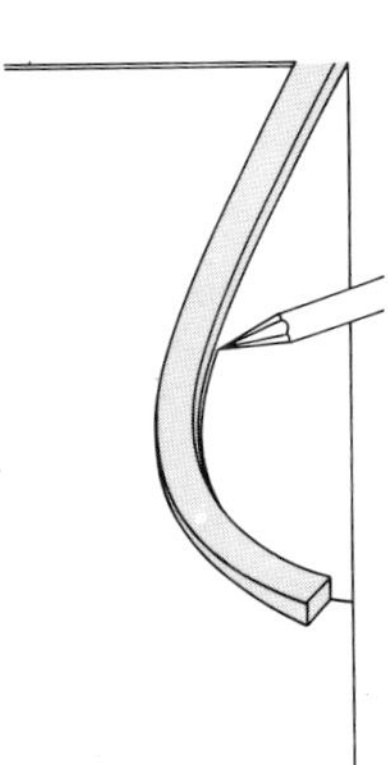

Continuous overlap opening
1 Stay-stitch around slash line, starting $\frac{1}{4}$in (5mm) from it at the raw edge and tapering to a point at the end. Slash along line to point.
2 Cut a bias strip of fabric to twice length of slash by $1\frac{1}{4}$in (3·5cm) wide. Open slash out straight and with RS together baste and machine-stitch strip to opening along line of stay stitching. Press seam onto strip.
3 Turn under outer edge of strip for $\frac{1}{4}$in (5mm), fold to WS and hem to stitching line. Press.
4 Turn front section completely to WS and baste at the top edge. Overlap the back section and stitch together at the bottom.

Keyhole opening
Using a flexible curve, draw opening to the required size and shape in position on your pattern. (The easiest way is to draw half the shape to the center fold.) Cut out along this line. Cut bias strips 1in (2·5cm) wide by the circumference of the keyhole and use to bind the opening, making a $\frac{1}{4}$in (5mm) seam allowance. Stretch the binding around the base of the opening for a smooth finish.

Band openings
These may be made to any length required on CF neck openings (e.g. to below the waist on shirt dresses) and fastened with buttons and buttonholes. The neck edge may be finished with a facing (see step **8** before starting) or with a collar. The bands may be made in fabric which matches or contrasts with the garment. If using striped fabric you can cut the bands with the stripes at 90° or 45° to the rest of the garment. Plaid fabrics can also be cut at 45°. For a finished band of $1\frac{1}{8}$in (3cm) wide cut 2 strips $3\frac{1}{2}$in (9cm) by the opening length plus $1\frac{1}{2}$in (4cm). Cut and apply interfacing to half the width of each piece. For sleeve openings with finished bands of $\frac{5}{8}$in (15mm) wide cut the strips to $2\frac{1}{4}$in (6cm) by the opening length plus $1\frac{1}{4}$in (3·5cm).

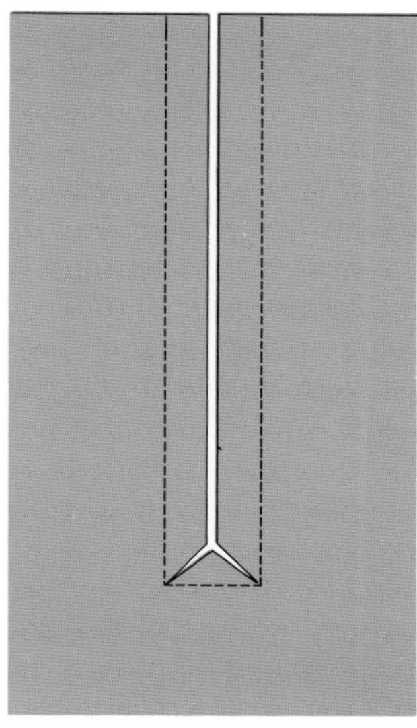

1 Mark position of opening and stay-stitch edge at half width of finished band to each side and below the mark. Slit the opening along the mark and into the corners.

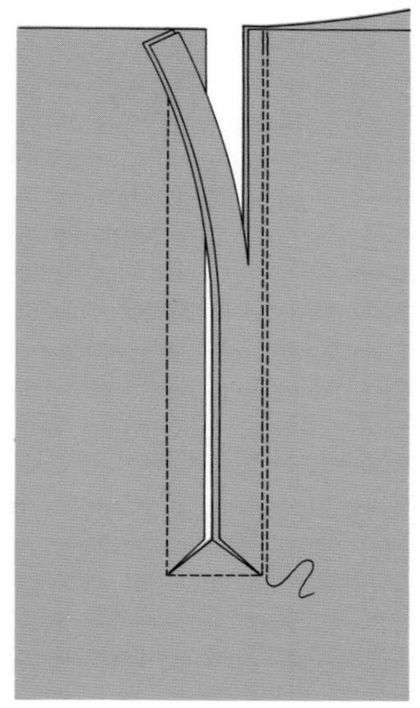

2 Pin the RS of one strip to the WS of the underlap edge of the opening. Baste and machine-stitch along the line of stay stitching to corner. Trim the edge.

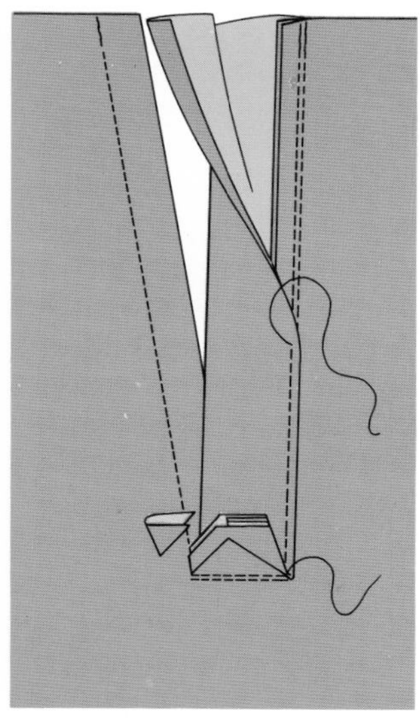

3 Press edge onto underlap, turn underlap to RS, fold under raw edge and stitch over seamline.
4 Stitch underlap to garment across triangle at end of opening. Cut across corners.

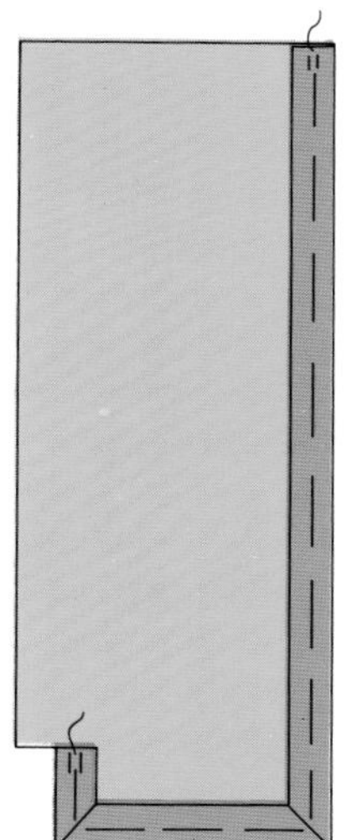

5 Mark length of opening from one end of inside edge of overlap band and clip seam allowance. Turn under remainder of seam allowances and baste, mitering corners.

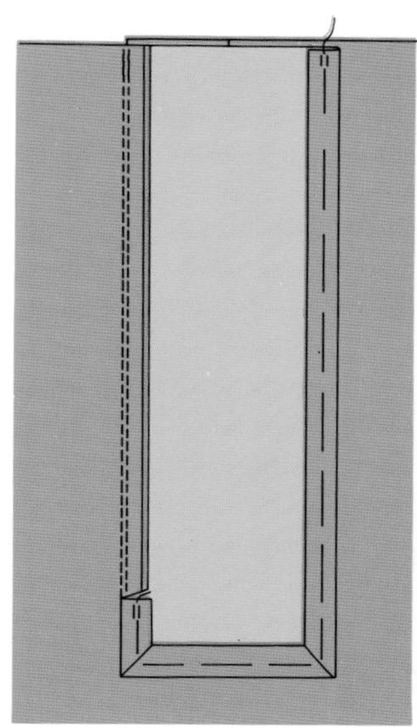

6 Baste and machine-stitch free edge of overlap band to free edge of opening with RS to WS. Press toward overlap and trim.

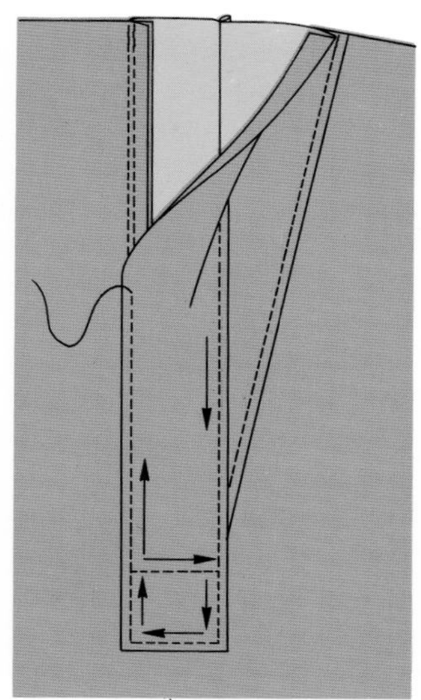

7 Fold band onto RS and then fold it in half. Baste over seamline. Top-stitch outer folded edge of band to base of opening. Stitch around base of band in a rectangle through all thicknesses then along inner edge of band to end.

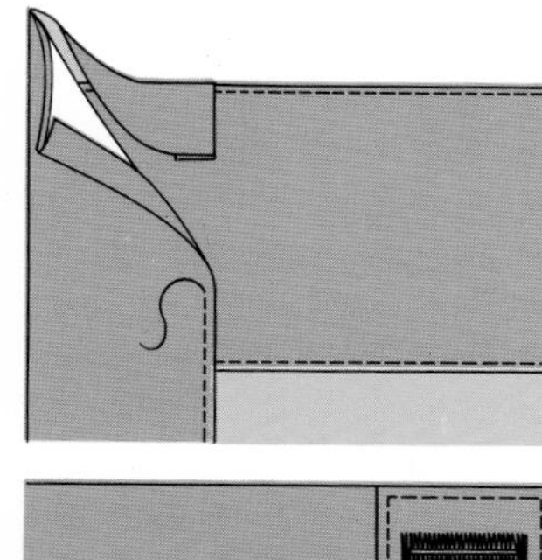

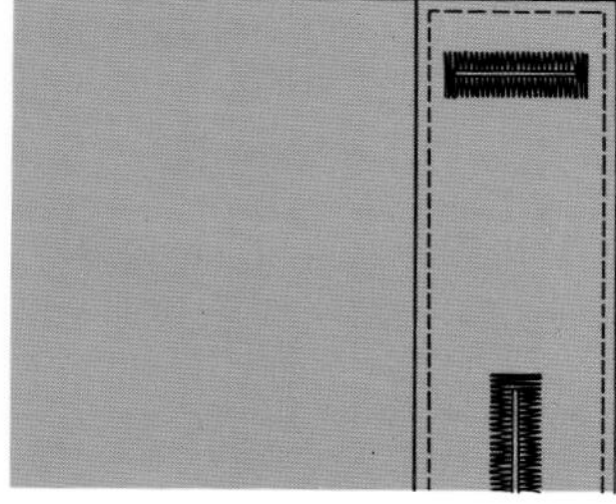

8 If finishing neck edge with a facing, apply facing before band. Fold under the bands and top-stitch at neck edge.

Sleeves

All set-in sleeves are cut with a sleeve cap slightly larger than the armhole, giving the extra fullness or ease necessary for the sleeve to fit over the arm and hang correctly. The fullness must be distributed evenly around the sleeve cap so that it is eased, rather than gathered, and appears quite smooth. On long tight sleeves ease is also included at the elbow, usually in the form of a dart, to allow room for the arm to bend.
On men's shirt sleeves the armhole is larger and the cap of the sleeve shallower with less fullness than set-in sleeves; it does not need gathering threads. The sleeve is cut quite wide to give an easy fit over the arm.
Puff sleeves are cut much larger at the sleeve cap than the armhole and this extra amount is gathered up to fit, giving the puffed shape.
Puff sleeves may be made from shirt-sleeve patterns. Other variations are shown on p64. You can also adapt armhole shapes for use with or without sleeves – see p66. All the patterns shown may be cut as short sleeves. Simply decide the length you would like the sleeve from the underarm, add a hem and cut across the pattern evenly.
Set-in sleeves are usually finished with plain hems and shirt sleeves are often gathered or pleated into cuffs. Some alternative finishes are shown here.

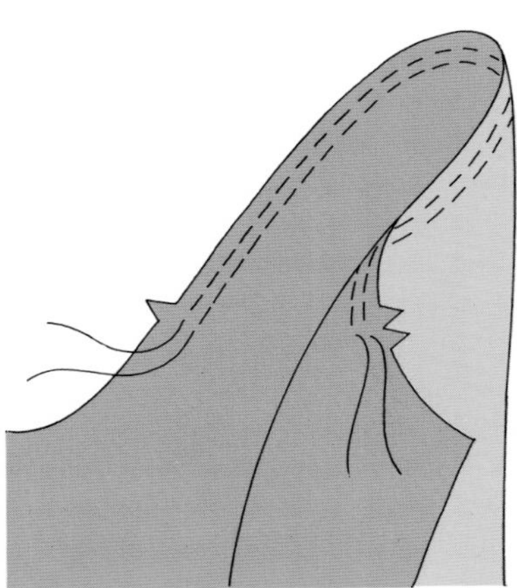

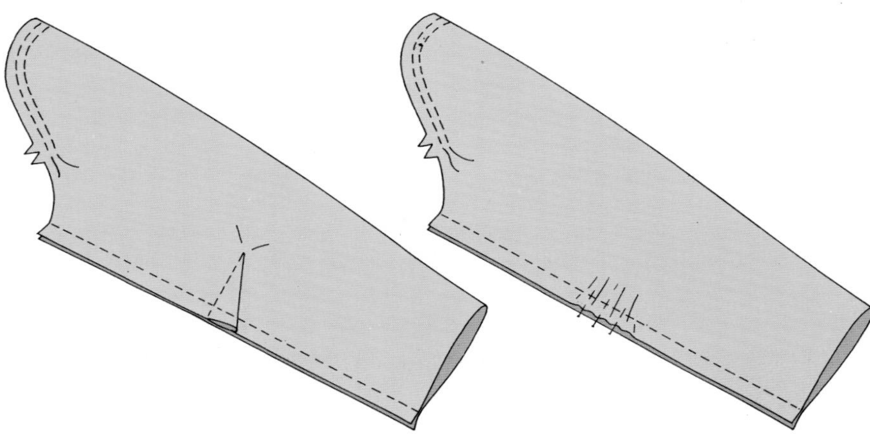

Set-in sleeves
1 Prepare the sleeve for easing into armhole by working 2 rows of gathering stitches around the sleeve cap between notches; place the first row on the seamline and the second row $\frac{1}{4}$in (5mm) above it.

2 On fitted sleeves construct the dart or ease in the elbow fullness. Check that the darts point toward the tip of the elbow or that the ease is distributed evenly over the elbow. Stitch the under-arm seam.

3 With RS together pin sleeve into armhole, matching underarm seams, notches and circle at sleeve cap to shoulder seam. Working on each side separately, pull up gathering threads until sleeve fits armhole. Distribute ease evenly. Baste and then machine-stitch, working with the sleeve uppermost.

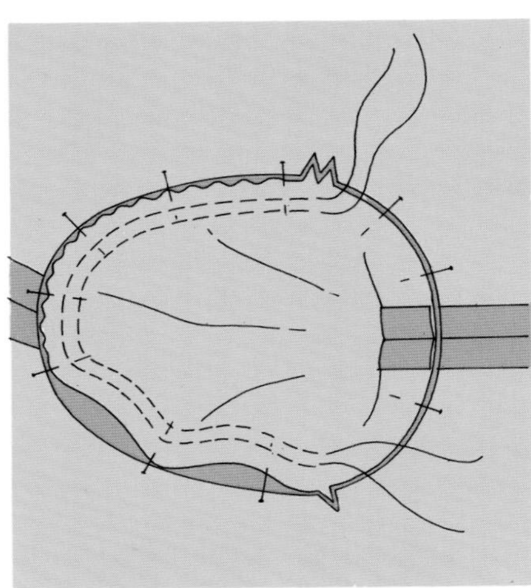

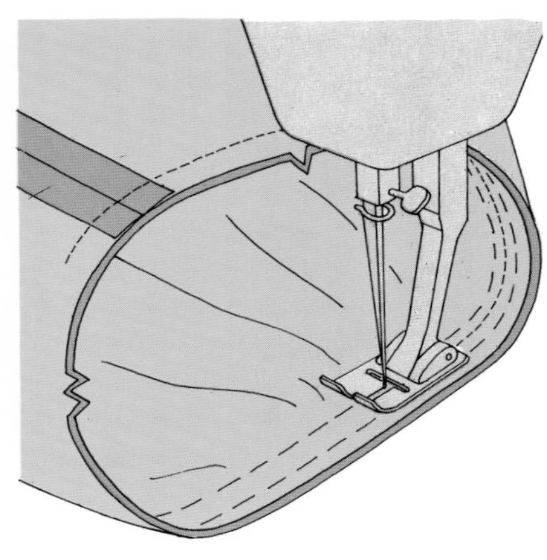

Puff sleeves
Prepare the sleeve cap as for a normal set-in sleeve. Stitch the underarm seam and finish the lower edge of the sleeve. With RS together matching underarm seams, notches and circle to shoulder seam, pin sleeve into armhole. Pull up the gathering threads until the sleeve fits the armhole, spreading the gathers evenly around the sleeve cap. Baste and then machine-stitch with the sleeve uppermost.

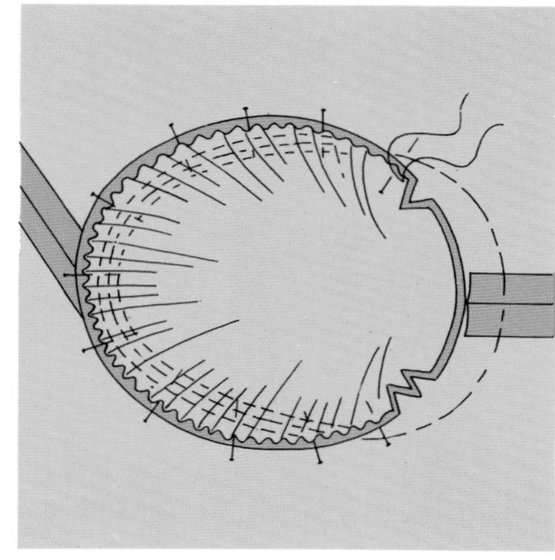

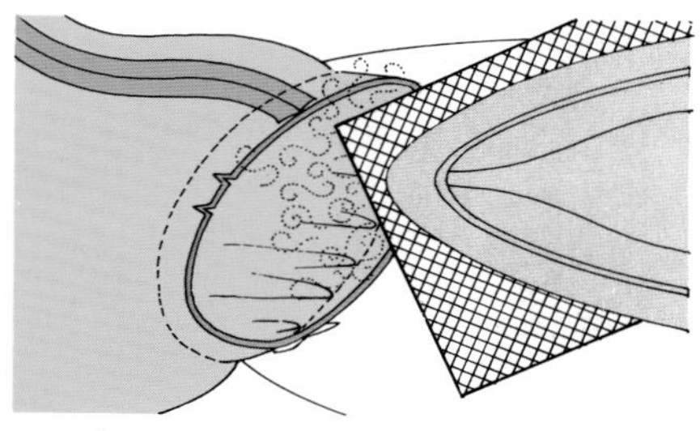

Pressing and finishing
Press the armhole seam over the narrow end of a sleeveboard using the point of the iron and pressing just up to the seamline. Turn the seam allowances into the sleeve and finish together.

Shirt sleeves
1 Construct the main part of the shirt but do not stitch side seams. With WS together, pin the sleeve into the armhole, matching notches, circles and underarm seamlines.
2 Ease in the fullness by hand across the sleeve cap. Baste and then machine-stitch seam. Press edges toward sleeve and complete like a flat felled seam.
3 Baste underarm seam and side seam in one with WS together. Complete as for a flat felled seam.

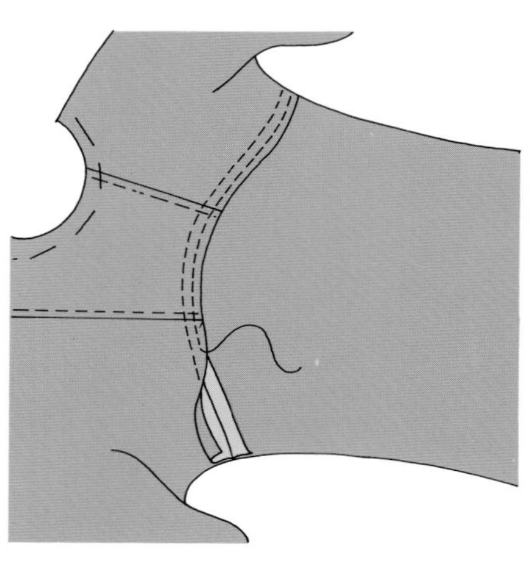

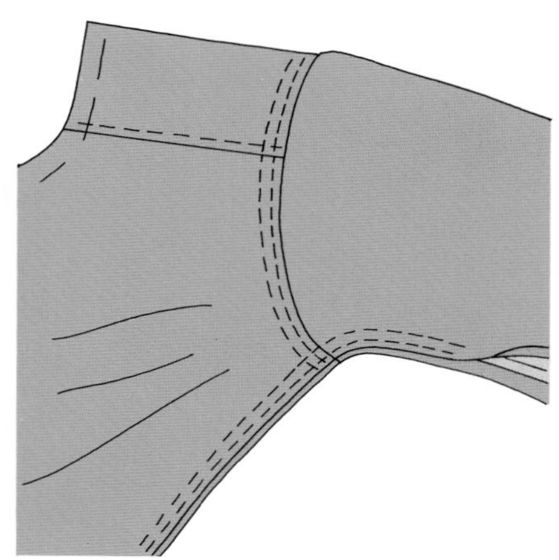

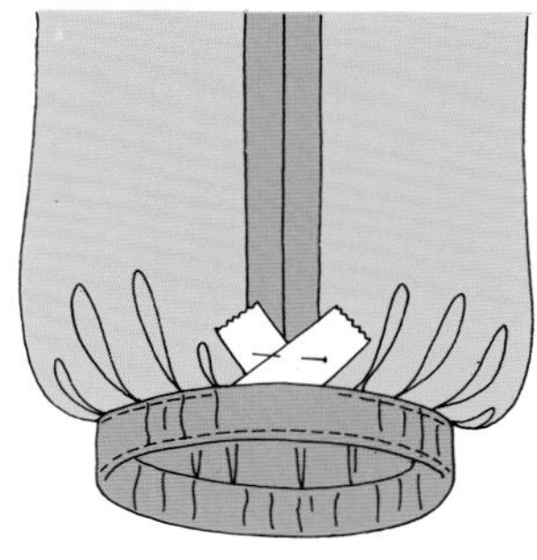

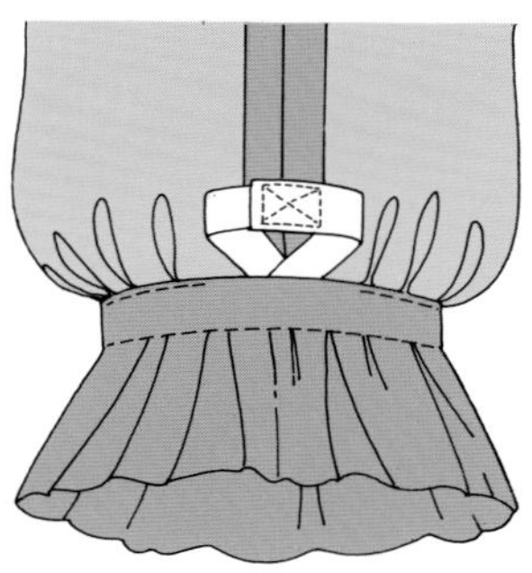

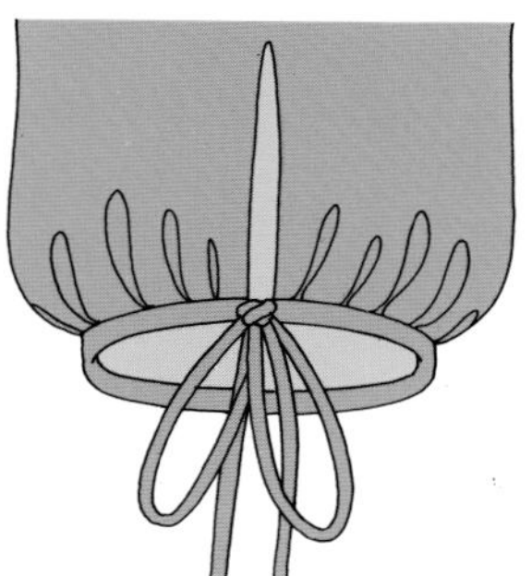

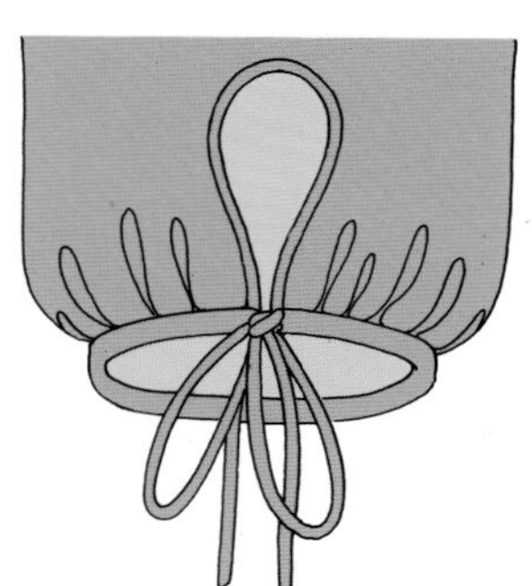

Elastic casing
Straighten the lower edge of the sleeve pattern and add $1\frac{1}{8}$in (30mm) for a hem. Turn up a double hem and machine-stitch, leaving a $\frac{5}{8}$in (15mm) opening. Machine-stitch lower edge. Insert elastic through hem to gather up fullness to fit. Stitch elastic ends together and then stitch opening.

Ruffle below casing
Start as left but add $4\frac{3}{4}$in (12·5cm) for the hem. Turn up the edge for 3in (7·5cm). Fold under $\frac{5}{8}$in (15mm) at the top of the hem and machine-stitch to the sleeve. Machine-stitch $\frac{5}{8}$in (15mm) below it to form a casing. Thread through elastic as left.

Binding with ties
Cut and face a slit opening at lower edge of sleeve (see p60). Bind the edge and continue binding to make rouleau ties (see p24).

Keyhole with ties
Cut and bind a keyhole opening at the lower edge of sleeve (see p60). Bind the hem edge and continue binding to make rouleau ties.

Sleeve variations

Bishop sleeve
Using shirt-sleeve pattern, divide the sleeve cap into 4 equal parts.
Draw lines from sleeve cap to hemline. Slash along these lines to within $\frac{1}{4}$in (6mm) of sleeve cap. Open each slash and spread pattern to fullness required. Re-shape lower edge.

Long sleeve gathered over sleeve cap
Using shirt-sleeve pattern, divide sleeve cap into 4 equal parts. Draw lines from sleeve cap to hemline. Draw horizontal line connecting underarm seams at armhole. Slash from center of cap of sleeve to horizontal line and across to both sides. Spread the sleeve cap raising the upper section of sleeve to amount required for fullness. If more fullness is required over top of sleeve, add to the cap of the sleeve tapering to side sections as shown by dotted line.

Tight short puff sleeve
Trace length of short sleeve from dress-sleeve pattern. Draw parallel line through center of sleeve. Divide sleeve cap horizontally into equal parts as shown.
Draw lines across to mark sections. Slash through center from top to within $\frac{1}{4}$in (6mm) of bottom edge, then across lines at top as shown. Spread pattern for fullness. Re-draw the cap of the sleeve.

Puff sleeve
Trace length of short sleeve from shirt-sleeve pattern. Divide sleeve cap into 4 equal parts. Draw lines from sleeve cap to hemline. Slash along these lines and spread pattern sections equally. Re-draw sleeve cap from side sections, and lower edge dropping hemline about 1in (2·5cm) in center. Mark grainline through center of sleeve. For a longer version, gathered in by elastic forming ruffle at lower edge, extend length of sleeve and spread the pattern more at the lower edge.

Bell sleeve gathered at cap
Trace short sleeve from shirt-sleeve pattern to length required. Divide sleeve cap into 4 equal parts. Draw lines from sleeve cap to hemline. Slash along these lines and spread each section equally at the top and bottom, allowing more fullness at the hemline for flouncing. Re-draw sleeve cap from side sections and lower edge dropping curve about 1in (2·5cm) in center. Mark grainline through center of sleeve.

Leg-of-mutton sleeve
Using dress sleeve pattern draw horizontal line to underarm seams 2in (5cm) above the elbow dart. Divide the upper section of sleeve into 4 equal parts. Draw lines from top to bottom for each section. Cut upper sleeve section away. Slash along lines and spread pattern sections equally for fullness. Re-draw sleeve cap from side sections and lower edge dropping curve about 1in (2·5cm) in center. Mark grainline through center of sleeve.

Unusual sleeve variations can be made by altering the line of the armhole and then adapting the sleeve to fit it (set it in as described on p62). Three of the most common armhole variations for sleeveless designs are shown on this page. Finish them with facings of the same shape (see p58). Their corresponding sleeve adaptations are shown opposite. All the sleeves shown can be made in short or three-quarter versions or varied once you have mastered the principle of adapting the pattern, in any other way, to suit a design.

Dropped-shoulder armhole
Measure down the side seam 1in (2·5cm) and square out from the armhole 1in (2·5cm). Curve between the 2 points for the underarm seam. Raise the shoulder seam $\frac{1}{4}$in (6mm) at the armhole and draw outer edge of sleeve to the required length of cap sleeve. Draw new shoulder line tapering into shoulder at base of neck. Add hem allowance to sleeve.

Cut-in armhole
Determine width of shoulder seam, measuring from neck edge. On the front and back bodice pattern draw a line from this point at the shoulder to the deepest part of the armhole curve.
Curve line in slightly for a smooth fit around the upper section of the armhole. If the shoulder width is narrow cut the armhole and neck facing in one piece for a sleeveless dress, as shown by lower dotted line.

Square armhole
On the front and back bodice pattern draw a horizontal line from the side seam at the armhole inward to depth of square required.
The new armhole line may be taken from any point of the shoulder seam. Decide the width of shoulder seam and from this point connect the shoulder to the inner corner to form square. The depth of the side seam may be dropped to lower the square if required.

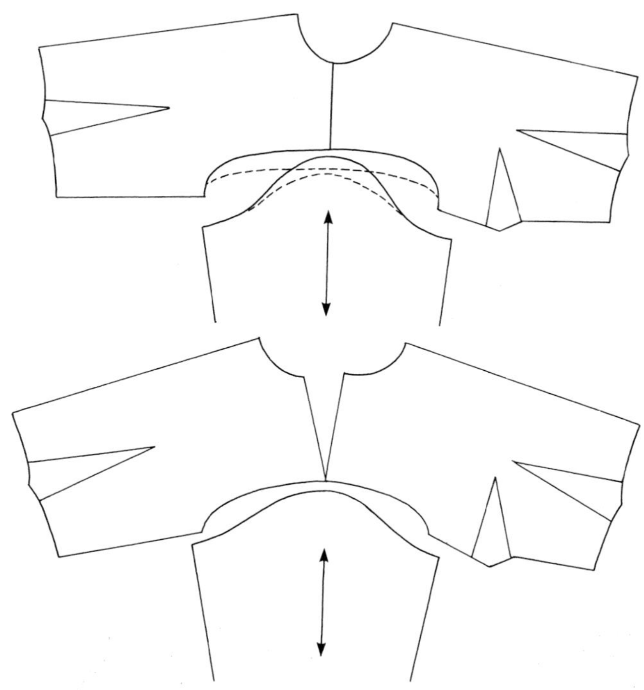

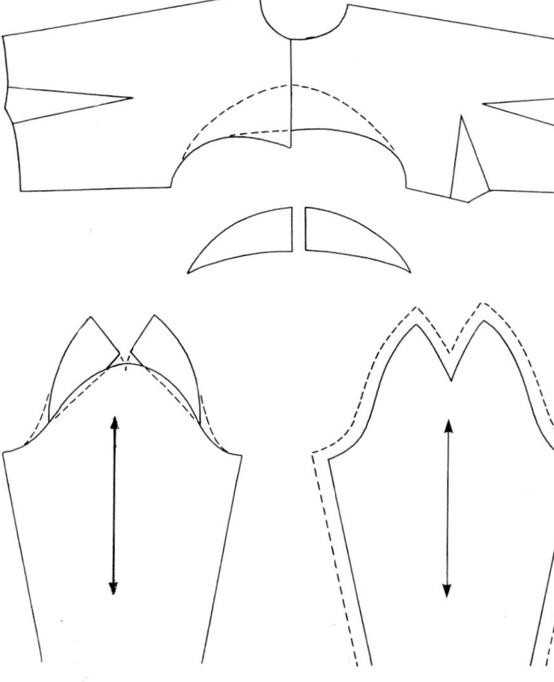

Dropped shoulder and sleeve
For this style, take off the cap of the sleeve the amount by which the shoulder is dropped.

1 Place the front and back shoulder seams together. Place center of sleeve cap to shoulder, the grainline being straight with the shoulder seam.

2 Drop the shoulder line to required depth and draw new armhole tapering into the deepest part of the armhole curve.

3 Cut a section of the same depth from the sleeve cap in a smooth curve over top of sleeve. Add seam allowances to new lines.

Cut-in armhole with sleeve
If the back bodice pattern has a shoulder dart, trim the same amount from the armhole edge as shown.

1 Place the front and back bodice pattern pieces shoulder to shoulder. Measure the required length of shoulder from base of neck and mark at shoulder line.

2 Draw lines of armhole from this point to curve at armholes. Cut away these sections from the bodices and attach to the sleeve cap, placing them $\frac{5}{8}$in (15mm) above the crown and $\frac{5}{8}$in (15mm) apart at the center. Spread the pattern to form a shoulder dart. Connect outer lines of sleeve and dart. Add seam allowances.

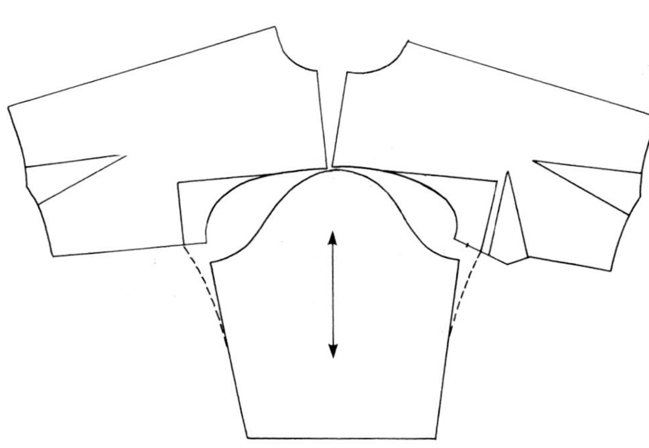

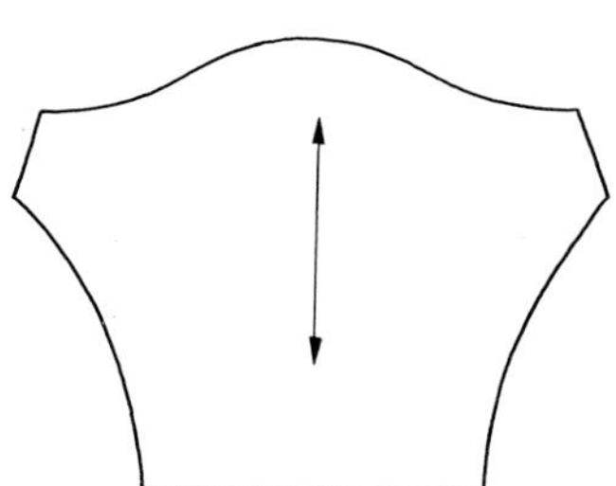

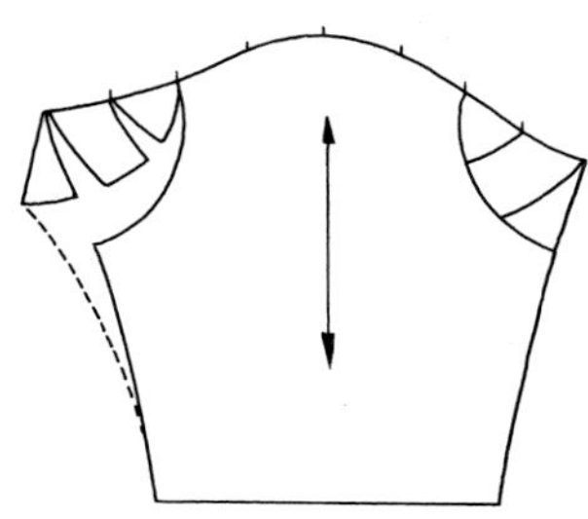

Square armhole with sleeve
To provide extra length on the sleeve at the top of the underarm seam so the arm can rise comfortably, lengthen the underarm seam by the amount that the armhole is deepened.

1 Place front and back shoulder points together with neck edge $2\frac{1}{2}$in (6·5cm) apart. Draw the square armhole $1\frac{1}{2}$in (3·8cm) deep from the underarm point and 2in (5cm) in. Connect to shoulder. Cut out front and back armholes along new lines. Place cap of the sleeve to shoulder point balancing sleeve evenly on either side. Widen top of sleeve from armhole to elbow. Draw new outline of sleeve cap between bodice and sleeve lines joining underarm and shoulder points.

2 Divide sleeve cap into 8 equal parts. To lengthen underarm seam $1\frac{1}{2}$in (3·8cm), draw slash lines as shown. Slash and spread each side of pattern to this amount. Re-draw underarm seams. Add seam allowances to new lines.

Basic dresses

Master pattern sheet
Using patterns and cutting out 16
Seams and edge finishes 20
Zippers 26
Hems 28
Darts 44
Facings 58
Sleeves 62
Collars 78

This is a basic pattern for a dress bodice which may be incorporated in a variety of dress designs. To alter the design, change the neckline, add a collar, adapt the sleeves or vary the type of skirt. You can also add pockets, belts and tabs. The basic techniques and method of making the dress, however, remain very similar for all styles.
The fabric requirements are for a dress with a high round neck, long fitted sleeves and flared skirt.

You will need

fabric 36in (90cm) wide:

bust size 34	38	42in
(85	95	105cm)
4	$4\frac{1}{8}$	$4\frac{1}{4}$yd
(3·60	3·70	3·80m)

matching sewing thread
interfacing: 8in (20cm) for all sizes
24in (60cm) dress zipper

Cutting out

Trace the pattern pieces in the size required from the master sheet. Add seam and hem allowances. If you are making a flared skirt from the wraparound (pattern pieces 4 and 5), omit wrap and facing from the front (piece 4) and place CF on a fold. Make a pattern for front and back neck facings and collar if required. Lay pieces on fabric as shown, and cut.

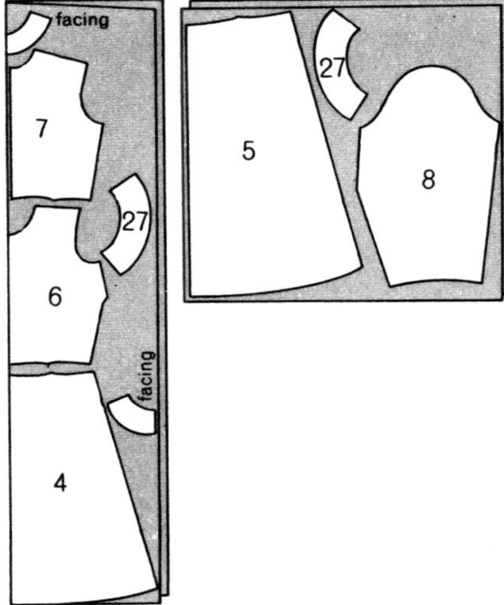

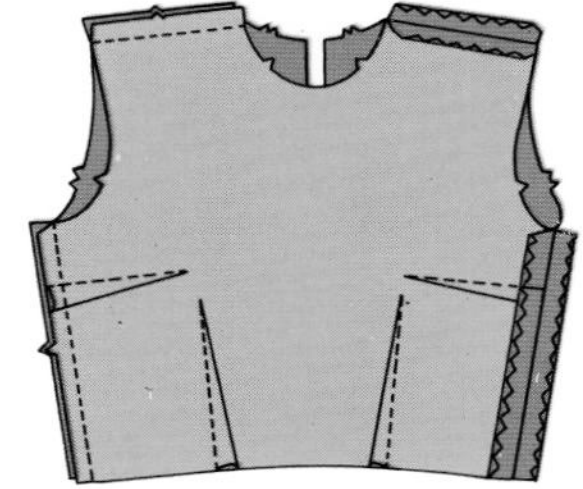

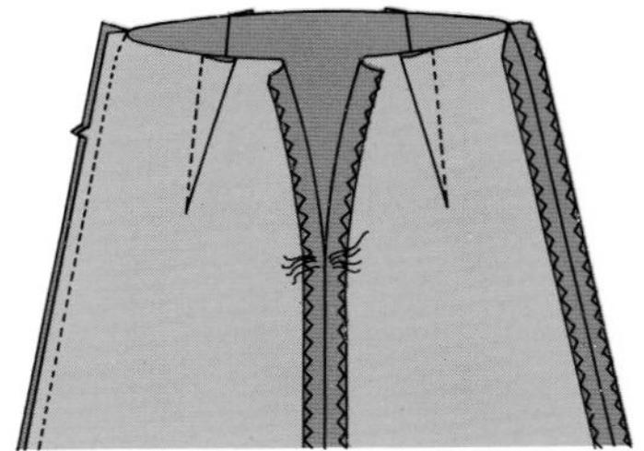

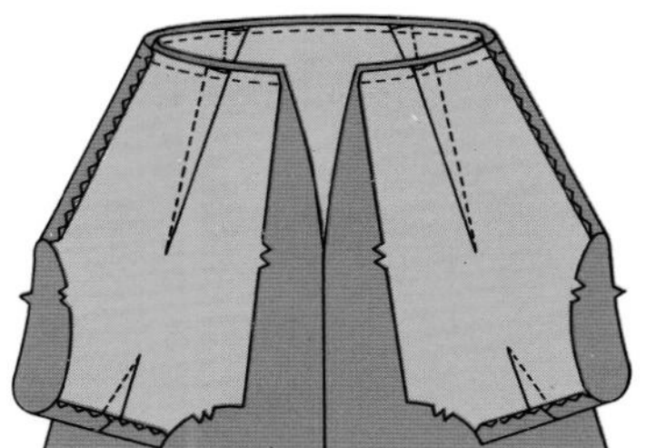

Making the dress

1 With RS together baste and stitch all the darts. Press darts downward or into the center. With RS together matching notches, join the front and back bodices (pattern pieces 6 and 7) at the shoulders and sides with plain seams. Finish seams and press open.

2 With RS together matching notches, baste and stitch the side seams and CB seam to circle on the skirt. Finish seams and press open.

3 With RS together matching CBs, side seams and CFs join the bodice to the skirt at the waistline edge with a plain seam. Press seam upward and finish edges together. Turn the seam allowance along the opening at CB to inside and baste. Insert the zipper into the CB opening.

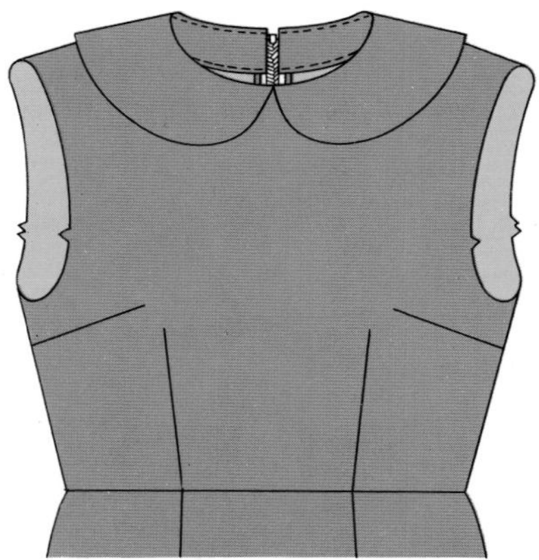

4 Finish the neck edge with collar (if you are putting one on) and facings.

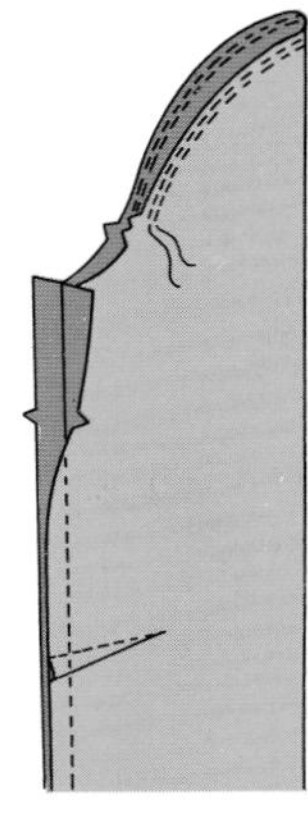

5 Prepare cap of sleeve (pattern piece 8) and apply like a set-in sleeve.

6 Try the dress on and mark the sleeve and skirt hems. Turn hems up and baste close to folded edges. Finish hems using the most suitable method for the fabric.

Sailor-collar dress with hipline pleated skirt

You will need
fabric, 45in (115cm) wide: $4\frac{1}{8}$yd (3·70m)
matching sewing thread
22in (55cm) zipper

Adapting the pattern Extend front and back bodice from side bust dart to hips so that the measurement between CF and CB to side edge is a quarter of hip size (including ease). Adapt the neckline and cut a sailor collar (see p80).

Making the dress Make the bodice like the basic dress but omit waist darts and join CB seam for 2in (5cm) from top so collar may be attached. Use remaining part of CB seam for zipper opening. Attach collar and make a pleated skirt (see p42) to fit lower edge of bodice. When fitting the dress curve the side seams in at the waist for a closer fit.

V-necked dress with circular skirt and bound edges

You will need
fabric, 36in (90cm) wide: $5\frac{3}{4}$yd (5·20m)
matching sewing thread
24in (60cm) zipper
bias binding to required length

Adapting the pattern Cut the V-neckline (see p56). Shorten the sleeves and slit the pattern to make bell shape as for bishop sleeves (see p64); cut out sleeves on the bias grain. Cut a circular skirt (see p46). Trim off seam allowances from neck and hems from sleeves and skirt.

Making the dress Make the dress like the basic dress but bind all raw exposed edges (see p25).

Tie-collar dress with gathered skirt

You will need
fabric, 45in (115cm) wide: 5yd (4·50m)
matching sewing thread
22in (55cm) zipper

Adapting the pattern Mark neck slit opening on CF. Cut a combined facing for the opening with the front neck. Adapt the sleeve pattern for bishop sleeves (see p64), adapt the flared-skirt pattern (see p54) to make a gathered skirt (omitting pockets). Cut the tie collar and cuffs (see pp80 and 38).

Making the dress Make like the basic dress but joining CB seam for 2in (5cm) at the top (use remaining part of seam for zipper). Make CF neck opening, attaching facing to slit only. Baste facing to neck edge with WS together and attach the tie collar. Make openings in sleeves and gather into cuffs.

T-shirt dress with tight skirt and side slits

You will need
fabric, 36in (90cm) wide: $3\frac{1}{8}$yd (3m)
matching sewing thread
24in (60cm) zipper

Adapting the pattern Extend front and back bodice to required dress length (including hem) so that hipline measurement between CF or CB and sides is a quarter of hip size (including ease). For side slits measure up seams from hemline for required length and increase seam allowance (see p60). Cut a new neckline (see p56) and shorten the sleeves (see p62).

Making the dress Make like the basic dress bodice but omit waist darts. Make side slits before turning up hem. When fitting the dress, particularly if using jersey fabric, curve the side seams in at the waist for a closer fit.

Fitting and altering patterns

All garments should fit comfortably without pulling or wrinkling; achieving this is an essential part of good dressmaking. Fitting should be done in two stages. Before cutting out, check your body measurements, including ease where appropriate (see p14), against the pattern measurements and adjust to size if necessary. If you know that your figure does not conform to standard sizing in any way it is much easier to adapt the pattern than to alter the garment.
Minor alterations, which may be necessary because of the type of fabric and the garment you are making rather than because of figure problems, can be made when you try on the garment (see pp74–77).
If you are adapting the design of a garment you can save disappointment by making a trial version in cheap fabric. Note any alterations and adjust the pattern accordingly before cutting out the real fabric. Basic alterations for bodices, sleeves and skirts are given here; for fitting and altering slacks see p98.

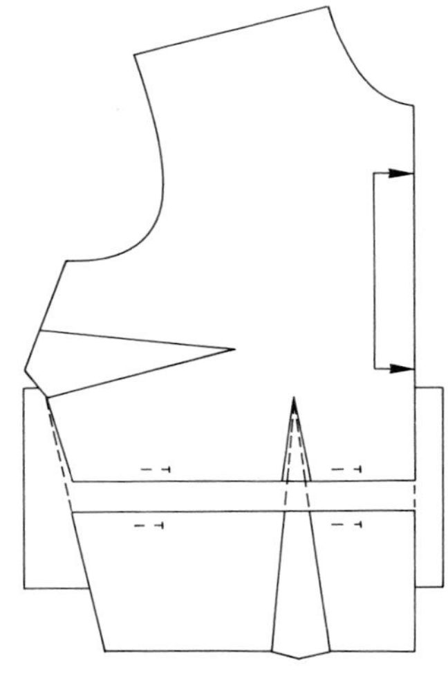

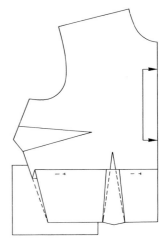

Long waist
This causes the bodice to ride above the waistline. To lengthen the bodice cut across the pattern horizontally. Spread it by the required amount and pin the pattern to paper. Straighten the side seams and re-draw the darts. This applies to both the front and back bodice pieces.

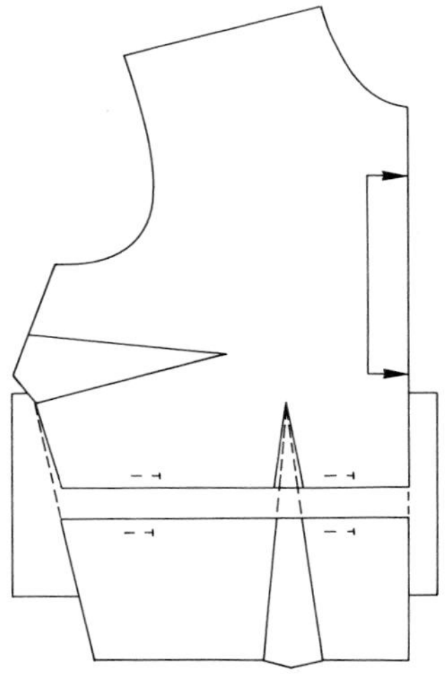

Short waist
This causes creases above the waistline. To shorten the bodice make a horizontal tuck to take out the required amount in the pattern, and pin it down to paper. Straighten the side seams and re-draw the darts. This applies to both the front and back bodice pieces.

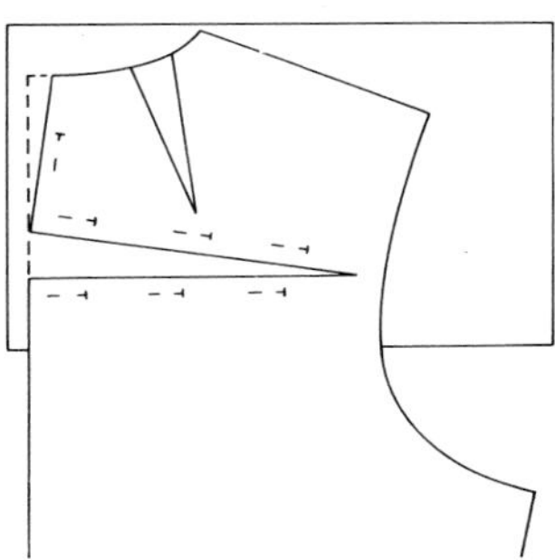

Round shoulders
These cause the neckline and collar to stand away from the back neck. Cut the back bodice pattern about $4\frac{1}{2}$in (12cm) down from the CB neck to the armhole. Raise and pin onto paper. To obtain the original neck measurement use the lengthened curved line if there is a CB seam. If the pattern is cut on a fold, use the straight line, taking the extra fullness into a dart at the neckline.

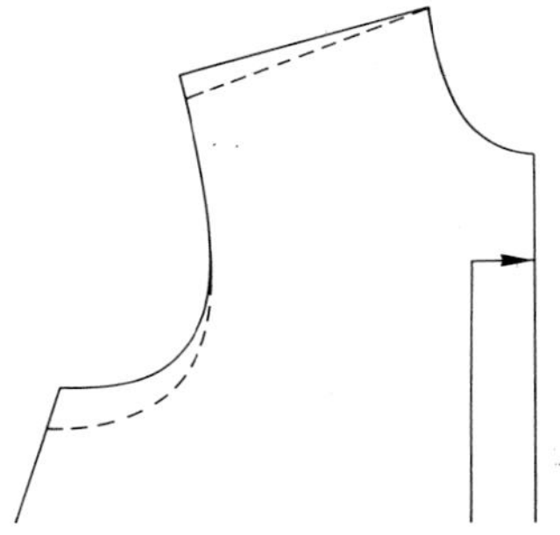

Sloping shoulders
These cause folds at the armhole. Draw a line from the armhole tapering down to nothing at the neckline and cut away the required amount. Cut away the same amount at the underarm to retain the original armhole size for the cap of the sleeve. This applies to both front and back bodice pieces.

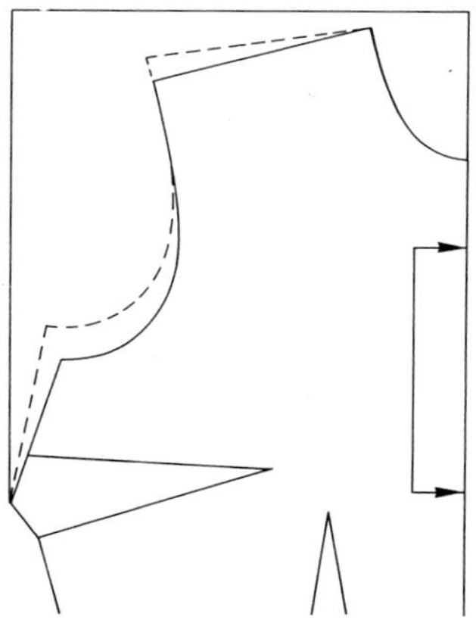

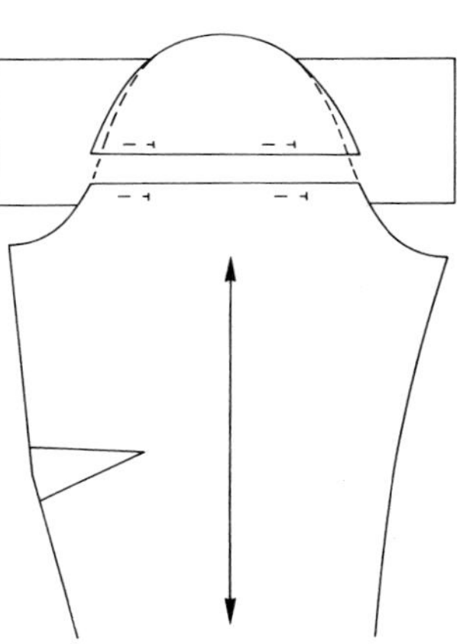

Square shoulders
Square shoulders cause creasing across the front and back neckline. Pin the front and back bodice pieces down onto paper to armhole level. Draw the new shoulder line allowing the required amount at the armhole tapering down to nothing at the neck. Raise the line at the underarm to maintain the original size and shape of the armhole. If the figure requires a larger armhole omit the addition at the underarm but increase the sleeve cap to make it fit into the larger armhole with the correct amount of ease.

Measuring figure 14
Using patterns and cutting out 16

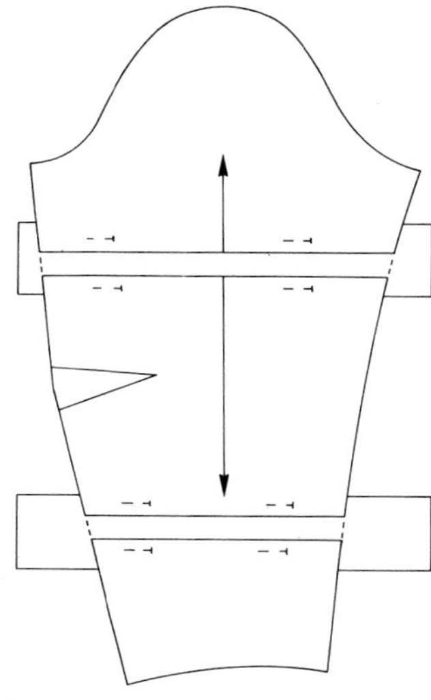

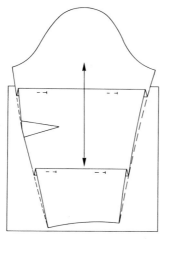

Long arms
To lengthen the sleeve, cut across the pattern horizontally. Spread it by the required amount and pin the pattern onto paper. Straighten the underarm seams.

Short arms
To shorten the sleeves, make horizontal tucks in the pattern and pin it down to paper. Straighten the underarm seams.

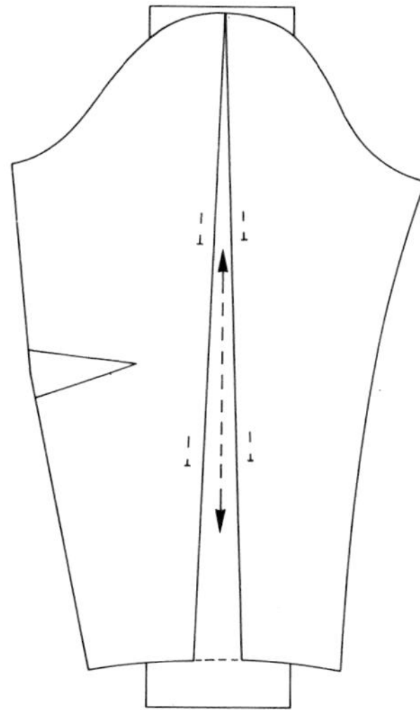

Fat arms
Slash center of pattern to cap of the sleeve. Spread it by the necessary amount at the hem tapering to sleeve cap. Insert and pin paper in slash. Re-draw grainline through center and straighten the lower edge.

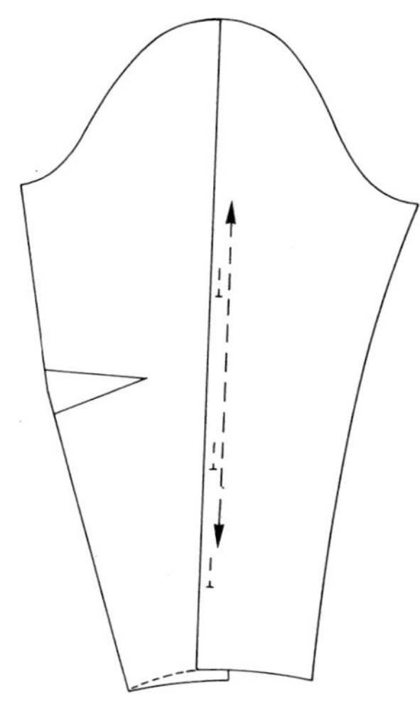

Thin arms
Slash center of pattern to cap of the sleeve. Overlap the slash edges and decrease the necessary amount at the hem tapering to sleeve cap. Pin in place.
Re-draw grainline through center and straighten the lower edge.

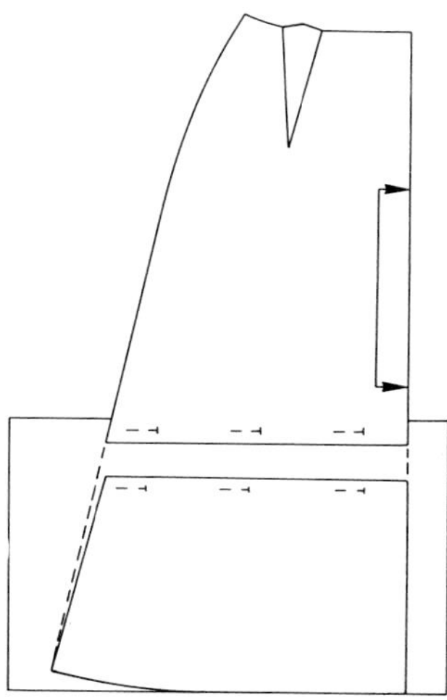

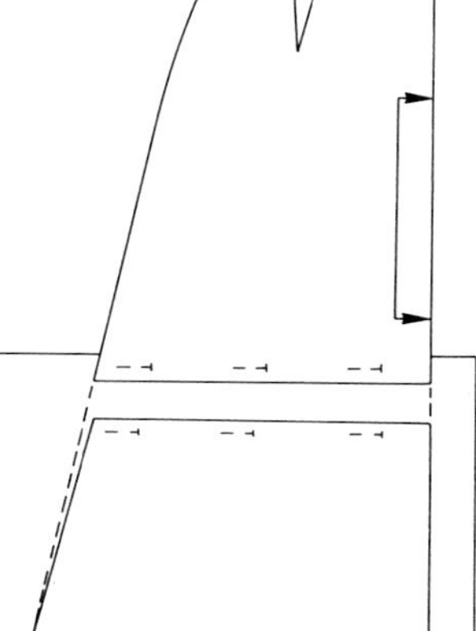

Short skirt
To lengthen the skirt, cut across the pattern horizontally. Spread the pattern to the required amount and pin it to paper. Straighten the side seams. This applies to both front and back skirt pieces.

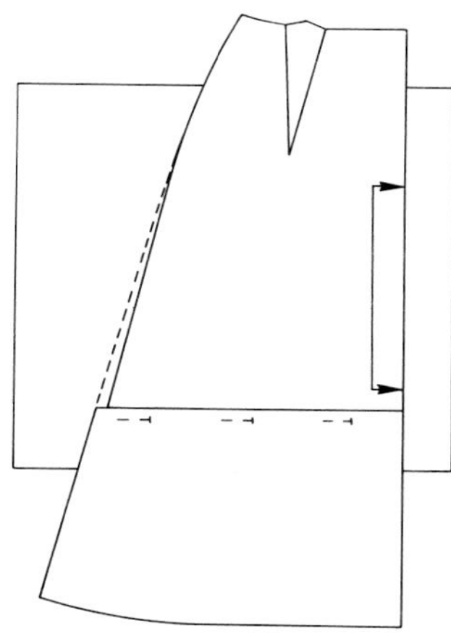

Long skirt
To shorten the skirt, make a horizontal tuck in the pattern and pin down to paper. Straighten the side seams. This applies to both front and back skirt pieces.

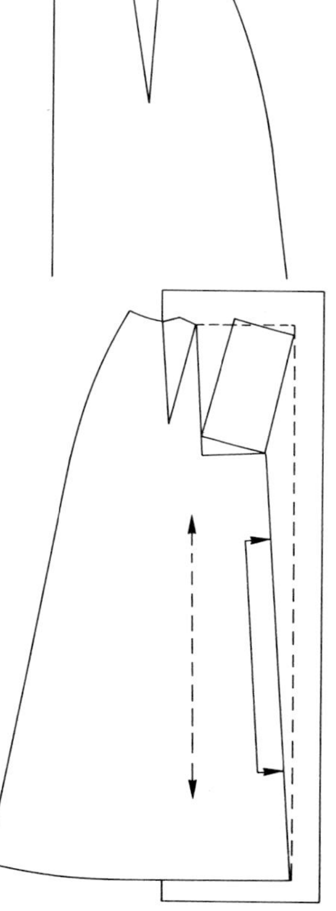

Hollow back
This causes wrinkles below the back waistline. On the back skirt pattern, mark and cut away the required amount from the CB tapering to nothing at the side seam.

High abdomen
This will cause the skirt to crease horizontally around the hips. Cut down from the center of the front waistline and across to the CF of the pattern at approximately hip level. Spread the section toward the CF to give extra width and height. Re-draw the waistline and CF line to straighten.

Fitting and altering bodices

Basic stitches 18
Darts 44

You should always try on a garment to check its fit several times while making it. This is necessary even when using a pattern which you know fits well because of the differences between types of fabric and the minor differences which can occur during cutting out.

To prepare the garment for its first fitting, stay-stitch any edges which are likely to stretch (e.g. neck and armholes) and then, with WS of fabric together, pin darts and main sections. Place the pins so that they point along the seamlines. Try on the garment and check for overall fit; make any adjustments by re-pinning.

For the second fitting, baste all the seams with RS together and incorporating any earlier adjustments. Try on and pin edges of openings together. Look at yourself critically in a full-length mirror and, if possible, ask someone else to look at your back view. Move your arms around to check the fit of sleeves and armholes, and sit down to check waistline and bodice length. Look at center and side seams to make sure they hang vertically. Check the positions of all darts and if the garment wrinkles or bulges locate the cause and remedy as described here and overleaf.

Have subsequent fittings after basting on major sections, such as sleeves or collar, and when determining the hemline.

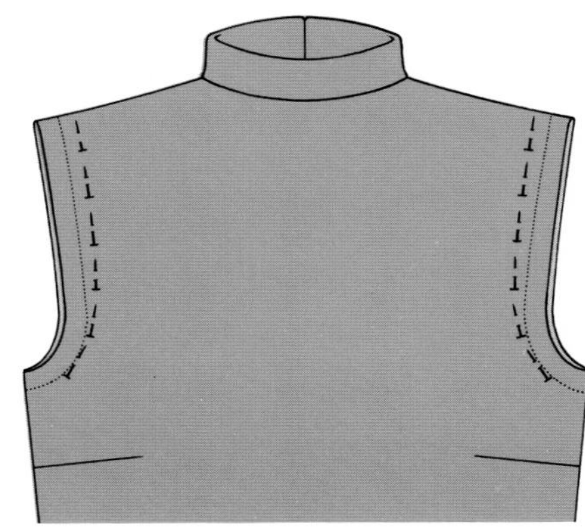

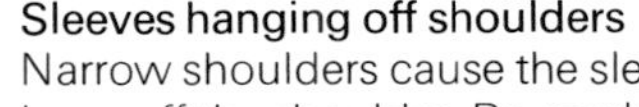

Sleeves hanging off shoulders
Narrow shoulders cause the sleeve to hang off the shoulder. Re-mark the correct shoulder line with pins. Remove the sleeves and set them into the higher armhole line matching notches, shoulder and underarm seams.

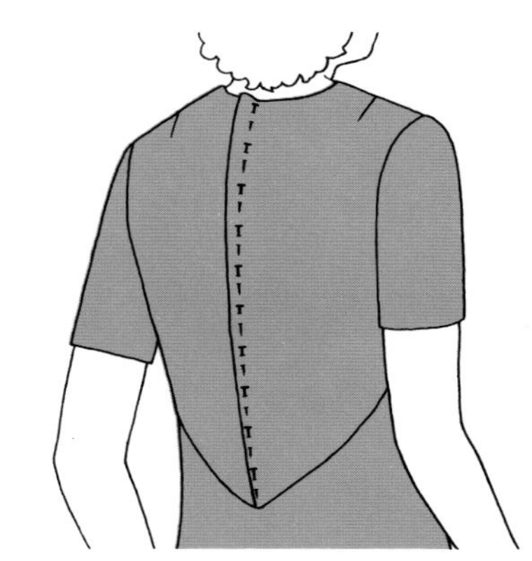

Back of dress too wide at neck
This often occurs on a heavy-busted figure where the back above the armholes is relatively narrow. Take in the surplus in the CB, creating a seam or removing zipper if necessary.
Carefully match striped or plaid fabrics.

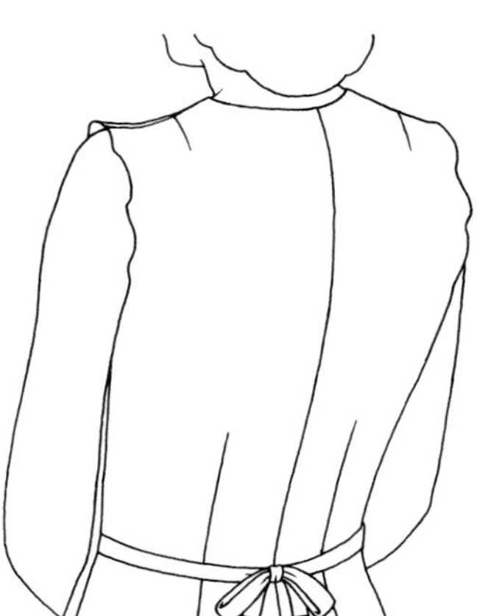

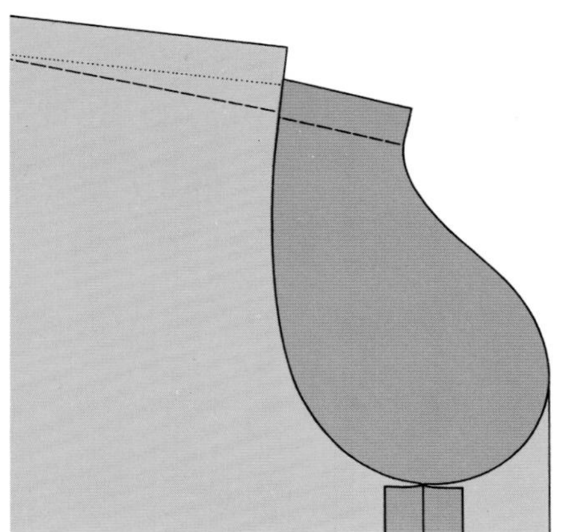

Gaping armhole at back
This is usually found on sleeveless dresses, caused by prominent shoulder blades. Lift the back shoulder seam slightly and also take in the back bodice at the underarm seam if necessary. Remember to make the same adjustment to the sleeve facing or sleeve cap.

Gaping neck at front
This is normally found only on low-cut necklines and is often caused by a full bust. Increase the bust shaping by inserting darts or gathers into the front neckline. Re-cut the neck facing to this new shape.

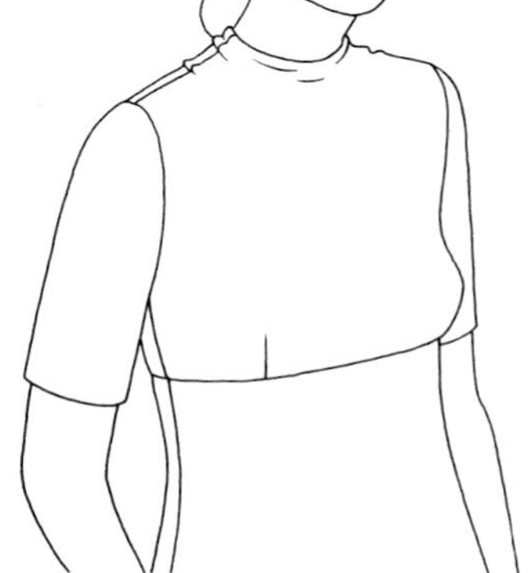

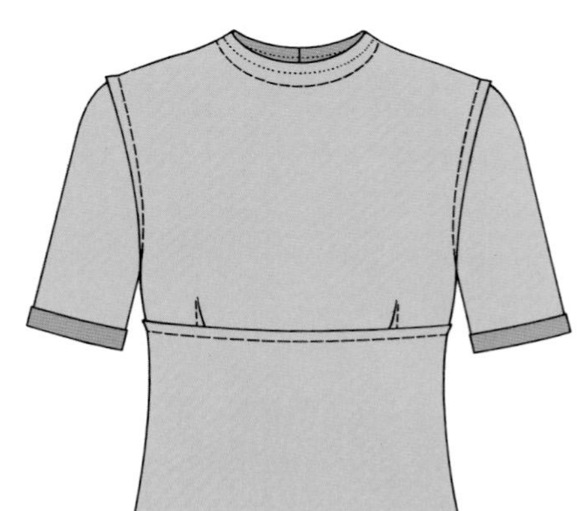

Neckline too high and tight
Remove the neck facings if already applied and lower the neckline, cutting new facings to this shape. Mark in new balance points and match shoulder seams before applying facing.

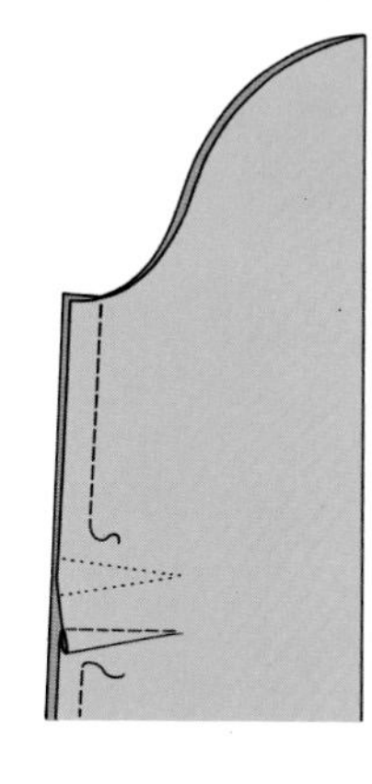

Uncomfortable fitted sleeve
This is usually caused by the darts being in wrong position for the elbow. Unpick the darts and press flat. Pin in new darts at elbow. Stitch, making the dart the same length as the original.

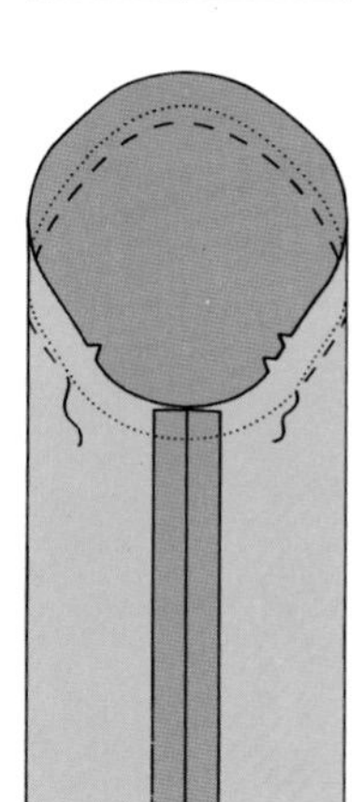

Too much ease in cap of sleeve
This causes the fabric to ripple or pleat. Fullness needs to be taken off the sleeve cap. Remove the sleeves from armholes. Smooth out sleeve cap. Run a row of gathering stitches around sleeve cap $\frac{1}{8}$–$\frac{1}{4}$in (3–6mm) below the seamline. Re-baste sleeve into armhole aligning new ease line with armhole seamline. Stitch.

Fitting and altering skirts

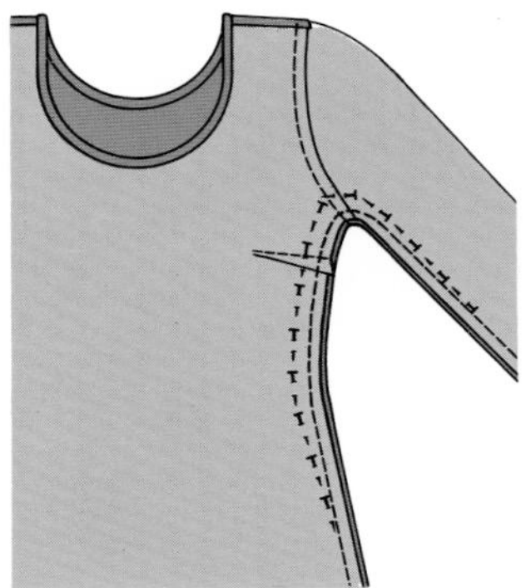

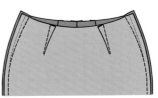

Stretchy garment too big around the middle
Try the garment on and pin in larger allowances at the side seams for a closer fit. Also pin larger allowances on the underarm seam of sleeves so that the sleeve and bodice armholes match.

Skirt waist too big
Remove the waistband and take in the side seams, tapering the new line into hip level. If this is not enough increase the darts.

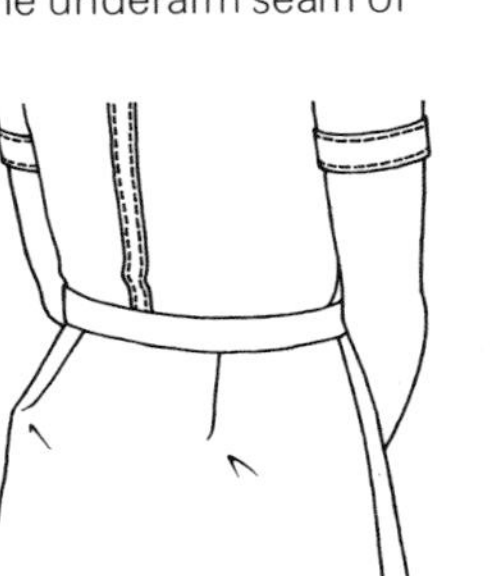

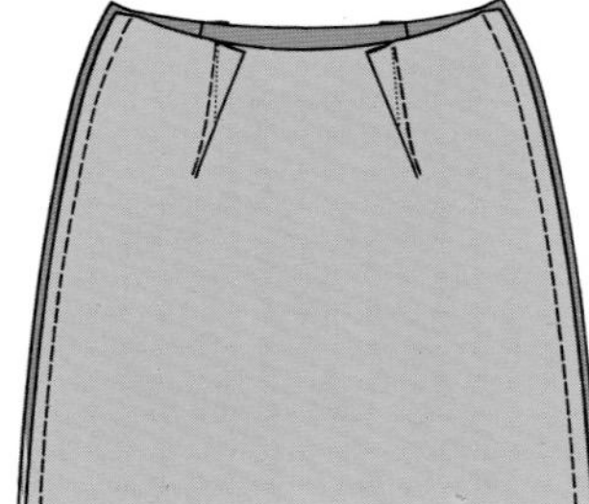

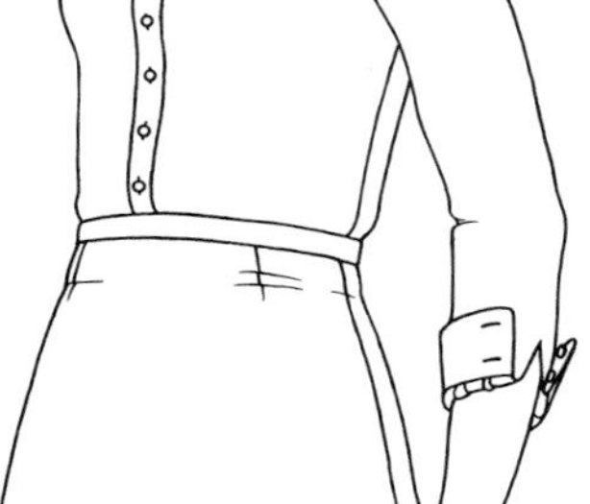

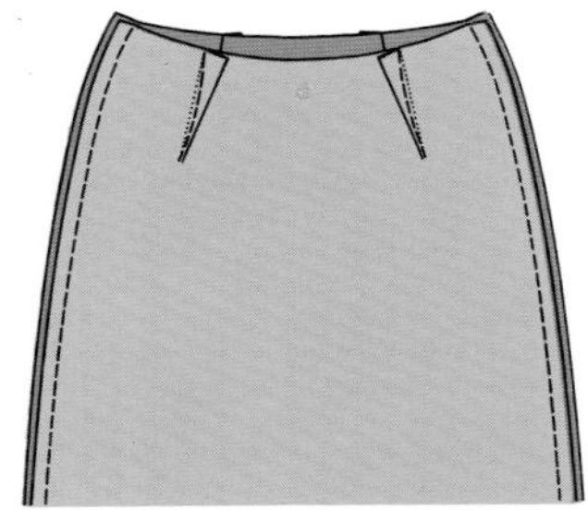

Fabric bulges below darts
The darts are probably too short or the dart has not been tapered smoothly to a point. Either re-stitch the points or try the garment on and pin darts to a longer length. Stitch to this length, maintaining the original width.

Wrinkling at darts
Darts may be too straight and therefore not molding to the figure shape. Try the garment on and pin in the darts to conform to the figure. The darts will probably be slightly curved. Re-stitch darts tapering to points.

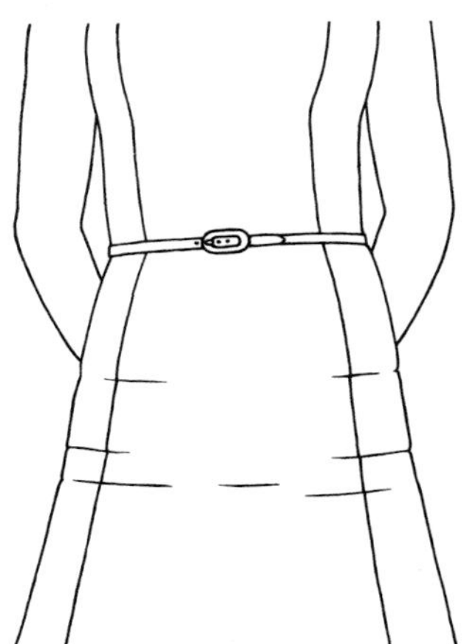

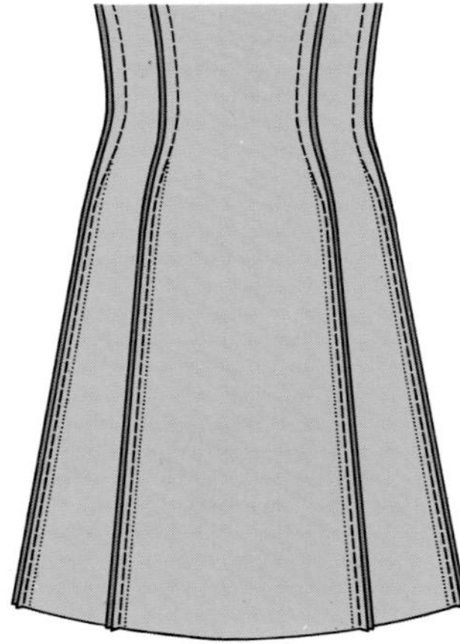

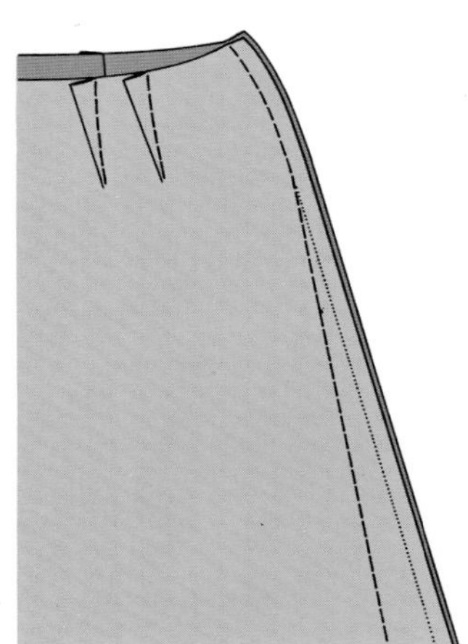

Panelled dress or skirt tight over thighs
Let out each seam by the same amount, tapering into seam just below waist. If this is a large amount finish the seam edges together for strength.

Skirt too loose over thighs
Take in the skirt side seams tapering into hipline.

Basic stitches 18
Darts 44

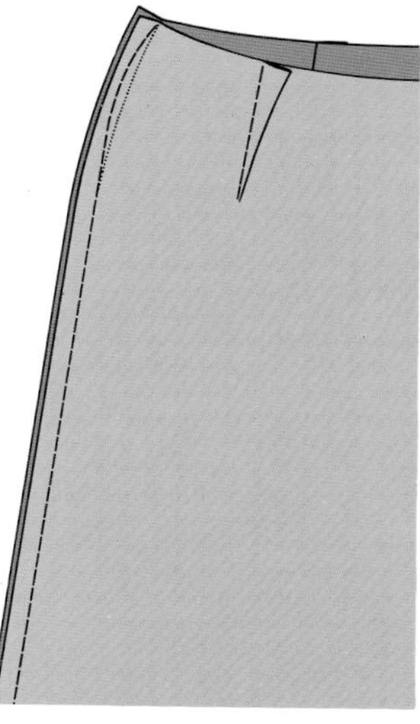

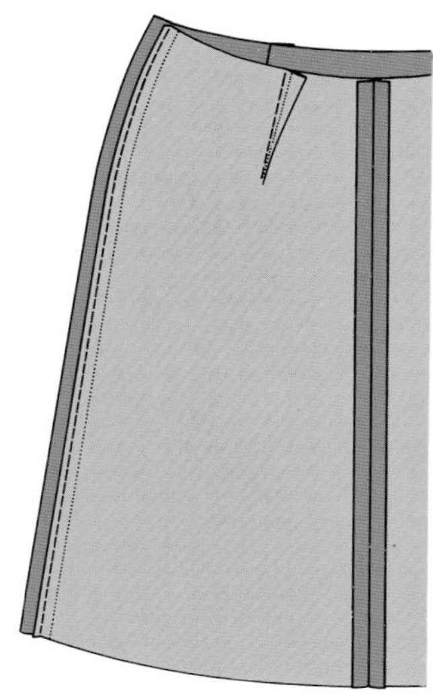

One hip higher than the other
If the hip bone does not affect the hang of the skirt, the seam need only be let out slightly over the hip bone in order to accommodate the higher curve. If it does affect the hang of the skirt, adjust both side seams by lifting the skirt into the waistband.

Skirt pulls in below seat
This is caused by the skirt being too tight over the seat. The side seams must be let out on the skirt back only. Pin new side seams on the back section of the skirt and take any extra width at the waist into the back darts.

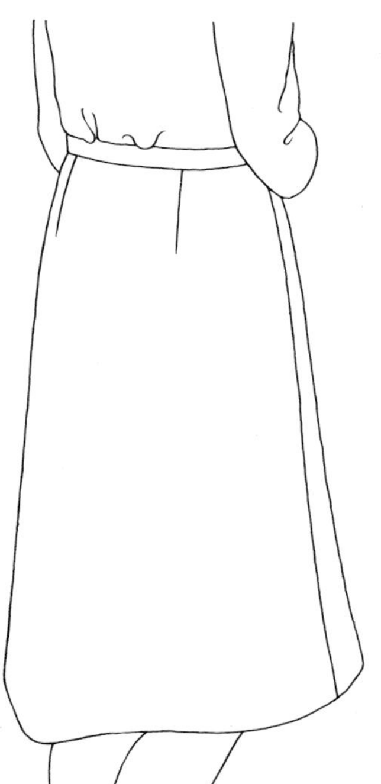

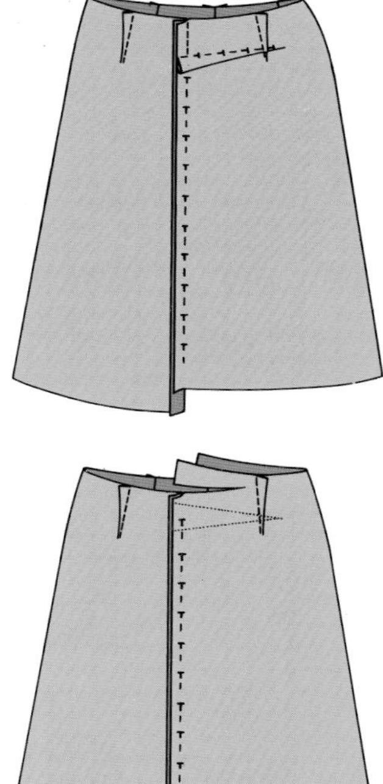

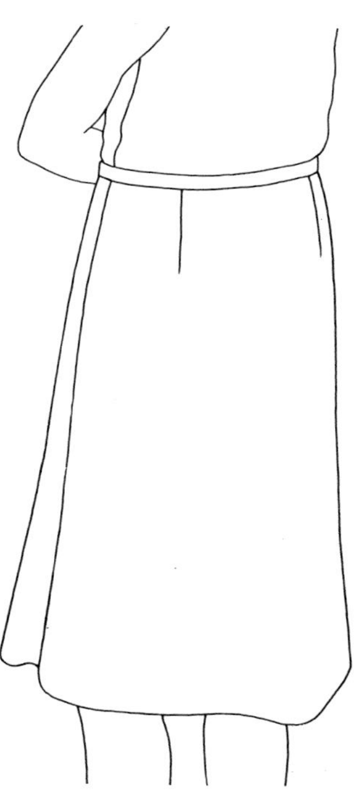

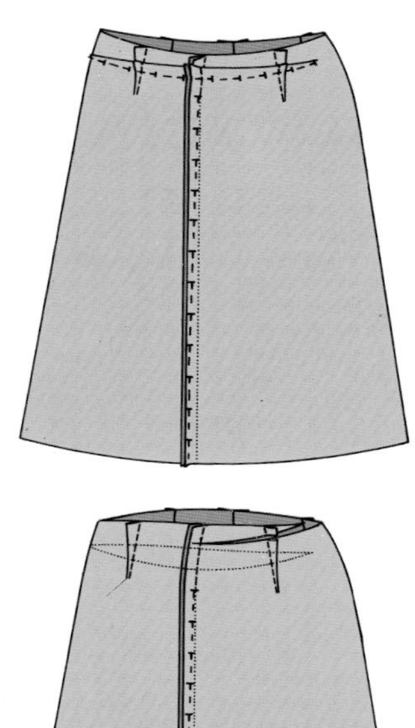

Skirt juts out at the front and back hem
This is probably caused by a high abdomen or seat. Try on the garment with the side seams open to just below the waist. Pin a small tuck toward the side seam on the section which juts out, lifting this section to the correct position for the hang. Measure the amount of tuck and take the same amount off the waistline edge. Re-pin new side seam and mark new waistline at side, tapering into waistline at CF.

Skirt juts out at front and back hem and side seams hang inward
This is usually caused by the waist being the same size as or larger than the hips. Make a tuck in the fabric below the waistline and across the side seams so that the skirt hangs straight. Re-pin side seams. Take the amount of tuck off the waistline. After making this alteration the skirt may be too big at the hips. Correct this by pinning the extra amount into the side seams.

Collars

There are two main types of collar: flat and stand-up. A flat collar is cut with an inner edge which follows the shape of the neck so that it lies flat against the garment. The shape of the outer edge may vary from a traditional round Peter-Pan style to a square. (The method of cutting flat collars is described on the next page.) The inner edge of a stand-up collar is straighter in relationship to the shape of the neck and it is this which causes it to stand up against the neck before rolling over. Sometimes there may be a separate section to give a neat strong finish, as on a shirt collar.

With the exception of bias-cut cowl collars (see p80), collars should always be interfaced. You should usually apply the interfacing to the under collar section to enable the edge of the upper collar section to roll easily. However, if using fine fabric, cut and apply the interfacing to the upper collar section to prevent the seam from showing through on the finished collar.

To check the fit of stand-up collars before stitching, cut out the upper collar from spare fabric before cutting the rest of the garment. Fold under the seam allowances and try the collar on.

If the collar is loose, alter the curve of the front neck on the bodice pattern by raising it between the shoulder and CF. Measure the new length between these points and shorten the inner edge of the collar to correspond. If the collar is too tight, lower the curve of the front neck on the bodice pattern from shoulder to CF and lengthen the inner edge of the collar to correspond. Always alter the under collar to correspond and, on shirt collars, alter the stand-up section and collar the same amount.

When making up the garment attach the collar as soon as possible so that the neckline does not become stretched during construction. It is advisable to stay-stitch the neck edge of the bodice immediately after removing the paper pattern.

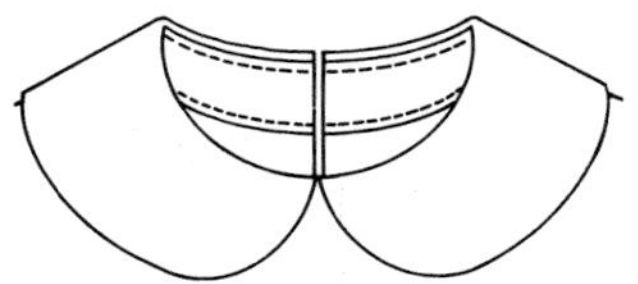

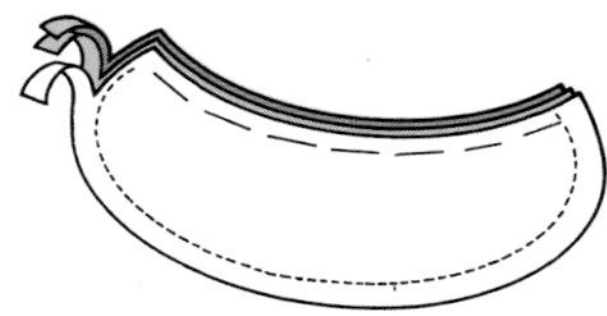

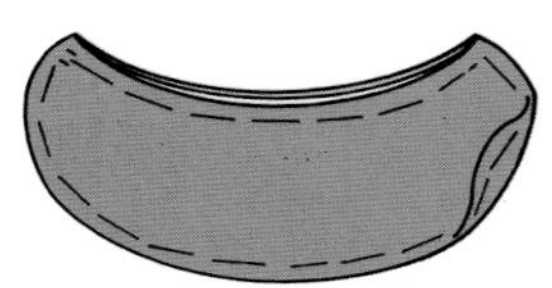

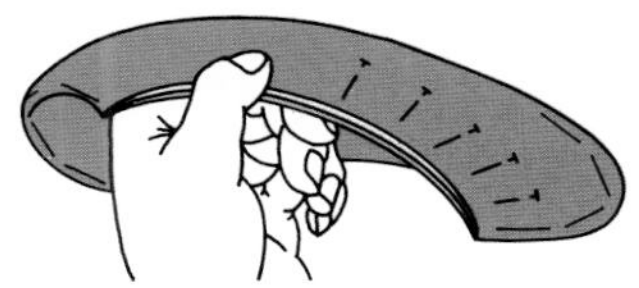

Flat collar with neck facing

1 Baste interfacing to WS of under collar. With RS together, baste and stitch upper collar to under collar, leaving neck edge open. Trim interfacing close to stitching and grade seam allowances as shown. Cut across corners.

2 Turn collar RS out. Press flat and baste around stitched edge.

3 To make collar fit snugly around the neck, roll its neck edge over your forefinger, pushing back the upper collar slightly. Pin.

4 With RS of under collar to RS of garment's neck edge, pin and baste collars in position, matching notches, CF, CB and circle to shoulder. Assemble facings and baste over collar with RS together and matching CF, CB and shoulder seams.

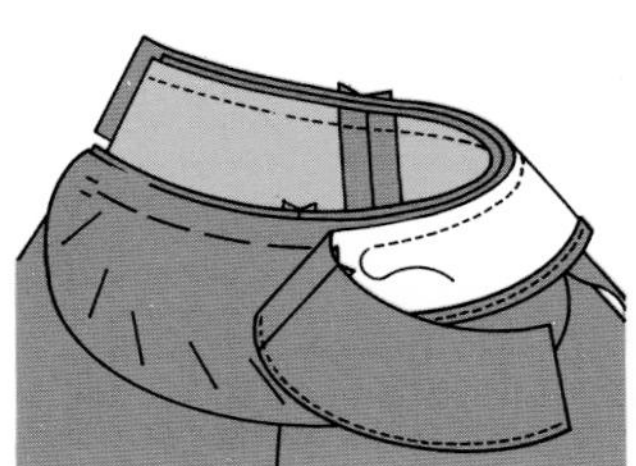

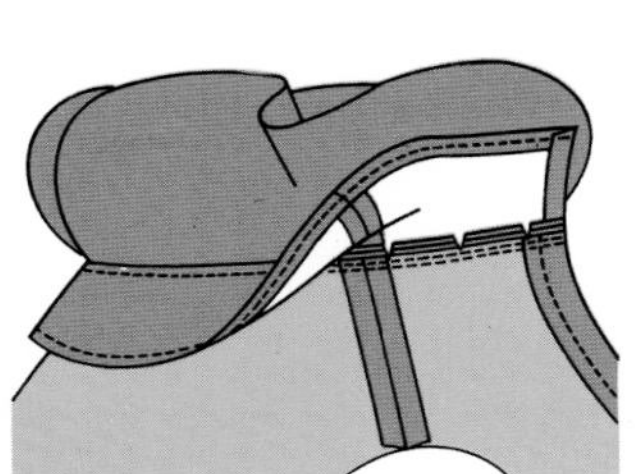

5 Machine-stitch through all thicknesses; grade seam and clip curves. Press seam allowances toward facing, under-stitch and turn facing to WS of garment. Slip-stitch to shoulders and CB seam.

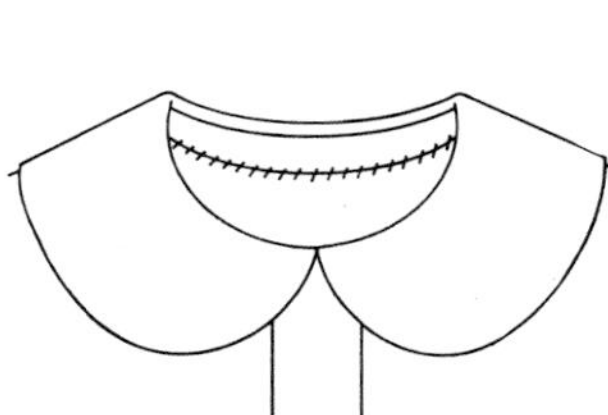

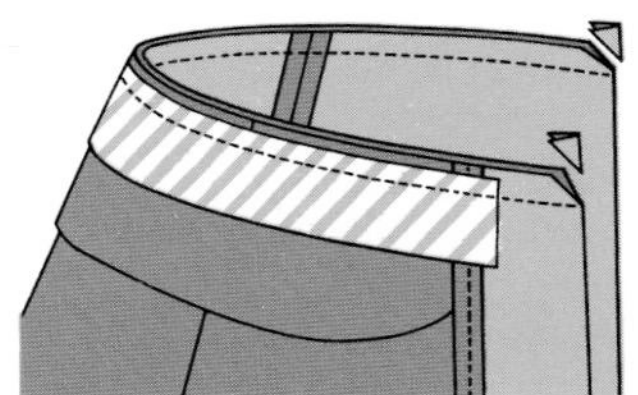

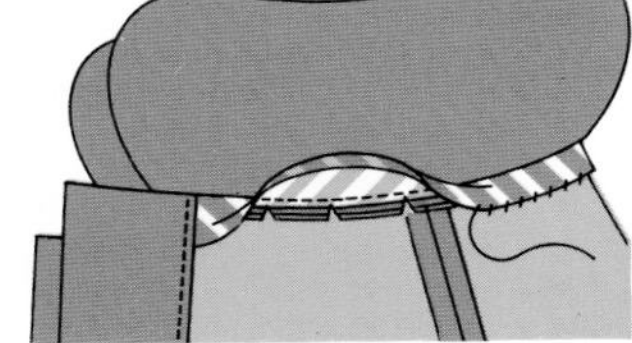

Flat collar with binding

Use this method with a front facing.

1 Make up collar and baste to neck edge as before. Finish outer edge of front facing, fold facing to RS along foldline and baste to neck edge over collar. Cut a bias strip of fabric 1in (2·5cm) wide to fit neck edge and overlap facing by $\frac{5}{8}$in (15mm).

2 With RS together baste and machine-stitch strip to neck edge over collar and overlapping facing. Grade seam, clip curves and cut across corners. Turn facing to WS, press seam toward bodice. Turn binding to WS, fold under raw edge and slip-stitch to seamline around neck.

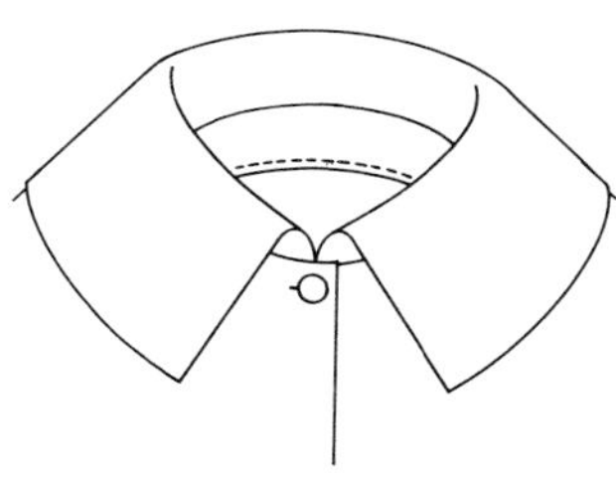

Stand-up collar

To make a pattern for this draw the inner edge with a straight line to the neckline length from CF to CF. Draw the outer edge twice the required collar depth from the inner edge and then the corners to the desired shape. Add turnings all around.

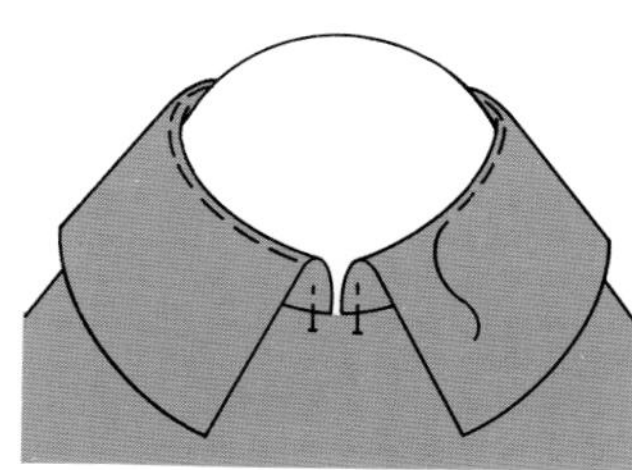

1 Assemble the collar as a flat collar. Place the collar around a tailor's ham and pin into position. Roll the collar down and baste along roll line to hold shape.
2 Attach the collar to the garment as a flat collar.

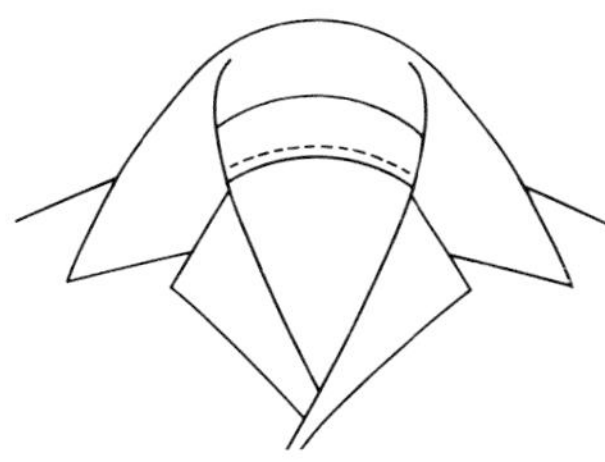

Straight collar with all-in-one facing

1 Assemble collar like a stand-up collar. With RS together and matching notches, CF, CB and circles to shoulders, baste collar to neck edge.
2 Assemble facings and with RS together, matching notches and shoulder seams, baste to neck edge over collar and down front edges. Machine-stitch through all thicknesses, trim interfacing close to stitching, grade seam, clip curves and cut across corners. Turn facing to WS of garment and press. Slip-stitch to shoulders.

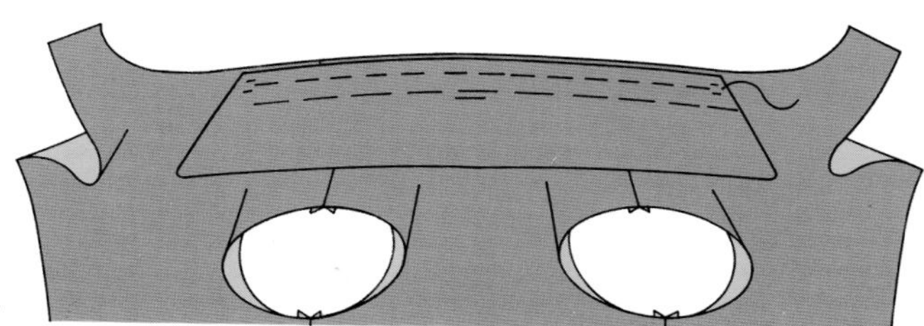

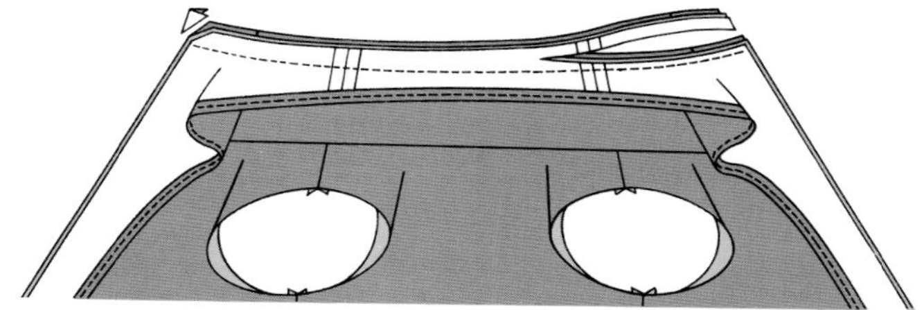

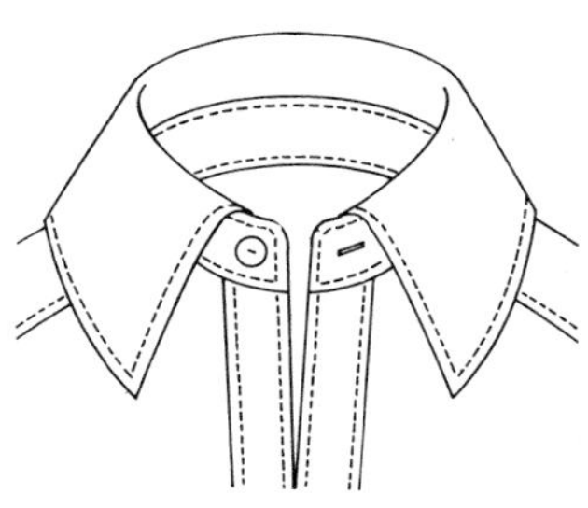

Shirt collar

1 Assemble collar like a flat collar and top-stitch $\frac{1}{4}$in (5mm) in from outer edges. Baste interfacing to WS of under collar band.
2 With RS together and matching notches, baste collar bands to each side of corresponding collar section and machine-stitch, continuing stitching to front edges of band.

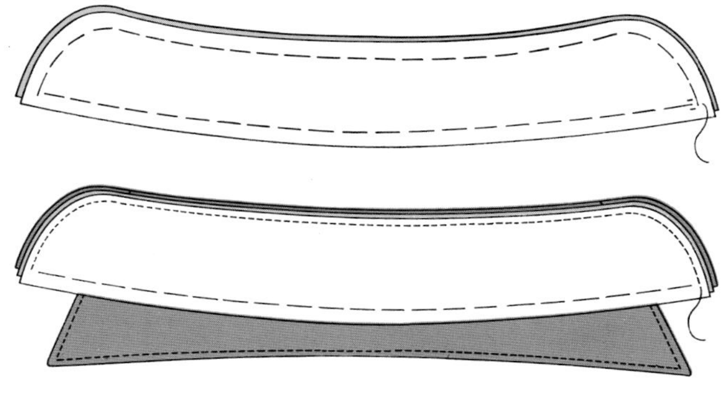

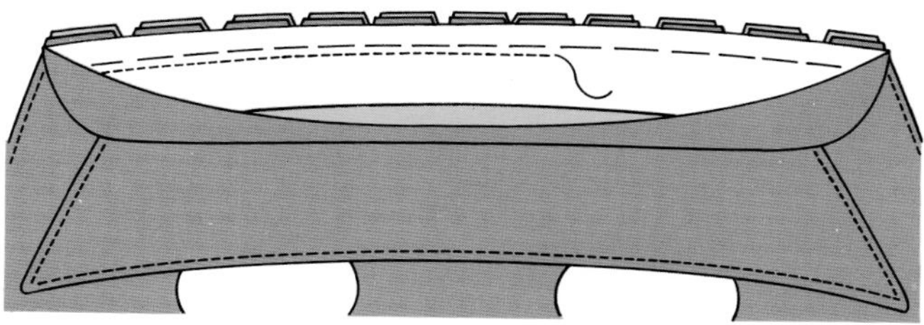

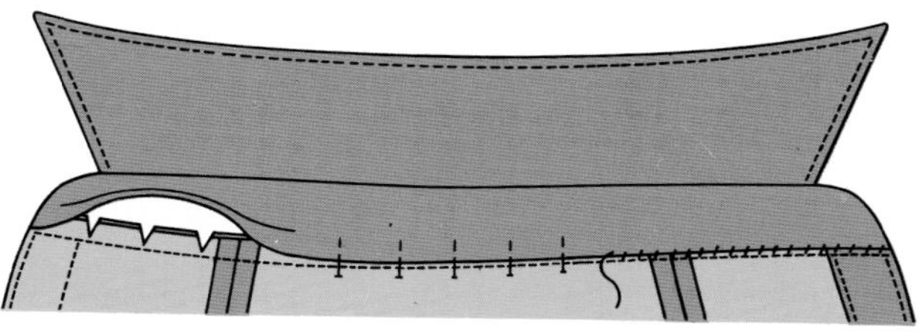

3 Trim interfacing, grade seams and clip curves. Turn bands down and press. With RS together and matching CF, CB, notches and circles to shoulders, baste and machine-stitch under band to neck edge. Trim interfacing, grade seams, clip curves and press seam toward band.

4 Turn seam allowances of upper band to WS and slip-stitch to seamline. Top-stitch band $\frac{1}{8}$in (3mm) in from neck seam, continuing stitching $\frac{1}{4}$in (5mm) in from collar seamline around top edge to front band of shirt.

Collar variations

A good way of adapting the neckline of a plain bodice or shirt is to alter the style of collar.
With the exception of the sailor collar (see opposite) you can add all the collars shown here to plain high necks or interchange them with the standard collars shown on p78. You can add the tie, cowl and variations of flat collars to boat-shaped and U-necks and the tie collar to a V-neck.
Make the collars in fabric to match or contrast with the rest of the garment, perhaps teaming them with matching cuffs, belt or pocket. Take neck measurements along the seamline – not the raw edge – after joining the shoulder seams of the garment.
Mark the CF and CB and position of the shoulder line with a circle and mark notches to correspond with those on the neck edge.

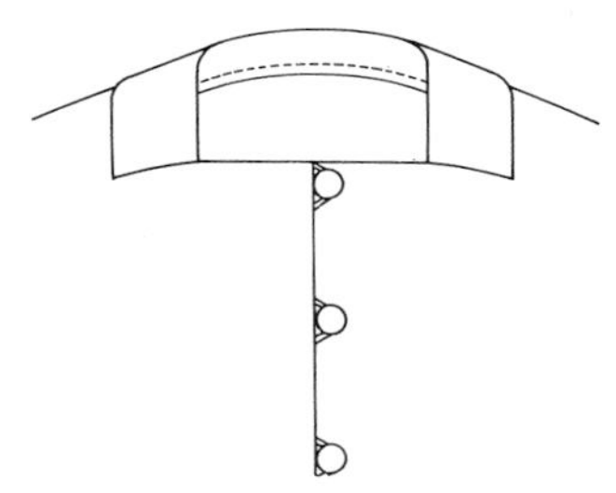

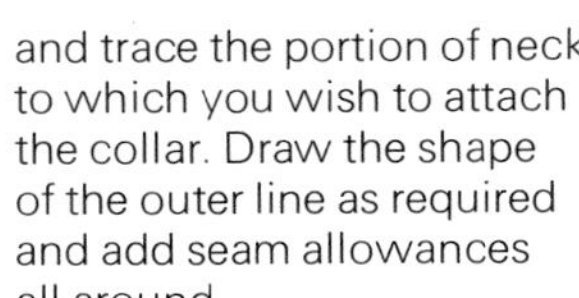

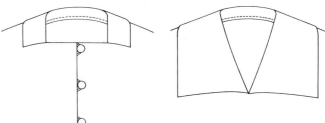

Flat collars
Flat collars may be drawn in many styles and also to fit any shape of neckline. The collars may be made in 1 or 2 pieces and need not fit the whole neckline.
To make a pattern, place the shoulder lines of the front and back bodices together and trace the portion of neck to which you wish to attach the collar. Draw the shape of the outer line as required and add seam allowances all around.

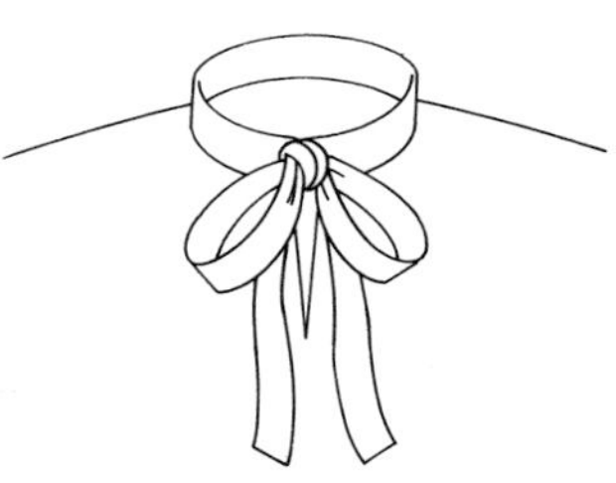

Tie collar
This is a narrow straight collar that stands up from the neck and ties at the CF. Calculate the length of the ties by tieing a tape measure in a bow.
1 Cut the collar to length of ties plus circumference of the neck edge by twice the required width (e.g. $1\frac{1}{2}$in/4cm). Add seam allowances all around.
2 Mark the section of the collar which will be attached to the neck edge and interface it. Fold the fabric in half lengthwise with RS together, stitch across short ends and along ties up to the marks.
3 Attach remaining section to the neck as a waistband to a waistline (see p38), turn the ties RS out, fold under the remaining raw edge of the collar and slip-stitch to the seamline.

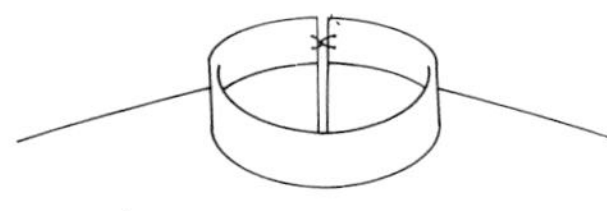

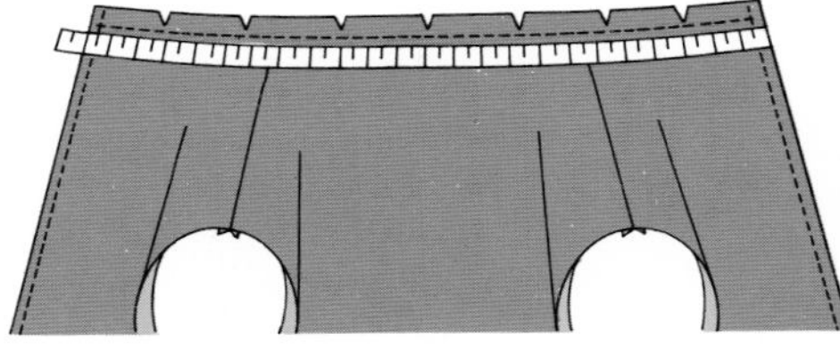

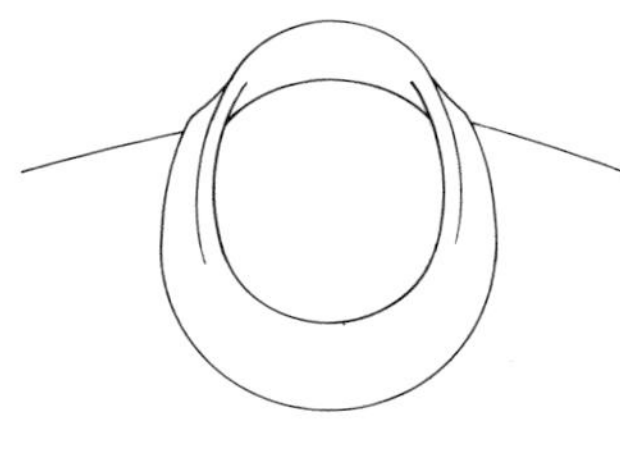

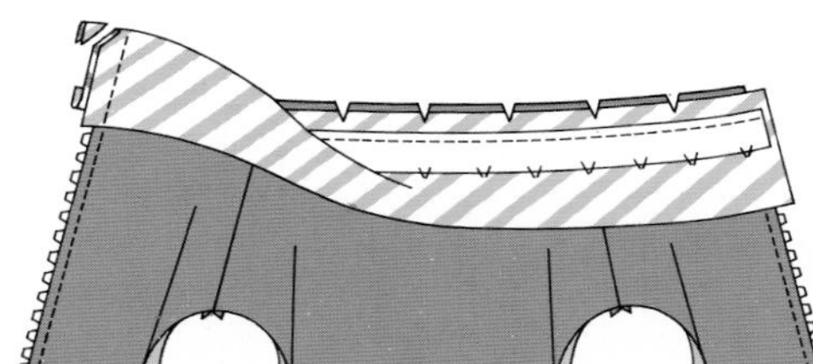

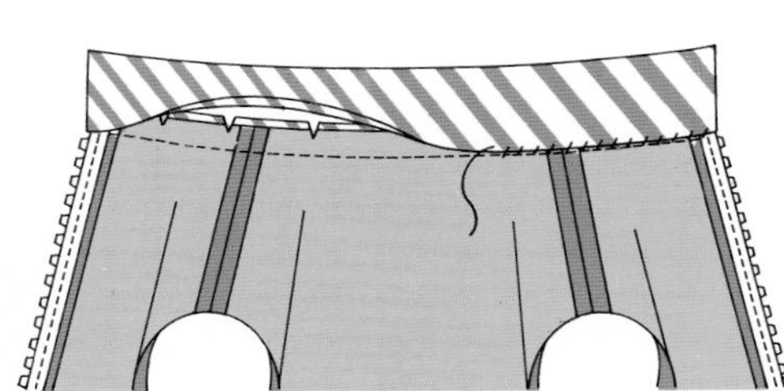

Band or cowl collar
This is a bias-cut band that stands up from the neck edge and fastens at the CB. It may be made twice the required finished width to turn over to form a cowl collar.
1 Cut the collar on the bias grain to the circumference of the neck edge by twice the finished width for a straight band or 4 times the finished width for a cowl. Add seam allowances all around. Cut interfacing to the same length by half the width of the fabric.
2 Baste interfacing to WS of fabric and catch-stitch to center line. With RS together matching CF and CB, baste and machine-stitch interfaced edge of collar to neck. Trim interfacing close to stitching. Grade seam, clip curves and press edges upward.
3 With RS together, fold collar along center line, baste and machine-stitch across short ends. Cut across corners close to stitching. Turn collar RS out and press.
4 On inside of garment fold under seam allowance of open edge and slip-stitch to seamline. Sew hooks and eyes to inside at CB of collar.

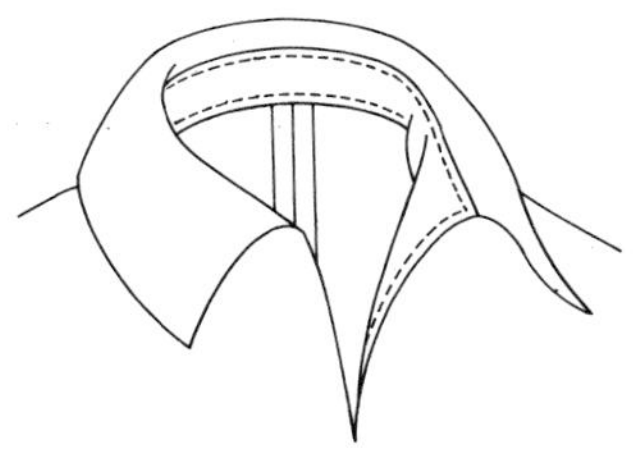

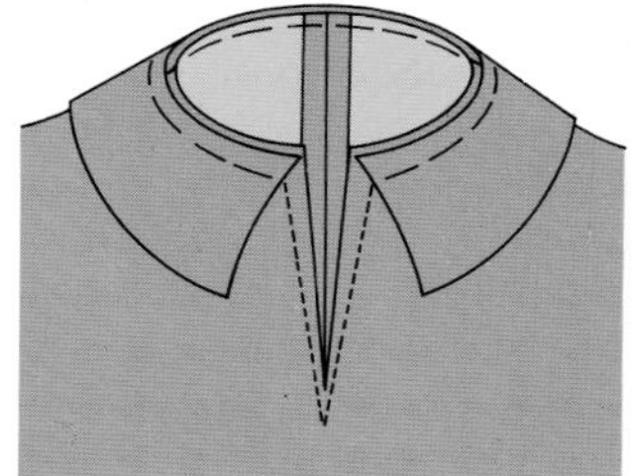

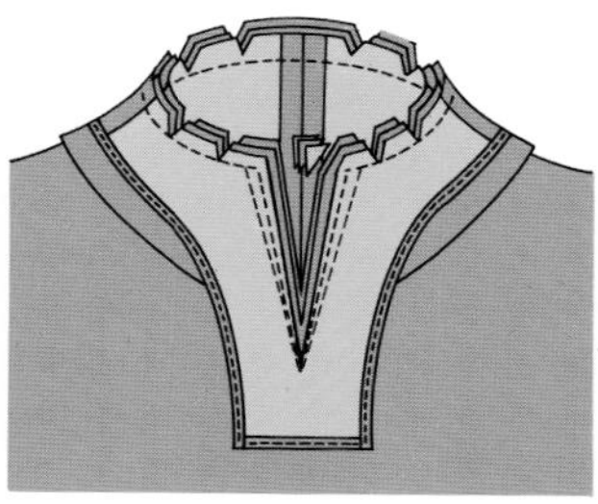

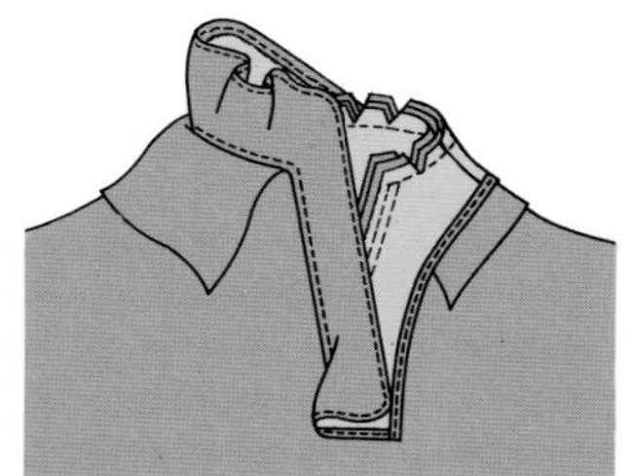

Collar with slit opening
Use the collar pattern from a shirt (omitting the band section) and combine with a faced slit opening on a regular round neckline.
Compare the length of the inside edge of the collar with the circumference of the neck and shorten or lengthen it to fit if necessary. Increase the collar width by 2in (5cm) from the outside edge and alter the angle of the front points if you wish.
Finish the collar as a stand-up collar.
1 On the front bodice and facing stay-stitch $\frac{1}{4}$in (5mm) in from either side of slash line, tapering stitching at the end.
Baste collar to neck edge, matching front edges of collar to stay-stitched line at CF. Slash along center of opening to point.
2 Attach facing to neck edge, checking that you pivot the stitching at the top of the opening exactly at the edge of the collar. Turn the facing inside the garment, under-stitch and press.

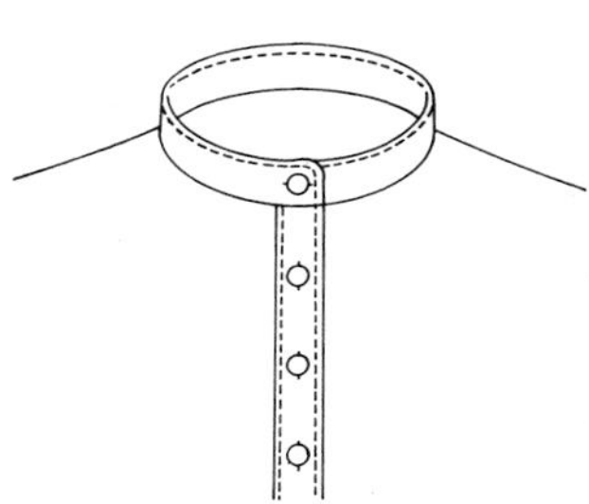

Collar band
Use the band pattern from a shirt collar and combine with a band opening on a high round neckline.

1 Interface the collar band as if making a regular shirt collar. Stitch the band pieces together along the outer edge (omitting the collar) and then stitch interfaced edge to neck edge with RS together.

2 Grade seam, clip curves and press edges upward. Turn under the free edge inside the garment and slip-stitch to seamline. Top-stitch from the outside all around edge of collar.

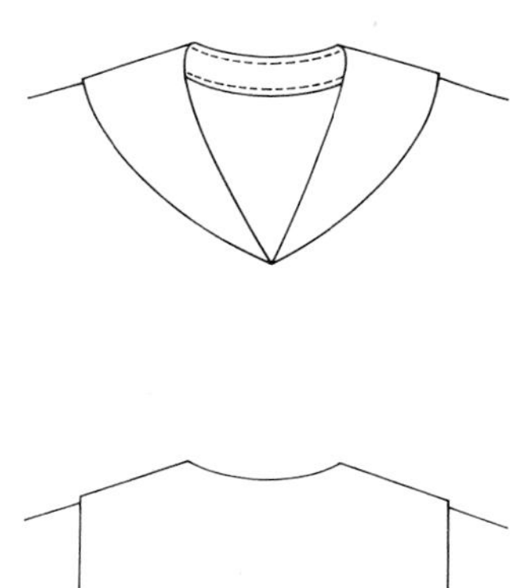

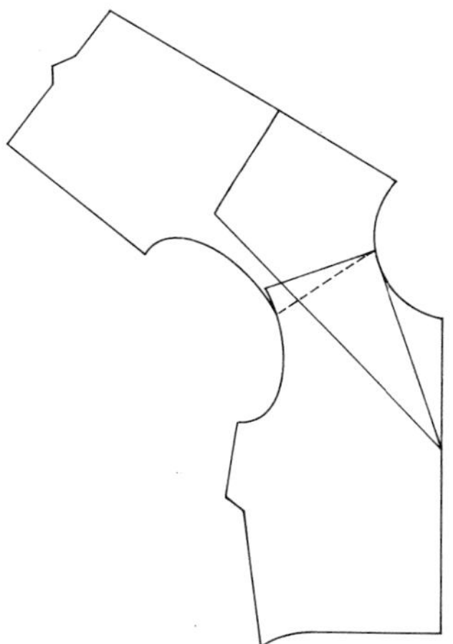

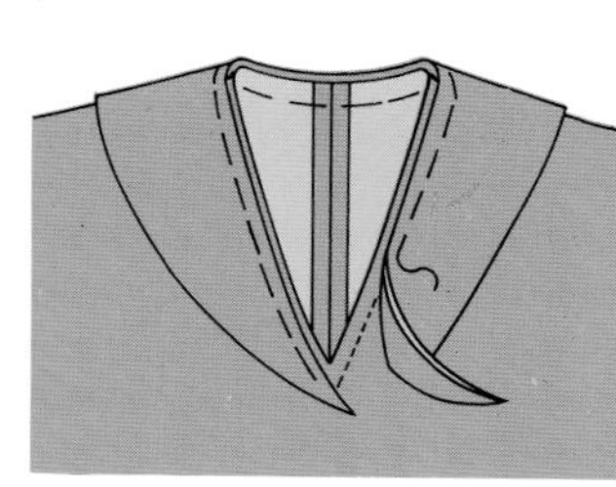

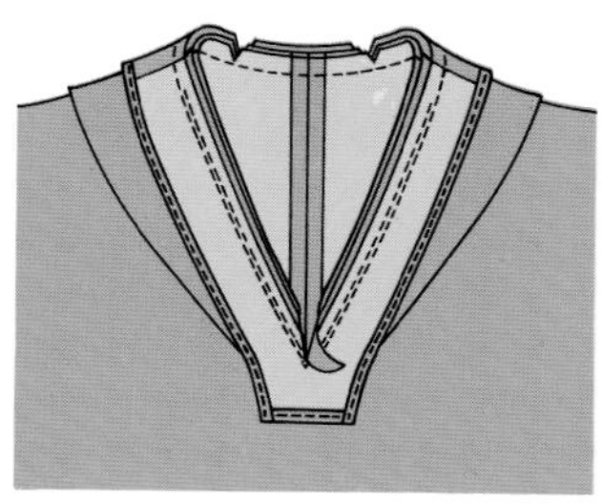

Sailor collar
Cutting the pattern
1 Place the front and back bodice neck points together and overlap shoulder points by $\frac{5}{8}$in (15mm). Lower CB neck by $\frac{1}{2}$in (1cm) and draw a new curve from shoulder. Draw the front neck in a V.

2 Measure down the CB to required depth of collar and draw in width of back collar at 90°. Join in a straight line to base of V at CF. Trace off the new collar shape and add seam allowances all around.

3 Cut the collar double with CB to a fold. Cut away the front and back bodice along inside lines of collar and add seam allowances. Cut facings to fit the edge.

Attaching the collar
1 Finish collar as a round collar. Stay-stitch neck edge of garment and facing to prevent stretching, clip to point of stitch at CF. Join bodice at shoulders and baste collar to RS of neck edge so that the ends of the seam allowances extend over the CF point.
2 Prepare the facing and baste over the collar with RS together and keeping the ends of the collar free. Stitch around neck through all thicknesses, grade seam, clip curves.
Press edges toward facing and under-stitch. Turn facing to inside of garment and catch to shoulder and CB seam allowance.

Basic shirt

These patterns for a classic shirt in all sizes can be made with simple adaptations such as a yoke, cut with double thickness (illustrated here and described on p84) or with different sleeves or collar. Add finishing touches such as pockets (see p92) or tucks shown on p84 or extend the pattern pieces to make a dress (also p84), a light coat or jacket (p86).

You will need
fabric 36in (90cm) wide:
$1\frac{3}{8}$yd/1·20m (sizes 22, 24, 26)
$1\frac{1}{2}$yd/1·30m (sizes 28, 30, 32)
$2\frac{1}{4}$yd/2m (size 34)
$2\frac{3}{8}$yd/2·10m (sizes 38, 42)
$3\frac{3}{8}$yd/3m (sizes 36, 40)
$3\frac{1}{2}$yd/3·10m (size 44)
interfacing:
$\frac{5}{8}$yd/50cm (children)
$\frac{3}{8}$yd/70cm (women)
$\frac{7}{8}$yd/80cm (men)
matching sewing thread
buttons

Cutting out
Trace appropriate pattern pieces in required size from the master sheet and make any adaptations. Add seam allowances and $\frac{3}{4}$in (2cm) hem turnings. Lay the pieces on the fabric as shown and cut out. From remaining fabric cut out cuffs. Cut interfacing to length of front bands by their full width on the man's shirt or half their width on the woman's and child's shirt. Cut interfacing for collar and collar band.

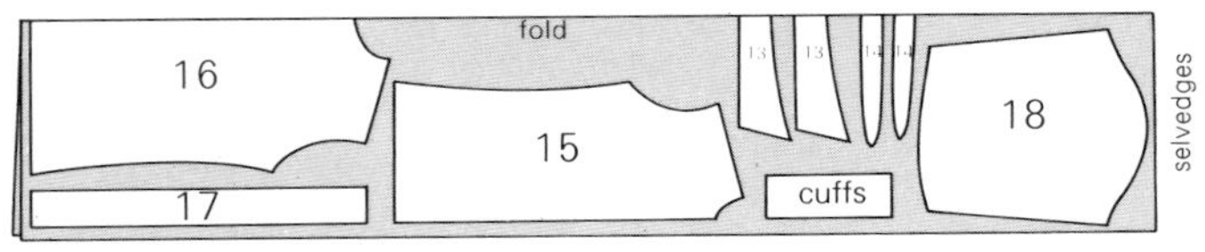

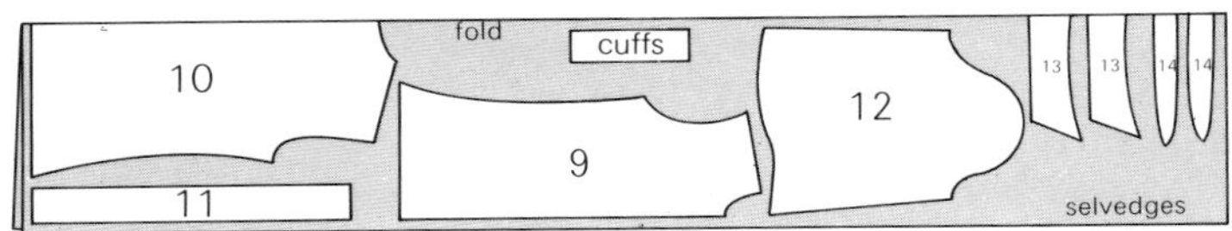

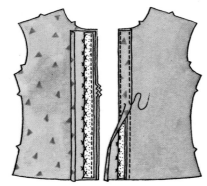

Woman's shirt
1 Baste interfacing to WS of notched edge of front bands (pattern piece 11). Catch to foldline. Turn in seam allowance along unnotched edge and baste. With RS together, matching notches, baste and stitch bands to shirt fronts (pattern piece 9). Trim interfacing close to stitching. Grade seam and press toward band.
2 Fold bands to inside along foldlines and slip-hem to stitch line. On the RS top-stitch $\frac{1}{4}$in (5mm) in from either side of bands. Press.
3 Using flat fell or French seams baste and machine-stitch shoulder and side seams.
4 Make shirt collar and collar band (pattern pieces 13 and 14) and attach to neck edge. From the inside top-stitch all around.

5 Make a continuous overlap opening at the ends of the sleeves (pattern piece 12). Run 2 rows of gathering threads around sleeve cap between notches. Using flat fell or French seam stitch underarm seam of sleeves.
6 Make cuff and attach to lower edge of sleeve, pleating or gathering sleeve to fit. Top-stitch around entire cuff $\frac{1}{4}$in (5mm) from edge.
7 Set in sleeves with a flat fell or French seam.

8 Turn under $\frac{1}{4}$in (5mm) around lower edge of shirt, then a further $\frac{5}{8}$in (15mm). Baste and machine-stitch $\frac{1}{2}$in (1cm) in from lower edge.
9 Make 6 vertical buttonholes at 3in (7·5cm) intervals on CF of RH front band, placing the first $2\frac{1}{2}$in (6·5cm) below the neck seam. Make a horizontal buttonhole along the center of the collar band beginning at the CF. Make 2 buttonholes on each cuff. Attach the buttons.

Child's shirt
Cut out using pattern pieces 27–32. Make the shirt as a woman's shirt but placing buttonholes on LH front band and pleating sleeves into cuffs for a boy's shirt.

Master pattern sheet
Seams 20
Hems 28
Fastenings 32
Cuffs 38
Pleating 40
Yokes 56
Openings 60
Sleeves 62
Collars 78

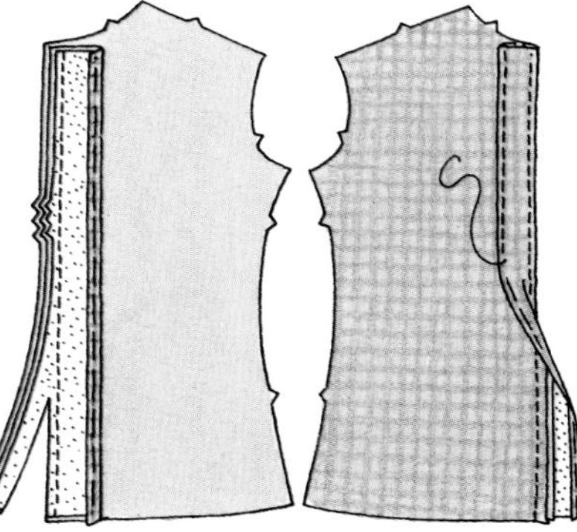

Man's shirt

1 Baste interfacing to WS of front bands (pattern piece 17). Turn in the seam allowance of the unnotched edge and baste. With RS of band to WS of shirt, matching notches, baste and machine-stitch bands to the shirt fronts (pattern piece 15). Trim interfacing close to stitching. Grade seams and press toward bands.
2 Fold bands to RS of shirt along seamlines and baste folded edges to fronts. Top-stitch $\frac{1}{4}$in (5mm) in all around the edge of the bands. Press.
3 If you have cut yokes, join to main sections.
4 Baste and machine-stitch shirt front to back (pattern piece 16) along shoulders using a flat fell seam.
5 Make the shirt collar (pattern pieces 13 and 14) and attach to neck.

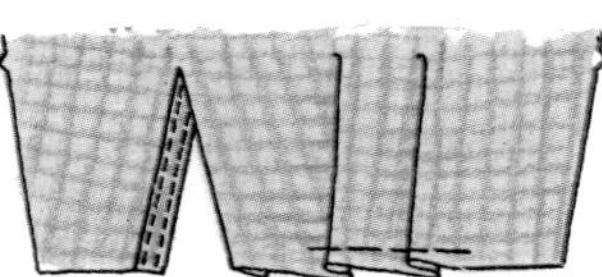

6 Make a continuous overlap opening on each sleeve (pattern piece 18) and pleat sleeve fullness to fit cuffs.
7 Using flat fell seams stitch sleeves into armholes and join the underarm and sides in one continuous seam.

8 Make up cuffs and attach to lower edge of sleeves. Top-stitch around entire cuff $\frac{1}{4}$in (5mm) from edge.
9 Make the hem as on the woman's shirt.
10 Make vertical buttonholes down CF line of LH front band at even intervals and a horizontal buttonhole at the center of the collar band from the CF. Make buttonholes on the cuffs. Attach the buttons.

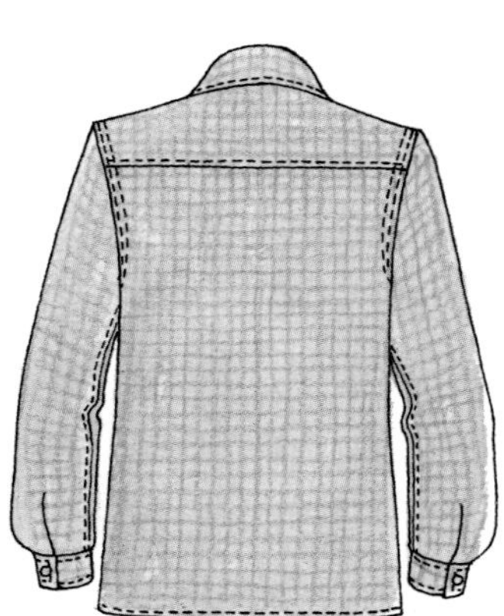

Shirt variations

Gathering 29
Tucks 44
Yokes 56
Belts 90

The pattern for the woman's basic shirt given on p82 can be adapted to make a dress as shown here or a light-weight coat as shown on p86. Both dress and coat may be made to any length, so estimate the amount of fabric required by making a cutting layout (see p16) after you have adapted the pattern.
The man's shirt may be adapted to make an evening shirt by adding a band of tucking into the shoulder seam, as shown here, or into the neck to give tucks nearer the front opening. It can also be used to make a jacket by enlarging the pattern slightly as described on p86.
Other simple variations may be made by adding different collars, cuffs, belts or pockets.

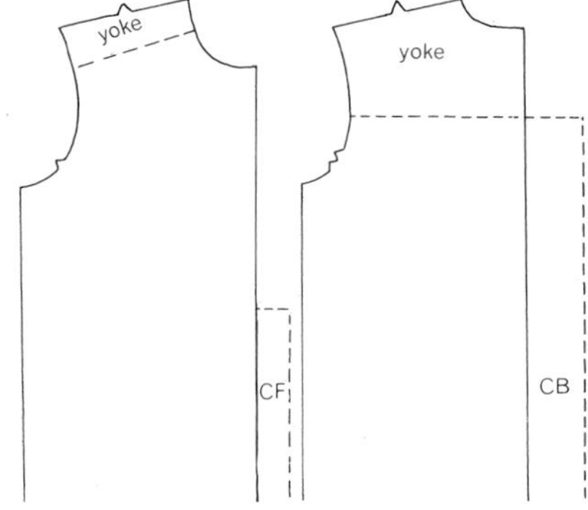

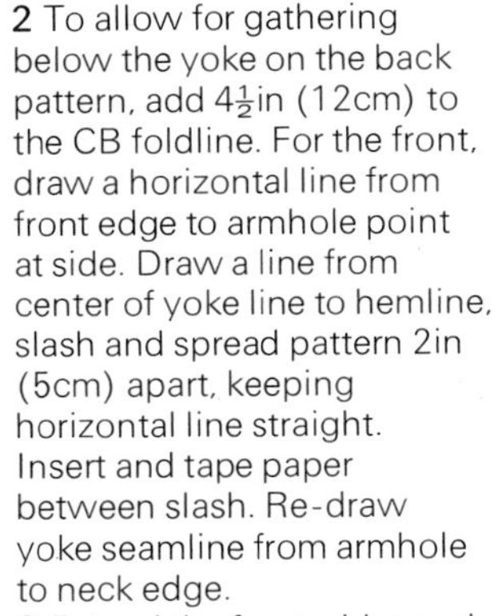

Dress
Adapting the pattern
1 Cut a yoke on the shirt front from armhole to neck, and on the back straight across from armhole to armhole.
Tape the yokes together at the shoulder line to eliminate the shoulder seam.
2 To allow for gathering below the yoke on the back pattern, add $4\frac{1}{2}$in (12cm) to the CB foldline. For the front, draw a horizontal line from front edge to armhole point at side. Draw a line from center of yoke line to hemline, slash and spread pattern 2in (5cm) apart, keeping horizontal line straight. Insert and tape paper between slash. Re-draw yoke seamline from armhole to neck edge.
3 Extend the front, sides and CB edges to length required (including hem) ensuring that the width of lower edge will fit fabric width.
4 Measure down front edge of dress $22\frac{1}{2}$in (58cm) and mark position for bottom of band. Extend front band to this length. For remaining length of front edge add $\frac{3}{4}$in (2cm) – place this edge to fold when cutting out.
Add seam allowances to new seamlines and cut out, including a lining for the yokes.
Making the dress
1 Apply front bands to dress as for a band opening (see p60) but working from the RS to the WS and slip-stitching the second edge of bands in position. Work buttonholes on RH band and attach buttons to correspond on LH band.
2 Gather top edges of dress onto yokes and stitch in position. With WS together, place yoke lining onto yoke. Fold under bottom edges and baste to seamline and around armholes and neck.

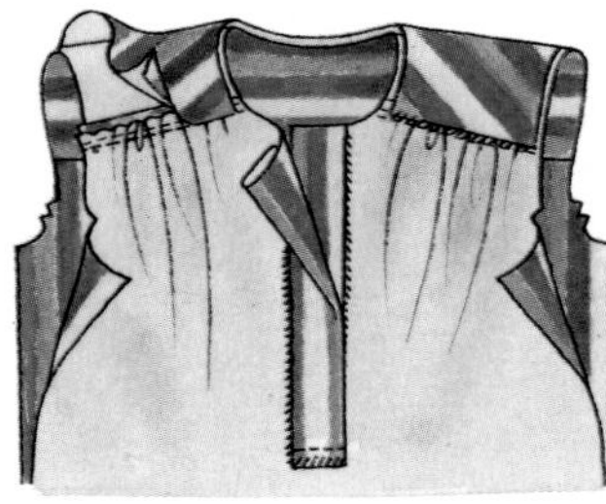

Slip-stitch lower edge of yokes in position.
3 Finish dress as for shirt but hand-stitch the hem.

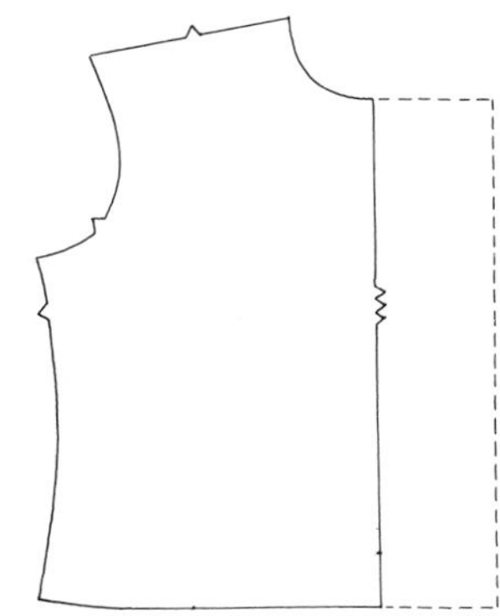

Dress shirt
Adapting the pattern Omit front bands and add $3\frac{1}{2}$in (9cm) to front edge of shirt for a fold-back facing. Decide on the style and number of tucks and mark their position on the shirt front.
Mark out length of fabric required for shirt fronts and cut away from main fabric length. Make tucks in required position, pin front pattern piece onto tucked fabric and cut out each piece separately.
Making the shirt Baste interfacing to front shirt facings and catch-stitch inner edge in position. Finish outer edge of facing, working stitching over interfacing. Fold facing to WS of garment along inner edge of interfacing. Complete as basic shirt.

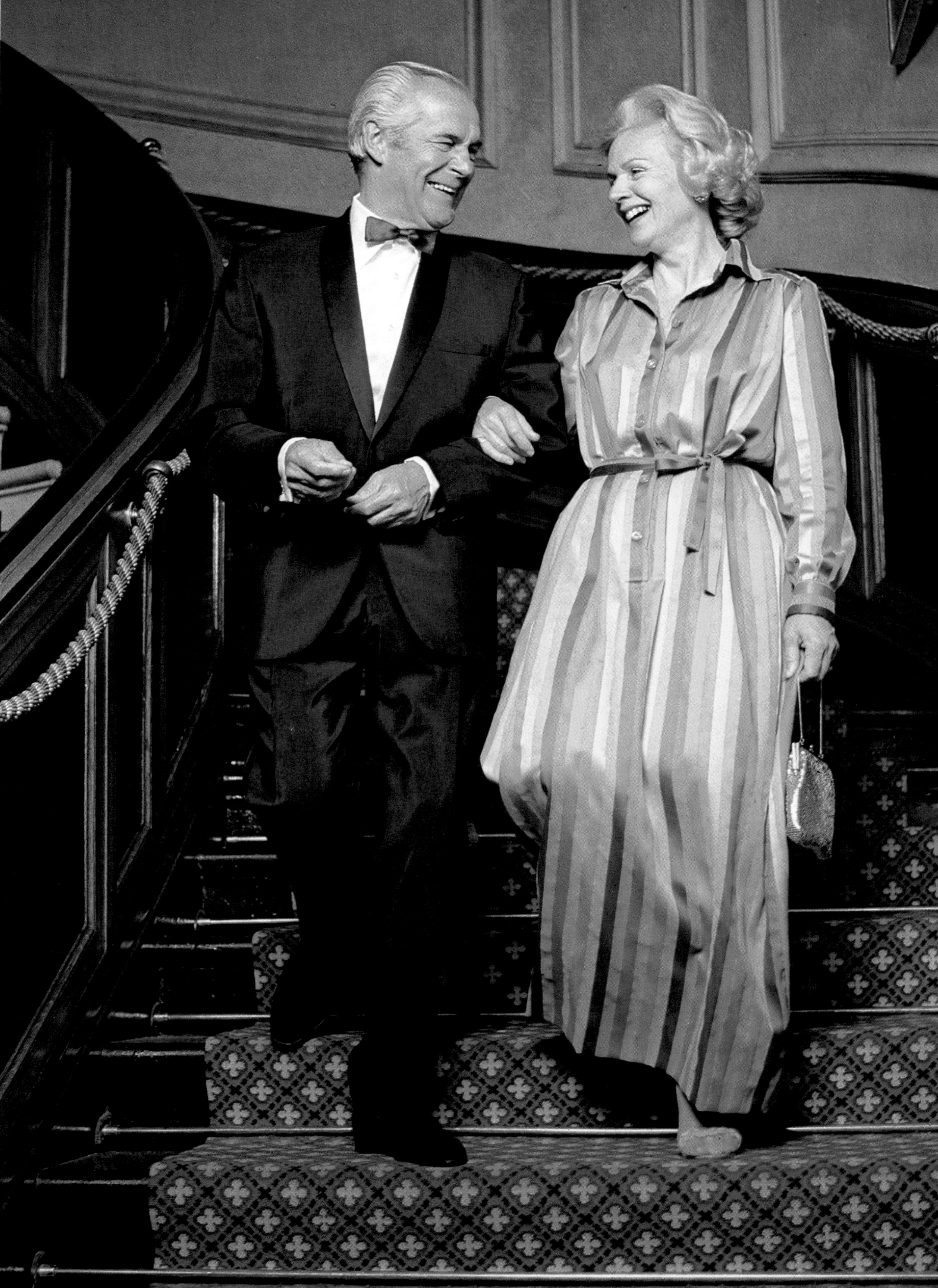

Jacket and light-weight coat

Belts 90
Pockets 92
Difficult fabrics 94

By enlarging the shirt patterns on p82 to add ease, you can adapt them to make a jacket or light-weight coat. Both may be made in fabric or in vinyl or suede as shown here, in which case you might wish to substitute snap fasteners for buttonholes.

You will need
fabric or vinyl to required amount (making a cutting layout with adapted pattern pieces) or suede to fit pattern pieces
matching sewing thread
buttons or snap fasteners
clear adhesive (vinyl or suede only)

Raincoat
Adapting the pattern Drop the front and back armhole at sides by $\frac{5}{8}$in (15mm). Extend and lift front and back shoulder line at armhole by $\frac{1}{4}$in (5mm). Re-draw shoulder line to original point at neck. Cut front and back yokes and join at shoulders (see p84) and add gathers to pattern pieces below yokes. Extend pieces to length required, and front bands. Alter sleeve cap to fit armhole. Measure sleeve width at top of armhole and straighten sides so bottom measures the same; straighten lower sleeve edge. Cut belt, straps for sleeves (like belts but smaller) and pockets.
Making the raincoat Work as the basic shirt but gather the fabric into the yokes and add pockets, sleeve straps and belt. If you are using vinyl, glue edges with an adhesive and attach snap fasteners.

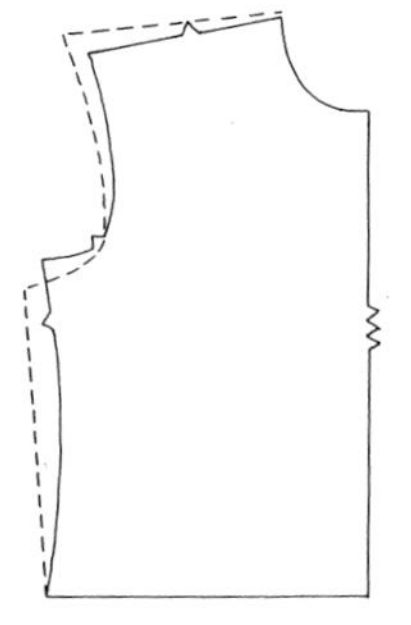

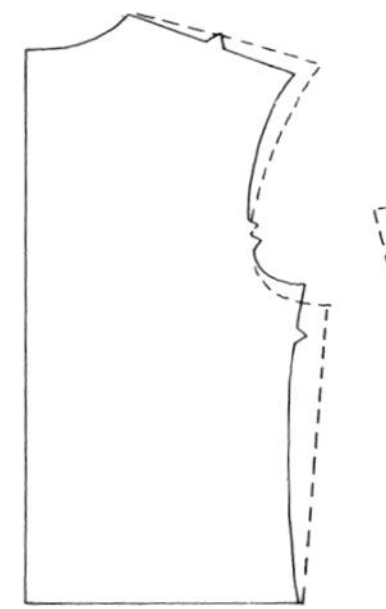

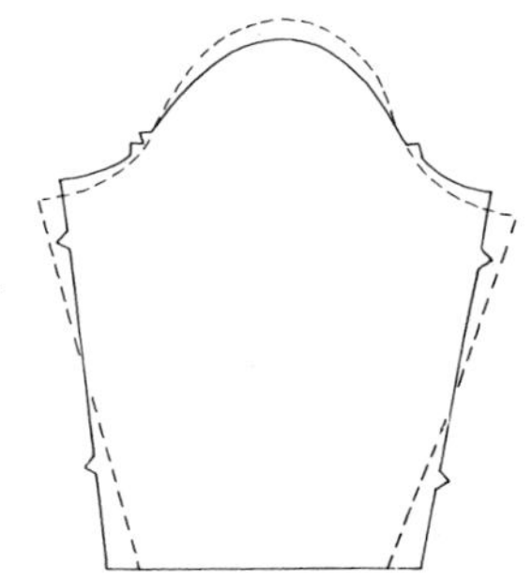

Jacket
Adapting the pattern
Measure CB length to hip bone and cut off front and back shirt pattern pieces to this length. Straighten side seams. Drop the front and back armhole and extend the sides by $\frac{5}{8}$in (15mm). Extend and lift the front and back shoulder line at the outer edge by $\frac{1}{4}$in (5mm). Re-draw the shoulder line to base of neck. Drop the underarm curves of the sleeve and extend underarm seams out by $\frac{5}{8}$in (15mm). Add $\frac{1}{4}$in (5mm) to sleeve cap, tapering lines into deepest part of armhole curve. Taper underarm seam of sleeve in from point of armhole curve to hem so that width at hemline is $9\frac{1}{2}$in (25cm). Cut cuffs 11 × 4in (28 × 10cm), plus seam allowances all around. Add seam allowances to all other pieces.
If you are making the jacket in suede, cut front band along foldline and add seam allowance to this edge. Cut band to the same length as the jacket. Cut a hip band to fit the lower edge of the jacket × $1\frac{1}{2}$in (4cm)
Add seam allowances to edges of all pattern pieces.
Making the jacket If you are using fabric, work as for a shirt but attach the hip band to the bottom edge as a reverse facing, and omit tucks from the lower edge of the sleeves.

If you are using suede, work as follows:
1 Trim off 1in (2·5cm) from lower edge of front bands. Turn under and glue the seam allowances along both side edges. With WS of bands to RS of jacket fronts, glue the bands so that front edges are level.
2 With RS together, stitch fronts to back at shoulders. Open turnings and glue.

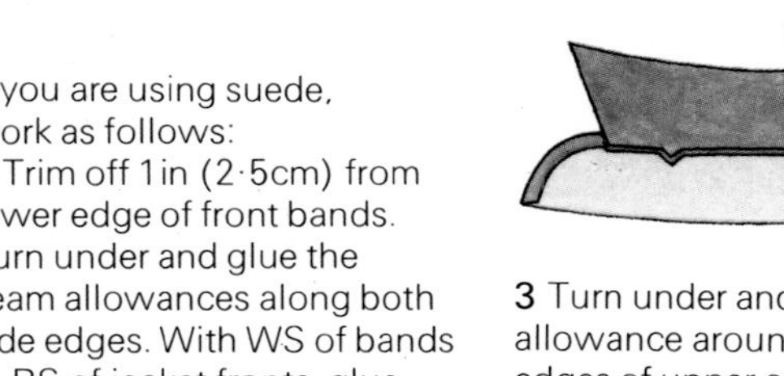

3 Turn under and glue seam allowance around outer edges of upper collar and curved edge of under collar band. Trim the seam allowance from upper collar band and outer edges of under collar. With WS together glue under collar to upper collar.

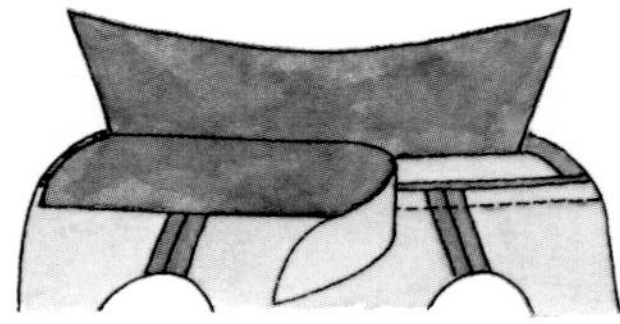

4 With RS together glue under collar band to collar and then stitch under collar band to neck of jacket. Glue turnings to band.
5 With WS together and matching outer edges, glue upper collar band to under band and stitch.

6 Set sleeve into armhole, stitching to within 2in (5cm) of side seams. Stitch side seams and sleeve seams to within 2in (5cm) of bottom. Open turnings and glue. Complete stitching at underarm curves.
7 Trim seam allowances from cuffs on one long edge and from half each short edge. Stitch the other long edge to sleeve, placing overlap toward back. Glue remaining seam allowances,

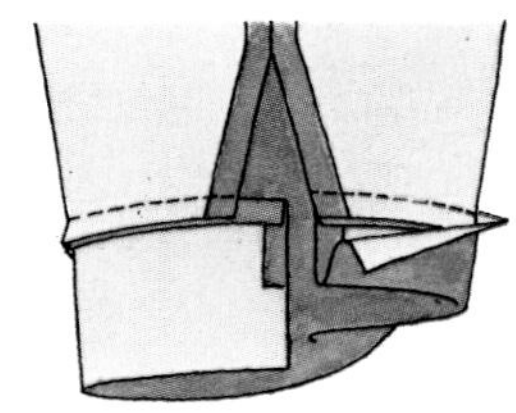

fold cuff in half with WS together and glue.
8 Turn under seam allowances of hip band and glue. With WS of band to RS of jacket, matching outer edges, glue band in place.
9 Top-stitch $\frac{1}{4}$in (5mm) from outer edges of front and hip bands, cuffs, collar and collar band.
10 Attach snap fasteners to front bands at CFs and cuffs. Pleat hip band at side seams to fit and attach snap fasteners to hold pleat.

Linings

Linings give the finishing touch to garments, making them neat inside and easy to put on. They also help to prevent the outer fabric from stretching and losing shape (although very loosely woven fabrics should also be underlined). In some cases, using a lining makes facings unnecessary, as on necklines and armholes of sleeveless dresses or vests. Garments may be fully lined or you may wish to line only part of them. For example, you could line the main body of a dress but not the sleeves. You could line slacks from the waist to the knee and the back of a skirt to below the seat.
Fabrics which should usually be lined are wool, rayon, many silks, some woven synthetics and any fabric which frays a lot. Knitted fabrics should not usually be lined unless you wish to prevent a certain area from stretching.
Fabrics suitable for linings are mostly synthetic and are smooth and slippery, making the finished garment pleasant to wear. They are made in a variety of weights suitable for different outer fabrics and garments. Choose one which has the same care requirements as the outer fabric and is slightly lighter in weight. If in doubt about weight, ask the shopkeeper's advice. Generally for a full lining you will need the same amount as the outer fabric. In most cases you should match the lining color to the garment but occasionally you may wish to use a contrasting color – in a jacket, for example – or even a non-lining fabric to make a garment reversible. Check that the lining fabric does not show through to the right side of the outer fabric by holding the two together. If necessary underline either the outer or the lining fabric before finishing.
Cut the lining from the same pattern as the outer garment (unless a lining pattern is included in your bought pattern), making any alterations specified. Make up both lining and outer garment to basting stage and try them on together to check for a smooth fit. On garments made in very heavy fabrics you may need to make the lining slightly smaller to allow for the roll of the outer fabric at the edges.

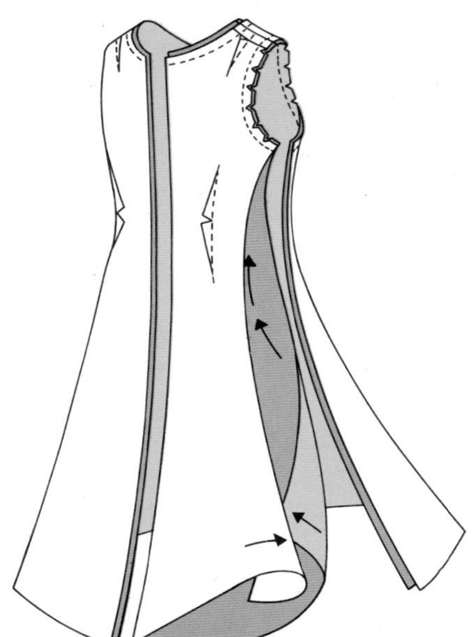

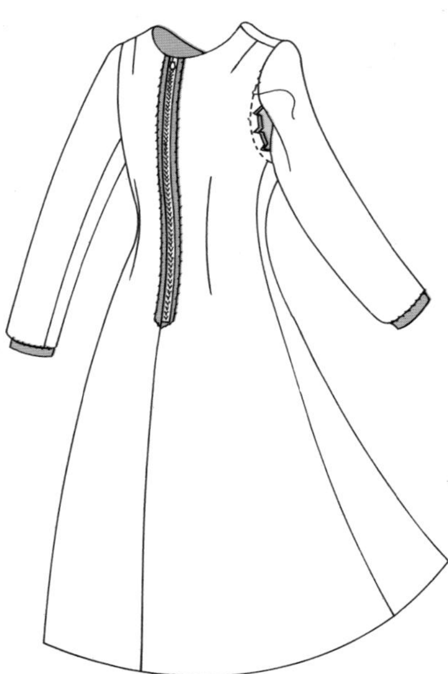

Dresses

Sleeveless dress Stitch any darts and join the front to the back along the shoulders only on both lining and outer fabric. Place lining onto the outer fabric with RS together and seamlines matching. Stitch along seamline around the neck and armholes.
Pull through shoulders to the RS, press and baste the edges carefully so that the lining does not show. Stitch the side seams of the outer fabric and lining in one, carefully matching the armhole seamlines. Stitch the back seams separately, insert the zipper into the opening of the outer fabric. Turn under the lining edges and slip-stitch to the zipper tape.

Dress with sleeves Make the dress and lining separately. If you wish you can use the lining as a facing for the neck edge by stitching with RS together and then turning lining to the WS. Place lining and outer fabric with WS together and baste around the armholes. Apply the sleeve to the double layer. If lining the sleeves, place sleeve linings over outer sleeves with WS together and matching seamlines, balance points and notches. Turn under seam allowances of lining around the armhole and pin the fold to the seamline. Hem in place, easing in the fullness by hand as you stitch. Finish the bottom sleeve edge by turning up the lining hem for $\frac{3}{4}$in (2cm) more than the hem of the dress. Slip-hem the lining hemline 1in (2·5cm) from the dress hemline to allow ease.

Basic stitches 18
Seams 20
Hems 28
Underlinings 37

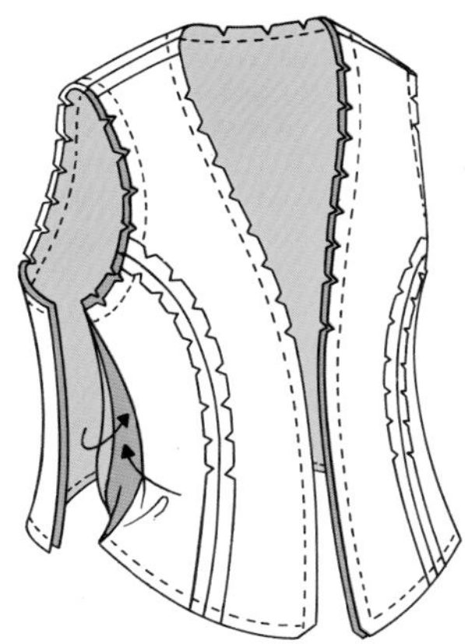

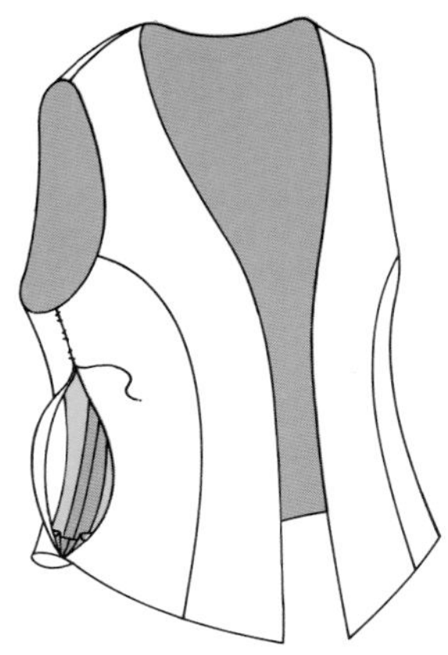

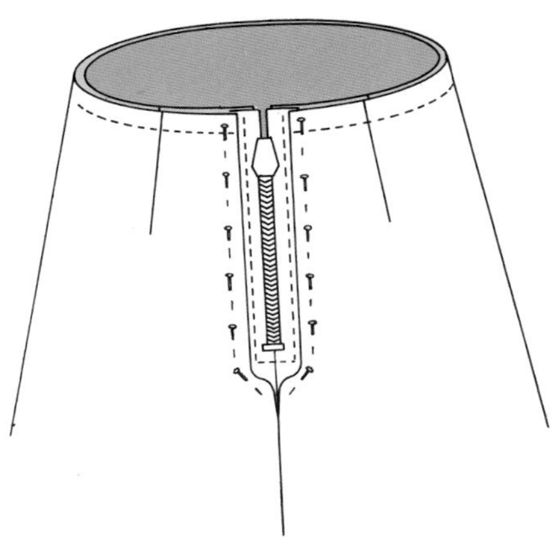

Vests

1 Stitch any darts and join the front to the back at the shoulder only on both lining and outer fabric. Place lining onto outer fabric with RS together and stitch along hemline, front and neck edge and armholes. Turn through to RS at the front side edges and pull through the shoulders and out at the back edges.

2 Baste the edges carefully and press so that the lining does not show. Stitch the side seam of the outer fabric, turn under and slip-hem the lining edges together.

Skirts

Make skirt as far as inserting zipper. Make lining in the same way leaving an opening slightly longer than zipper. Place lining onto skirt with WS together, matching seamlines. Baste along waist edge. Fold under edges of lining along the opening and hem to zipper tape. Apply waistband. Turn up skirt hem and then lining hem to finish 2in (5cm) above skirt hemline.

Jackets

1 Cut the lining for the front, back and sleeves allowing 1in (2·5cm) extra at the CB for a pleat to give ease. Trim the width of the facing less twice the seam allowance from the front and neck edges of the lining. Make the jacket to the point of applying the facings. Join the side and shoulder seams of the lining and insert the sleeves. Form the CB pleat and stitch across the seamline at the top.

2 Join the shoulder seams of the facings. With RS together stitch the lining to the facings along the neck and front edges. Open out and press the edges onto the lining. Place the lining onto the jacket with RS together and seamlines matching. Stitch along the seamlines of the front and neck edges, leaving 3in (7·5cm) unstitched at the bottom of the front for the hem.

3 Turn to the RS and press. Turn up the jacket hem and then turn up the lining hem for $\frac{3}{4}$in (2cm) more and slip-hem the lower fold to the jacket 1in (2·5cm) from the hemline. Repeat on the sleeves.

Belts, bibs and shoulder straps

Soft tie belts

Cut fabric to twice required belt width plus $\frac{1}{2}$in (10mm) by waist size plus 1yd (1m). Use light-weight interfacing (optional) cut to the same size and apply to WS of belt. Fold belt in half lengthwise with RS together and stitch from each end to within 2in (5cm) of the center, taking $\frac{1}{4}$in (5mm) turnings.
Re-fold with seam along center and press edges open. Shape the ends if you wish and stitch, taking $\frac{1}{4}$in (5mm) seams. Turn RS out and press again with the seam along the centre. Slip-hem folds of opening together.

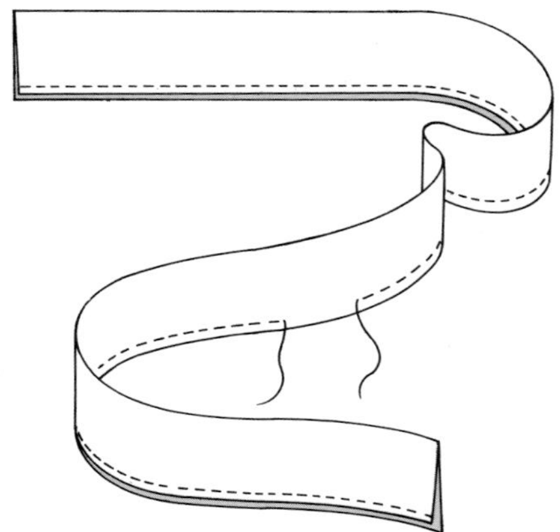

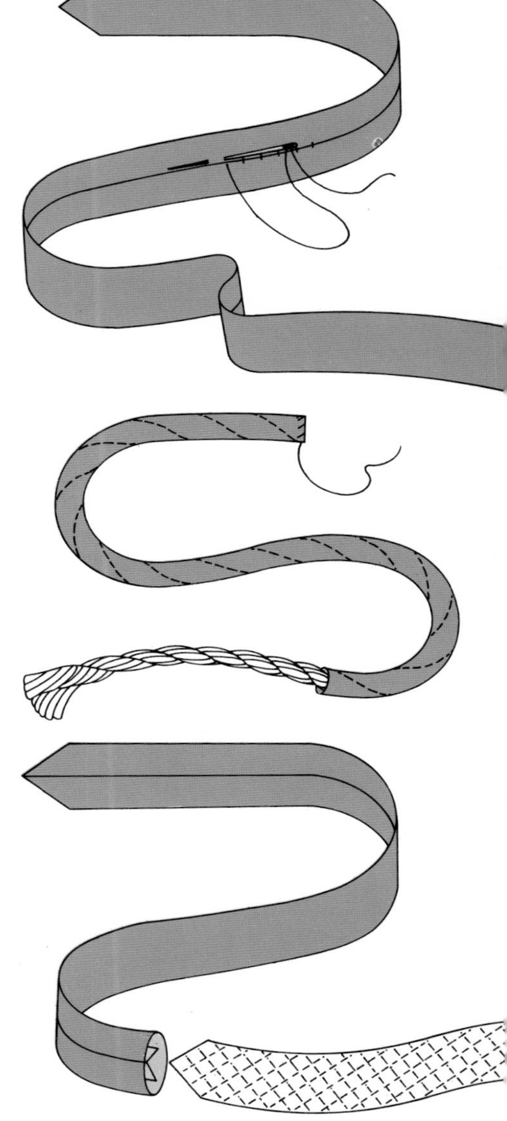

Firm rouleau belt

Buy a piece of piping cord of the required diameter by the waist measurement plus 1yd (1m) for tieing. Cut a strip of bias fabric to the same length plus $\frac{3}{8}$in (1cm) and wide enough to fit around the cord plus $\frac{1}{2}$in (1cm).
Fold the strip in half lengthwise with RS together and stitch along the long edge taking $\frac{1}{4}$in (5mm) seam allowances. Turn through to the RS. Thread the cord through the strip using a bodkin. Turn under $\frac{1}{4}$in (5mm) at each end neatly over the cord and slip-hem firmly.
To form a wider belt with a clasp, cut 2 lengths of cord to fit the waist, minus the clasp width, and 2 bias strips $\frac{3}{4}$in (2cm) longer. Make a belt with each length, leaving $\frac{3}{8}$in (1cm) of rouleau empty at each end. Slip-stitch the belts together along their length and thread ends through the clasp; overcast on WS.

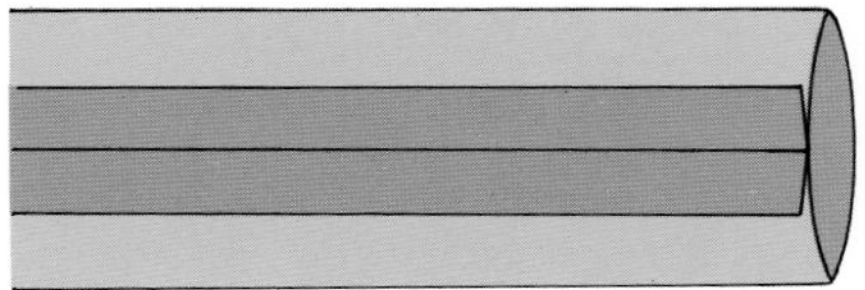

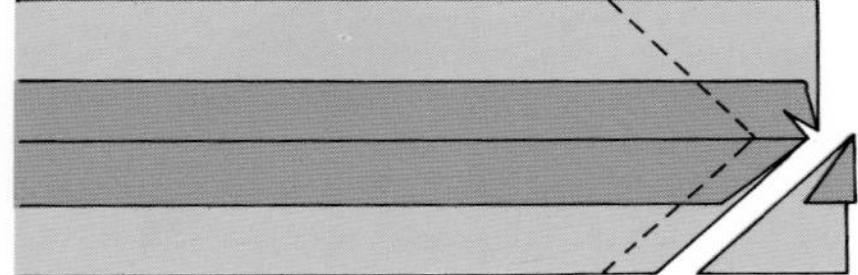

Stiff belt with bought buckle

Buy a piece of belt stiffening measuring slightly less than the buckle width by the waist length plus about 9$\frac{1}{2}$in (25cm) overlap. Cut a piece of fabric to the same length by twice the width of stiffening plus $\frac{1}{4}$in (5mm) all around.
1 With RS together fold the fabric in half lengthwise and stitch $\frac{1}{4}$in (5mm) in from the long raw edges. Re-fold the fabric so that the seam lies in the center and press the edges open.

2 Trim the end of the belt stiffening to a point or curve and mark the end of the fabric in the same way, using the stiffening as a template. Stitch along the mark, trim the seam and turn the fabric RS out. Press again so that the seamline is exactly on the center of the reverse side of the belt.
3 Insert the stiffening and overcast the edges of the plain end together.

4 If the buckle has a prong, insert a metal eyelet in the center on the RS about 1in (2·5cm) from the plain end of the belt. Thread the end through the buckle and insert the prong in the eyelet. Insert eyelets, 1in (2·5cm) apart, in the right position to fit the waist at the opposite end. Alternatively work the eyelets by hand by punching a hole with a holepunch, working around it with a running stitch and then with a buttonhole stitch.

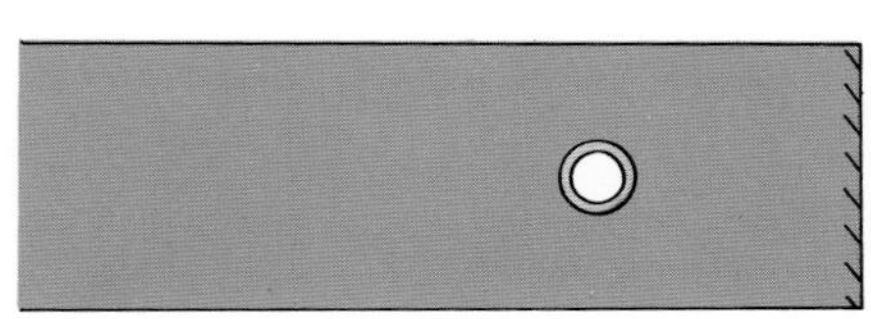

If there is no prong, insert the plain end through the buckle and wrap around the center bar.

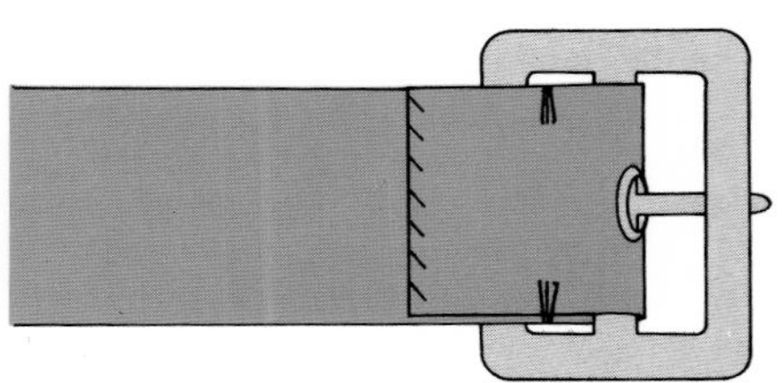

5 Overcast the end firmly to the back of the belt at each edge. Add belt loops if required.

Fastenings 32
Interfacings 36
Waistbands 38

Tabs

Use tabs to fasten slit openings or front openings on casual garments like car coats, or to decorate pockets, shoulders and cuffs.
Make them like short belts with one straight end to be stitched to the garment and a shaped end to fasten with a button and buttonhole or snap fasteners.

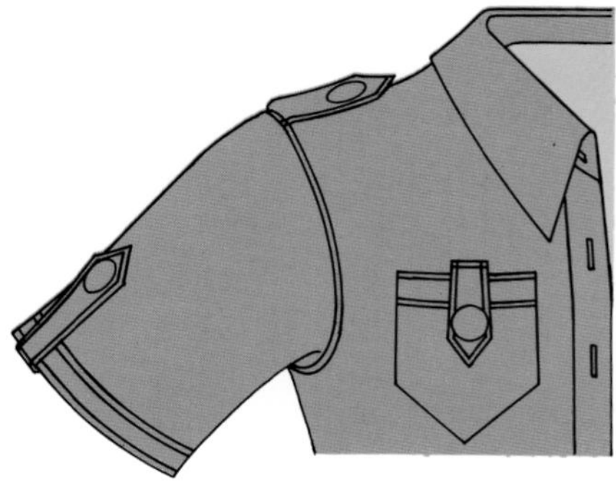

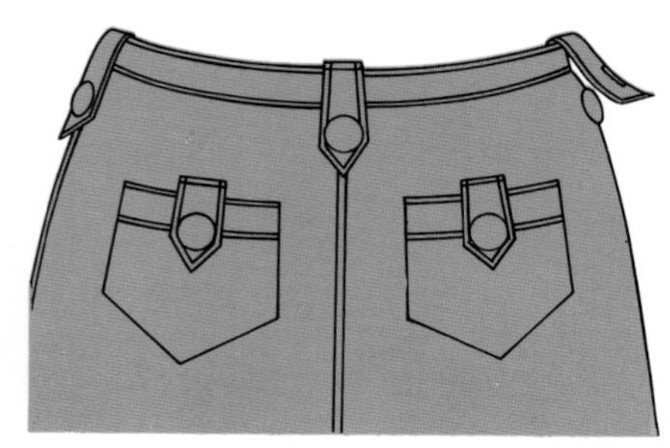

Shoulder straps

Measure from back waist or top of garment diagonally (or straight) across shoulders to front waist or to top of garment. Add 1in (2·5cm) for fastening with buttons or 2in (5cm) for fastening with buckles. Cut strips of fabric to twice required width (e.g. 1in/2·5cm) × required length plus $\frac{1}{4}$in (5mm) all around for seam allowances. Cut interfacing to the same size and apply to WS of strips. Make the straps as for the soft tie belts.

Try garment on with straps in position and pin at the back. For button fastenings, mark button positions on garment and then mark vertical buttonholes in center of straps so that the lower end of the buttonhole is at the correct length for the strap. Work buttonholes and stitch straps and buttons in position.

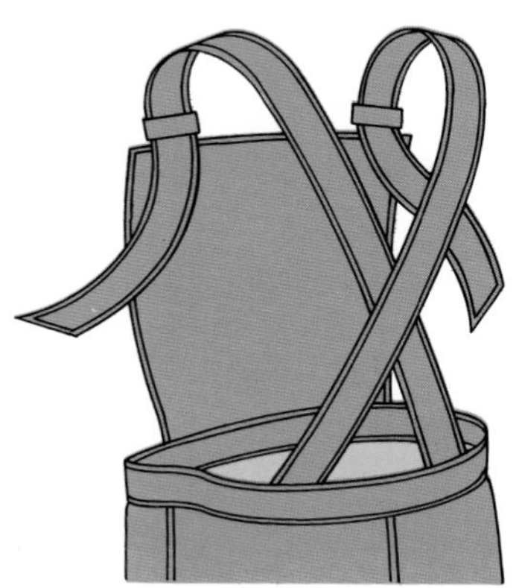

Belt loops and carriers

Cut 1in (2·5cm) wide strips by twice the belt width plus $\frac{1}{2}$in (12mm) for loops or by the belt width plus $\frac{5}{8}$in (15mm) for carriers. Fold strips in half lengthwise with RS together and stitch $\frac{1}{4}$in (5mm) from the fold. Turn to the RS and press so that the seam lies along the edge.
For loops, place the ends together and overcast firmly; turn RS out. For belt carriers either hem firmly or machine-stitch each end in position on garment so that belt slides through easily.
To attach carriers with a waistband, sandwich one end between the garment and waistband before attaching the band. Complete the band, press the carrier up, turn under the free end and stitch to the band.

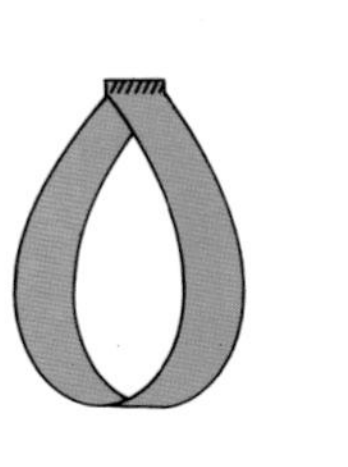

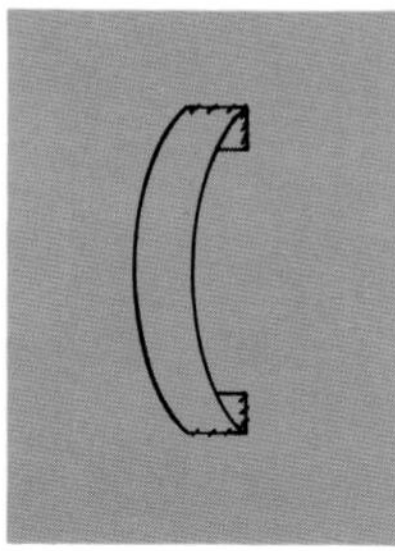

Bibs

Decide width of bib and measure for length from top of armpit to waist. Cut 2 pieces of fabric (on bulky fabrics cut 1 from fabric and 1 from lining) to the required size and shape plus seam allowances all around.
Make bib before attaching waistband to garment. Cut waistband in 2 sections so that it has a separate facing.
Stitch bib pieces with RS together along sides and top edge. Turn to RS and press so that seam lies along edge.
With RS together pin and baste bib to waistband so that its bottom edge is flush with the top of the band and the center of the bib corresponds with the CF of the band.

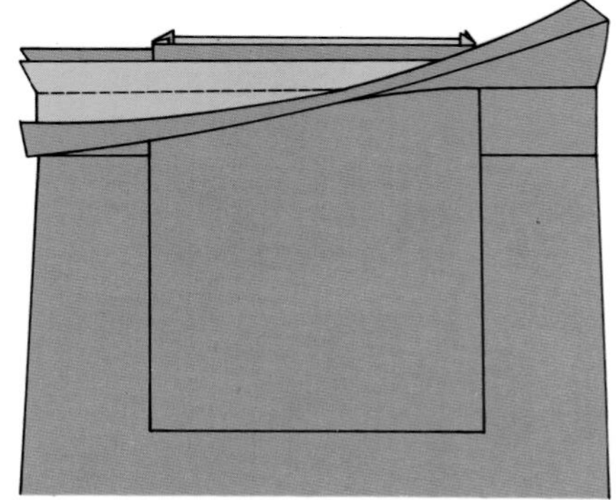

Attach the band to the garment so that the bib is sandwiched between the layers. Finish with shoulder straps or bought suspenders.

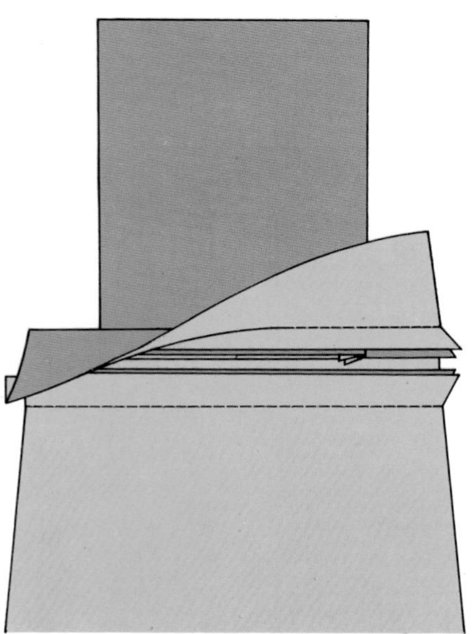

Pockets

Basic stitches 18
Seams and edge finishes 20

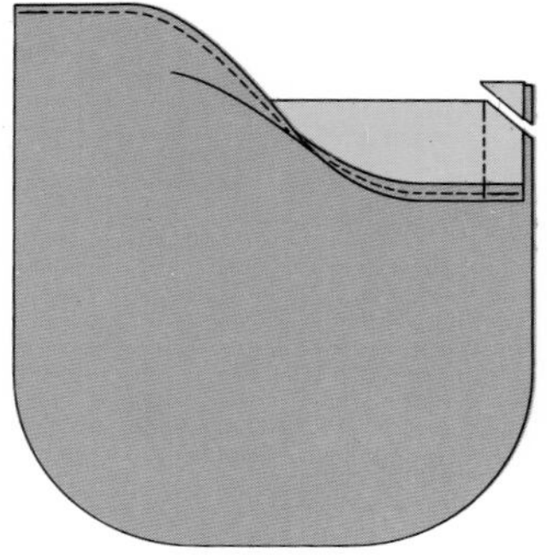

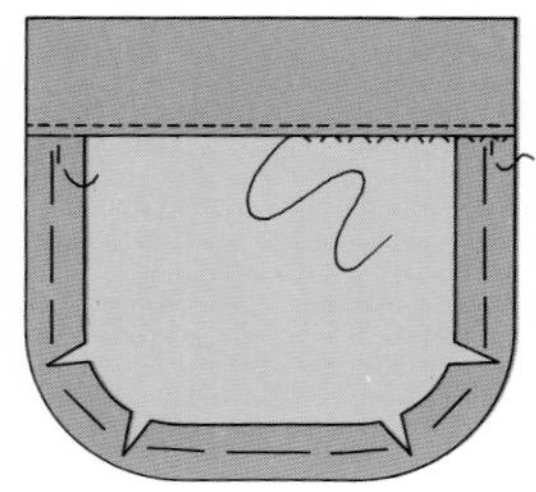

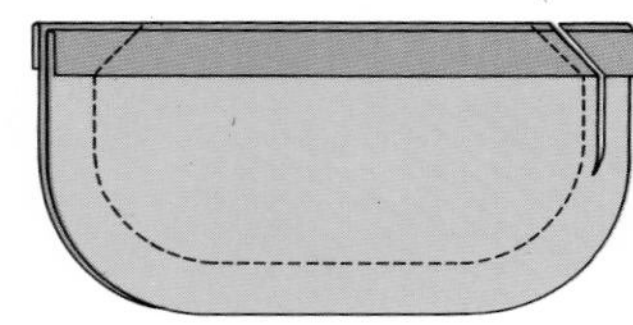

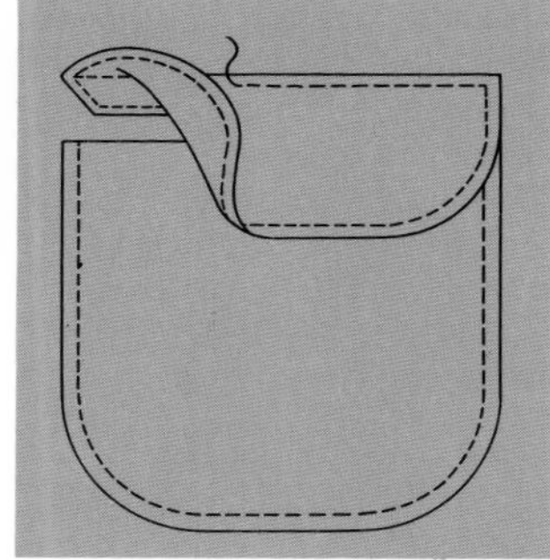

Patch pocket
Making the pattern Decide the position of the pocket and the shape and size most suitable for the garment. Draw it in position on the pattern, using a flexible curve for curved edges. Trace the shape of the pocket off the pattern; add 2in (5cm) to the top edge for facing, and seam allowances around side and lower edges.
Attaching the pocket
Finish top edge of pocket by turning in $\frac{1}{4}$in (5mm) and machine-stitching. Fold facing to RS, baste and stitch ends. Cut across corners. Turn facing RS out and press folded edge.
Slip-hem facing to pocket. Turn in the seam allowance around the outer edge of pocket and baste. For rounded pocket cut small notches in the seam allowance on curved edges. Baste pocket in position on garment and then top-stitch or slip-stitch.

Patch pocket with separate flap
Making the pattern Draft a patch pocket pattern. Decide on the depth of flap, keeping it in proportion with the pocket, and draw it to the same width as the pocket. Cut the flap pattern adding seam allowances at sides and bottom and a double allowance at the top. Cut flap double.
Attaching the pocket
1 Make and apply pocket to garment as for patch pocket. To make flap, fold under half seam allowances at top edge to neaten. Baste and machine-stitch around side and bottom edges with RS together leaving top edge open. Trim and clip seam. Turn flap RS out. Baste close to stitched edges. Press.
You may want to top-stitch around curved edge of flap.
2 With RS together baste flap to garment $\frac{5}{8}$in (15mm) above pocket. Stitch in place, fastening ends securely. Stitch turned-in edge to garment and press flap down. Top-stitch to hold flap down if necessary.

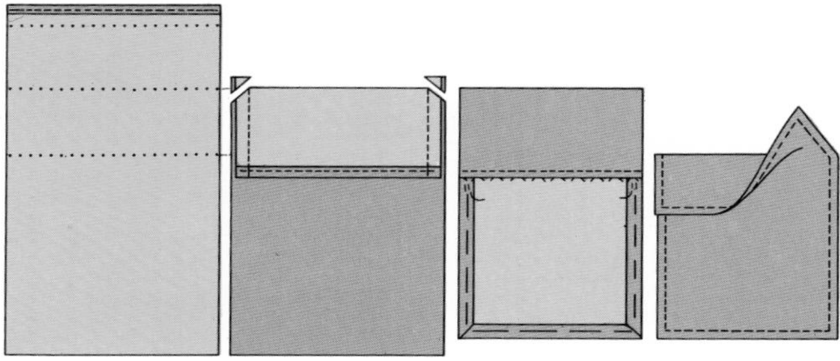

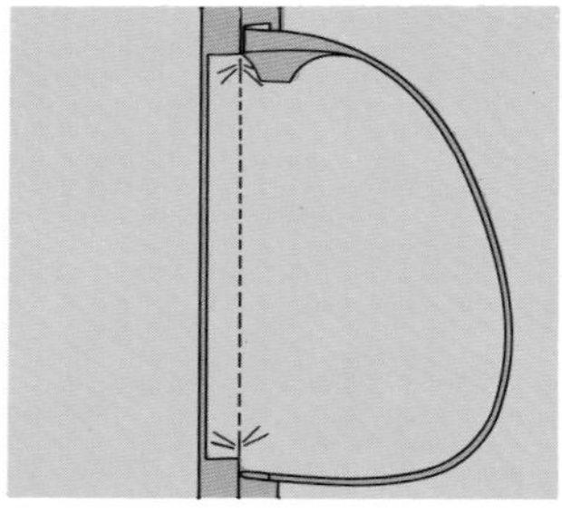

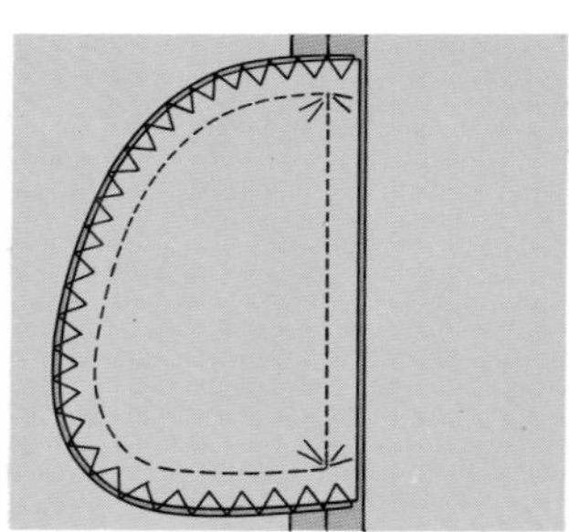

Patch pocket with self flap
Making the pattern The flap is cut with the pocket. Draw a patch pocket. Decide the depth of the flap and add double the measurement to the top edge of pocket. Mark the foldline and flap foldline. Add a further 2in (5cm) for facing. Add seam allowances to side and lower edges.
Attaching the pocket
1 Finish top edge of pocket by turning in $\frac{1}{4}$in (5mm) and machine-stitching.
2 With RS together fold flap along flap foldline. Baste and stitch ends. Cut across corners. Turn flap RS out, press folded edge. Slip-hem facing down to pocket. Turn in seam allowance around outer edge of pocket and baste. Top-stitch around outer edge of flap to foldline if desired.
3 Baste pocket into position on garment and top-stitch around outer edge. Press flap down.

Pocket in side seam
Making the pattern Mark the pocket position at the side seam of pattern, or at the front panel seam, to required length (e.g. 6in/15cm). Using flexible curve, draw the outline of the pocket pouch on the pattern at opening, ensuring the inside depth of pocket is the right size for your hand. Trace this shape off pattern and add seam allowances to all edges. For each pocket cut the pocket section double.
Attaching the pocket
1 With RS together baste and stitch 1 pocket section to front of garment and 1 to back of garment between opening marks. With RS together baste and machine-stitch the seams above and below pocket. Press seams open. On the inside clip the front pocket seam allowance to stitching line. Press front pocket seam allowance toward back and the pocket to the front.
2 With RS together baste and machine-stitch around outer edge of pocket pieces. Finish raw edges of pocket together.

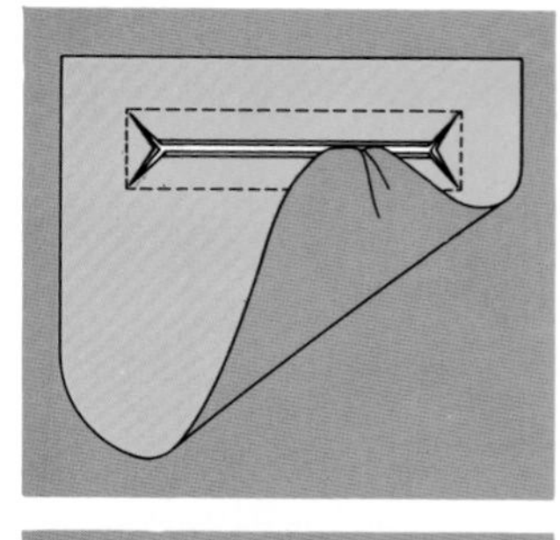

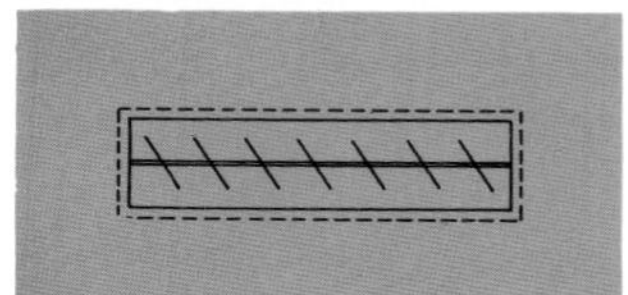

Bound pocket

Making the pattern Mark length of pocket opening on pattern. Draw pocket pouch to required depth, making the top edge 1in (2·5cm) higher and wider than opening. Trace shape off pattern and add seam allowances to side and lower edges. For each pocket cut pocket section double.

Attaching the pocket

1 With RS together and with top edge of pocket section 1in (2·5cm) above opening mark, baste 1 section of pocket to garment. Stitch $\frac{1}{4}$in

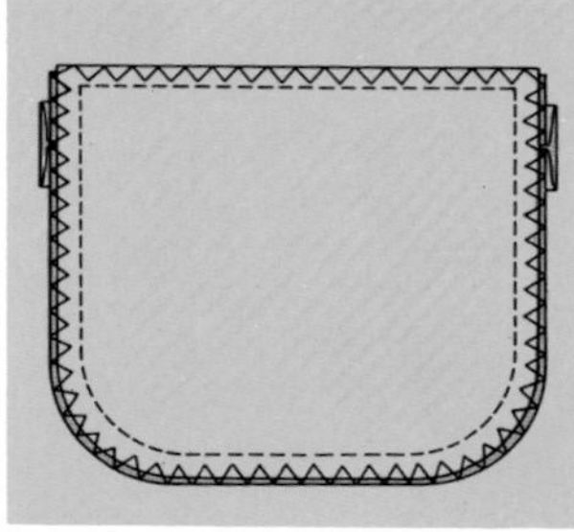

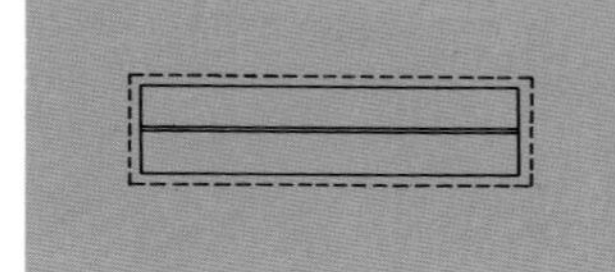

(5mm) all around mark. Cut along center and clip diagonally into corners. Draw pocket through opening to WS. Bring folded edges together, forming a binding on each side of opening. Pleat ends and press.

2 On the RS overcast folds together and top-stitch around close to binding.

3 On the WS, with RS together, place second pocket section over first and trim to the same size. Baste and stitch sections together around outer edges. Finish raw edges together.

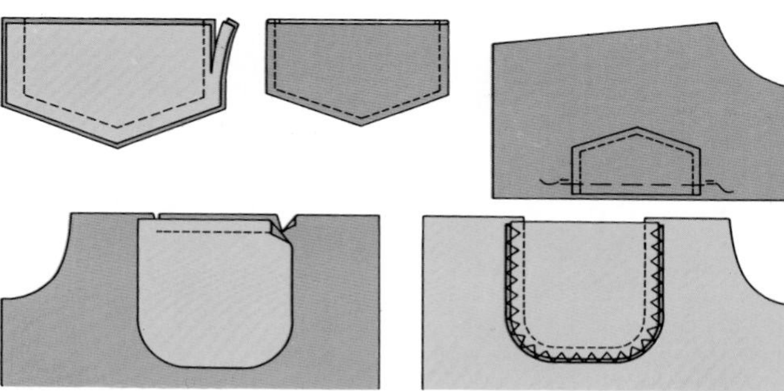

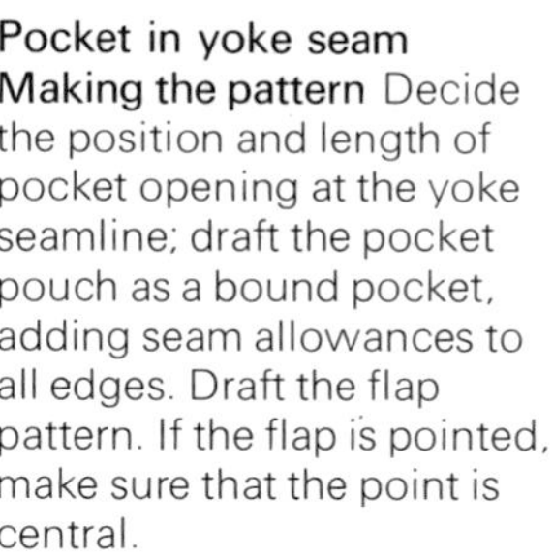

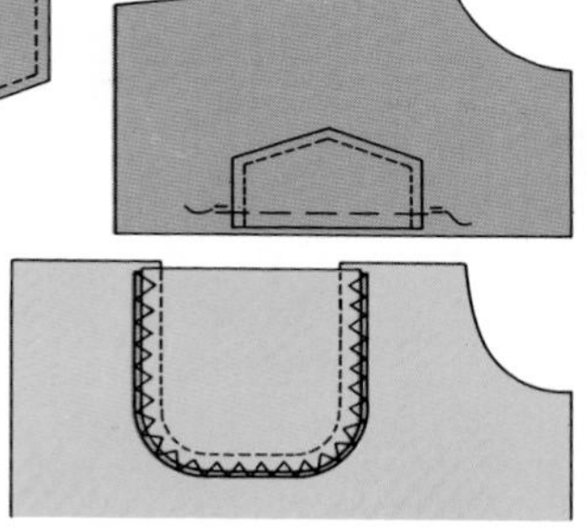

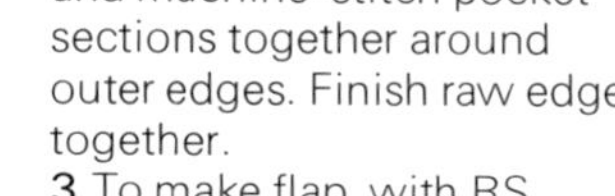

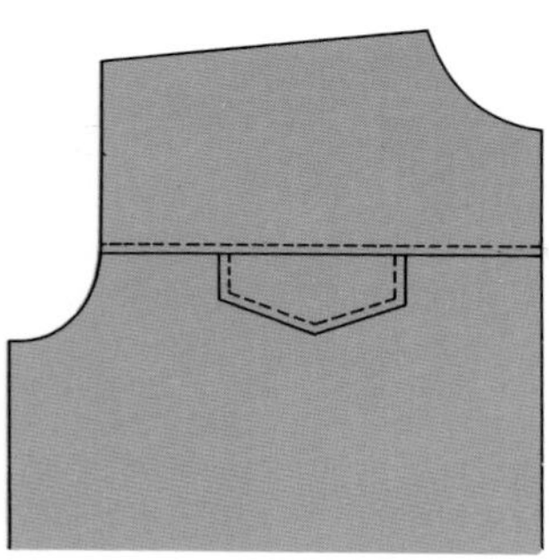

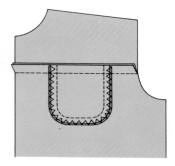

Pocket in yoke seam

Making the pattern Decide the position and length of pocket opening at the yoke seamline; draft the pocket pouch as a bound pocket, adding seam allowances to all edges. Draft the flap pattern. If the flap is pointed, make sure that the point is central.

Attaching the pocket

1 With RS together, baste and machine-stitch one pocket section to bodice seamline between pocket opening. Clip bodice seam allowance on both sides of opening to stitching. Turn pocket section to WS. Press stitched edge.

2 With RS together, baste and machine-stitch pocket sections together around outer edges. Finish raw edges together.

3 To make flap, with RS together, baste and machine-stitch around edges leaving top edge open. Trim seam allowance and turn flap RS out. Press. Top-stitch around outer edge of flap.

4 With RS and raw edges together, baste flap to yoke at opening position. With RS together, baste and machine-stitch yoke seam through all layers. Press seam upward and flap down. Top-stitch above seam.

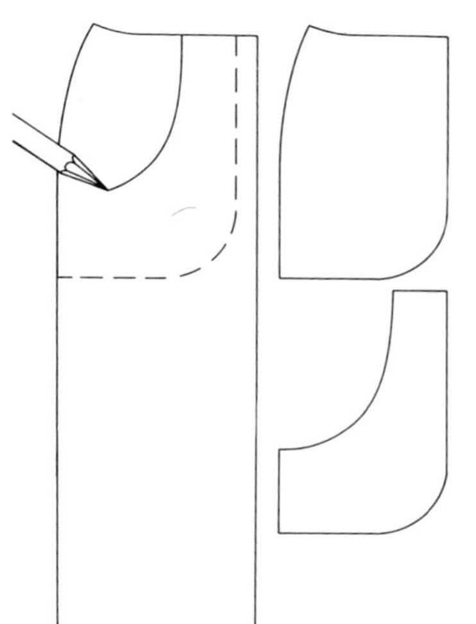

Curved hip pockets

Making the pattern For the pocket position measure 3in (7·5cm) in from side seam at waistline, and 6in (15cm) down side seam. Draw the pocket curve on pattern from waist to side using flexible curve. Draw the outline of pocket facing (bottom left) and back pocket section (top left) making the lower edge of pocket pieces 2in (5cm) below the curve at side seam. Trace off the pocket facing and back pocket section separately. Add seam allowances where necessary. Cut away pattern for curve.

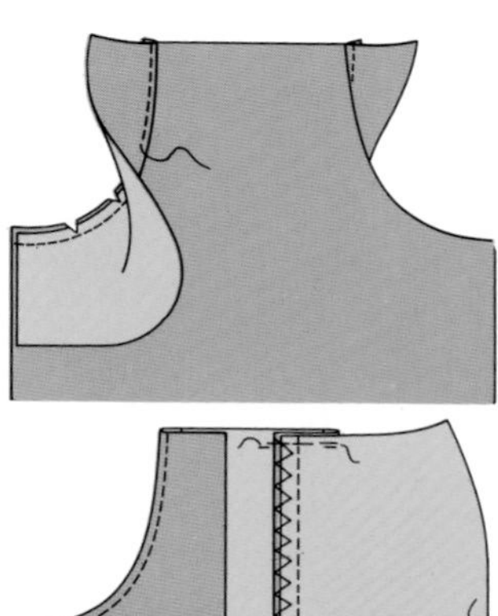

Attaching the pocket

1 With RS together baste and machine-stitch the pocket facing to garment front. Trim and clip seam allowance, turn facing outward and stitch facing to seam allowance around curve. Turn facing to WS.

2 On the WS overlap the back pocket section over the facing, matching top and side edges. Baste and machine-stitch around outer edge of pocket. Finish raw edges together. Press.

Difficult fabrics

Fabric glossary 11
Basic stitches 18
Seams and edge finishes 20
Hems 28

As fabrics vary tremendously in weight, thickness and texture, some are more difficult than others to work with. This may be because they fray during cutting or are thick and therefore hard to cut; some slide or stick and are awkward to stitch or cause the needle to become blunt. If you take certain precautions and test stitches and pressing on spare fabric first, however, you will find it is quite easy to achieve success with so-called difficult fabrics. Here is a list of fabrics and the problems they present, together with the best ways to overcome them.

Brocade
Woven and Jacquard knits; if they contain metallic threads handle as metallics (see below).
Styles to choose Evening coats, tunics or simple dresses look best in this stiff fabric.
Cutting Brocade frays so leave large seam allowances. Make sure fabric runs in the same direction if it has a sheen and match motifs where they occur.
Stitching Finish seams with overcasting or zigzag stitching. Avoid bound buttonholes. Do not use a zipper on metallic brocades.
Pressing Press lightly with a cool iron and a towel underneath fabric.

Metallics
Any fabric that has metal threads knitted or woven into it—from sheer silks to lamés and brocades.
Styles to choose Draped or tailored depending on fabric.
Cutting Place pattern pieces in the same direction. Leave large seam allowances if fabric frays.
Stitching See Brocade. Use synthetic thread and fine needle; metallic threads make needles blunt so change them when necessary. On coarse fabric use satin piping (see p56) on necks and armholes or line complete garment (see p88).
Pressing Iron only if absolutely necessary with dry iron on WS and a dry cloth on top. Finger-press seams, protecting your fingers with a thimble.

Jersey
Any machine-knitted fabric; varying degrees of stretchiness; single- or double-sided.
Styles to choose Simple, soft-fitting, clinging designs, avoid complicated details.
Cutting Avoid patterns falling on center crease in synthetic fabrics as it may be difficult to press out.
Stitching Use fine synthetic thread and ballpoint machine needle with zigzag or multiple machine stitch. Stitch any strain-bearing seams twice or reinforce with tape. Hang garment overnight before hemming to let it reach its natural length.
Pressing Press lightly with steam or dry iron and damp muslin pressing cloth. Place brown paper under seams to avoid press marks.

Lace
Machine-made lace comes in light, medium and heavy weights.
Styles to choose Simple styles with few seams and darts which break up fabric design. Lace cannot bear much strain, so avoid close-fitting waists or armholes. Collars are difficult to work; instead of buttonholes use loops.
Linings and underlinings Use underlining to support fragile lace and to prevent scratching. Suitable underlinings are silk organza, fine net, marquisette or chiffon; match fiber with that of lace. For a more sculptured style use taffeta or satin lining. You can vary the effect by making long sleeves in unlined lace with the rest of the garment mounted or by making a separate lining (see p88).
Cutting Make sure pattern motifs run in the same direction and are not broken up by seams. Make use of any scalloped edges by positioning pattern pieces so they fall on hemlines.
Stitching Stitch fragile laces as sheers and underlined lace in the normal way. Some heavy laces must be hand-stitched. Reduce seam allowances to $\frac{1}{4}$in (5mm) and overcast raw edges to finish. Face hems with fine organza. On delicate laces use an overlap opening (see p60) instead of a zipper.
Pressing Use steam or dry iron with slightly damp muslin pressing cloth on top and pressing pad or towel underneath to prevent design flattening.

Sheer fabrics
Transparent fabrics classified as crisp or soft. Crisp sheers include voile, organdy and net; soft are batiste, chiffon, China silk, cheesecloth, georgette and gauze.
Styles to choose Airy, floating, full not fitted.
Cutting To prevent fabric sliding, pin to thick blanket or sheet fastened to cutting surface. Allow large seam allowances if fabric frays.
Stitching Place pins within seam allowance to avoid marking fabric. Use fine needle and silk or synthetic thread. Stitch between layers of tissue paper, using French seams and narrow hand-sewn or machine-stitched hems; with an underlining you can make a normal hem. Bind edges of net.
Pressing Press lightly with a steam or dry iron; press embroidered sheers face downward on a towel.

Beaded or sequinned fabrics
Beads or sequins can be applied to knitted or woven base fabric; fabrics may be heavily encrusted or lightly sprinkled.
Styles to choose Fabrics are difficult to work, so choose styles with a minimum of seams and darts.
Cutting Lay pattern pieces in one direction, matching motifs if necessary. Pin within seam allowance and try to avoid cutting beads: cut through single thickness only. If the beads are close together remove the appropriate amount with small scissors before cutting fabric; fasten threads to stop the rest from unravelling.
Re-apply spare beads or sequins if necessary when the seaming is finished.
Stitching Slip-baste seams and darts (see p18) on RS. When you are sure of the fit remove beads from final seam allowances and dart areas. Use zipper foot for all stitching. Remove beads from hem allowance and from seam allowance if using a zipper. Use small press studs instead of buttonholes.
Pressing Use a cool dry iron only and cover fabric with a dry cloth. Press on WS on padded board.

Velvet and corduroy
Silk or rayon velvets are difficult to use; cotton or synthetic corduroy, velveteen and panne velvets are easier.
Styles to choose Heavy velvets are most suitable for suits and evening skirts. Choose simple styles and handle velvet as little as possible; avoid gathers, darts and pleats.
Cutting Lay pattern pieces so pile runs upward on finished garment for a richer look. If possible use fine pins or needles to prevent permanent marks.
Stitching To prevent velvet slipping, baste with silk thread, using small stitches and back-stitching at 2–3in (5–7·5cm) intervals. Machine-stitch in direction of pile with tissue paper strips between fabric layers to prevent wrinkling; finish seams with overcasting or zigzag stitch. Panne velvet requires no finishing.
Insert zipper by hand and substitute loops for buttonholes (see p32).
Use straight or bias seam binding for hems, or overcast raw edge and hem in place, picking up one thread of fabric at a time.
Pressing Remove basting and hang garment in steamy bathroom to remove slight wrinkles. Press pile-side down on an ironing board, flat but lightly and with a damp cloth. For seams, use pressing cloth made from a velvet scrap placed pile-side down on seam, or purchased velvet pressboard.

Coated fabrics
These include vinyl-coated, bonded or laminated fabrics.
Styles to choose Vinyl-coated fabrics can be made into raincoats, ponchos, aprons and all-purpose bags. Bonded and laminated fabrics make simple, casual coats.
Cutting If the finish is slippery, lay fabric WS down. Attach pattern pieces with steel pins placed within seam allowance to avoid making holes.
Stitching To prevent fabric slipping use a roller foot or insert tracing paper between seam foot and fabric. Seams on vinyl fabrics can be top-stitched. Prevent foam-backed fabrics from sticking to machine by basting straight seam binding or a strip of lawn over foam.
Pressing Do not press vinyl- or polyurethane-coated fabrics. If they crease, roll them around a cardboard tube and leave overnight.

Satin
Cotton satin is easy to work but synthetics fray and are slippery.
Cutting and stitching Handle as little as possible. Leave large seam allowances. Prevent seams puckering by using polyester thread.
Pressing Your iron must be smooth and not discolored; use a pressing cloth or tissue paper and always press on WS. On delicate satins, finger-press seams; otherwise press seams over brown paper.

Fur fabrics
Various types and depths of pile, with knitted, woven or foam backing.
Styles to choose Aim for simple lines, intricate seaming is lost in pile of fabric.
Cutting As with leather, check the fit before cutting your fabric. Make a sample first. Lay out pattern pieces so that pile runs downward. Cut fabric pile-side down on single thickness only. Depending on backing fabric, pin pattern pieces or secure them with transparent adhesive tape. With soft pencil or chalk, mark outline of pattern pieces and draw arrows in direction of pile. Cut through backing only and ease pile apart.
Stitching This also depends on the backing fabric. Stitch firm-backed fur by hand. Trim seam allowance to $\frac{1}{4}$in (5mm), hold edges together with clothes pins and overcast, with fine, sharp needle and silk or synthetic thread.
On jersey-backed fabrics use small zigzag machine stitch, or blanket-stitch by hand. Use a roller foot for vinyl-coated backings. On foam-backed furs, place strips of lawn over seamline or stitch between layers of paper. After stitching, shave pile from seam allowances. Tease out pile with a pin from seams on RS.
Finishing touches Cut darts open and grade enclosed seams, such as collars, to reduce bulk. For hems, shave $1\frac{1}{2}$in (4cm) of pile along hem edge and stitch a grosgrain ribbon of same width onto it; turn up hem and slip-stitch ribbon to backing. On heavier fabrics turn up hem and glue in position. Buttonholes are difficult to make so use hook or frog fastenings or simulate a buttoned effect by stitching buttons on top and snap fasteners underneath.
Pressing Finger-press seams and with a cool, dry iron carefully press garment pile-side down on velvet pressboard or towel to prevent flattening.

Leather and suede
Fine, smooth leather, suede and chamois are most suitable; usually sold in speciality shops.
Styles to choose Simple skirts, tunics and vests are easiest; on first attempt avoid facings, set-in sleeves, buttonholes. Size of pattern pieces must fit into size of skin.
Discuss requirements with shopkeeper and take pattern along if in doubt. If necessary, join pieces so that the maximum amount of skin is used.
Cutting Needles and pins leave permanent holes, so make a sample and make adjustments on that. Always lay pattern pieces on flat skin, with nap running downward. Note any blemishes on RS of skin and mark position on WS. Cut left and right pattern pieces separately. Secure pattern to skin with transparent adhesive tape and mark outlines of edges and darts lightly with ballpoint pen.
Stitching Don't baste. Use transparent adhesive tape, paper clips or clothes pins to hold seam allowances together; use pure silk or synthetic thread. On plain seams or darts a few dabs of glue under the seam allowances produce a neat, flat effect. For hand-sewing use a glover's needle and for machining a spearpoint needle; replace when blunt. A roller foot will prevent material sliding. Use plain or overlapped seams; leave hems raw or glue down. Tie off thread ends (back-stitching can tear fabric).
Finishing touches If they are bulky, cut darts open and pare away undersides of seam allowances with razor blade; practice this first.
If using bound buttonholes, sew small reinforcing buttons on WS of buttons; otherwise insert metal eyelets.
Instead of facings turn under edges and top-stitch. If lining, stitch tape to seam allowance and slip-stitch lining to this.
Pressing Finger-press seams on fine skins; on heavier skins use a mallet or rolling pin to flatten seams.
Press carefully on WS with medium-hot dry iron and dry pressing cloth.

Basic slacks

Master pattern sheet
Zippers 26
Hems 28
Waistbands 38
Darts 44
Pockets 92

These slacks, given in a wide range of sizes for men, women and children, are a classic shape with straight legs. They can easily be adapted to other shapes and styles as shown on p100. The smallest children's sizes (waist 20–24in/52–60cm) are made with an elasticized waistband. All other sizes have a conventional waistband with a front fly or overlapped opening – this opening could, however, be moved to another seam. Instructions for fitting slacks are given on p98.

You will need
fabric, 45in (115cm) wide:
- 3yd/2·70m (men's sizes)
- 2⅝yd/2·40m (women's sizes)
- 1⅛yd/1m (children's sizes 20–24in/52–60cm)
- 2⅜yd/2·10m (children's sizes 25–26in/63–65cm)

matching sewing thread
8in (20cm) zipper (not sizes 20–24in/52-60cm)
waistband stiffening and fastenings (not sizes 20–24in/52–60cm)
1in (2·5cm) wide elastic (sizes 20–24in/52–60cm only)

Cutting out
Trace the appropriate outlines from the master sheet. Extend lines to give required leg length plus hem allowance. Add seam allowances to the other edges. Cut out the waistband, forming it in two sections if adding a bib and straps.

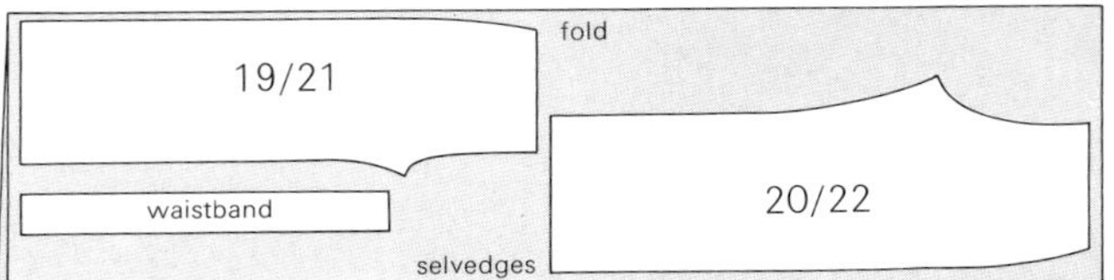

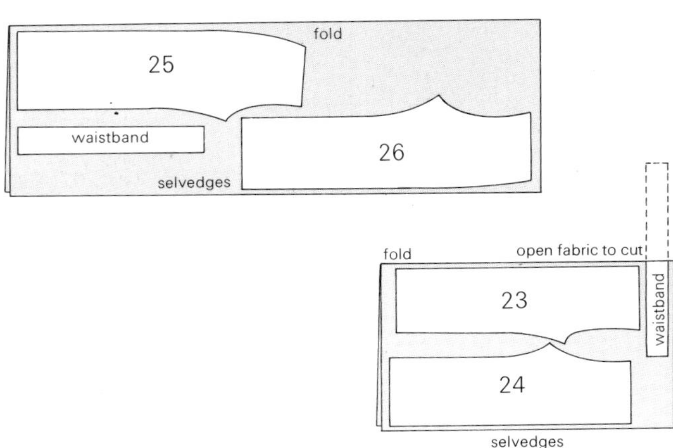

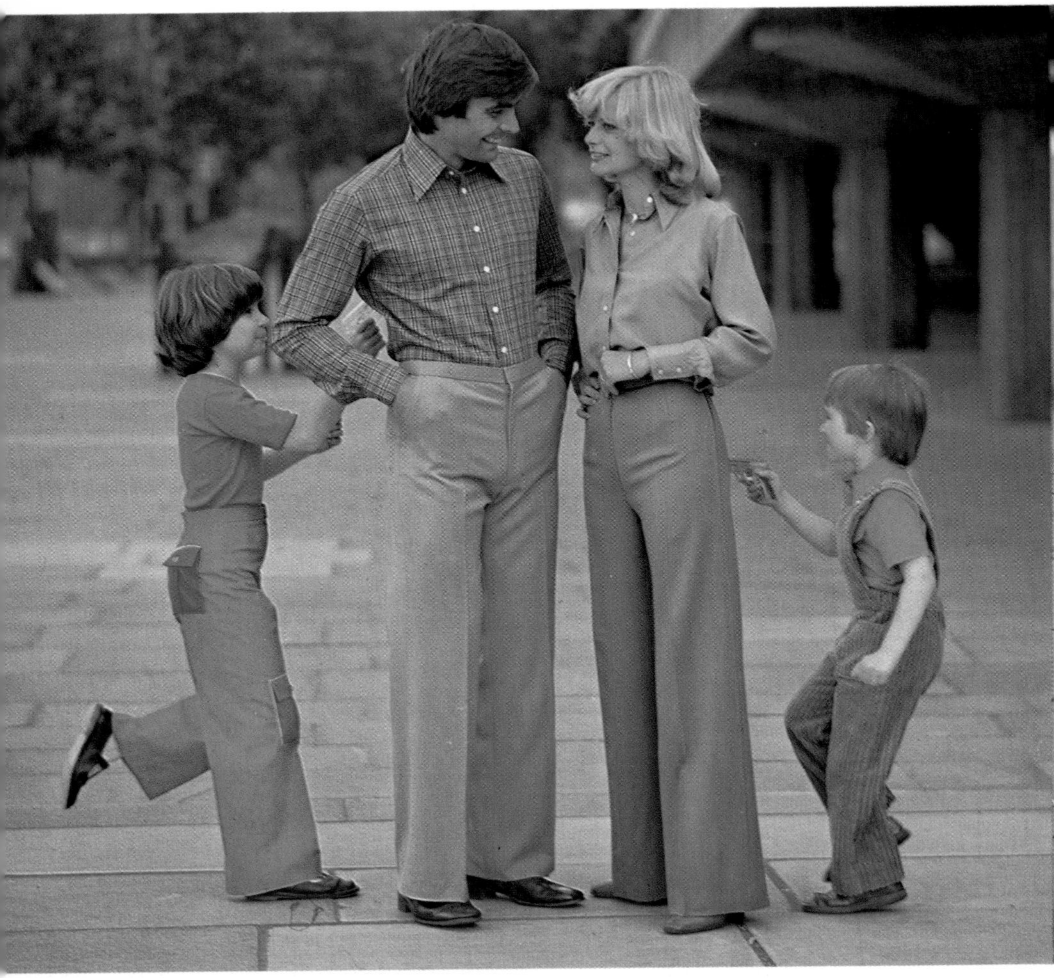

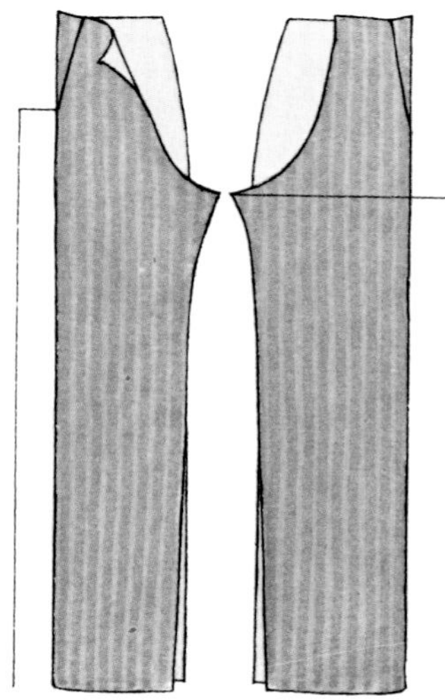

Making the slacks

1 Fold each piece in half lengthwise with WS together. Press the folds firmly, so that the front creases end at the dart point and the back creases taper beyond the level of the crotch (see diagram above). Keep side seams vertical.

2 (Not sizes 20–24in/52–60cm) Insert zipper into CF seam (pattern pieces 19/21/25) using overlap or fly method. (If using an overlapped fastening, join seam by machine-stitching 1in/2·5cm only below base of opening before inserting zipper.)
Fold, baste and stitch all darts.
3 (All sizes) With RS together matching notches join slack front to backs (pattern pieces 20/22/24/26) at side seams and inside leg seams. Finish and press seams open.
4 (All sizes) Turn one leg inside out, and with RS together slip one leg inside the other. Matching notches

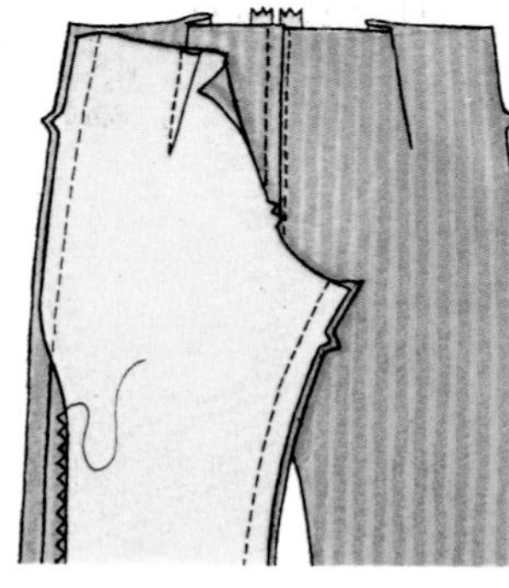

and inside leg seams, baste and stitch the crotch seam from the back waist to the front. Finish seam, clip curves and press seam open.
5 (Sizes 20–24in/52–60cm

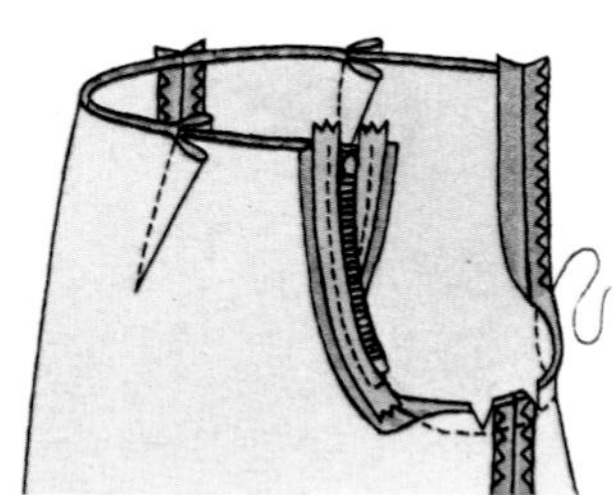

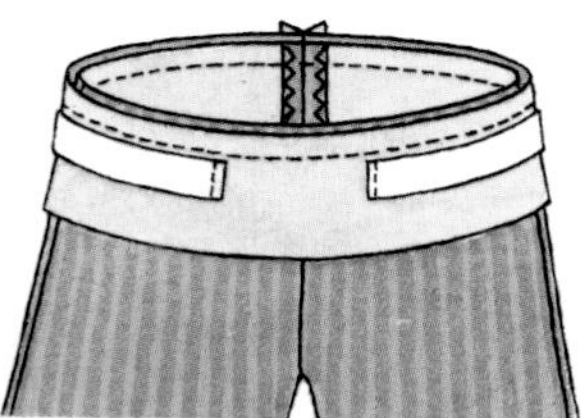

only) Omitting any form of stiffening, attach one edge of waistband to slacks. Cut elastic to fit around waist, beginning and ending 3in (7·5cm) from each side of CF seam.
Stitch elastic to WS of front edge of waistband at these points. Stitch free edge of waistband to seamline on WS.
(All other sizes) Try on slacks to check that creases hang straight. If they hang inward, raise the slacks at the waistline on the appropriate side to correct the line. Make and attach waistband to slacks.
6 (All sizes) Turn up and press hem.

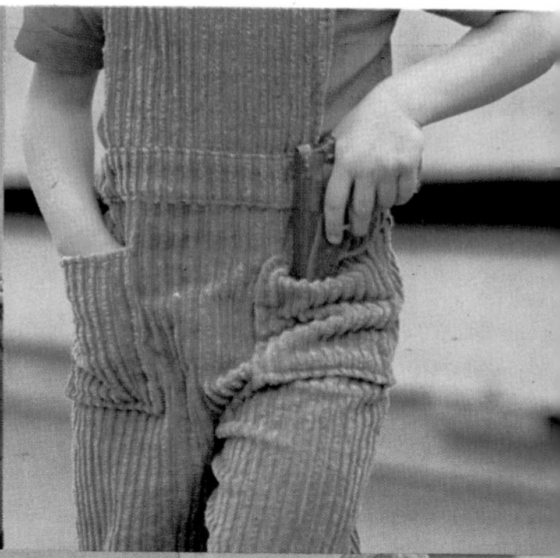

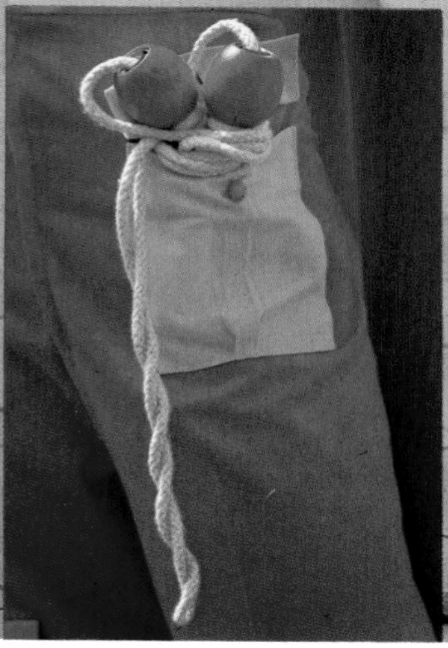

Fitting and altering slacks

Measuring the figure 14
Using patterns and cutting out 16
Darts 44

Slacks are probably the most difficult garments to fit well because of the difference in figure types.
It is advisable to make a sample so that you can see where the difficulties occur before you tackle good fabric. Many problems can be solved in advance by checking all the measurements – particularly the crotch – on the pattern before cutting out. This is because these measurements can differ on people who otherwise have the same waist and hip measurements. When you are making slacks for yourself, ask someone else to check the fit when you try them on. If you are making slacks from the master pattern sheet without adaptation, check that they hang straight from the rounded part of the seat. After some of the pattern alterations you may have to correct the straight-grain line. To do this, fold the pattern to establish the crease line (see p97) and draw the new grain line parallel to it.

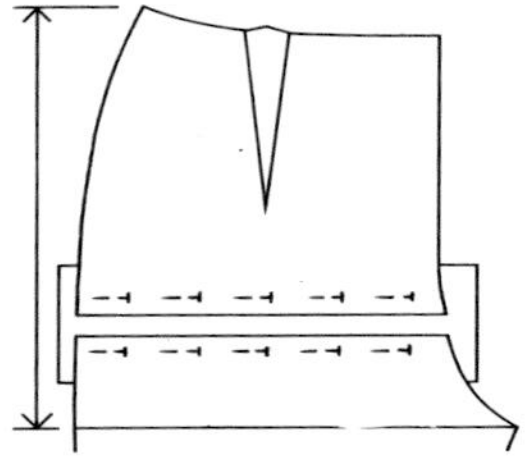

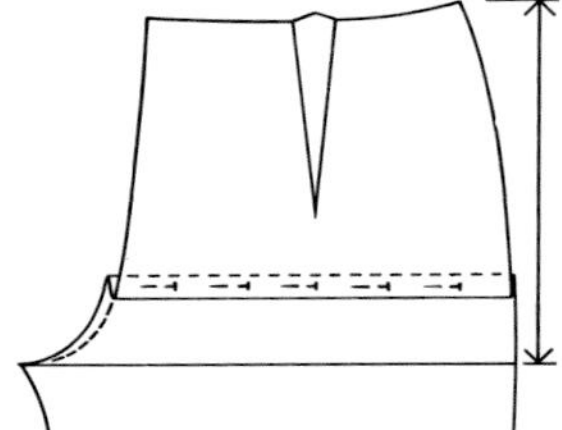

Long or short crotch
Draw a horizontal line across the pattern at the base of the crotch. Measure vertically between the waistline and the drawn line. If your crotch depth is different you should lengthen or shorten the pattern by the appropriate amount.

To lengthen the crotch, cut across the pattern horizontally. Spread the pattern to the required amount and pin onto paper. Re-draw the seams.
To shorten the crotch, make a horizontal tuck in the pattern taking out the required amount. Pin down. Re-draw the crotch seam.

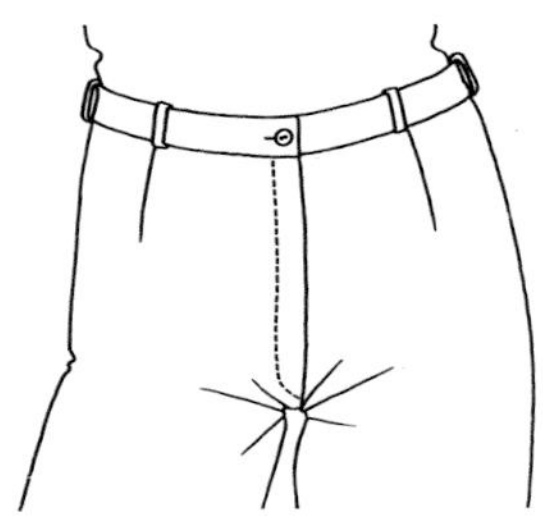

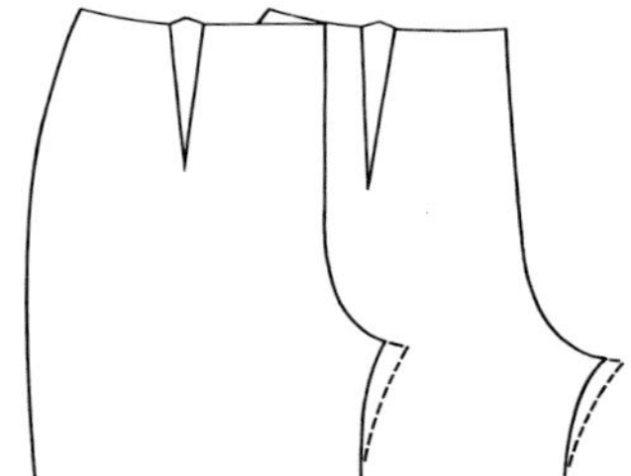

Long crotch (2)
Measure the CF and CB seams along the seam lines between the top and bottom seamlines (use a tape measure on its side). If the crotch depth is correct but this length too short, divide the extra amount by two and extend the front and back crotch point by this amount, tapering new line into inside leg seam.

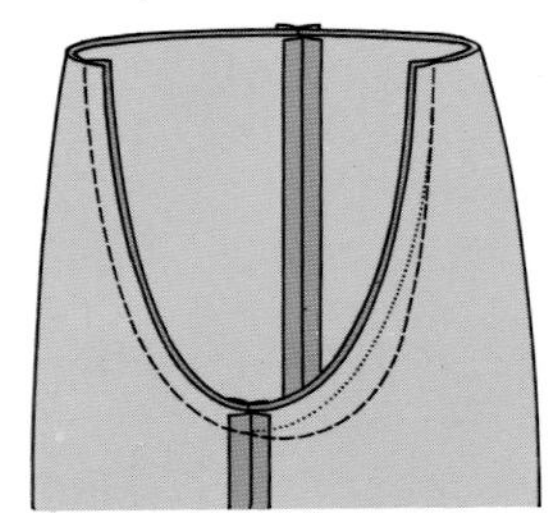

Baggy at back below seat
Take in the crotch seam. Turn slacks inside out. Slip one leg inside the other. Starting just below the hipline of the CB seam, baste the new seamline taking out the excess fabric from the crotch, tapering the stitching to the crotch point at the inside leg seam. Try on the slacks to check fit and if necessary lift them at back waist to re-position waistline. Stitch seam. Cut away surplus fabric.

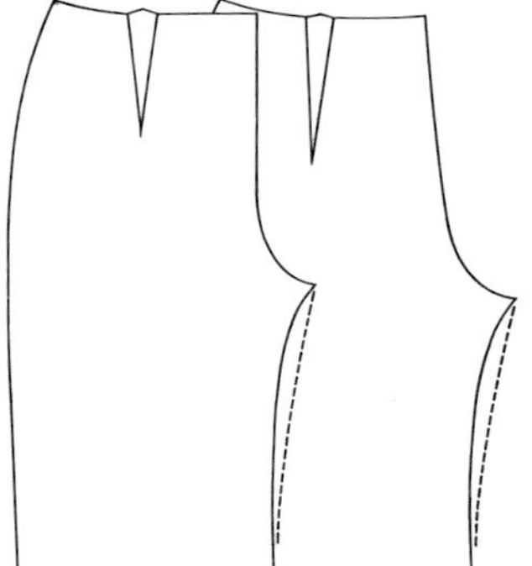

Large thighs
Halve the extra amount required and add to both front and back inside leg seams at the thigh, tapering into the crotch point and seam below the thigh.

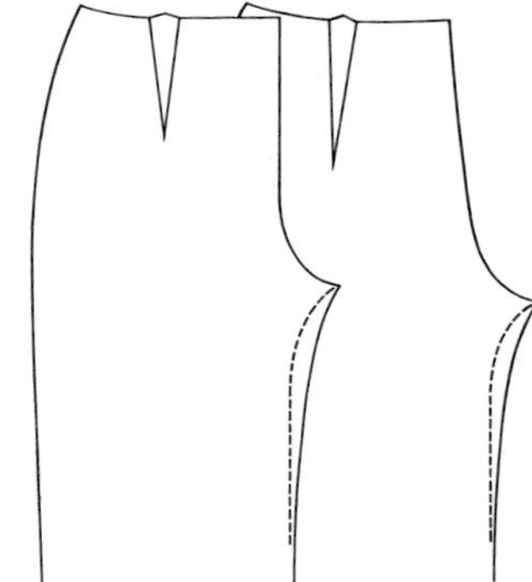

Thin thighs
Decrease the thigh width. Try on the slacks WS out. Pin in the required amount on the inside leg seams at the thigh, tapering to crotch point. Baste and try on the slacks RS out. Stitch seams, tapering the stitching above and below the thigh area into the original seamline. Trim away excess fabric. Press seams open.

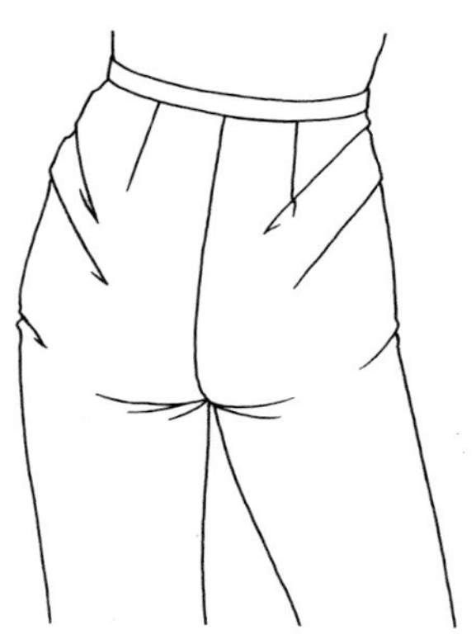

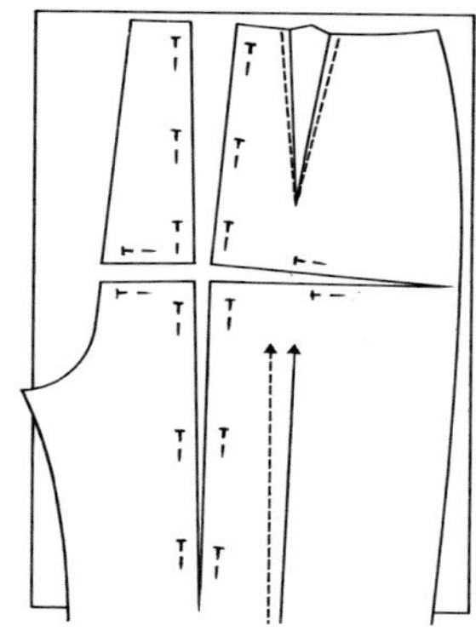

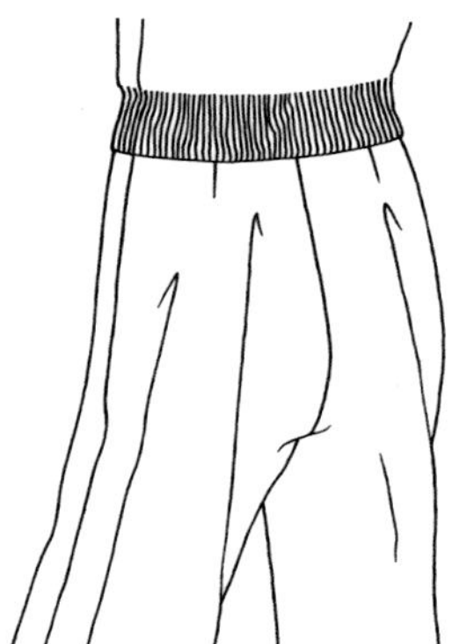

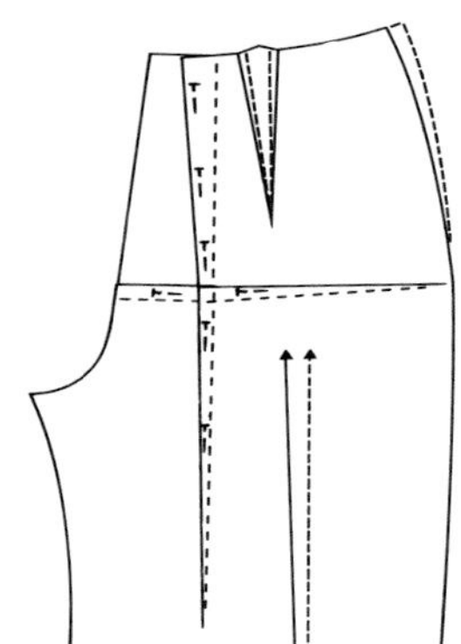

Large seat
Cut the back pattern between the CB and dart vertically to the knee.
Measure 8in (20cm) below the waistline and cut the pattern horizontally from the CB to the side seam.
Open the slashes each to a quarter of the amount required on the hipline, keeping the CB straight. Insert a piece of paper and pin in place. Re-draw the grain and outer lines. If the waistline becomes too large, increase the darts.

Flat seat
Cut the pattern as for a large seat, but instead of opening the slashes, overlap them each by a quarter of the amount required on the hipline. If the waistline becomes too small, decrease the back darts. If this is not sufficient add the remaining amount to the waistline at the side seam and taper into hipline.

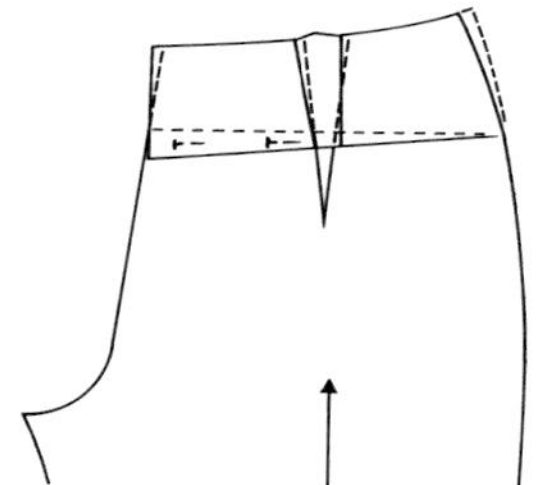

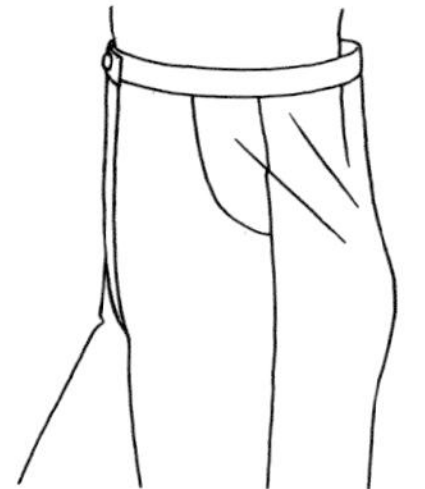

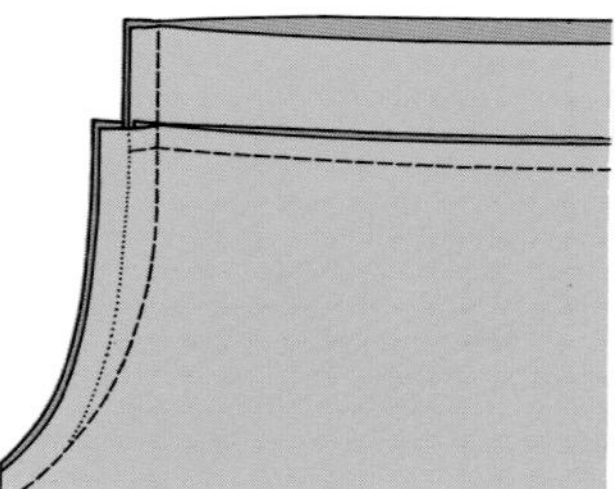

Sway back
This will cause folds in the slacks below the back waist. To remove the extra fullness at the CB, cut straight across the back to the side seam about $3\frac{1}{2}$in (9cm) below the waistline. Overlap the pattern to remove the necessary amount. Re-draw the CB seam and also the dart if it has been affected. To regain the original waistline width, add the amount trimmed from the CB to the side seam at the waistline tapering to hip level.

Waist too big at the back
Take a larger turning on the CB seam. To make the alteration if the waistband is attached, open the inner edge of the band and the CB seam to hip level. Cut through the waistband exactly at the CB. Try on the slacks inside out and pin in the amount required at the CB. Baste and machine-stitch seam, continuing stitching through the waistband. Press seam open. Finish waistband.

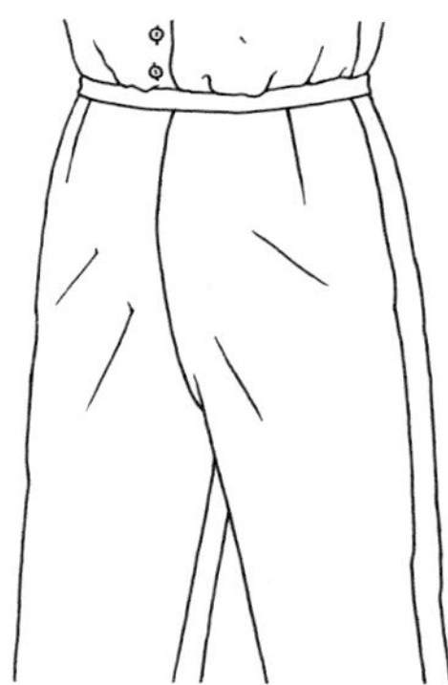

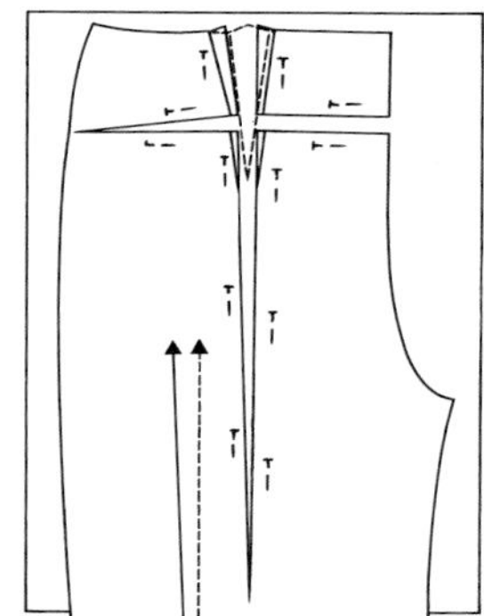

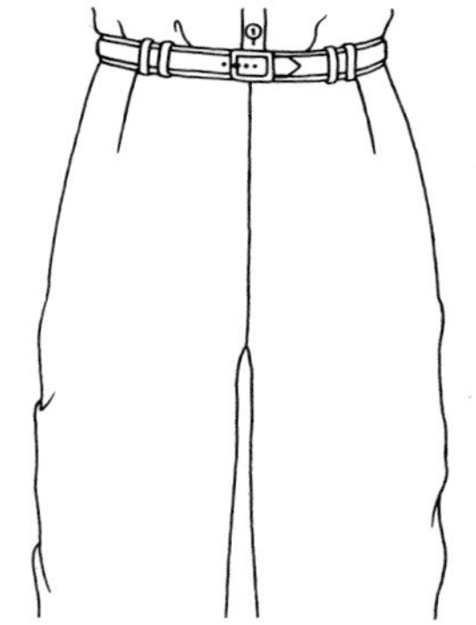

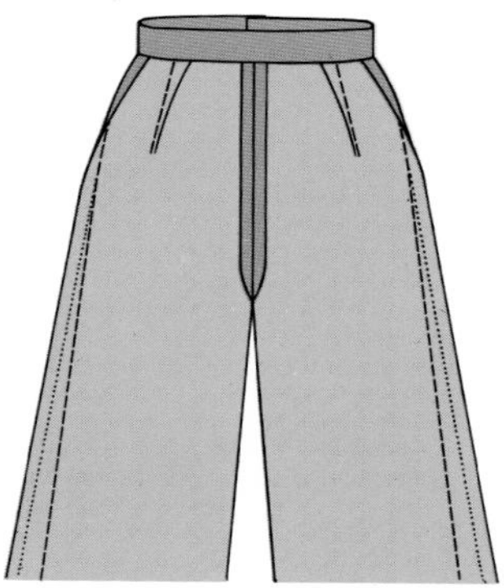

Large stomach
Cut vertically through the center of the front dart to knee level and horizontally from CF to side seam about 3in (7·5cm) below waistline. Spread the pattern equally on each side to the required amount as shown. Keeping the CF straight, insert and pin paper behind slashes. Re-draw the grain line and the waist dart to the original size in the center of slash.

Slack legs too baggy at sides
Take in the side seams. Try on the slacks WS out and pin in the side seams the required amount. Baste and try on the slacks RS out. Stitch new seams. Cut away excess fabric. Press seams open.

Slack variations

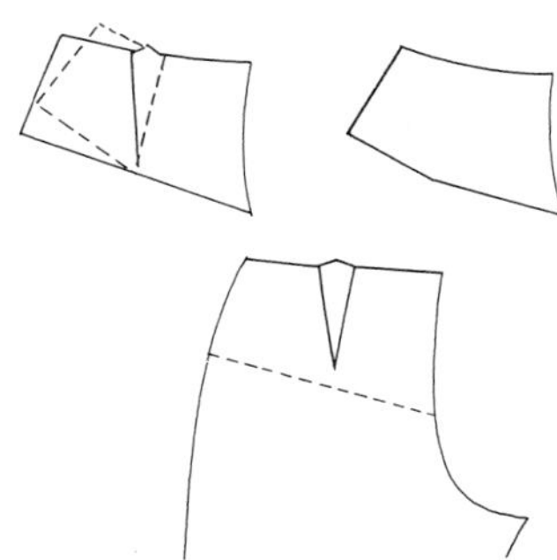

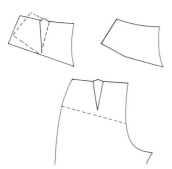

Slacks with yokes

Adapting the pattern Draw the yoke to required shape on the pattern so that the lines touch the dart point. Cut along line and add seam allowances to both edges. Cut away the dart and tape the edges together to form a curved lower line.

Making the slacks Join the slacks to the yokes and then make them as basic slacks but omitting darts.

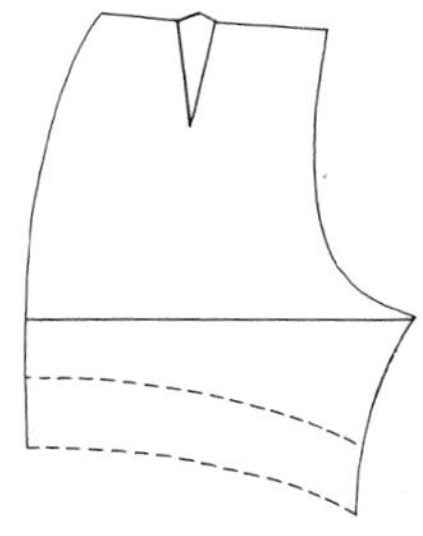

Shorts

Adapting the pattern Trace pattern pieces to required length, making the side seams 1 in (2·5cm) shorter than inside leg seams. Curve hemline and add hem allowance. For a slight flare at sides add 1 in (2·5cm) to front and back at hemline tapering to hipline.

Making the shorts Make them as slacks, moving the zipper to side or CB seam and adding cuffs if you wish.

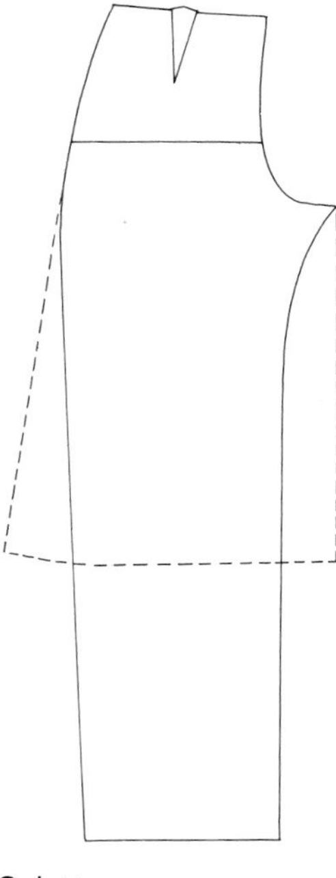

Culottes

Adapting the pattern Trace pattern pieces to required length and draw a line parallel to grainline from crotch points to hemline. Decide how much flare you

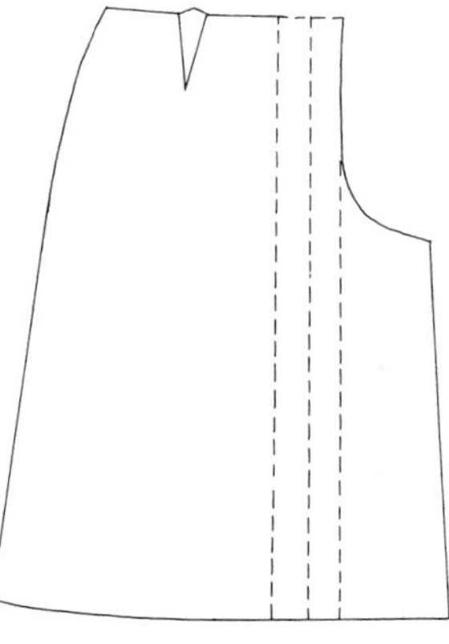

want at the hem and add this amount to the outside leg seam, tapering to hipline. Curve the hemline up by $\frac{5}{8}$in (15mm) at the outside leg. To add pleats draw a straight line from CB and CF to hem, slash and open out for depth of pleat. Insert paper and mark pleat foldlines.

Making the culottes Make them as basic slacks. Form the pleats to face toward the center seams.

Cuffs 38
Pleating 40
Basic slacks 96

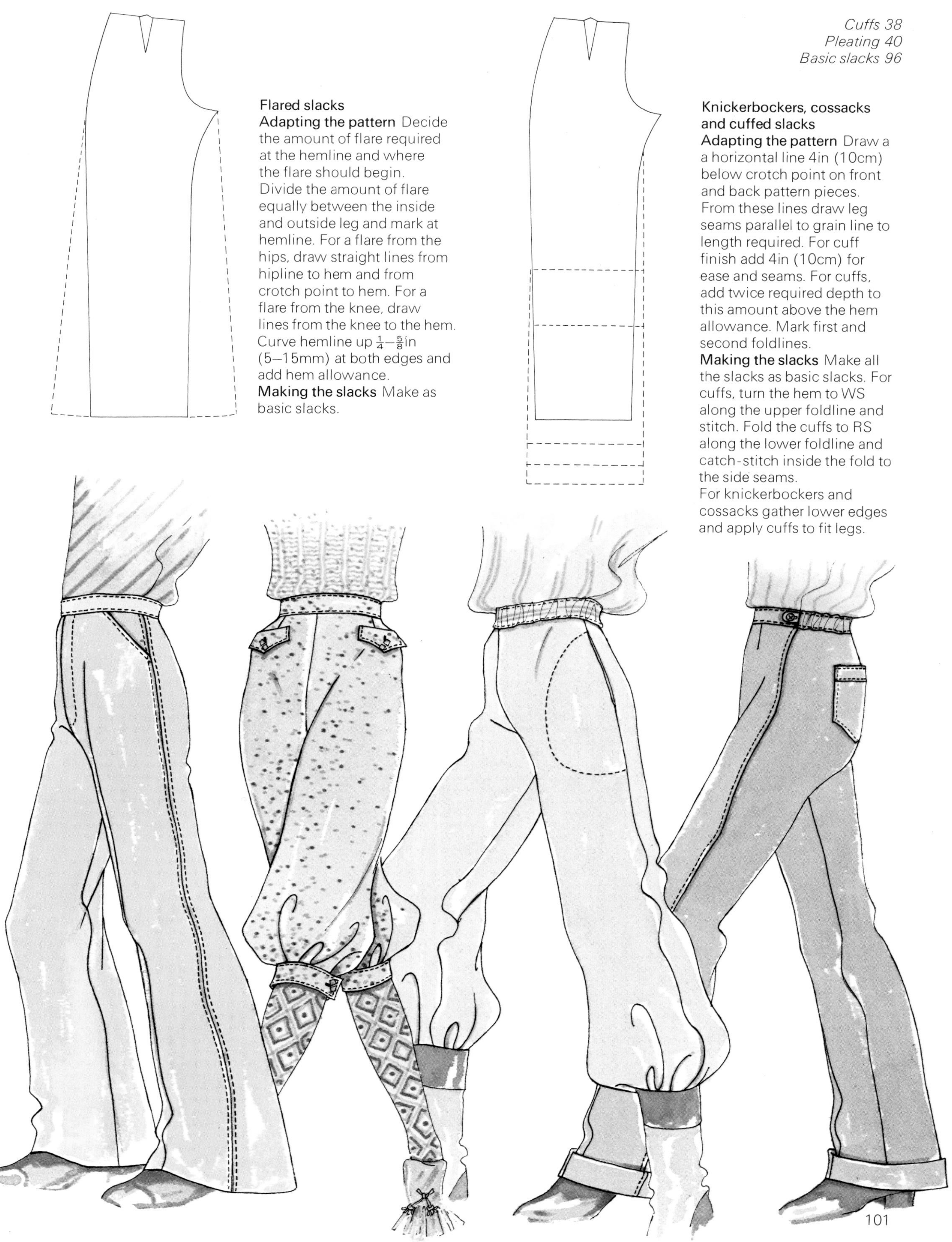

Flared slacks

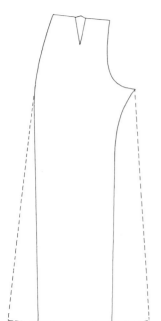

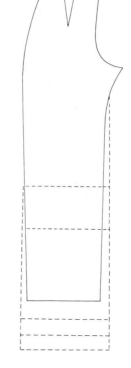

Adapting the pattern Decide the amount of flare required at the hemline and where the flare should begin. Divide the amount of flare equally between the inside and outside leg and mark at hemline. For a flare from the hips, draw straight lines from hipline to hem and from crotch point to hem. For a flare from the knee, draw lines from the knee to the hem. Curve hemline up $\frac{1}{4}$–$\frac{5}{8}$in (5–15mm) at both edges and add hem allowance.

Making the slacks Make as basic slacks.

Knickerbockers, cossacks and cuffed slacks

Adapting the pattern Draw a a horizontal line 4in (10cm) below crotch point on front and back pattern pieces. From these lines draw leg seams parallel to grain line to length required. For cuff finish add 4in (10cm) for ease and seams. For cuffs, add twice required depth to this amount above the hem allowance. Mark first and second foldlines.

Making the slacks Make all the slacks as basic slacks. For cuffs, turn the hem to WS along the upper foldline and stitch. Fold the cuffs to RS along the lower foldline and catch-stitch inside the fold to the side seams.

For knickerbockers and cossacks gather lower edges and apply cuffs to fit legs.

Decorative finishes

Basic stitches 18
Hems 28
Facings 58

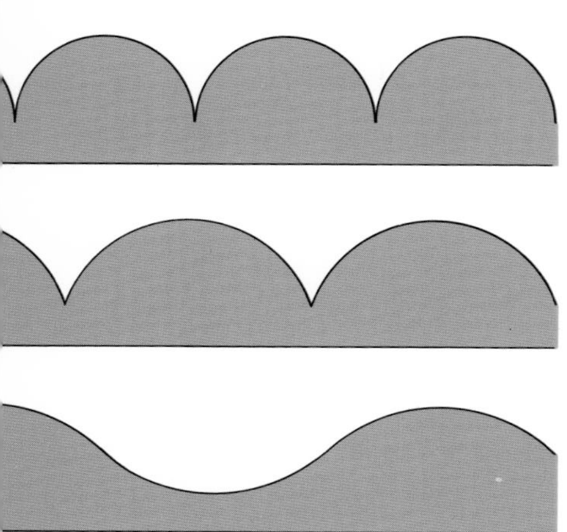

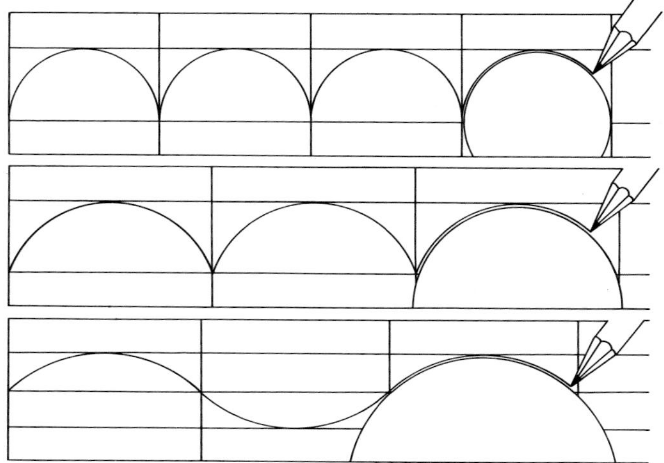

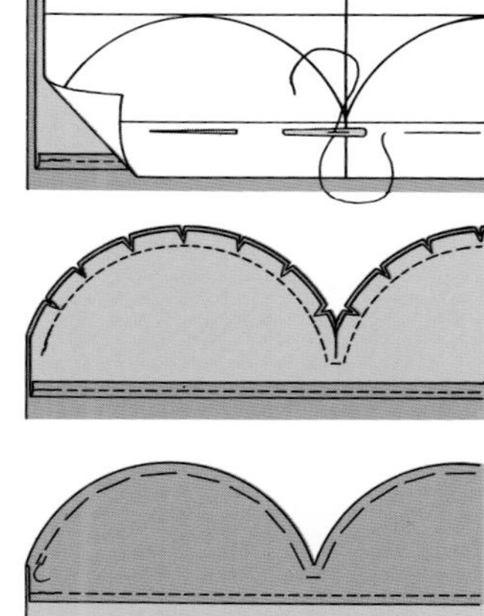

Scalloped edging
Use this on an opening or around a neckline, collar, hem or armholes. This method incorporates the facing or hem, so make the scallops at least $\frac{5}{8}$in (15mm) shallower. Make up the garment to the stage of preparing, but not sewing, the facing or hem.
1 Decide the width of the scallops and check whether this divides exactly into the length of the edge. Adjust if necessary.
2 Cut tissue paper to length and shape of edge by depth of hem or facing. If you trace the facing pattern, trim off edges where there would be seams (e.g. at shoulders) and butt the edges together.
3 Divide paper into sections of scallop width. Mark the seamline and draw another to the depth of the scallops from this. If making shallow scallops, calculate the circle and how much overlap there should be to give the required effect.
4 Draw a circle to size on cardboard and cut out. Use this as a template to draw the scallop pattern on the edge.
5 With RS together, place facing onto edge or fold back hem turning. Lay paper pattern in position on top and baste along both edges. Machine-stitch along line of scallops through all thicknesses.
6 Tear away paper carefully and trim fabric to within $\frac{1}{8}$in (3mm) of stitching. Notch curves and clip into angle between scallops. Turn RS out and baste so that seam lies exactly on the edge. Finish the hem or facing.

Twisted cord
You will need someone else to hold one of the pencils. Allow just over $2\frac{1}{2}$ times the required finished length by half the number of strands you need to give the thickness.
1 Start by each holding a pencil. Tie one end of yarn around one pencil, loop it around the second pencil and continue to wind yarn to required number of strands.
2 Hold the end of the yarn just below the pencils, keep the yarn taut and twist the pencils in opposite directions.
3 While your helper now brings the pencils together, still keeping the cord taut, hold center of yarn and remove the pencils. Shake vigorously to keep a permanent twist. You can knot the ends or add tassels.

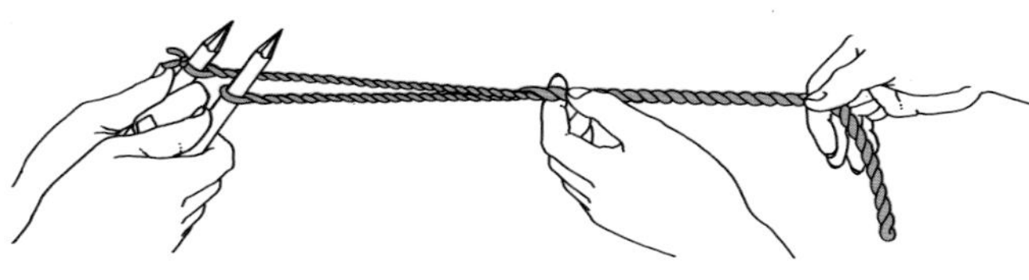

Frog fastenings
Use fine cord and form into loops of required size as shown, stitching each as it is formed. Apply to garment with tiny hemming stitches.

Chinese ball buttons
Use with frog fastenings and make from matching cord, $5\frac{1}{2}$in (14cm) long. Weave the cord as shown, pull the ends, easing and shaping to form a tight ball. Trim the excess and sew down the ends to secure.

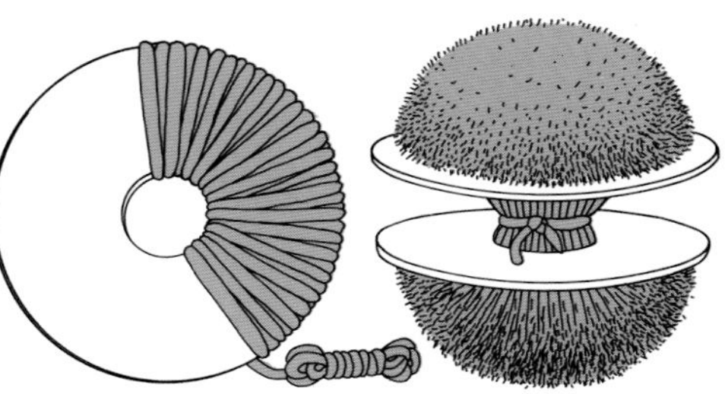

Pompons
Make from soft cotton yarns or knitting worsted.
1 Cut 2 circles of cardboard to required diameter of pompon. Cut a small circle in the center of each disc.
2 Twist a length of yarn into a figure-eight.
Wind yarn over discs until center hole is filled, threading the yarn into a bodkin to finish.
3 Cut through the loops at the edge of the discs and pull them slightly apart. Tie a short length of yarn firmly around the loops between discs, then pull the discs away.

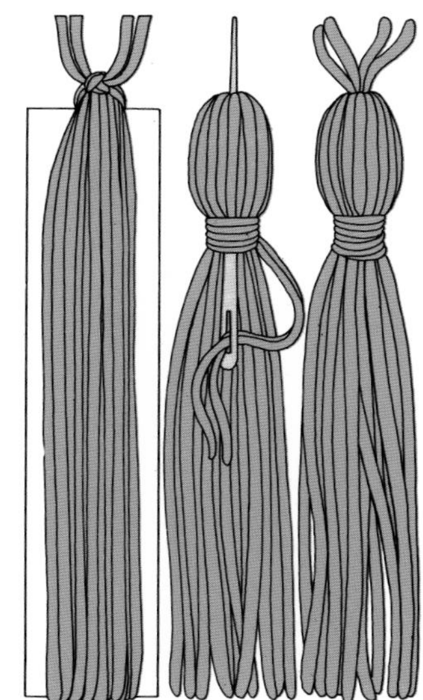

Tassel
Wind yarn around cardboard strip of tassel length.
Tie loops at top with length of yarn threaded onto needle.
Remove card and cut lower loops. Fold threads over knot and bind with yarn $\frac{5}{8}$in (15mm) from top. Slip needle under binding and bring out at top.
Attach to garment.

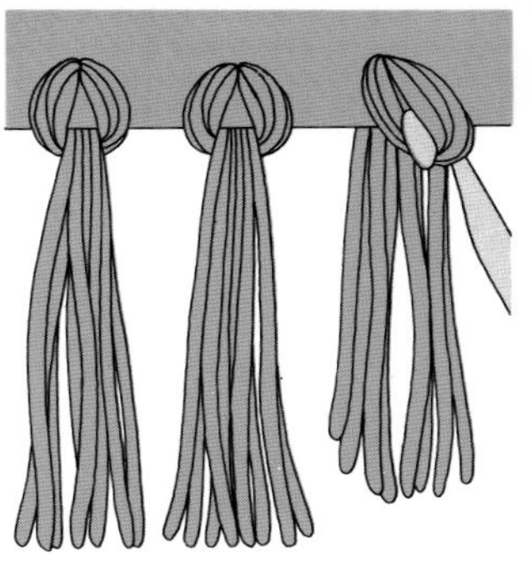

Fringing
Wind yarn 3–4 times around a cardboard strip of fringe depth. Cut bottom loops. Make a hole in required position with a crochet hook, pull top loops through edge, pass cut ends through and pull tight.

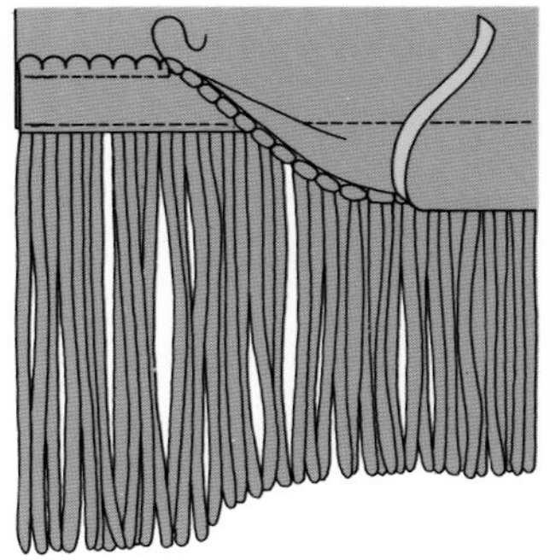

Bought fringe
Trim the seam allowance of fabric to slightly less than fringe heading. With WS together stitch the lower edge of heading to the seamline. Turn heading to RS and stitch upper edge to fabric.

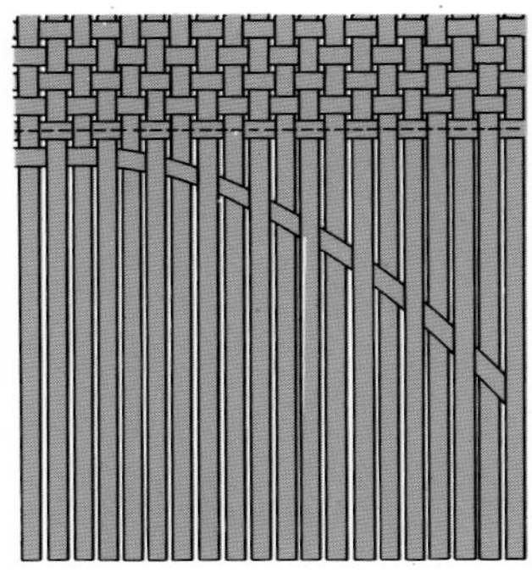

Self-fringe
Use on soft loosely woven fabrics.
Machine a row of stay-stitching across the fabric at the upper edge of the fringe. Working from the lower edge inward remove one thread at a time up to the stay stitching.

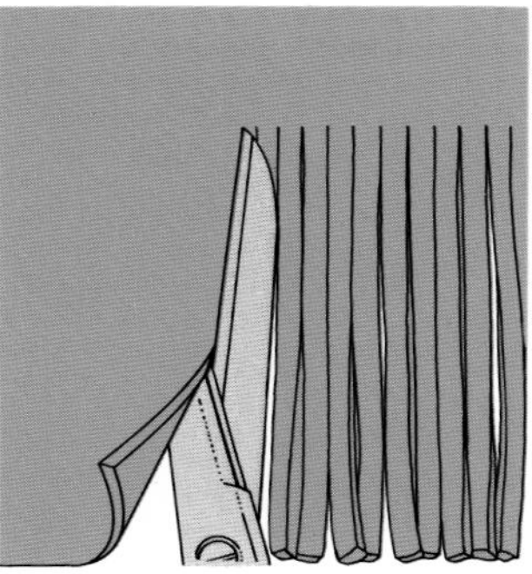

Leather fringe
Using very sharp scissors, cut evenly into the edge to the depth required at $\frac{1}{8}$–$\frac{1}{4}$in (3–5mm) intervals.

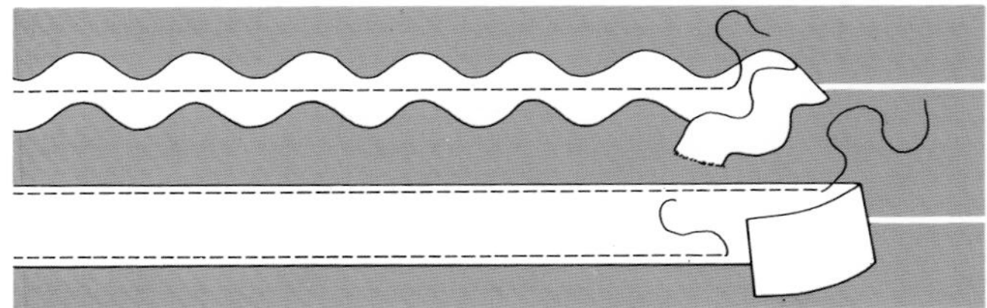

Applying flat braids
Narrow braids (e.g. rickrack)
Mark position on the fabric with tailor's chalk, pin the braid centrally over the line and machine-stitch in a matching color.

Wide braids and lace borders
Position and pin as narrow braids but machine-stitch or whip-stitch along both edges.

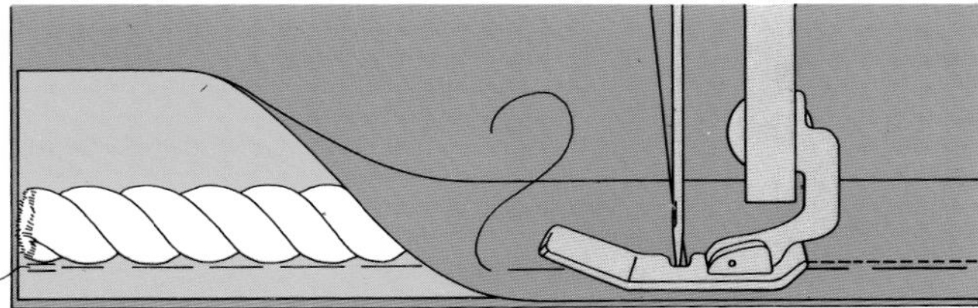

Piping
Cut bias strips of fabric wide enough to cover piping cord with seam allowances on both edges. Apply strips to edge as binding, lay cord centrally along them, place second edge of strip flat over first, thus enclosing the cord.
Fit piping foot to machine and stitch as close to edge of piping as possible. When applying next layer of fabric (e.g. a facing) stitch it over the first line of stitching.

Mending and recycling

Basic stitches 18
Binding 25
Facings 58
Decorative finishes 102

A garment can appear to have outlived its usefulness for a number of reasons: it may need mending, the style or color no longer appeal or the fit is wrong. However, it can be surprisingly useful to take stock of old clothes to see what can be revitalized.
Mending should be tackled as quickly as possible, using the appropriate techniques. On children's or casual clothes you might want to make a feature of the mending with a decorative patch or some embroidery.
When a garment looks outdated or it simply doesn't fit, you can often improve it by recycling or remodeling. You could change the look of a dress entirely, for example, by altering the sleeves, neckline, length of the skirt or, more dramatically, making it into a skirt and bolero top. Whatever alteration you make, the less apparent it is the more effective it will be. If you need to add new material choose a color that goes well with the original and a fabric of equal weight and durability; always check for color-fastness first. Remember also to match thread colors.
Prolonging the life of a home-made garment starts when you first make it. Particularly on children's clothes, leave large seam and hem allowances so that they can be enlarged or let down at a later time.
It is also useful to keep scraps of material for patches, ruffles or insertions.

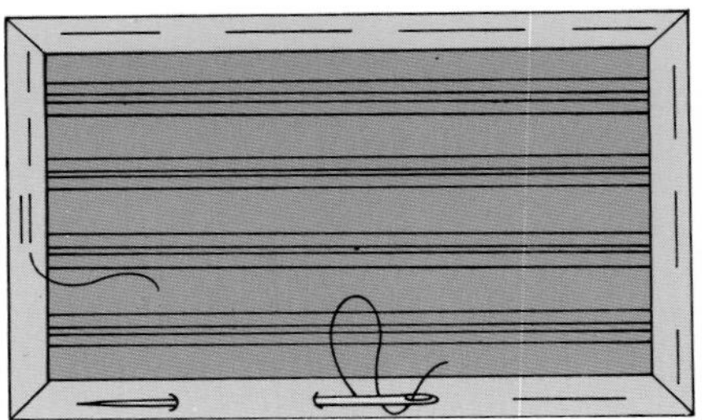

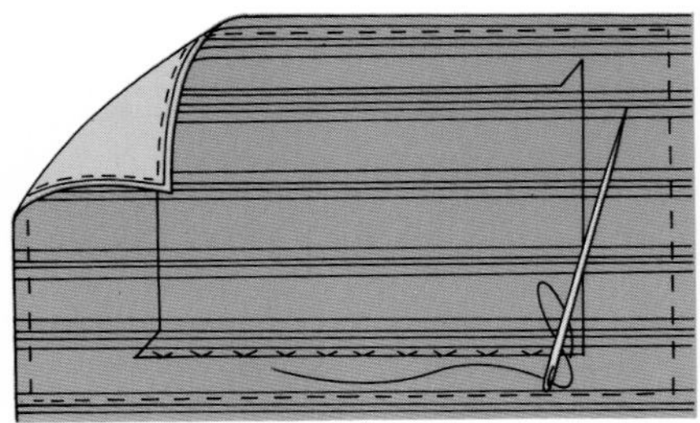

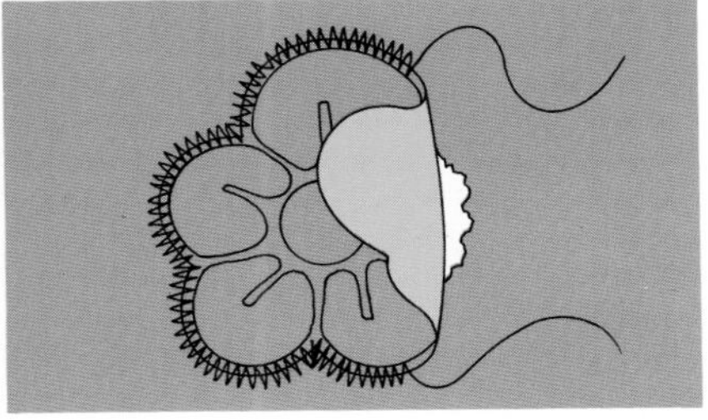

Inserted patch
Use an inserted patch to mend holes. To make the patch, use a matching scrap or fabric taken from an inconspicuous part of a facing, hem or pocket. Cut a rectangle for the patch about 1in (2·5cm) larger all round than the hole to be repaired, plus a $\frac{1}{4}$in (5mm) seam allowance. Match the grain and any pattern on patch to fabric of garment so that the patch will not show. Turn in a $\frac{1}{4}$in (5mm) hem to RS of fabric and baste, mitering corners as shown. Trim hole in garment to a neat rectangle. Pin, baste and sew patch to WS of garment, either by machine or hand. On RS, turn in raw edges of rectangle and slip-hem as shown.

Applied patch
This is a decorative way to cover a damaged area on a garment. You can use ready-made motifs or cut motifs or shapes from a firm fabric. If necessary, reinforce the fabric with iron-on interfacing on WS before applying patch. Apply motif with close zigzag stitch or with buttonhole stitch. Leather patches can be applied in the same way.

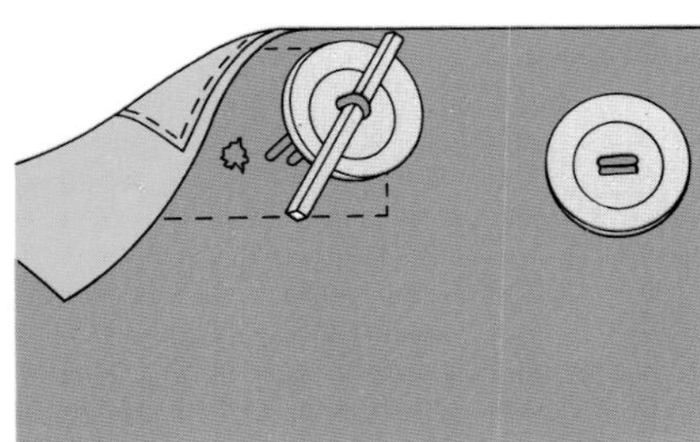

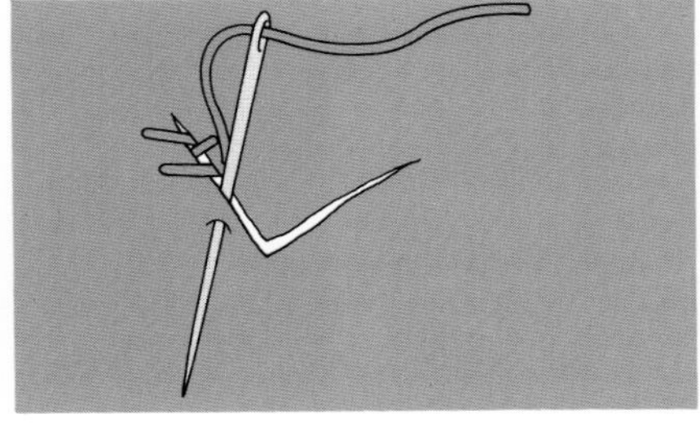

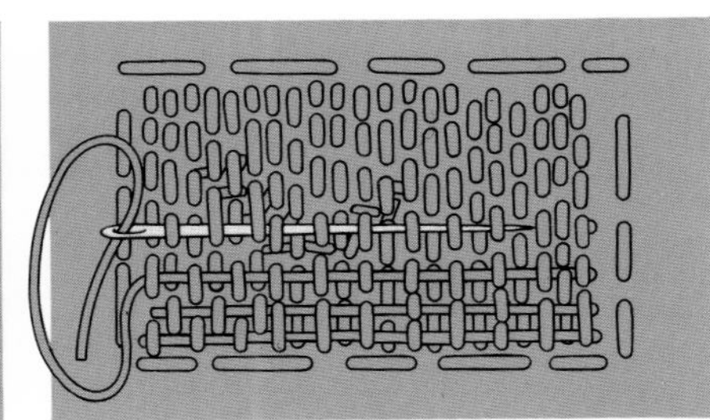

Fabric torn behind button
If fabric behind button is torn, reinforce the button position with a small patch applied on the inside of the facing. Use fabric for patch from garment, as for an inserted patch, or from a piece of tape. Replace button when patch is completed.

Straight or angled tears
Draw edges of fabric together with fishbone stitch, as shown, working from side to side across tear. Use a weft thread drawn from garment for greatest strength on woolens or an exactly matching sewing thread.
If fabric around tear is weak, mark the area with basting and reinforce with darning making the stitches as small as possible; remove the basting when finished. If the tear is large, reinforce it with a strip of material on WS and darn through both thicknesses.

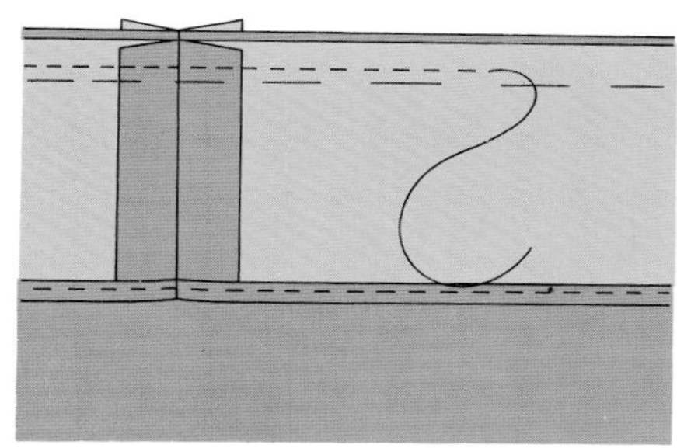

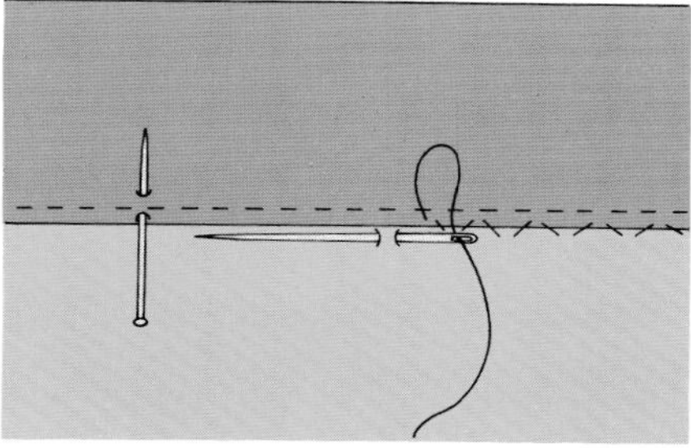

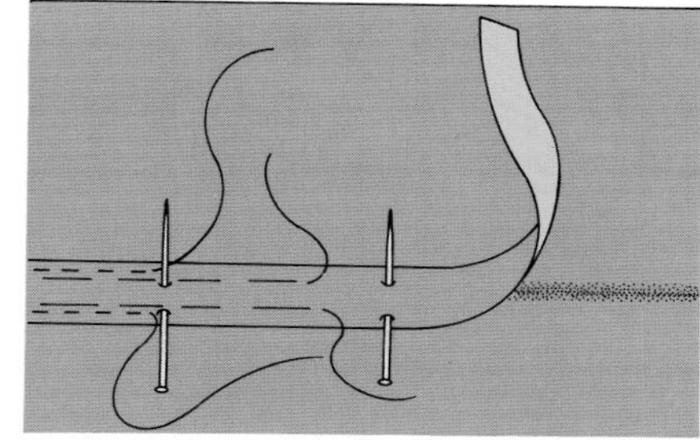

False hem
With this method you can lengthen a hem to the utmost. Cut a facing of matching fabric to the width of hem and depth required, plus seam allowances. Make joinings if necessary, matching seams to those on garment. With RS together, stitch new hem facing to garment. Press seam allowances upward and turn facing to WS. Finish hem by hand as shown. (Circular hems are too shallow to be extended in this way.)

Concealing old hemlines
If, after lengthening a hem, you find there is a permanent line on RS of garment, you can disguise it by applying a decorative braid. You can also disguise a seamline in this way if a strip of fabric has been added to a garment.

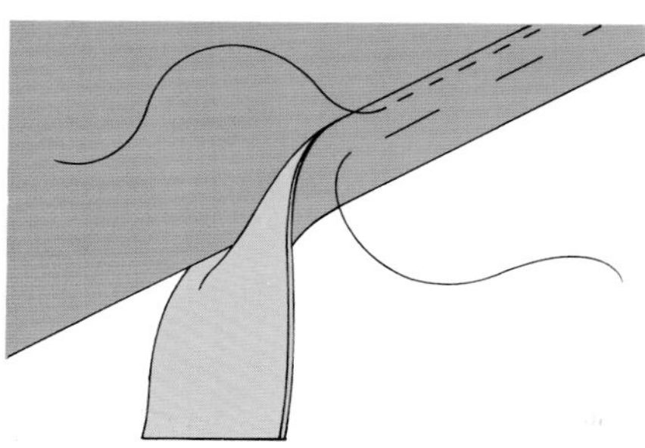

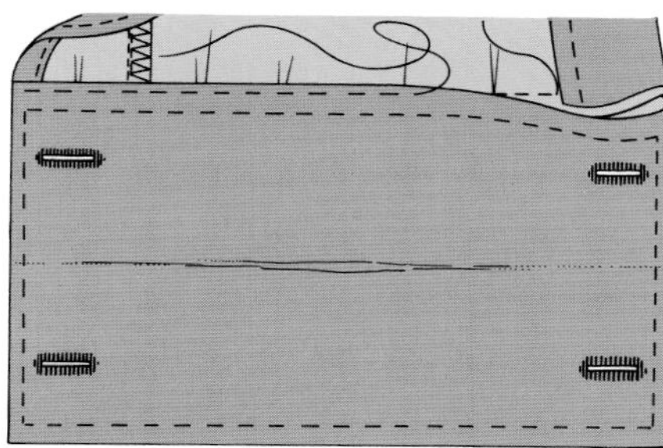

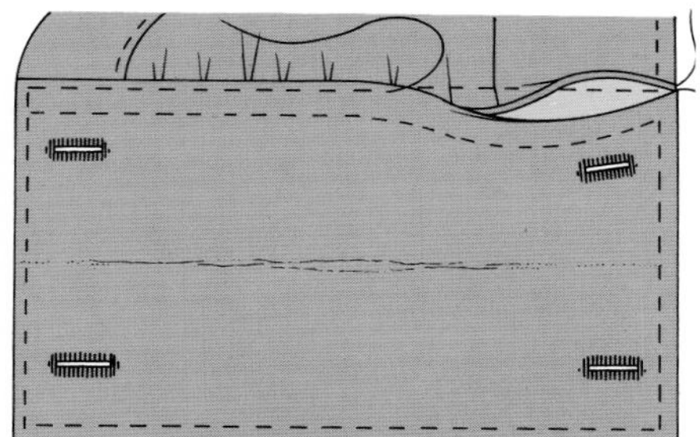

Frayed edges
On woolen garments cover frayed front or cuff edges with a matching or contrasting leather binding. Use bias binding or a decorative braid or ribbon on cotton garments.

Turning a cuff
This repair is only possible on a shirt that has linked fastening on the cuffs. Iron sleeves. Separate the top of the cuff from the sleeve, and reverse it so that the worn part is on the outside when unfolded. Replace interfacing if necessary and attach the turned cuff to the sleeve, sewing along original stitching line and folds in sleeve.

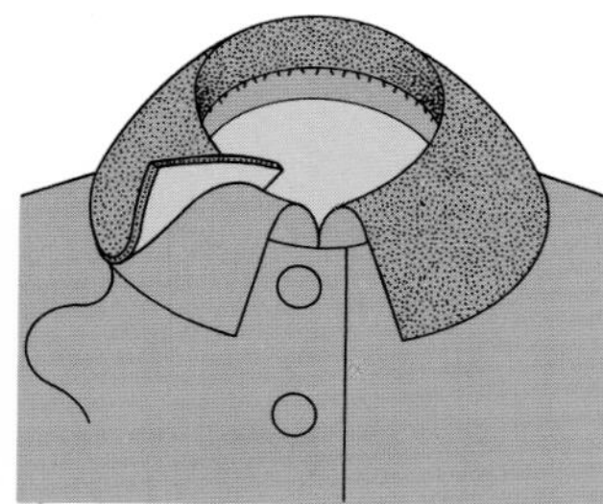

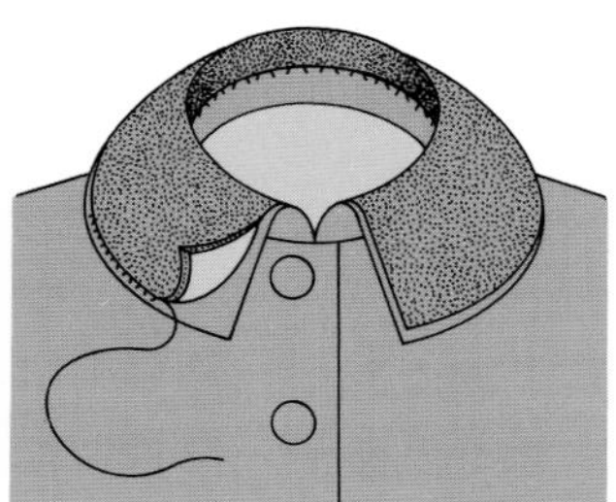

Frayed pleats
When pleats or vents burst open at the top, mend with a stitched arrowhead. Mark the outline of the triangle lightly in pencil. With thread fastened on the underside, bring the needle out at LH point and go up to apex, taking a single small stitch underneath from right to left. Then bring needle down to RH point and insert it across and underneath so that it comes up next to first stitch at LH point.
Repeat this pattern until the triangle is completely filled in, keeping stitches close to each other.

Trimming a collar
Using the original collar as a pattern, cut trimming in velvet, fur or leather (see p94) leaving a seam allowance all around. Fold under edges and miter corners. Slip-hem edges to original collar.
If you would like a margin of the original collar to show, cut to exact size of original, fold and miter corners as before. Stitch the inner edge to neck seamline, place remainder flat over original collar and slip-hem all around.

Basic stitches 18
Binding 25
Zippers 26

Hems 28
Shirring and gathering 29
Necklines 56

Hole or tear
Insert or apply patch, or embroider over a small hole. To embellish add decorative pockets.

Worn pocket edges or elbows
Bind pockets with leather; blanket-stitch or overcast leather patches on elbow in matching color.

Worn collar, cuffs, turn-ups
Turn if possible. Otherwise make new ones in contrasting material, opening original to use as pattern.

Worn coat cuffs, collar, hem
Cover with fur or bind with matching velvet or leather trim.

Sleeves too long
Gather loose sleeves with a drawstring or elastic drawn through narrow hem. On sleeves with a cuff, take a tuck above cuff and upper part of sleeve.

Sleeves too short
Cut to a new length or eliminate sleeve altogether and bind, face or hem armhole as necessary.

Skirt too short
Add ruffle in contrasting or matching material or a deep eyelet trim to suggest a petticoat. Otherwise add a false hem.

Frayed skirt hem
Shorten to mid-calf or knee-length or cover with border or braiding in contrasting material.

Worn neckline
Re-shape into a lower neckline, adding binding or a decorative trim. Or add a hood (see p22) in contrasting material.

Re-styling empire-line dress
Re-make bottom half into a skirt and save top for a sash or pockets.

Pinafore dress too small
Make into tabard top. Shorten to the length you want, open sides and bind all edges, adding ties to match.

Dress too small at waist
Re-make into bolero top and skirt, using one of the lengthening techniques if necessary.

Slacks too short
Add false hem or cut off into pedal pushers or shorts. Otherwise gather just below knee for wearing inside long boots.

Shirt too short
Re-make into a boy's baseball jacket. Cut off cuffs and shirt to waist, leaving narrow seam allowance. Add a 1–2in (2·5–5cm) elastic band at waist and sleeves. Insert a zipper down front. Remove buttons and buttonhole band first.

Frayed pleats
Make arrowheads by hand where pleat begins. For a decorative effect, use different colors.

Skirt too long
Re-make floor-length skirt into a sun dress. Remove zipper and waistband. Adjust fit across top and cut about 6in (15cm) from old waist. Adjust seams and add shirring or finish top with a ruffle or band of leftover material; add straps.

Baby clothes

Seams 20
Binding 25

The pattern pieces for this simple baby outfit are based on rectangles; to add the shaping you just need a ruler and flexible curve. You can make the outfit to fit any baby by adjusting the measurements as required.
As well as simple adaptations to the pattern pieces such as shortening sleeves and altering the neckline, you can make the top with the opening at the front so that it becomes a coat; substitute rouleau loops for the ties and add buttons for a more substantial fastening. Vary the pants by adding a bib and shoulder straps or by shortening the legs to make knickers. You can also make a dress and a robe (see below).

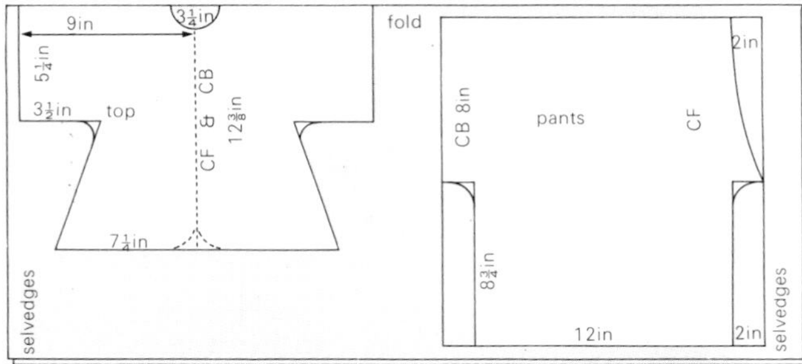

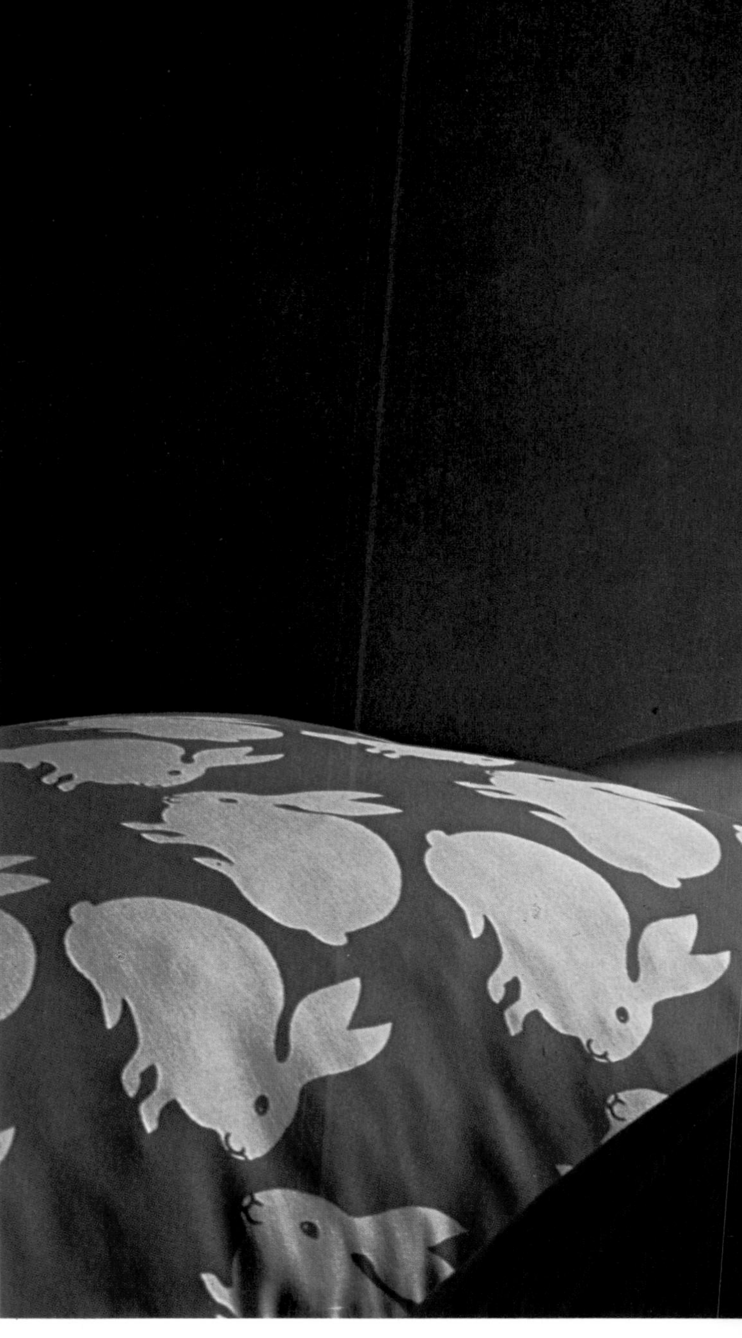

You will need

stretchy fabric, 36in (90cm) wide: ¾yd (0·80m)
matching sewing thread
elastic, ⅝in (15mm) wide
contrasting fabric for binding (optional)

Making the pattern and cutting out

Draw the pattern as shown in the diagram and cut out on double fabric, placing shoulder lines to fold.
From spare or contrasting fabric cut bias strips 2in (5cm) wide for binding plus a patch pocket 4 × 3in (11 × 8cm) (optional).

Making the top

With RS together, join the front to the back at the underarms and sides. Press. Bind the hem and CB edges with a long continuous strip. Bind the ends of the sleeves and then the neck, continuing the binding to make ties (see p24). Make 2 more ties and attach halfway down CB. Bind the edges of the pocket and stitch it in position on the front of the top.

Making the pants

With RS together, stitch the inner leg seams of each pants leg. Turn one leg to RS and slip it inside the other leg with RS together. Stitch the seam from CF waist to CB waist and press. Turn up ¼in (5mm) and the 1½in (4·5cm) hem at the bottom of each leg and stitch leaving ⅝in (15mm) open to insert elastic. Work a second row of stitching below the first.
At the waist turn under ¼in (5mm) and then ⅞in (20mm) hem and stitch, leaving ⅝in (15mm) open. Work a second row of stitching along the top fold.
Insert elastic into each casing, draw up to fit, stitch the ends together and close the opening.
If you are making the pants for wearing with other tops you could add a bib to them (see p90). Remember to cut the waistband in 2 pieces and to sew the bib to the top of the waistband only so that the elastic can be inserted.

Variations

Dress Increase the length of the side seams if necessary and cut out as the top, slitting the CB for 3in (7·5cm) only (you could cut this into a keyhole shape). Join front to back at underarms and sides and bind the hem and neck, including the opening.
Robe Increase the length of the sleeves and side seams and cut out as for the top but slitting the CF instead of CB. From spare fabric cut out cuffs. Make the robe as the top but gathering the sleeves into cuffs instead of binding them and inserting a double-ended zipper at the CF.

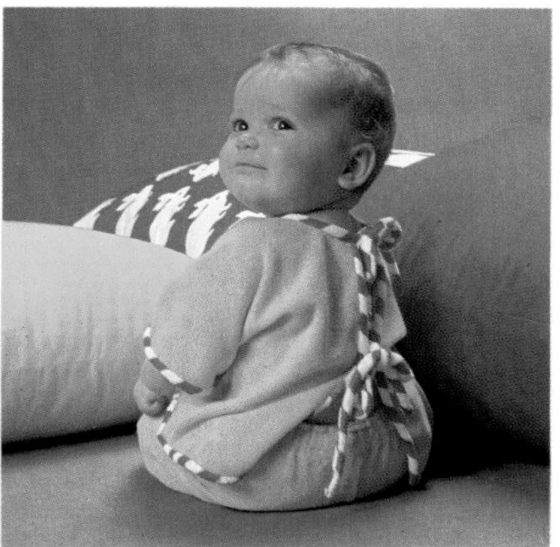

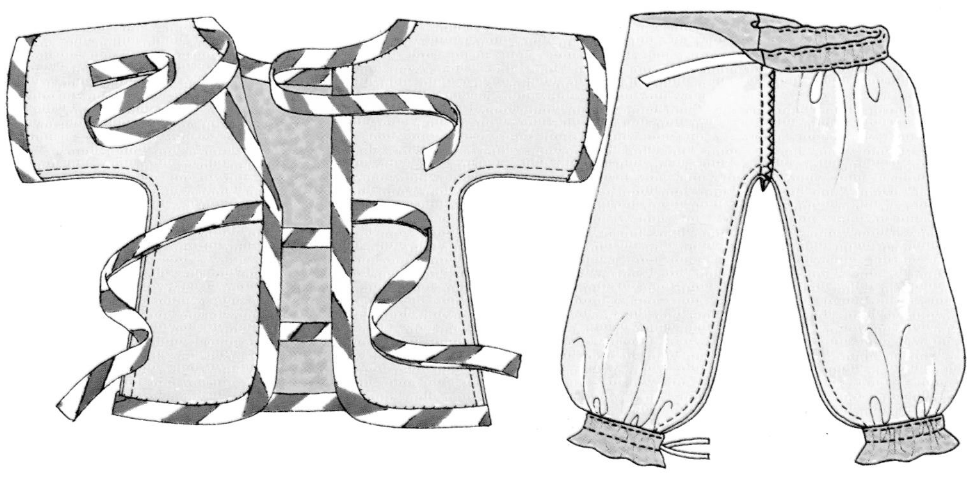

Basic stitches 18
Seams 20
Binding 25
Belts 90

Baby carrier

This practical carrier for a small baby incorporates a padded head rest and quilted bound edges to prevent chafed legs. Make the carrier from a strong fabric, such as cotton canvas. Machine-stitch all seams twice for security.

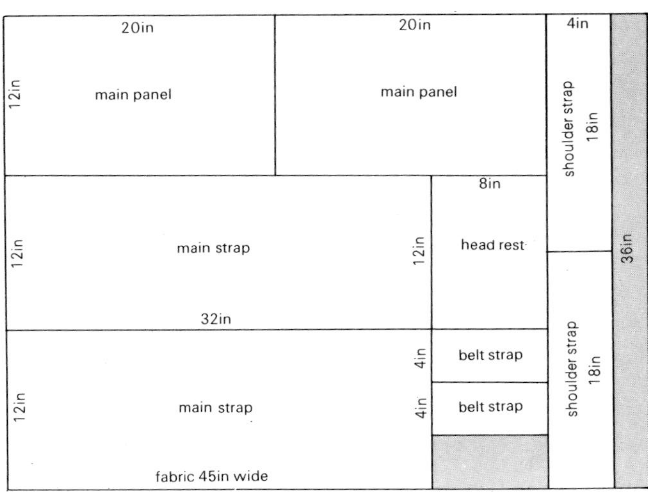

You will need
fabric, 45in (115cm) wide: 1yd (0·90m)
quilted fabric, 45in (115cm) wide: ½yd (0·50m)
matching thread
buckle, 2in (5cm) wide
metal eyelets

1 Cut the pieces to the sizes shown on the cutting chart. Cut a second head rest piece from the quilted fabric. Shape the center panels by curving each short edge in by ¾in (2cm) at the center. Baste pieces together with WS facing.

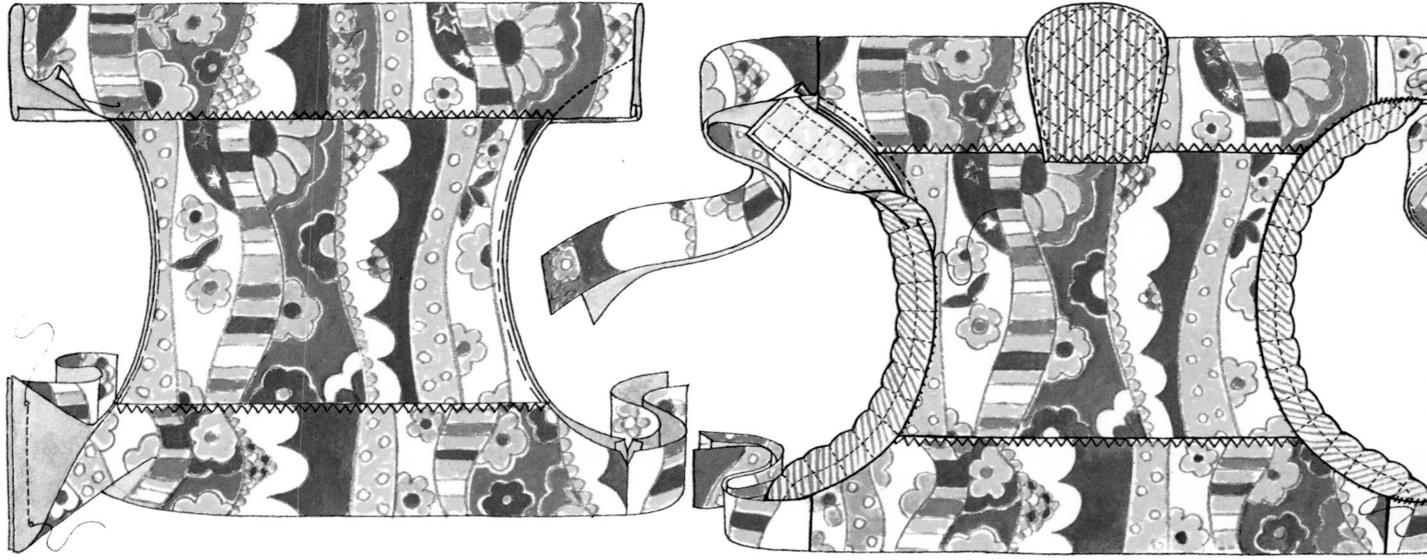

2 Mark the center of each long edge on the main straps. Fold under a ½in (1cm) turning for 10in (25cm) to each side of the center, then fold each strap in half lengthwise with WS together.

3 Place the straight edges of the center panel between the folded edges of the main straps, baste and zigzag-stitch.

4 Curve the remaining length at each end of the main straps to reduce them to 2in (5cm) when folded. Open them out and with RS together stitch the shoulder straps to each end of the top main strap and the belt straps to the ends of the bottom main strap. Re-fold straps as before.

5 Cut bias strips 4½in (12cm) wide from quilting and bind the curved edges of the center panel up to the seams on the straps. Fold under remaining raw edges of straps for ¼in (5mm), enclosing the ends of binding, and machine-stitch the folds together.

6 Attach a buckle to LH belt strap and insert eyelets on the RH strap to form a belt. Try on the carrier and fasten the buckle. Bring the shoulder straps over your shoulders and loop around the belt straps. Adjust to allow room for the baby. Turn in the ends and machine-stitch firmly in a rectangle to the WS of the shoulder straps.

7 Shape the pieces for the head rest by curving in the long edges so bottom edge measures 6in (16cm). Round off the top corners. Stitch the pieces with RS together taking ¼in (5mm) turnings and leaving the bottom edge open. Turn RS out and fold under the bottom edges for ⅜in (10mm) and baste together. Top-stitch ⅜in (10mm) from the edge.

8 Place the head rest, with quilted side facing up onto the WS of the carrier so that the bottom edge is ⅝in (15mm) below the main strap and the centers are aligned. Zigzag-stitch firmly in position across the bottom.

Toys

Some of the most attractive and individual toys can be made simply and inexpensively at home. With basic sewing skills (see the first chapter) you can produce original finger and glove puppets, animals and dolls, from scraps of leftover fabric or at very little cost. The patterns given here are so easy to make that they are very good first projects for a child learning to sew.

The basic equipment you will need is the same as for dressmaking (see p10). Try to keep all fabric scraps when you have finished making larger items; if they do not come in useful for main toy pattern pieces, you may well want to use them for features or trimmings. Felt is probably the easiest fabric to work with since it doesn't fray and can be stitched or glued. However, there are many other possibilities and the pictures on the following pages suggest some different ways to experiment.

All the basic patterns are given here; with a little ingenuity they can be adapted indefinitely. Although the instructions are complete in themselves, you may well want to make use of information given in other chapters. Sewing, knitting and crochet projects that are based on measurement are all suitable for dolls' clothes, and embroidery techniques are very useful for adding the finishing touches.

Simple shapes

All the toys shown opposite are made very simply out of circles and squares. By sewing many different colored squares together in a diamond pattern you make a snake, or by making a circle in shiny black and adding huge eyes and pipe cleaner legs you have a long-legged spider.

Snake

You will need

felt in different colors or patterned cotton fabrics
stuffing
cardboard

1 Draw a 3in (7·5cm) square on cardboard and use as a template. Cut out 10–15 pairs, according to length of snake, from different colored fabrics. Cut out 2 triangles of another color for the mouth (using half the square but with an extra $\frac{3}{8}$in/8mm all around). Sew the mouth pieces RS together across the diagonal.
2 With RS together, sew each mouth to top and bottom head squares, then sew head together on other 2 sides leaving the corner open for turning and stuffing. Sew each pair of squares together leaving one corner open. Trim and turn, including head. Stuff each square separately. Turn in seam at open corner of head, parallel to diagonal, and insert the closed corner of the first stuffed square. Pin and sew together all around. Repeat until all the squares have been sewn together in this way. Sew on button or felt eyes and add a long forked felt tongue between the open mouth. If the snake opens its mouth too widely sew a few stitches at either side.

Alligator

You will need

$\frac{1}{3}$yd (30cm) green velvet
pieces of red and white felt
2 white 2-holed buttons
stuffing

1 Draw a 4in (10cm) square and a triangle 4 × 7 × 7in (10 × 18 × 18cm), narrow point rounded, and add $\frac{3}{8}$in (10mm) seam allowance. Cut out 4 pairs of squares for the body, 2 pairs of triangles for the head and tail, in velvet. Cut out 2 red felt triangles for the mouth, approximately 1$\frac{1}{2}$in (4cm) shorter, and 2 similar white ones. Cut white pieces into zigzag teeth as shown.
2 With RS together sew mouth to head, placing white teeth between. Sew together sides of the head for the remaining length, leaving the back open for stuffing. Trim and turn. With RS together, sew triangle pairs and each square around 3 sides. Trim and turn. Stuff the head, tail and each square separately. Turn in open end of head and insert 1 side of the first square. Pin and sew together. Repeat with other 3 squares, then tail piece. Sew on eyes with black thread to make a horizontal slit. Stitch mouth at sides as for snake.

Chicken

You will need

about $\frac{1}{3}$yd (0·30m) yellow terry cloth for an 8in (20cm) diameter chicken
pieces of red, white, orange and black felt
stuffing

1 Using graph paper draw features to scale as in diagram. Draw circle 8in (20cm) in diameter. Trace each pattern piece and, using double-thickness fabric, cut out circles and wing in yellow terry cloth, red felt comb and orange felt beak. Using single thickness cut the white of the eye and red wattle with $\frac{3}{8}$in (8mm) for seams on perimeter only. Cut a black circle for eye.
2 Sew white eye piece to front of circle, then the red wattle slightly overlapping the white circle and then the black eye. With RS together sew around coxcomb, beak and wing pairs. Trim and turn. With RS together join circles, pinning beak and coxcomb in between with points to the middle; leave an opening for stuffing. Trim, turn and stuff. Sew up the opening. Put a little stuffing into the wing, sew up the opening and sew to the body around the front and sides only.

Spider

You will need

$\frac{1}{3}$yd (0·30m) black velvet
8 black or colored pipe cleaners
2 buttons and stuffing

1 Draw a circle on paper with a compass or around a plate. Place on double-thickness fabric and cut out allowing $\frac{3}{8}$in (10mm) seam allowance all round.
2 With RS of fabric together, place the pipe cleaners, spaced 4 on either side, between the circles, so that only the ends show around the rim. Sew the circles together, leaving an opening for stuffing. Carefully turn to the RS pulling the pipe cleaners through first, and stuff. Sew up the opening. Add either buttons or felt circles for eyes.

Tortoise

You will need

graph paper
pieces of dark green, light green, gray and 5 other colors of felt
stuffing

1 Using graph paper draw each pattern piece to scale as in diagram, making the head, tail and legs long enough to sew $\frac{3}{4}$in (2cm) in from the rim. Draw an 8in (20cm) diameter circle and cut out 2 in dark green, 1 in light green with scalloped edges and 10 shapes as shown with 2 of each color – all without seam allowance. Cut out 2 gray head pieces, 2 tails and 8 leg pieces, all with $\frac{3}{8}$in (8mm) seam allowances.
2 Sew head, tail and pairs of legs together, leaving tops open. Trim, turn and stuff. Sew scalloped circle to top of 1 dark green one. Machine-stitch other pieces onto body as illustrated using white cotton. Place the 2 dark circles WS together, pin the head, tail and legs in position between them. Sew together on RS, about $\frac{1}{4}$in (5mm) from the edge, leaving an opening. Stuff and sew up opening. Glue or sew on felt eyes.

Cow

You will need

$\frac{1}{2}$yd (0·50m) brown and white herringbone tweed
pieces of pink, brown and white fabric or felt
black and white felt for eyes and nostrils
black and brown knitting worsted
stuffing

1 Draw 2 adjacent 8in (20cm) squares and draw in features to scale as shown. Trace patterns and cut out 4 squares in tweed, 8 rectangles (about 1$\frac{1}{2}$ × 2$\frac{1}{2}$in/3 × 6cm) for legs, 4 ear pieces, 2 pink udders, 4 horn pieces, 1 each pink and brown nose piece, 2 large white and 2 smaller black circles for eyes and 2 small black circles for nostrils.
2 With RS together, sew pairs of ears, horns, legs, and the udder together, leaving tops open. Trim and turn. Stuff legs and udder. Sew top and bottom nose together across center. Turn in seams and sew to front of 1 square. Sew front head and body square together at center line placing 1 ear between. Sew back 2 squares together.
3 Sew front body to back body, inserting legs, other ear, udder and horns between them. Sew around leaving opening in back. Trim and turn; stuff front. Machine-stitch or sew front to back down center. Stuff back and sew up. Sew on eyes, nostrils and black wool mouth. Braid brown wool for a tail, and sew to body.

1 sq = ¾in
Add seam allowances all around

Using patterns and cutting out 16
Basic stitches 18
Seams and edge finishes 20
Hems 28

Finger puppets

Finger puppets are a really simple way of making your own toys and involve very little sewing so that they can be done either by hand or machine. This makes them ideal toys for children to create for themselves.
A variety of characters can be sewn from the basic shape just by changing a face or a detail. You can either follow the illustrations as a guide or invent your own characters.

You will need
pieces of different colored felts
rubber cement
thin cardboard
tweezers
pleated ribbon trim for dog's ruff

1 Cut a finger-shaped template to required size from cardboard, about 3in high by 1¾in wide (7·5 × 4·5cm). Use this as a basic pattern to work from, adding shape changes, such as the seal's snout, the horse's head and Punch and Judy's nose and chin.
2 To make the basic finger puppet, draw around the template onto a double thickness of felt and cut out without seam allowances. Cut features out from different colored felts and glue on with rubber cement, using tweezers to help hold the small pieces. Insert ears, arms, etcetera between the front and back body pieces.
3 Machine-stitch the front and back together, leaving the bottom open for the finger. To stop additional parts flopping over, as with the seal's ball, you can use a stiffener such as thin cardboard.

Liberty horse Add a horse's profile to the basic template. Use double thickness of white felt for the body. Cut out and glue on black eye and nostril, red bridle and brown reins, yellow trimmings including feathers on forehead (red ribbon trim can be used to decorate the bridle). Cut out and glue on gray felt fringe and mane. Cut the mane with pinking shears so it is wide enough to allow for insertion between front and back body. Add ear. Machine-stitch along edge, leaving end open.

Dog Make the body and ears from beige felt, the features from white, black and pink felt. Make the ears quite large and insert between body pieces, then turn over and glue down after stitching the body. Make the ruff from a short length of pre-pleated ribbon, or you could use white felt instead.

Seal Use gray felt for the body, adding a pointed snout. Cut out one flipper and glue it to the front. Glue on a small black circle for the snout, black and white felt circles for the eye. Cut out 5 felt segments of a circle and glue onto a complete felt circle for the ball. Attach ball to seal with a narrow strip of cardboard glued to the back of the ball and the inside of the body. Machine-stitch a little way in from the edge, leaving the bottom open.

Punch and Judy Add a profile nose and chin to basic template. Cut the main body from double thickness pink felt. Use purple and red with yellow trim for Punch, and purple and white for Judy, shaping the hats as shown and glueing them onto main body. Add a blue circle for an eye and a red mouth and machine-stitch around edge, leaving the bottom open.

Strong man Use pink for the body and arms, yellow for the leotard, black for the weight. Insert arms between body with a drop of glue to keep in place. Strengthen the bar of the weight by a thin piece of cardboard at the back extending to the circle on either side; it also helps to extend the cardboard at the center by a small T-bar glued between the body pieces at the top of the head. Double thickness for the arms and the weight circles again helps to strengthen the puppet and keep it from flopping over.

Ringmaster Use pink felt for the body. Glue on white shirt, red jacket, black mustache, lapels, eyes and nose and 2 thicknesses of black felt for the hat (to strengthen it). Insert the hand and ears between front and back body pieces. Machine-stitch around edge, leaving end open.

Glove puppets

This is a basic pattern for a clown glove puppet which can be made in a variety of ways by combining scraps of different fabrics and altering the features and accessories. The puppet fits an average-sized adult hand but you can easily reduce the size for a child by making the body narrower and shortening the length of the arms.

hat brim
hat crown
head
ear
finger stall
hand
body
1sq = $\frac{3}{4}$in
Add seam allowances all around

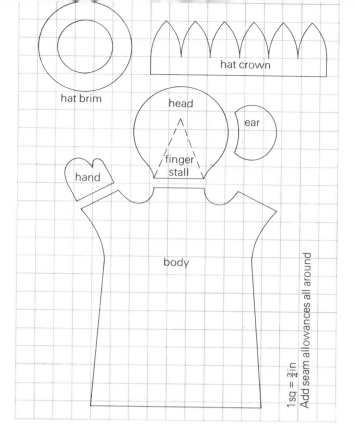

You will need
graph paper for making pattern
scraps of felt and fabric for body, features and accessories
unbleached muslin for face and hands
wool for eyes and hair
cotton batting or kapok stuffing
fabric glue
accessories such as buttons, pleated ribbon trim for a ruff or a shoe lace for a tie; ribbon for the suspenders

1 Using graph paper draw each pattern piece to scale with a $\frac{3}{8}$in (10mm) seam allowance all around. Using double-thickness fabric cut out the head, ears (if using), hands and triangular insert, to allow fingers to manipulate head, in unbleached muslin: cut out the body in other fabric, using more than one color or pattern if desired.

2 With RS together, sew front hands to front body and back hands to back body across wrist with the thumbs pointing toward the neck. With RS together sew front to back body, with bottom and neck open. Trim. Turn RS out.

3 To make ears, sew each pair together, leaving inner curve open. Turn RS out. Place on the RS of back head with raw edges even. Ease in and tuck. With RS together, sew front to back head, with neck open. Turn RS out.

4 Stitch triangles together on 2 long sides to form a cone. Stuff head and insert cone into neck opening; sew head and cone together around neck.

5 Insert neck into body opening and sew together. Turn up a hem along the bottom edge of the body.

Hair Cut 6in (15cm) pieces of wool. Lay side by side and stitch across the middle. Sew to head just behind head seam.

Eyes For eyelids cut semi-circles of felt and glue in place. Sew eyes and eyebrows with wool.

Mouth and cheeks Cut from felt and glue in place.

Bowler Cut out 1 crown and 2 brims from black felt. Butt edge and sections of crown and glue together with strips of felt on inside. Join tops of crown by glueing a small piece of felt inside. Join remaining length of sections by glueing to narrow strips inside. Glue brim and sew to crown.

Using patterns and cutting out 16
Basic stitches 18
Seams and edge finishes 20
Linings 88

Adaptable animals

Stuffed animals made from a simple shape and a variety of materials can be quite easy to do once you have mastered the technique of drawing and cutting out the relevant shapes, sewing them together and stuffing them firmly with kapok or any other suitable material. By altering the shape of a nose, the length of the legs, ears or face you can make a number of different animals from one basic shape.

Elephant
You will need
graph paper for making pattern
approximately 1yd (0·90m) of patterned cotton fabric
white and black felt scraps for eyes and tusks
matching wool for tail
fabric glue
kapok or cotton batting

1 Using graph paper draw pattern and cut from double thickness fabric allowing an extra $\frac{3}{8}$in (10mm) seam allowance all round.
2 With RS together pin and sew back gusset to both body pieces from head to tail. Sew inside leg gussets to body as for pig and continue as for pig, leaving feet and trunk end open. Trim and turn. Stuff firmly. Sew circles to feet and trunk openings as for pig; sew up gusset opening.
3 With RS together sew pairs of ears leaving an opening. Trim and turn to RS. Sew up openings and sew to head. Cut out eyes from black and white felt and glue to face. Make tusks from cone-shaped pieces of white felt, leaving wide ends open; sew together and stuff lightly. Sew to head at broad end and along inside. Make tail by braiding lengths of wool together: sew to body.

Pig
You will need
graph paper for making pattern
28–36in (0·70–0·90m) pink floral quilted fabric (or floral cotton fabric)
small quantity pink or white cotton for ear linings
pink or red pipe cleaner
scraps of felt for eyes
fabric glue
kapok or cotton flock stuffing

1 Using graph paper draw each pattern piece to scale. Cut patterns from double thickness fabric, with an extra $\frac{3}{8}$in (10mm) for seam allowance. Cut out 4 circles for feet and 1 circle for nose. Cut 2 outer ears from quilted fabric and 2 inner ears from lining.
2 With RS together sew each inside leg gusset to body, leaving ends of legs open. Sew head and back body together leaving snout open. Sew gussets together at center, leaving an opening for stuffing. Trim seams and turn RS out. Stuff body firmly. Turn in edges of circles and sew to leg and snout openings. Sew up gusset opening. With RS together sew white inner ears to outer ears leaving straight ends open. Trim and turn to RS. Sew openings and sew to head. Cut out eyes from felt and glue to face. Twist pipe cleaner for tail and attach.

Rabbit
You will need
graph paper for making pattern
1yd (1m) fur fabric
piece of white fur fabric (or felt) for inside ears and tail
black felt for nose
2 brown button eyes
stuffing

1 Using graph paper draw each pattern piece to scale, allowing an extra $\frac{3}{8}$in (10mm) for seam allowance all around. Place pattern pieces onto back of fabric and cut out making sure the pile brushes towards the feet on all pieces.
2 With RS together sew gusset to body pieces. Fasten button eyes into position. Sew body together around head and back, leaving an opening at the base for stuffing. Trim and turn RS out. Stuff firmly and sew up opening. With RS together, sew white inner ears to outer ears, leaving ends open. Trim and turn. Turn ends inside, pinch ends together, and sew to head. With RS together sew tail pieces, turn and sew to back of body. Cut out a circle of black felt, gather and stuff as for glove puppet's nose. Sew to head with thread doubled.

Kangaroo
You will need
graph paper for making pattern
$\frac{2}{3}$yd (0·60m) dark green corduroy
$\frac{1}{3}$yd (0·30m) light green corduroy
pair of brown button eyes
black and white felt for nose and eyes
stuffing

1 Using graph paper draw patterns to scale as for pig, allowing $\frac{3}{8}$in (10mm) seam allowance all around. Cut patterns out of double thickness fabric, using light green for gusset and inner ears. Cut the gusset in 2 pieces so that the bottom half overlaps the top thus forming a pouch.
2 Fix eyes in position. Turn in top of lower gusset. Lay on RS top gusset to overlap and stitch together at side seams. With RS facing sew gusset to body pieces. Sew the end of the top gusset across neatly to the bottom of the pouch so the stuffing will not come through later on. Continue to sew up body as for the rabbit, leaving an opening for stuffing. Trim seams and turn. Stuff firmly, and sew up opening.
3 With RS together sew inner ears to outer ears leaving an opening. Turn and sew to head as illustrated.

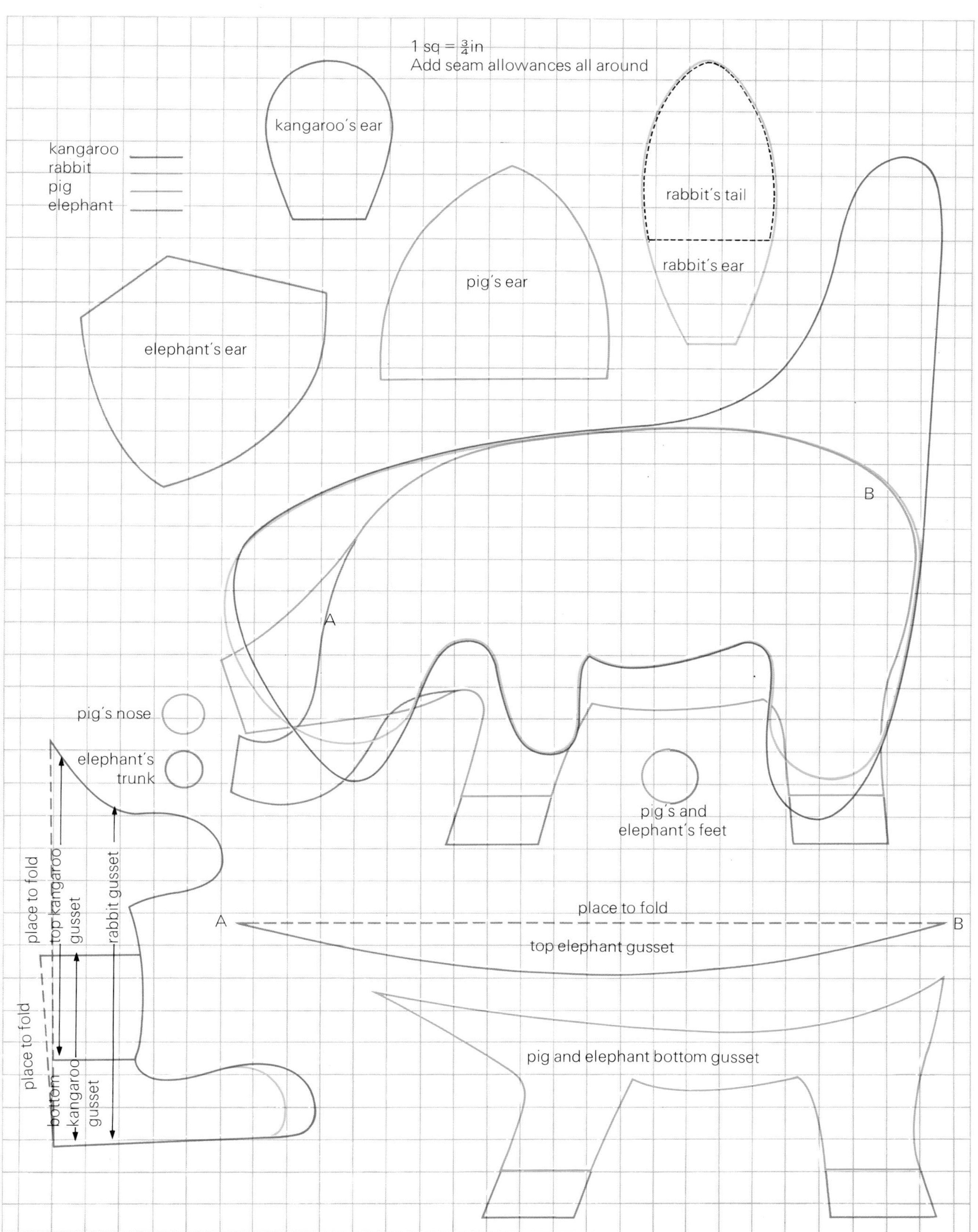
1 sq = $\frac{3}{4}$in
Add seam allowances all around
kangaroo
rabbit
pig
elephant
kangaroo's ear
rabbit's tail
rabbit's ear
pig's ear
elephant's ear
B
A
pig's nose
elephant's trunk
pig's and elephant's feet
place to fold
top kangaroo gusset
rabbit gusset
place to fold
bottom kangaroo gusset
A
place to fold
B
top elephant gusset
pig and elephant bottom gusset

Dolls

Using patterns and cutting out 16
Basic stitches 18
Seams and edge finishes 20
Hems 28
Shirring and gathering 29
Sleeves 62
Linings 88

These dolls have all been made from one simple, basic shape, but by changing the hair, clothes and faces they have been made to look completely different. The body is cut out from muslin or strong cotton fabric and stuffed with kapok. It is important to remember that the size and shape of the doll can alter considerably depending on the fabric used and how firmly it has been stuffed, so do measure the clothes against your doll before cutting out to ensure a good fit.

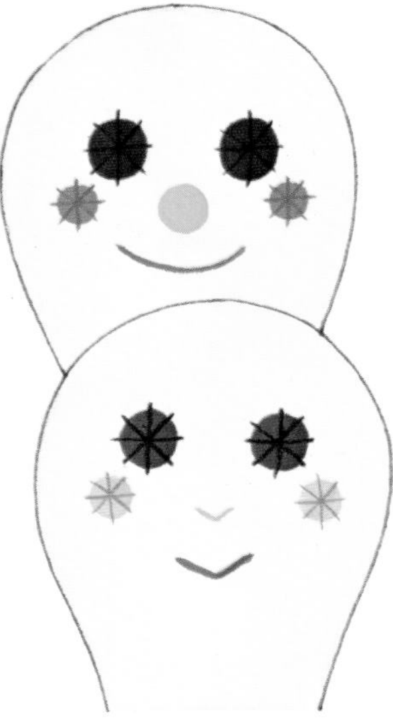

Basic body
You will need
graph paper for making pattern
about ½yd (0·50m) pink cotton fabric or unbleached muslin
cotton batting or kapok stuffing

1 Using graph paper draw each pattern piece to scale. Add ⅜in (10mm) seam allowance all around. Cut out the pattern pieces.
2 Cut out pattern from double thickness fabric – 2 body and 2 head pieces, 4 arm and leg pieces. With RS together, sew front head to front body across neck and back head to back body. Sew up pairs of legs and arms leaving the tops open. Trim seam allowances, turn to RS and stuff. To make the arms and legs more flexible, stitch elbow and knee joints as shown in diagram; stitch lines to indicate fingers. Place stuffed arms between front and back body, so that the thumbs point upward. Sew around body and head, leaving bottom open. Trim seam allowances and turn body RS out; stuff firmly. Turn in bottom seam; insert tops of legs making sure both feet face forward and hand-stitch across.

Features Make eyes and cheeks for all dolls, and nose for boy, from circles of felt and glue into place. Embroider mouth. Sew 6- or 8-point stars over eyes and cheeks.

Hair
You will need
about 1oz (30g) knitting worsted

Doll with pony tails Cut brown wool into lengths – measure against doll's head and allow a little extra. Machine-stitch across the middle of the wool so that the finished length of the stitching measures about 5in (12cm). Sew the wool to the head along the machine stitching to form center part. Tie pony tails on either side of head. Trim ends. Stitch hair to head in one or two places.

Doll with braids Cut approximately two-thirds of yellow wool into lengths as for the other doll. Cut the rest into slightly shorter lengths for the bangs. Sew the shorter lengths about 3in (8cm) from one end and sew this to the head just behind and parallel to the seam with the bangs at the front. Attach long hair as for doll with pony tails. Make braids at each side. Fasten with thread. Sew braids to head just above end to keep in place. Trim.

Boy doll Cut orange or brown wool into equal lengths against doll's head. Tie tightly around middle and, using this as the crown, sew to head. Arrange lengths around head and sew to head to keep in place. Trim.

Victorian doll's clothes

You will need

graph paper for making pattern
$\frac{2}{3}$–1yd (60–90cm) floral cotton fabric
wide, medium and narrow velvet ribbon to match
2yd (2m) white trimming $\frac{3}{4}$in (2cm) wide
elastic for sleeves, $\frac{1}{8}$in (3mm) wide
3 snap fasteners
matching felt for shoes
white cotton fabric, white lace trimming and elastic for petticoat and pants (optional)

1 Using graph paper draw pieces for dress pattern to scale, adding $\frac{3}{8}$in (10mm) seam allowance all around, marking all the foldlines on the pattern.
2 Cut out patterns from double thickness of fabric. In addition to top tier shown, cut 2 rectangles 4 × 15in (10 × 46cm) for middle tier of skirt and 2 rectangles 4 × 27in (10 × 68·5cm) for bottom tier, allowing extra for seams.
3 Make darts in front and back bodice as indicated on pattern. With RS together, join bodice front to back at shoulders. Gather top of each sleeve to match arm opening from front to back. Pin and sew sleeves to arm openings from front to back. Trim seams. Sew up underarms and side seams.
4 Join top tier of skirt at sides, leaving back open, and middle and bottom tiers at sides to form a circle. Gather top tier around the top to match bodice waist and with RS together sew together. Gather the top of the middle tier and with RS together sew it to the bottom of the top tier. Gather the top of the bottom tier and sew to the middle tier in the same way. Trim all seams. Turn the edges of the back opening to the WS and stitch in place.
5 Sew medium velvet ribbon to trim neck opening. Turn sleeves under as marked on pattern and sew 2 lines of stitches wide enough to take elastic, leaving an opening. Insert elastic and fasten (alternatively use shirring elastic). Turn to WS and stitch in place. Sew on white trimming all around hem and ends of sleeves. Sew on snap fasteners to back dress opening. Dress doll, tie wide velvet ribbon round her waist and narrow ribbons around her pony tails.

Petticoat and pantaloons

Make petticoat as for short skirt, adjusting length. Trim with white lace trimming. Adapt boy's slacks pattern to short legs for pantaloons; turn in seams at waist and leg openings and insert elastic. Trim with lace.

Skirt and bolero doll

You will need

graph paper for making pattern
$\frac{1}{2}$yd (0·50m) blue denim or cotton fabric for bolero and skirt $\frac{1}{4}$yd (0·30m) floral cotton fabric for blouse, blue lining for bolero
eyelet or other white trimming
3 snap fasteners
elastic

1 Using graph paper draw each pattern to scale. Cut skirt and bolero from double thickness of blue denim (but only 1 waistband) and a second bolero pattern from lining fabric. Cut blouse bodice and sleeves from floral fabric.
2 To make the skirt, sew front to back with RS together. Gather top edge to fit waistband. With RS together sew waistband to top of skirt. Fold band over and sew to inside of skirt, leaving opening for elastic. Insert elastic, measure to fit waist and fasten. Turn hem under and sew in place.
3 To make the bolero, join front and back bolero bodice at shoulders and sides with RS together. Repeat with bolero lining. Trim and press. With RS together sew lining to bolero around neck and front openings. Turn RS out. Turn in armhole seams and sew denim armholes to lining. Turn bottom of bolero under and sew denim to lining; press.
4 To make the blouse, sew front bodice to back at shoulders with RS together. Gather sleeves, sew to armhole opening and continue as for dress bodice including elasticated sleeves. Trim neck with eyelet. Turn in back openings to WS and attach snaps. Hem bottom edge.

Boy doll's clothes

You will need

graph paper for making pattern
$\frac{1}{4}$yd (0·30m) brown denim
2 scraps blue or other color fabric for patches
$\frac{1}{4}$yd (0·30m) brown and white plaid cotton
8in (0·20m) yellow felt
triangle of red and white polkadot cotton
white bias binding
3 snap fasteners

1 Using graph paper draw each paper pattern to scale.
2 Cut slacks out of double thickness brown denim, shirt (with straight sleeve) out of plaid fabric and waistcoat from yellow felt allowing extra for seams all around, but omitting them on neck, front opening, armholes and bottom of vest.
3 To make slacks, sew CF seams together and CB seams together with RS together. Trim and press. Sew patches to front of each leg. With RS together sew front to back slacks at sides and round inner leg from ankle to ankle. Turn RS out. Sew waistband to slack tops as for doll's skirt and insert elastic. Check slack length; turn up hems.
4 To make the shirt, sew front to back shirt pieces at shoulders with RS together. Pin and sew sleeves to armhole openings. Sew up underarm and side seams. Turn edges of back openings to WS and sew in place. Trim neck opening with white bias binding. Turn hems of sleeves and shirt bottom to WS and sew in place. Sew on snap fasteners – if opening is at front, you could also add 3 buttons.
5 Make the vest as for girl's bolero but without lining. Hem the raw edges of the red and white neckerchief and tie round the boy's neck.

Shoes (all dolls)

Cut out 2 pairs of shoe pattern, omitting seam allowance on top edges. With RS facing, sew together, trim and turn RS out. By extending the shoes upward you can make boots as shown. Stitch around and leave the front open above the foot. Insert eyelets or punch holes and cut laces from narrow cord or tapes.

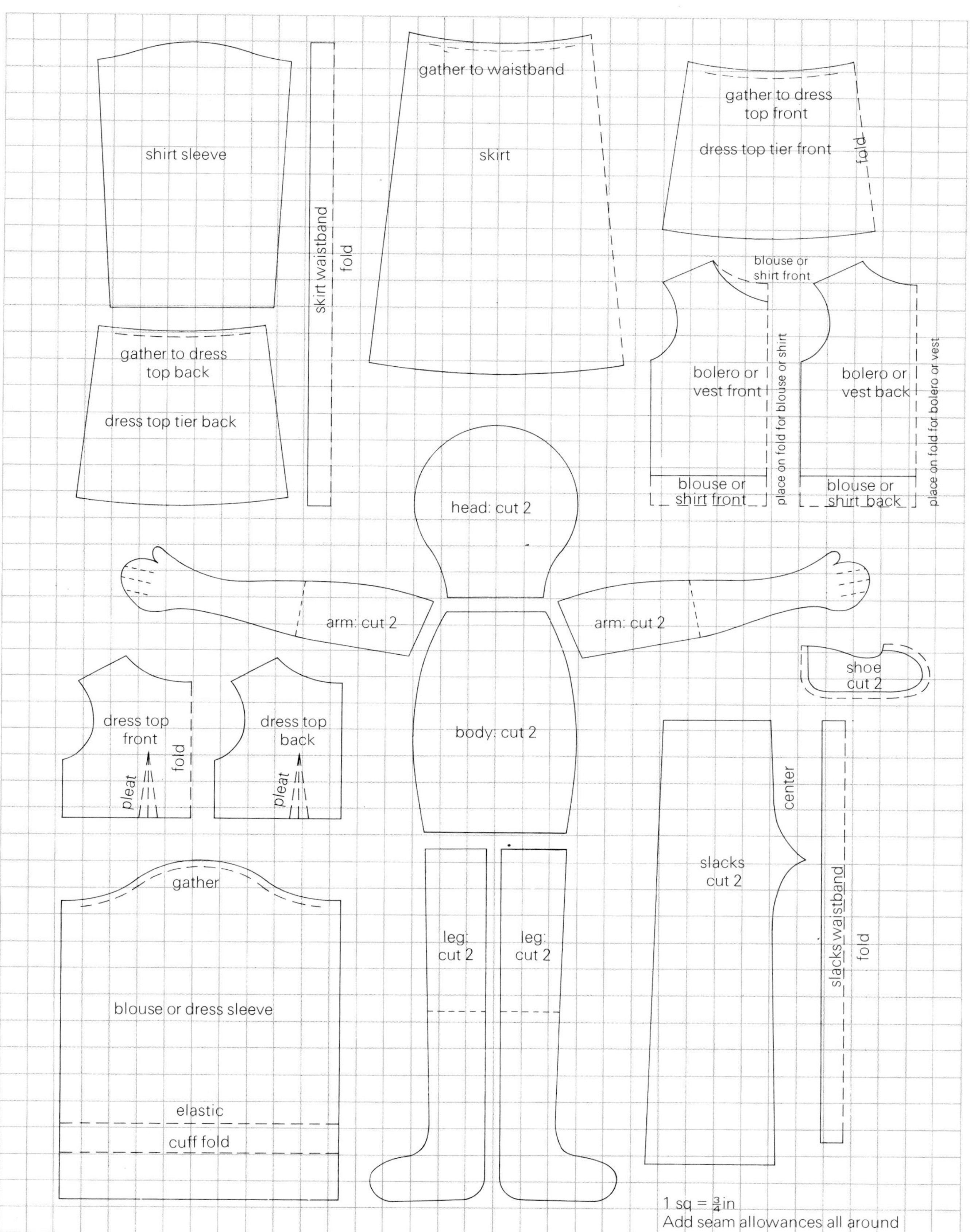
shirt sleeve
skirt waistband
fold
gather to waistband
skirt
gather to dress
top front
dress top tier front
fold
gather to dress
top back
dress top tier back
blouse or
shirt front
bolero or
vest front
place on fold for blouse or shirt
bolero or
vest back
place on fold for bolero or vest
blouse or
shirt front
blouse or
shirt back
head: cut 2
arm: cut 2
arm: cut 2
shoe
cut 2
dress top
front
pleat
fold
dress top
back
pleat
body: cut 2
center
slacks
cut 2
slacks waistband
fold
gather
leg:
cut 2
leg:
cut 2
blouse or dress sleeve
elastic
cuff fold
1 sq = ¾in
Add seam allowances all around

Home sewing

Using the sewing techniques introduced in the first chapter you can make a wide range of items of soft furnishing for the home. These vary in complexity from simple pillows and bedthrows through articles such as lampshades, curtains and shades, to major undertakings like tailored slipcovers. You can incorporate decorative techniques from the chapters on embroidery and on crochet to make your creations original. Finally, the rugmaking techniques offer you a pastime that is more long-term but which can be extremely rewarding.

As well as the obvious advantages of economy, making your own soft furnishings enables you to solve the problems presented by an oddly shaped chair or an irregularly sized window. It also gives you unlimited scope to match colors and fabrics and create a coordinated and entirely individual furnishing style in your home. You can even consider the luxury of making a second set to ring the changes in color and style.

While it is less expensive to make your own household items than to buy them ready-made, don't be tempted to over-economize in your choice of fabric. Use materials that are recommended by the manufacturer for your purpose. Furnishing fabrics are often heavier and more durable than dress-weight fabrics, so make sure that your sewing machine is robust enough to cope with the types of fabric you want to use.

Curtains

Gathers

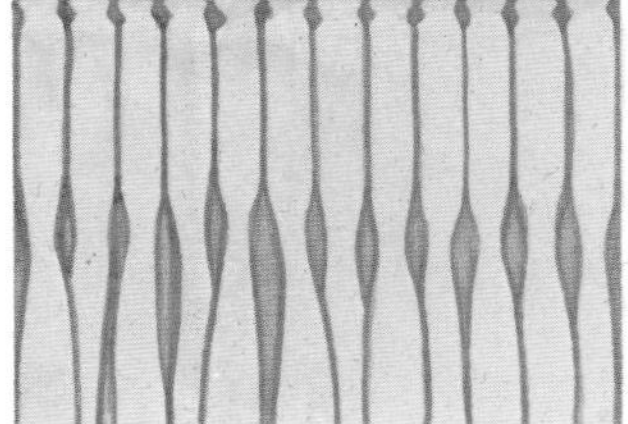

Pencil pleats

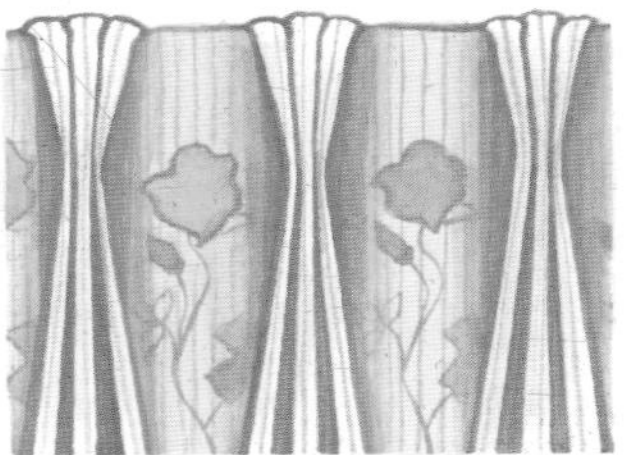

Pinch pleats

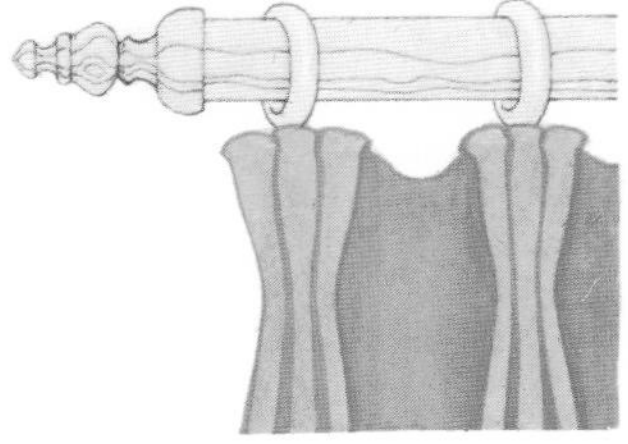

Underslung pinch pleats

The processes involved in curtain-making are all basically simple—seaming the fabric, turning hems and forming the heading. This last process may be worked by hand for a special effect or it may be simplified by the use of a tape which gathers or pleats the heading and provides pockets for the hooks to hang the curtains; you can also buy a special tape for making detachable linings. The success of your curtains, however, depends on careful measuring and calculating before cutting out the fabric. For drawstring curtains, start by deciding the style of heading you wish to make because this determines the amount of fabric you will need overall. There are three main styles of curtain tape, producing gathers, pencil pleats or spaced pinch pleats. All are suitable for use on tracks without a valance (use the simple gathered style with a valance) and all can be attached so that the curtains either cover or are underslung from the curtain track or the curtain pole.

Buying curtain tape
When you buy the tape, ask for an instruction leaflet because the method of attaching it and forming the heading differs with each manufacturer.

Taking measurements
If you are using washable fabric that has not been pre-shrunk it is advisable to allow extra fabric for shrinkage. Decide where you wish the top edge of the curtain to be (in line with either the top or bottom of the track) and whether the bottom hem should rest on the sill, or drop below it or down to the floor. Take all measurements carefully and accurately (you will need help if the curtains are very long or wide).
Length Measure from the required position of the top edge to the bottom; add 2in (5cm) for the top hem and 6in (15cm) for the bottom hem.

Width Measure from one end of the curtain track to the other. Divide by the number of curtains required at the window and calculate the amount for each one separately as shown on the chart. The chart also shows the number of standard fabric widths necessary to make up the required curtain width. These calculations include allowances of 2in (5cm) on each side of the curtain and ⅝in (15mm) for seaming. The track lengths given are for full and half standard curtain widths—use this as a simple way to calculate as most types of heading will allow for slight adjustments.

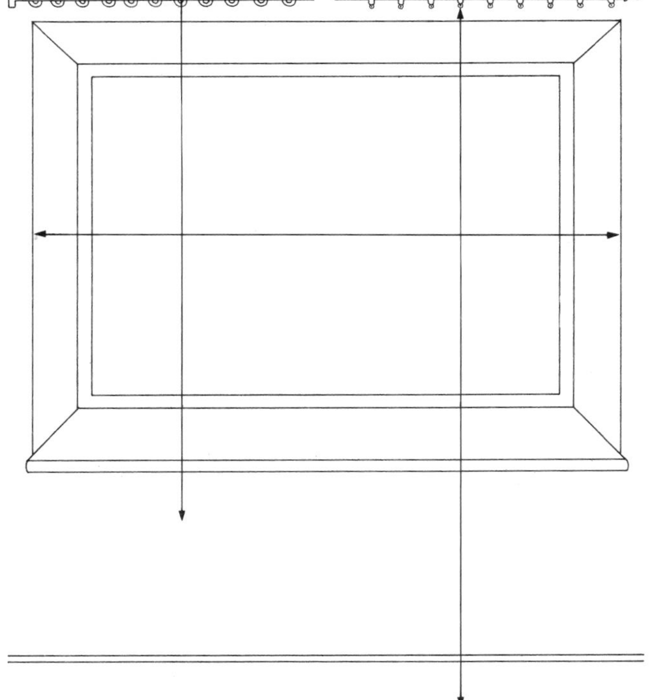

Chart to calculate fabric amounts

Per curtain	Gathered heading (min. 1½ times fullness)				Pinch-pleat heading (double fullness)				
Track length	12in	28in	60in	90in	10in	22in	45in	70in	94in
No. of 48in fabric widths	½	1	2	3	½	1	2	3	4
Heading tape length	22in	1⅜yd	2⅝yd	4yd	22in	1⅜yd	2⅝yd	4yd	5½yd

Basic stitches 18
Seams 20
Hems 28
Pleating 40

Curtain fullness
The amount of fullness required in curtains is determined by the style of heading as shown below. Except for pinch pleating by tape and drawstring (as opposed to pleat hooks), these amounts can be slightly adjusted each way if it is more convenient.
Simple gathers $1\frac{1}{2}$–2 times fullness.
Tape pinch pleats 2 times fullness.
Hand-stitched pinch pleats 2–3 times fullness.
Pencil pleats $2\frac{1}{4}$ times fullness (heavy fabrics); $2\frac{1}{2}$ times fullness (medium-weight fabrics); 3 times fullness (fine fabrics).

Calculating the number of standard widths
1 Multiply the length of track to be covered by each curtain by the required fullness for the style of heading chosen.
Example (for simple gathers): $60\text{in} \times 1\frac{1}{2} = 90\text{in}$.
2 Add 4in for side hems.
Example: $90\text{in} + 4\text{in} = 94\text{in}$.
3 Divide total by fabric width and round up to next half width.
Example: $94 \div 48\text{in} = 2$ (rounded up).
4 Add $1\frac{1}{4}$in for seam allowances for each full or half width after the first.
Example: $94\text{in} + 1\frac{1}{4} = 95\frac{1}{4}\text{in}$.
5 Compare the total with the rounded up measurement of curtain widths and increase by a half width if necessary (in which case allow an extra $1\frac{1}{4}$in).

Total fabric amount If you are using fabric with a distinct pattern you may have to add extra fabric to match the repeat on the seams and to allow for the repeat to be even on each curtain.
1 Divide curtain length by pattern repeat and round up to a whole figure.
Multiply the figure by the pattern repeat.
Example: $68\text{in} \div 12\text{in} = 6$ (rounded up).
$6 \times 12\text{in} = 72\text{in}$.
2 Multiply this figure by the number of widths required in one curtain.
Example: $72\text{in} \times 3$ widths $= 216\text{in}$.
3 Multiply by the number of curtains required for the total amount.
Example: $216\text{in} \times 2$ curtains $= 432\text{in}$.

Lining
If the lining fabric is the same width as the main fabric, allow the same amount less 2in from each length. Otherwise, calculate the amount following the same procedure as for the main fabric.

Curtain tape
See the amount on the chart. Allowances are included for hems and for accurate positioning of pinch pleat tape. If you are making detachable linings, buy the same amount of lining tape as heading tape.

Cutting out the curtains
1 Press the fabric to remove all creases and lay it out, RS up, on a large flat surface. You must be able to see a complete curtain length at one time, so use the floor if you do not have a table large enough.
2 Straighten the top edge of the fabric, measure the total length of the curtain down the selvedge and cut across the fabric at this point.
3 Place the top edge of the cut length alongside the next length so that you can match the pattern and trim off any excess fabric from the top edge. Cut the second length. Cut subsequent lengths in the same way. For a half width, fold one length in half, selvedge to selvedge, and cut down the fold. It is advisable at this point to trim selvedges by about $\frac{1}{4}$in (5mm) to prevent the finished curtain from puckering.

Joining the fabric
1 For plain fabrics, pin the pieces with RS together and edges even. Place half widths on the outside of each curtain.
2 Baste and machine-stitch making $\frac{5}{8}$in (15mm) seams. Press both seams to one side and clip them if they are tight.
3 For patterned fabrics, slip-baste the pieces together from the RS with the pattern matching exactly. Machine-stitch them from the WS and press the seams to one side.

Pencil-pleat heading
($2\frac{1}{2}$ times fullness)

6in	18in	36in	56in	74in	94in
$\frac{1}{2}$	1	2	3	4	5
22in	$1\frac{3}{8}$yd	$2\frac{5}{8}$yd	4yd	$5\frac{1}{2}$yd	$6\frac{2}{3}$yd

Pencil- or pinch-pleat heading
(triple fullness)

15in	31in	47in	62in	78in	94in
1	2	3	4	5	6
$1\frac{3}{8}$yd	$2\frac{5}{8}$yd	4yd	$5\frac{1}{2}$yd	$6\frac{2}{3}$yd	8yd

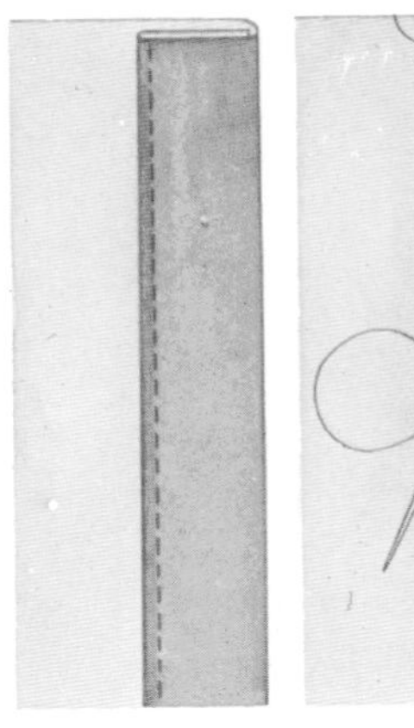

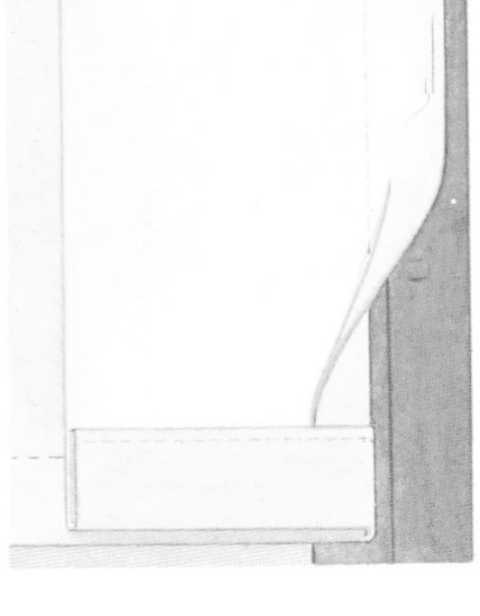

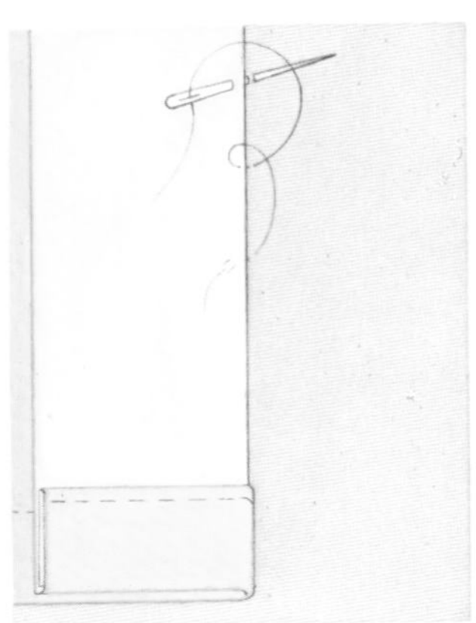

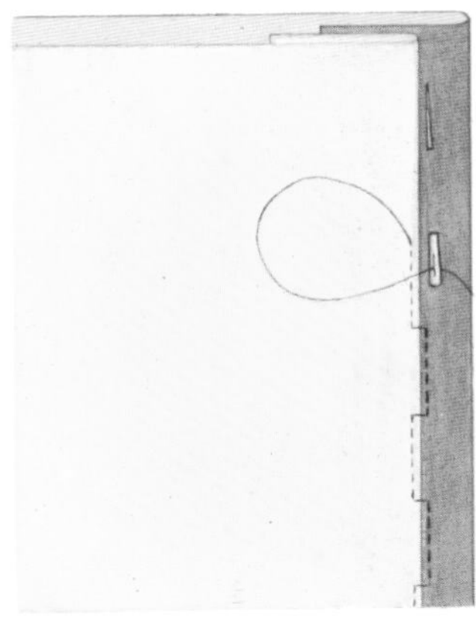

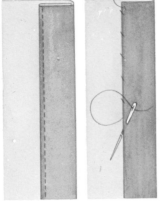

The side hems

1 For unlined curtains or curtains with detachable linings, make 1in (2·5cm) double hems down each side of the curtain; machine-stitch or slip-stitch in position to within 12in (30cm) of the bottom.

2 For curtains with fixed linings, fold over the 2in (5cm) allowances once on each side and loosely hem in place with large stitches to within 12in (30cm) of the bottom.

Fixed linings

1 Cut out the lining 2in (5cm) shorter than the main fabric. Join any sections together and make a double 3in (7·5cm) hem on the bottom edge.

2 Lay out the curtain flat, WS up, and place the lining WS down on top matching seamlines and top edges.

3 If the curtains have more than 1 fabric width, fold the lining back with RS together and baste the lining and curtain hems together to within 12in (30cm) of the bottom. Continue as **4**.

4 If the curtains are made from 1 width, fold back the lining down the center. Start from the top edge and attach the lining to the curtain with 4in (10cm) long blanket stitches; pick up 1 thread of the curtain in each stitch so that it does not show on the RS. Finish 12in (30cm) from the bottom edge.

5 Keeping the curtain and lining flat, turn under the side edges of the lining $1\frac{1}{2}$in (4cm) from the edge of the curtain. Slip-stitch to the curtain to within 12in (30cm) of the bottom.

Hand-stitched headings

With hand stitching you can pleat or gather the curtain fullness to any depth of heading (e.g. 6in/15cm on very long curtains) and place the groups of pleats or gathers to suit your fabric design. Smocking (p206) across striped or plaid fabrics can also be effective.

To hang the curtains you need sew-on brass hooks. Allow 1 hook per group of pleats plus 1 at each side. You will need iron-on interfacing to stiffen deep headings.

Hand-stitched pleats

1 Decide the space required between each pleat (e.g. 4–6in) and divide into finished curtain width. Example: 60in ÷ 6in = 10.

2 Subtract 1 to give number of pleats (there is a space at each edge of curtain). Example: 10 − 1 = 9 pleats.

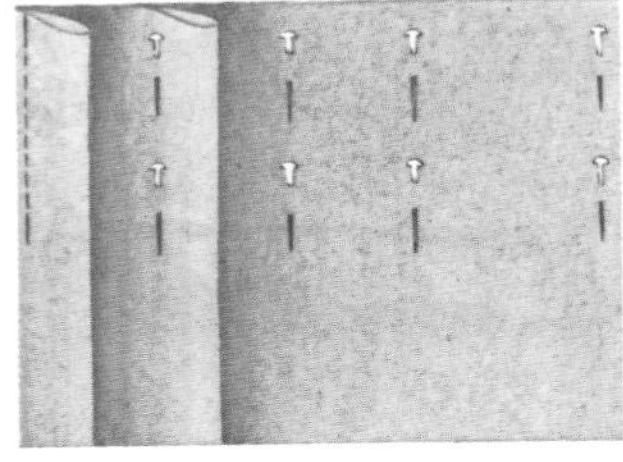

3 Subtract finished width from total width allowed (less side hems and seams). Example: 120in − 60in = 60in.

4 Divide by number of pleats to give amount for each pleat. Round up or down and allow any margin at end spaces. Example: 60 ÷ 9 = 7 (rounded up).

Making the heading

1 Apply iron-on interfacing cut to required heading depth (e.g. 4–6in/10–15cm) to WS of top edge of curtain, placing it $\frac{5}{8}$in (15mm) below raw edge.

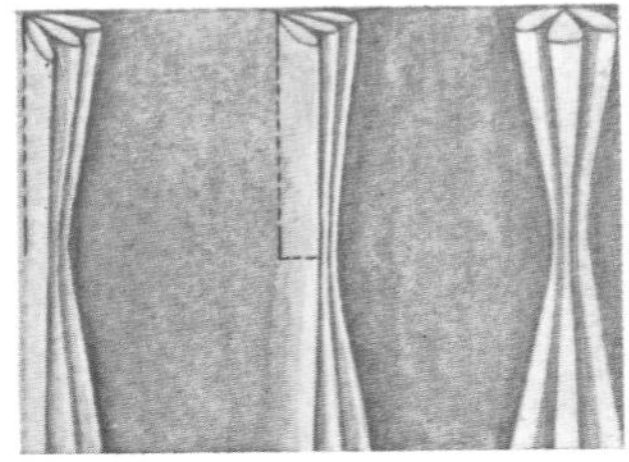

Turn edges of curtain and lining separately for $\frac{5}{8}$in (15mm) to inside and slip-stitch together.

2 Working on the RS and starting with a space, mark the positions of the pleats.

3 Bring the marks with WS together and machine-stitch for the depth of the heading.

Making pinch pleats

Divide the pleat equally into 3 and finger-press the folds firmly. Stitch across the bottom through all the folds and overcast each pleat at the top.

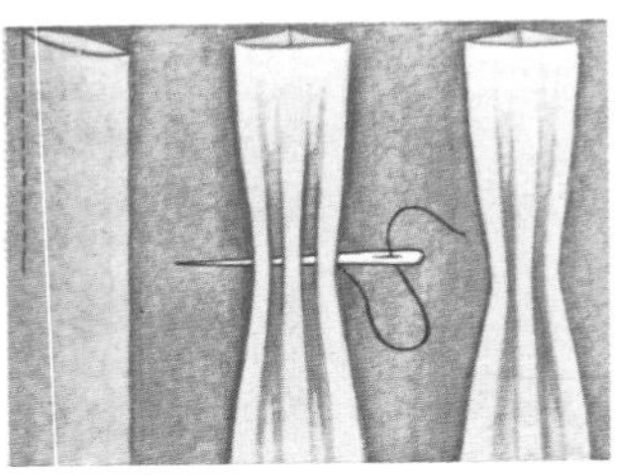

Making trumpet pleats

Divide the pleat equally into tiny pleats and back-stitch through all thicknesses. Leave the top loose.

Sewing on the hooks

Place each hook onto the WS of the curtain in line with a group of pleats so that the top of the hook is the required distance below the top edge of the curtain.

Using sewing thread overcast the bottom hole of the hook to the curtain, work up the stem of the hook and work more overcasting stitches at the top.

Detachable linings

1 Cut out the lining as the main fabric making each length 2in (5cm) shorter. Join the sections and make a double hem down each side and then along the bottom edge.
2 Attach the lining tape, following the manufacturer's instructions.

Forming the heading

1 Fold over 2in (5cm) at the top of the curtain (if you have fixed linings, treat the 2 fabrics as a single layer).
2 Attach the curtain tape, following the manufacturer's instructions, and form the pleats or gathers to the required width.

Making the hems

Hang the curtains for 2–3 days before turning up the hems as the fabric may drop a little.
1 Mark the required length of the curtains with pins across the width while they are still hanging.
2 Take the curtains down and mark the hemline with basting. Trim the raw edge if necessary so that it is an equal distance from the basting across the width of all the curtains.
3 To miter the corners, turn up half the depth of the hem allowance and press lightly. Mark the depth of the hem above the hemline on the side edge.
4 Unfold the side and bottom hem completely and fold over the corners diagonally in a line which passes from the mark on the side edge, through the junction of the side foldline and the hemline to the raw edge of the curtain.

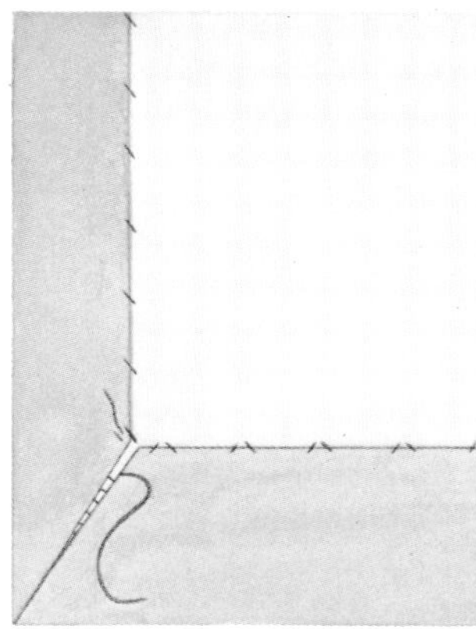

5 Fold down the side hem and slip-stitch the remaining section in place, including lining.
Turn up the bottom hem along the original fold and along the hemline and slip-stitch along the complete curtain. Slip-stitch the folds of the miters together, and then the remaining part of the lining in position. Re-hang the curtains, including detachable linings if you are using them.

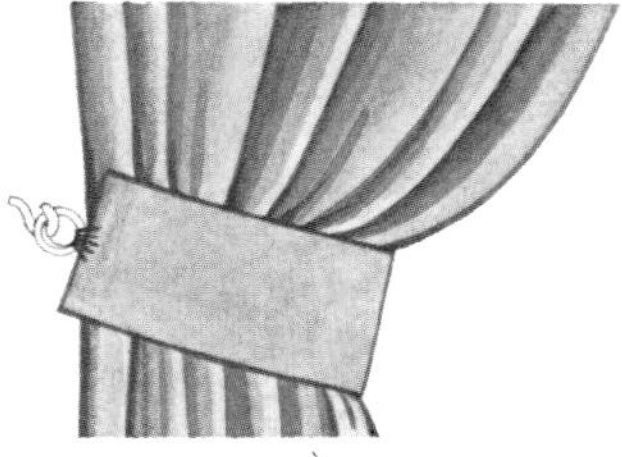

Tie backs

Taking measurements

Decide the depth and width of your tie back (in proportion to the depth of your curtain). To calculate the length, loop a tape measure around the open curtains and adjust the size of the loop until you have the best effect.

Making a straight tie back

1 Cut out a piece of fabric twice the width of the tie back by the length plus $\frac{5}{8}$in (15mm) all around for seams.
Cut out iron-on interfacing to the exact tie back size.
2 Fold the fabric in half lengthwise with RS together and finger-press the fold.
3 Apply the interfacing so that 1 edge is level with the fold and the seam allowances extend on the other 3 sides.
4 Baste and machine-stitch close to the edge of the interfacing on the 3 sides, leaving a 2in (5cm) gap in the stitching on the long side for turning RS out.
5 Trim the seam allowances diagonally at the corners and turn the tie backs RS out. Fold the seam allowances to the WS along the opening and slip-stitch together. Press.

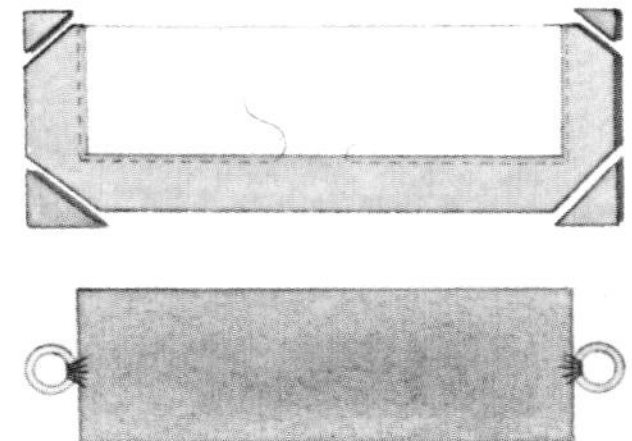

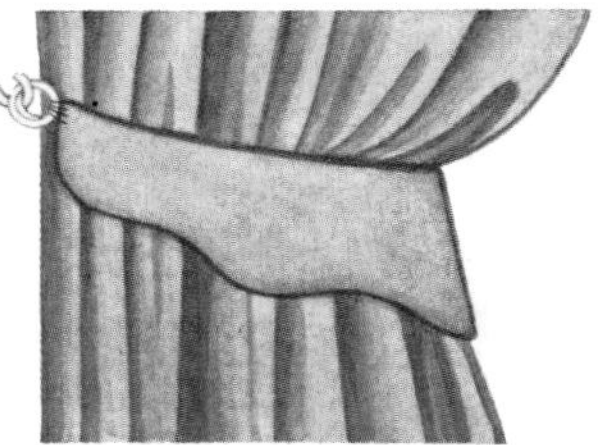

Shaped tie backs

1 Start by making a paper pattern of required shape. To insure that the shape is symmetrical, draw shape of half the length of tie back on folded paper, placing center to the fold. Cut around the shape, open it out and loop around the open curtain to judge the effect. Adjust if necessary.
2 For each tie back cut 2 pieces of fabric from pattern allowing $\frac{5}{8}$in (15mm) all around for seam allowances. Cut out interfacing to exact size of pattern.
3 Apply interfacing centrally to WS of fabric. Place fabric with RS together and stitch around edge of interfacing, leaving a 2in (5cm) gap.
4 Trim corners, clip curves and turn RS out. Fold under the seam allowances along the opening and slip-stitch together. Press.

Hanging tie backs

To hang each tie back you will need 2 rings of 1in (2·5cm) diameter and a hook.
1 Overcast the rings to the short edges of the tie back.
2 Screw the hooks in position at the side of the window and hang the tie back in place.

Café curtains and window shades

The scallop and strap is the traditional heading for café curtains; they are hung from a rod and are made in a similar way to conventional unlined curtains. The most attractive way of hanging café curtains is from a decorative rod, which can be bought complete with fittings, or you can use a wooden dowel and buy the fittings separately. Fix the rod in position halfway down the window (or in line with one of the cross bars) before taking measurements.

Window shades are simple to make from a kit by following the instructions supplied using special shade fabric or some kind of soft furnishing fabric. To prepare the fabric and to add a scalloped hem, see below. If you wish you can substitute a decorative rod for the supplied slat to use with either scalloped or other unusually shaped hems. The rod can be wood or metal, about 1in (2·5cm) diameter, and fitted with decorative ends if there is room for them at each side of the shade.

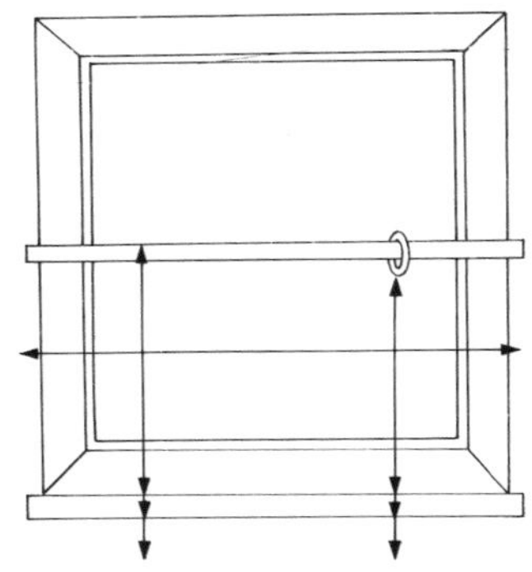

Café curtains – unlined

Taking measurements For the scallop and strap curtain hung from rings, first slide a ring onto the rod and measure from its base to the required length. Add the facing allowance, e.g. the scallop depth plus 2in (5cm) (see below), and 6in (15cm) for the bottom hem. If you are hanging the curtains simply from the strap casings, measure the length from the top of the rod. Add the scallop facing and hem allowance, as before, plus casing allowance of $1\frac{1}{2}$ times the rod diameter.

Fabric amounts Calculate the amount of fabric as for unlined curtains (see p126), allowing a fullness of $1\frac{1}{2}$ times the width. You will also need interfacing to the depth of the heading by the total fabric width.

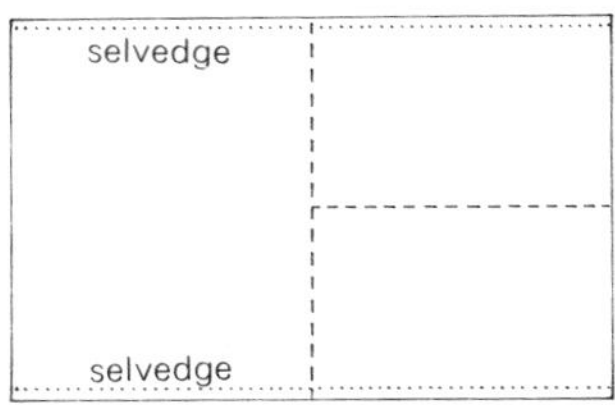

To join narrow fabric to the required width, cut in half widthwise, then cut one of the pieces in half lengthwise. Matching any pattern, join selvedges of half-pieces to the full piece. Trim excess fabric equally from each side.

Making café curtains

1 Cut out and join any seams necessary (see left).
2 Make a paper pattern for the heading (see below), make the heading and turn RS out.
3 Machine-stitch double hems on the outside edges – finish the raw edge of the facing.
4 Finish the straps by making rod casings or inserting eyelets (see below).
5 Check the length of the curtain, turn up the bottom hem and hang in place.

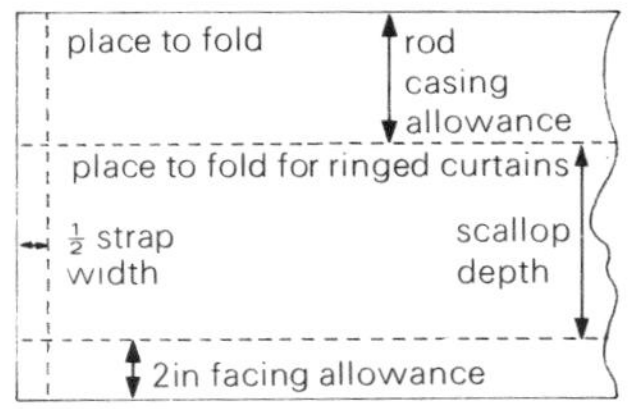

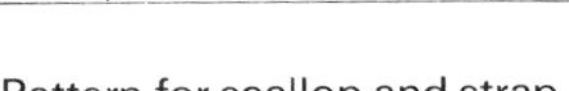

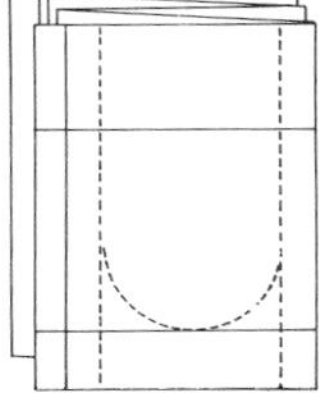

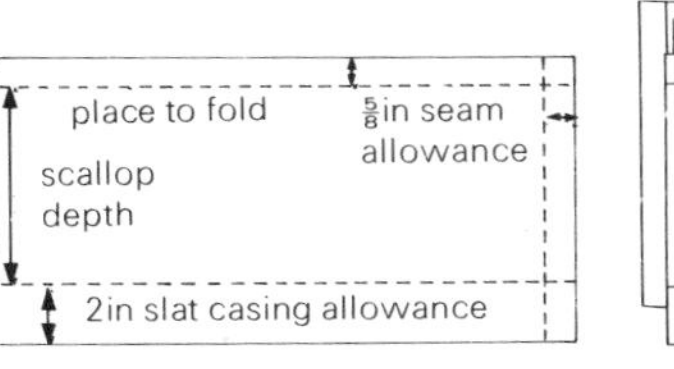

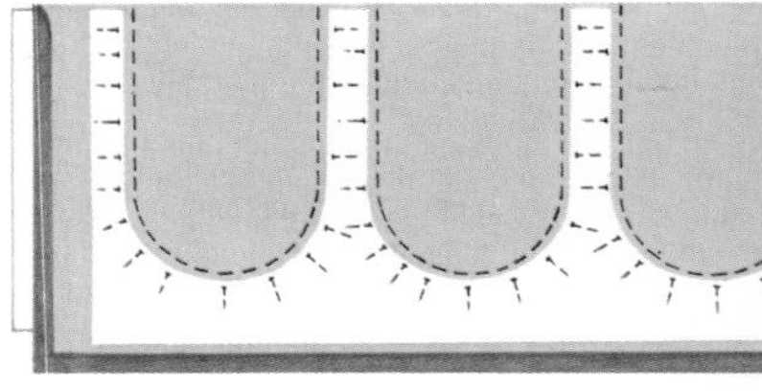

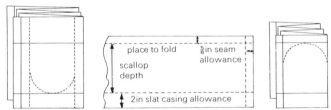

Pattern for scallop and strap

1 Decide scallop depth (e.g. 4–6in/10–15cm) and add casing and facing amounts.
2 Cut paper to this depth by the curtain or blind width. Draw lines across it to mark the casing allowance and scallop depth. Decide the scallop width (e.g. 3–4in/7–10cm) and strap width ($\frac{3}{4}$–$1\frac{1}{2}$in/2–4cm). Mark half strap widths at each end of the pattern.
3 Add together 1 scallop and 1 strap width and divide this measurement into the remaining width of pattern; round the measurement up or down as necessary.
4 Divide paper into sections alternately with straps and scallops; divide each strap in half. Fold paper accordion-wise on half strap lines. Draw scallop shape. Cut out through all folds and open out pattern.

Using the pattern

1 Finish the raw edge of the facing and fold back with RS together. Place interfacing underneath. Pin the pattern in position to the fold (on café curtains the side hem allowances will project). Baste around scalloped edge of pattern through all thicknesses. Unpin the pattern and machine-stitch along the basted lines.
2 Cut out the scallops to within $\frac{1}{4}$in (5mm) of the stitching; do not cut along the fold at the top of the straps. Clip into the curves and trim the top corners. Turn RS out and baste around edge of the scallops. Press on WS.

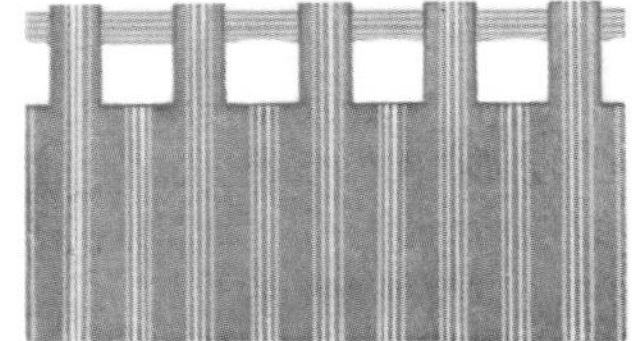

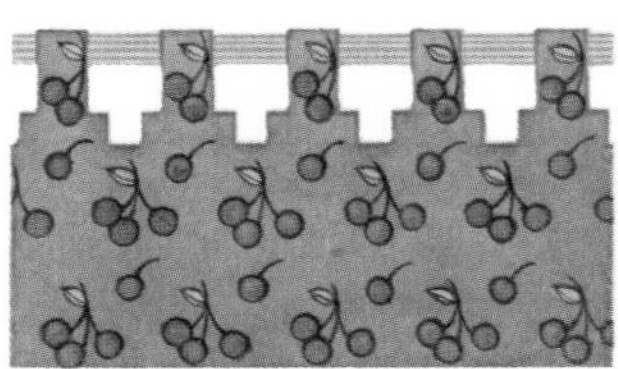

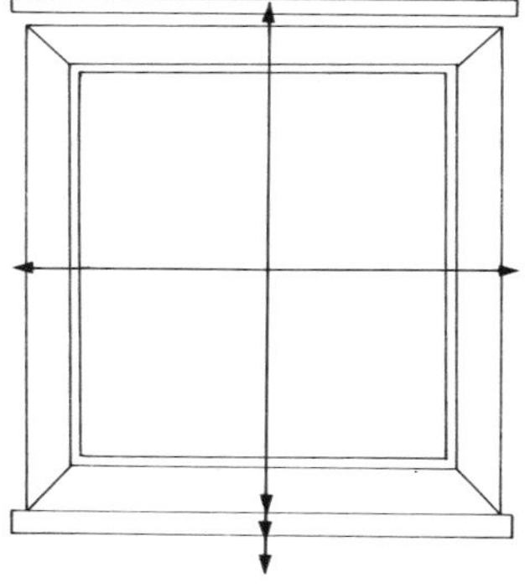

Window shades

Taking measurements If the blind is to hang inside the window frame, add seam allowances of $\frac{3}{4}$in (2cm) to the width and 6in (15cm) to the length. If it is to hang outside, add 2in (5cm) to the width and 8in (20cm) to the length. For a scalloped hem with the kit slat add a facing allowance, of the scallop depth plus 2in (5cm) below for the slat and $\frac{5}{8}$in (15mm) above for seam allowance. If you are using a decorative rod add the facing allowance plus casing allowance of $1\frac{1}{2}$ times rod diameter.

Fabric amounts If the fabric is wider than you need, allow a piece the same as the measured length. If narrower allow twice the measured length. For scalloped hems allow interfacing as deep as facing by finished shade width

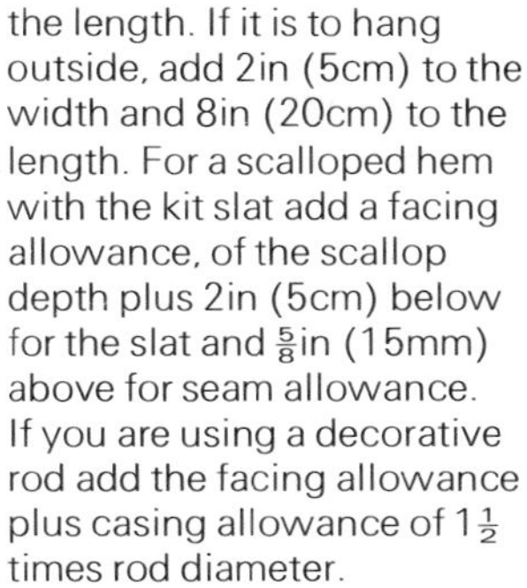

Making the blind

Note that since special blind fabric does not fray, hem allowances on the outside edges are not necessary.

1 Measure the roller and cut the fabric to size. Join narrow fabric to the required width (see diagram opposite).

2 On soft furnishing fabric machine-stitch $\frac{1}{4}$in (5mm) double hems on each side.

3 To finish the shade with the kit slat, use either a plain hem (right) or a scalloped hem (below).

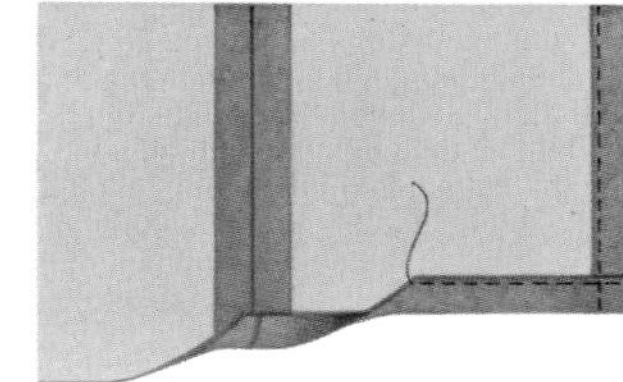

Plain hem If you are using the bottom wooden slat supplied and a plain hem, turn up and stitch the hem so that it is deep enough for the slat to be inserted.

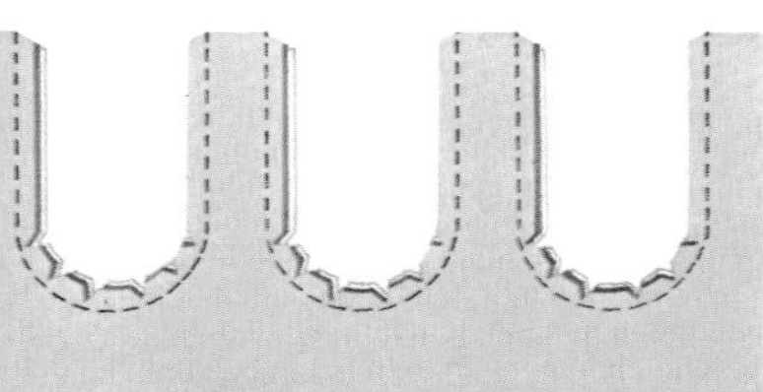

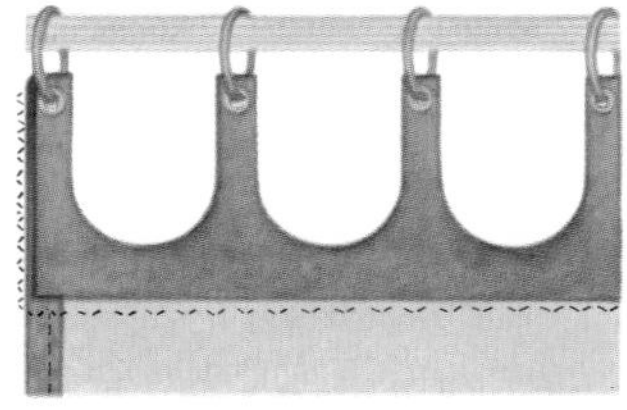

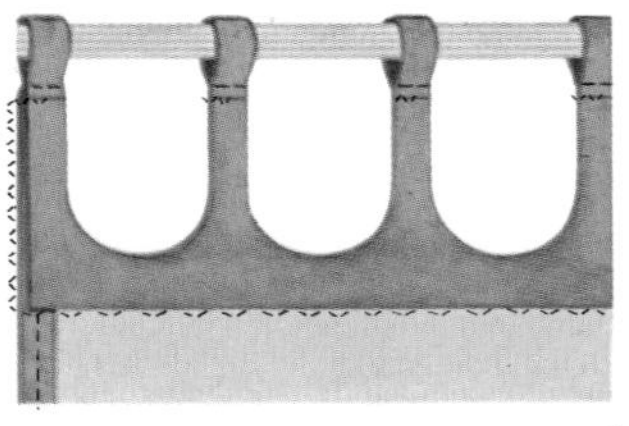

Finishing café curtain headings

Fold under the side seam allowances of the facing and slip-stitch to the curtain, enclosing the interfacing. Either slip- or machine-stitch the lower edge of the facing to the curtain.

Attaching rings You can use split curtain rings with metal eyelets as in the diagram, inserting the eyelets $\frac{1}{4}$in (5mm) from the top of each strap. Alternatively, overcast closed curtain rings firmly to the top of each strap.

Rod casings If you are making casings for the rod, fold over the straps to the WS of the curtain for the appropriate amount and machine-stitch or hem in position. Thread the casings onto the rod.

Finishing shades

Scalloped hem To make a plain scalloped hem using furnishing fabric, first make a paper pattern (see opposite). Cut paper to facing depth by shade width plus seam allowances. Mark seam and casing allowances and scallop depth. Divide pattern equally into scallop widths, adjusting size if necessary. Fold paper accordion-wise on lines, draw scallop, cut out and open pattern. Place interfacing and pattern to facing fold and continue as for scallop and strap. Turn facing to RS, finish and stitch to shade. Stitch a second line leaving space for the slat to be inserted.

Decorative rods Use these instead of slats. Finish the straps with casings as for café curtains, but at lower edge of shade (see examples at bottom of page).

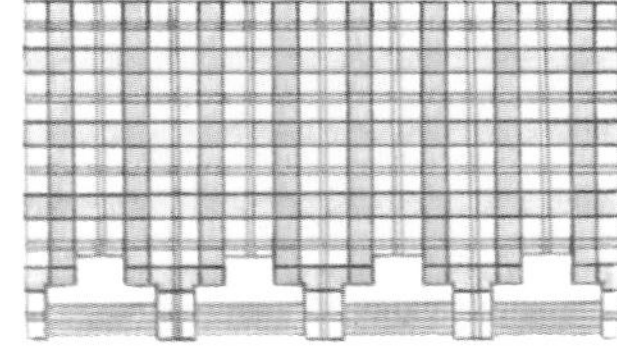

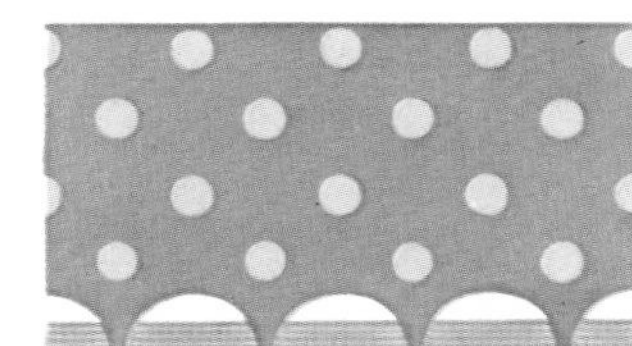

Household linen

Seams 20
Hems 28
Decorative finishes 102

Flat items of household linen, such as plain bedspreads, sheets, tablecloths, tablemats and napkins are all simple to make, involving only straight seams and hems after cutting out. It is possible to buy suitable fabric wide enough to fit most items for average-size tables and beds. However, if you do have to join it to obtain the right width, try to position the seam so that it is unobtrusive or so that it adds to the overall design. You can, for example, cover the seamline with braid or with bands of contrasting fabric. Alternatively you could seam lace or a crocheted insertion between the edges.
You can add interest to the edges by using one of the methods illustrated below.

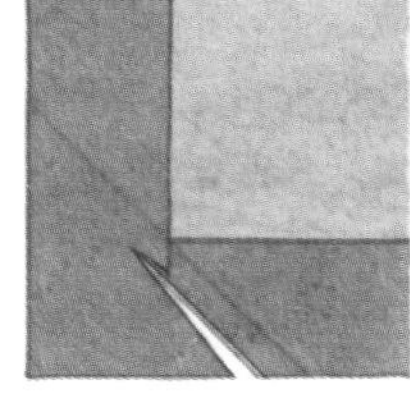

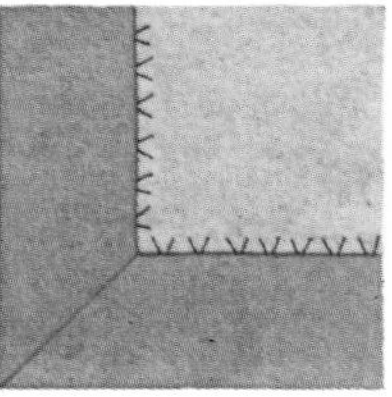

Mitered corner
1 Turn the hem on each side of the corner to be mitered and press.
2 Open out the second folds and turn in the corner on a diagonal line through the meeting point of the foldlines and at an equal distance from the corner on both sides.
3 Leaving the first folds turned, trim off the corner $\frac{1}{4}$in (5mm) outside the diagonal crease, cutting through the folded edges.
4 Fold the corner with RS together at the center of the diagonal so that the sides of the fabric are level.
Stitch on the diagonal, press seams flat and trim protruding corners. Turn RS out, gently easing out the point with a knitting needle. Turn under hem and stitch.

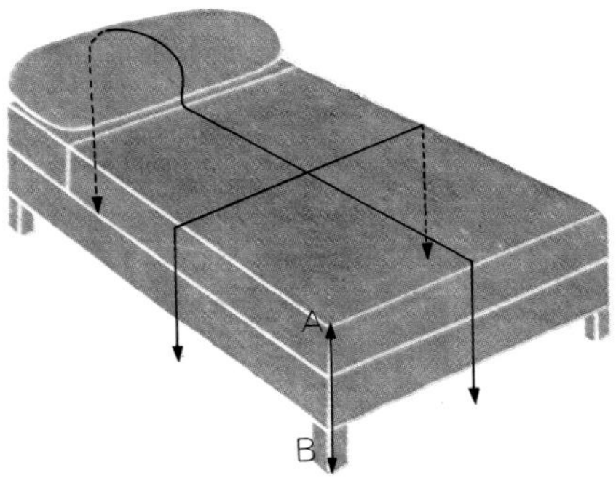

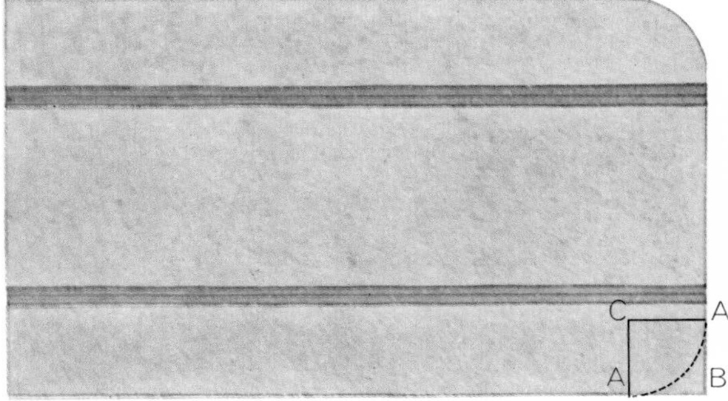

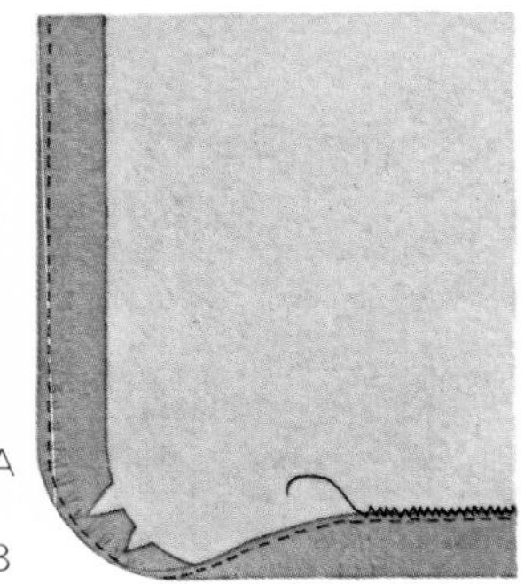

Bed throws
Measuring the bed Take measurements over bedclothes and pillow. Measure the length from the mattress at the top, over the pillows to the floor at the base; add 2in (5cm) for hems. Measure width from the floor on one side to the floor on the other side; add 2in (5cm) for hems. If you intend to make rounded corners, note the height of the bed from the top of the mattress to the floor (A–B); add 1in (2·5cm) for hems.

Calculating the fabric If the total width is the same or less than your fabric, allow the total length. If the width is more, allow twice the total length.

Making plain bed throws
1 If using more than 1 fabric width, cut the fabric in half widthwise; cut one piece in half lengthwise.
2 Join the selvedges of the half pieces to each side of the full piece with RS together taking $\frac{5}{8}$in (15mm) seams.
3 If needed trim fabric from each side to required width.

4 Square corners Make double hems all around, mitering corners.
Round corners Measure the depth of A–B and mark in on both sides (ABA). Measure the same amount inward from A to C.
Using C as the center, draw a quarter circle as shown. Cut along this line. Make a double hem all around the edge, mitering the top corners.

Self fringing

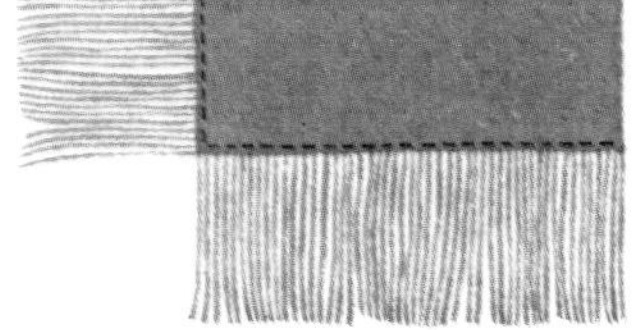

Applied fringing

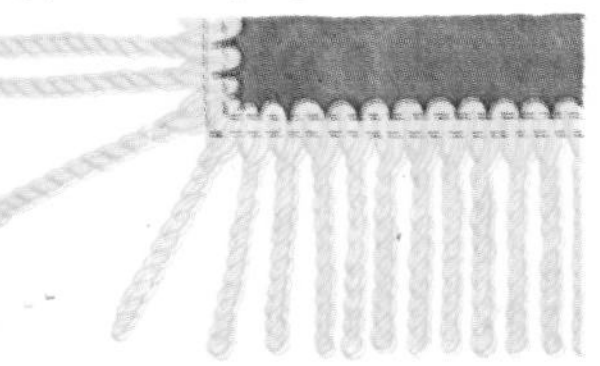

Applied rickrack

Applied lace

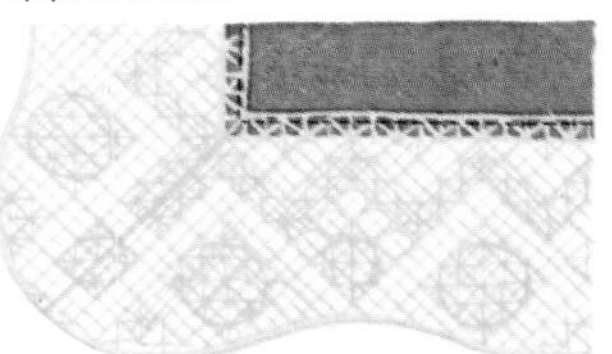

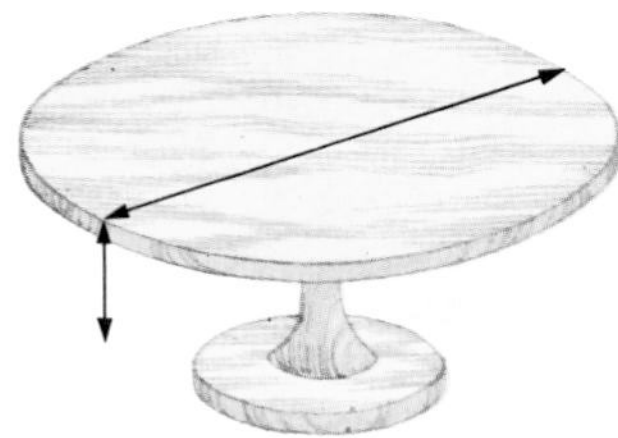

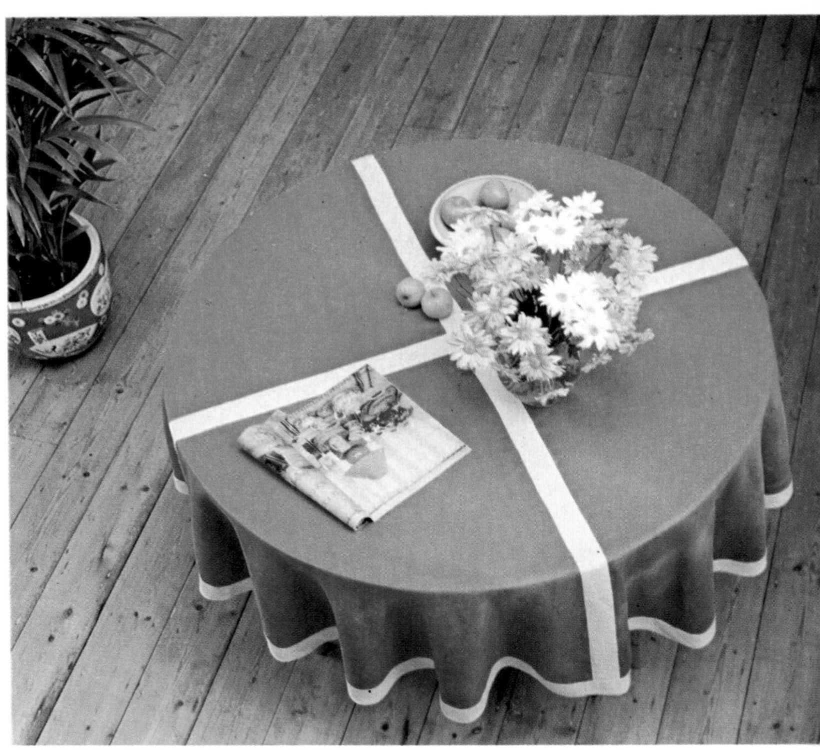

Tablecloths

Taking measurements

Decide on the depth of the overhang – usually to half the table height or to the floor. Measure the diameter or the length and width of the table-top and add the total overhang allowance plus 2in (5cm) for hems, on square or rectangular cloths, to both measurements.

Calculating the fabric See plain bed throws.

Making square or rectangular cloths

Follow the method for plain bed throws, making all corners round or square.

Making round cloths

Cut and join the fabric as for a plain bed throw, then fold in half and cut into a semi-circle, using the radius of the table plus overhang. Finish the edge with binding.

Napkins and tablemats

Choose tablemat sizes to suit your requirements and the fabric width. Napkins are usually square, ranging from 12 to 20in (30cm to 50cm).

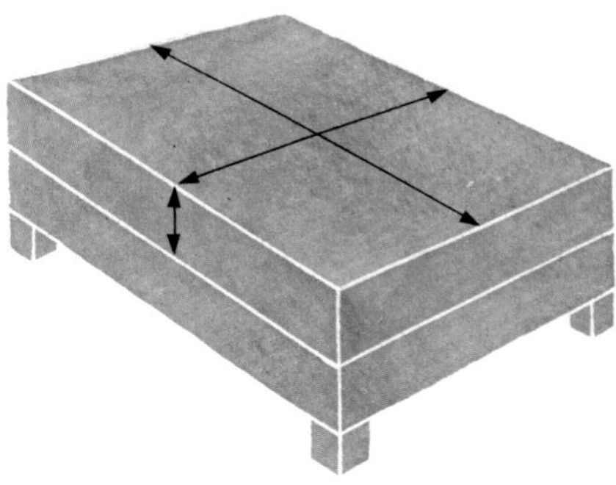

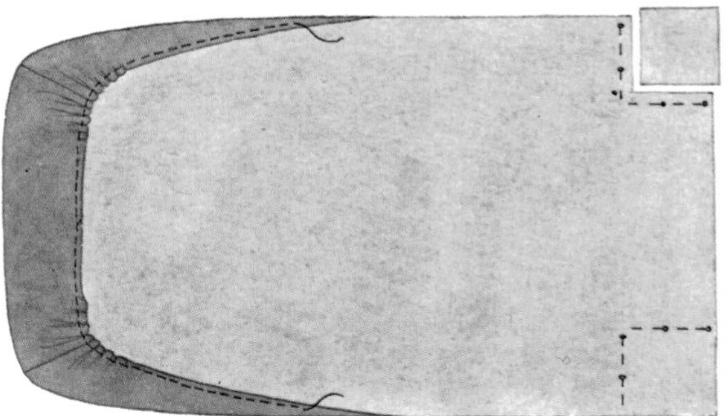

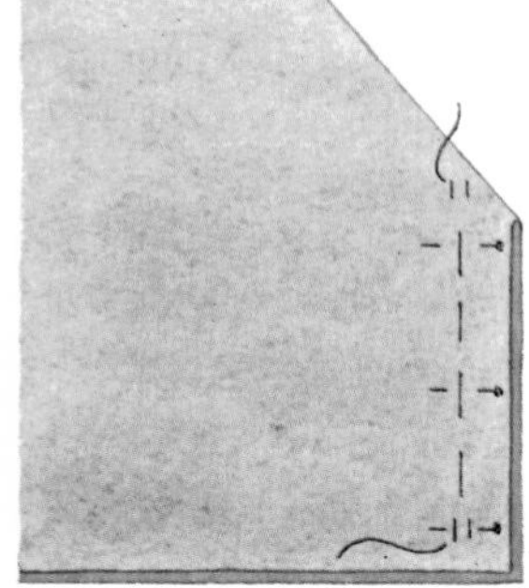

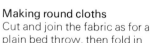

Sheets

Taking measurements Measure the length and width of the mattress and add twice the depth plus 8–12in (20–30cm) to both measurements – add 4in (10cm) seams for flat sheets. Buy the width of sheeting nearest (or larger than) your width to required length. For fitted sheets you will also need 1yd (1m) of $\frac{5}{8}$in (15mm) elastic.

Making flat sheets

Machine-stitch a hem along the top edge of the sheet, making 1in (2·5cm) for the first fold and 2in (5cm) for the second. Hem the bottom edge, making $\frac{1}{4}$in (5mm) and then $\frac{3}{4}$in (2cm) folds. There is no need for hems on the sides if you have not trimmed off the selvedges.

Making fitted sheets

1 Measure the depth of the mattress plus tuck-in along the edges from all the corners. Measure in the same amount on the straight grain at 90° to the edges, marking the lines with pins.

2 Cut out a square from each corner $\frac{1}{4}$in (5mm) outside the pinned lines. Pin the cut edges of the corner with RS together and machine-stitch, making $\frac{1}{4}$in (5mm) seams. Finish the edges.

3 Make a hem all around the edge, making $\frac{1}{4}$in (5mm) and then $\frac{3}{4}$in (2cm) folds and leaving $\frac{3}{4}$in (2cm) openings in the stitching, 6in (15cm) to each side of the corner seamlines.

4 Thread elastic through the hems between the openings at each corner. Stitch the elastic ends level with the openings so that the corners of the sheet gather. Stitch up the openings.

Ruffle

Zigzag scallops

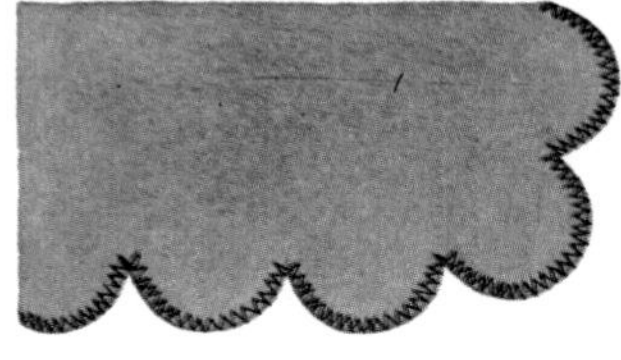

Binding

Facing

Pillows and quilt covers

You can make pillows to any shape or size, using any fabric from carpet or needlepoint to patchwork or lace. The front and back (or top and bottom) of the covers need not be the same and you can add piping to match or contrast if you wish.
If you want a conventionally shaped pillow – i.e. a rectangle, square or round – you can usually buy a ready-made pillow and make a cover to fit it. For unusual shapes you will have to make your own pillow. You can make pillows with the padding put straight into a cover but generally it is better to make an inner casing from a firmly woven fabric so that the main cover can be removed for cleaning.
Pillows may be filled with feathers (you will need a wax-coated casing fabric to prevent them from working through), solid or shredded foam, or a synthetic or kapok filling. Larger pillows may be filled with styrofoam granules to make bean-bag seats.
You can make pillows to varying depths by inserting a band or gusset between the two main sections. This type of pillow – known as box-sided – is often used for seating (it is more comfortable) and for intricate shapes (so they do not become distorted when filled).
Make covers for quilts like those for plain-edged pillows, using sheeting or any washable fabric.
For covers made from several pieces of fabric such as box-sided pillows and pillowcases (see next page) estimate the amount required by drawing the sections to scale on a cutting layout (see pp140–41).

Making pillows
Make the casing in the same way and to the same size (but without piping) as the cover (see below). Insert the stuffing, poking it into the corners well, and filling the case so that it is neither too soft nor too hard. Fold under the raw edges of the opening and overcast, using firm stitches, or machine-stitch together.

Openings and fastenings
Position the opening in a convenient place along the back, side or bottom edge of the casing or cover and make it long enough to insert the pillow.
For covers which will be removed frequently for cleaning, the opening may be fastened by a zipper, a touch-and-close strip (e.g. Velcro), buttons or by snap fasteners (the no-sew type is ideal).
Alternatively, after the padding has been inserted, you can machine-stitch or whip-stitch the openings on casings or slip-stitch those on covers (slip-stitching can easily be removed for laundering).
For quilt covers use sewn-on ties or finish as for a pillowcase (see p138).

Plain-edged pillows
Simple shapes To make a simple cover without piping for a square or rectangle, allow fabric of the pillow width by twice its length (or to twice the width by the length if easier) plus seam allowances on the raw edges. Cut out, fold in half across the width (or down the length) with RS together and machine-stitch both sides. Turn RS out. Fold under the seam allowances on the remaining side and finish with a fastening.
Other shapes Decide on the shape and size of the pillow and if complicated draw a paper pattern. Allow fabric of twice the overall size, plus seam allowances all around. Cut out to shape on double fabric. With RS together, join the pieces around the edges, including piping if you wish, and leave an opening in one side. Turn RS out and finish as for simple shapes.

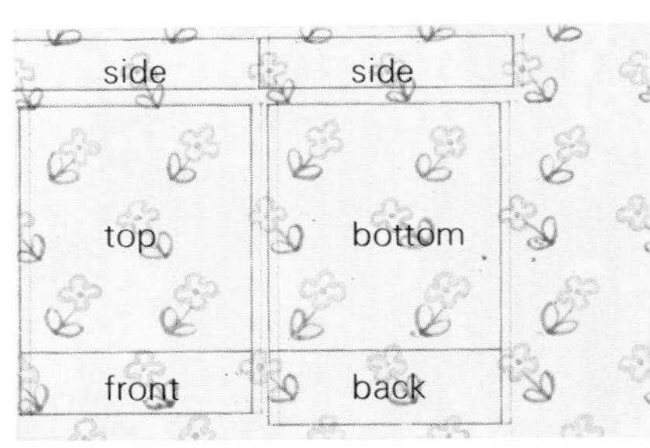

Box-sided pillows
Taking measurements For simple shapes measure the length, width and depth of the pillow. For more complicated shapes, draw a full-size paper pattern and measure the overall width and length.
For the top and bottom sections of the pillow allow 2 pieces of fabric of the required size allowing $\frac{5}{8}$in (15mm) seam allowances all around.
Rectangles and squares For the strip to fit the depth of the pillow, allow fabric to fit the depth by each side and the front plus $\frac{5}{8}$in (15mm) seam allowances all around. Allow a fourth strip to fit the depth plus $2\frac{1}{4}$in (6cm) to allow for a center opening by the back plus $1\frac{1}{8}$in (3cm).

Box-sided circles For the strip to fit the depth of the pillow allow 1 piece to fit the depth by two-thirds the circumference, plus $\frac{5}{8}$in (15mm) seam allowances all around, and, to allow for an opening, 1 piece to the depth plus $2\frac{1}{4}$in (6cm) by one-third the circumference plus $1\frac{1}{8}$in (3cm).
Other shapes Decide the position and length of the opening and allow a strip of the length plus $1\frac{1}{8}$in (3cm) by the pillow depth plus $2\frac{1}{4}$in (6cm). Allow strips to fit each remaining side, or the remaining length of the perimeter, by the pillow depth plus $\frac{5}{8}$in (15mm) seam allowances all around.

Making box-sided pillows
1 Cut out the pieces to size.
2 Prepare the opening, cut the wider strip in half lengthwise. With RS together, stitch the pieces for $\frac{5}{8}$in (15mm) from both ends along the cut edge. Insert a zipper into the remaining section (alternatively, slip-stitch the edges together after inserting the pillow).
3 With RS together and starting and ending each seam $\frac{5}{8}$in (15mm) from the ends, join the strips on the corresponding short edges to make a continuous piece. Apply piping to the RS of each edge if you wish. Clip the seam allowances of the strip on curves and at points where angles of the cover meet the strip where there is no seamline. A false seamline may be made on either the RS or WS of the continuous strip to accentuate a corner.

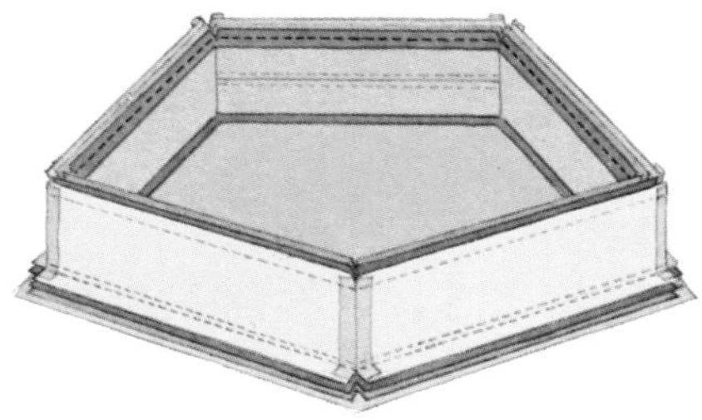

4 With RS together and matching clips join the strip to the main pieces (use a cording foot on the machine if including piping). Turn the cover RS out and press.

Quilt covers
Taking measurements
Measure the width of the quilt and add 4in (10cm) for ease and seam allowances. Allow fabric of this width by twice the quilt length plus 5in (13cm) for ease and hems. You will also need sufficient snap tape or alternative fastening.

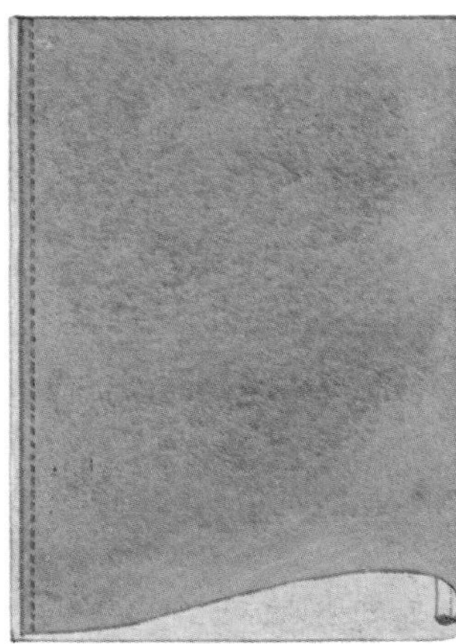

Making quilt covers
1 Cut out the fabric to size.
2 Fold the fabric in half across the width with WS together. Make French seams down each long side.
3 Make a hem around the opening making a first fold of $\frac{3}{8}$in (10mm) and then one of $1\frac{1}{2}$in (4cm).
4 Sew on fastenings to finish.

Basic stitches 18
Seams 20
Hems 28

Pillowcases

You can make pillowcases like plain-edged pillow covers (p134) but it is more usual to make them slightly larger than the pillow for ease in putting them on and to incorporate an extra pocket piece to hold the pillow in place instead of a fastening. As well as plain pillowcases, you can make them with a matching or contrasting gathered ruffle or with a flat border. You could also substitute a decorative edge for plain hems.

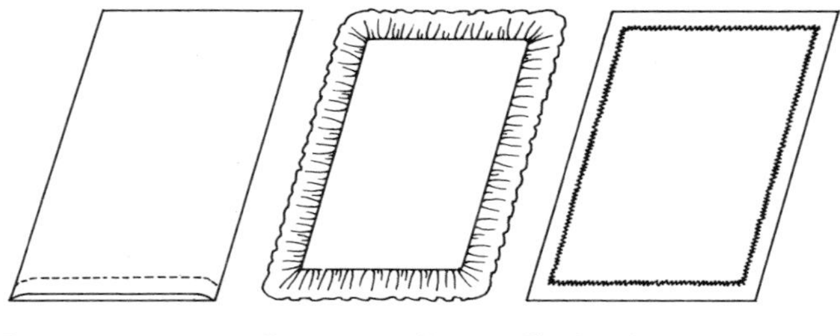

English-style   Gathered ruffle   Flat border

English-style pillowcases

Taking measurements Measure the width of the pillow (i.e. from side to side), double it and add 12in (30cm) for a pocket, ease and seam allowances. Allow fabric of this width by the pillow depth (i.e. from top to bottom) plus 2in (5cm).

Making pillowcases

1 Cut out the fabric to size; place 1 short side on the selvedge if possible.

2 Make a hem across the raw edge of one short end, making first a $\frac{1}{4}$in (5mm) fold and then a 2in (5cm) one. If the opposite end is not a selvedge, hem across it making $\frac{1}{4}$in (5mm) folds each time.

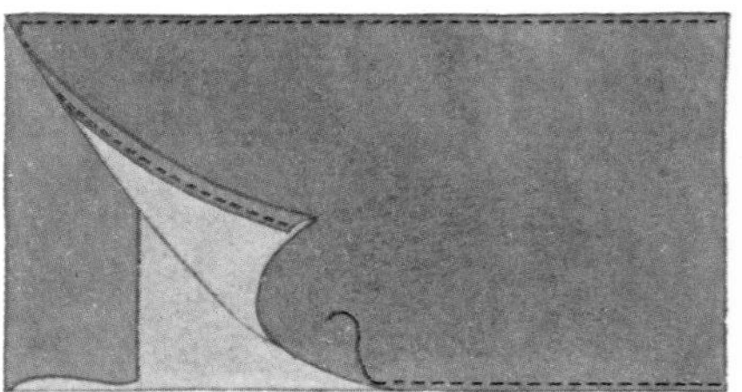

3 With WS together, fold down the short side with the selvedge or narrow hem for 6in (15cm). Fold the remaining section in half so that the pocket is enclosed and stitch taking $\frac{1}{4}$in (5mm) seams. Trim seams to $\frac{1}{8}$in (3mm).

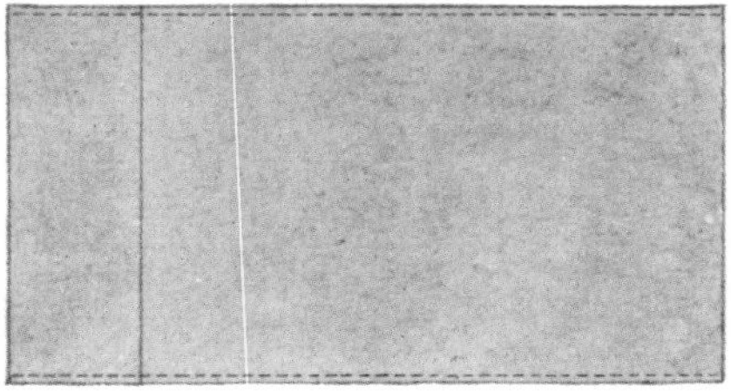

4 Turn WS out, refold as shown and stitch taking $\frac{1}{4}$in (5mm) seams. Press, turn pocket and pillowcase RS out.

Ruffled pillowcases

Taking measurements

Measure the width and depth of the pillow and allow 1 piece for the top section of these measurements plus 2in (5cm) each way for ease and seam allowances, 1 piece for the bottom section of the width plus $2\frac{3}{4}$in (7cm) by the depth plus 2in (5cm) and 1 piece for the pocket 8in (20cm) wide by the depth plus 2in (5cm).

To calculate for the ruffle, measure the perimeter of the pillow and allow strips of $1\frac{1}{2}$ times this by the required ruffle depth plus $\frac{3}{4}$in (2cm) for hems and seams. Alternatively you can make one from double fabric with a fold on the outer edge. Calculate as for the single ruffle by twice the depth plus $\frac{3}{4}$in (2cm).

Making ruffled pillowcases

1 Cut out the fabric to size; place 1 short side to a selvedge.

2 Make a hem across 1 short end of the wider piece, taking a first fold of $\frac{1}{4}$in (5mm) and a second fold of $\frac{5}{8}$in (15mm).

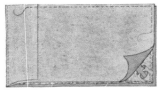

3 Make the ruffle and join the short ends to form a continuous piece. Make a narrow hem along the bottom edge. With RS together and raw edges even, gather and baste the ruffle to the top section of the pillowcase, easing around corners and taking $\frac{3}{8}$in (10mm) seams.

4 With the ruffle in position place the bottom and pocket sections on top as shown. Stitch making $\frac{3}{8}$in (10mm) seams. Finish the seams with overcasting or zigzagging and turn the pocket to the underside. Turn the pillowcase RS out.

Flat-border pillowcases

Taking measurements Measure the width and depth of the pillow – allow 1 piece for the bottom section to these measurements plus 2in (5cm) each way for ease and seam allowances, 1 piece for the top section plus 10in (25cm) each way for ease, seam allowances and border, and 1 piece for the pocket 8in (20cm) by pillow depth plus 2in (5cm).

Making flat-border pillowcases

1 Cut out the fabric to size, placing one long side of the pocket at a selvedge.

2 Make a $\frac{1}{4}$in (5mm) double hem along a short edge of the bottom section.

3 Fold under $\frac{3}{8}$in (1cm) and then 2in (5cm) onto the WS all around the top section and press. Open out the second folds and miter the corners. Re-fold the hems.

4 Place the pocket at one end of the top section WS together and insert the raw edges under the hem of the border. Baste and zigzag-stitch through all layers along the edge of the hem on the short edge of the pillowcase only. Work an inner row $\frac{1}{4}$in (5mm) from the first.

5 Place the bottom section on the pocket side of the top section with WS together so that the hem of the bottom section is level with the zigzag stitching. Tuck the raw edges under the hems of the top section. Baste and zigzag-stitch in position.

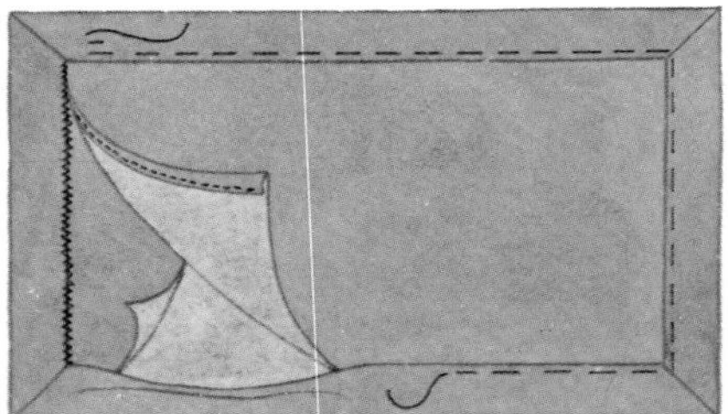

Fitted bedspreads and valances

Basic stitches 18
Seams 20
Hems 28
Gathering 29
Pleating 40
Scallops 102

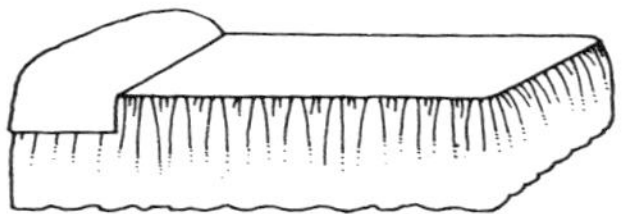

Gathered flounce

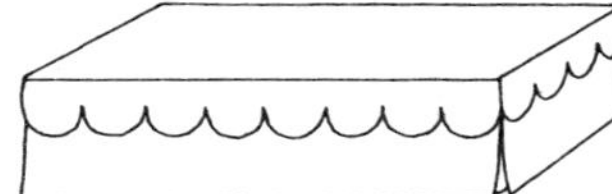

Valance with corner pleats and short bedspread

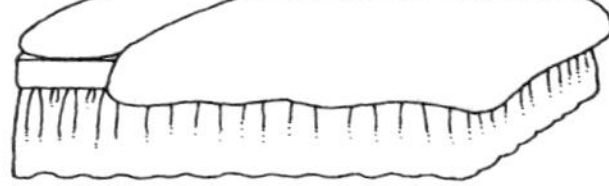

Dust ruffle with quilt

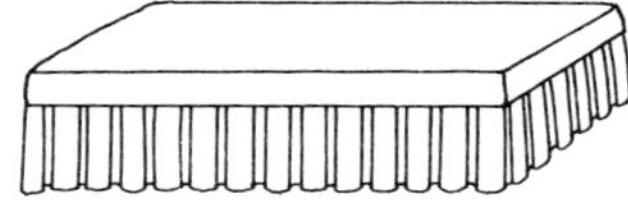

Box-sided dust ruffle with box pleats

Fitted bedspreads have one panel of fabric for the top of the bed with a plain, gathered or pleated flounce. You can make a more tailored version by adding box sides to the top panel so that the flounce begins at the base of the mattress. Valances which are put on the bed with the top panel below the mattress are also made as fitted bedspreads, often from matching fabric.

Decide which sides of the bed are to be covered by the flounce. If the head of the bed is placed against a wall you will probably need to fit the flounce to the sides and foot, or to the sides only if there is a foot board. For divan covers you may wish to include the head of the bed too. High pillows can distort the shape of the bedspread; to avoid this you can incorporate a pillow flap on the top edge of the bedspread as long as you are not attaching the flounce to this edge.

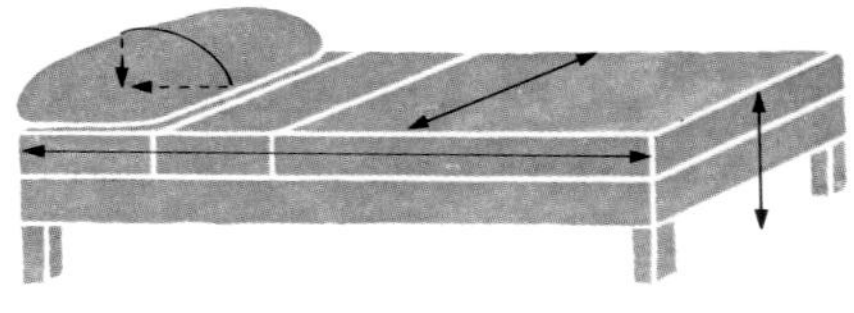

Taking measurements
Measure bed with usual bed dressing (without pillows if making a pillow flap).

Top panel Measure the length and width of the mattress and add $\frac{5}{8}$in (15mm) all around for seam allowances. For box sides, measure the depth of the mattress and add $1\frac{1}{8}$in (3cm).
Flounce Measure from top or bottom of the mattress to the floor, according to style, and add $\frac{5}{8}$in (15mm) to the top edge and $1\frac{1}{8}$in (3cm) to the bottom edge.

Pillow flap Replace the pillows. Measure across the pillows, from one side of the bed to the other, by the length from the head of the bed to the base of the pillows. Add 6in (15cm) to both measurements for ease, hems and seams.

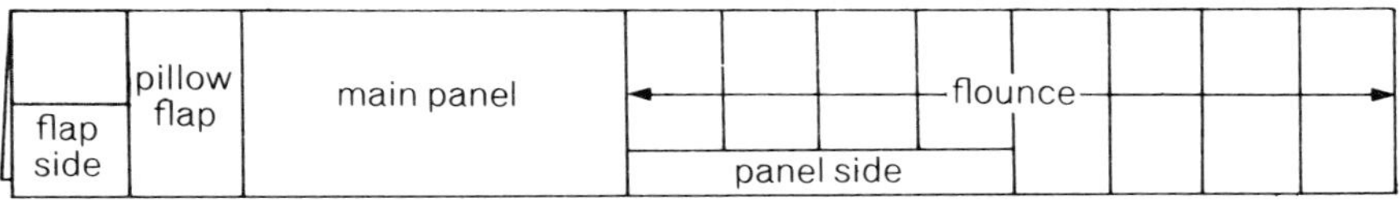

Fabric amounts
Make a cutting layout to scale (see p141) showing each required size and shape.
Top panel Calculate amount required for this and flap as for a plain bed throw.
Flounce Calculate the amount of fabric to fit the required edges of the top panel using the same principles as for a gathered or pleated skirt.
For plain sides and pleated corners, calculate as for a slipcover skirt (p140).
Box sides Attach box sides in 1 continuous strip (the seams may not necessarily fall at the corners). To attach these to the sides and foot of the bed only, add the width of the mattress to twice its length. If you are also attaching it to the head of the bed, add twice the mattress width to twice its length. Divide the width of the fabric you are using into the total length of the box side to give the number of complete fabric widths required. Multiply this number by $1\frac{1}{8}$in (3cm) (seam allowance) and add to the remaining figure plus $2\frac{1}{4}$in (6cm) (side hem allowance) for the width of the remaining panel. Draw all these panels to the required depth on the cutting layout.

Making the bedspread
1 Cut and join the fabric for the top panel and flap as for a plain bed throw (p132). Make a double $\frac{3}{8}$in (10mm) hem along the bottom edge and for twice the mattress depth from the end on each side if you have a footboard.
2 If you are having box sides, join the panels on their side edges. Mark off the length of the top panel edges along the top of the strip and clip into the seam allowance at each mark.
3 With RS together and matching the marks on the strip to the corners of the top panel, stitch the pieces together.
4 Join the panels for the flounce, make hems along the bottom edge and also at the side edges if you are not including it on the head of the bed. Gather or pleat the top edge of the flounce according to your chosen style. For sewing inverted pleats see p145. Attach it to the top panel making $\frac{5}{8}$in (15mm) seams and leaving $\frac{5}{8}$in (15mm) from the top edge on each side if not attaching the flounce to this edge.

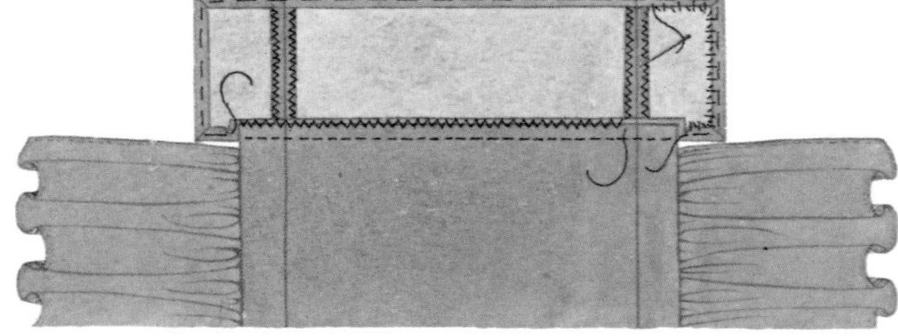

5 To attach the flap, place the RS of the top edge of the flap centrally on the WS of the top edge of the bedspread. Stitch for the width of the top panel only, taking $\frac{5}{8}$in (15mm) seams. Turn under and make hems along the remaining raw edges, mitering corners.
6 When putting the bedspread on the bed, place the pillows on the bedspread, fold back the flap over them and tuck it in underneath.

Slipcovers

Slipcovers are removable covers fitted over the original upholstery of armchairs and sofas. With the exception of those covered in velvet or leather, almost any upholstered furniture can be fitted with them. Modern furniture is sometimes upholstered in muslin so that a slipcover in the customer's choice may be fitted. Slipcovers are an excellent way of extending the life of shabby furniture although you should not regard them as an inexpensive form of re-upholstery, since they will not disguise lumpy padding or sagging springs. Their main benefit is that you can remove them easily for cleaning, but other advantages are that you can vary the decor of a room by having two sets of covers in different fabrics and you can replace worn panels easily.

Choose a fabric which is recommended for slipcovers by the manufacturer. It should be tough, firmly woven, color-fast and pre-shrunk. Avoid thick fabrics as these can be awkward, particularly on piped seams.

The sections
In most cases the sections and seams of the slipcover should correspond to those on the original upholstery. The main exception to this is on scroll arms where the slipcover should be seamed on the guide line—an imaginary line on the outside arm (B-I). It is placed here, rather than below the arm as on the upholstery, for ease in putting the cover on.
Tuck-in allowances are added to some sections of the cover so that they can be pushed into the crevices of the upholstery where the inside back joins the arms and seat. This anchors the cover and helps to prevent strain.

Finishes
Piping It is advisable to pipe all the main exposed seams of the cover to give it a professional finish and to add strength. Allow $1\frac{5}{8}$yd (1·40m) fabric for cutting bias strips for piping seams on chairs and $2\frac{5}{8}$yd (2·40m) for sofas.
Plain bottom For a plain bottom to tie underneath the chair or sofa, allow fabric to cut 4 strips, 4in (10cm) deep by the width of each side between the legs.
Skirt For a tailored skirt with inverted corner pleats, measure the width of each side of the furniture 6in (15cm) above the floor and allow pieces of fabric of these widths plus 7in (18cm) by $6\frac{3}{4}$in (17·5cm) deep. For corner pleats allow 4 strips $7 \times 6\frac{3}{4}$in ($18 \times 17{\cdot}5$cm).

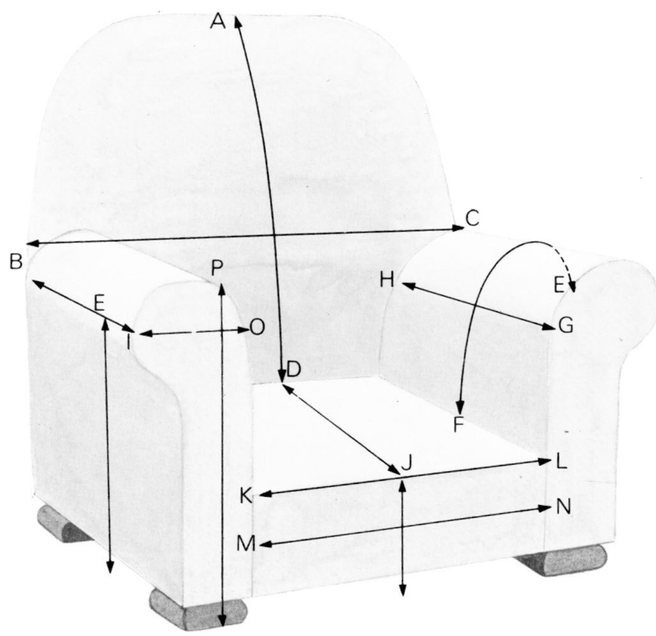

Taking measurements
Scroll-armed furniture
Remove any cushions and using a fabric tape measure, measure each section including cushions horizontally at the widest and vertically at the longest points. If your particular chair or sofa sections are not shown, measure them by the same principle.
If you intend to finish the cover with a skirt, subtract 6in (15cm) from the length measurements of the outside arms and back and the front arms and border.
Outside back: from A to floor; from B to C.
Inside back: from A to D plus 6in (15cm) for tuck-in; from B to C.
Inside arm: from E to F plus 6in (15cm) for tuck-in; from G to H plus 6in (15cm) for tuck-in.
Outside arm: from E to floor; from B to I.
Seat: from J to D plus 6in (15cm) for tuck-in; from K to L plus 6in (15cm) each side for tuck-ins.
Border: from J to floor; from M to N.
Front arm: from I to O; from P to floor.
Add $1\frac{1}{8}$in (3cm) seam allowance to each measurement.

Seams and edge finishes 20
Zippers 26
Hems 28
Fastenings 32
Pleating 40
Openings 60
Piping 102
Pillows 134

Taking measurements
Box-armed furniture
Measure all sections excluding the arms as scroll-armed furniture.
Outside arm: from A to floor; from B to C.
Inside arm: from D to E plus 6in (15cm) for tuck-in; from F to G plus 6in (15cm) for tuck-in.
Box sections: measure the width and length of each section as for a box-sided pillow. Add $1\frac{1}{8}$in (3cm) seam allowance to each measurement.

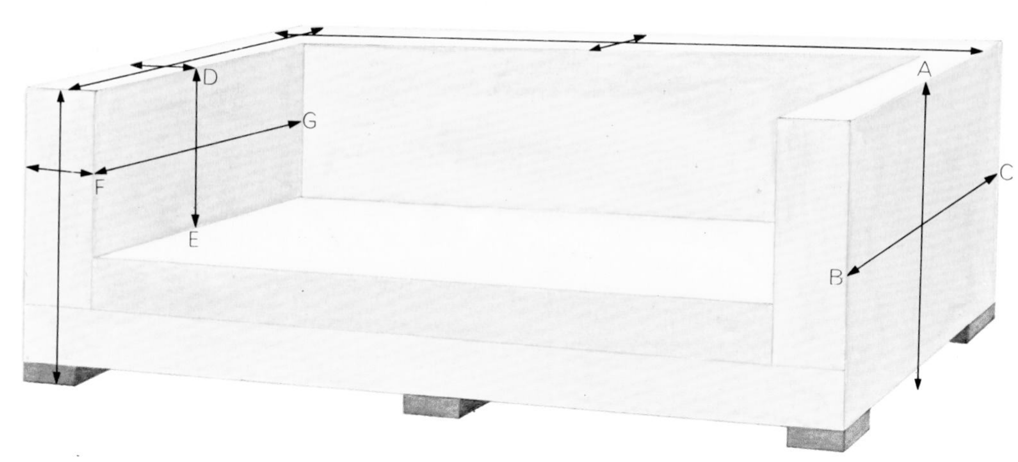

Sofas You will probably have to join the fabric to make sections wide enough for the inside and outside back and the front borders. The best way of doing this is to position a complete fabric width in the center and join narrower strips to each side. To calculate the width of the strips, subtract the fabric width less $1\frac{1}{8}$in (3cm) for seams from the total width of the section and halve the remainder. Add $\frac{5}{8}$in (15mm) to each edge of the strips for seams. Join the sections before fitting the cover.

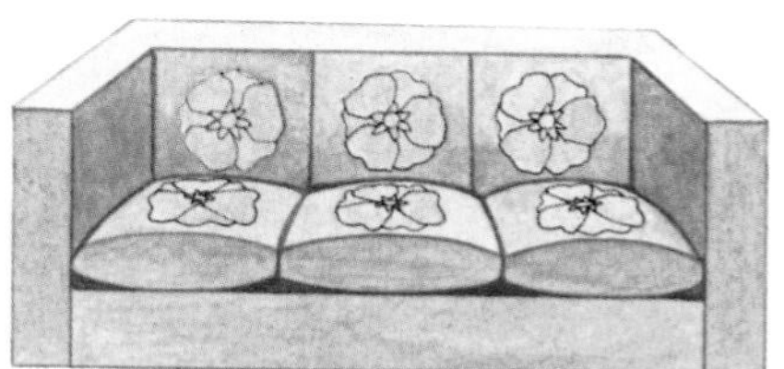

Alternatively if your fabric has a large single motif you could cut the fabric into strips to display it attractively and join them to make the required width. If you have seat cushions try to cut them out to display the motifs in a similar way, placing them centrally on the main sections.

Use the remaining fabric to cut the box strips on the straight grain and the piping casings on the bias grain of the fabric.

Fabric amounts
No paper pattern is needed for slipcovers because you shape the fabric on the furniture from rectangles cut to the overall dimensions of each section. Before buying fabric, calculate the amount required from the measurements of each section. From these draw a cutting layout using the fabric in the most economical way. Mark the size of the pattern repeat on the layouts as a position guide.

The cutting layout
Using a simple scale, e.g. $\frac{1}{16}$in to equal 1in (1mm = 1cm) draw 2 parallel lines to represent the width of fabric. On another sheet of paper draw rectangles to the same scale to represent each section of the cover. Label each rectangle and mark its dimensions. Cut out these rectangles and arrange them closely together on the fabric layout with the lengthwise measurement parallel to the fabric edges. Pin in place. Measure the length of the layout, convert back in scale and add on the piping allowance to give the amount of fabric required.
For displaying a large motif, add one extra repeat to allow for any layout adjustments.

Cutting the fabric
Before cutting out, lay the fabric on the furniture to check your position and cutting plan. Make changes in the plan if necessary. Following your layout cut out each rectangle.

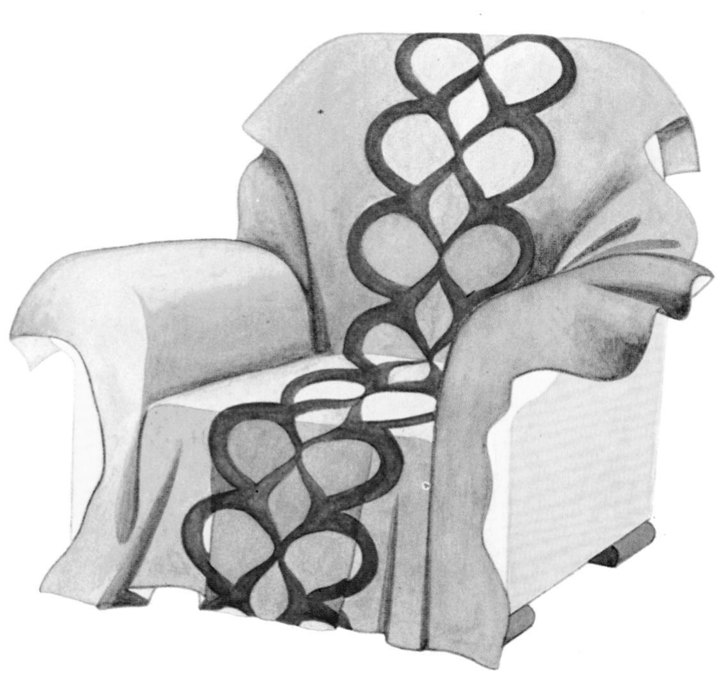

Seams and edge finishes 20
Zippers 26
Hems 28
Fastenings 32
Pleating 40
Openings 60
Piping 102
Pillows 134

Fitting slipcovers
The method of fitting the sections on the chair is to fold them in half with WS together and then, working from the center out to the side, fit, pin and trim. The fabric is then opened out and the sections seamed together.
Start by marking a line with straight pins placed into the old cover up the center of the outside back, down the inside back and along the seat from back to the front border and then to the floor.

Outside back
Fold the fabric in half lengthwise and place the fold level with the pins down the back of the chair so that the seam allowances project at the top, side and bottom. Pin the fold to the old cover, then smooth the fabric out to the side and pin again at the line of the joining, placing the pins at 90° to the edge. Keep the fabric smooth and taut and with the grain straight in both directions.

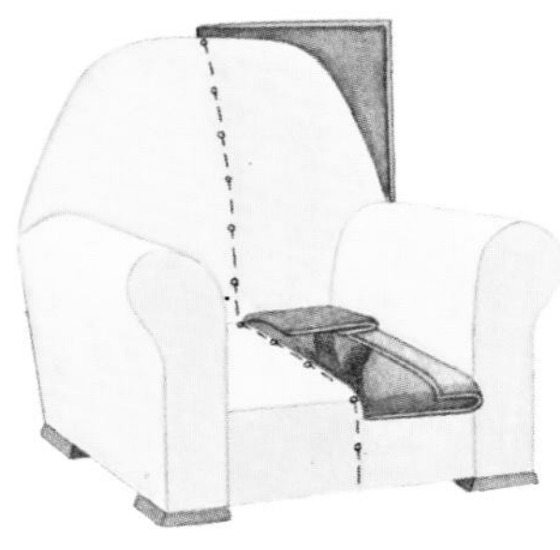

Seat
Fold and pin the section in position on the corresponding side of the chair so that the allowance for the tuck-in lies at the back and side and the seam allowance projects at the front. Fold back the tuck-in onto the seat and leave for now.

Inside back
Fold and pin to the old cover in the same way, then pin to the outside back at the top of the chair following the shape and joining line of the upholstery. The fullness of some shapes can be eased in but with others you may

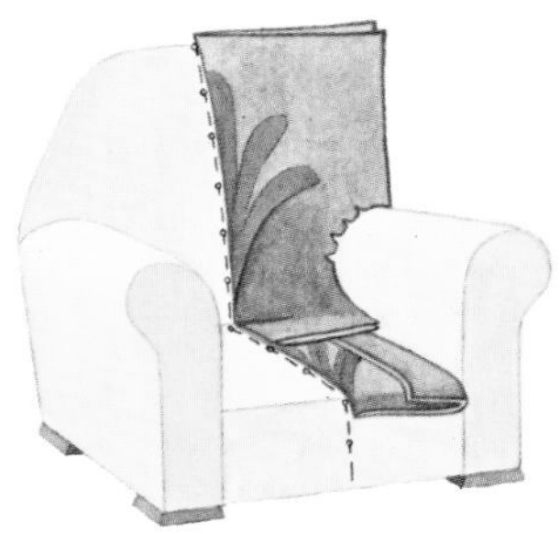

have to fit it with small darts at the corners. Pin the pieces together down the sides, working from the top down, along the line of the upholstery joining. At the arm, cut into the fabric from the sides so that the inside back can be wrapped around smoothly.
Carefully cut the curve over the arm, extending it outward at the bottom to the full width of the tuck-in allowance. Clip seam allowance on the crown of the curve. Pin edges of tuck-ins together.

Inside arms
Place the pieces with WS together on the inside arm so that the seam allowances project at the front, and the top edge overlaps the guide line at the front edge. Keep the crosswise grain straight on the inside arm and let the rest overlap the guide line. Pin the front edge to the old cover first, smooth the fabric across the arm and then pin it to the guide line. Pin the bottom edge to the tuck-in edge of the seat and cut the back edge to correspond with the inside back.

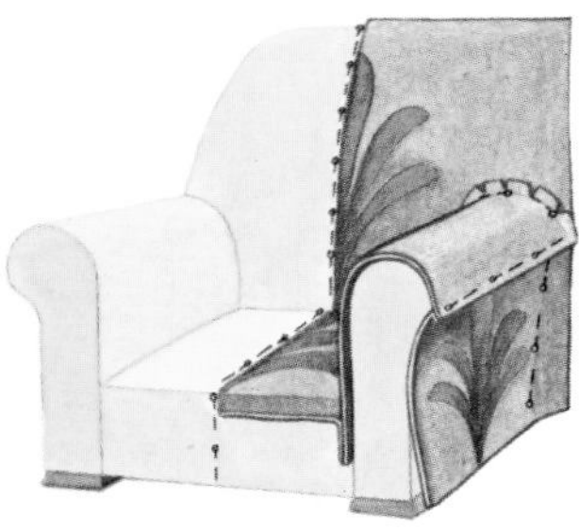

Outside arms
Place the pieces with WS together in position, with the seam allowances projecting at the front and the top edge overlapping the guide line by $\frac{5}{8}$in (15mm) at the front edge. Keeping the grain straight, pin it to the inside arms on the guide line, making larger seams as necessary toward the back of the arm if the padding is less rounded.
Pin the back edge to the outside back.
Leave the front edge free but pin the bottom edge to the old cover.

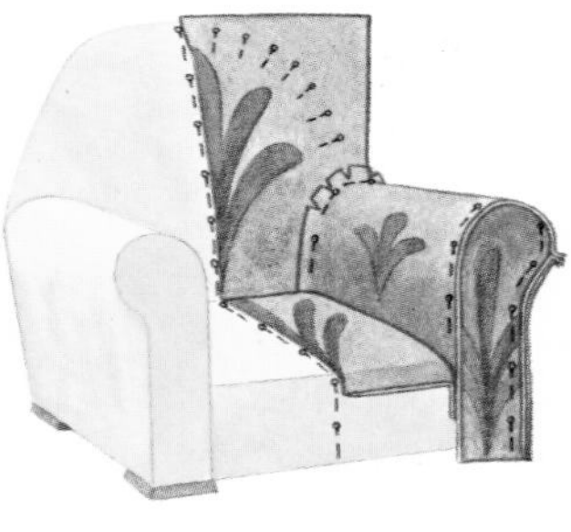

Front arms
Push the tuck-ins in position, then place the pieces for the front arms with WS together in position, pinning to the inside and outside arm sections, following the shape and original joining line. Pin to the inside arm tuck-in.

Front border
Leave this and fit it when you have seamed the other pieces.

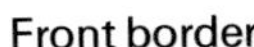

Cushions
Fit and assemble as described for pillows on pp134–5.

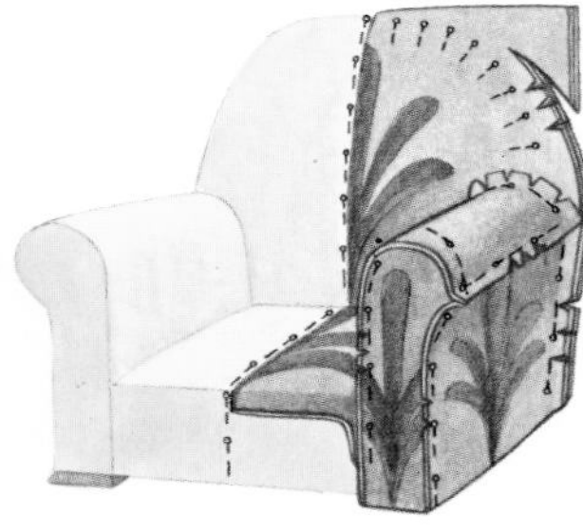

Notching seams
Trim all the seams exactly to within $\frac{5}{8}$in (15mm) of the pinned seamlines. Cut notches in the corresponding seams in groups of 2 or 3 so that you can fit the pieces easily together again.

Fitting and making box-armed covers
Follow the same method as for scroll-armed covers, but insert the box pieces between the inside and outside arms and the inside and outside back. Join the box sections of the arms and back with either a straight or a mitered seam.
When making the cover apply piping to both edges of the whole length of the box strip, to the sides of the outside back and to the seat front.

Assembling scroll-armed covers
Remove all the pins, take the sections off the chair and open them out. Note that as cotton piping cord shrinks when washed it is advisable to boil and dry it twice before using it. In soft furnishing a medium thick piping cord is recommended.
The bias strips should be cut $1\frac{1}{2}$in (4cm) wide. Use a cording foot in the machine for all seams which include piping. Make up the required lengths of piping and baste to the sides and top of the outside back, front arm, the top of the outside arm and the seat front, including tuck-in, so that the stitching is $\frac{5}{8}$in (15mm) from the raw edges. Stitch all seams in the order shown, placing the pieces with RS together and making $\frac{5}{8}$in (15mm) seams. Press all seams away from the front of the chair as soon as they are stitched and finish the edges with zigzag stitch or by straight-stitching $\frac{1}{4}$in (5mm) from the edges and then trimming with pinking shears. Leave an opening at the back by stitching the seam to within 4in (10cm) of the arm.

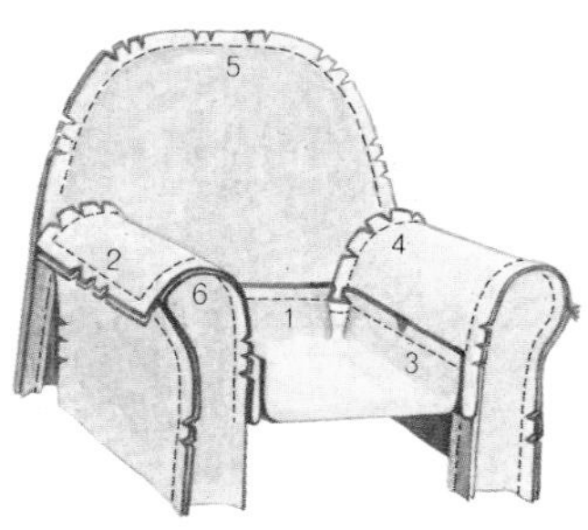

Front border
Put the cover on the chair with the RS out. Tuck in the sides and back and leave the seam allowance protruding at the front edge of the seat. Place the front border in position and pin it to the front of the seat and to the seam allowance of the tuck-in with WS together. Pin it to the front arms below the seat tuck-in. Trim the seams to $\frac{5}{8}$in (15mm); remove cover from chair. Stitch the border to the cover with RS together.

Back opening
The opening may be finished with a zipper touch and close tape such as Velcro, or hooks and eyes. If using hooks and eyes, prepare the opening by binding with a straight strip of fabric 3in (7·5cm) wide. Fold the binding on the outside arm to the inside of the cover and sew the hooks to the cover level with the fold. Leave the binding on the outside back so that it extends and sew on the eyes level with the inner edge of the binding so that the binding forms an underlap.

Finishing the bottom
Cut a bias strip for piping to fit the bottom edge of the cover plus $1\frac{1}{8}$in (3cm). Fold under $\frac{5}{8}$in (15mm) at each end and make the piping. Attach to the cover so that the stitching is $\frac{5}{8}$in (15mm) from the edge and the ends fall at the back opening.
Plain finish In order to tie the cover underneath, trim the short ends of the strips so that they clear the inside of the leg. Make a narrow hem on the angled ends of each strip and then a casing $\frac{5}{8}$in (15mm) wide on the inner long edge. Stitch the raw edges of the strips to the bottom of the cover. Insert a long piece of tape through the casings, place the cover on the chair (after fitting the back opening) and tie in one corner.

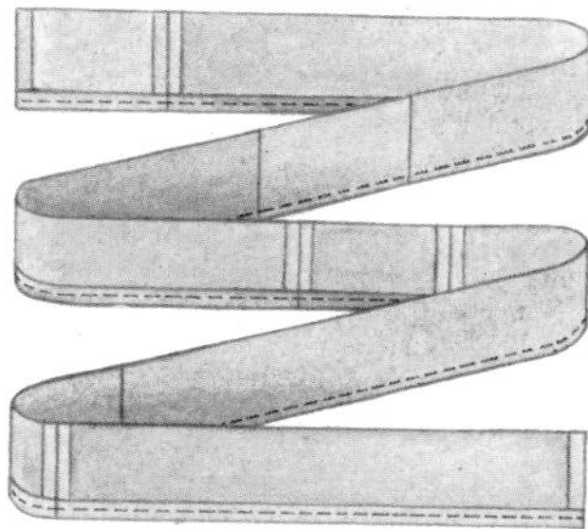

Skirt Join the skirt pieces together placing a short piece between them at the corners and leaving the back corner open to correspond with the opening on the main part of the cover.
Make $\frac{5}{8}$in (15mm) double hems along the bottom edges of all skirt sections and narrow hems at the opening. From the RS make an inverted pleat at the corners so that the seams are on the inside fold of the pleat.
Stitch the skirt to the cover, incorporating the piping into the seam. Attach hooks and eyes to secure the pleat at the opening.

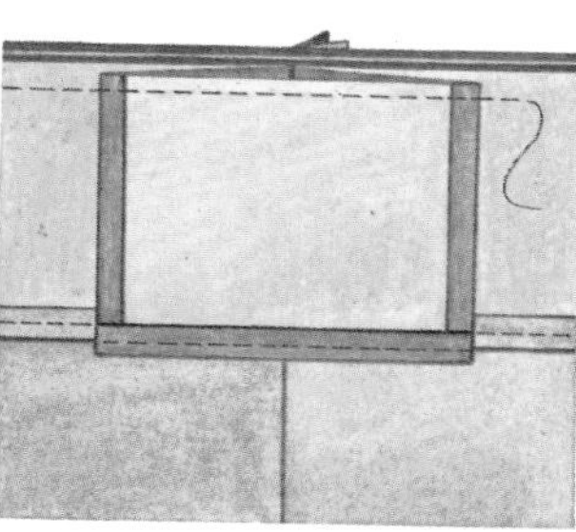

Lampshades

Lampshades made with slip-on covers may be removed easily for washing. The fabric is gathered and the cover overlaps the rings of the frame. A second method with permanent covers sewn or glued to the frame gives a more tailored finish and does not overlap the frame. (Details of the gluing method are given on pp148–9.)

Both methods can be used for all lampshade shapes except for the more difficult curved empire shape.

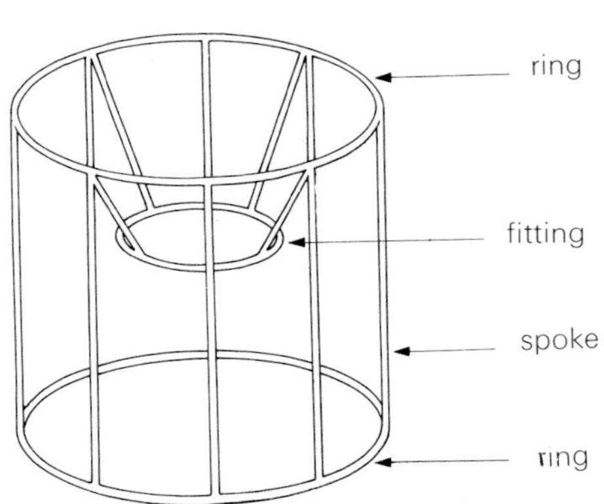

Choosing your frame

Check the frame for correct suspension or table lamp fitting – make sure joints are securely soldered.

Choosing fabrics

Choose a translucent fabric which will not be affected by heat from the light bulb. Dark colors or heavy fabrics can be lined with a light color to reflect light. Interline sheer fabrics to hide spokes.

Calculating amounts

Measure circumference of frame at its widest part and add $\frac{3}{8}$in (10mm) for seams. If total is narrower than width of fabric you are using, allow fabric the length of the spokes plus 4in (10cm) If it is more than the fabric width, allow fabric twice the spoke length plus 8in (20cm). For lining use a light-weight plain fabric and allow the same amount.

Preparing the frame

Unless your frame is plastic-coated, it is advisable to prevent rusting by painting it with a coat of enamel – leave to dry until hard before making the lampshade. If you are sewing the cover to the frame you will also need plain weave cotton tape $\frac{3}{8}$in (1cm) wide for binding the rings; double the circumference of each ring to give the amount.

Trimmings

The raw edges of sewn-on covers are usually finished by covering them with a trimming. This may be narrow ribbon, braid or fringe. Allow enough trimming to fit around both rings plus about 2in (5cm) for seams.

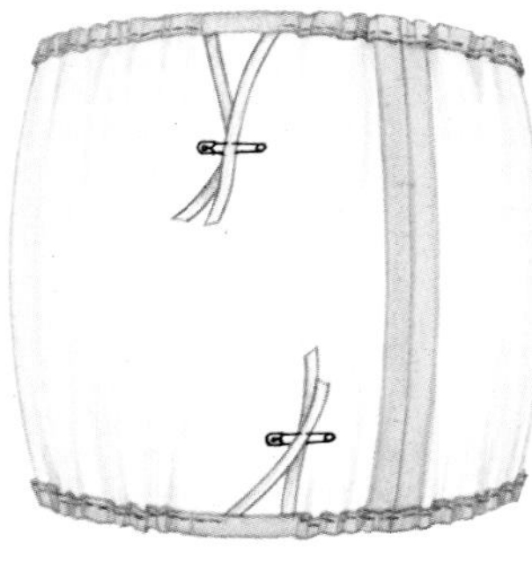

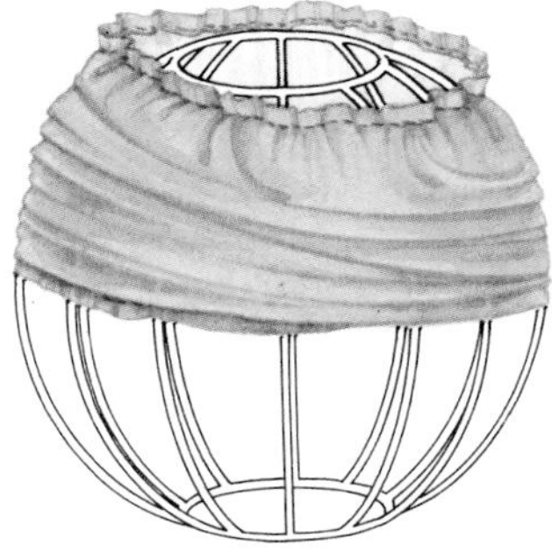

Slip-on covers

You will need

frame
fabric in calculated amount
matching sewing thread
cord elastic, the length of each ring

Making the cover

1 Cut the fabric to the size calculated. If you have to join the fabric to make the width required, cut each section to half the circumference of the frame plus $\frac{3}{8}$in (10mm).

2 With RS together and making $\frac{1}{4}$in (5mm) seams, join the vertical edges of the fabric. Trim and press seams open.

3 Make a hem along both edges, taking $\frac{1}{4}$in (5mm) for the first fold and $\frac{3}{8}$in (10mm) for the second fold. Machine-stitch, leaving $\frac{5}{8}$in (15mm) openings in the stitching.

4 Thread elastic through the hems and pin the ends together. Place the fabric RS out over the frame so that it overlaps equally at top and bottom. Pull up the elastic to draw the fabric over both edges of the frame. Knot the elastic ends together and insert the ends neatly into the casings.

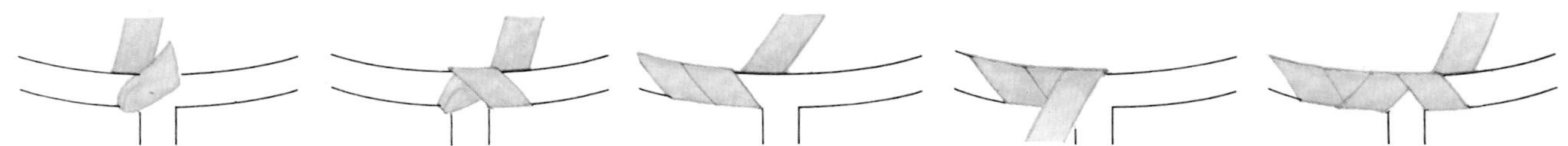

Sewn-on cover

You will need

frame
tape for binding
fabric in calculated amount
matching sewing thread
trimming
glue

Binding the frame

1 Cut pieces of tape to twice the circumference of each ring. Place one end of the tape under the ring at a joint with a spoke, bring the tape over the joint and bind over the end of the tape. Continue binding the ring as tightly as possible, keeping the tape at an acute angle and slightly overlapping the previous wrap.
2 At each spoke, wrap the binding around the ring an extra time before you reach the spoke and then continue binding on the other side of it.
3 To finish pull the tape end through a previous loop and secure with a few stitches. Cut off any excess tape.

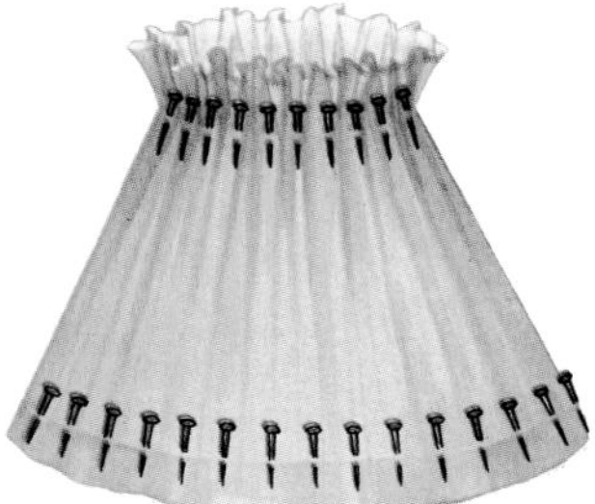

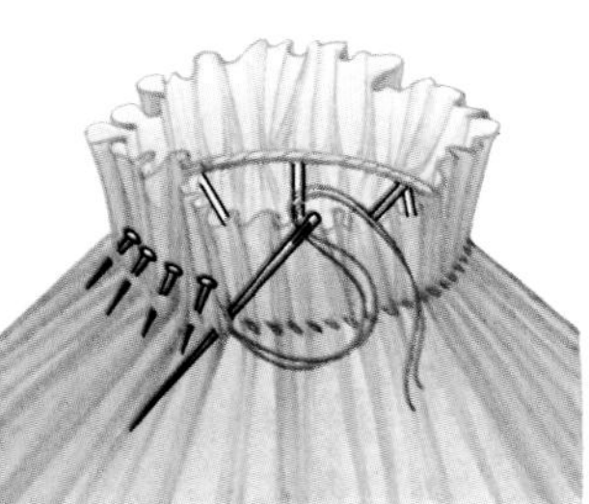

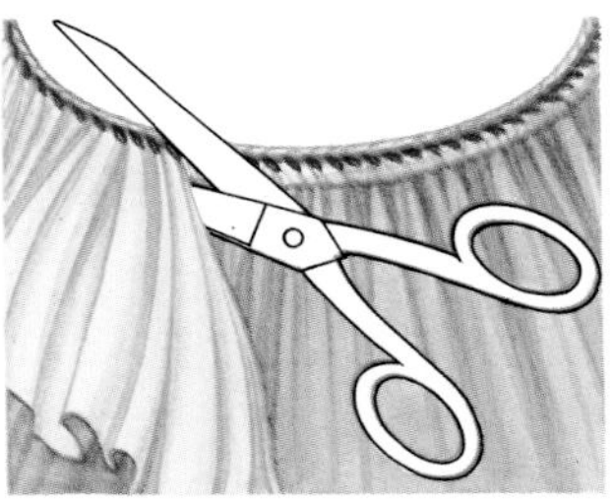

Attaching the cover

1 Cut and join the fabric as for a slip-on cover.
2 Place the fabric RS out over the frame so that the seams align with spokes and an equal amount extends at top and bottom.
3 Pin the fabric to the binding around the bottom ring, easing or pleating any fullness evenly.
4 Smooth the cover up the line of the spokes to the top ring, keeping the grain straight, and pin to the binding at the top of each spoke. Fold any fullness between spokes into tiny pleats and pin them down.
5 Using double thread, overcast the fabric to the binding on the outside of the rings, making sure that you catch-stitch the pleats.
6 If you are not lining the fabric, turn the surplus fabric back over the stitching so that the fold is level with the outer edge of the rings and stitch to the binding again through all thicknesses.
7 Trim off the surplus fabric close to the stitching. Apply the lining if using one.
8 Cover the raw edges by gluing on the trimming. To do this, fold under one end of it, place the fold in line with one of the cover seamlines and with the outer edges of the trimming and rings level. Cover the WS of trimming with glue, and smooth the trimming down on the cover, keeping it as straight as possible. At the end, fold it under to meet the first fold and press down securely.

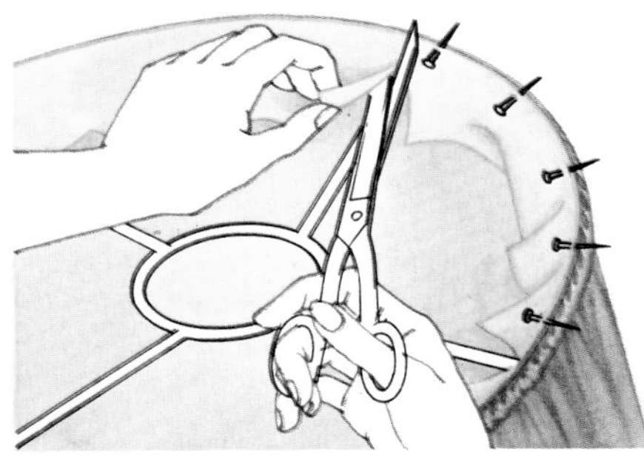

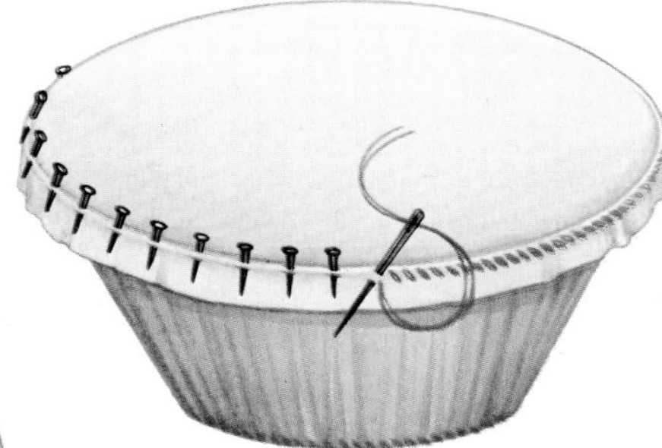

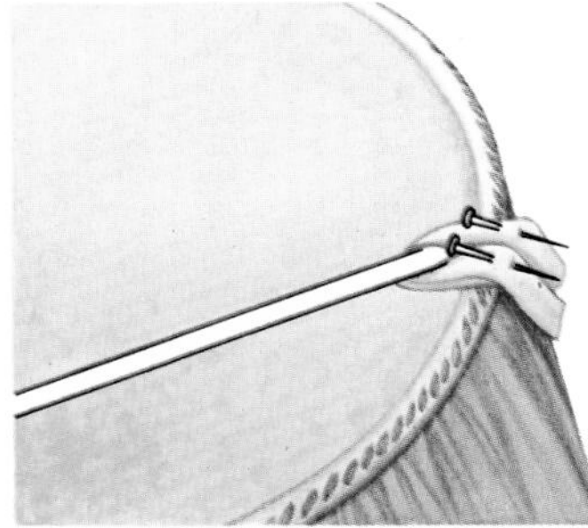

Lining the shade

1 Make the lining as for the main cover. After attaching the main cover, place the lining with RS facing inside the frame and pin it to the rings in the same way as the outer cover, slitting the fabric to fit it around the bars of the frame.
2 Roll the fabric over the top ring to the outside of the frame and fold it under at each side of the slits. Stitch the lining to the frame, placing the stitches over those of the main cover. Cut off the excess fabric close to the stitches.
3 To finish the slits, cut bias strips 2 × 1 in (5 × 2·5cm). Fold in the raw edges to meet in the middle with WS together, and fold the strip in half again. Slip-stitch the folds lightly together.
4 Loop each strip loosely around the bar of the fixture so that it covers the slit. Stitch the ends to the ring and trim off any surplus length.

Glued lampshades

Gluing the fabric to the frame is a quick and easy way of making a lampshade, particularly if you use ready-backed fabric (see below). For your first attempt at making one, choose a straight drum shape (i.e. with top and bottom rings of equal diameter) so that you do not have to make a paper pattern.

The fabric

With the glued method of making lampshades the fabric is first applied to a stiff backing. You can buy fabric which is already bonded to the backing or you can buy the backing and apply it to the fabric yourself. Buy enough fabric to fit the circumference plus $\frac{1}{4}$in (5mm) overlap by the height of the shade or the overall size of the paper pattern if you have to make one (see below).

The frame

Although standard frames with spokes can be used for glued lampshades, all you actually need is a ring for the top and bottom – the structure between them is formed by the stiffness of the fabric. The rings are sold in a wide range of diameters so that you can vary the size and shape of the lampshade and decide its height to suit yourself. Check when you buy them that the top ring has the right attachment to suit your light bulb fixture.

You will also need sufficient self-bonding parchment and fabric to cover, $\frac{5}{8}$in (15mm) self-adhesive cotton tape to fit around both rings, a tube of clear glue, a cardboard tube and some snap clothespins.

When using commercially bonded fabrics it is possible to prevent the white edge of the cut cardboard from showing. Add an extra $\frac{1}{4}$in (5mm) to the pattern on the edge to be joined. Cut away $\frac{1}{4}$in (5mm) of backing and turn the soft fabric over the cut edge and glue to the back. This finished edge then forms the overlap.

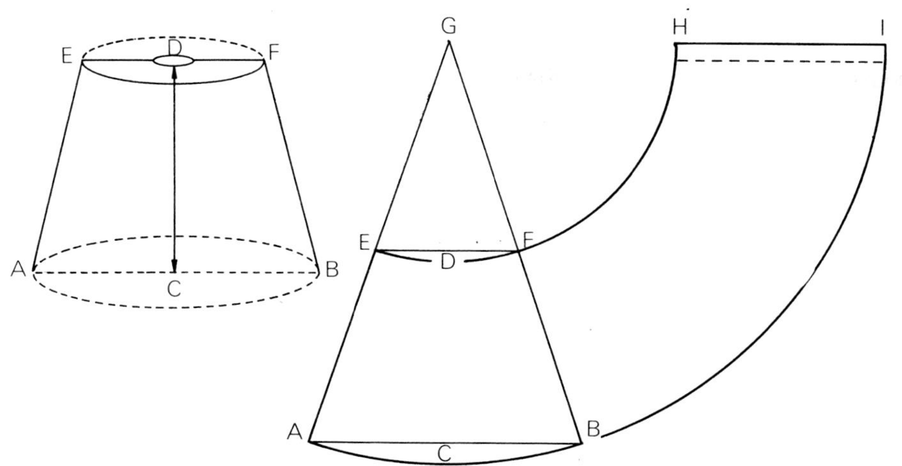

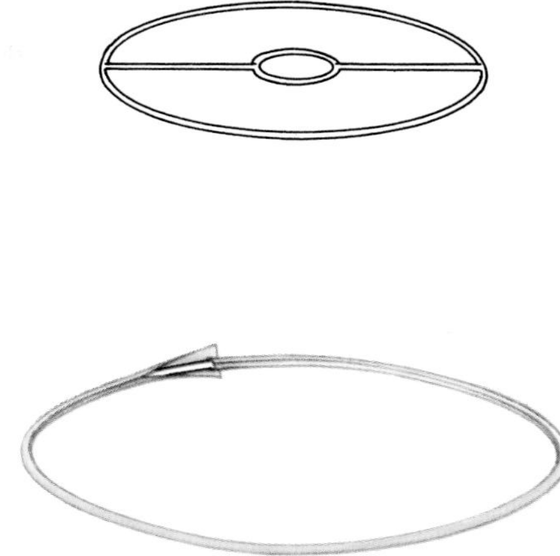

Making a pattern

If the diameters of the top and bottom rings are different, you will have to make a paper pattern for the cover, using a large sheet of graph paper.

1 Starting at the bottom left-hand corner of the paper draw a line (A–B) equal to the diameter of the bottom ring. Draw a perpendicular line upward from the center of A–B to the required height of the shade (C–D).

2 At D draw another line, E–F, to the diameter of the top ring with D as the center. Join A–E and B–F and extend the lines to intersect at G.

3 Using G–E as the radius, draw an arc from E which is equal in length to the circumference of the top ring (measure length of the arc with a piece of string).

4 Using G–A as a radius, draw another arc from A equal to the circumference of the bottom ring. Add $\frac{3}{8}$in (10mm) to each arc for turnings and then join them (H–I). Cut around A–E–H–I for the paper pattern. Fit pattern to rings to check for accuracy.

Preparing the frame

Cut a piece of self-adhesive tape to fit each ring. Press the center of the adhesive side to the outside of the ring, then turn over one edge to the outside of the ring and press down. Turn over the other side in the same way and press down so that it overlaps the first edge smoothly.

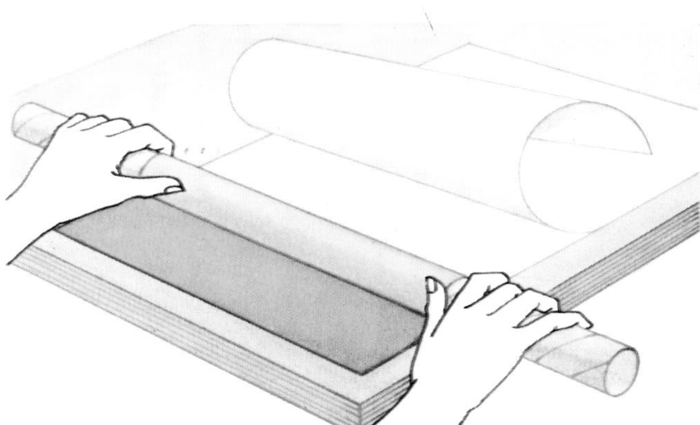

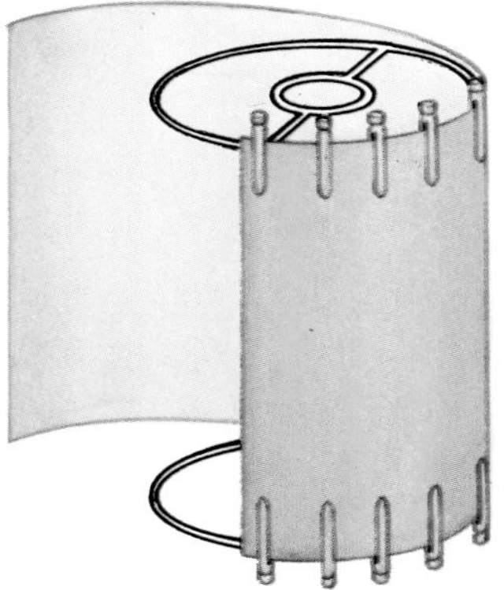

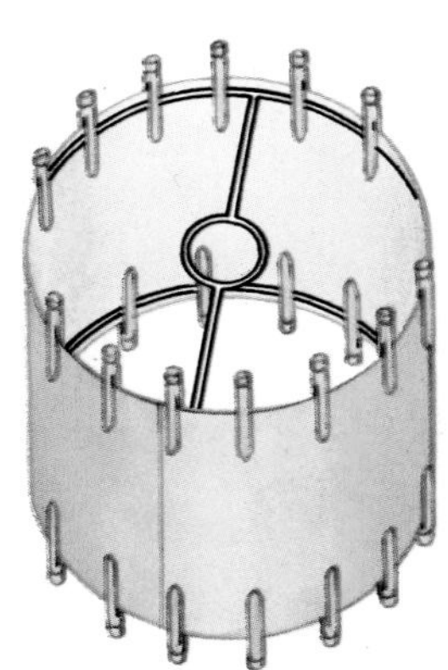

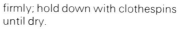

Preparing the fabric

1 If you are using a paper pattern, cut out the fabric from it allowing $\frac{1}{4}$in (5mm) hems on the curved edges only. Otherwise cut out a piece of fabric on the straight grain to the height of the lampshade by the circumference of the rings allowing $\frac{1}{4}$in (5mm) hems all around.

2 Fold the turnings along the top and bottom edges onto the WS, baste and press. Remove the basting.

3 Cut out the stiffening to the same size as the fabric and trim off $\frac{1}{3}$in (7mm) from the top and bottom edges.

4 Roll the fabric, WS out, onto the cardboard tube. Unpeel the backing from the stiffening and place the fabric WS onto it so that $\frac{1}{12}$in (2mm) of fabric extends at the top and bottom. Unroll the fabric and press it onto the stiffening, peeling off the backing as you do so.

5 Keeping the stiffened fabric with the RS out, overlap the side edges by $\frac{3}{8}$in (10mm) and hold together with clothespins at top and bottom. Insert the rings to check that the size is correct; adjust the amount of overlap if necessary. Check that the seam is straight, then mark inside the shade the points where the fabric overlaps. Remove the rings and clothespins, apply adhesive along the overlapping section of the stiffening and press down firmly; hold down with clothespins until dry.

6 Apply adhesive around the outer edge of the top ring and insert it into the shade so that it is just below the top edge. Press it firmly to the cover and hold in place with clothespins until dry. Repeat the process for the bottom ring.

Braided, hooked and pegged rugs

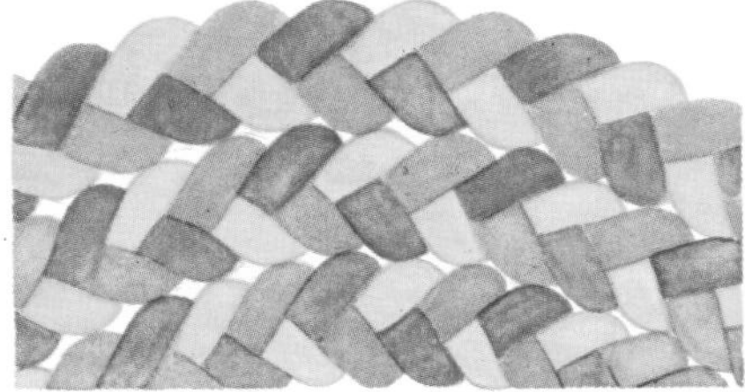
Braiding

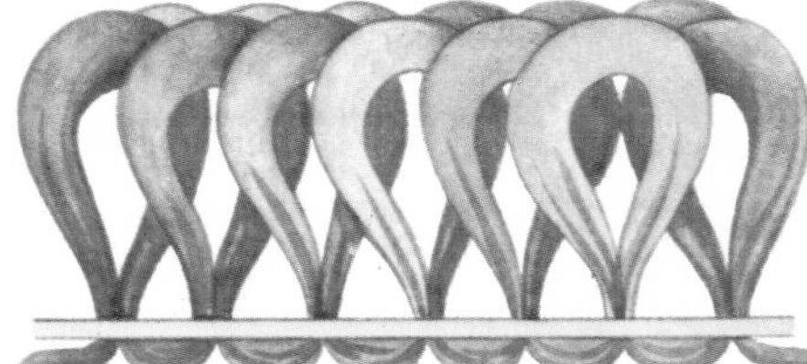
Hooking

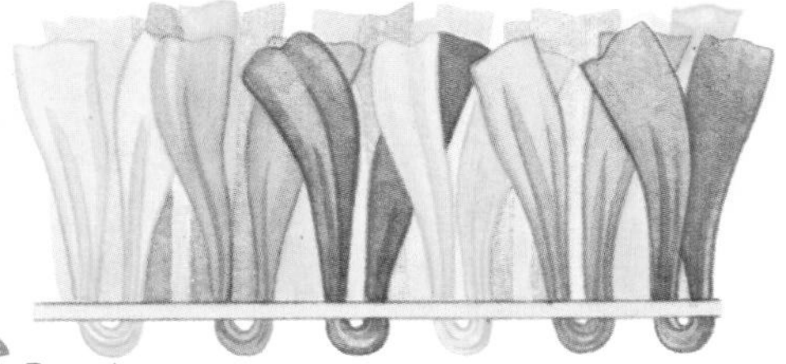
Pegging

Braiding, pegging and hooking are all traditional methods of making mats and rugs from rags. You need a minimum of equipment and the rags may be pieces of fabric left from a dressmaking project or good areas cut from discarded clothing or household items. You can use any type of fabric, although if you are combining different fabrics ideally they should be of similar weight and fiber for even texture and maximum wear. For braided rugs you can also use the leg sections of old panty-hose and stockings. The finished rugs are durable and surprisingly attractive. For braided rugs you simply make a braid several yards long from three fabric strips which you coil into shape and lace to hold together. For pegged and hooked rugs you hook or prod the strips through burlap to make the surface. All the methods are time-consuming so start with something small, such as a tablemat, to practice technique and build up rhythm.

Braided rugs

Fabric amounts The precise amount you will need depends on the weight and the width of the strips, but as a guide you should allow about 1 square yard of cotton fabric for a circle of 16in (40cm) diameter and about 7 square yards for an oval of 36 × 24in (90 × 60cm).

Equipment You can buy a device to prepare the strips but you can easily do it by hand. You simply need pieces of cardboard, scissors, needle and thread, and a bodkin and fine twine for coiling and lacing the braids.

Preparing the strips

1 Cut or tear strips of fabric 1–3in (2·5–7·5cm) wide on the straight grain and as long as possible.

2 Fold the raw edges of the strips to the center with WS together, then fold the strip in half lengthwise to enclose the raw edges completely. Keep the strips folded by winding them around pieces of cardboard. Make a slit in

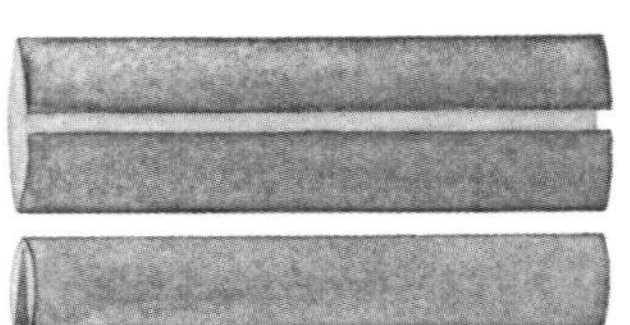

the edge of the cardboard to hold the working end. Make 2 more strips the same way.

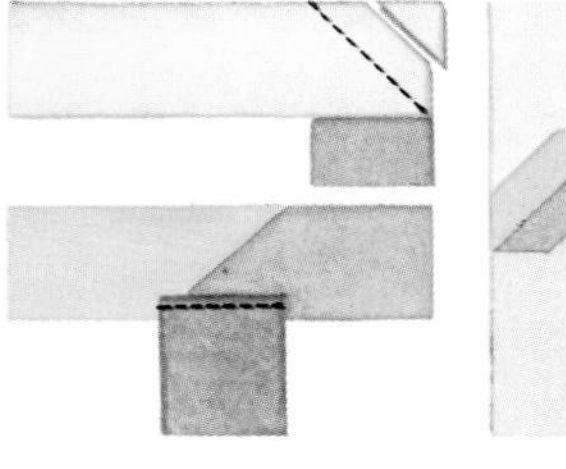

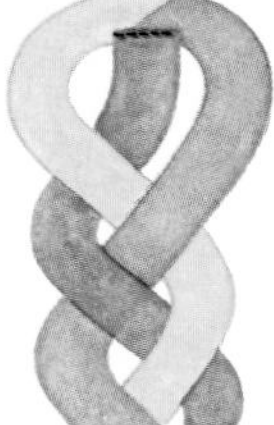

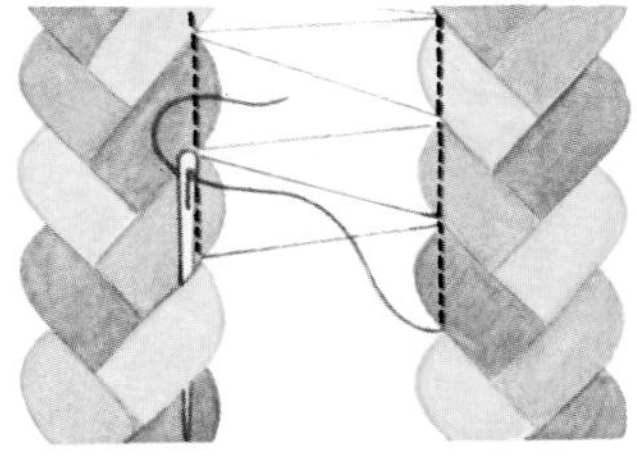

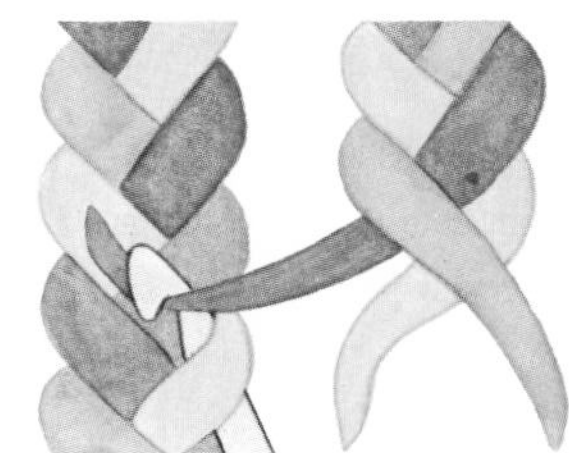

Making the braid

1 Unfold the ends of 2 strips and with RS together join them on the bias grain. Trim off the corner and re-fold the strip as before. Attach the third strip with a few stitches to form a T shape.

2 Loop the T end over a hook or door handle to give tension while you braid. Start braiding evenly, keeping the folded edges toward the center of the braid and pushing the work up to the top. As you finish a strip, join on a new one with a bias seam. Try to hide the joining by braiding over it.

3 When you have braided about 1yd (1m), take it off the handle and start coiling and lacing. For a circle, wind the braid around and around, keeping the shape tight but flat and easing in the fullness on the curves. It may help to draw a circle on cardboard and to work on this as a guide for shaping. You can then pin the coils to it.

4 Thread the bodkin with fine twine and knot the end neatly at the center of the coil. Lace through the loop on the inside coil, then through the corresponding loop of the outer coil. Work back and forth between the coils, drawing them together as firmly as possible.

5 Continue braiding and coiling, to form the required size. To finish off, taper the width of the strips to make the braid narrower. Weave the ends into the outer ring of the braid and slip-stitch the ends to secure them.

Hooked rugs

Fabric amounts Allow about 2oz (50g) mixed rags per 5in (12cm) square of rug and a piece of burlap 4in (10cm) longer and wider than the required rug size. If you are making the rug as a floor covering, buy double the amount of burlap for backing it.
Equipment To make the holes through the burlap and pull the fabric strips through, you need a strong hook. Traditionally these are made from steel with a wooden handle, but you can also buy more elaborate versions designed to speed up the process. You will also need a large frame (either a needlepoint or a picture frame) for mounting the burlap, a large-eyed needle and carpet thread.

Preparing the strips

Cut or tear the strips on the straight grain as long as possible by $\frac{1}{2}$–$\frac{5}{8}$in (12–15mm) wide. If you are combining fabrics of different weights, cut them wider from the lighter fabric and fold them to provide the same width and bulk as the heavier fabrics.

Making the rug

1 Fold up the burlap hems onto the RS and baste them. Mount the burlap onto the frame RS up. Lay the frame horizontally for working the rug, by supporting it across 2 chairs if it is not a floor-standing frame.
2 You can work the hooking across the burlap in horizontal rows or you can work the main motifs first and then fill in the background. Loop

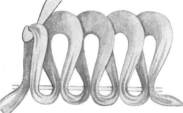

the end of the first strip over for about 1in (2·5cm) and hold the loop below the burlap in your starting place.
3 With your free hand push the hook through the burlap from the top and insert it into the loop. Pull it back through the burlap and draw up the loop to the required height (e.g. 1–1$\frac{1}{2}$in/2·5–4cm).
4 Still holding the strip under the burlap, make another loop, push the hook through the burlap about $\frac{1}{4}$–$\frac{3}{8}$in (5–10mm) from the first hole and pull the loop through.
5 Continue in this way using strips of appropriate colors for your design.
6 To back the rug, remove from the frame, fold under the edges on the backing piece and place it with WS together onto the rug. Pin and overcast firmly around the edge.

Pegged rugs

Fabric amounts Allow the same amount of rags and burlap as hooked rugs.
Equipment To make the holes in the burlap and poke the fabric strips through you need a round awl or wooden peg about 4in (10cm) long by $\frac{3}{8}$in (1cm) diameter. You can make your own wooden peg by shaping the end of a piece of dowel rod with a file. You will also need a large frame, cardboard, a large-eyed needle and carpet thread.

Preparing the strips

1 Cut or tear the strips on the straight grain as long as possible by $\frac{1}{2}$in (12mm) wide for double pegging or 1in (2·5cm) wide for single pegging (the quicker but less durable method).
2 Cut the strips into tabs by winding them around a piece of folded cardboard 2$\frac{1}{2}$in (6·5cm) wide and then cutting along the open side with shears.

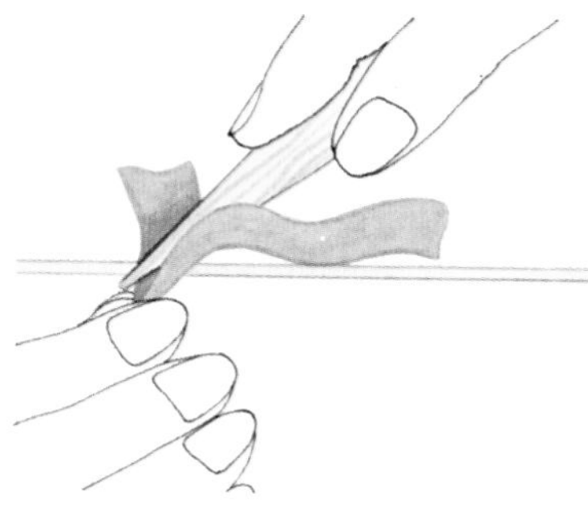

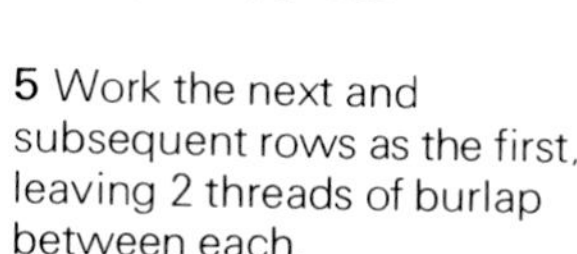

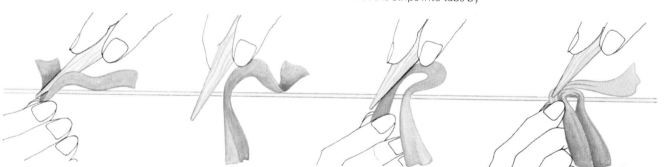

Making the rug

1 Prepare the burlap as for hooked rugs but mounting on the frame with the WS facing up.
2 Push the point of the peg through the burlap to make a hole in the position of the first tuft. Fold the end of the first tab lengthwise and push it through the hole with the peg. Put your free hand under the burlap and pull the tab halfway through.
3 Make a second hole with the peg 2 threads of burlap farther along the row and prod the other end of the tab through. Use your free hand to pull the ends of the tab on the underside evenly into place.

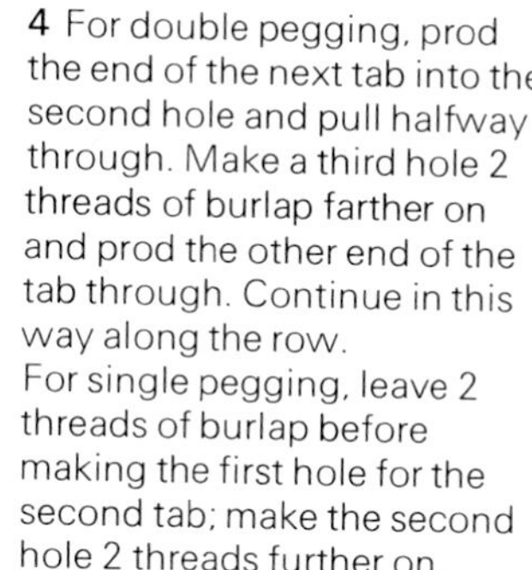

4 For double pegging, prod the end of the next tab into the second hole and pull halfway through. Make a third hole 2 threads of burlap farther on and prod the other end of the tab through. Continue in this way along the row.
For single pegging, leave 2 threads of burlap before making the first hole for the second tab; make the second hole 2 threads further on.
5 Work the next and subsequent rows as the first, leaving 2 threads of burlap between each.
6 Finish the rug as a hooked rug.

Stitched and latch-hooked rugs

You can make a pile rug on a canvas foundation using a needle and long lengths of yarn or with a latch-hook and cut pieces of yarn. Both methods make durable, attractive rugs and require similar quantities of yarn – it is a matter of personal preference as to which is easier and quicker. The advantage of using Ghiordes stitch is that it can be made on a finer gauge canvas, using a 2-ply rug yarn.

Materials for stitched rugs

Yarn You can use hanks of 6-ply rug wool for a bulky pile or 2-ply rug yarn for a finer pile; this is available as odd lots from carpet mills as offcuts from the loom and is one of the least expensive ways of making rugs. If you can not obtain your wool this way, you can purchase specially manufactured rug wool from a store specializing in yarn.

Canvas For working with thick yarn you can use rug canvas with either 8 or 10 holes per 3in (7·5cm) – available in different widths from 14in (36cm) to 48in (122cm). Alternatively with 2-ply yarn only, use double-mesh canvas with 4 or 5 holes per 1in (2·5cm) or a special jute backing which has threads woven in blocks of 4 so that the stitching is worked into the holes between. Using 2 strands of yarn in the needle for good coverage, you will need about 9oz (225g) yarn per 12in (30cm) square. Using 1 thickness of 6-ply or 3 thicknesses of 2-ply in the needle, you will need about 12oz (300g) yarn per 12in (30cm) square on the coarsest canvas.

For square or rectangular rugs, buy the exact width by 4in (10cm) longer than the required size.

For round rugs buy a square 4in (10cm) larger than the required diameter. For finishing round rugs you will also need 1in (2·5cm) carpet tape to fit the circumference, a carpet needle and linen thread.

Equipment

Needles Use a large-size rug needle or tapestry needle which can easily be threaded with the yarn.

Frames Jute can be mounted in a frame if preferred – stiffened canvas can easily be worked on your lap or on a table.

Making stitched rugs

1 If using a canvas foundation, prepare it as for latch-hooked rugs (see opposite).

If using jute, fold the selvedges to the RS for $\frac{5}{8}$in (15mm) and herringbone-stitch. Then turn up the top and bottom edge for 2in (5cm) and herringbone-stitch.

2 Work braid stitch around all sides (see opposite). Then work the pile stitches (see below) in horizontal rows from the lower edge. Have several needles threaded with the appropriate number of strands in each color to avoid wasting time as you change color to fit the design. Cut the loops and trim the pile after each row.

3 Finish the rug as for latch hooked rugs.

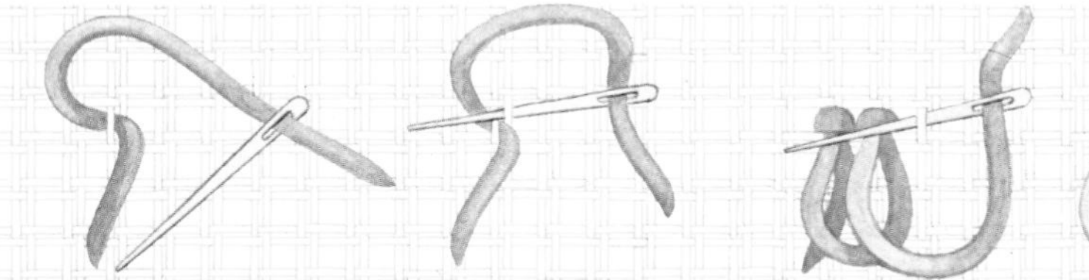

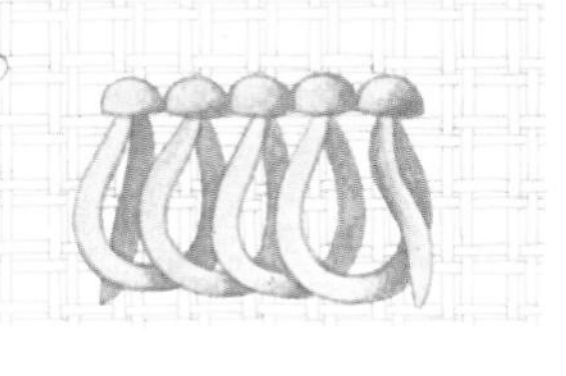

Ghiordes stitch

Use Ghiordes stitch on fine mesh rug canvas. Work from left to right.

1 Insert the needle from left to right, splitting the first warp bar. Pull through, leaving an end of the desired pile length.

2 Loop the yarn around to the right and insert the needle from right to left into the same split bar. Pull the yarn firmly to secure the knot.

3 Cut the yarn leaving a tail of the pile length or leave a loop of the same length and go on to the next stitch.

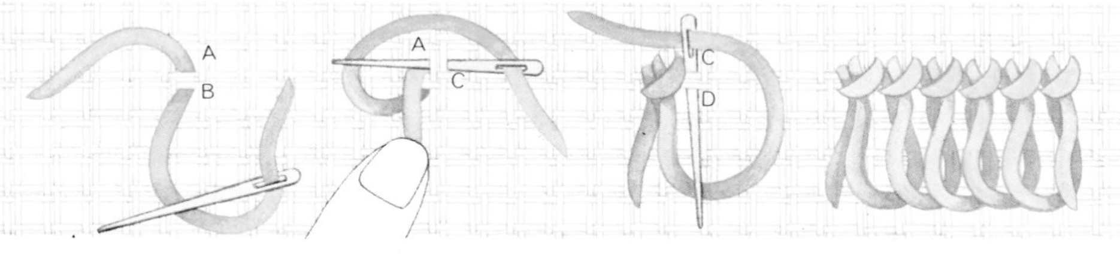

Surrey stitch

Use Surrey stitch on coarse rug canvas. Work from left to right.

1 Bring the needle through under the first double weft bar. Pull through from A to B, leaving an end of 1–2in (2·5–5cm) according to required pile length.

2 Loop the yarn around to the left and bring down the end over the bar. Hold with your left thumb. Insert the needle at C and bring out at A, passing the needle over the loop. Pull the needle toward you to form a knot.

3 If you are making a single stitch, cut off the yarn leaving an end of the required pile length. If you are making more stitches in the same yarn, loop it around to the right, re-insert the needle at C, bring it out at D over the loop, pulling through until the right length.

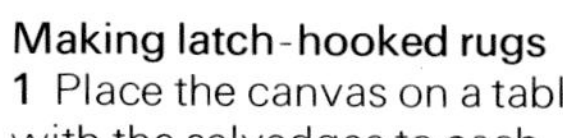

Materials for latch-hooked rugs

Yarn For making a short-pile rug you can buy a special coarse 6-ply rug wool or a 3-ply acrylic yarn. These are sold in packs with about 300 pre-cut pieces 2$\frac{3}{4}$in (7cm) long. Each piece makes 1 knot with 2 strands of pile about $\frac{3}{4}$in (2cm) long; 1 pack of yarn with this number of strips covers just over 3 canvas blocks 3in (7·5cm) square on the coarsest canvas.

You can buy matching uncut yarn by the hank for finishing the edges of the rug.

For a long pile (rya) rug you can buy 2-ply woolen rug yarn sold in hanks or pre-cut packs containing 170 pieces approximately 7in (18cm) long. Three lengths are used in each knot, making 6 strands of pile 2$\frac{3}{4}$in (7cm) long. Each cut pack covers slightly more than 3in (7·5cm) square on coarse canvas.

Canvas You can use the same coarse rug canvas as for stitched rugs (allow the same amount). For rya rugs, which are worked less closely than short-pile ones, you can buy a specially woven canvas in a range of widths from 24–45in (60–115cm) with the appropriate spacing (allow the same amount).

Equipment Latch-hooks look like crochet hooks but have a wooden handle and a hinged latch which closes the hook to prevent it from being caught in the canvas as the knot is formed.

Making latch-hooked rugs

1 Place the canvas on a table with the selvedges to each side and the full length away from you. As you progress, turn under the worked section so that you do not have to lean over to reach the row on which you are working.

2 To make a neat edge on square or rectangular rugs only, turn up the 2 cut ends for about 2in (5cm) and fold down so that the holes correspond with those on the layer beneath. Baste in position.

Work the first rows of knots through this double thickness, leaving the first 2 rows from the folded edge and, on finer canvas, 1 hole on each side unworked.

On circular rugs mark the area to be covered and leave the margin on the canvas until finished.

3 Work the knots (see below)

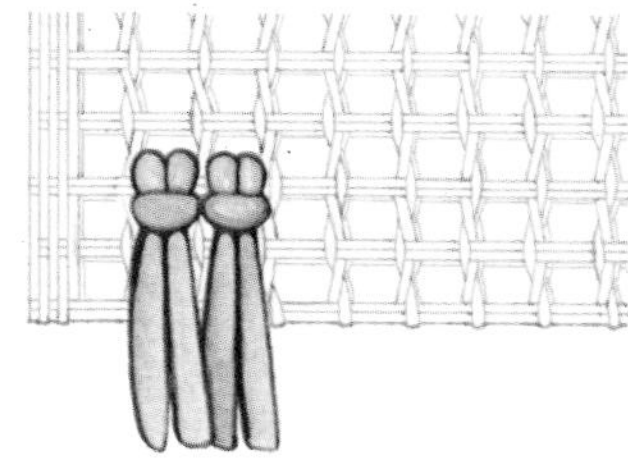

from left to right (or *vice versa* if you are left-handed) on every weft thread or on alternate weft threads for rya rugs worked on ordinary canvas.

4 Complete square or rectangular rugs by knotting through the double thickness at the end of the canvas.

To compensate for the directional fall of longer pile, turn the rug around about 5 rows from the end and work in a few knots in the opposite direction gradually increasing the number until the last row is completely reversed.

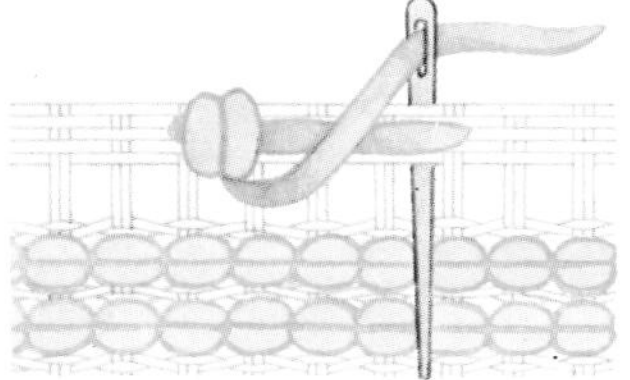

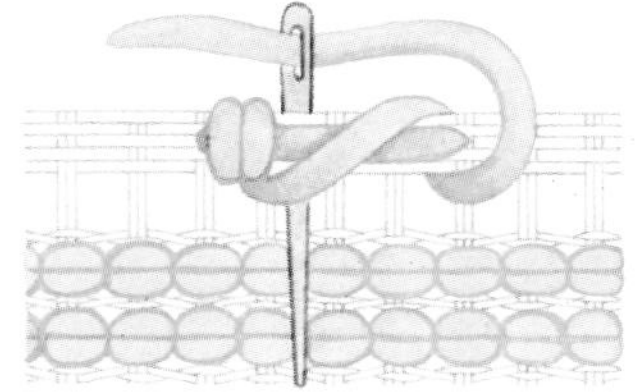

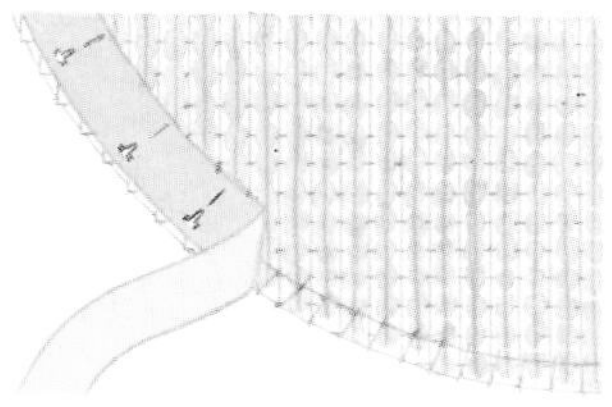

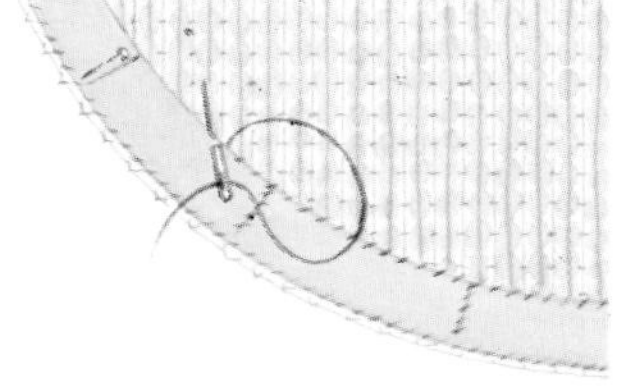

Finishing squares and rectangles You can add a fringe to both folded ends and finish the selvedges by stitching or you can work braid stitch on all sides.

Work the stitching from left to right with the WS of the rug facing up.

1 Hold the end of the yarn to the right so that it will be covered by the stitching, insert the needle into the first hole and work a few overcasting stitches over the outside thread of canvas or the selvedge into the same hole.

2 Move to the fourth hole to the right, taking the yarn over the edge and through the hole toward you. Take the yarn over the edge, return to the second hole and pull through. Go on to the fifth hole, back to the third and so on along the edge.

Finishing circles Trim spare canvas to within 1in (2·5cm) of the pile. Fold the margin to the WS and pin and overcast the carpet binding on so that it is $\frac{1}{4}$in (5mm) from the fold. Smooth out the slight fullness along the inner edge of the tape into pleats and overcast the edge to the canvas.

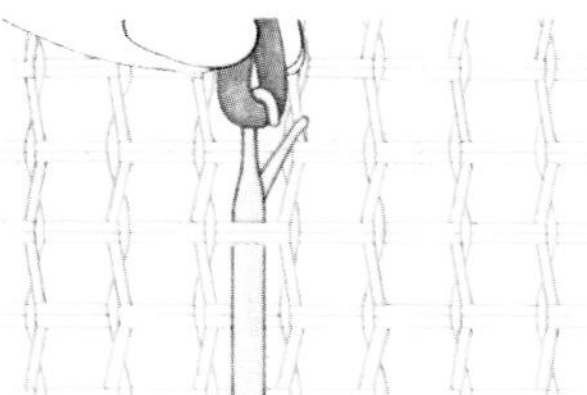

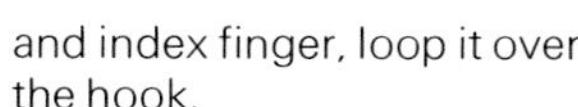

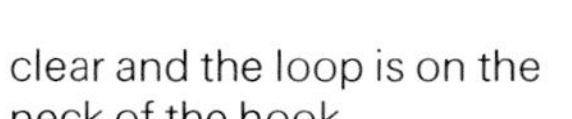

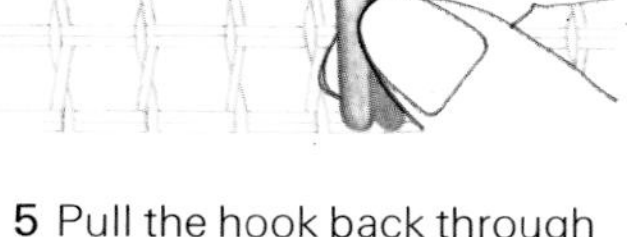

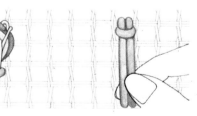

The knots

1 Insert the hook under the first weft thread and open the latch. Fold the cut length of yarn in half and, holding the ends between your thumb and index finger, loop it over the hook.

2 Pull the hook back through the canvas.

3 Push the hook through the loop of yarn until the latch is clear and the loop is on the neck of the hook.

4 Place the cut ends of yarn into the crook of the hook from below so they are enclosed by the latch.

5 Pull the hook back through the loop of yarn until the ends are clear.

6 Pull the ends of yarn tightly to secure the knot.

Embroidery

Embroidery is needlecraft in its most decorative form: the stitching is almost always the focal point. You can use stitching to cover the background material completely, thus giving the effect of a new fabric altogether, as with needlepoint, or you can use stitches to add color and texture to specific areas of a fabric.
In some techniques, such as patchwork, the stitches themselves recede in visual importance and the piecing together of fabric shapes serves to create a new effect.

In the following pages you will find all the basic techniques with clear instructions and diagrams together with a discussion of their uses and design possibilities. Accompanying most of the methods are projects carefully chosen to show you the full extent of each technique. As you acquaint yourself with the techniques, you will want to discover your own variations and find the tremendous satisfaction to be gained from working out your own design.

General instructions are also given for preparation of materials, methods of finishing garments, accessories or wall-hangings and general care of embroidered fabrics. You will find these helpful both as a practical reference and as an introduction to the enormous scope for creativity that embroidery offers.

Basic equipment

Needles
The needle should make a hole in the material large enough for the thread to pass through but not so large that it alters the mesh of the fabric. Its eye should accommodate the thread easily without roughening it. All needles are graded from fine to coarse, the higher numbers being the finer needles.
Tapestry needles are used for needlepoint and pulled and drawn thread work. They have an oval eye and a blunt end.
Crewel needles are long and sharp with a large eye and can be used for surface stitches.
Chenille needles are sharp with a large eye and are suitable for thick threads and tapestry wool.
Beading or straw needles are very fine and long, and are used for beadwork.

Threads
In addition to the list of threads below, you can use weaving yarns, knitting yarns, crochet yarns, raffia and metallic threads. For machine work you can buy special machine embroidery thread (see p190).
Soft embroidery cotton is a matt, fairly thick, medium-weight, single-thread cotton.
Embroidery floss is slightly shiny; you can separate the strands (usually 6) and thread any number through a needle.
Pearl cotton is a loosely twisted cotton with a lustrous finish forming a single thread.
Coton à broder is a tightly twisted thread which is softer and finer than pearl cotton.
Crewel wool is a fine 2-ply, hard-wearing yarn which may be used in more than 1 strand.
Persian yarn is a 3-ply wool slightly thicker than crewel wool.
Tapestry wool is a thick 4-ply yarn, used as a single thread.
Rug wool comes in varying thicknesses.
Silk thread is either 6-stranded or twisted, and sometimes difficult to use.

Background fabrics
These fall into two basic categories: counted-thread and non-counted-thread.
Counted-thread fabrics For counted-thread work such as needlepoint and Bargello, you need a background fabric of canvas or closely woven linen. Most canvas is stiffened cotton but plastic canvas is also available. Canvas is available in both single and double mesh, the former being easier for beginners, and contains on average 14 to 16 threads per inch but the range spans from as coarse as 3 to as fine as 32 threads.
Non-counted-thread fabrics The choice of background fabrics is much wider for non-counted-thread embroidery: cottons, wools and wool mixes, evenweave linens, silks and burlap all lend themselves to embroidery. The fabric should be firmly woven and the threads should separate easily as the needle passes through. Try to match the weight of the thread with that of the background fabric to avoid puckering.

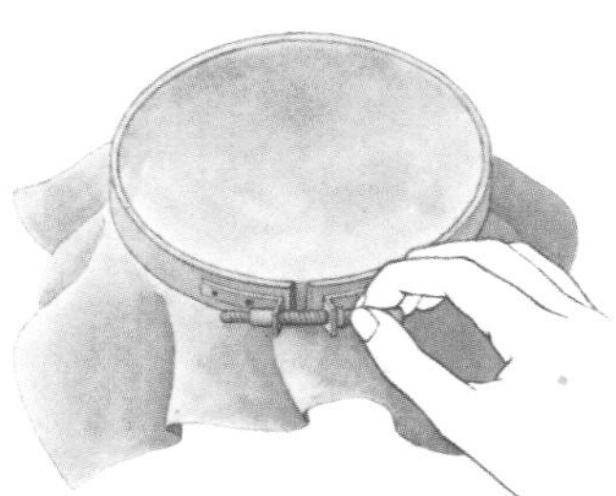

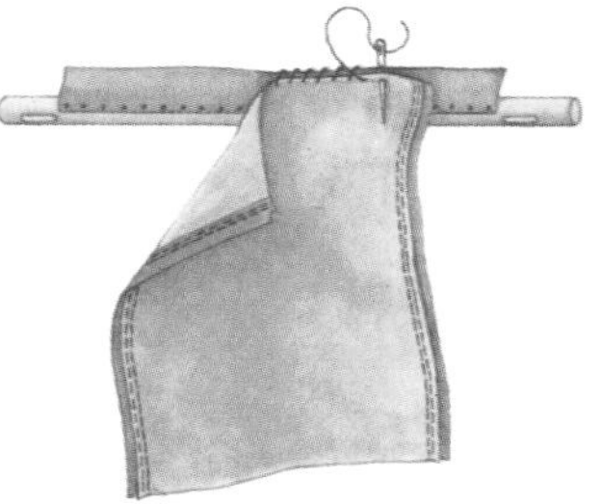

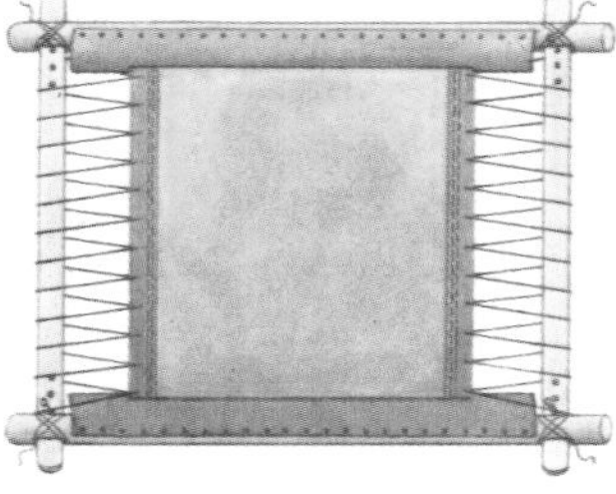

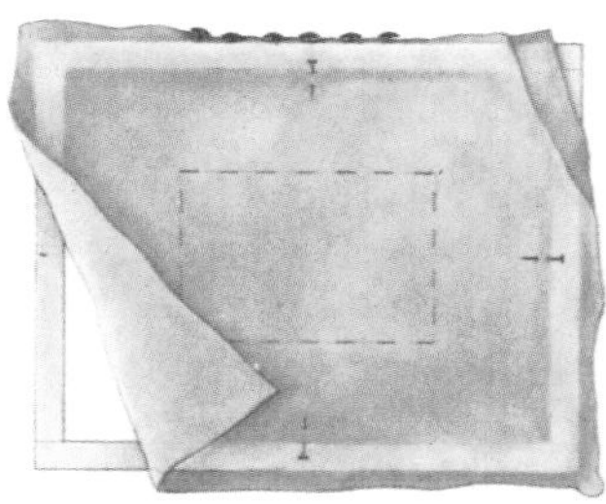

Frames
These keep the fabric under tension, enabling the embroiderer to make even stitches.
Embroidery hoops
which are used on fabrics such as cotton and wool consist of an inner and outer ring of metal, plastic or wood, with a screw for adjusting tension on the outer ring.
To mount the fabric lay the area to be embroidered over the inner ring and gently press the outer ring over it. Adjust the tension screw so that the fabric is smooth and the grain is straight. To prevent the fabric from slipping or marking, you can bind the inner ring with bandage or masking tape.

Stretcher frames are useful for working large areas. The 4-sided wooden frame consists of 2 runners or rollers at the ends for winding excess ground fabric around, 2 stretchers at the sides and 4 split pins, pegs or screws. The runners have slits at either end and a strip of webbing firmly attached along the edge. Stretchers are flat with holes at the ends for the pins. To mount the fabric, cut a rectangle of fabric on the straight of grain, turn a ⅜in (1cm) hem top and bottom and machine-stitch a 1in (2·5cm) wide tape to the sides. Pencil vertical half-way marks on both strips of webbing and top and bottom of fabric. Starting from the center overcast edges of webbing and fabric with RS together. Repeat with the opposite end. Wind excess fabric around roller if necessary, fit the stretchers into the ends of the rollers as far apart as they will stretch keeping them equally spaced at both ends. Wind a strong length of carpet thread or fine string into a knot around the top of each lath. Using a chenille needle sew it through the tapes on the ground fabric and lace it around the stretcher at intervals of about ¾in (2cm) for the length of the fabric. Pull fabric taut, keeping grain straight.

Simple wooden frames differ from slate frames in that they can not easily be dismantled or adjusted. You can either make your own or use a firm wooden picture frame, canvas stretcher or silk screen. It must accommodate the fabric plus a 3in (8cm) border fully stretched. To mount the fabric first mark half-way points on all sides of frame and fabric. With central points aligned on one side and starting from the center, staple or tack the fabric to the outside edge of the frame. Repeat on the opposite side and then top and bottom, keeping fabric straight.

Transferring designs

Unless you have a working design already stenciled onto your ground fabric, you will need to know how to transfer a design from paper to fabric. Designing your own embroidery offers enormous scope so it is well worth learning the various methods of transferring designs. More detailed patterns transfer best directly from tracing paper to fabric, whereas simple motifs are best transferred with a template.

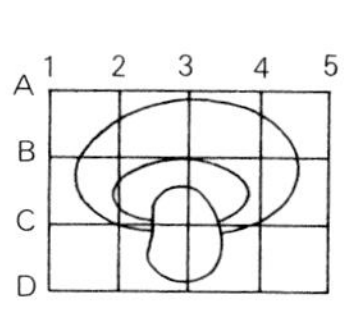

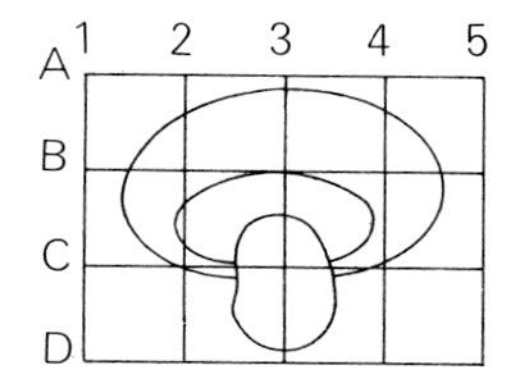

Enlarging or reducing a design

Trace the design onto plain paper and enclose it with a rectangle or square, as close to the design as possible. Using letters and numbers to identify the lines, divide the design into squares to form a grid. On graph paper or another sheet of plain paper draw a separate rectangle or square to the size required and divide it into the same number of squares as the original. Copy outlines from smaller to larger squares for enlarging and the reverse for reducing.

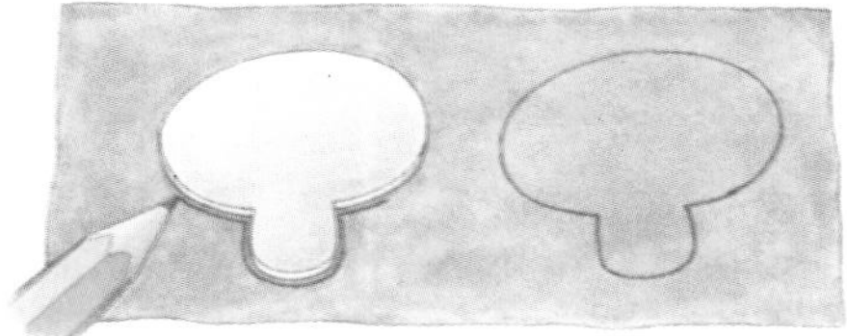

Templates

A template is a piece of plastic, metal or cardboard which has been cut, or manufactured in the case of plastic or metal, to a specific shape for use as a tracing guide. To make your own template, accurately measure, draw and cut out the required shape from lightweight cardboard. Register the template on the background fabric and either baste or draw around with tailor's chalk or a hard pencil.

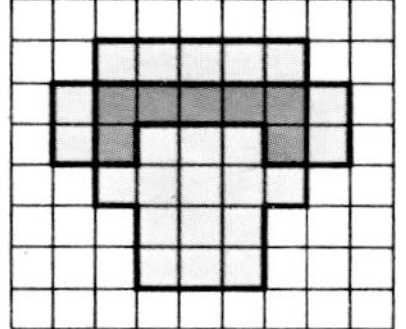

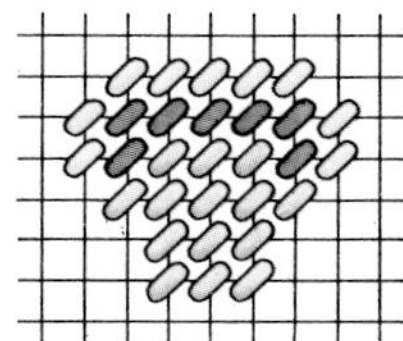

Working from a chart

Use this method for counted-thread techniques. Draw the design on graph paper so that one square on the paper represents one stitch or ground fabric unit and color it in accordingly. Work the center of the design by drawing vertical and horizontal lines across the chart.

To work from the chart begin at one end and embroider the design and the background in rows. On larger works, you may find it more satisfying to tackle the central motifs first.

Tracing and basting

This method is suitable for heavier fabrics such as velvet, wool and burlap. Place the background fabric on a hard flat surface or in a frame to transfer the design. Baste central horizontal and vertical lines onto fabric for registration. With a felt-tipped pen transfer main lines of design onto tissue or tracing paper. Lay the paper RS up over fabric, center it and baste it along registration lines through paper and fabric. Using small running stitches and with a contrasting thread stitch the design outline through paper and fabric. Carefully tear all the paper away from the fabric.

Dressmaker's carbon paper

Transfer detailed designs onto tracing paper with a fine felt-tipped pen or soft pencil. Iron the background fabric, baste registration lines on it and place it on a hard, smooth surface. Register the tracing over the fabric and slip the carbon paper, shiny side down, between the two. Pin the tracing to the RS of the fabric, but don't pin through the carbon paper as it would mark the fabric. Alternatively, tape all 3 layers to the working surface. Trace the design with a hard pencil or tracing wheel, pressing firmly and evenly. If working a border design, move the tracing along and repeat the process.

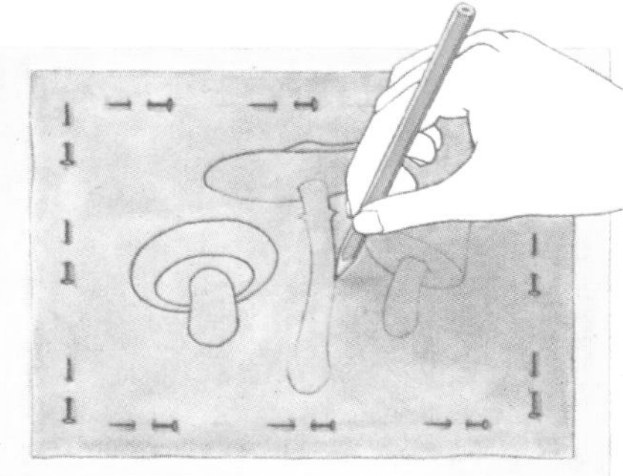

Tracing from paper

Use on semi-transparent fabrics such as silk, fine cotton or canvas where the stitching will completely cover the tracing lines.

Using a fine felt-tipped pen, outline the design clearly on paper. Pin the fabric over the design and trace through onto RS of fabric with a hard pencil for cotton and silk and black waterproof ink and a fine pen or brush for canvas.

Finishing

Hand-washing

You should always wash finished embroidery by hand, particularly if it has been worked on cotton or linen. With the exception of canvas, it is also advisable to wash fabric before embroidering it. Dissolve soap flakes in very hot water and when hand-hot, gently squeeze the work first in the lather and then in clear water of the same temperature. Rinse finally in warm, clear water. Spread the work out smoothly to dry on an absorbent towel and leave until ready for pressing.

Ironing

If the work is cotton, linen or wool, iron while still damp; if silk, iron when just dry. Always press embroidery at once; never leave it damp or rolled up for future pressing. Place the article RS down on a towel or blanket folded into 4 layers and cover the embroidery with dry muslin to press; use a cool iron.

Cleaning wall-hangings

Unglazed wall-hangings have a tendency to collect dust. A flick with a feather duster or soft brush is usually sufficient to keep most work clean. If it really needs cleaning, seek the advice of a specialist cleaner or embroidery restorer.

Dry-cleaning

To prevent uneven shrinkage you should dry-clean embroidery which contains a mixture of threads and fabrics. This includes wool worked on cotton canvas, and indeed anything which has been worked on canvas because washing canvas causes it to become limp.

Damp-stretching

If your finished object shows signs of puckering or warping, you should damp-stretch it.

1 Cover a drawing board or piece of fiber board at least as large as the finished work with a damp towel.

2 Place the work RS down on the board and dab the WS with a soft, cool, damp cloth.

3 Remove embroidery and thoroughly dampen the towel on the board with a sponge.

4 Return the work RS up to the board. Align one of the selvedges with the edge of the board, measuring this distance so that the other selvedge stretches to the same length.

5 Pin firmly into position with rust-proof thumbtacks, upholstery nails, dress-maker's pins or staples, depending on the weight of the fabric, at least 1in (2·5cm) from the edge of the embroidery and about 1–2in (2·5–5cm) apart.

6 Repeat for the other selvedge and then the remaining sides, so that the corners are at right angles and the grain of the fabric is straight.

7 Leave until completely dry, 24 hours or longer. Closely worked embroidery takes longer to dry.

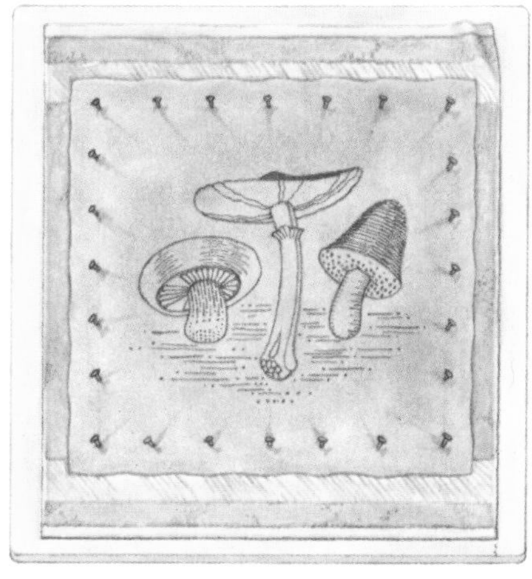

Covering a pillow

These instructions are for a pillow which will be covered on both sides by embroidery but the same assembling principles apply if only the top side has been embroidered. Remove the work from the frame leaving a 1in (2·5cm) border all around for seams. Damp-stretch it if necessary.

1 Place the 2 pieces of fabric with RS together, making sure that the patterns on both sides match.

2 Pin, baste and machine-stitch around 3 sides, leaving the remaining side open for the filling.

3 Overcast the seam edges and gently poke out the corners with a pencil. On canvas snip across the corner just outside the stitching.

4 Insert the pillow, turn in seam allowance and slip-stitch opening. On needlepoint and Bargello, where there is a chance of the canvas showing through at the seams, work whip stitch (p18) or cross stitch (p170) in a toning yarn along the seam on RS, picking up opposite threads of the canvas from each side as you proceed. Alternatively you can cover the seams with a twisted cord (p102) using one or more of the yarns or threads used in the work.

Covering a 4-sided chair seat or stool

If you are covering a chair which needs re-upholstering, you must see that this takes place before you embroider the cover. In any case, always remove the existing outer cover to avoid a bulky double-thickness of fabric.

1 Make a paper template of the parts of the chair to be covered, including sides.

2 Place the template on the ground fabric and baste around the outline, allowing a border of at least 2–3in (5–8cm). Check to see that the corners are at 90° to facilitate mitering.

3 Work the embroidery on a frame, remove and damp-stretch.

4 Miter the corners and join them with whip stitch in a toning yarn.

5 Attach base of cover to seat with slip stitch or upholstery tacks.

Covering a drop-in seat

1 Make a paper template of the area to be covered, allowing an additional amount of canvas for the padding which will be underneath.

2 Work the embroidery on a frame, remove and damp-stretch.

3 Fasten the embroidery to the back of the seat with chair tacks, beginning from the center of each side and working outward, checking to see that it is taut and that the filling is even.

Scroll wall-hangings

1 Overcast the edges of the embroidery and then turn under to WS and herringbone-stitch the edges to it (see p170).
2 Cut out a cotton lining the same size as the hemmed work. Press, then turn in the edges to about $\frac{5}{8}$–$\frac{3}{4}$in (15–20mm) and baste them.
3 Baste the lining to the hanging, beginning with the vertical and horizontal lines to hold the two in position.
4 Pin, baste and then slip-stitch the lining edges onto the base.
5 For an article larger than a yard in either direction, catch the lining to the middle of the work with loose slip stitches at 12in (30cm) intervals.
6 For the batten you will require a flat length of wood, section of dowelling, brass or glass rod, depending on the weight of the hanging and the effect you want. To attach the batten, either turn the top hem over to form a channel for it or insert tabs to backing fabric before it is hemmed. These could be finished strips of the ground fabric, assuming it is not canvas, and should be at least 1in (2·5cm) wide.

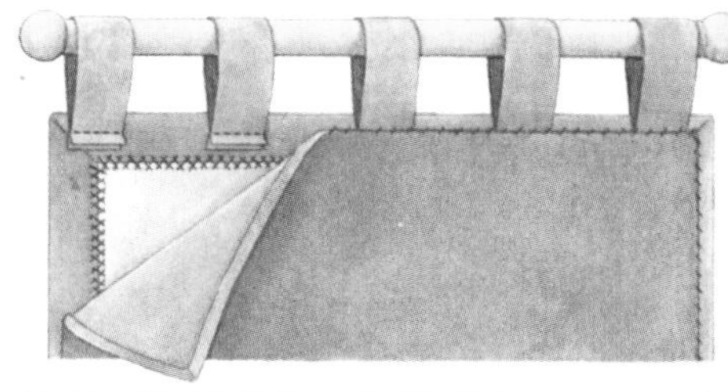

Framed wall-hangings

A simple frame will give a wall-hanging a professional finish. Glazing embroidery detracts from its tactile qualities, but as it does provide protection from dust, you might find it preferable. If you are having your work framed professionally, you can save yourself some expense by mounting the embroidery first.

Lace-backed mounting If your work is larger than 12in (30cm) sq you should mount it on hardboard $\frac{1}{4}$in (6mm) thick. Use thick cardboard for smaller objects.
1 Cut a piece of board the same size as the embroidery, plus $\frac{1}{4}$in (6mm) border.
2 Overcast or machine-zigzag the embroidery edges to prevent fraying.
3 Place embroidery RS down on a flat surface and place board over it.
4 Using a darning or chenille needle and a long length of carpet thread, thin string or twine knotted at the end, lace the fabric onto the board. Begin from the centers of the top and bottom and work outward to the sides to give an evenly stretched effect.
5 Join more thread where necessary with a non-slipping knot and occasionally turn work over to RS to check that the design is straight.
6 On completion of each side pull the lacing taut and secure firmly to give a smoothly stretched surface on RS.

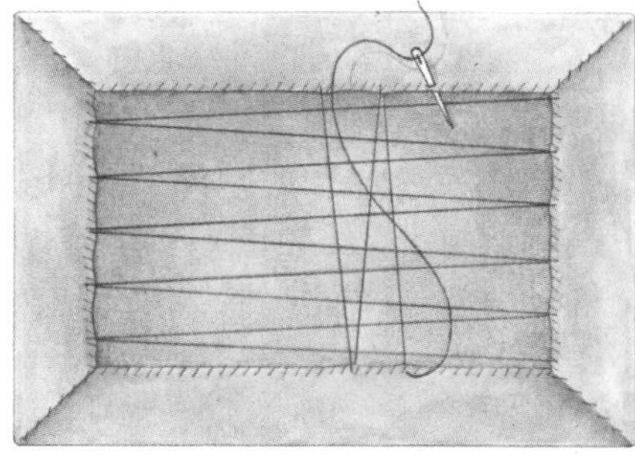

Stretch-mounted wall-hangings If you are buying your stretcher you should select it before you start your embroidery to insure that the two are the same size.
1 Buy or assemble a canvas stretcher the same size as your embroidery, plus a $\frac{1}{4}$in (6mm) border for the frame.
2 Place embroidery RS down on a clean surface.
3 Beginning from the center of each side pull the fabric over the stretcher and secure to the outside edge with thumbtacks spaced about 1in (2·5cm) apart, checking that edges are straight on RS.
4 Replace each thumbtack with an upholstery tack or staple and neaten the corners. Rectify any errors in alignment at this stage.
5 Complete by slip-stitching a matching tape or velvet ribbon to the frame.
If you are not having your work framed professionally, you can make your own frame simply by attaching laths of wood to the outside edges, making sure that they are equal in width to those of the stretcher. Do any painting or staining of the wood before nailing laths to the frame.

Finishing rugs

As a general rule, it is better not to line rugs. To finish rugs, overcast the edges, turn them under about 2in (5cm) to WS, and herringbone-stitch the borders to WS. To prevent the rug from sliding, attach an iron-on non-slip binding to the edges on WS.

Embroidering clothes

Wherever possible work the embroidery before making the garment to reduce the risk of puckering. Baste the outline of the area which will be embroidered and cut out the garment leaving at least 3in (8cm) around the edges. Alternatively, mount a large piece of fabric on a frame, baste the outline of the garment, embroider it and then cut it out.
If the WS of the embroidery is rough line it with a finer fabric of the same fiber as that of the garment. Most reputable embroidery threads are color-fast so there should be no problem with hand-washing. If in doubt, dry-clean.

Basic needlepoint stitches

One of the oldest types of embroidery known, needlepoint is particularly noted for its hard-wearing qualities. Occasionally people mistakenly refer to needlepoint as tapestry; this is because it was done originally to imitate expensive woven tapestries. It is also called canvas work sometimes, because of the background fabric which it covers.

The distinguishing feature of needlepoint is the square-based construction of the stitches, a result of the warp and weft pattern of the canvas on which they are worked and which they must cover. The grid pattern of the canvas means, further, that the stitches can only move vertically, horizontally or diagonally. Despite this seeming limitation there are more than 60 needlepoint stitches.

Instructions are given here for right-handed people. If you are left-handed simply hold the diagrams up to a hand mirror and follow the mirror image.

Equipment needed

Choose your canvas to suit the design and purpose of the article you plan to make; on fine work you can use a very closely woven linen, designed for this purpose. Tapestry wool, Persian wool, crewel wool, weaving wool and odd lengths of carpet wool are the most durable threads to use and are therefore best for items that will receive a lot of wear, but cotton and linen threads are also effective as long as they suit the object. The most important consideration is that the thread is thick enough to cover the background fabric completely. Tapestry needles with their blunt ends are essential for working needlepoint.

Needlepoint has a tendency to warp so you should mount any canvas larger than 12in (30cm) on a stretcher or simple wooden frame. Otherwise work with the canvas in your hand.

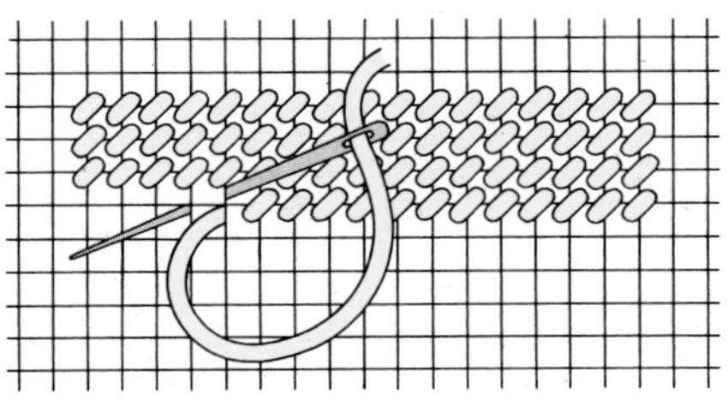

Tent stitch Work this stitch over 1 crossing thread of single-mesh canvas. You can work it horizontally, as shown, diagonally or vertically, but over a large area you should work it diagonally to prevent pulling the canvas out of shape and to give strength to the work. The needle always goes back over 1 thread and forward 2 threads.

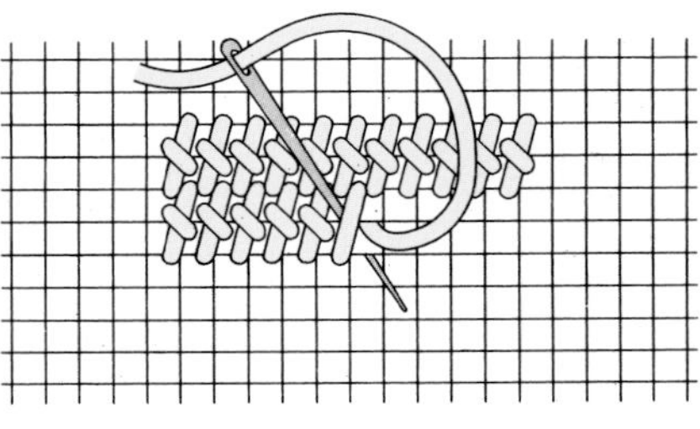

Knotted stitch Work this horizontally in overlapping rows of slanting stitches over 3 horizontal threads tieing each down in the center.

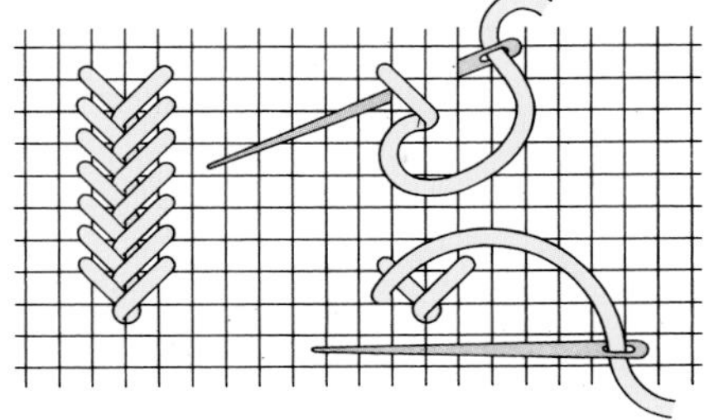

Fern stitch Work each row from the top downwards. You can vary the number of threads covered according to the mesh of the canvas.

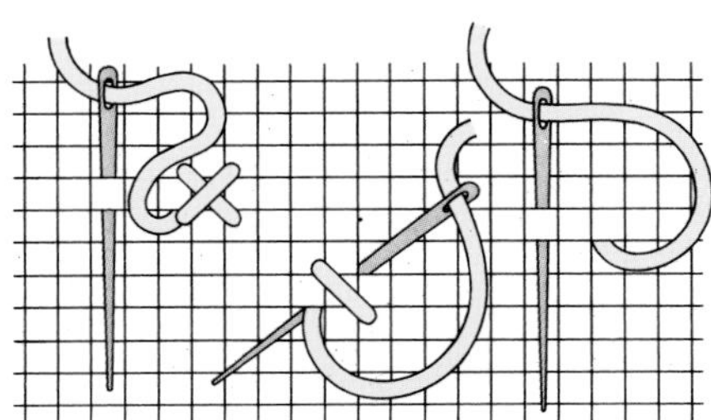

Cross stitch Work each cross separately with all the stitches crossing in the same direction and the line from lower left to top right always uppermost.

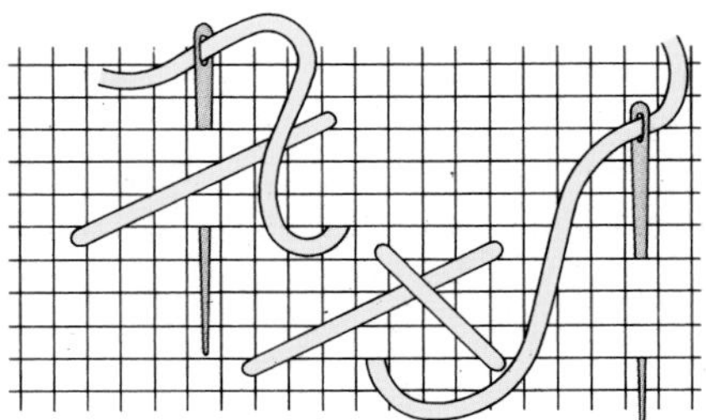

Long-armed cross stitch Work this in horizontal rows, first making a long slanted stitch and then crossing it with a shorter stitch slanted in the opposite direction. This covers large areas quickly.

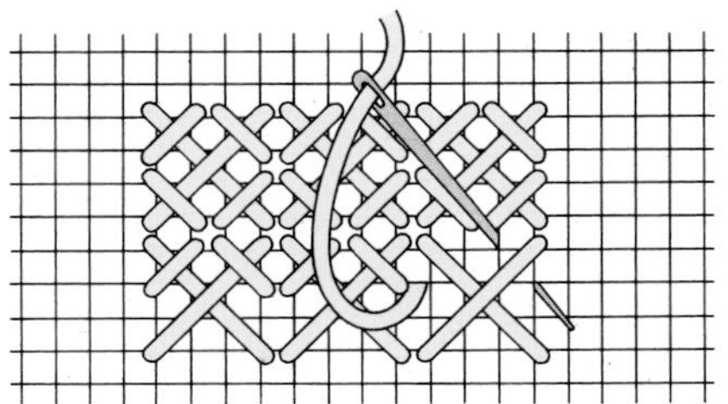

Rice stitch This is also known as William and Mary stitch and crossed corners. Work it in 2 steps. First work a large cross in a thick yarn over 4 crossing threads, then work a half cross in a thinner yarn over first the top corners and then the lower ones.

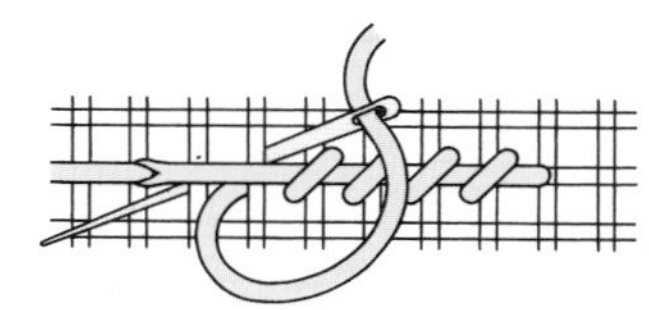

Design
Although the warp and weft structure of the canvas imposes certain limitations there is still great scope for designing needlepoint. As a technical guide, use only a few stitches on complicated designs, allowing the colors and shapes to give the work its interest; on simpler designs or on a single-color piece, you can vary the stitches so that the textural variety becomes the focal point. You can achieve further variation by combining threads of different finishes, such as matt and gloss, or by using two colors in a stitch that lends itself to this, such as rice stitch. You can sketch your own design or adapt one from something which inspires you.

Stitches
Before you begin, try out some stitches on a sampler to establish an even tension and to see their effects.
To secure the thread run it across the back of the canvas a short distance away from the starting point; after working a few stitches weave the loose end through the back of the stitching. Start and finish subsequent threads by weaving them underneath existing stitching.
Pass the needle from the right hand on top of the canvas to the left hand underneath, and back again.
If you are working a straight stitch which doesn't cover the canvas completely, such as upright Gobelin, you can lay a background of tramming stitch first in the same wool as that used for the stitch. This raises the surface stitches so that they cover any canvas that shows through, producing a padded effect. It is often worked on double-mesh canvas. To do tramming, work a series of split horizontal stitches of mixed lengths, as shown above right, to cover the same amount of area as the stitches to follow. Then work the stitch over the trammed thread, catching the loose end of the tramming thread on the WS as you come across it. If you do more than one row of tramming stagger the stitches.

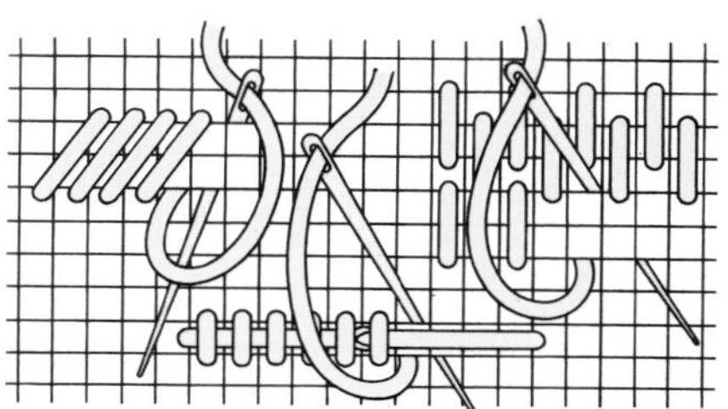

Gobelin stitch This has many variations.
Slanted: Work over 2 vertical and 3 horizontal threads.
Interlocked: Work an upright stitch over 3 horizontal threads leaving 1 vertical thread between so that the next row can interlock.
Trammed upright: Lay a tramming thread first and work an upright stitch over 2 horizontal threads.

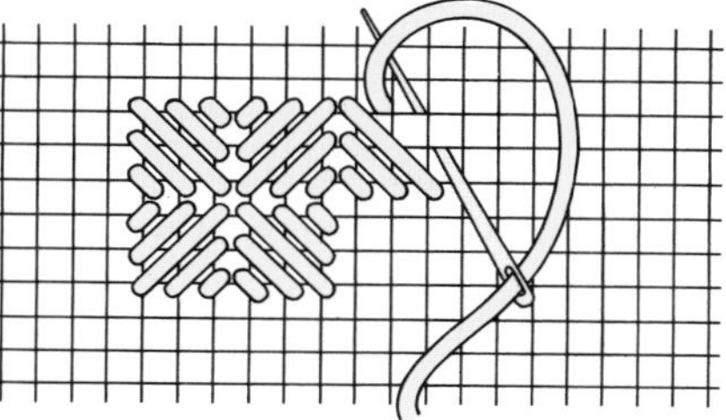

Flat stitch or satin stitch squares Work a series of diagonal stitches over 1, 2, 3, 2 and 1 crossing threads. Then work the adjacent square so that the stitches slant in the opposite direction, and continue alternating in this way.

Square eyelet stitch Work stitches to radiate from a central point, each extending over the same number of threads, the number depending upon the area you want the stitch to cover. To fill in the outside edge of the stitch, use small back stitches (p18).

Smyrna stitch Work a diagonal cross and then work an upright cross on top.

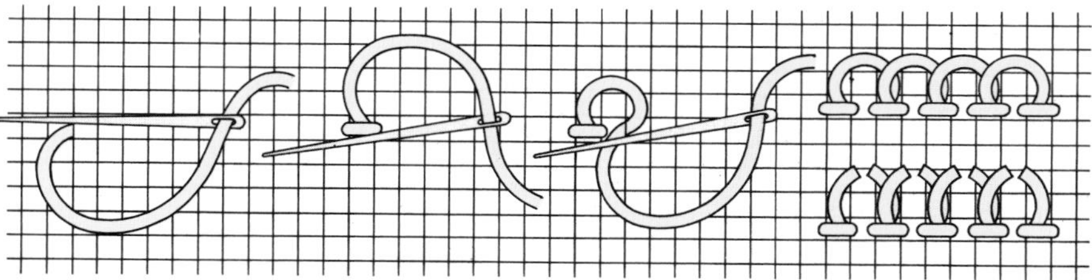

Turkey work Holding the end of the yarn at the back of the canvas, bring the needle out and over 1 vertical thread to the right. Repeat process, leaving the thread to make a loop above the needle. Hold this in position with your thumb and make another stitch to the right over 1 vertical thread and draw up firmly to make a holding stitch. Work the rows either 1 or 2 horizontal threads apart from the bottom to the top of the area. Work each row from left to right across the width of the canvas, completing it before beginning the next. Cut the loops as each row is completed and fluff them out.

Tent stitch bag and pin

Tent stitch is one of the most commonly used needlepoint stitches. Its simplicity and the small area which it covers make it an excellent stitch for pictorial representations. Here are two projects in tent stitch which are visually lively and which you can use to great effect as fashion accessories. The pin would look equally eye-catching in another simple shape, such as a fish.

You will need (for the bag)
soft embroidery thread,
10 skeins for grass; 2 skeins for river and sky; 1 skein each for remainder of landscape (in 9 colors)
canvas 12 × 20in (30 × 50cm) with 12 holes per 1in (2·5cm)
tapestry needle
stretcher frame
stiff cotton and interlining, both same size as canvas
sewing thread to match grass
2 snap fasteners

Preparing the canvas
Leaving at least a $1\frac{1}{2}$in (3cm) border all around, mark out in pencil the working area of 9 × 16in (23 × 40cm). Because of the diagonal pull of the stitches it is essential to frame the canvas before working to prevent distortion.

Method of working
The front of the bag is in tent stitch worked diagonally over 1 thread and the back is in half-cross stitch worked diagonally over 2 threads. When stitching, use both hands and work the stitches in up and down movements to avoid distortion. The half-cross stitch not only gives a contrast in texture but it is much faster to work. To prevent the light colors from getting dirty it is best to deal with them last, working all the dark colors first. Work the rows of each shape from the bottom diagonally upward (see chart) to ensure a smooth, flat surface.

Front Using a length of thread approximately 32in (80cm) with a knot at one end, start by outlining the trees, mountains and river in tent stitch, filling in the shapes afterward. Complete by stitching the background of grass and sky.

Back Work as for front using half-cross stitch. The river on front and back should meet when the bag is folded.

Finishing the bag
The clutch bag is a simple envelope without a gusset, which snaps shut. If you prefer, you could secure the bag with ties in a matching fabric.

1 Damp-stretch the canvas if required.

2 Machine-stitch interlining to WS of lining.

3 Pin RS of lining and canvas together.

4 Fill in any canvas showing through, using the appropriate embroidery thread and stitch.

5 Machine-stitch 3 sides, turn RS out and overcast remaining side.

6 Fold bag twice as shown in diagram and overcast side edges of top and middle sections.

7 Sew the first two halves of the snap fasteners (p32) onto the positions indicated by circles on the stitch diagram (opposite page). Then, making certain that the alignment is correct, attach the other halves of the fasteners to lining. Alternatively sew fabric ties. in the positions marked.

Basic equipment 156
Transferring designs 157
Basic needlepoint stitches 160

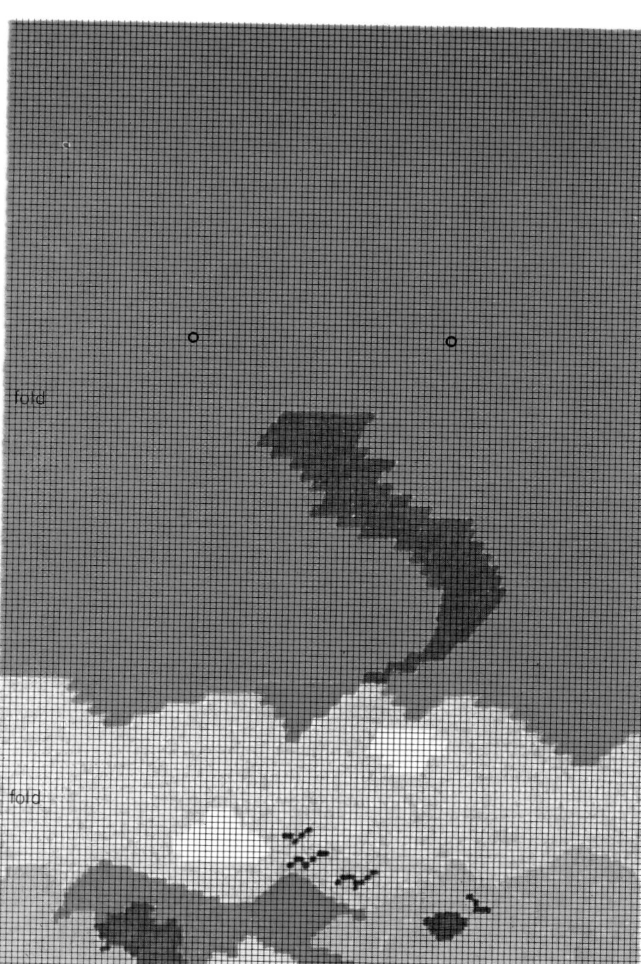

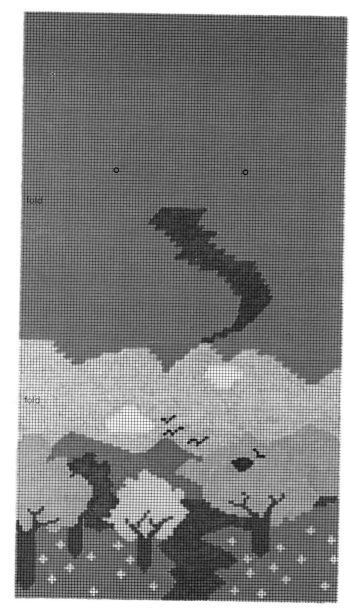

You will need (for the pin)
linen canvas, 8 × 8in (20 × 20cm) with 24 threads per 1in (2·5cm)
ring frame, 6in (15cm) wide
coton à broder, 1 skein each in red, green and off-white
tapestry needle
small piece of cardboard
2 pieces of red felt, each 2 × 3in (5 × 7·5cm)
sewing thread in green and red
sewing needle
medium-sized safety pin

Method of working
Place the canvas in the hoop so that it is very taut. Work the entire strawberry in tent stitch. Start the foliage of the strawberry in green, following the chart. Then fill in the red areas and complete filling in the off-white speckles and reflection marks. Remove the work from the hoop and cut around the edge, leaving a ½in (12mm) canvas border. Be careful not to cut the stitching between stalk and fruit.

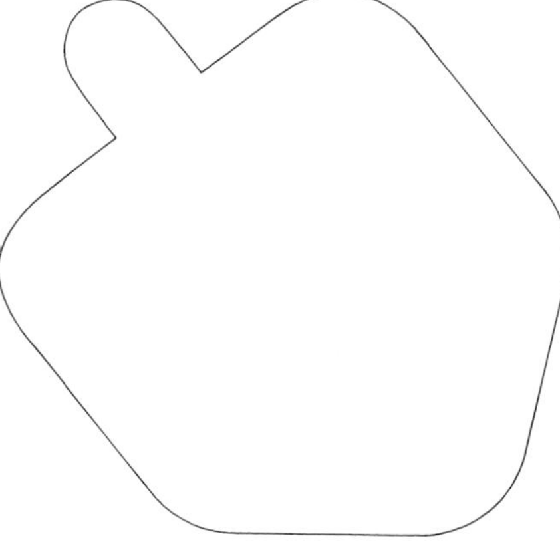

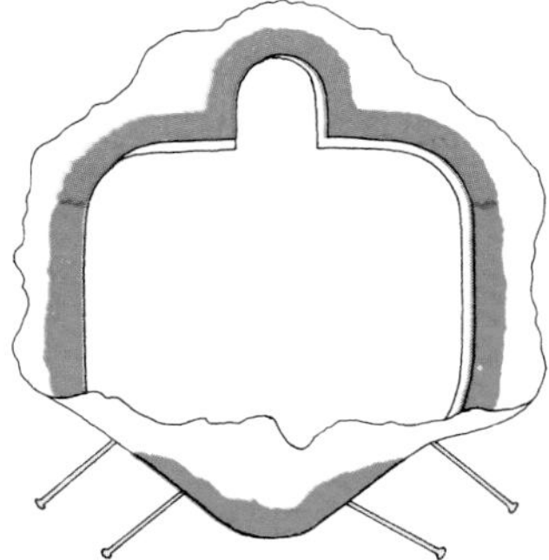

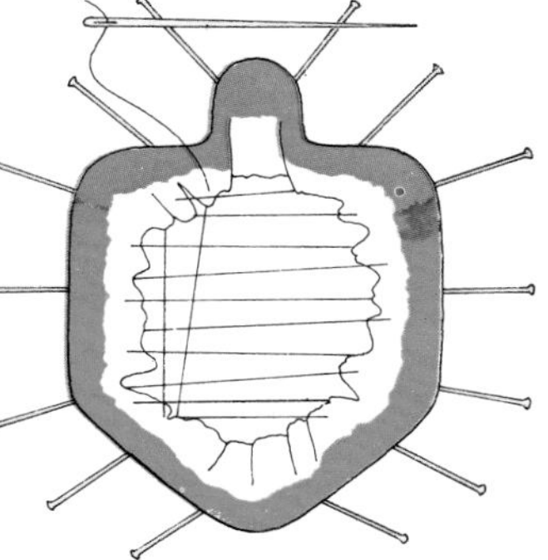

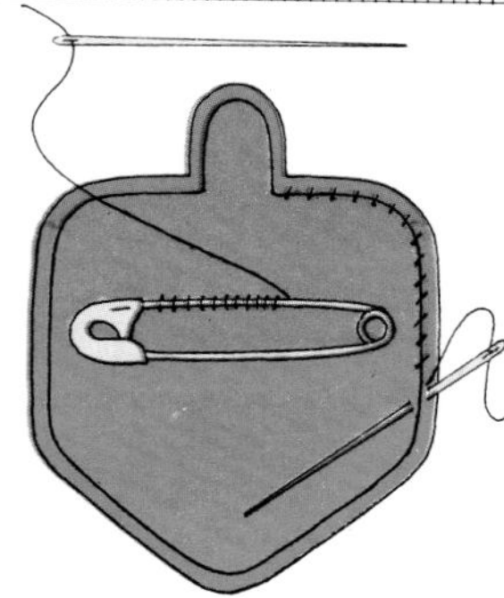

Finishing the pin
1 Cut out the cardboard into the strawberry shape, using the template above.
2 Overcast a thick piece of felt no larger than the template to the cardboard.
3 Stretch the embroidered piece over the cardboard and felt and pin all around the edge through the cardboard and embroidery, being careful not to fray the sides of the stalk.
4 Secure the material to the cardboard by stitching back and forth across the over-lapped edges.
5 Cut a piece of red felt to the same shape as the strawberry cardboard and baste it to the back, being careful to cover all the canvas and stitches underneath.
6 Overcast the felt to the side edges of the embroidery with matching thread.
7 Overcast a safety pin to the center of the felt, using a double thickness of red sewing thread.

Textural needlepoint rug

The needlepoint rug opposite demonstrates the textural qualities which you can produce by using the same color throughout a work with a number of different stitches. If you prefer more regular shapes than those shown you could work the stitches in stripes or squares. Equally you can achieve textural variation using the same stitch throughout; simply change the stitch direction according to the pattern you wish to create.
The instructions given are for a rug with finished canvas measurements of 40 × 25½in (100 × 63·5cm); with the fringe the rug will of course be longer.
Work from one end of the rug to the other, and roll canvas not being worked.

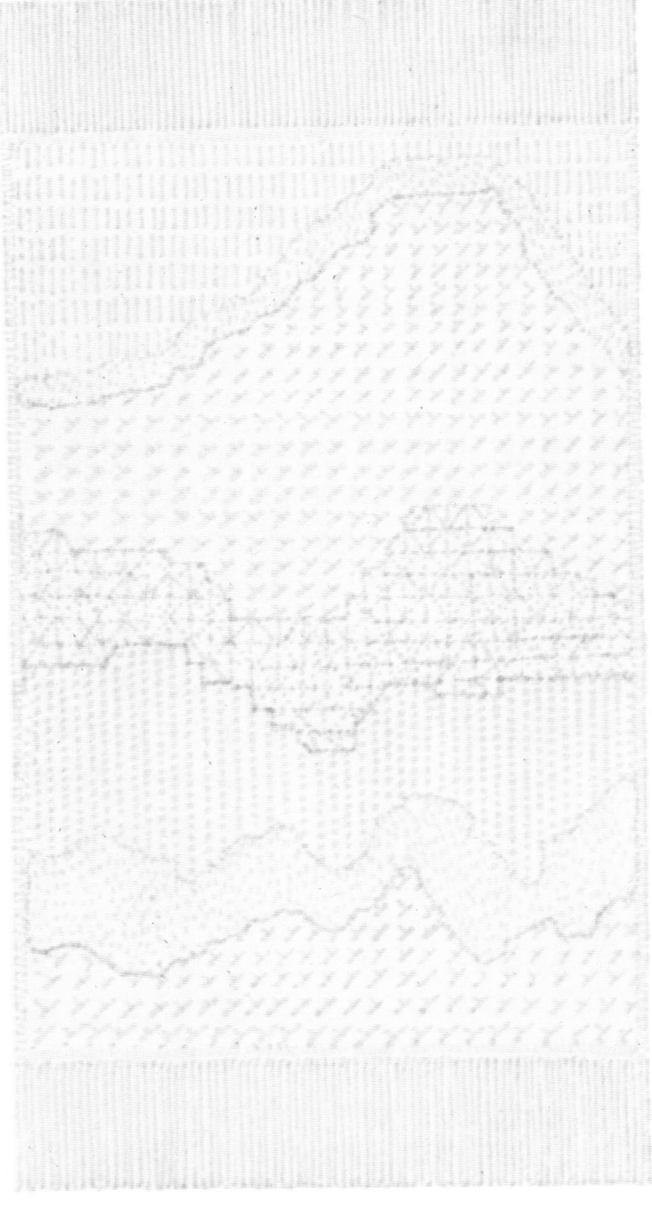

You will need
24 × 2oz (50g) balls rug yarn (uncut), about 27yd (25m) each
rug canvas 45 × 30½in (10 × 73·5cm) with 10 holes per 3in (7·5cm)
large tapestry needle
graph paper
felt-tipped pen

Preparing the canvas
Before you begin, turn all the edges of the canvas in 2in (5cm) along a thread so that the holes on top match those underneath. Then overcast the side edges with buttonhole stitch (p18) using single yarn and 2 stitches in each hole. This step is important because it prevents fraying and provides a strong finish. When you come to stitch the remaining folded areas treat them as if they were a single layer.

Transferring the design
On sheets of graph paper taped together at the back, or on one large sheet if available, enlarge the design to full size. Then place the prepared canvas over the design and trace it onto the prepared canvas with a felt-tipped pen.

Working the rug
It is important throughout not to pull the stitches too tightly as this distorts the canvas and spoils the finished appearance.
Using the chart on this page as a guide, work all the stitches in horizontal rows across the rug except the knotted stitches which you should work vertically. The stitches as they appear from top in the diagram are:
Upright Gobelin using double yarn and worked in rows alternating between 2 and 3 threads of canvas. Between every row work back stitches in single yarn.
Turkey work using double yarn.
Long-armed cross stitch using double yarn, worked over 2 threads vertically and 4 threads horizontally.
Flat stitch using double yarn and worked up to 3 threads in each direction.
Knotted stitch worked vertically using double yarn.
Turkey work as above.
Long-armed cross stitch as above.

Key to chart

Upright Gobelin

Turkey work

Long-armed cross stitch

Flat stitch

Knotted stitch

Finishing
If after you have done all the stitching any canvas threads are still visible, cover them by working small tent stitches or back stitches (p18), using single or double yarn as appropriate. Trim all loose ends at the back of the work and make sure they are securely fastened.
Make a simple fringe (p103) at either end of the rug with double strands of yarn which are about 10½in (26cm) long before being folded. Trim all the ends to 5in (12cm) when fringe is completed.
If necessary press the WS of the rug on a well-padded ironing board. Press very lightly but avoid the areas of Turkey stitch which must not be flattened.

Bargello

Bargello or Florentine embroidery is the general name applied to all needlepoint designs worked in a straight stitch, which is also known as flame stitch or Hungarian point. Beautiful historical examples of this work are on display at the Bargello Palace in Florence – this is how the technique got its name. Despite the fact that all the stitches are straight, you can work them in several ways to form curved or geometric designs and sometimes a combination of the two.

As with other forms of needlepoint you need to count the threads of canvas as you work, but the advantage of Bargello is that it covers several threads at a time (most stitches are worked over at least 4). Because it is quick to work, Bargello is often used for soft furnishings such as chair covers and pillows. You will find working instructions for three pillows on p168.

Designs

In terms of color, Bargello is typified by subtle shaded gradations. In traditional work, generally used for furnishings, dull greens, pinks and browns prevailed but today there is no reason to be confined to these limited ranges. For beginners, however, it is better to use only two or three colors, incorporating as many intermediate shades of these in a work as possible and working each line in a darker or lighter shade than the last. The basic Florentine stitches used lend themselves to a variety of patterns, both curved and geometric. The stitches shown here will give you some idea of the scope, and you can experiment to create your own.

Materials

As Bargello is a form of needlepoint the materials required are the same. Wool is traditionally used. Strands of crewel wool cover the canvas well and are durable, but you can also use tapestry wool. The canvas should be single-mesh.

General hints

Before you begin, experiment with the yarn to see how it covers the canvas and to determine how many strands (if you are using crewel wool), you will need. From this you can estimate the quantity required. If you are working with a closely related color scheme, sort out your skeins of wool first and assort them in the appropriate shaded sequence. All embroidery threads are labeled with a number to designate color. By keeping these tags visible on the skeins throughout the work, you will reduce the risk of using the wrong color.

If you do make a mistake of any kind, it is quicker to cut the stitches than to pull them out. (It is an unwise economy to work with used yarn which tends to fray.)

On square or rectangular objects, where precision is essential, begin the work at the marked center lines unless otherwise indicated, stitching outward from the center. You can then stitch remaining rows straight across.

Patterns for development

The scale of the pattern depends upon the type of yarn and size of canvas used. The stitch patterns shown opposite would appear slightly larger than this size on canvas with 12 holes per 1in (2·5cm). To get some idea of what the scale would be on any other size of canvas try one repeat of the design.

Stitches

Whether straight or angular, Bargello patterns depend for their success upon an accurate foundation row of stitches. The simple straight stitch is repeated over the same number of threads in a straight row with the back looking similar to the front. Do not make the stitches too long, otherwise they will snag with handling. Three stitches are shown below.

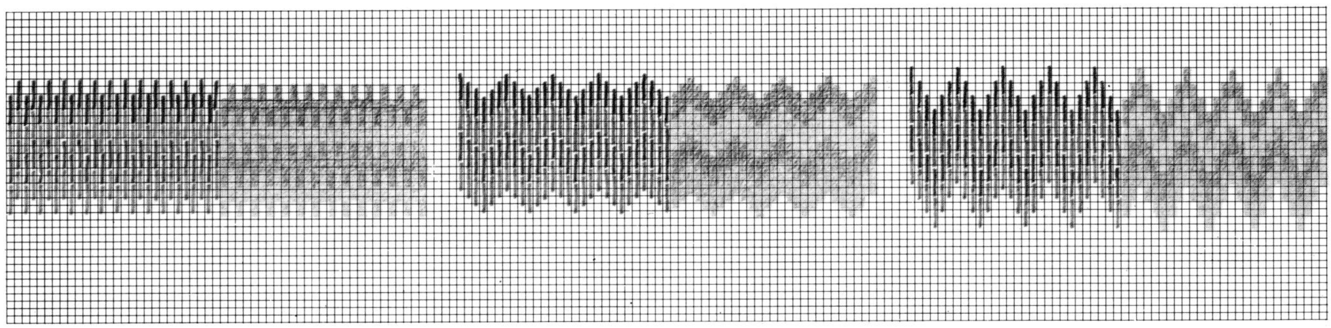

Florentine stitch A Work each stitch over 4 horizontal threads and back 2, according to the pattern. Interlock the rows of stitches as shown above left.

Florentine stitch B Work all the stitches over 4 horizontal threads, starting each adjacent stitch 1 horizontal thread above or below the previous stitch, as shown above.

Florentine stitch C This is similar to the previous stitch, except that this stitch steps up or down by 2 horizontal threads at a time.

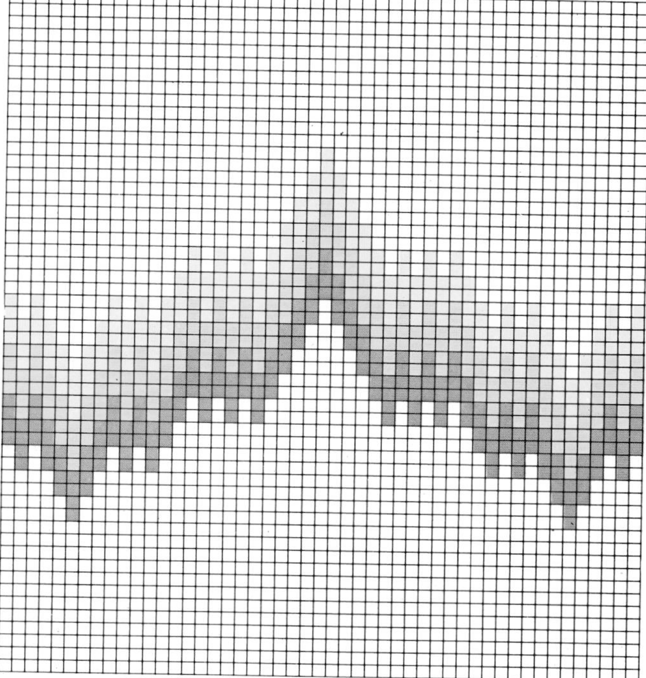

Chevron trellis Work the outer trellis in 2 rows of 4 threads and back 2. Fill remaining areas in the same stitch, or shorter ones, according to the graph. Shown above is one trellis repeat.

Honeycomb Work the outline over 4 horizontal threads and back 2, except at sides where you work 2 vertically adjacent rows, each over 4 threads. Fill the centers as indicated in the pattern below.

Aurora Borealis Work this over 4 threads and back 2, staggering the pattern as shown above to form a curved geometric pattern. You could add a paler shade of pink to the bottom line.

Fountain brocade Work this pattern over 6 threads and back 2 in alternating sequence as shown below. Toward the bottom of the motif work adjacent horizontal rows in groups as shown.

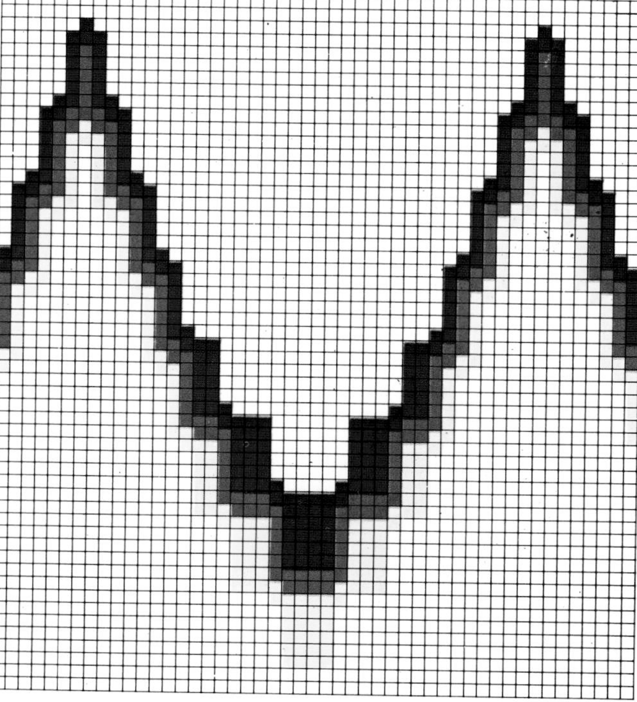

Pillows
Bargello is a popular form of embroidery for soft household furnishings, and any of the designs shown here could equally well be used for chair covers and other items. The pillows on this page are based on three zigzag formations. Instructions are given for each pillow and the colors are coded alphabetically according to the working sequence in each. An attractive backing fabric for the pillows would be a soft wool, such as the one used, burlap or velvet. You can finish the edges, as shown, by attaching a twisted cord made from yarns used in the work, or by adding piping (p102).

Preparing the canvas
Mount the canvas on a frame. Find the exact center of canvas 2 and 3 and baste a horizontal and vertical line through it. Baste the borders of the 12in (30cm) sq for all 3 pillows. On pillow 1 where the stitching begins at the top of the canvas, you only need to baste a vertical line through the center, since the top edge of the pillow can act as the horizontal guide. If you are experienced in canvas work you might find a frame unnecessary, in which case you can work free-hand, with the areas not being worked rolled loosely.

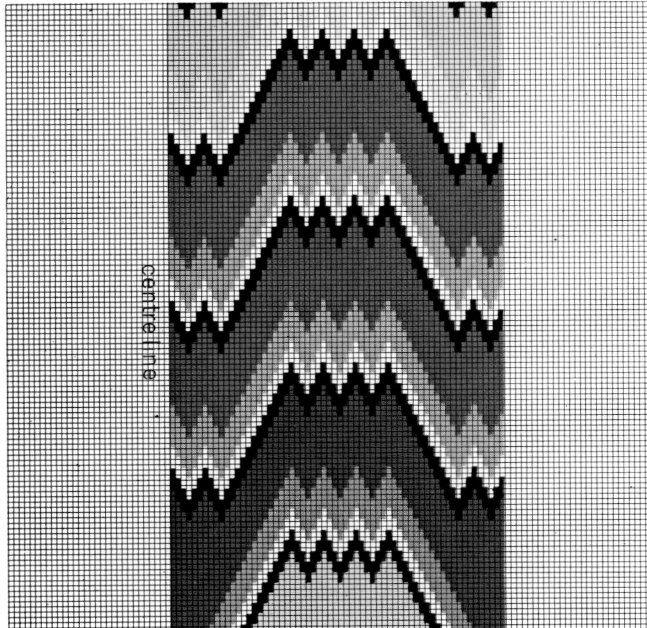

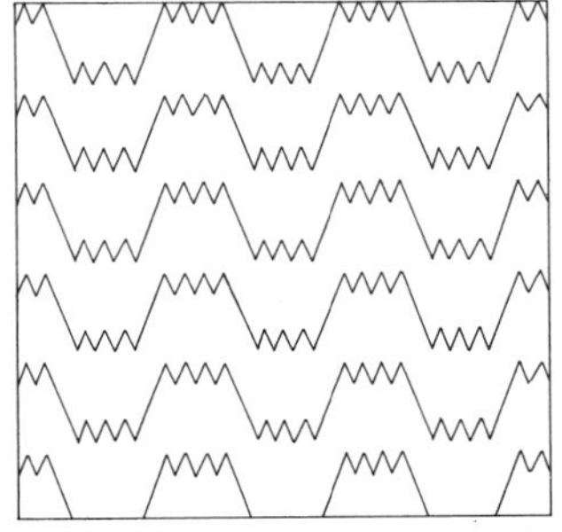

You will need (for pillow 1)
- crewel wool in colors coded A–H: 3 skeins A,B,C,F; 2 skeins D; 4 skeins E; 5 skeins G; 1 skein H
- tapestry needle
- canvas 18 × 18in (45 × 45cm) with 14 threads per 1in (2·5cm)
- stretcher frame

Method of working
Prepare your canvas as described. Use 4 strands of wool and work over 4 horizontal threads of canvas throughout, dropping 2. Start by working the top line of color A from the center across, first to one edge and then to the other. Carefully counting the rows of stitches between, work the 5 remaining rows of color A. Stitch the remaining colors in sequence, working row by row from the bottom edge and leaving any spaces for new colors to be filled by subsequent rows. When finished, remove the basting threads.

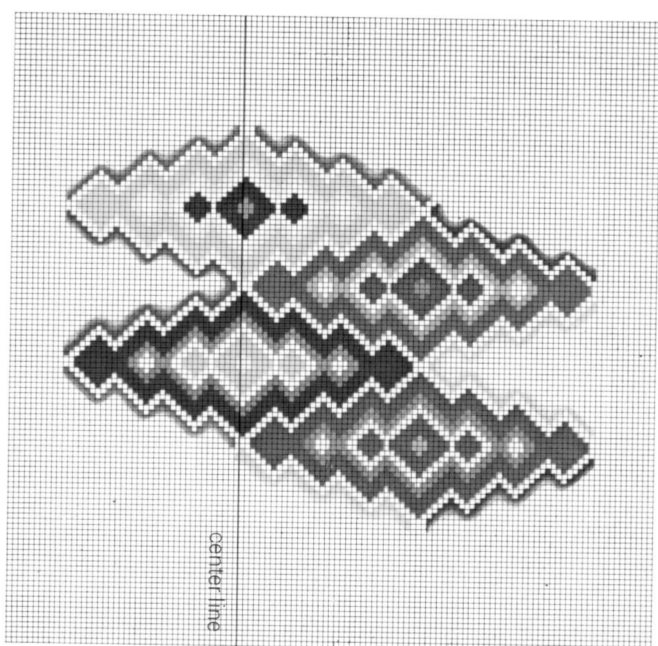

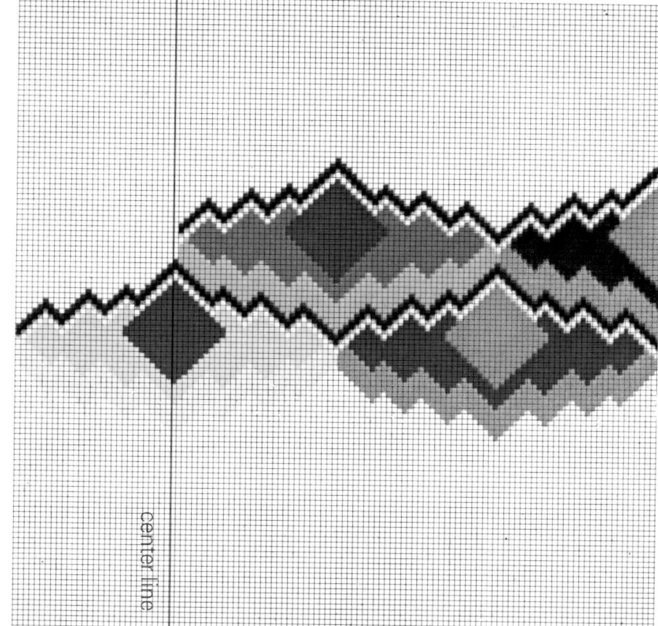

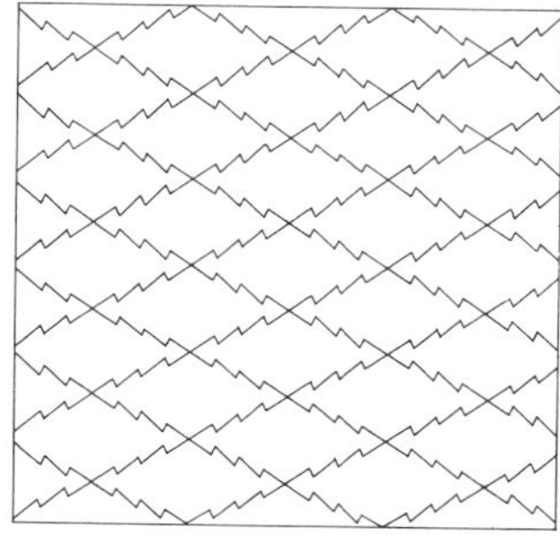

You will need (for pillow 2)
crewel wool in colors coded A-I: 9 skeins A; 5 skeins B, D, F, H; 1 skein C, E, G, I
needle, canvas and frame as pillow 1

Method of working
Prepare the canvas as described and baste further vertical lines every 33 canvas threads from both sides of the center. Work over 2 threads of canvas, dropping 1, with 4 strands of wool.
Begin by working the outer trellis foundation in color A, starting the 1st row 15 threads above the center of the canvas; stitch first to one side and then to the other, counting very carefully against the graph. Complete the foundation trellis in color A, working the remaining motifs outward from the center. The top (and bottom) stitch of every motif should fall on the basted vertical lines. If they do not you should make any adjustments at this point.
Allow for the fact that some of the stitches are common to upward and downward rows of adjacent motifs.
There are 4 separate color schemes running through the motifs. It is easiest to work through all of the motifs of one color scheme before beginning the next and so on.
To work each motif, begin with the predominant dark shade and work 2 rows of this inside the trellis foundation, filling in the diamonds which remain at the far ends in the same color. Within this, work 1 row of the lighter predominant shade. Then in color A, work a small cross in the space left at the far ends and 1 row which forms an inner trellis. All that remains of the motif now is to work 2 dark rows of the 2nd color, working a small cross of its paler shade in the center.

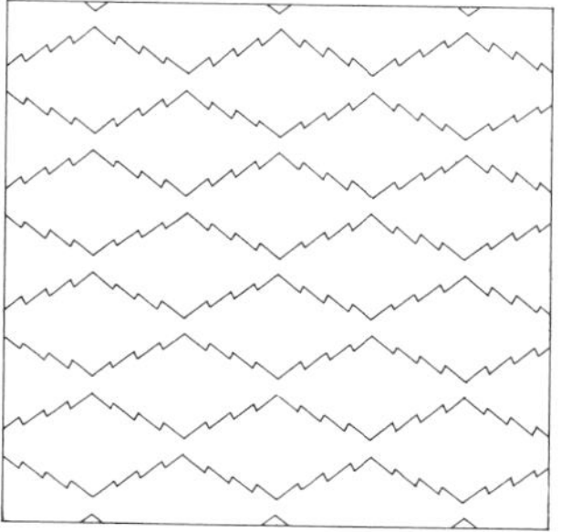

You will need (for pillow 3)
crewel wool in colors coded A-H: 5 skeins A, 3 skeins B, 6 skeins C, 2 skeins D and E, 4 skeins F and G, 8 skeins H
needle, canvas and frame as pillow 1

Method of working
Prepare the canvas as described. Use 4 strands of wool together and work over 2 threads dropping 1. Consult the graph and find the zigzag line closest to the horizontal center.
Work this line in color A, from center toward one side edge and then the other. Carefully checking that the foundation stitches match those on the graph, work all the other outline rows of color A, starting from the left side of the canvas. Now work all the rows of color B, again from left to right. When you have completed the rows of foundation stitches, work the blocks starting from those running down the center and continuing outward in both directions. The best way of working each block is to stitch the central diamond first, then the color adjacent to it and finally the color at the bottom of the block. The color sequence of the central blocks, for example, would be C, D, E. The blocks between the central ones would be C, F, G; those on the side edges would alternate between H, A, H and H, C, H.
Remove the basting threads when all the blocks are completed.

Basic surface stitches

Unlike needlepoint stitches which are geometric and worked on a counted-thread canvas or fabric, surface stitches can move in any direction and on any type of fabric. Because of this they lend themselves to a wide variety of shapes and textures. Based on the simple motions of running, looping and knotting, surface stitches can be used to follow the line of a design, to fill an enclosed shape or to produce random decoration.

It is better, initially, to learn just a few stitches and to use them well rather than to attempt to use them all. To see what sort of variations you can achieve it is worth experimenting with stitches. Take different types of fabric and try the stitches on spare scraps; vary stitch sizes and shapes and use different types of thread.

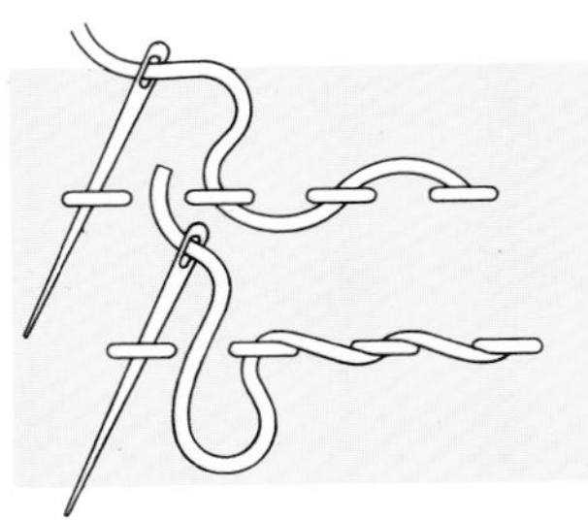

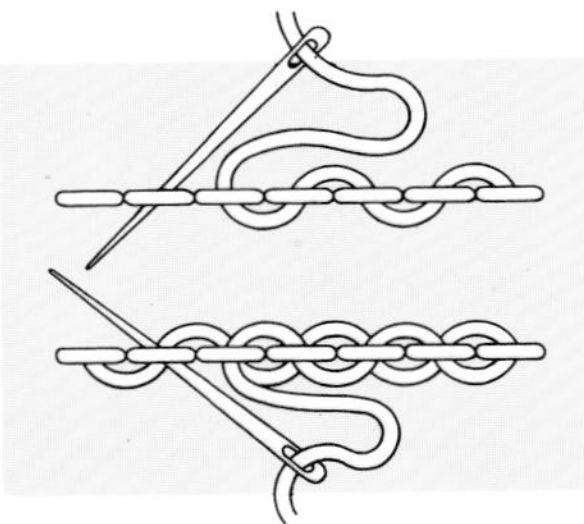

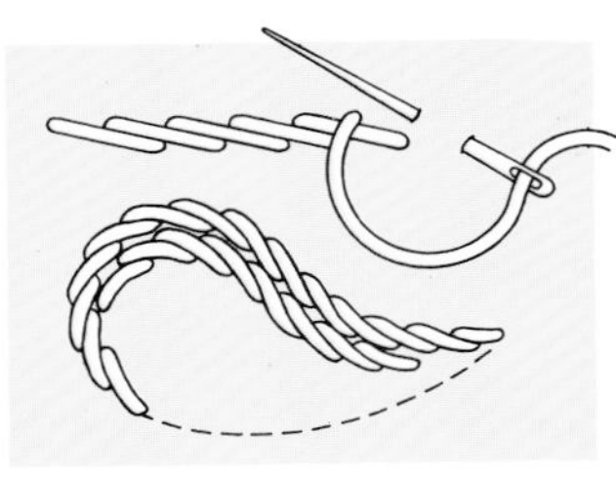

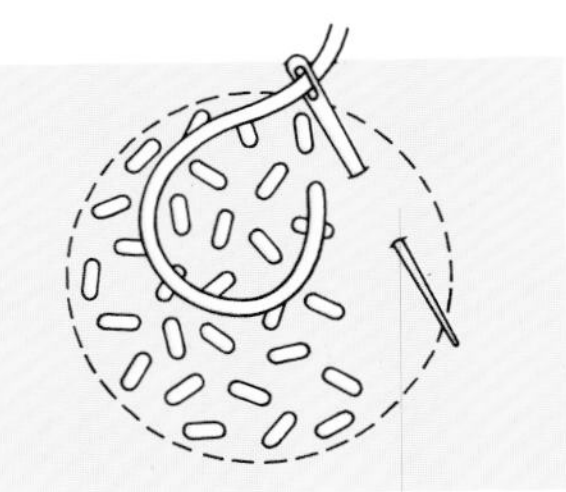

Running stitch (see p18)
Threaded running stitch: First work a line of running stitches with small intervals. Then thread the same or a contrasting yarn under the line of running stitches, as shown.
Whipped running stitch: Work the line of running stitches. Then pass the yarn over and under the stitches without piercing the fabric. To avoid splitting the yarn you can use the eye of the needle to thread the whipped stitch through.

Back stitch (see p18)
Threaded back stitch: Like threaded running stitch, this stitch produces a raised effect. First work a line of back stitches. Then thread the back stitches alternately up and down, working from right to left. Repeat the threading if you like, working through the back stitches in the opposite direction. You can use the same or a contrasting thread.

Stem stitch This is useful for any line or outline of shapes and attractive as a filling if the stitches are worked in close rows. Work from left to right, taking regular, slightly slanting stitches along the line. Keep the thread below the needle. The WS of the stitch should look like back stitch.

Seeding This is an interesting filling stitch. Make tiny straight stitches at all angles and in any direction, keeping their lengths basically the same. For a heavier effect, work 2 stitches over each other.

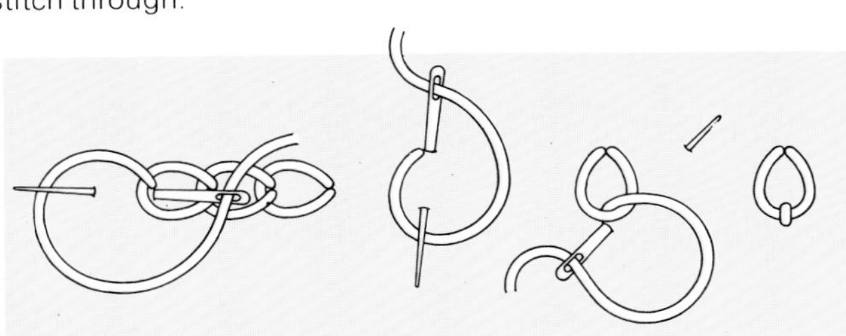

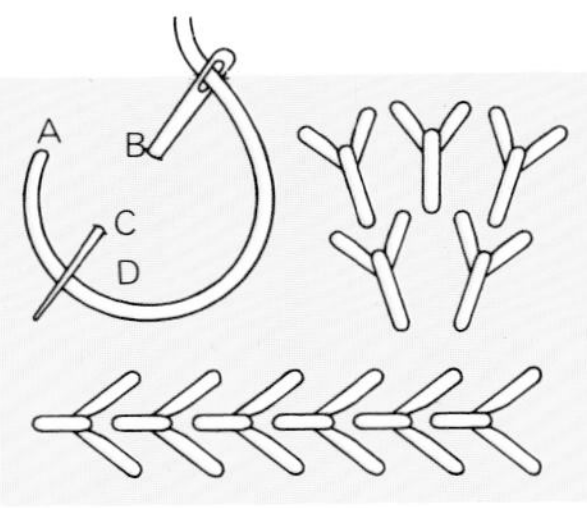

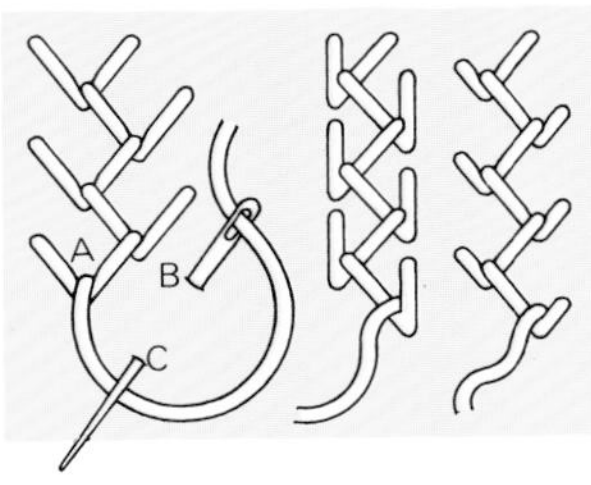

Chain stitch Work this singly in a straight line or as a filling. Bring out the thread at the top of the line leaving a loose end on the WS and hold it down with your free thumb. Insert needle where it last emerged and bring it out a short distance away from where it entered. Pull the thread through, keeping the loop under the needle. Check to keep the length and tension of the stitches even. Work the loose end under the stitches and overcast tiny stitches into back of first chain to secure.

Detached chain stitch: Fasten each chain with a small stitch at the base of the loop. Vary the angles of stitches and group them together to form shapes.
Filling chain stitch: Work lines of chain stitch closely together. The effect is that of a knitted surface.

Fly stitch Bring the thread up through the fabric at A and hold it down with your thumb. Insert needle at B and bring it out below at C. Pull through the loop and tie down with a small stitch. The length of this may be varied. Try working this stitch in all directions, including arranging them in patterns, overlapping them and so on.

Feather stitch This is useful for borders, outlines and light fillings for shapes. Bring the needle out at A and hold thread down with free thumb. Insert needle to the right on the same level at B and take a stitch into the center at C. Keeping the thread under the needle point, pull through to make the characteristic Y-shape. Looping the thread towards the left side, repeat process and work these movements alternately.

Preparation
Using the correct needle, thread and fabric makes all the difference in your enjoyment of stitching. It is a good plan to start off with a yarn similar in scale to the weft thread of the background fabric; the needle should be slightly thicker in size. You can choose other thicknesses of yarns for a more varied surface.

Begin by using one stitch only in shades of one color from light to dark; then try changing the scale in both width and depth, overlapping some lines, curving others and simply discovering your own variations. Keep these stitch doodles for reference in a folder or notebook.
When planning a work, think of its purpose. If the article is likely to receive hard wear and washing, work small firm stitches to make a strong bond with the background fabric. On more decorative objects you can use larger stitches.

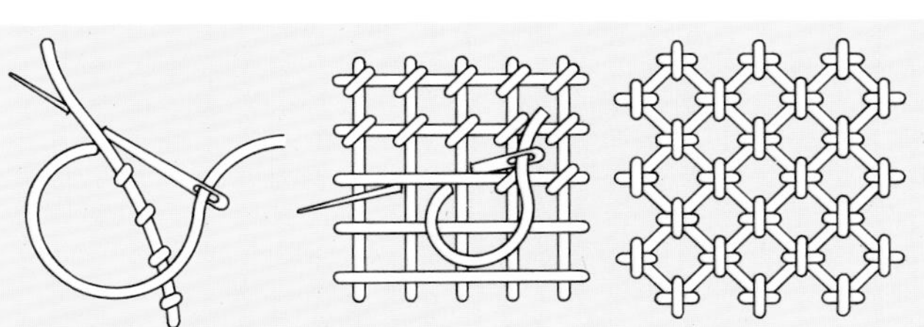

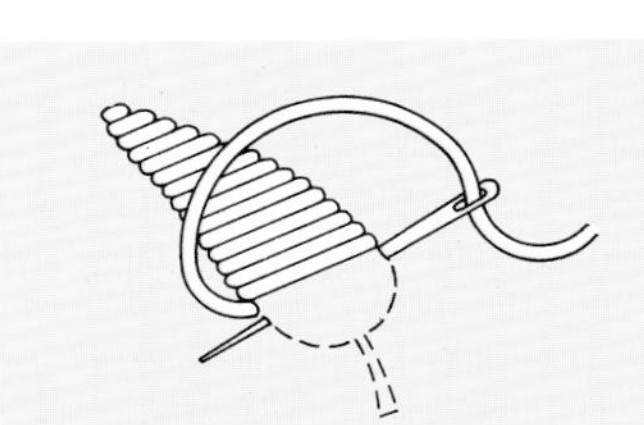

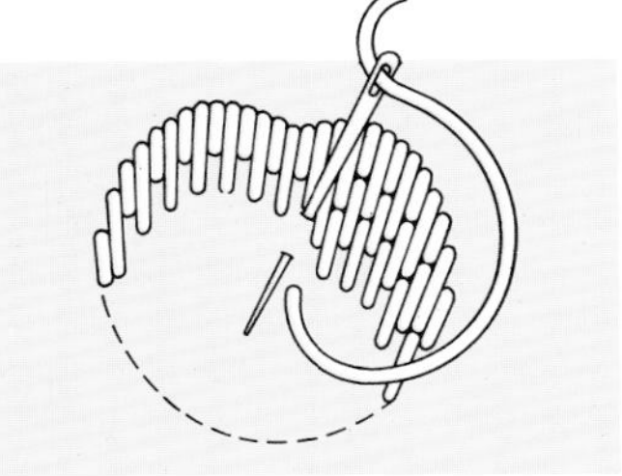

Couching Lay a thread on the surface of the fabric. Catch it in place with a new thread using small stitches at regular intervals. When you work the couching stitches, hold the laid thread firmly in place on the fabric. This is often used for thick yarns and metalic threads.

Jacobean couching: This stitch is useful for filling the centers of flowers and other enclosed shapes. Lay long evenly spaced threads across the area horizontally and vertically or diagonally as on a trellis. Tie down intersecting threads, with a small, slanting stitch in the case of the horizontally and vertically laid threads, or with an upright cross stitch.

Satin stitch This consists of straight stitches worked side by side across a shape. In counted-thread embroidery, the stitches are usually kept to the same length but in freer surface work they can vary. Keep the stitches short so that they do not pull out of shape. A frame is advisable for this and all variations of satin stitch.

Long and short stitch This is a variation of satin stitch which is frequently used for shading in crewel work in various colors or textures of thread, and for filling areas which would be too large or irregular for satin stitch alone. Work the 1st row in alternating long and short straight stitches starting at the outside edge, and the 2nd and all subsequent rows in equal-sized satin stitches between the gaps.

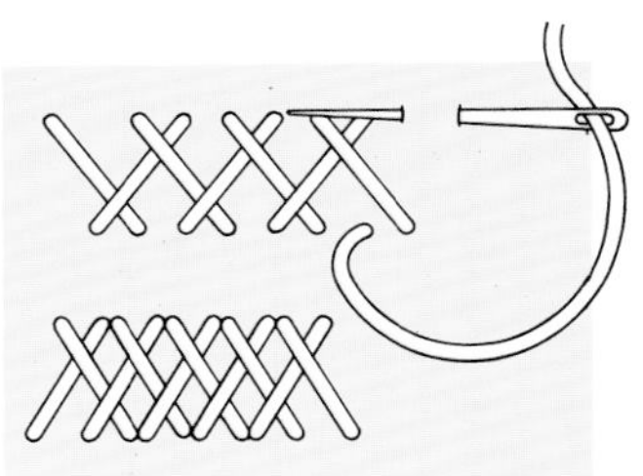

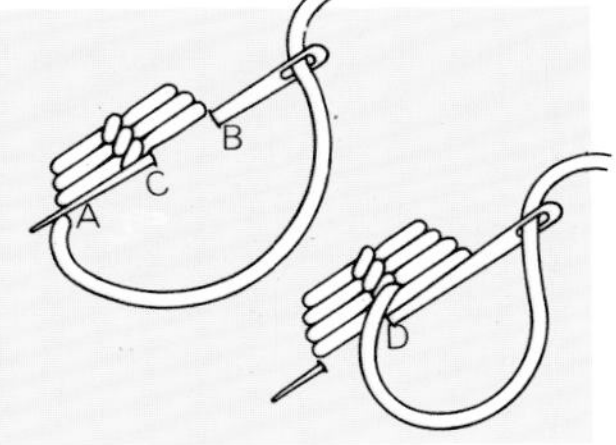

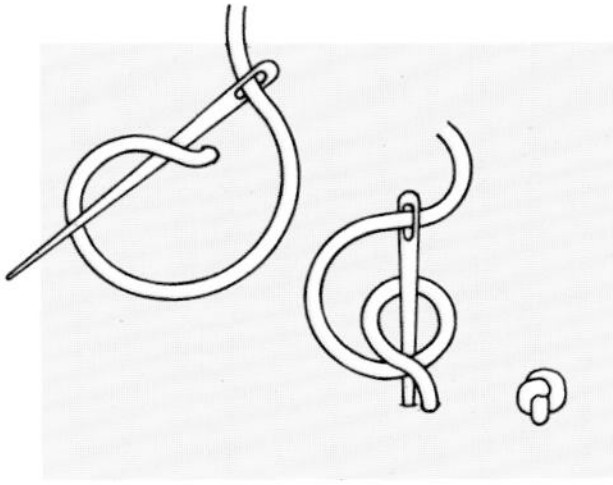

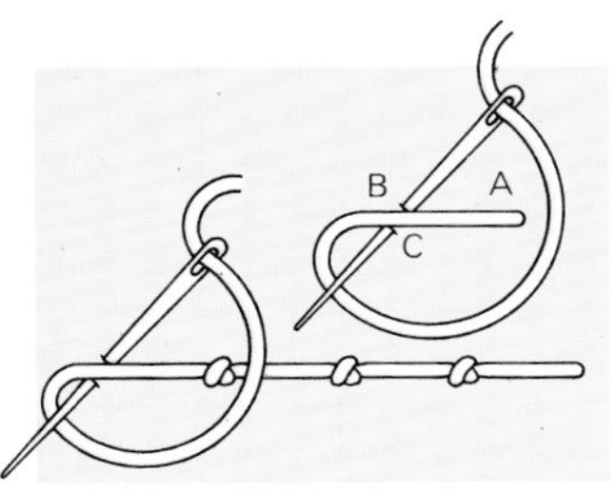

Herringbone stitch Work from left to right between imaginary parallel lines. Bring the needle out on the lower line and insert it to the right on the upper line taking a small horizontal stitch to the left with the thread below the needle. Draw through. Then insert the needle on the lower line a little to the right and take a small stitch to the left with the thread above the needle. Repeat. For a closed effect, leave no spaces between stitches.

Romanian stitch This stitch, which is used for broad outlines and fillings, is similar to satin stitch but is tied down in the center. Work from the top downward. Bring thread out at left side of the shape at A, enter at B with thread below the needle and emerge at C. Take a small diagonal stitch over the laid thread to D and emerge on the left side of the shape. Continue working these two movements until the shape is filled.

French knot Bring thread up to point where knot is required. Hold thread taut between left thumb and first finger and with the needle under the thread twist it away from you once. Still holding the thread taut to avoid any loose looping, insert needle close to the point at which the thread first emerged. For a more nubby texture twist the thread 2 or 3 times.

Coral stitch You can use this knotted stitch for straight or curved lines and for fillings. Bring the thread out at A. Hold the thread down along the line to be covered with the other thumb, insert the needle just above the thread at B. Then take a small slanting stitch to just below the line to emerge at C. Pull through the loop to make the knot. Repeat process, making the knots at short regular intervals.

Fashion embroidery

With fashion embroidery you can be as free or as stylized as you choose, depending on the effect you wish to create on the garment. You can plan and work the embroidered sections beforehand if you are making a garment, but there is still plenty of scope for embroidering clothes already made. Embroidery is a marvelous vehicle for adding life and color to fading, tired-looking clothes – or, indeed, to new clothes that could do with decoration. The outfits on this page show that whether you choose a specific floral motif or a mixture of freely worked filling stitches, the result will give the garment a distinctive look. You will find stitching and making-up instructions for the garments shown on pp 174–7.

Ready-made clothes

Take stock of your wardrobe and see what there is. A pair of jeans, a summer T-shirt, a scarf, even knitted garments (see p229) are potential candidates for embroidery. You can stitch directly onto the garments or you can add embroidered details, such as pockets and cuffs.
Embroidery can be used to inject humor. An idea for a sweater or T-shirt is to embroider a necklace or pin directly onto the relevant position. Very few necklaces hang straight; the outline can be slightly crooked to convey this. Or you could embroider a pocket watch on a chain on the hip pocket of a pair of jeans.

Children's clothes

Because children's clothes have a fairly short life, they might not seem worth embroidering. This need not be the case if you confine the embroidery to simple stitches or appliqué. A good reason for embroidering children's clothes is that it is an attractive form of mending (see pp 104–7). On a less practical level, children derive great pleasure from colorful decorations; even if you don't embroider their clothes, you can always apply needle and thread to their toys (see pp 112–23). You could portray pictorial scenes reflecting their interests or monogram their names (p178).

Hand-made garments

On the whole it is more advisable to embroider clothes before making them, for the simple reason that you can work any part of a garment before it is cut. Also you can work it in a frame, which is frequently not possible on finished garments. Decide what type of stitch and arrangement of stitches would be appropriate. The jacket shown here, for example, is fairly angular in shape; so too are the stitches on its embroidered sections. The skirt, on the other hand, is flowing and this quality is echoed in the stitching.
You should also consider the fabric. On linen where the threads are visible you can use a counted-thread stitch such as cross stitch (p160) which looks effective in either the same color or a multi-colored arrangement of threads. Linen also lends itself to blackwork (p182), which looks attractive on borders and collars.

Free-hand embroidery

Experiment with traditional surface stitches to see what effects you can achieve. You can extend a stitch, shorten it, superimpose one upon another. You can make the stitching sparse in some areas, dense in others. For further variation, alter the color and type of thread.

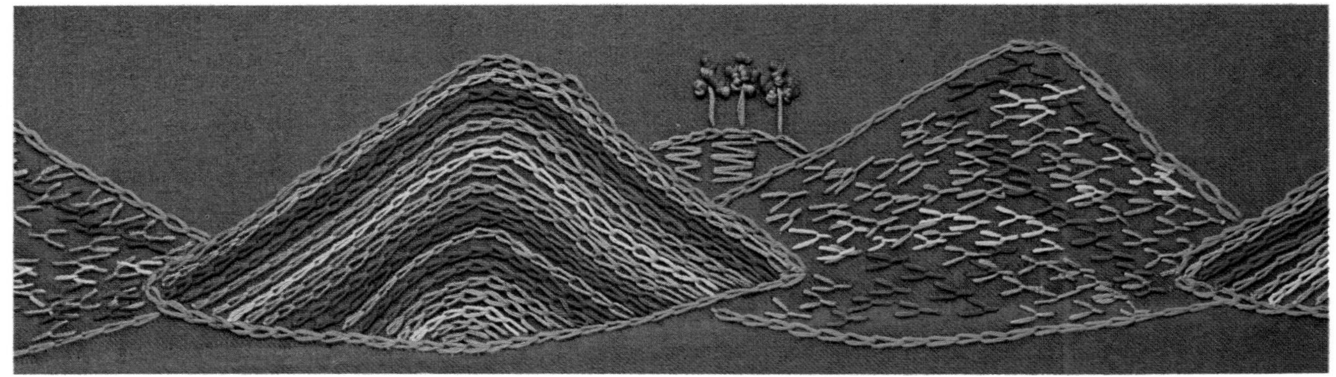

Dirndl skirt
The skirt pattern, fabric requirements and finishing instructions are exactly the same as for the dirndl skirt on p30. Sew together skirt before embroidering but leave it unhemmed. It is important to keep the fabric smooth and free from puckering when embroidering each area as it is usually inadvisable to damp-stretch a garment once it has been finished.

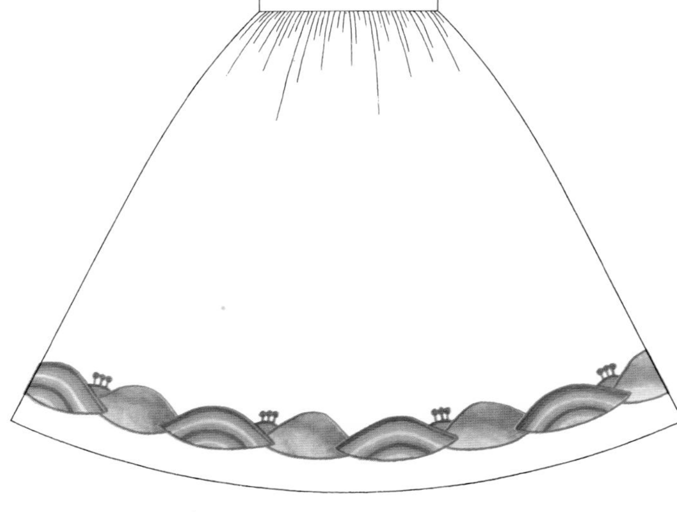

You will need
fabric and interfacing, as for dirndl skirt
embroidery floss: 3 skeins each in coordinating colors, 2 skeins in skirt color
embroidery hoop
crewel needle

Preparing the fabric
1 Press side seams flat and baste hemline.
2 Enlarge the design to size from pattern given and transfer to skirt using the dressmaker's carbon method, with base of design 4in (10cm) above basted hemline.

Working the embroidery
Use the embroidery hoop with the fabric held reasonably taut and the grain straight. Work all areas of embroidery within hoop before removing and re-positioning it over new area to be embroidered. Use 3 strands of floss throughout and stitch across seamlines.
Hills In the same color thread as skirt, work the hill outlines in chain stitch; do the larger hills first and then the small ones.
Filling stitches Working through each stitch, fill in the hills following color and contours shown in diagram. The stitches are overlapping fly stitch, chain stitch and zigzag satin stitch.
Trees Work the trunks in stem stitch and foliage in multi-colored clusters of French knots.

Finishing
1 Steam-iron on WS of embroidery, gently smoothing fabric and easing out any puckering.
2 Hem.

Dirndl skirt 30
Dirndl blouse 34
Basic equipment 156
Transferring designs 157
Finishing 158
Basic surface stitches 170

Key to stitch diagram

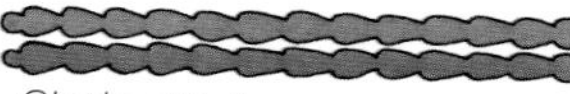
Chain stitch

Fly stitch

Zigzag satin stitch

Stem stitch

French knots

Satin stitch

Couching

Whipped chain stitch

Long-and-short stitch

Seeding

Dirndl blouse

Use the pattern, fabric requirements and finishing instructions given for the dirndl blouse on p34, but disregard the embroidery details on that page.

In satin stitch embroider flowers and leaves on front and again on sleeves, and herringbone-stitch the sleeve edges and shoulder seams. Try to use a regular-weave smooth fabric to allow the satin stitch to lie evenly on it.

You will need

fabric and other materials, as for dirndl blouse
embroidery floss: 4 skeins each in 4 co-ordinating colors
embroidery hoop
crewel needle

Preparing the fabric

1 Cut out pieces, leaving the front slit un-cut. Baste hemlines and seamlines to indicate borders of stitching areas.

2 Enlarge and transfer the floral design with dress-maker's carbon.

Working the embroidery

The working order depends on personal preference.

Shoulder and sleeve edgings Following diagram, work without the hoop all the herringbone stitching in the same color, using 3 strands of thread. Start sleeves $\frac{3}{8}$in (1cm) above basted hemlines. (You can embroider additional seams if you wish.)

Floral patterns Place the area to be embroidered within the hoop making sure the grain is straight and the fabric reasonably taut. Using the motif given, work flowers down either side of basting at at un-cut neck opening and down center of sleeves. Work the flower stems in stem stitch, using 3 strands of floss; leaves and flower petals in satin stitch, using 1 strand; and leaf veins in stem stitch, using 2 strands.

Finishing

1 Dampen the embroidery and press lightly on WS.

2 Complete cutting and finish making the blouse.

Jacket

Embroidered with French knots, stem stitch and couching, the jacket shown is based on the woman's shirt (p82). The collar has been omitted so that the neckband becomes a mandarin collar; patch pockets (p92) have been added to the jacket and slip-stitched with side openings. For a yoke as deep as the one in the photograph, add 1in (2·5cm) or more to the front yoke and subtract the same amount from the front sides. Add interfacing to all the pieces before embroidering them to facilitate stitching and work all the embroidery before finishing.

You will need

fabric, thread and buttons (optional) as woman's shirt
interfacing as woman's shirt plus extra for pockets, cuffs and yoke
lining fabric for yoke and pockets
crewel needle
tapestry yarn: 2 skeins each in 3 colors
embroidery floss: 2 skeins in 1 color

Preparing the fabric

1 Cut out all the pieces and add interfacing.
2 Baste seamlines on all pieces to be embroidered.
3 Baste a 1in (3cm) square grid using basted seamlines as border for grid.
4 Transfer the design if you feel you will be unable to work freehand; otherwise omit this step.

Working the embroidery

The stitching on all the pieces is the same throughout the jacket, except at inside cuffs and back yoke where the stitches slant in the opposite direction.
Referring to the design diagram, work the French knots in one color of tapestry yarn, positioning them correctly within the basted grid. Work the lines of stem stitch in a 2nd color of tapestry yarn followed by the outer lines which are couched. The upper line is 6 strands of embroidery floss couched at regular intervals; the lower line is a double length of tapestry yarn using the 3rd color. Work through each grid square at a time until all areas of embroidery are completed.

Finishing

1 Damp-stretch the embroidered pieces.
2 Finish jacket in the usual way. Line yoke and pockets and slip-stitch pockets in position.

Crewel shawl

Stitched entirely in tapestry yarn, this shawl is a modern interpretation of crewel work. Traditionally, crewel is wool embroidery worked on a linen twill in bold patterns using bird, leaf and other natural motifs outlined in stem stitch with intricate filling stitches such as Jacobean couching.
The shawl makes use of filling stitches within a mountainous landscape. Fabric requirements are for an adult size.

You will need

$1\frac{3}{8}$yd (1·20m) soft woolen fabric, 45in (115cm) wide
tapestry yarn: 3 skeins each in 6 colors; 1 skein in same color as fabric
crewel needle
$5\frac{5}{8}$yd (5m) fringe (optional)

Preparing the fabric

1 Cut 2in (5cm) off length of fabric to make it square. Overcast edges to prevent fraying.
2 Fold shawl in half, press lightly and baste along folded line. Fold again in the other direction and repeat so that basting divides the fabric into quarters.
3 Enlarge the design and transfer it to 3 corners, using the tracing and basting method.

Working the embroidery

The method of stitching is very similar to that for the skirt on p174. Work one corner at a time.
Hills Work the outlines of the hills in whipped chain stitch, using the fabric-colored wool for the chain stitch and another color for the whipping (or vice versa). Remove basting threads.
Filling stitches The stitches used to fill the hills are: chain stitch, long-and-short stitch, zigzag satin stitch, fly stitch and seeding. Work through one type of stitch at a time, in colors and directions shown in stitch diagram.
Trees and leaves Finally work the trees in stem stitch and leaves in French knots.

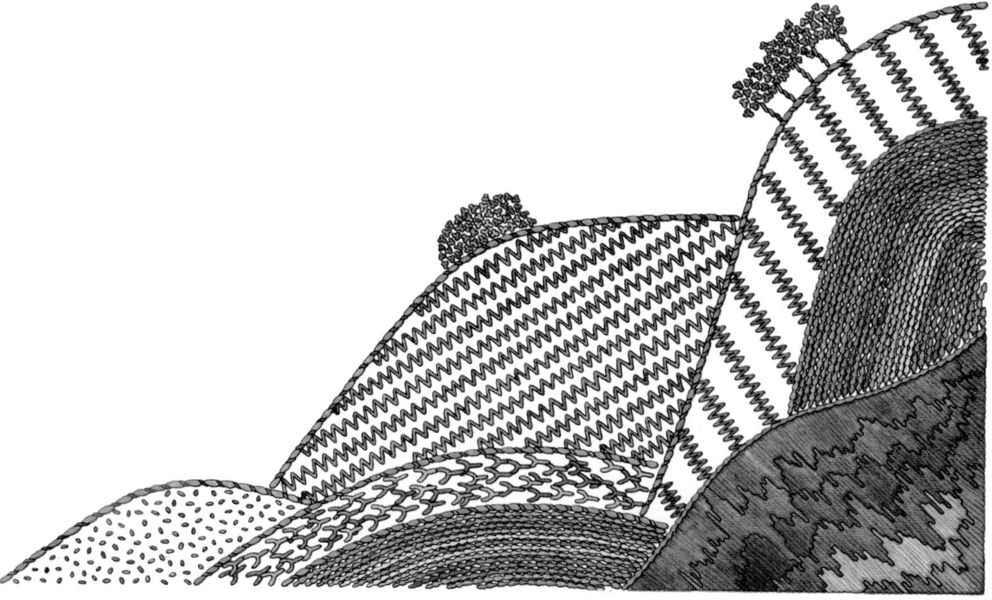

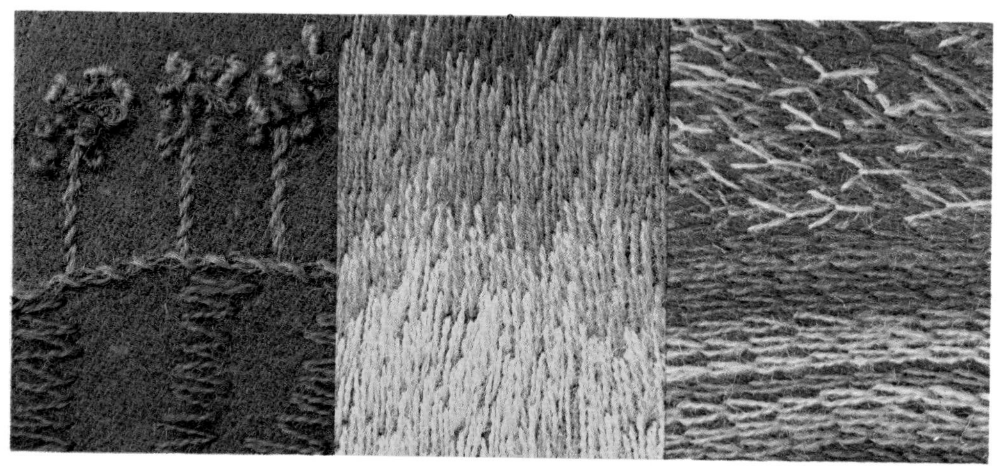

Finishing

1 Damp-stretch on a large flat surface, and leave until completely dry.
2 Hem the edges about $\frac{3}{8}$in (1cm) all around.
3 Add fringe (p102).

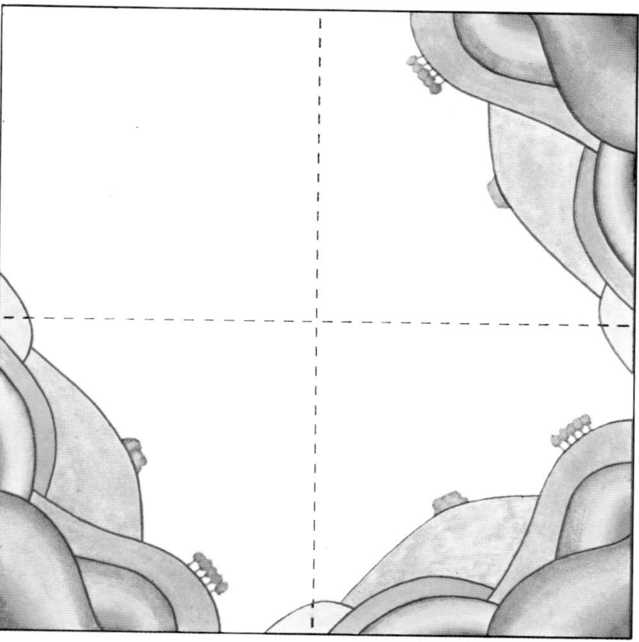

Monograms

The use of monograms or stitched letters on clothing, accessories and household items such as pillows, placemats, sheets and towels will personalize an article. Traditionally, monograms on an object represent the initials of the owner; equally you can use monograms as a label, for example, the words 'tea towel' stitched boldly across kitchen toweling or 'jeans' on the pocket of same.
The variety of techniques and the style and design of the monogram which you can use will be determined by the fabric to be embroidered. Simple machine or hand appliqué work is easier on thicker fabrics whereas intricate, detailed hand embroidery is more suitable for finer fabrics. The piece to be embroidered is another consideration; on an expensive silk shirt you would probably choose formal lettering; primitive characters would be a more likely choice for a casual T-shirt.
If your monogrammed article will need frequent washing choose a method which will withstand this.

Design
Collect different styles of lettering cut from magazines, newspapers and posters to use as a design source. From these you can create your own monograms.
When designing monograms which are to be cut out and applied to the fabric, keep the letters simple and fairly bold.
If you are working monograms in surface stitchery you can afford to include a certain amount of detail such as the curves and slopes that would appear in handwriting.
First cut out the basic monogram shape in paper and pin it in place to check size, position and proportion.
If the monogram is to be seen at a distance, stand well back and scrutinize to make sure it is legible.

Transferring the design
For simple cut-out letters use dressmaker's carbon paper to trace the outline onto the fabric. Use graph paper for planning your monogram design for all forms of counted-thread work, such as needlepoint and cross stitch (p160). For plain surface embroidery (p170) draw your monogram first on tracing paper and with carbon paper underneath trace through to the fabric below. For transferring designs to semi-

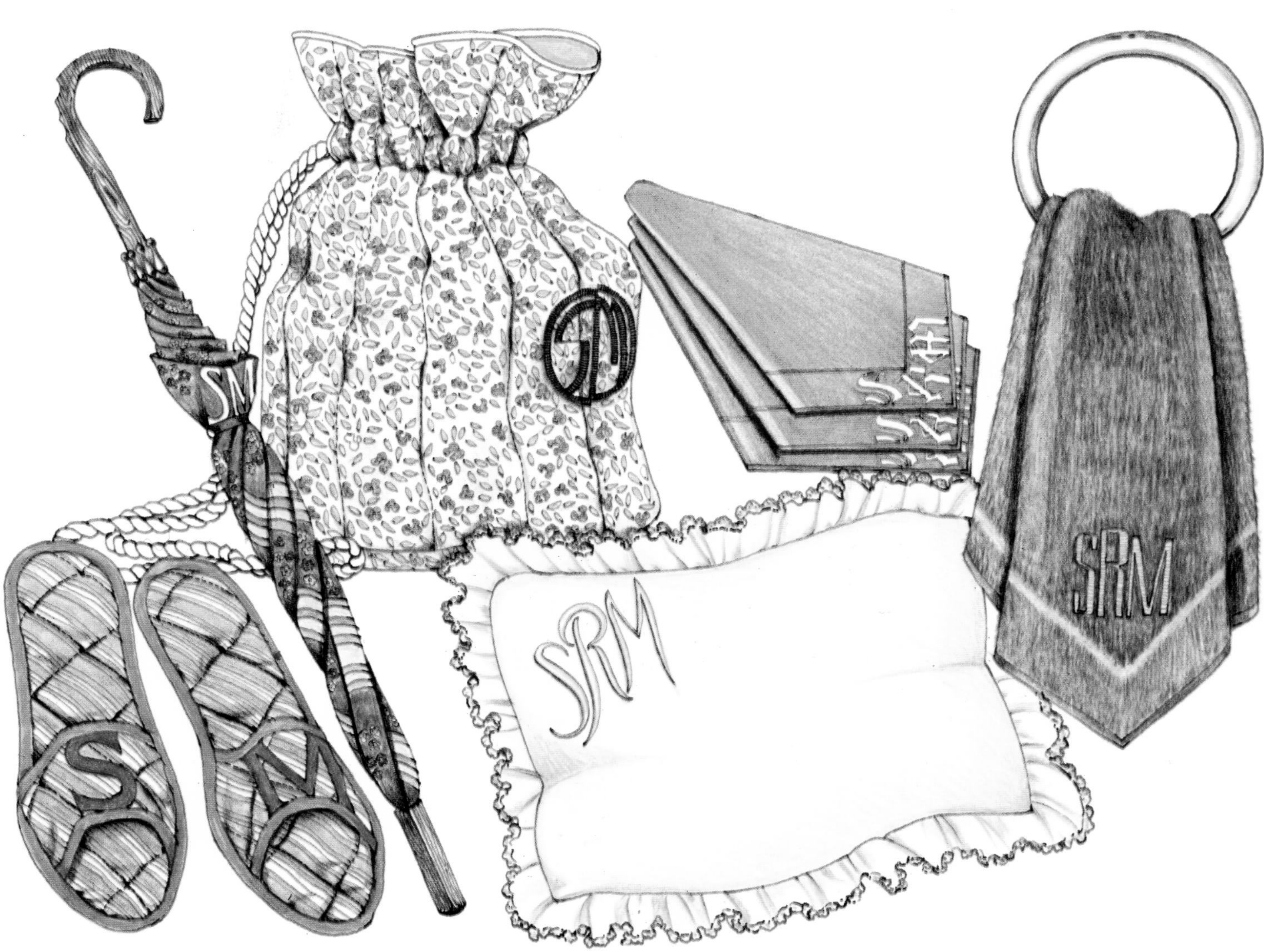

transparent fabrics, such as silk, pin the fabric over the design and trace through with black waterproof ink and a fine pen or brush.

Stitching techniques

Before you cut out your letters it is advisable on some fabrics to back them with iron-on interfacing (p36). This not only prevents them from fraying but it gives them a much firmer surface and reduces unsightly creasing. This would be an advisable step on the monogrammed canvas shoes, for example.
Using either a matching or contrasting thread, machine a closed zigzag stitch (p190) around the edges of the character outline or hand-sew around them with buttonhole stitch (p18). Cut out the letters close to the stitching and apply by hand-sewing to shoes, bags or knitted fabrics, or to bulky items where it is not possible to work under the machine foot.
On some items, like T-shirts, it will be possible to stitch your cut-out monogram in place at the same time as machining the edging stitch. This is possible because the object to be monogrammed is flat enough to fit under the machine needle.
On stiff fabrics such as canvas, leather or vinyl, spread a thin coat of fabric glue before stitching it to the object. This will prevent the letters from puckering.
Another idea for needlepoint canvas would be to embroider a letter in tent stitch, cut it out, hem it and then apply it as described here.
A plain knitted fabric with its regular stitching can be treated in the same way as a counted-thread canvas. On knitted fabrics you can embroider initials directly using chain stitch, cross stitch or satin stitch (p229). The easiest of these would be satin stitch, but for variety you could use a combination of stitches.

Alphabet samplers

In the 18th and 19th centuries it was customary for embroiderers to work stitch samplers on even-weave linen. These often contained an alphabet, the numbers 1 to 10 and a floral or pastoral scene for decoration. Surviving examples of this work now bring high prices and make very attractive wall-hangings. Try making your own alphabet sampler; it is an excellent form of monogram practice.

Blackwork

Blackwork is a counted-thread embroidery worked in black thread on a white background fabric; the design emphasis is on the creation and arrangement of geometric patterns. The characteristic geometric pattern of blackwork can be adapted to make individual motifs or border designs for pillows, pillowcases, curtains, wall-hangings or fashion accessories. In addition to the conventional black-and-white color scheme, you can use other dark colors on light fabric, or light threads on dark. The important thing to aim for is contrast between thread and fabric so that the patterns are bold and visible.

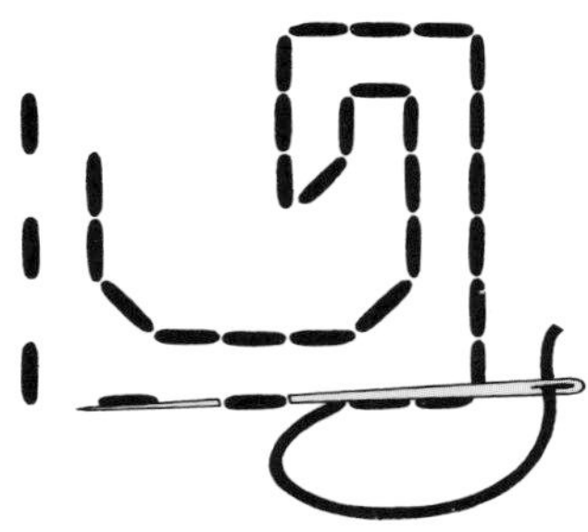

Double running stitch Work over 2, 3 or 4 threads in running stitch (p18) with stitches and spaces between them covering the same number of threads. When you have completed a motif or reached the end of a line, work back with the same thread, filling in the spaces between stitches already worked. To avoid an uneven line, insert the needle at a slight angle.

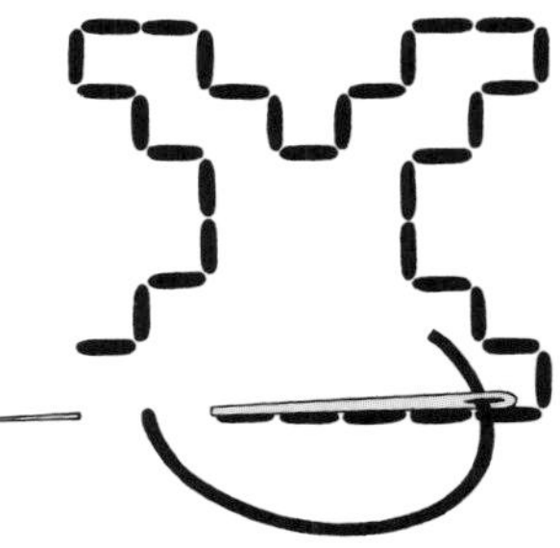

Back stitch (p18) When working the stitches, make sure that the thread between patterns does not show on RS of the work.

Design

Blackwork is open to freer interpretation now than it was in the past when a heavy black outline usually enclosed naturalistic shapes filled with geometric patterns. Today, the outline is often omitted altogether and more use is made of tonal variations which you can achieve by using different weights of thread or by altering the density of the pattern. The shapes themselves tend to reflect the angular nature of the work. To plan your design beforehand work it out on graph paper or make a paper collage to establish pattern areas. With a little practice you can design as you stitch, building up the patterns a little at a time. Transfer designs by tracing and basting.

Fabric

An even-weave fabric is essential, because all the stitches are counted. The fabric may be coarse or fine; 18 to 20 threads per 1in (2·5cm) is most usual. Linen is the traditional choice, but you can also use cotton, woolen or synthetic fabrics; if so, give careful thought to the scale of the work and choose the type of embroidery threads accordingly.

Thread

Generally speaking, the thread should be the same thickness as the woven threads of the background fabric. You may, however, introduce thinner or thicker threads in order to achieve tonal variation. Embroidery floss is particularly useful since you can vary the number of strands. Other threads include fine pearl cotton, coton à broder and sewing silk. If working on even-weave woolen fabric, use a single strand of crewel wool. Metal threads can add interest, but use them only in small amounts. If you do introduce another color thread, choose it to enhance the design; beware of the new color undermining it.

Other equipment

Use a tapestry needle to avoid splitting the thread of the fabric; size 24 is suitable for most work. Use an embroidery hoop to help you count threads and stitch evenly, although you can work freehand if you prefer.

Stitches

Traditionally blackwork relies on two stitches: double running or Holbein stitch and back stitch. However you can use virtually any stitch to form the pattern outline: stem, chain, whipped and coral stitches (p170) are all effective. If you use other stitches work a small sample first to ensure that they will be successful. If the stitching itself is too decorative and complex it may detract from the overall design. Use the double running stitch if both sides of the finished work will show. Whatever stitch you use, count the threads of the background fabric accurately.

Basic equipment 156
Transferring designs 157
Finishing 158

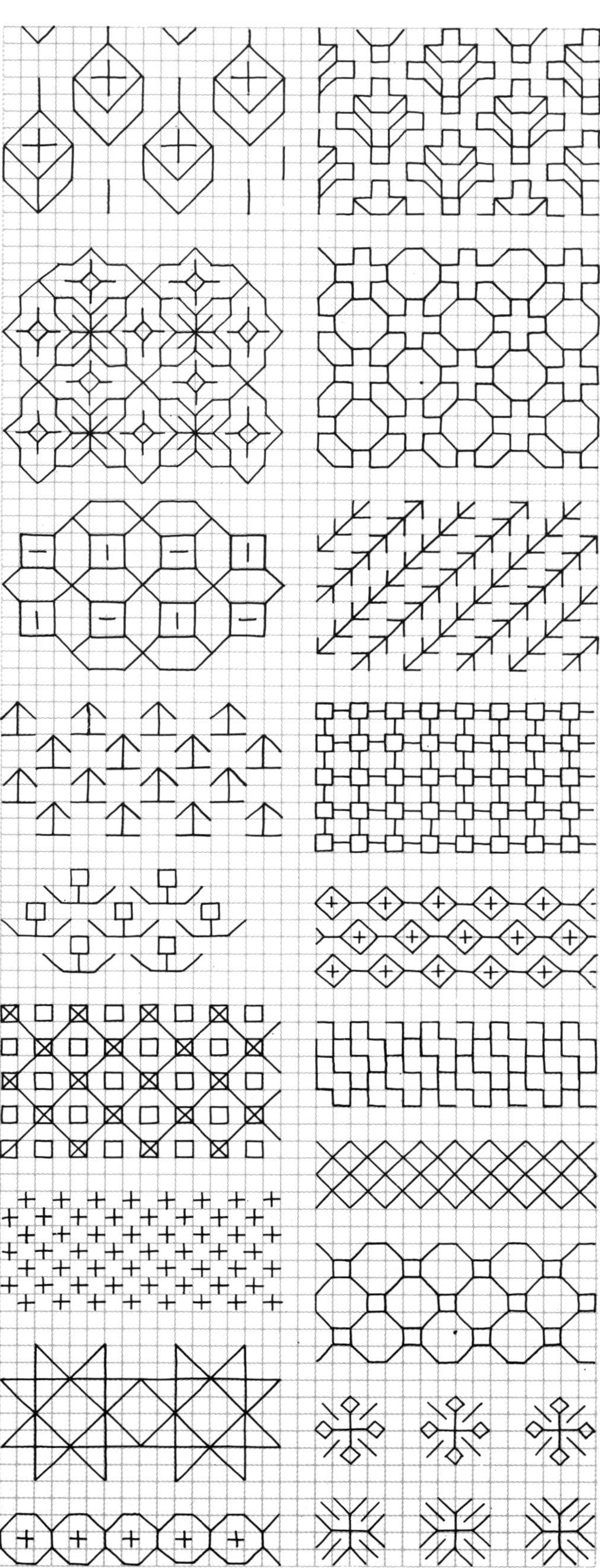

Blackwork sampler

This traditional blackwork sampler, based on a tree of life motif, could be made up into a wall-hanging or pillow cover. It demands a great deal of patience, so do not try to rush it.

You will need

even-weave linen ½ × ½yd (50 × 50cm) with 25 threads per 1 in (2·5cm)
embroidery hoop (optional)
2 skeins black embroidery floss
tapestry needle

Preparing the fabric

Take a tracing of the pattern outline; place this over graph paper. Using grid lines enlarge design onto second sheet of graph paper. Transfer by tracing and basting (p157).

Working the embroidery

Back-stitch the outline of the design in 2 threads and then work the filling stitches, one at a time, varying the number of strands to produce or relieve contrast. Each grid line represents 1 thread of linen. There are 19 filling stitches shown and all have been used in the sampler. Choose the ones you feel most comfortable with and incorporate them to suit your own preference.

Cutwork

Traditionally worked in white thread on white fabric, cutwork is an embroidery form in which the outlines and details of motifs are buttonhole- or machine-stitched and the areas of fabric between the stitching are then cut away. If done by hand it can be rather time-consuming; with a zigzag machine and practice you can achieve similar effects in half the time. With either method, try to choose small, simple motifs for the design. You can then add decorative stitching (p170) to surrounding fabric, using stem stitch, French knots, or any other stitch that would enhance the design.

Hand cutwork
Use a crewel needle with coton à broder or embroidery floss with 2 or 3 strands depending on the thickness of the fabric you are working. Instead of white thread, you could use another color; equally you could vary the color of the fabric. Choose fine, stiff, firmly woven fabric such as linen or cotton.

Preparing the fabric
Transfer the design onto RS of fabric using dressmaker's carbon paper or fabric-marking pencil if you are working freehand. Cutwork designs frequently have lines running across the center of shapes, called bars. These are inserted to strengthen the shape and normally occur at about $\frac{1}{2}$in (1·5cm) intervals; remember to transfer them with the rest of the design.

Stitching the design
1 Work small running stitches (p18) just inside the design outline, using a double row of stitches or 2 or 3 strands of thread and a single row. As soon as you come to a bar fasten the running thread with a back stitch on RS, pass it across the bar to the other side picking up 2 or 3 threads of fabric and back again to the starting point (where the running stitch left off).
2 Continue running stitches and bars as they appear. This preparation strengthens the fabric and provides a strong edge when the fabric is cut away.
3 Work over the running stitch outline and bars in buttonhole stitch. Place the loops of the buttonhole stitch so that they face the area to be cut away and loops on the bars so that they all face the same way. The sequence is the same as **1** and **2**, with a slight variation when you come to a bar. Run a thread across to the opposite side and start buttonhole stitch at this point, working toward (not away from) the previously stitched outline, as on diagram. Complete stitching.

Picots
As a further decoration you can make picots. Work as an ordinary buttonhole stitch until picot is required. Form picot as shown by twisting the thread around the needle.

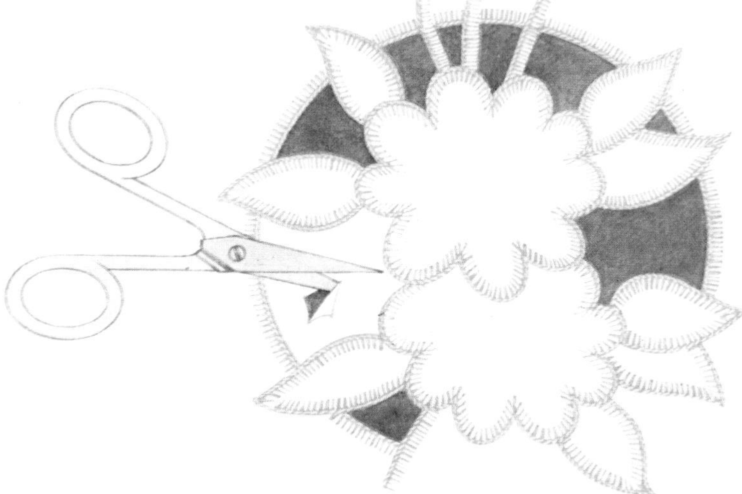

Cutting away background
1 Press the embroidery carefully on WS.
2 Cut away the areas between stitching with small, sharp-pointed scissors. Start in the center of fabric area; work toward one corner and then cut as close to the stitching as possible. Take great care not to cut the stitching itself, otherwise it will unravel.

Machine cutwork
If you have a zigzag machine, you can produce very professional looking cutwork. (You can not do machine cutwork on a straight-stitch machine.) The working order is basically the same as for hand-sewn cutwork; for the precise technique refer to the embroidery instructions opposite for the nightdress shown.

Master pattern sheet
Basic stitches 18
Bikini 50
Basic equipment 156
Transferring designs 157

Nightdress
The nightdress shown on p185 has a cutwork bodice and hem with a large motif worked on the skirt front. The bodice is an adaptation of the bikini top on p50. The skirt is a dirndl type. Embroider the bodice before cutting it out and the skirt after finishing it and marking the hemline. It is advisable to make a muslin pattern first for a proper fit. You can use the embroidery technique for any machine cutwork you do, adapting it as necessary.

You will need
$2\frac{1}{4}$yd (2m) fabric, 36in (90cm) wide
large spool matching machine thread
embroidery hoop
small, sharp-pointed scissors
bias binding to fit across top of skirt back and front, $\frac{1}{2}$in (1·2cm) wide
rolled elastic, $\frac{1}{4}$in (6mm) wide to fit snugly below bust
$1\frac{3}{4}$yd (1·5m) satin ribbon for straps, $\frac{1}{2}$in (1·2cm) wide

The dress pattern
The skirt has rolled elastic at the top and is attached to the bodice just below the bust.
The bodice Draw the bikini top as instructed on p50, omitting the darts.
Skirt Draw 2 rectangles each as wide as the measurement of the bodice by the required length. The CF and CB will be on the fold of each piece. Add $\frac{1}{2}$in (1·2cm) seam allowances for sides and top.

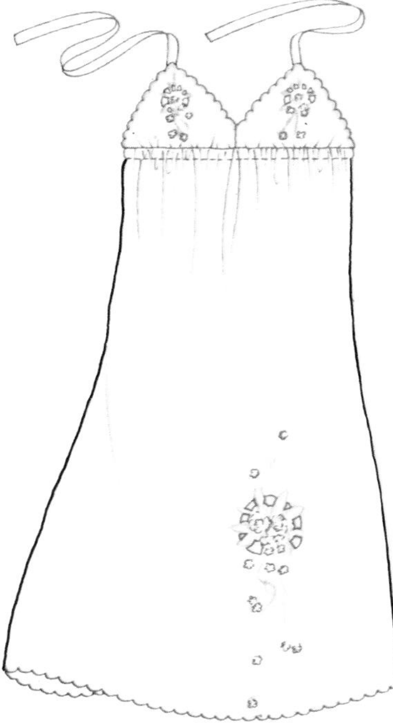

Preparing the machine
Set machine to a $\frac{1}{16}$in (2mm) zigzag stitch, remove presser foot and lower the feed control. Work with presser foot lever down, as this controls the tension of the top thread. Practice first on some left-over dress fabric in an embroidery hoop (p191) to get a freely worked line of satin stitching.

Preparing the bodice
1 Mark cutting lines of bodice fronts on RS of fabric, with pattern aligned with straight grain of fabric. Do not cut.
2 Enlarge the bodice design shown (top center) to the correct size on stiff paper with washable ink. Place under the right front of bodice fabric and trace through onto RS with sharp, hard pencil; hold fabric firmly when tracing design. Reverse the design for the left front of bodice.
3 Place the first bodice piece in the hoop so that the design is centrally placed. Pull fabric taut and make sure grain is straight.

Embroidering the bodice
1 Work the design on each bodice front, along the circle first, then the leaves, then the lines going out from the motif. Finish all loose ends by taking them through to WS, and secure them.
2 With sharp scissors, cut out the areas marked, cutting close to but not into the line of stitching.
3 Remove from the hoop and press on WS.
4 To make separate flowers, transfer the small motifs to a spare piece of fabric and place it in the hoop, pulling it taut as before.
5 Work several small flowers, remove from the hoop and cut around outside edges.

6 Arrange embroidered flowers on cutwork and sew in place, decorating the center of each with a French knot.
7 Cut the bodice pieces and pin with RS together.
8 Re-set machine to straight stitch and join bodice pieces along CF seam.
9 Press open, trim and finish raw edges.

Scalloping the bodice
If your machine has a scallop stitch, set it to this and work scalloping directly onto the bodice, $\frac{1}{2}$in (1·5cm) away from arm and neck edges. If not, re-set machine to satin stitch and lightly pencil the scallop outline directly onto RS of fabric. Start scalloping in either case from central seam, working in a continuous line up around point and down side of one half. Work other half of bodice the same way.

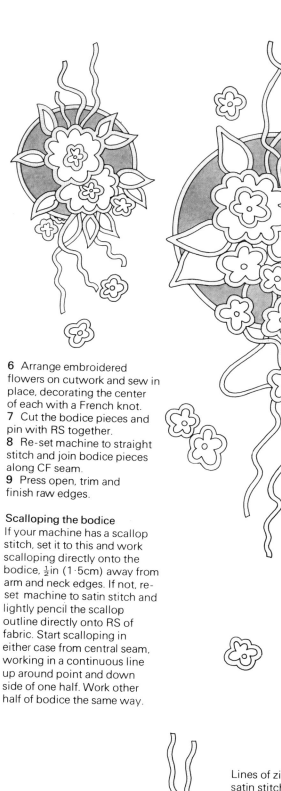

Lines of zigzag satin stitch

Fabric to be cut when stitching is complete

Small flowers worked separately and applied to the dress.

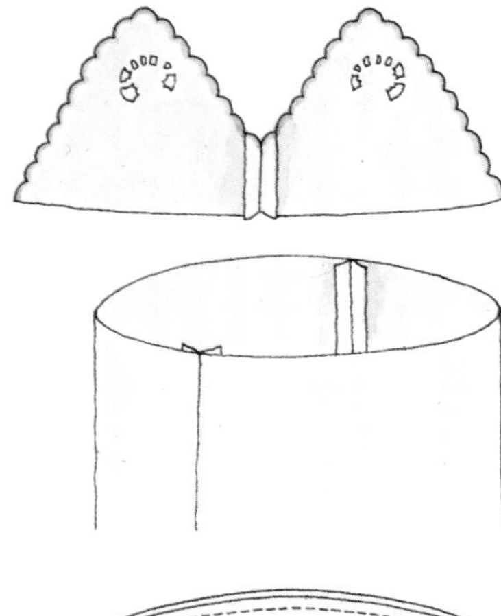

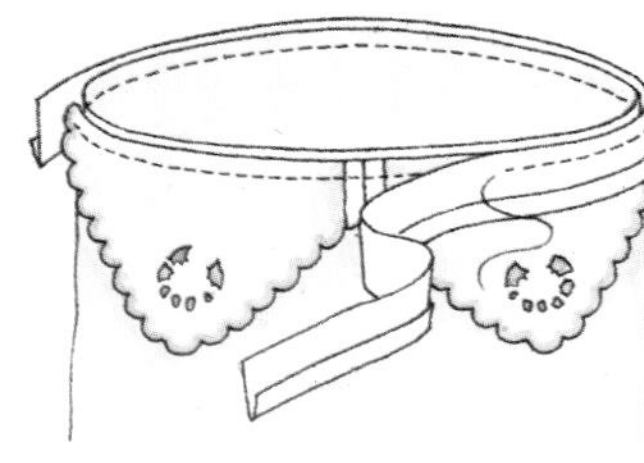

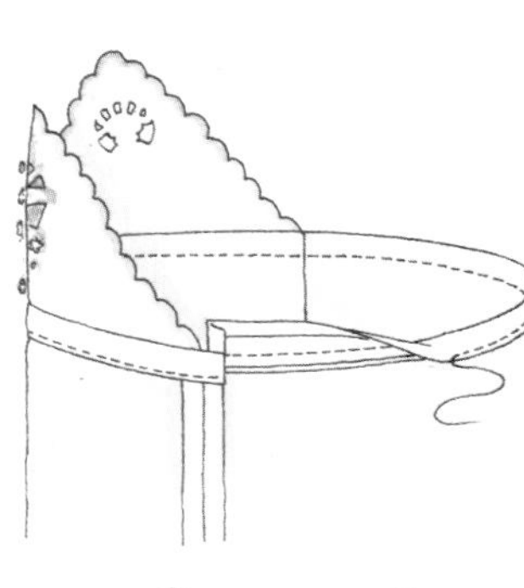

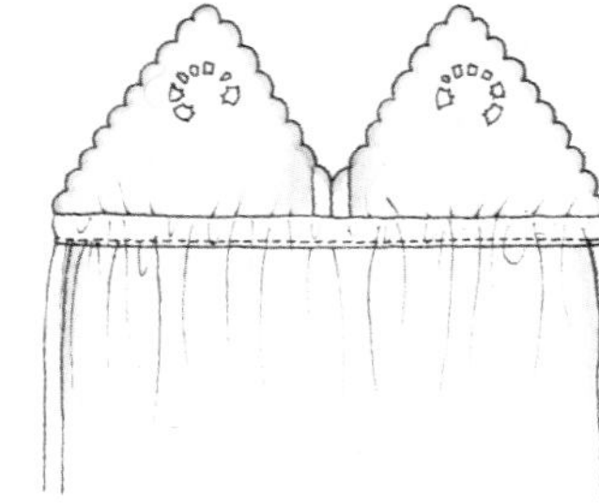

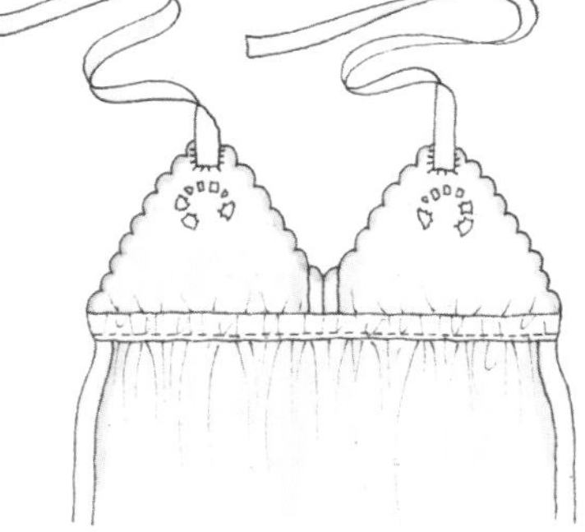

Preparing skirt embroidering cutwork

1 Cut the skirt front and back. With RS together pin side seams and stitch along them. Press seams and finish edges.

2 Transfer cutwork motif to the skirt front in position marked, using transferring technique referred to in bodice. Place motif area in a hoop.

3 Work the embroidery as for the bodice and remove from the hoop. The skirt is ready to be attached to the bodice.

Attaching skirt to bodice

1 With RS together join skirt front to bodice.

2 Stitch bias binding along seamline in front and along seam allowance on back.

3 Trim seam to $\frac{1}{4}$in (6mm), press it flat downward and stitch remaining edge of binding all the way around.

4 Cut elastic to fig snugly but comfortably all around below bustline and thread through casing. Secure ends at side seams.

5 Cut ribbon, finish loose ends and sew each piece to right and left inside of top.

6 Measure and mark hemline.

Scalloping hemline

To save time, you can use a larger scallop for the skirt than for the bodice.

1 Mark the hemline with straight basting stitches.

2 Set machine and work scalloping as for bodice, working all the way around.

3 Remove any basting that shows and cut carefully around the scalloping to finish.

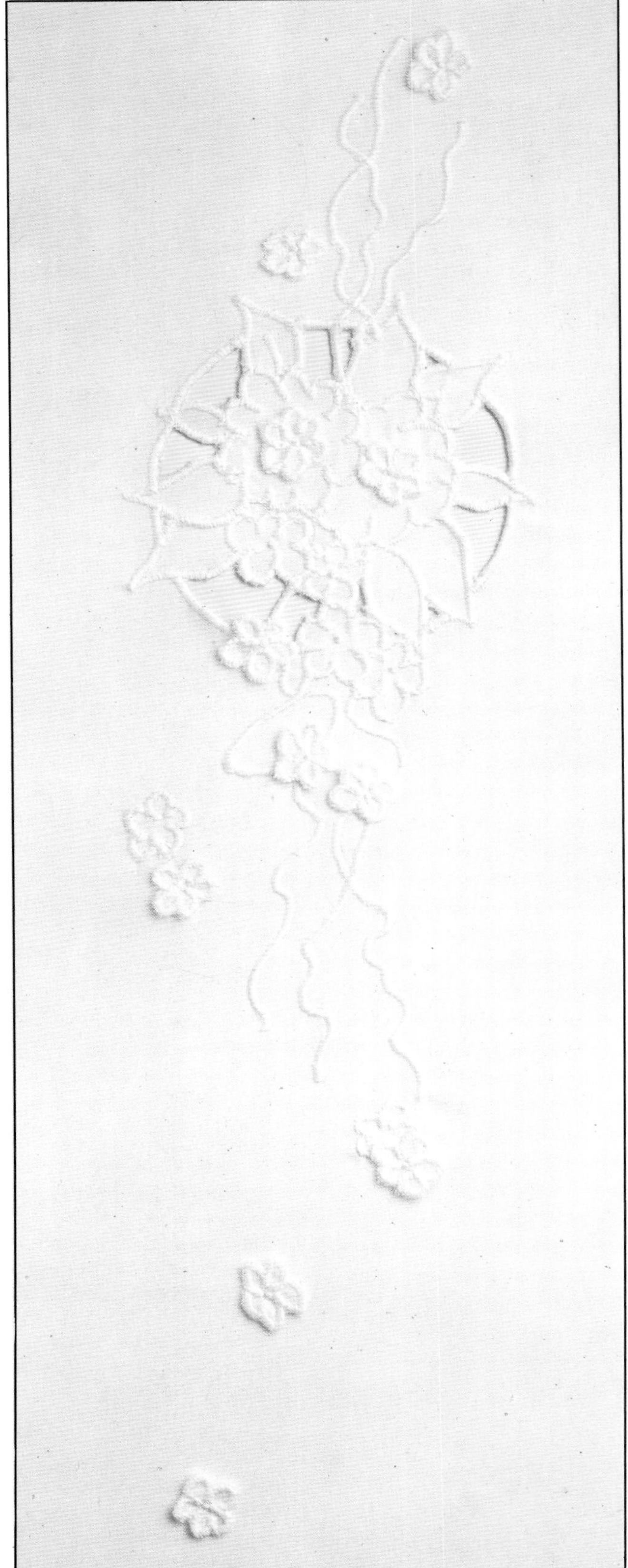

Pulled and drawn thread

Pulled thread work and drawn thread work are two separate techniques but they can be combined, as shown in the window shade. Pulled thread refers to the stitching together of the warp and weft threads of a fabric to create open patterns; drawn thread refers to the drawing out of warp or weft threads from the fabric and stitching the warp or weft threads, whichever remain, together in small groups. Since no threads are withdrawn from the fabric in pulled thread work, this is a stronger technique and is therefore more suitable for items that will be worn and washed frequently.
Both techniques produce delicate-looking results and the materials needed are very similar. White even-weave linen is the traditional fabric used, with thread of the same color and thickness as the fabric. If you choose not to use linen you can use a loosely woven synthetic or natural fiber fabric; such fabric is also useful for less traditional, contemporary designs. The looser the weave, the more open-looking the finished work will be. For both methods you should use a tapestry needle, a thick one in the case of pulled work to help emphasize the perforations. An embroidery hoop makes it easier to count the threads in pulled work but is not necessary for drawn work.

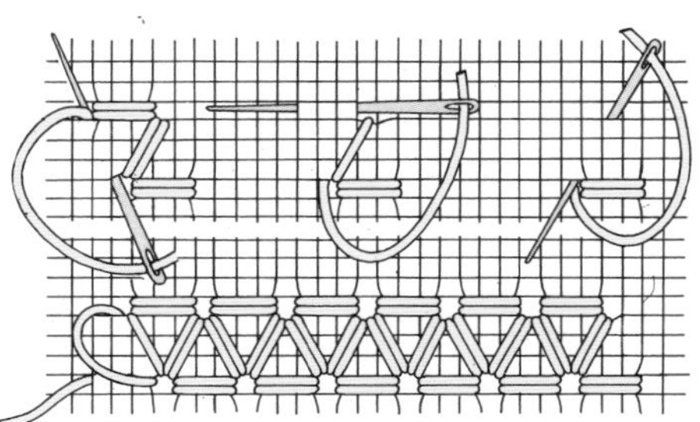

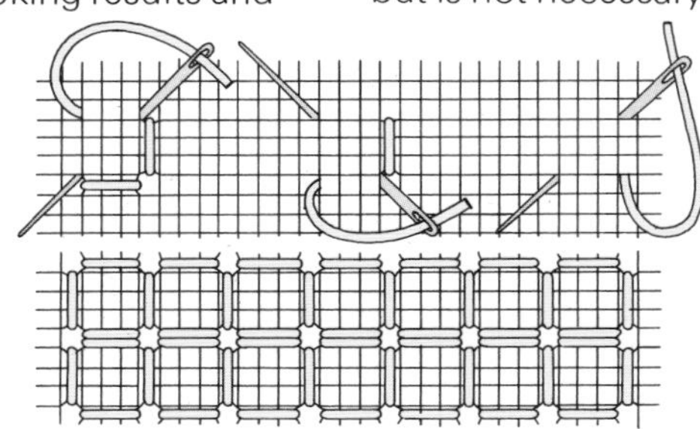

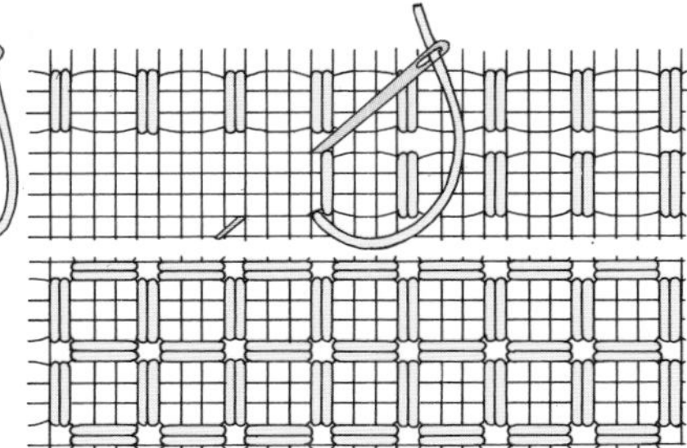

Pulled thread
The working thread is used to make the stitches which pull the warp and weft threads together to form perforated patterns and contrasting textures.
Preparation Usually you will not need to transfer a stitch design as this will be worked by counting the threads, but if you are filling areas of naturalistic shapes, e.g. flowers or birds, it is helpful to baste the outlines first.
Stitches There are a number of pulled work stitches including square eyelets (p161), 3-sided stitch, 4-sided stitch and punch stitch (shown above from left to right). All produce different textures and degrees of openness.
When embroidering a design that has an outline it is usually better to do the filling stitches first but there are exceptions, such as the filling on the window shade which was done after the outline was stitched. With each needle movement, pull all stitches tightly with the exception of satin stitch and any stitches made with it, where the stitches should be pulled more or less tightly depending on the effect required. The satin stitches which produce a solid line provide contrast to the more open ones.
Begin work with a knot on RS (some way from where the needle emerges for the 1st stitch) which you can cut off and weave in at the back of the work when convenient. You should not take any threads across the back of the work as these will show through the pulled holes, or make a shadow. It is important when finishing off at the end of a row to pull the last stitch as tightly as the others.

Drawn thread work
The threads are withdrawn from either the warp or the weft of the chosen material; the threads that remain are then decorated with hem-stitching. The most important thing when planning a drawn thread design is to pay close attention to the spacing of the lines. Count the number of threads you need to remove, but do not withdraw so many that you weaken the pattern. There should be an equal number of remaining threads so that when stitched together they form a regular pattern.
Withdrawing the threads
For the simplest kind of border which has threads withdrawn across the full width or length of the fabric, mark the required width with 2 straight lines of basting. Ease out the first thread with the tip of a needle or pin for an inch or so, and then pull it gently the rest of the way. Continue until the border is the required width. If you plan to work a border which continues around the 4 sides of a piece of fabric, mark the points where the corners will be. Count an even number of threads that will remain for each side and withdraw as above to the corners.

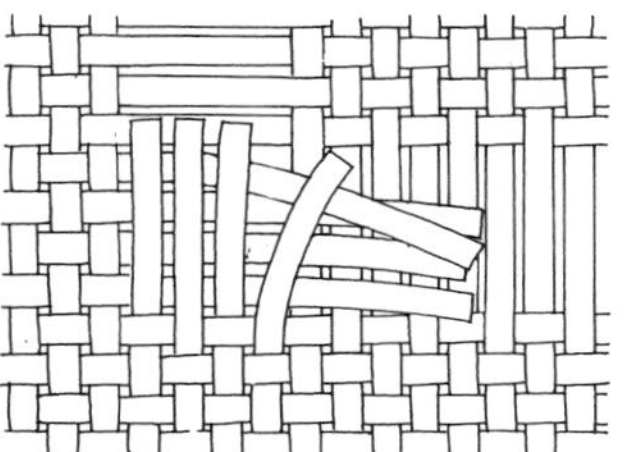

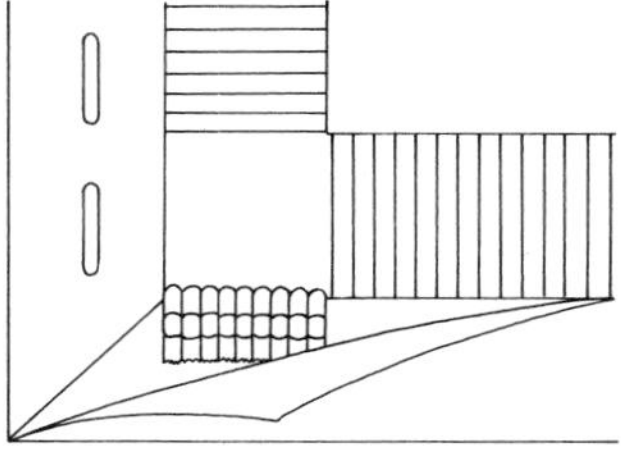

Finishing corners Leave the threads hanging until you have withdrawn the required amount. There are 3 possible methods of finishing the raw edges on corners. The strongest is to turn the threads back on themselves, baste them down and cut away the surplus so that they will be hidden in the hem when it is turned. Otherwise you can cut off the threads and secure the raw edge of the border with buttonhole stitch (p18) or you can darn the threads back (p104) into 4 or 5 threads of the fabric. When you have cleaned up the excess threads, miter the corners if necessary; the object is ready for stitching.

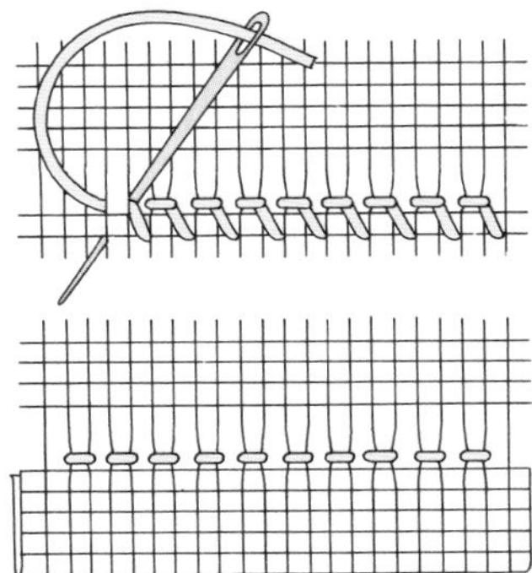

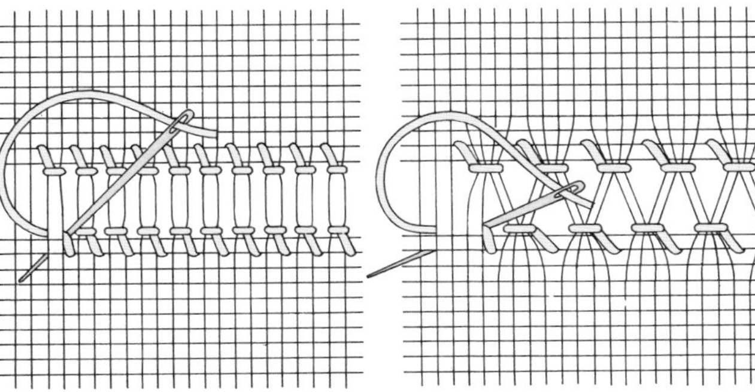

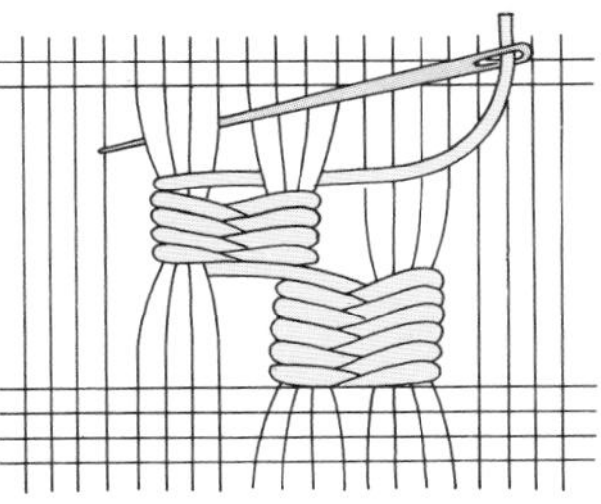

Stitching Hem-stitch the borders; this not only secures the hem if there is one, but at the same time it ties the remaining threads into tidy bundles. You can use several variations of hemstitch including antique – just like hemstitch except that the stitching is hidden inside the hem – ladder and serpentine or zigzag hemstitch, all shown above from left to right.
You can also use needle-weaving (top right) to decorate drawn thread borders. Since it replaces the threads which have been removed it lends strength to the work, but its appearance is not as delicate.
At corners where warp and weft threads have both been withdrawn, there will be a space which you can fill after you have stitched the borders, with spider's webs or wheels.

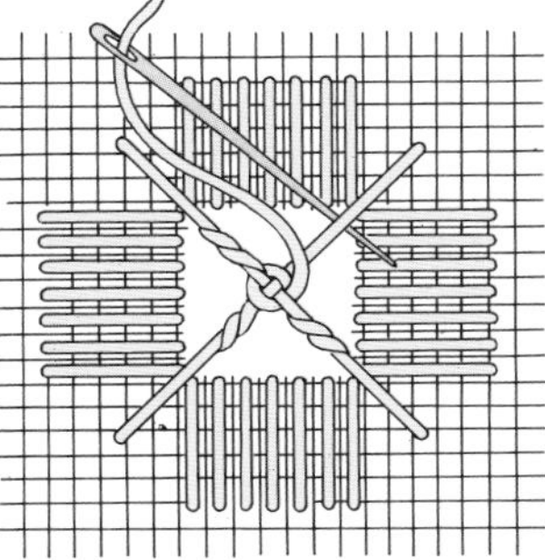

Window shade
The shade shown incorporates pulled and drawn thread work. It measures 40 × 31in (100 × 77·5cm) on even-weave linen with 26 threads per 1in (2·5cm). If you use a coarser linen, you can adapt the pattern accordingly; the stitches will appear bolder.

You will need
linen the size of your finished window shade, plus allowance for side hems and for finishing as on p130
pearl cotton to match the fabric
tapestry needle
basting thread
embroidery hoop for pulled work window shade kit, as p130

Preparing the fabric
1 If the fabric frays, overcast the edges by hand or use a machine zigzag stitch.
2 Mark the finished area of the shade with basting.
3 Lightly mark the drawn thread borders at the sides.

Drawn thread work
1 Withdraw a suitable number of threads from the sides for the borders (12 were taken out here).
2 Work ladder hemstitch along the borders over 4 threads at a time.

Pulled thread work
1 Decide how far from the bottom of the finished shade the border is to be.
2 Measure the distance between the two drawn thread borders and mark the center of the square eyelets with basting. (The eyelets will be worked over 6 threads in all directions from the center.)
3 Work through all the square eyelets (p161), pulling them fairly tight.
4 Work satin stitch over 6 threads to form the 2 complete and 5 open-ended rectangles. Count threads carefully so that the number inside each rectangle is a multiple of 4.
5 Fill in the rectangles at the sides with punch stitch worked over 4 threads.

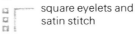

Key to stitch diagram
ladder hemstitch
square eyelets and satin stitch
punch stitch
satin stitch with 3-sided stitch filling

6 Now work the borders above and below the line of rectangles. For each border work 2 rows of satin stitch over 6 threads, leaving 6 threads between these rows.
7 Work 3-sided stitch over the rows of 6 threads that remain.

Finishing
1 Remove from the frame.
2 Place RS on a towel, press with a hot iron and damp cloth.
3 Remove basting, finish side edges with zigzag stitch or overcasting and hem to edge of drawn thread borders.
4 Finish as for the window shade on p130.

Beadwork

You can embroider beads on clothes, knitted garments, fashion accessories and household items such as lampshades and room dividers. Available in a wide assortment of materials—wood, metal, glass, stone, pearl, plastic, papier mâché—beads can add not only texture but also a reflective, luminous quality to an object. (The lampshade shown is a good example of this.) You can use beads as solid clusters or as single units placed at random or along the outline of a shape. As well as working with beads alone, you can combine them wito other forms of embroidery.

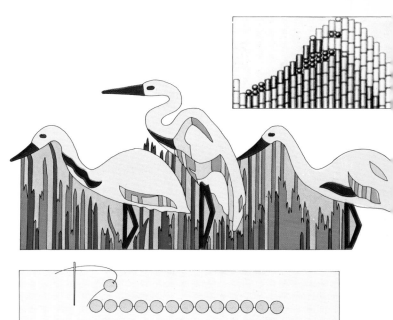

Suitable fabrics

The garment or object will determine the type and weight of bead you use. If you would like to use heavy beading, use firm, closely woven fabrics. You can strengthen light-weight fabrics by mounting them on muslin or an interfacing.
Nap is another consideration. Choose fabric which will show the beads off to their greatest advantage; small beads would probably not be visible on deeply piled velvet or corduroy.

Types of bead

Beads can be rounded, square, cylindrical or spherical. It is important when combining different shapes in a work that they fit together well. Beads should lie flat on a fabric, and not pull or stretch it. Beads are available from department stores and speciality shops. If in doubt, take a rough sketch with you and discuss your beading requirements with the shop-keeper.

Estimating quantities It is difficult to make a precise estimate but you can buy a small amount of beads to begin with and work a sample. Make your estimate from this. If a design includes several repeats, lay beads together as they will appear, count the number of beads used (or weigh them) and multiply this figure by the number of repeats. It is better to over-estimate, when making your purchase, since you are likely to lose some beads, possibly through breakage.

Other equipment

A velvet or felt pad is useful to keep the beads in place when you plan a design. Special beading, or 'straw', needles are available; these are long, straight, very fine and usually sold in packets of mixed sizes. Choose a needle that will fit the hole of the bead. For beads with larger holes you can use a small crewel needle.
The best type of thread is polyester as it is not likely to break and beads will slide easily along it. If you use cotton, silk or linen thread you will need to draw it through a block of beeswax first to strengthen it and prevent knotting. The thread should not show on RS of the work, but a certain amount will be seen along the side of the bead so choose a color that tones in with the fabric.

Working order

Baste the finished area, transfer the design to the fabric and mount the fabric onto a frame. Take beading just up to the hem or seamline and when you have finished, stitch by hand or machine, using a zipper foot. If there are any gaps in the beading fill them in at this stage.

Beading methods

There are various methods of embroidering with beads; for those given here use a polyester thread; otherwise work with a waxed single thread about 12–16in (30–40cm) long. To secure heavier beads you can use a double thread.

Method A Draw the needle through to RS of fabric and pick up one bead, passing it off the needle just onto the thread. Following the design line, pass the needle to WS of fabric a bead's length away from the beginning. Draw needle through and secure the bead in position. Bring the needle to the RS, re-entering the fabric one single thread along the line. Repeat the process.

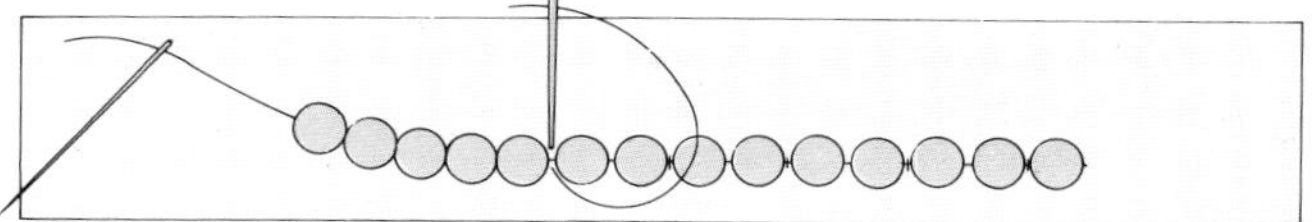

Method B You will need two needles threaded with the same colour. With needle 1, the beading needle, pick up several beads at a time and lay the threaded beads along the line of the design. Then with a crewel needle catch down the thread between each bead with small couching stitches (p170). Finish couching the line and pass needle 1 to WS to secure or to work another line.

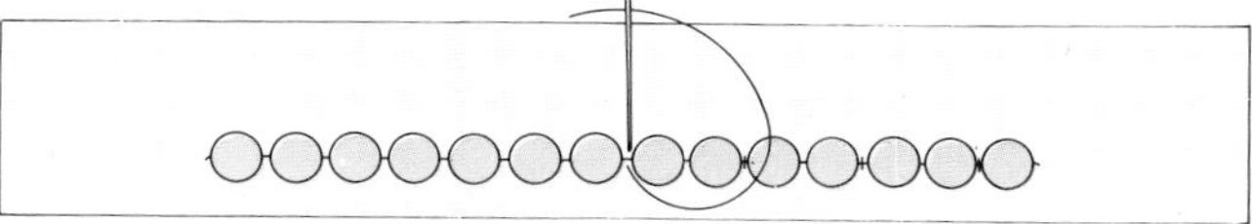

Method C Using about 3 times as much thread as the line of beads, assuming it is not longer than 6in (15cm), back-stitch to secure and insert the needle from WS to RS of fabric. String the beads along the thread and re-insert needle at the end of the line of beads. Bring needle out between 1st and 2nd bead and couch down. Couch (p170) between each or every other bead depending on size.

Finishing

With sheer fabrics and net always work one line at a time and finish off the thread on WS behind the line of beads so that it will not show on RS. You should line all areas of beadwork to prevent catching. Press gently with a warm iron and a soft pad placed on WS of fabric. It is advisable to dry-clean beaded garments.

Lampshades 146
Basic equipment 156
Transferring designs 157

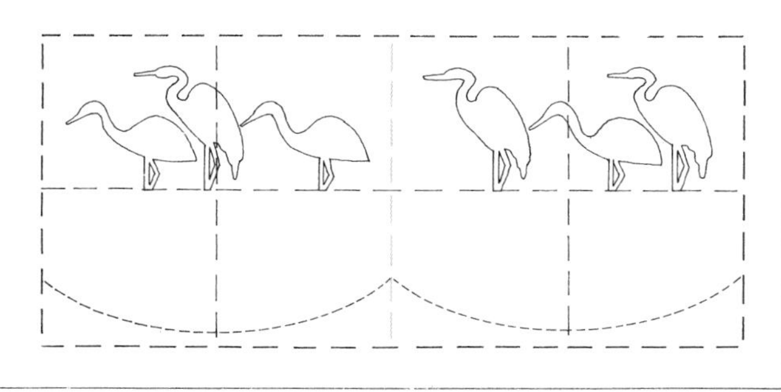

You will need

frame, fabric and lining as p146 (allowing extra for fringe area and framing)
tracing paper
dressmaker's carbon paper
stretcher frame, 27in (68cm) wide
2 spools polyester thread to match fabric
basting thread in 2 colors
beading and crewel needles
glass beads: $\frac{1}{4}$in (5mm) – long bugles – 3oz (75g) each in opaque white and transparent blue, pale blue, green; $\frac{1}{3}$in (7mm) – long bugles – 1oz (25g) black; 1$\frac{1}{4}$in (30mm) – long bugles – 4 packs of 100 clear; small round – 12 individual terracotta beads (for the eyes), 2oz (50g) each white, black, gun-metal

Lampshade

The lampshade shown combines embroidered beadwork with a beaded fringe. You could achieve a similar effect with a half-drawn window shade. The beads are glass and two basic shapes have been used: long cylindrical, known as bugle, and round. Instructions and bead quantities are for a sewn-on oval lampshade 10 × 8in (25 × 20cm). Embroider the lampshade before lining and finishing it.

Preparing the fabric

1 On the straight of grain, cut lining and fabric as described on p146 for a slip-on lampshade. Remember to allow extra fabric for framing and fringe area.
2 In one color thread, baste an outline of the finished lampshade and vertical guide lines along straight of grain. The foldline indicating the base of the shade must be absolutely straight. Below it repeat the vertical lines and outline of the lampshade area, making it deeper if you want the fringe to have more depth than the lampshade.
3 Lightly pencil a curved line to indicate depth of fringe. Work this line in small double running stitch (p180).
4 In another color thread, baste a central vertical line from top to bottom to indicate division between front and back of lampshade.
5 Enlarge the design onto tracing paper and transfer with dressmaker's carbon or by basting onto central areas of front and back.
6 With grain straight, mount the fabric onto a frame.

Embroidering the shade

For ease of working, you can embroider about 4in (10cm) of the lampshade and then go back and do the fringe to the same point.
1 Thread a beading needle with polyester thread and back-stitch to secure. Insert it from WS to RS just to the right of the basted seamline on the left-hand side.
2 Pick up a line of beads for the grass and stitch using Method C. Work each line in this way.
3 When you reach a motif where the beading order is very important, string the beads on from bottom to top of the design. Continue stitching as before.
4 Complete the motif, fill in beading in the center of the lampshade and then complete the other half; work the final line of beading to the left of the right-hand seamline.

Beading the fringe

The most efficient method of working the fringe is to whip the beaded thread under the line of double running stitch which marks the fringe length. (Do not go through the fabric.) This holds the fringe in place and prevents tangling.
1 Secure the thread with a backstitch and bring the needle through to RS on the foldline. String the beads from top of the reflection down, following the reverse color order of the line of embroidered beading above; continue to the double running stitch with plain blue beads and finish with a long clear bead followed by a round black bead.
2 Take the needle and thread through the black bead and pass it back through all the beads.
3 Secure the thread at the foldline directly beneath the embroidered bead of the same color.
4 Repeat with every line until the fringe is complete.

Finishing

1 Take fabric off the frame, and remove any visible lines of basting and the line of double running stitch.
2 Cut away excess fabric, leaving a $\frac{1}{2}$in (15mm) seam allowance.
3 Make up lampshade as described for sewn-on lampshades.

Machine embroidery

The sewing machine can be used to create interesting linear and textural effects quite unlike those of hand-embroidery. It can also be used to imitate the effects of hand-embroidery with such techniques as appliqué, patchwork, cutwork and free-hand embroidery. To get the best results from your machine, experiment to see what it can and can not do. When using it for embroidery you can work in one of two basic ways: with the presser foot or without it. You will get a regular stitch with the foot; without it you will have a much greater freedom of movement, but you will probably need to practice this technique. Both techniques are described here.
The various types of machines, listed on p10, range from simple straight-stitch models to sophisticated ones which you can set to work individual embroidery stitch patterns. It is usually the case, however, that you will be creating your own embroidery stitches by changing stitch size, tension or bobbin thread.

Needle, thread and bobbin
As with other forms of embroidery, the needle and thread should suit the thickness of the fabric. You can use ordinary sewing thread or a more expensive machine embroidery thread which gives a lustrous finish. For interesting variations you can use coton à broder, pearl cotton, lurex, knitting yarn and other textured yarns. Wind such threads onto the bobbin by hand. (The textured stitching will be on the underside of fabric as it goes through the sewing machine.)

Frames
For free-hand embroidery without the presser foot you will need an embroidery hoop to keep the fabric taut. Wooden hoops should be used in preference to plastic, since they are more rigid, and they should have a screw adjustment. A hoop should be no more than $\frac{3}{8}$in (1cm) deep and about 8in (20cm) in diameter, but for small areas and eyelets 5–6in (13–15cm) is a good size. By binding one or both rings with masking tape, you will be able to pull the fabric taut, which is essential for machine work.

Fabrics
Use non-stretch material. Firm fabrics such as cotton, denim and organdy are easier to work with than loosely woven ones.

Machine care
As embroidering can put extra strain on the machine, it is important to see that it is kept in good working order and to arrange for a service if necessary. There are some problems, however, which you can prevent before stitching.
Thread and needle breakage Check tension and change the needle if it is blunt. Thread can snap or the needle can break when the machine is running too fast and the hoop moving too slowly.
Jammed thread This can happen when you are working without the foot and have forgotten to lower the lever.
Missing stitches Check that the fabric is pulled as taut as possible on the frame and that you are not moving the hoop too quickly under the needle.

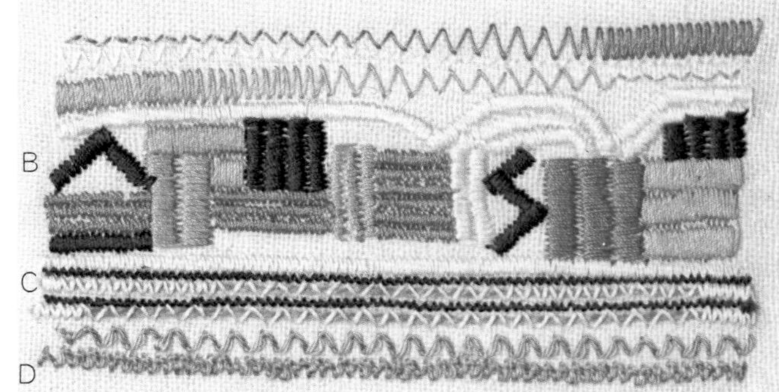

Embroidery with a presser foot
To begin with, experiment with firm, closely woven fabrics. These will pass smoothly and evenly under the presser foot. If you use a flimsy fabric, back it with cotton and place tissue paper underneath it to prevent it from puckering.
Straight stitching Use straight geometric outlines. Here are some possibilities:
A: Stitch parallel lines of running stitch in one or more colors. Change the stitch length for each line. You can add further decoration by stitching textured yarns, ribbons or braids to the fabric. Take all thread ends through to WS.
B: Make a small textured area by building up patterns in different colors.
C: For a heavier texture, wind a thicker yarn onto the bobbin and slacken the tension. Turn the fabric over and work straight lines on what was the WS.

Zigzag stitching Thread the top and bobbin with the same or different colors. Run the machine to make sure that the zigzag stitches interlock and that none of the bobbin thread shows through on RS.
A: Work lines of stitches in varying widths and lengths. When the stitching is very close together it becomes satin stitch.
B: Build up blocks of satin stitch worked close together. Change the stitch direction to form a new pattern.
C: Lay wool onto the fabric and couch it down with zigzag stitches of varying lengths. You can also use zigzagging for appliqué: stitch about $\frac{1}{4}$in (5mm) in from raw edge and trim off excess fabric.
D: Wind a thicker thread such as pearl cotton onto the bobbin. Tighten the top tension slightly and stitch from WS.

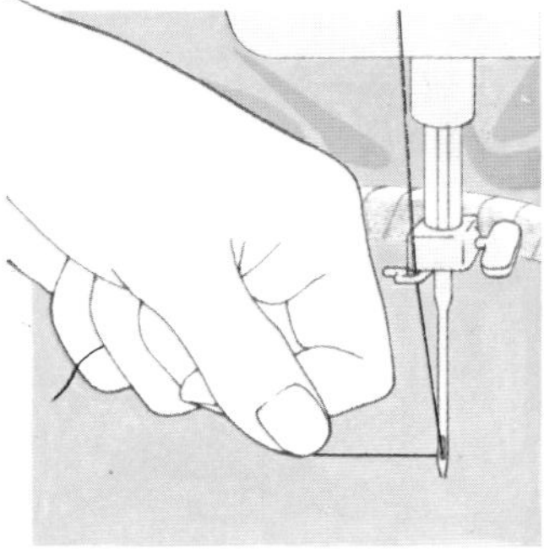

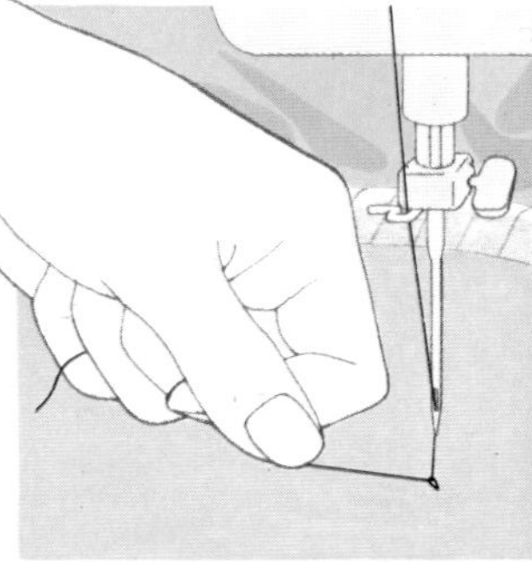

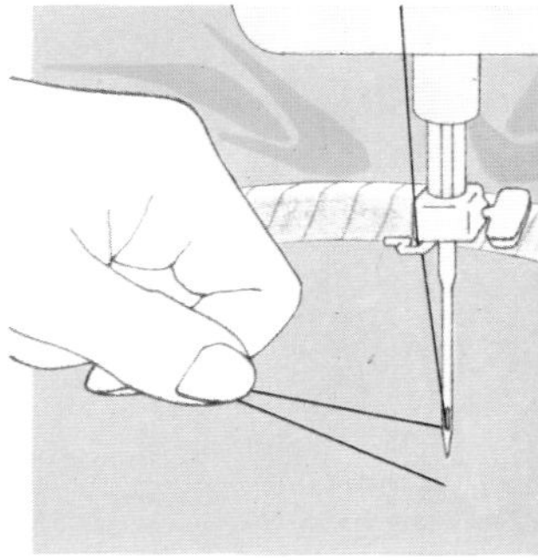

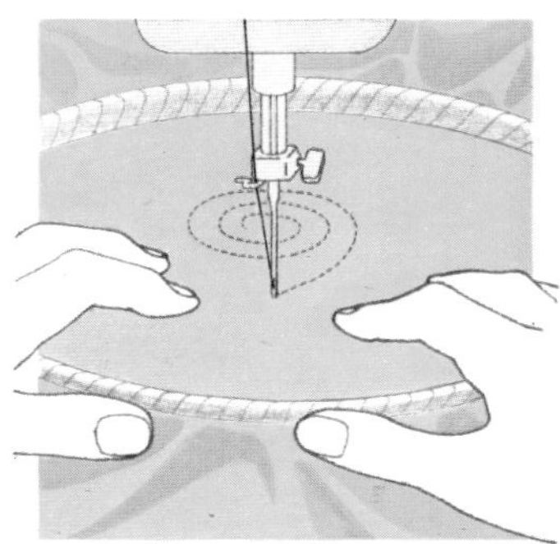

Embroidery without a presser foot

With this method, which requires a great deal of practice, you can move the fabric in any direction but you must work it in a circular hoop.

1 With WS up and grain of fabric straight, place the fabric over the inner ring; place the larger, outer ring in position and pull fabric taut (it should fit tightly and require only a slight amount of further adjustment).

2 Remove the presser foot and lower or cover the feed control (see manufacturer's instructions if you are in doubt about these parts). Set the tension to normal and thread the top and bobbin.

3 Place the framed fabric RS up so that the fabric lies flat on the machine.

4 Lower the presser foot lever (even though you have removed the foot itself) to engage the top tension.

5 Hold the top thread in one hand and bring the bobbin thread through to RS by turning the machine wheel with the free hand.

6 Hold both threads in one hand and work two or three stitches by slowly moving the hoop under the needle.

7 Holding the hoop with both hands, and keeping the fingers well away from the needle, practice making lines, small spirals and circles in running stitch. The speed of the machine and movement of the hoop will determine the stitch length. Move the hoop smoothly; jerky motions can cause finger injuries.

Pillow cover

If seen from a distance the photograph below looks like a patterned fabric; in fact it is a detail from an exquisitely embroidered floor pillow. Long narrow strips and small squares of fabric have been worked separately without a foot, using a build-up of straight stitches, and then joined together like a patchwork.

Variations

When you feel confident using the machine without the foot, you can change the thread tensions for the following:

A: Two possible straight-stitch variations are whipped and corded stitches.

For whipped stitch, worked here in pink and blue rosettes, tighten the top tension and loosen the bobbin tension so that the lower thread is drawn up onto the RS of the fabric. Move the hoop slowly in circles and spirals, and use a fine lower thread with a thick upper one.

To make a corded stitch (see the heavy dark blue areas) loosen the bobbin tension slightly so that the thread is more controlled when drawn up by the top thread.

B: Alter zigzag stitch by changing the stitch length and width. By running the machine quickly and moving the hoop slowly you can build zigzag up into a satin stitch as seen in the pink and cream stitching. In contrast you can achieve a more open effect by running the machine slowly (see the dark blue lines).

Appliqué

Appliqué is the technique of stitching pieces of fabric onto a background fabric by hand or machine. It can be as simple or as elaborate as you choose to make it. Either way its interest lies in the combination of different fabrics to produce areas of contrast or harmony in color, texture and pattern. It is a technique which works as well for practical items such as clothes and household articles as for purely decorative banners, panels or wall-hangings. However, it is important to consider the use of the finished article as this will influence the design, the method of working and the type of fabric to be used. If the appliqué is on an article of clothing, attach it securely to the background fabric so that it will withstand washing and ironing.

Design

Plan your design carefully in order to achieve maximum effect. You can build your design as you work or plan one beforehand. An interesting way to create your own patterns is to fold a sheet of paper and cut or tear away areas to form an interesting shape; further folds and cuts or tears will produce more elaborate patterns.

Equipment

You can work appliqué on stretcher or embroidery hoop, or freehand with the article laid upon a flat surface or on a sewing machine. The size and the complexity of the design will determine whether a frame is necessary or not. If you use a frame, make sure the fabric is not too taut so that the tension of shapes and background fabric remain equal. If you are working freehand, make sure the fabrics are smooth and flat against one another.

In addition to a frame, you will need 2 pairs of scissors, one for paper and one for fabric (use a small sharp-pointed pair for intricate shapes); paper for preparing the shapes and templates; tracing or dressmaker's carbon paper for transferring the design; tailor's chalk or a hard pencil; needles and pins.

Fabrics and threads

The background fabric and patches should be closely woven and not likely to fray, stretch or pucker. If you use a flimsy fabric, you should back it first with an interfacing, firm cotton or similar fabric, in order to strengthen it.

For articles that will require washing or cleaning, choose fabrics which are pre-shrunk and color-fast, of equal weight and similar type. For children and beginners felt is a useful fabric. It cuts cleanly, doesn't fray and can be applied directly to the background fabric.

The choice of thread depends upon the design and type of appliqué. If you don't wish to make a feature of the stitching, use a matching sewing cotton, otherwise use a contrasting thread. You can use anything from machine thread to tapestry wool as long as it is suitable for the fabric.

Finishing

When you have applied all the shapes, press the article carefully on the WS if necessary. Finish as appropriate.

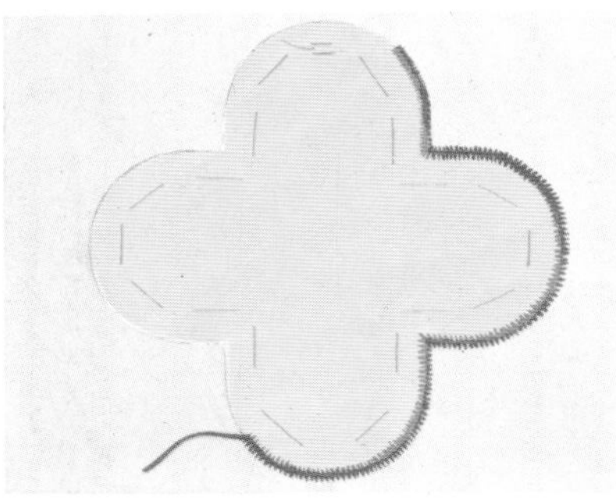

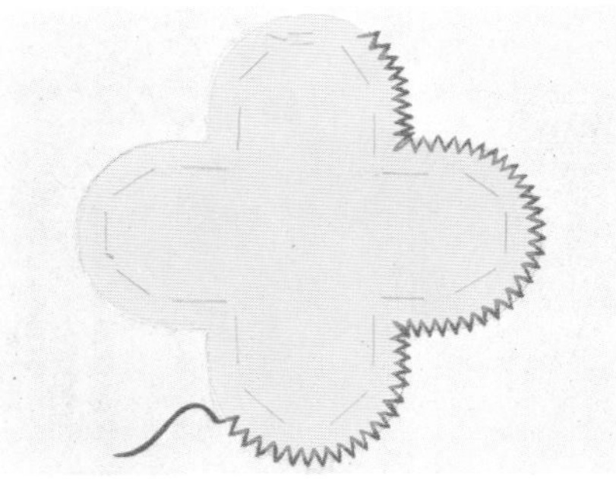

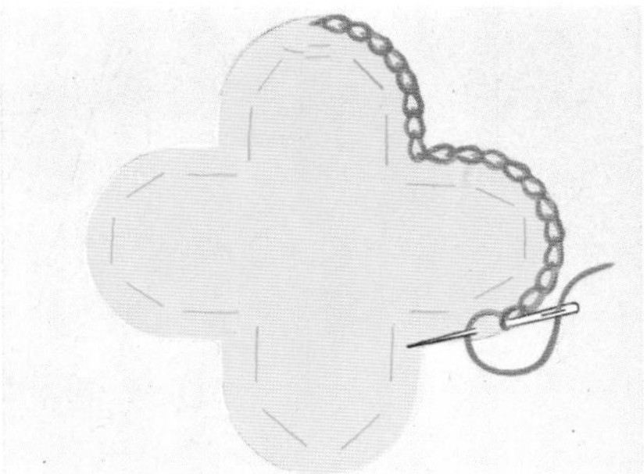

Working methods

There are two main types of appliqué. The first is applying shapes with raw edges in such a way that the edges are covered totally or partially in order to prevent fraying. The second type is applying shapes with hemmed edges. Each method creates a different effect. The basic procedure is the same for both methods; prepare the patch, pin it to the background fabric and baste it securely in preparation for the final stitching.

Raw-edge appliqué Cut the shape to the exact size required with a paper pattern or template or freehand if it is being used in a random design.

Here are three methods of covering the edges.

Satin stitch: Cover the raw edge completely with a line of closely and evenly worked machine (p190) or hand-sewn satin stitches (p170). The line of stitching prevents fraying at the same time as it attaches the patch to the background fabric.

Open zigzag or buttonhole stitch: You can apply the patch with machine zigzag (p190) or evenly spaced hand-sewn buttonhole stitches (p18). This is suitable for non-fraying fabrics or for an article requiring little or no cleaning.

Decorative stitches: You can apply the shape to the background fabric by working over the raw edge with a decorative stitch (p170) such as herringbone, chain stitch or rows of couching. Use this method only when it will enhance the design.

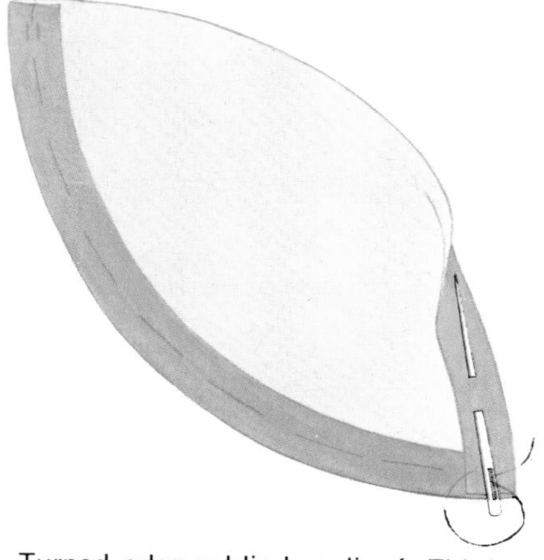

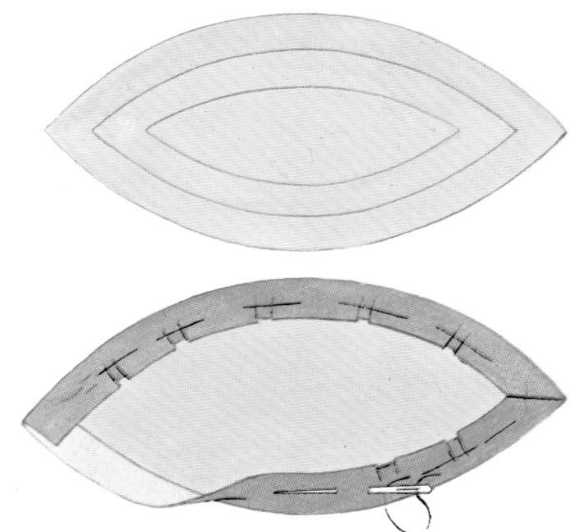

Turned-edge or blind appliqué This is useful for applying loosely woven fabrics to those which are liable to fray easily. When using this method always allow a turning of $\frac{1}{4}$–$\frac{1}{2}$in (6–12mm) when cutting out the appliqué shape. After preparing the shape according to its type as described below, apply the shape to the background fabric with slip stitch, back or running stitch (p18) or machined straight stitch. There are three basic shapes.
Simple shapes: Cut these out as described for raw-edge appliqué, remembering to allow for the hems. Baste the raw edge to WS of the shape to form a hem. Press if necessary.
An alternative method is to pin and baste the shape directly onto the background fabric and turn under the hem allowance as you stitch.
Intricate shapes: For these, use an iron-on interfacing (p36) cut to the exact size of the shape required; iron it to the WS of the appliqué fabric. Snip all turnings on concave edges, nick out small wedges of fabric at intervals on convex edges and miter any corners. Turn edges to WS and baste.
Alternatively, use a cardboard template or non-stick interfacing as a temporary guide. Turn fabric edges over the template and baste. Press well and remove basting to release template before applying the shape in position.

If you use an interfacing template you can leave it under the fabric to give it a slightly raised effect; remember to remove basting.
Padded shapes: These create a further dimension to the work but are more suited to decorative appliqué which won't need washing. To form the pad use batting or layers of felt cut progressively smaller in size. Cover the padding with the chosen fabric and baste the raw edges to the underside of the pad.

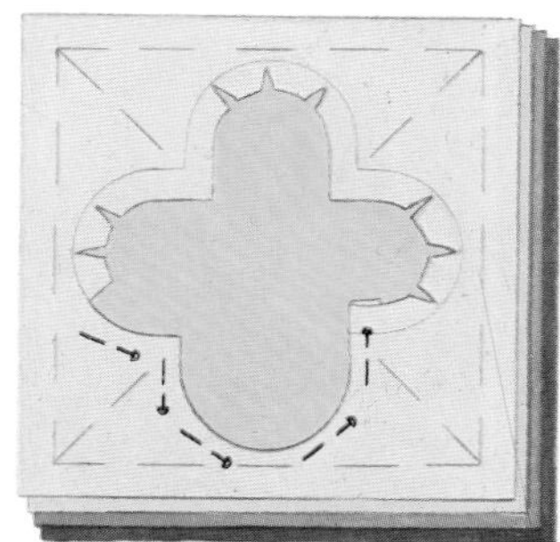

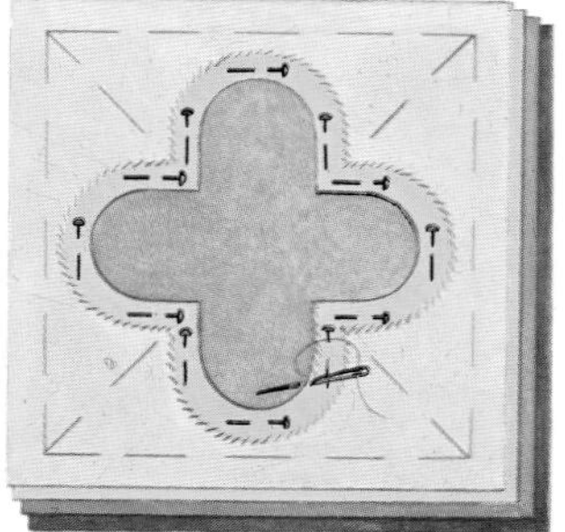

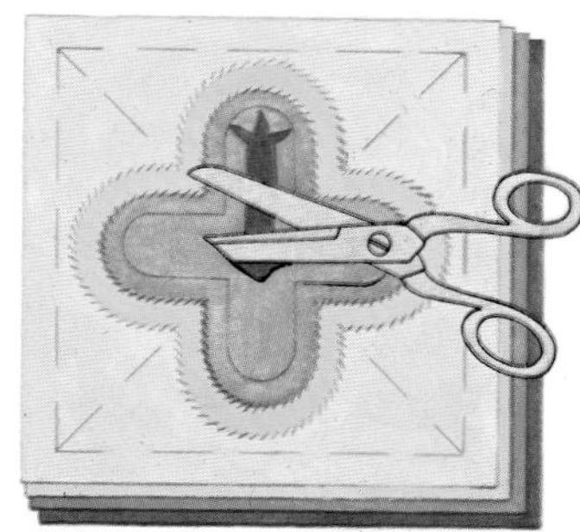

Reverse appliqué
This is a method of appliqué in which layers of fabric are cut away to expose other layers underneath. It is also known as San Blas appliqué because the Cuna Indian women of the San Blas Islands are noted for their skills in this technique. You can use reverse appliqué on clothes or on soft household furnishings. Choose firm, light-weight, closely woven fabrics in bright, contrasting colors or in various shades of one color. Beginners should only use 2 or 3 layers; more than 5 are difficult to handle. Choose a simple design outline with inner contour lines to correspond with the number of layers of fabric.
Working method Transfer the design outline onto the top surface and, allowing $\frac{1}{8}$in (3mm) for hems, cut out the center of this layer only. Baste the layers together with RS up. Use a pair of sharp-pointed scissors; take care not to cut through more than one layer at a time. Clip curves and points, fold under hems and pin if necessary. Sew with matching thread, using small running or slip stitches through all layers of fabric. Repeat this process of tracing the design, cutting, and stitching under edges on all layers until the design is complete.

Variations You can also cut openings in the top layer and slip small pieces of fabric underneath to form an extra layer. Instead of turning under the edges on each layer you can cut along design lines and satin-stitch over the raw edges by hand or by machine.

Appliqué curtains

Curtains 126–9
Appliqué 192

The curtains shown here and on p200 demonstrate that appliqué can transform a plain fabric into one with an all-over pattern. The finished size of each curtain is $1\frac{1}{8} \times 1\frac{3}{8}$yd (1 × 1·22m) and the appliqué design is based on these dimensions. To adapt the design to your own curtains, draw an outline on graph paper based on the scale of your curtains (or the appliqué area in the case of curtains already made); extend or reduce the ribbon trellis and borders accordingly and estimate the quantity of ribbon required. Then determine how many flower shapes there will be and estimate fabric for these using the template shape. Because the fabric requirements will vary from curtain to curtain, quantities are not provided.

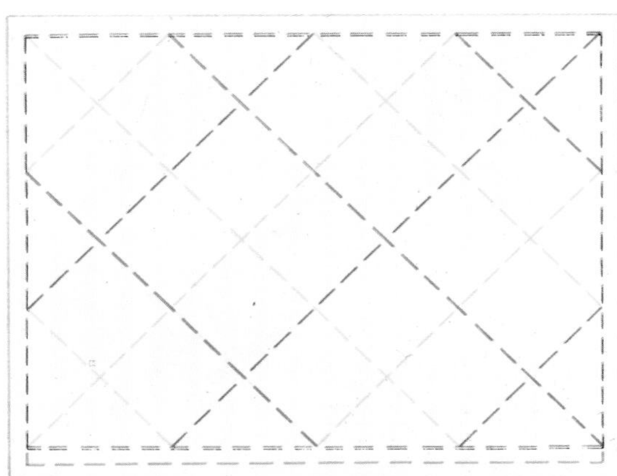

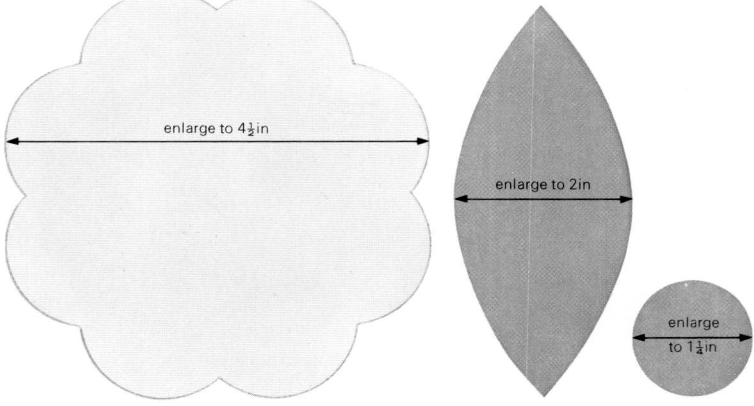

You will need
pencil
graph paper
thin cardboard
ruler
curtain fabric and lining
satin ribbon, 1in (2·5cm) wide in yellow and blue
satin ribbon, $1\frac{1}{2}$in (4cm) wide in pink and green
floral cotton, 54in (140cm) wide in pink and green
matching machine thread in the 4 colors above

Preparing the fabric
If you are doing the appliqué on finished curtains, clean them first; then take out the hem and lining to facilitate stitching. You can leave the heading in and regard the area just below it as the top of the appliqué area.
1 Measure and baste the lines of the finished size of the curtain, or appliqué area in the case of ready-made curtains. Leave a $3\frac{1}{2}$in (9cm) border at the bottom edge of each curtain where the pink and green ribbon will be stitched.
2 Measure and baste the diagonal guide lines for the ribbons. To measure the diagonals, mark 12in (30·5cm) intervals along the basted lines which represent the outline of the trellis area and join these points as shown.
3 Enlarge to actual size and trace onto thin cardboard the flower and leaf motifs. If you do not have a zigzag machine add $\frac{1}{4}$in (6mm) hems around motifs. Cut out the appropriate number, turning under the narrow hem if necessary, and press. When cutting out the incomplete flowers which fall on side edges and corners, as in photograph, allow $\frac{1}{4}$ in (6 mm) hem along these edges and blind-stitch them (p28) to the curtain fabric when in position.

Applying the shapes
1 Pin and baste flowers and leaves in position using the diagonal lines and the scale plan as a guide.
2 If you have a zigzag machine, set it to zigzag with a minimum length for satin stitch and a width of $\frac{1}{8}$in (2mm). Otherwise use normal machine stitch and prepare to top-stitch the hemmed shapes and ribbons.
3 Machine-stitch around each flower and leaf, ensuring that the satin stitch covers the raw edge to prevent fraying. Draw all loose threads to WS and tie to secure. Otherwise top-stitch close to edge of hemmed area. (Re-set zigzag machine to straight stitch.)
4 Center trellis ribbons along guide lines following the scale plan. Lay down the blue ribbons first and then the yellow. Turn under raw ends to prevent fraying. Pin and baste in place and machine-stitch, using a straight stitch in matching threads.
5 Place border stripes in position along bottom edge of curtain area, turn under raw ends and check length. Pin and baste in position and top-stitch close to the ribbon edges.
6 Using flower center motif and adding hem allowance if necessary, cut out enough centers from the green fabric. Hem if required. Pin and baste where the ribbons intersect.

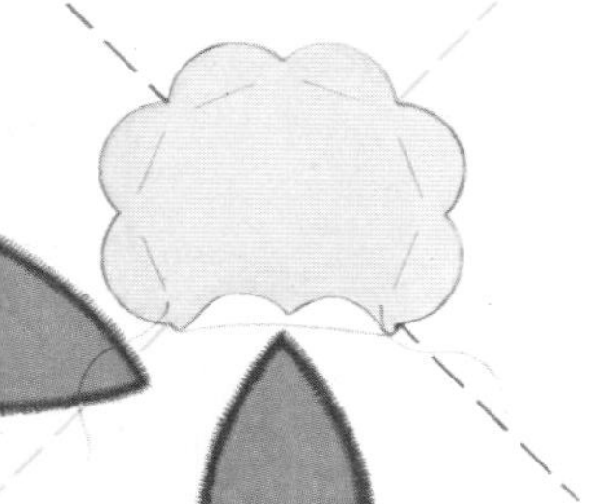

7 Re-set zigzag machine to satin stitch, as before, if appropriate. Zigzag- or top-stitch flower centers.

Finishing
1 Remove basting threads and press carefully on WS, easing and smoothing the fabric flat.
2 Replace hem and lining, or finish and line in the usual way.

Patchwork

Patchwork or 'pieced work' is the art of assembling and sewing together small shapes of material to create a whole fabric. It is a popular technique for recycling clothes and for making use of dressmaking and home-furnishing oddments. In addition to its economic value, it offers an exciting opportunity to design with colour, pattern and texture.

Suitable fabrics

Dress-weight or light furnishing cottons, velvets, corduroys, linens, silks, wools, wool and cotton mixes are all suitable. You should see that the fabric you choose folds well and doesn't stretch or fray. It is best to use the same type of fabric in a given work, but if you do mix them make sure they are of the same weight or thickness to avoid uneven shrinkage. Most patchwork items require backing or lining, preferably in the same or similar fabric. In addition to fabric, you will need templates and, for hand-sewn patchwork, paper.

Templates

These are the master shapes used to cut the fabric patches. You can buy them or make your own. Manufactured templates come in a variety of shapes - triangles, squares, diamonds, pentagons, hexagons and octagons. They are available as pairs, containing a solid metal shape for cutting the paper and a plastic window shape for cutting the fabric. Alternatively you can buy the two types of templates separately; if you do so, make sure the sizes correspond. The clear area of the window template is the same size as the solid template; bordering the clear area is an opaque surround, 6-10mm, which represents the fabric turnings. When cutting your fabric shapes, make use of the windows for selecting the pattern and fabric grain. To make your own, accurately cut a window template from medium-weight card, using a set square, metal ruler and craft knife. Mark a double-headed arrow along one side of the card to remind you to place this along the straight grain of fabric, and place transparent tape along all edges to prevent the card from wearing.

Paper

This is cut from the solid template and placed on the WS of the fabric patch as a guide for folding the turnings on hand-sewn patchwork. It should be absolutely straight on all sides and firm enough for the edges to be felt through the fabric. Stationery, magazine, cartridge paper and greeting cards are all suitable. **Interfacing** can be used instead of paper and left in the fabric shapes to give them a firm edge. Iron-on interfacing (p36) is good for this purpose. If you use any kind of interfacing you should line the patchwork to prevent wear.

Needle, thread and scissors

Use needle and thread to suit the thickness and fibre of the fabric. A sharp sewing needle is suitable for most hand-sewn patchwork; for machine patchwork use a standard needle. With natural fibre fabrics use cotton thread unless you are using silk, in which case use silk thread. Use a polyester thread for all synthetic and man-made fabrics.

Design

Items such as the bedspread on p198 require accurate planning on graph paper beforehand. However, when using the same or similar shapes throughout, you can design as you work. On the whole, regular designs are more pleasing than haphazard arrangements. Try to choose colours and patterns that blend well visually and texturally. Think not only of the units the patches will form but also of the overall impression of the work.

Mosaic patchwork

This comprises patchwork made up of the same or a combination of geometric shapes such as diamonds and hexagons, and is easiest worked by hand. The main thing is that the shapes should share sides of equal length so that they fit together like a jig-saw puzzle.

Preparing the patches

These instructions apply to all hand-sewn patchwork.

1 Trace the solid templates onto the number of papers required and cut with scissors. Draw an arrow on each paper shape to indicate grain direction.

2 Wash fabric to avoid shrinkage and iron while still damp.

3 Place the window template on WS of fabric, making sure that the grain runs parallel to one edge of the template. Trace round the outside and cut along this.

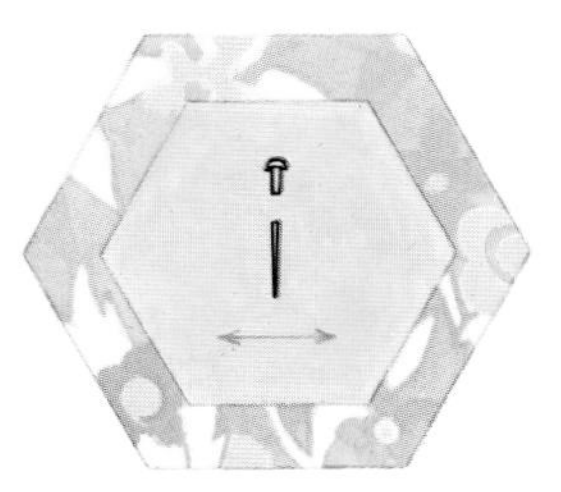

4 Centre the paper along straight of grain on WS of fabric and pin to prevent it slipping.

5 Fold the turnings over the paper and baste through both thicknesses making sure that corners are securely basted. It is essential at this stage to baste each patch accurately to the papers. If the patches vary in size they will not match one another when sewn together.

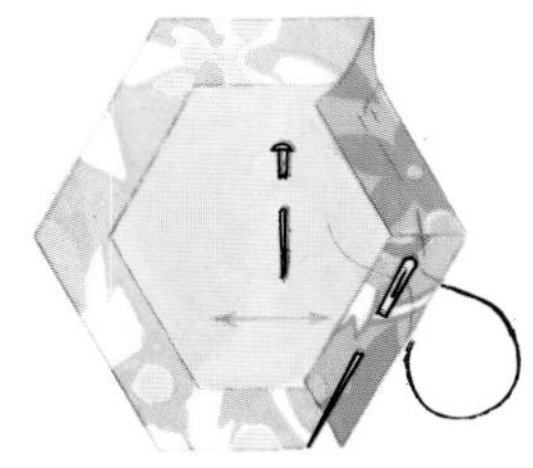

6 Arrange the prepared patches in piles according to colour and shape.

Basic equipment 156
Quilting 200

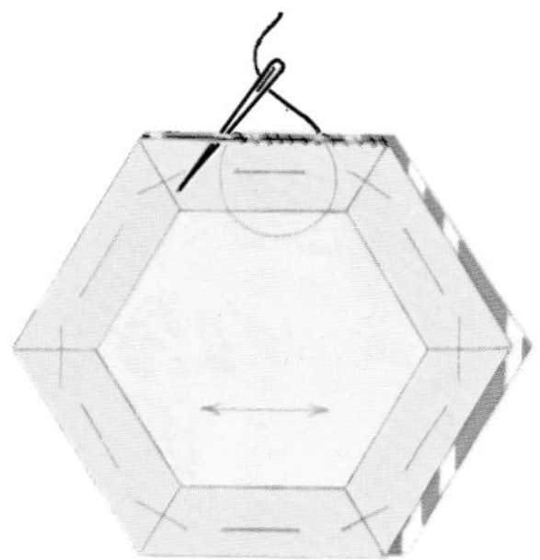

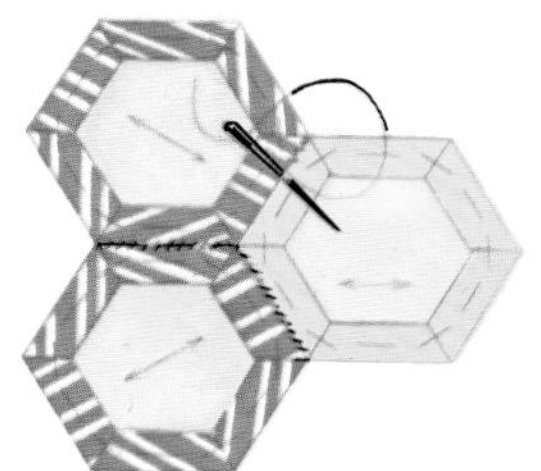

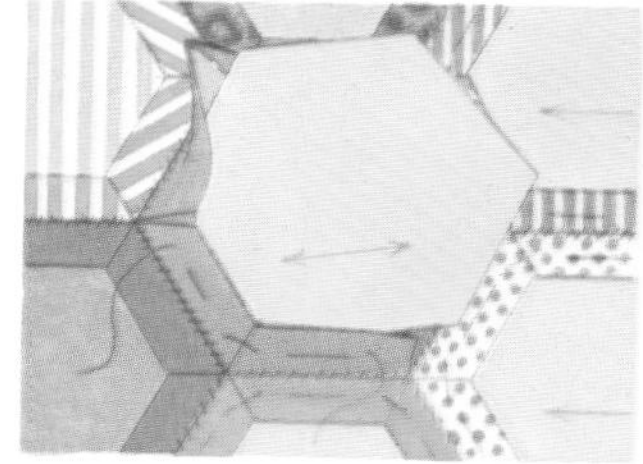

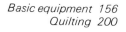

Sewing the patches
1 Starting with 2 patches from the center of the design, place with RS together, grain matching and edges equal. Securing the thread with a knot or tiny back stitches, overcast the central seam with small even stitches, just avoiding the paper patterns. Secure thread at the bottom of the seam.
2 Take another patch and repeat the process.
3 Continue to join patches in this way until you have units of roughly the same size. Keep these in a plastic bag so that they will stay clean and flat.
4 Piece together all the completed units.
5 Remove basting and papers from all of the patches and press gently on WS.
6 Finish patchwork as required, turning in any protruding edges if it seems necessary.

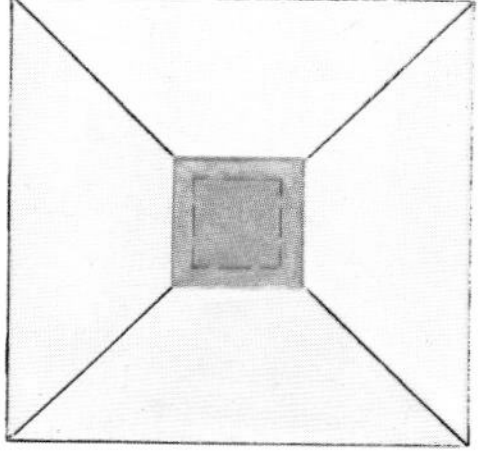

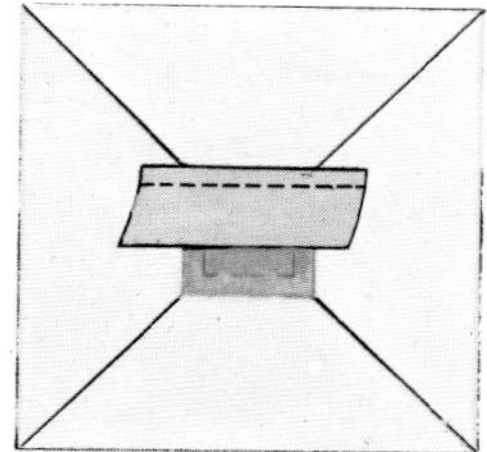

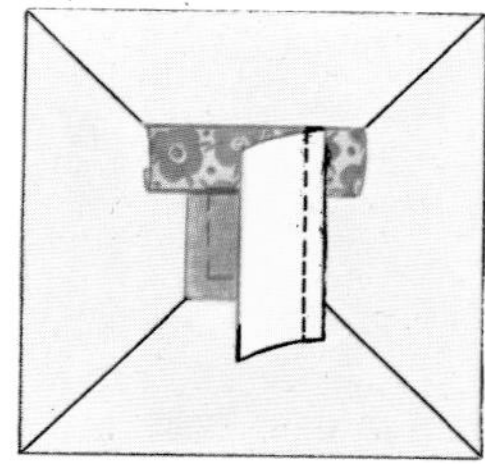

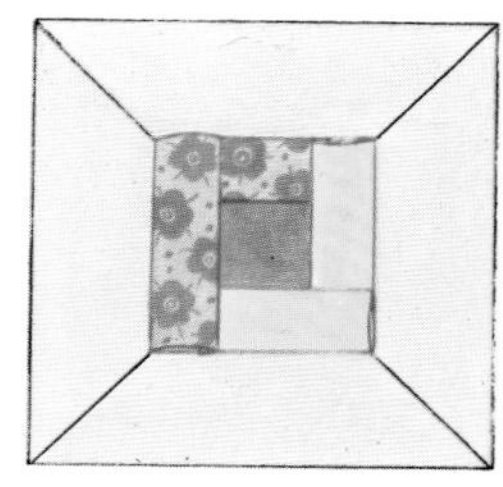

Log cabin
This patchwork design relies traditionally on the contrast of light and dark in each panel. A panel is made up of a central square surrounded on all sides by progressively larger square bands, which are usually divided diagonally into light and dark sides. Instructions here are for finished panels being pieced together so that light and dark sides are adjacent and diagonal divisions run in the same directions. (You could also arrange the light and dark sides to create a different type of effect.) To make each panel:
1 Cut a foundation square from monk's cloth or cotton sheeting; 9–12in (23–30cm) is a good size to work with.
2 Baste or lightly pencil 2 diagonal guide lines from corner to corner across the square.
3 Where the guide lines intersect place a 1in (2·5cm) square of fabric. Center it exactly and baste it, unhemmed, on all sides.
4 For the first band of the design cut 4 strips of fabric, 2 light and 2 dark. Each should be about 1in (2·5cm) wide and just long enough on the outside edge to cover the diagonal guide lines at either end.
5 With RS together pin the 1st strip over one edge of the central square and stitch by hand or machine $\frac{1}{8}$in (3mm) from the edge. Fold back and press flat.
6 Position the 2nd strip along an adjacent side of the square in the same way as the 1st strip (this time one end will overlap a folded end of the strip). Stitch, fold back and press.
7 Continue with the 3rd and then the 4th strip.
8 For the 2nd band, cut 4 more 1in (2·5cm) strips of light and dark, long enough to cover the diagonal lines now showing at the ends. Attach in the same way, treating the previous band as the central square.
9 Continue building up the logs to about $\frac{3}{8}$in (10mm) inside the edges of the square following the color sequence. Hem the outer edges of the logs.
10 When you have made the required number of panels, stitch them together along the panel turnings, making sure that none of the foundation fabric shows through.
11 Line work if required.

Machine patchwork
As well as the stitching involved, the technique for machine patchwork also differs from hand-sewn patchwork in that no backing paper is required. Use a window template and mark cutting lines of fabric only. Shapes that lend themselves most readily to machine patchwork are squares, rectangles and triangles; you can combine them or build them up separately into larger units depending on the article you are making. Diagonal or brick patterns are interesting variations which you can achieve with these shapes.
Working method Make fabric patches from window templates by tracing cutting lines directly onto WS of fabric. If you want seamlines, mark them at this stage with a ruler and hard pencil about $\frac{1}{4}$in (6mm) in from the cutting lines. Cut the patches.
Seam the shapes into strips so that grain runs in the same direction and then join the strips, matching seamlines (or staggering them in the case of brick patterns). Press seams as strips are completed and then join. Finish as appropriate.

Patchwork bedspread

This patchwork project combines the pieced-block technique, popular in our traditional American quilts, with appliqué. The applied flowers are optional and can be omitted without detriment to the design. The spread is made for a single bed, but by doubling the width you could make one for a double bed of the same height. The instructions apply to a bed with a surface area of 3 × $6\frac{1}{2}$ft (0·90 × 1·95m) and a 2ft (0·60m) drop to the floor on all sides. Calculate your own bedspread accordingly, remembering to include twice the measurement of the drop at the sides, and if it is not a simple case of doubling the width, sketch a new plan onto graph paper to work out the quantities of material. To give a flat finish, press seams as you complete each process. Instead of backing the bedspread as described, you could quilt it first. The simplest method for this would be to machine-quilt along border strips and square blocks, according to the instructions for English quilting (p202).

Fabric required
All the materials used are plain-weave cottons, 36in (90cm) wide. In a work of this size, it is essential that the materials are of the same weight and type. Remember to wash and iron fabric first.

You will need
for the top fabric:
4yd (3·60m) pink,
$3\frac{5}{8}$yd (3·30m) yellow,
$1\frac{7}{8}$yd (1·70m) green,
1yd (0·90m) blue
for the backing:
$9\frac{1}{3}$yd (8·40m) green (or any other) fabric used in patchwork or $3\frac{3}{8}$yd (3m) sheeting, $2\frac{1}{2}$yd (228cm) wide
graph paper (optional)
ruler
triangle or T-square
craft knife
cardboard
paper
scissors
transparent tape
white machine thread

Finished size of pieces
One measurement is given for each triangle. This represents the sides which form the right angle.

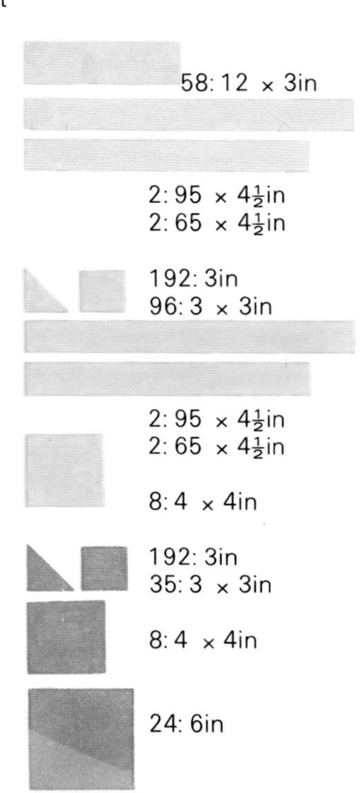

Preparing patchwork and border fabric
1 Using a triangle, ruler and craft knife make a solid cardboard template for all the patchwork and square border shapes. To allow for a $\frac{1}{4}$in (5mm) seam on all sides, make the templates $\frac{1}{2}$in (10mm) larger on each edge, $\frac{3}{4}$in (2cm) in the case of triangles.

2 Measure the border strips along the bottom of the fabric, so that each will be a complete length when cut. To get an accurate width for each of the strips, measure $4\frac{1}{2}$in (11·5cm) up from the bottom across the WS of fabric at regular intervals, and mark with dots; join the dots until you reach the required length. Mark the required length, plus a bit extra to allow for stretching which might occur after the patchwork is pieced together.

3 Still on the WS of fabric mark all the pieces by drawing around the solid templates. It is not necessary to mark seamlines; use a $\frac{1}{4}$in (5mm) machine guide or improvise your own seam guide.

4 Cut all the pieces carefully and assort them according to color and shape. Knot threads and draw one through each pile to keep the pieces together. As you need the pieces, take them from the top of the appropriate pile. (Remember to keep spare pink and yellow material for the appliqué which comes later.)

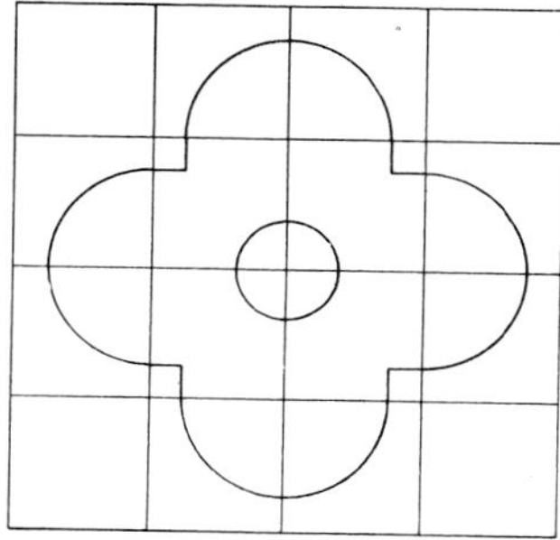

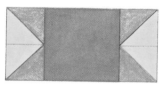

Making the patchwork blocks
1 Sew green and yellow triangles together so that you finish with 192 green/yellow squares.
2 Taking 2 green/yellow squares at a time with RS together and diagonal seams running in the same direction, join yellow sides together along one side to form a rectangle when fabric is opened up; then work through remaining squares.
3 Taking half (48) of the seamed rectangles, join a yellow square to both ends of each, with RS together, to form the top and bottom strips of each block.
4 Attach the remaining 48 rectangles to the 24 blue squares. With RS together and base of green triangle joined to the blue, stitch 2 rectangles to opposite ends of the square.
5 To the remaining 2 sides of each square, attach the top and bottom strips with RS together, matching all seams.

Making the flowers
1 For the applied pink flowers make a solid template from cardboard by enlarging the tracing pattern shown. Trace and cut 24 paper patterns.
2 With material left over from the patchwork shapes, cut rough squares of pink fabric, about $5\frac{1}{2}$in (14cm) on all sides. Pin paper patterns to WS of squares and allowing for a $\frac{1}{4}$in (5mm) seam, cut out the shapes. Clip curves within seam allowance (see p192). Baste or press over edges and remove thread and papers.
3 Make 24 flower centers the same way from 2in (5cm) squares of yellow fabric.
4 Pin or baste flowers to the center of each blue patchwork square and overcast with tiny stitches, small invisible running stitches, or top-stitch by machine. Pin yellow centers and sew as above.

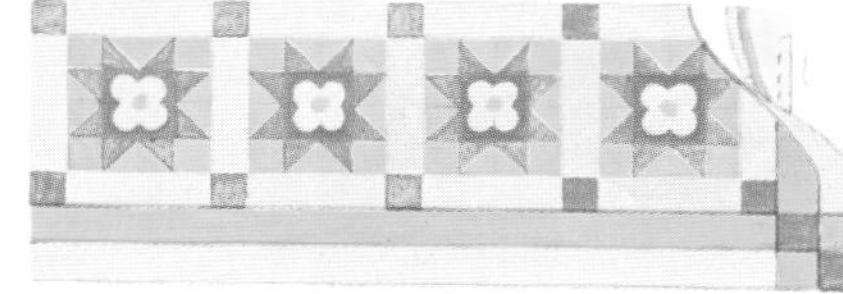

Piecing the patchwork blocks
1 Join the finished blocks into 6 horizontal rows, using 4 blocks and 5 pink rectangles in each. Connect and frame the sides of the blocks with the rectangles.
2 Now make the strips that will connect the rows of blocks at top and bottom, beginning and ending each row with a green square, using the 28 pink rectangles that remain and the 35 green squares. Make 7 strips, each one containing 4 pink rectangles and 5 green squares alternately placed.
3 Join these strips with the rows of blocks made in **1**. With RS together pin all the strips to the rows of blocks, matching seams. When all the strips are pinned, machine-stitch them together.

Making the borders
1 Matching lengths, seam together 2 of the long pink with 2 of the long yellow strips, and then 2 short pink with 2 short yellow.
2 Pin longer strips to patchwork sides first, making sure they match. Trim to correct length including extra for seam allowance at the corners, and stitch seams.
3 Make 4 large green/yellow squares for the corners, using 2 green and 2 yellow 4in (10cm) squares in each. Attach a large square to either end of the shorter pink and yellow strips, with a green square adjacent to a yellow strip and a yellow square adjacent to a pink one.
4 Attach these strips to the patchwork in same way as in **2**, joining corner seams.

Making the backing
1 Sew center seam of backing if using the 36in (90cm) wide fabric. Measure against the top fabric and trim, leaving $\frac{1}{4}$in (5mm) seam allowances.
2 With RS together, place top fabric and backing together making sure they match. Pin along 3 complete sides and part of the 4th side. Machine-stitch, clip corners and turn through the gap to RS. Press edges together and seams left at the opening. Overcast the remaining gap.

Quilting

Basic equipment 156
Transferring designs 157
Finishing 158

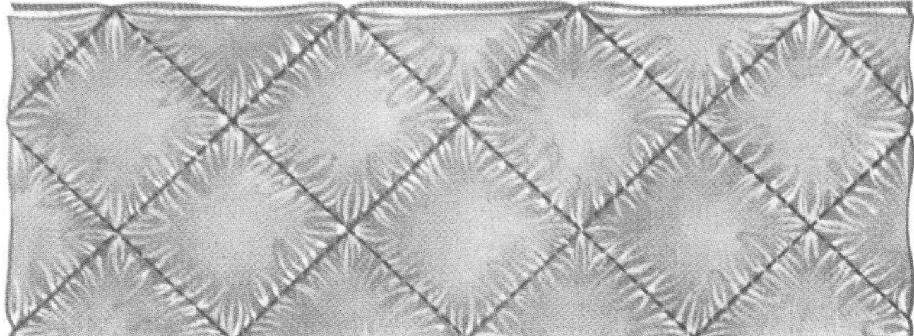

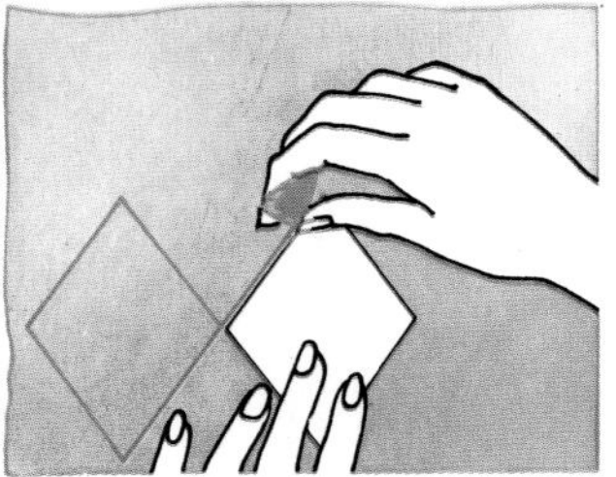

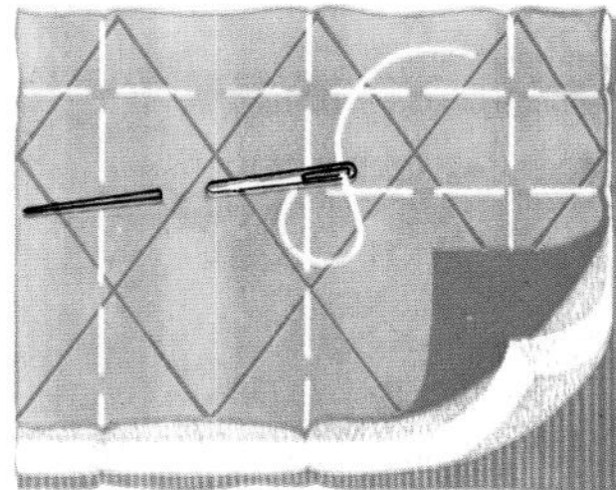

English quilting

English or padded quilting consists of 3 layers of material stitched together in a regular all-over pattern to produce a raised, warm fabric. The lines of stitching create a contrast of light and dark on the top fabric, and the padding, which lies between the top fabric and lining, produces the warmth. The main advantage of quilted garments and articles is that they are both warm and light-weight. Quilting is used mostly for bedspreads, outer-garments and vests, but it can be used as a decorative detail on items such as handbags.

Equipment
You will need top fabric, filling and backing.
Top fabric Choose a pliable, soft material such as cotton or flannel. Synthetics are also suitable.
Filling Fluffy kapok, flannel or an old blanket will give slight padding; but for lightness, washability and springiness polyester or Dacron batting (available in various thicknesses) is an excellent filling.
Backing This should be firm enough to provide support for the filling so that the quilted pattern is emphasized on the top fabric. Monk's cloth or cotton sheeting are both suitable.
On articles where both sides will show, such as bedspreads, you can use the same material as the top fabric or one in a blending color. If the top fabric on a bedspread is slippery choose a backing with a non-slip surface. Use cotton for backing garments and then line in the usual way (p88).
Thread This should match the fiber of the top fabric and should be in a matching or contrasting color.
Needles Use a crewel needle for hand-quilting. If you are quilting by machine, use a strong needle if the materials are heavy, but experiment if in doubt.
Templates Use a solid patchwork template (p196) if appropriate for the design, or cut your own from cardboard. For circular shapes you can use the base of cups or glasses.
Frame Use an embroidery hoop for small articles and a stretcher frame for large items. You do not need a frame for machine-quilting if you are using a presser foot.
Choosing a design
Quilting designs fall into two basic categories; all-over repeating patterns which are geometric or curved, and individual shapes such as large floral patterns in the center of an article. All-over repeating patterns are much simpler than detailed ones to quilt and look as effective, so beginners would be wise to start with them. Do not use a complicated design with a lot of stitching as this will not give the relief needed.
Preparing the materials
If you are quilting a garment baste around the outline of each piece allowing 2½–3in (6–7cm) extra all around for shrinkage, and quilt before cutting out and finishing. With the exception of the framing which is only applicable to hand-quilting, the basic preparation of materials is the same for both methods of stitching.

1 Work out the design on paper or graph paper
2 Wash and iron top fabric and backing to reduce shrinkage.
3 Cut and seam, if required, all the layers to the same size, allowing for extra backing if necessary – see Finishing (D).
4 Transfer the design to RS of top fabric with templates and tailor's chalk or by tracing and basting, if you are working a detailed design.

5 On a smooth, flat surface lay backing WS up, place the padding on top of that and finally, the top fabric RS up. Bind or hem the edges if you plan to work the article on a stretcher, using one of the methods below.
6 Baste the 3 layers together horizontally and vertically to prevent them sliding.
7 Attach the quilt to the frame, stretching the material evenly but not too taut, and roll the ends if required.

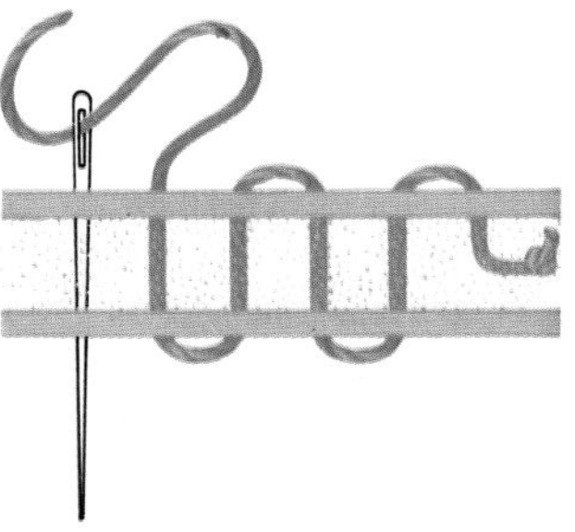

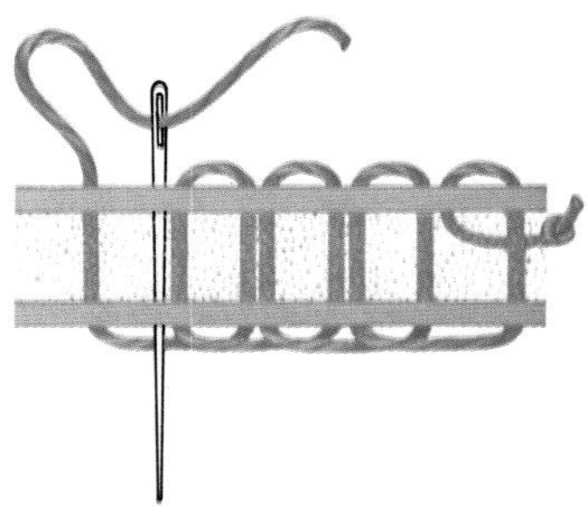

Hand-stitching
Depending on your frame, you can work either from the center outward or from the bottom to top edge. There are two basic stitches for hand-quilting. Use back stitch (p18) if the filling is thin and the reverse side is not seen and running stitch (p18) for more substantial fillings where the backing is seen.
To begin, knot the thread and bring the needle through to the surface, pulling gently but firmly until the knot lodges itself in the lower layer of the filling. To finish off, make a single back stitch and run the thread in through the filling. Cut the thread close to the surface and the end will be lost. Make sure each quilting stitch is short and even in length. With running stitch, make the spaces between each equal in length to the stitch. The best way to achieve this is to use a stabbing movement with one hand above the frame and the other below. To maintain an even tension, thread several needles at a time and stitch as many lines of the design as you can, working each a little way more forward and so on.

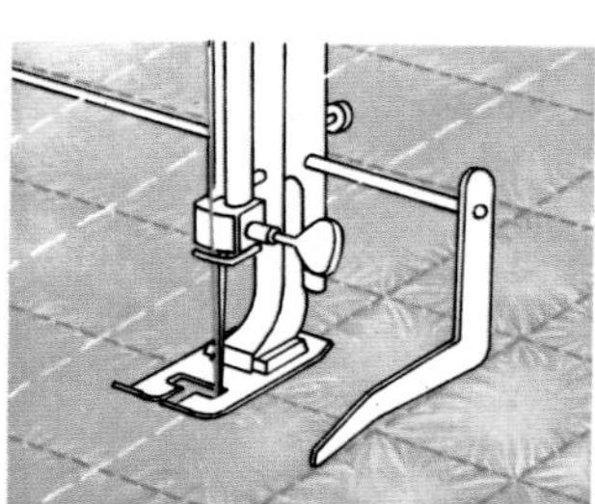

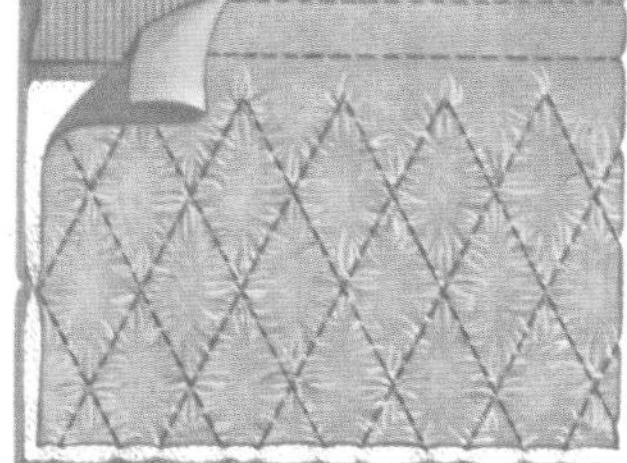

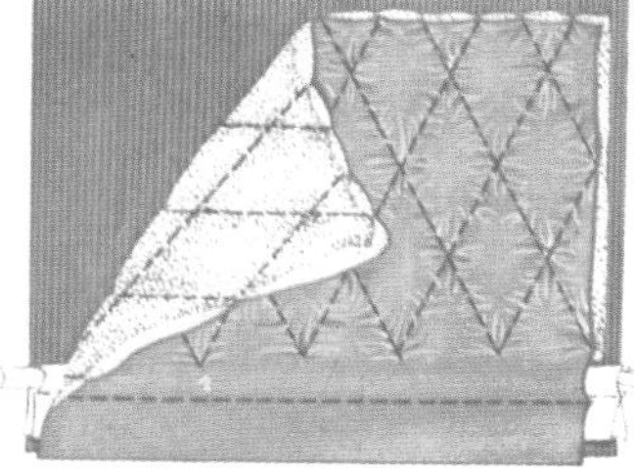

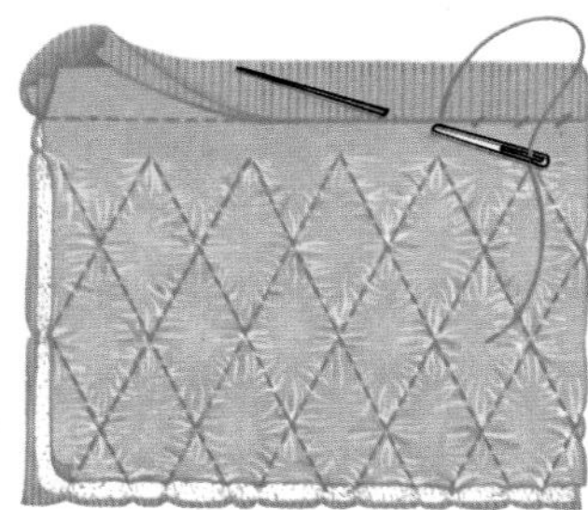

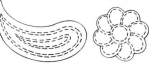

Machine-stitching
Straight-edged geometric designs are the easiest to work on a machine. To get the lines of stitching evenly spaced, use an adjustable gauge or edge-marker (quilting bar) attached to the foot. A medium-length stitch with a slightly loose tension is usually satisfactory. Work the stitching as shown in the diagram. You might find it necessary to clean and oil the machine as you work because the fluff from the batting tends to build up around the bobbin case; remove quilting from machine and refer to your machine instructions.

Finishing
When the quilting is completed, remove the basting and then take the quilt off the frame if appropriate. Finish garments in the usual way and line if necessary. Finish the edges of other items with one of the following methods:
A Trim the batting to the width of the seam allowance, and top-stitch together.
B Turn in the edges of the top fabric and insert piping (p102) to match the top fabric.
C Finish the edges with a bias binding (p25) made from the same material as the top fabric.
D Turn the backing over to the front and machine-stitch.

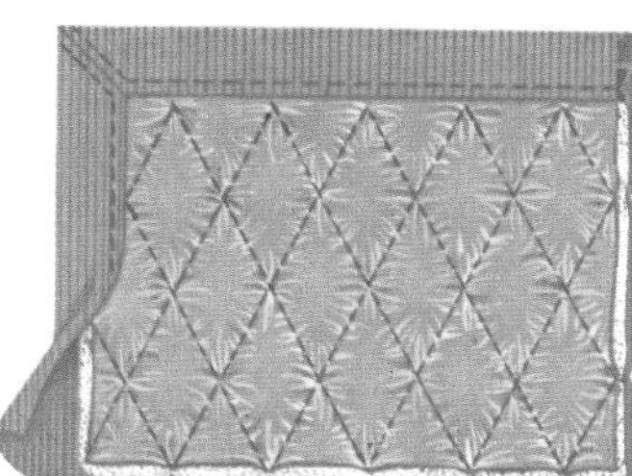

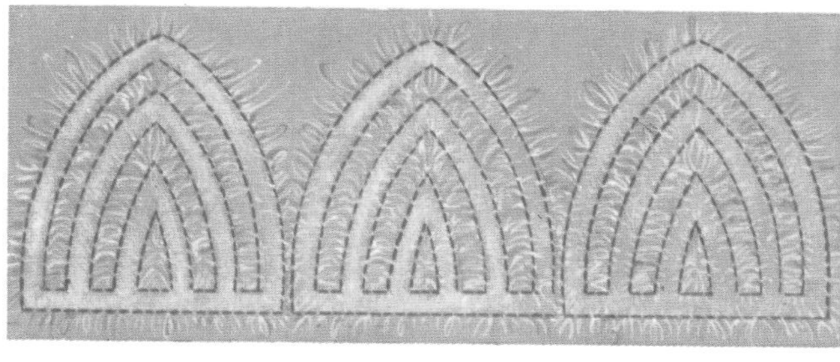

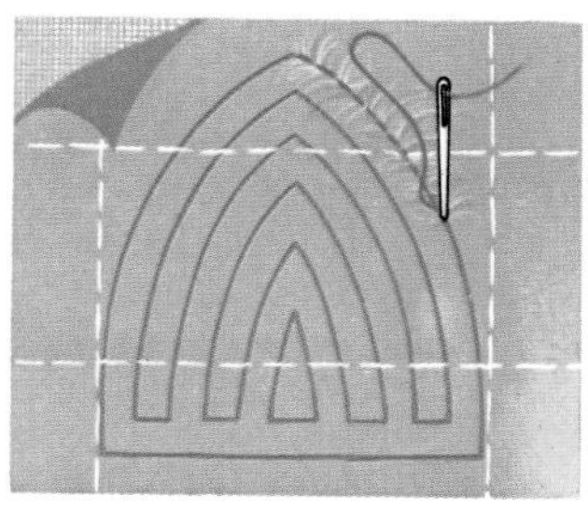

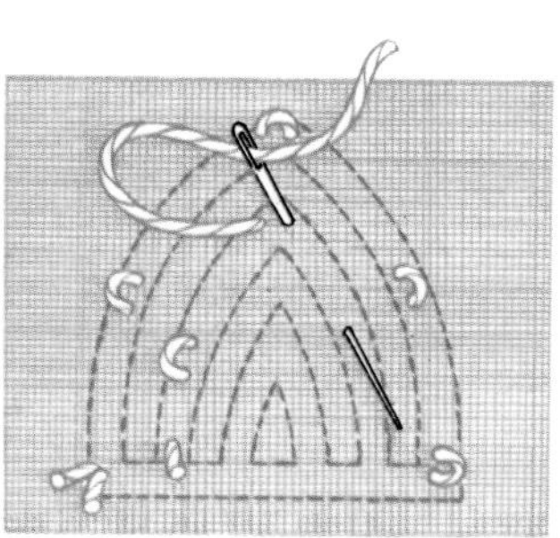

Italian quilting
Purely decorative, and not designed for warmth, Italian quilting is characterized by parallel lines of stitching between which cording is inserted to give an effect of high relief. The stitching lines can be straight, angular or curved; the space between lines is known as a channel. The materials needed are a muslin or loosely woven backing and the same sort of top fabric and lining as used for English quilting. For the cording you can use pre-shrunk cotton piping cord, quilting yarn, 8-ply rug yarn or knitting yarn. Cording should roughly be as wide as the channel. You will need a tapestry needle or bodkin for pulling the cord through the backing between stitching lines; use pliers to assist you if the cording does not pull through easily.

Method of working
1 Draw your design on paper, remembering to use parallel lines.
2 Wash and iron the fabric and lining, and cut to required shape, allowing extra lining if necessary.
3 Transfer design to RS of fabric.
4 Cut enough muslin to back the quilted area and place to WS of fabric. Baste securely horizontally and vertically.
5 Stitch along the lines of the design with small back stitches or straight machine-stitches first on one line and then on the one parallel to it.
6 Remove basting.
7 Turn work over to the backed side. Thread through the tapestry needle or bodkin slightly more cording than the length of the channel to be worked. Insert the needle between the 2 layers of fabric. To do this, carefully pierce the muslin at the starting point of a line and run the cording through the stitched lines. At sharp angles and curves take the needle out through the backing leaving a loop of wool (un-cut) and insert it again to proceed in the appropriate direction. This prevents puckering; for the same reason, do not pull the cord too tightly.
8 When quilting is complete mount the quilt on a stretcher (see p158) to give even ridges and trim the loose ends of cording. Remove from stretcher and attach the lining as for English quilting.

Trapunto jacket

Master pattern sheet
Interlining 36

Like Italian quilting, trapunto is mainly decorative, giving emphasis to certain parts of a design by padding between small stitched areas. Stuffing material, such as batting or kapok, is inserted after the stitching has been done to produce the relief. The important thing about trapunto quilting is that the raised surface should be absolutely smooth. For this reason, try to base your design on small enclosed shapes, either geometric or stylized, which are much easier to stuff evenly than large areas.

As shown in the jacket here, trapunto quilting lends interest to an otherwise plain fabric. Although trapunto is decorative and not strictly designed for warmth, this jacket has a wadding interlining so that it can be worn in cold weather. As an alternative to batting, you could use an interlining of soft wool or kapok. The jacket, which fastens at the front with ties, is an extended adaptation of the T-shirt given on p50.

Jacket pattern

To allow for the fastening, cut the front of the T-shirt pattern in half; extend the CF of the right front and add a seam allowance to the left front. Extend the sleeves to the required length and round the corners of the shoulders and sleeve caps slightly where they join. (See diagram of pattern pieces.) Determine the size of the remaining pieces, adding to the length of front and back if you wish (this jacket comes to just below the waist). Using the cutting pattern as a guide, calculate the amount of fabric you will need, remembering to allow for any extra length you might add.

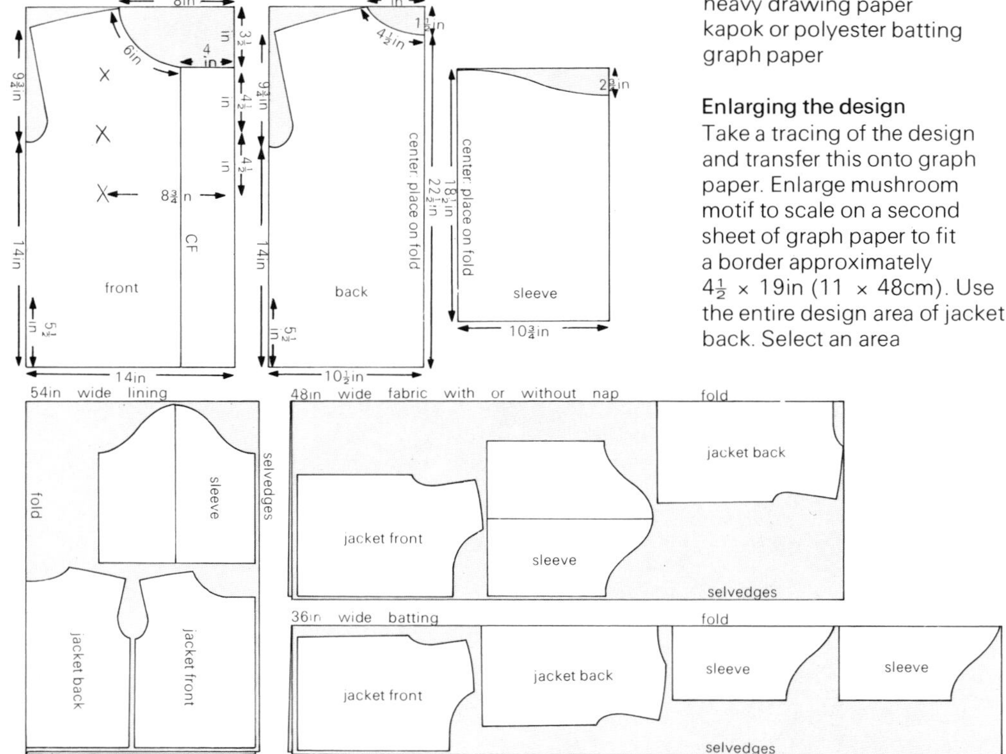

You will need

2⅜yd (2·10m) fabric 48in (122cm) wide
1⅝yd (1·40m) lining 54in (140cm) wide
2¾yd (2·50m) batting, 36in (90cm) wide
firm cotton backing, e.g. cambric, 24 × 45in (60 × 115cm)
matching and contrasting machine thread
paper-cutting scissors
small sharp-pointed scissors
heavy drawing paper
kapok or polyester batting
graph paper

Enlarging the design

Take a tracing of the design and transfer this onto graph paper. Enlarge mushroom motif to scale on a second sheet of graph paper to fit a border approximately 4½ × 19in (11 × 48cm). Use the entire design area of jacket back. Select an area approximately 9½in (24cm) wide for sleeves, and divide design to fit right and left fronts, allowing for central overlap.

Preparing jacket for quilting

1 Cut jacket fronts, back and sleeves in top fabric and padding. Baste padding to WS.
2 First prepare the sleeves for quilting. Cut 2 strips of backing fabric 12 × 8in (30 × 20cm) each. Place in a central position on WS of sleeve edge; baste to padding only.
3 Enlarge mushroom pattern for sleeve and make a paper template for the basic outline.
4 Position the template on RS of first sleeve so that the middle is slightly off-center toward the front half of the sleeve, and 1in (2·5cm) up from the hemline.
5 Slip cardboard between fabric and padding to give a smooth tracing surface. Lightly pencil around the design outline, filling in all other lines except gill lines.
6 Reverse template and repeat for other sleeve.
7 Cut strips of backing for jacket back and front sections: 8 × 10½in (20 × 26cm) for left front, 8 × 14½in (20 × 37cm) for right front and 8 × 20½in (20 × 53cm) for back.
8 Baste to padding and transfer design as for sleeves, using center front and center back as position guides for the center of the designs.

T-shirt 50
Lining 88
Quilting 202

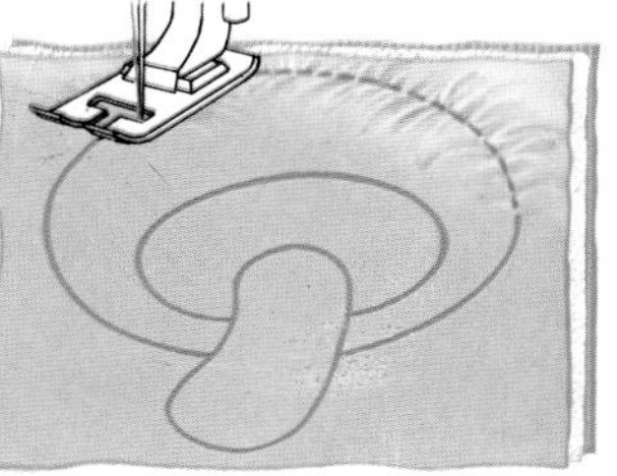

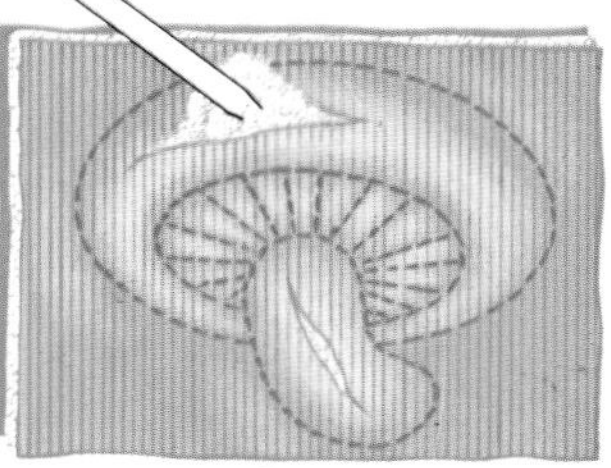

Quilting the mushrooms
Because of the padding, the quilting is a combination of English and trapunto quilting.

1 Machine carefully along the pencil lines, easing the fabric to achieve smooth and accurate lines.

2 When you have stitched all the lines, stitch by eye the gill lines in a darker or contrasting thread.

3 Draw all loose ends through to WS and tie to secure.

4 Make a small slit in backing fabric in areas representing mushroom caps and stems and insert stuffing. Do not over-pad the areas to prevent distortion of the garment pieces. Overcast the slits when padding is complete.

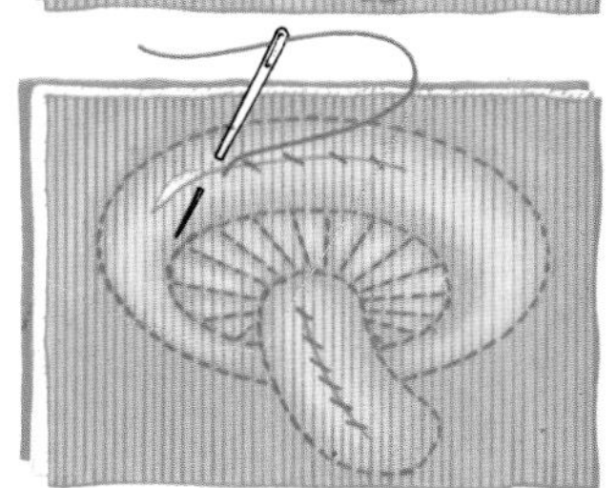

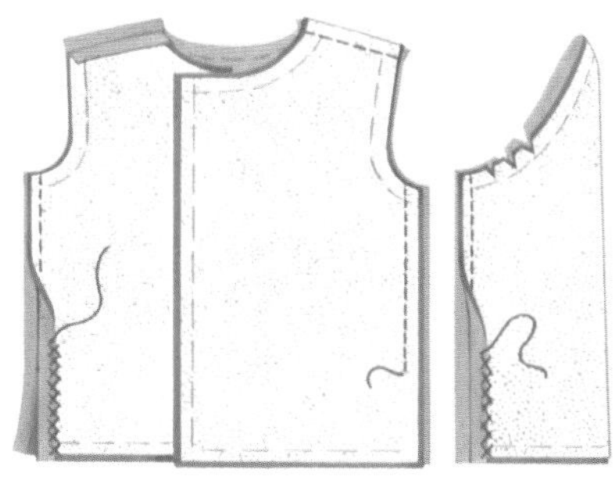

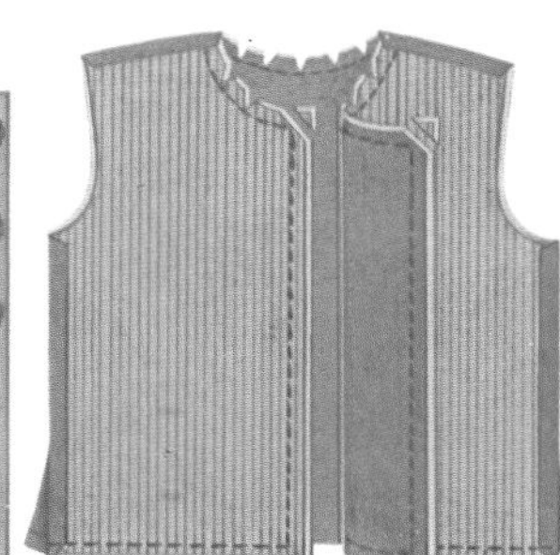

Finishing the jacket

1 With RS together baste and stitch shoulder and side seams to circles. Trim padding from seam allowance, press seams open and herringbone-stitch (p170) seam allowances to padding.

2 With RS together, baste and stitch underarm seam of sleeve. Trim, press and stitch as **1**.

3 Make 6 rouleau ties (p102), to finish $\frac{1}{4} \times 8\frac{1}{4}$in (6mm × 20cm) Baste and top-stitch 3 ties to RS of right front in positions indicated.

4 Finish lining as for jacket up to this stage. With RS together, matching outer edges and seams, baste and stitch lining to jacket around the neck, front and lower edges, leaving side slits open and 8in (20·5cm) open in center of back at lower edge. Trim padding at seams, clip neck curves and cut across corners. Turn jacket RS out through opening at back. Baste close to stitched edges and around armholes. Press.

5 At the side slits turn in seam allowance of lining and slip-stitch to jacket.

6 With RS together, baste and stitch sleeves into armholes with sleeves uppermost. Trim padding, press seams towards sleeves. With RS together, matching underarm seams and lower edges, slip sleeve lining over sleeve. Baste and stitch around lower edge of sleeve. Trim padding. Pull lining down and up into the sleeve with WS together. Baste around lower edge and press.

7 Turn in seam allowance around sleeve cap lining, pull over sleeve cap and slip-stitch to stitching line.

8 Turn in seam allowance at back opening and slip-stitch to close; slip-stitch the other 3 rouleau ties to left front in positions indicated in drawing.

Smocking

Smocking is a decorative form of embroidery used to control fullness on a garment; it makes an attractive feature on yokes, sleeves, pockets and necklines of dresses or shirts. The basis of smocking is the gathering of pleats onto which the smocking stitches are worked. The gathering reduces the garment to one-third of its original width, so allow for this when buying your fabric. Suitable fabrics for smocking are cotton, cotton/wool mixes, fine woolens and corduroy. Very fine fabrics such as voile, lawn and silk can look exquisite smocked but require practice; avoid very thick fabrics as these will not hang properly, and the smocking will not be as distinctive. Always complete smocking before you finish a garment, but if smocking a ruffle hem the edge first. The same applies to the hems of pockets.

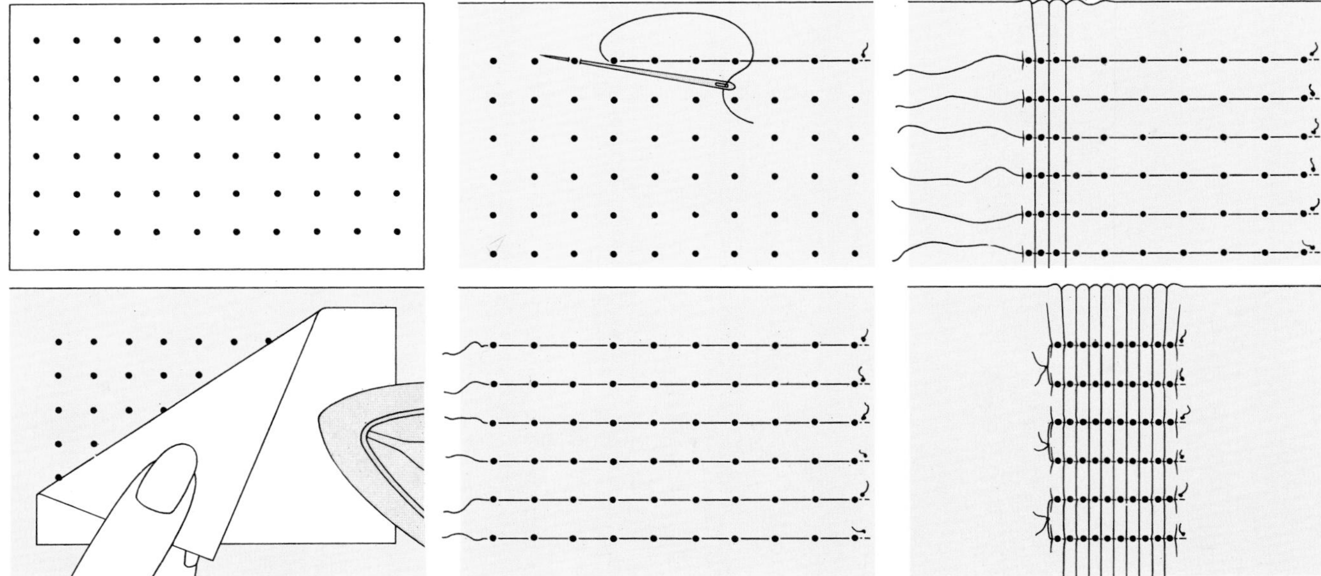

Smock transfers
To ensure regularly spaced, even pleats you should use a transfer on all fabrics except those which contain their own symmetrical design, e.g. checks, stripes. The transfer is a piece of tissue paper with a printed grid of dots which when ironed onto the fabric serve as a guide for the gathering threads. The average distance between dots is $\frac{1}{4}$in (6mm); this is suitable for all but fine fabrics which require a more densely spaced transfer to give smaller pleats.
Use a transfer with light-colored dots for dark material and dark-colored ones for light. The dots should disappear after the first or second wash.
Preparing the transfer Cut the transfer paper to the exact shape and depth required for the smocking area. Position it accurately onto the WS of fabric, leaving an allowance for seams or hems. Iron directly onto the paper with a dry iron at a temperature suitable for the fabric underneath, lifting up the paper after the iron has passed over it.

Making the gathers
With strong synthetic thread, work separate lines of gathering. With WS of fabric facing, starting at right-hand side secure the first stitch with a knot and back stitch. Pass the needle under each dot produced by the transfer, just lifting it, until you reach the end of the row and leave a little bit of loose thread at the end. Work each row in this way. When you have completed all the rows pull all loose ends together simultaneously and evenly, but not too tightly. Then knot the ends together in pairs and cut off the excess thread. Turn the garment over so that RS is facing ready for smocking.

Threads and needles
Pearl cotton is the most suitable thread for smocking, but embroidery floss can also be used. Use a smooth needle with a sharp point; a crewel needle is best for use on long stitches. The size of both needle and thread depends on the fabric used and the effect you want.

Choosing a design
As a rule smocking designs are based on a combination of stitches, although a single-stitch design can also be effective. Smocking stitches vary not only in appearance but also in degree of elasticity and ease of working; you should bear all three in mind. Sketch your proposed design on paper and work a small sample to see how it will look.

Finishing
When the smocking is complete, and with gathering threads still in place, lay the fabric WS up and press very lightly with a hot iron and damp cloth placed over the fabric. The steam sets the pleats and gives the work an even appearance. Remove the gathering threads and continue to finish the garment.

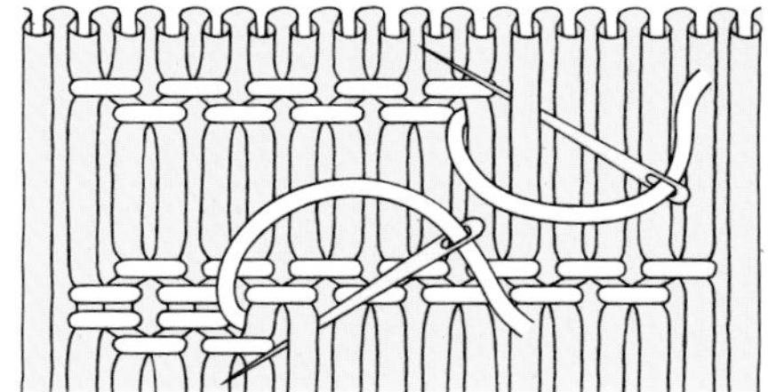

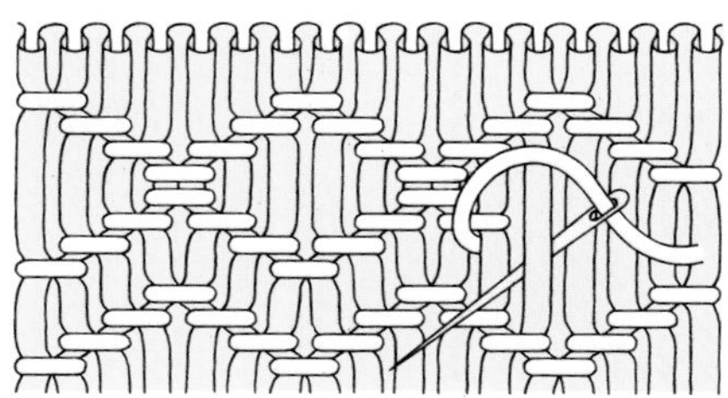

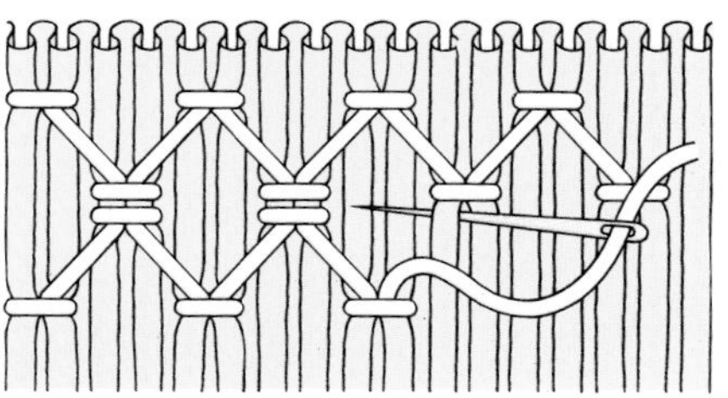

Cable stitch
This is a firm control stitch. Two rows worked closely together at the top and bottom of a band of smocking prevent it from fanning out. You can also use it between rows of more elastic stitches to add strength to the design. Bring needle up through 1st pleat, and draw it across to next pleat; have thread above needle for one stitch and below for the next, continuing alternately to end of row.
Double cable stitch If doing 2 adjacent rows in cable stitch, start the 2nd row with thread below the needle if the 1st row began with the thread above. The effect is that of the rows being inverted.

Trellis stitch
This is outline stitch done in opposite zigzag lines as shown in top drawing. Begin on 2nd gathering thread and work up to 1st gathering thread over 3 or 4 pleats and down again over the same number of pleats; keep thread below needle going up and above needle going down. Slant the needle slightly except at points where you should insert the needle horizontally. Make sure the points meet exactly to form the trellis.
Wave stitch This stitch is also a variation of outline stitch and is worked exactly like trellis except that the zigzags can move to form any number of designs. You can fill in the diamonds if they are large enough with French knots and cross stitch. Shown here is one row of single wave.

Diamond stitch
Bring needle up to left of 1st pleat on 1st row of gathering. With thread above needle take a back stitch through 2nd pleat. Then go down to 2nd row of gathering and take a back stitch through 3rd pleat; repeat on 4th pleat with thread below needle. Take needle up to left of 5th pleat on top row and repeat the process as from 1st pleat. Complete the line. This forms the first part of the stitch. For the second part start on the 3rd row of gathering so that the upper row of stitches is immediately behind the bottom stitches of the 1st row and work as for first part. When the diamond is complete 2 pleats should lie in the center. This is a very elastic stitch.

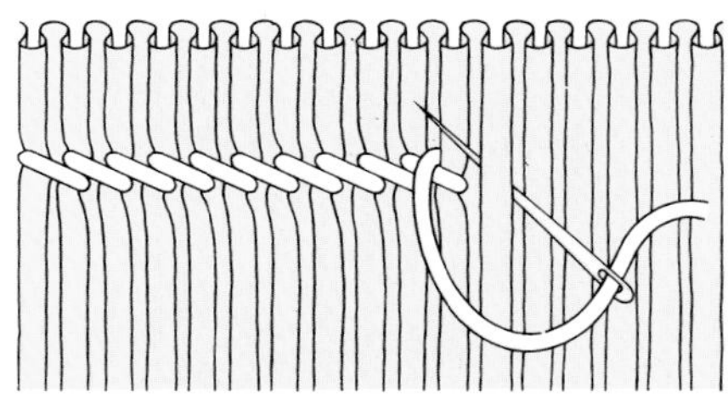

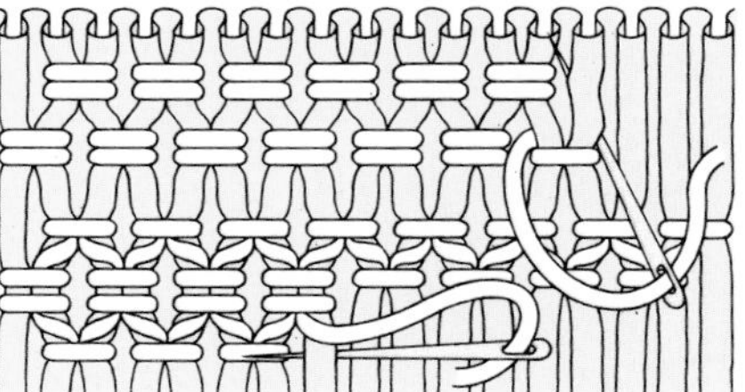

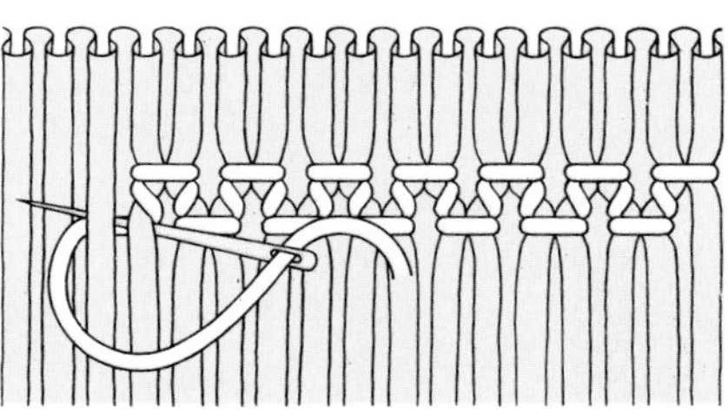

Outline stitch
This is a firm control stitch used at the top of smocking and sometimes at the base. Bring needle up on 1st pleat and into next one in a slanting position, keeping thread above needle with every stitch worked. If you are doing a 2nd row, alter the effect by keeping the thread below the needle with every stitch.

Honeycomb stitch
Bring needle up on 1st pleat on 1st gathering thread. Stitch this pleat and the next together. Take another stitch over same pleats and slip needle down back of pleat and bring it into 2nd gathering thread, and sew 2nd and 3rd pleats together. Take needle to back of pleat and go up to 1st gathering thread, stitching 3rd and 4th pleats together. Continue this pattern to end of row. Start the next row on the 3rd gathering thread, staggering it and all subsequent rows exactly as the 1st.
Surface honeycomb Work this the same as honeycomb, with thread on pleat surface instead of behind it.

Vandyke stitch
Bring needle up on 2nd pleat on 1st gathering thread, and back-stitch through 1st and 2nd pleats with thread above the needle. Go down to 2nd gathering thread, pick up the 2nd and 3rd pleats and back-stitch with the thread below the needle. Return to 1st gathering thread, connecting 3rd and 4th pleats and back-stitch with thread above the needle. Continue in this way to end of line. Start the next row on the 3rd gathering thread and work up to the 2nd row, and so on, starting each row alternately up and down.

Smocked dress

Smock dress pattern 34

The smocked dress shown here is based on the dress described on p34. The pattern requirements are very similar; sleeve ruffles and pockets have been added. To vary the pattern you could add full-length sleeves and smock the cuffs or reduce the length to make a top instead of a dress. If you are left with extra material you could make it up into an accessory, such as a simple draw-string bag, smocking the top with some of the same stitches.

You will need
thread and fabric as p34, allowing for 3 times the width of bottom edge of yoke for skirt front
lining for yoke
3 skeins pearl cotton or embroidery floss in shades A and B
smock transfer

Cutting the fabric
Cut out the skirt back and the yoke (plus yoke lining) as described on p34, and the skirt front to 3 times the width of the bottom edge of the yoke. Cut out patch pockets (p92) and shoulder ruffles as described.

Shoulder ruffles To make a pattern for these draw a straight line $2\frac{1}{2}$ times the distance of the armhole between the lower edges of front and back yoke. Mark a point $1\frac{1}{2}$in (4cm) above this line at each end and a point $2\frac{1}{2}$in (6cm) above the line at the center. Join these points with a slightly curving line, add seam allowances all around and cut out the pattern.
Cut out 2 pieces.
Pockets Cut 2 patch pockets 3 times the required width and about $5\frac{1}{2}$in (14cm) deep.

Smock pattern

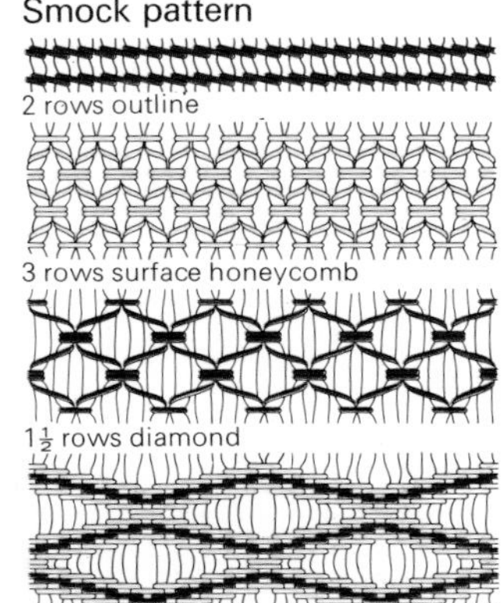

Smocking skirt front
On WS of the skirt front iron on smocking transfer to a depth of $4\frac{1}{2}$in (12cm) (the smocking itself is $3\frac{1}{2}$in/9cm deep). Gather the pleats for smocking. On heavier fabrics such as corduroy single knots rather than double ones are sufficient.
Stitches Work the stitches in the order shown in smocking pattern, starting $\frac{3}{4}$in (2cm) down from raw edge of fabric. Make sure that you keep the stitches at an even tension and that the needle enters the fabric absolutely straight. Progress through the stitches, keeping the same proportion of space between the rows as shown in the diagram. When the smocking is complete, remove the gathering threads and pin out the skirt to the required width. Steam press the smocking very light with a damp cloth, barely keeping the iron on the fabric to prevent the pleats from flattening.
Smocking pockets
Hem and smock the top edge, using the same pattern as for the front skirt, adding $1\frac{1}{2}$ rows of diamond stitch in A and 1 row outline stitch in B at the base. (The extra rows add an extra $\frac{3}{4}$in/2cm to the smocking depth.)

Smocking shoulder ruffles
Iron the smocking transfer onto the WS to a depth of $1\frac{1}{4}$in (3cm). Turn in a narrow double hem on the curved edges and stitch. Draw up the smocking pleats and work 1 row of diamond stitch in color A. Remove the gathering threads and press to the correct length, i.e. the distance from one yoke to the other.

Finishing
Because of the smocking the order of finishing is slightly different from the procedure on p34.
1 Mark pocket position on skirt with pins. Place seamline of pocket base with RS down to position required and stitch across.
2 Turn the pockets RS up, turn edges under, allowing a little extra smocking on the outside edge, and baste to the skirt. Top-stitch in position.
3 Stitch the front yoke to the front skirt. Turn under seam allowance on lower edge of front yoke. Place yoke centrally over RS of front skirt, baste and slip-stitch picking up a pleat with each stitch.
4 Stitch the back yoke to back skirt in the usual way.
5 Join yoke shoulder seams and shoulder seams on yoke lining.
6 Attach lining to yoke around neck edge.
7 Join side seams of skirt.

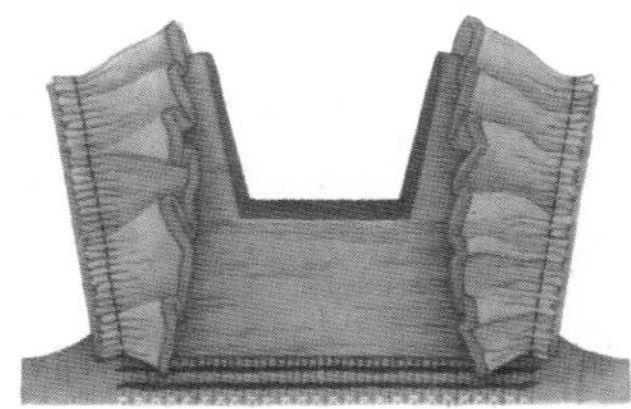

8 Attach ruffle to the yoke with RS together, keeping the smocking even.

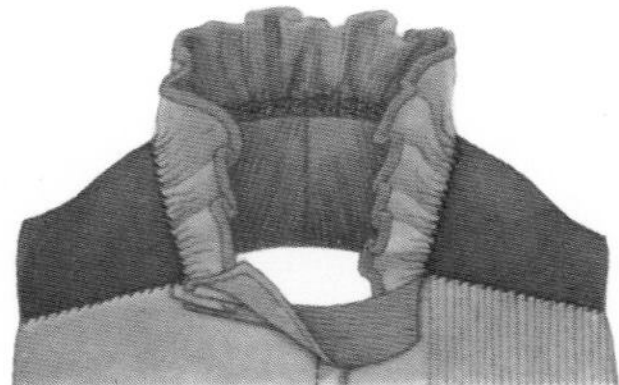

9 Turn in lining edges and slip-stitch to WS of lining.
10 Cut facings (p58) for remainder of raw armhole edges and apply, placing raw edges of ruffle between facing and skirt.
11 Hem skirt.

Knitting

Knitting is a satisfying craft where you create the shape and texture of your fabric as you work. It is also a money-saving pastime because buying yarn to knit yourself is much less expensive than buying a ready-made garment in the equivalent yarn, particularly if you want to use expensive natural fibers.

This chapter forms a thorough introduction for beginners as well as a useful reference for more experienced knitters. Technique is built up from casting on and working the simplest stitches through shaping and patterning to the more advanced stages of designing your own knitting. The aim is to give knitters the confidence to adapt and transform existing patterns, and to know how and when to substitute different yarns and stitches. Diagrams of all the component shapes of each pattern show you exactly what you are going to knit and make it easy to introduce your own adaptations and variations.

The projects are graded so that you can try out new techniques as you learn them but even the simplest designs offer scope for the practiced knitter to adapt.

Instructions given are primarily for hand knitting although many of the projects can be adapted for working on a machine – if you want to use a machine see your manufacturer's instructions.

Needles

Plastic- or nickel-coated, light-weight aluminum is a popular material for knitting needles but plastic, wooden and steel ones are also available. Buy good-quality needles and take care of them: a bent needle can distort your fabric or gauge; a sharp plastic point can split yarn; an old, blunt needle can fray yarn. Old-fashioned steel needles are heavier than the modern light-weight ones and can slow you down.

Sizing of knitting needles is by their diameter. The metric range goes down in size from 10mm to 2mm, and the table below shows the equivalent sizes under the system used in the US and that formerly used in the UK.

Pairs of needles
For most items, where you knit back and forth in rows, use a pair of needles each with a point at one end and a knob at the other. You can buy pairs from 10 to 15in (25 to 40cm) long. If your piece of knitting becomes very wide at some stage and has a large number of stitches, use the longest needles; otherwise you will find knitting most comfortable with shorter needles, which by definition are lighter.

Sets of needles
Knitting 'in the round' with double-pointed needles (see p250) produces a tubular fabric without seams and is widely used for gloves, hats, socks and for neckbands and armholes; sets of needles can also produce flat circular motifs. Sets of 4 or 5 needles are sold together in a pack.

'Circular' needles
A circular needle (see p250) consists of 2 small, pointed needles connected by a flexible strip of thin nylon wire. Use one when more stitches are being knitted in the round than can easily be handled on a set of needles. Circular needles are also helpful in distributing the weight more evenly when working back and forth in rows on a large number of stitches.

Cable needles
In cable patterns and Aran knitting a shorter double-pointed needle is used to hold the stitches that are being twisted in front of or behind the work. Use a cable needle that is the same size as, or smaller than, the needles you are using for the main piece of work (see p258).

Equivalent knitting-needle sizes

US	Metric	Old UK
000	1·75	–
00	2	14
0	2·25	13
1	2·5	–
2	2·75	12
3	3	11
–	3·25	10
4	3·5	–
–	3·75	9
5	4	8
6	4·25	–
7	4·5	7
8	5	6
9	5·5	5
10	6	4
–	6·5	3
$10\frac{1}{2}$	7	2
–	7·5	1
11	8	0
–	9	00
13	10	000

Yarns

The word 'yarn' was once synonymous with wool; nowadays a wide range of synthetic yarns which imitate wool but have other qualities is also available. In addition to wool and its synthetic counterparts you can knit with cotton, silk, metallic yarns, string, ribbon or raffia. When choosing yarn for a pattern it is essential to find one appropriate to the effect you want. To test that the yarn will make an item of the right size and weight, first work a swatch using the needles and stitch pattern of your choice. As long as you always do this test, you are free to substitute yarns other than the ones recommended by the manufacturer of a pattern (see Gauge, p220).

Ply

Ply refers to the number of single threads spun from either natural or man-made fibers which combine to make up a specific yarn. Note that ply is not an indication of the thickness of a yarn, and that, for example, the 4-ply yarns that different manufacturers produce can vary considerably in weight.

Texture

Originally the texture of yarns was totally dependent on the quality of the woolen fleeces available; a fine wool hair was long, smooth and wavy and was spun into a soft, delicate yarn, while short, coarse fibers were used for cheaper yarns. Modern technological advances and the advent of synthetic yarns have made it possible to create different textures deliberately. Some of today's textures have a practical quality, like the harsh Aran wool that is oiled to keep out damp, but others are purely decorative, like the gleaming metallic yarns. Fancy and unusual textures are created in the spinning or twisting process, when the plies are combined into one thread.

Bouclé Loops of varying size are produced as one ply is fed into the machine at a faster speed than the other plies.

Tweed Either little knobs of wool in different colors are thrown in during the spinning process, or more than one ply is fed unevenly into the machine (as with bouclé) and one is released at intervals so that it winds back on itself and forms a knot.

Crêpe The strong corded appearance is produced by an extra twisting process.

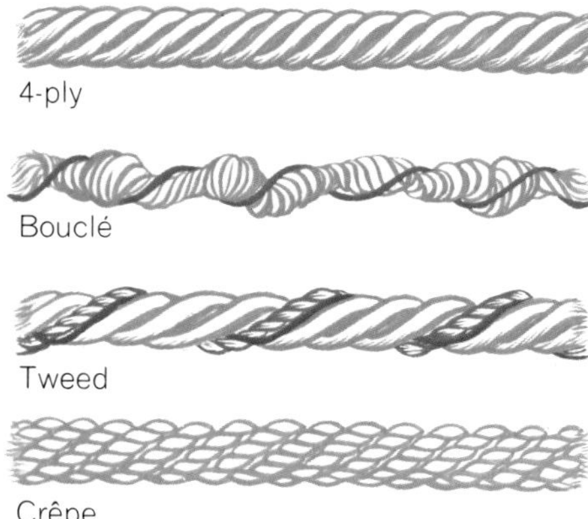

Fibers

Wool is warm, elastic and hard-wearing and, being a soft fiber, retains its surface texture. Natural wool needs careful hand washing to prevent shrinkage and felting, but you can now buy machine-washable wool which is coated with a resin to make it more resilient. The bulk and soft texture of wool combines effectively with the strength and washability of man-made fibers to make a wide variety of yarns that obviate the cost and care problems of pure wool.

Mohair, alpaca and angora – from goats, llamas and rabbits respectively – are expensive because their supply is unpredictable. Their long hair is spun into light, soft yarn much in demand for fashion garments; it is often blended with man-made fibers for greater durability and cheapness.

Cotton has less elasticity than wool, but in varying weights makes a useful yarn for hot-weather wear.

Linen is similar to cotton in its properties, but is expensive and more often used in conjunction with other threads than on its own.

Man-made fibers are spun into yarns of a very wide variety of thickness and texture. They are on the whole cheaper than natural ones, although some fashion yarns can be as expensive as pure wool; they have the advantages of washing easily and of not shrinking, but tend to be less elastic than wool and to soil more easily. Acrylics, for example, are soft and light-weight, but a loosely knitted fabric can stretch. Nylon, polyamide and polyester yarns are very hard-wearing, but are altogether tougher and less elastic in feel than the acrylics.

Buying yarns

Yarn comes in balls, hanks and spools. Since most balls of yarn are sold by weight not by length, some yarns that are thicker-spun or are made heavier by greater dye content have less yardage per ball than others.

To wind yarn into balls you need someone cooperative to hold a hank firm over two outstretched wrists while you wind it; otherwise use the backs of chairs to prevent tangling. Wind yarn into balls over your fingers, and not too tightly; when you remove your fingers, the yarn will not be stretched around the ball.

Manufacturers' wide range of yarns are of standard quality, though lines can be discontinued and color still varies slightly between dye lots. Manufacturers' pattern leaflets designed with a specific yarn in mind are easy to follow.

Chain stores often market own brands, of good quality because they are made by major manufacturers. The range offers less choice, and the weight can need careful gauge checking.

Markets can offer bargains in remnants, but labels can be inaccurate or missing, so that yarn composition is difficult to identify and you have no recourse to complaint.

Mail order firms whose addresses you can find in craft magazines, often have a wide range of own brands and manufacturers' yarns. Although postage can increase cost, this source is particularly useful if local supply is limited.

Estimating quantity

A reliable method when dealing with a manufacturer's yarn is to find a published pattern of approximately the same style (size, long sleeves, high neck, etc) and see how much yarn is required for that. Another is to knit up a ball of yarn in the gauge you intend using, work out the area it covers, estimate the approximate surface area of the item you are making and calculate how much you will need to complete it.

Casting on and binding off

Making a slip loop on the needle

All knitting begins with a row of loops being cast on to one needle, and subsequent rows are worked into these loops. At the end of a piece of work the knitted stitches are secured by binding off so that they do not unravel. There are a number of different methods of casting on, and you can choose the one that produces the type of edge you want—e.g. the thumb method gives a sturdy elastic edge for cuffs and waistbands. If you experiment, you may find one method more natural than others; or you may already have been taught one way with which you are comfortable. As with casting on, there are different positions for knitting, and the important thing is to find one where you can keep your hands comfortable and relaxed so that you knit evenly. Stitches are normally knitted from the LH needle onto the right. The diagrams show methods for right-handed knitters. If you are left-handed and wish to reverse the positions of yarn and needles, use a mirror to reverse the diagrams.

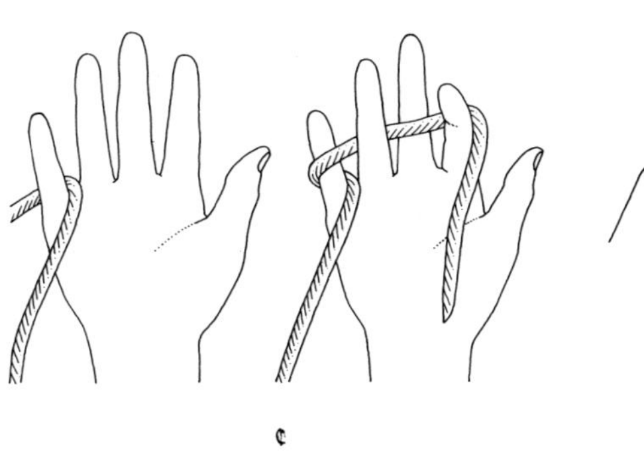

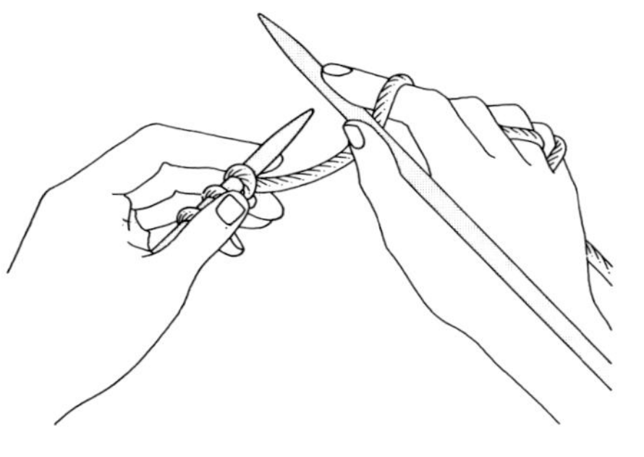

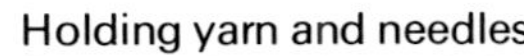

Holding yarn and needles
The yarn from the main ball winds round the fingers of the right hand to control the tension. Take the needle which forms stitches in your right hand and the needle holding the stitches to be worked in your left. When making a stitch, carry the yarn round the needle point with the RH forefinger only; don't let go of this needle to wind the yarn round the point.

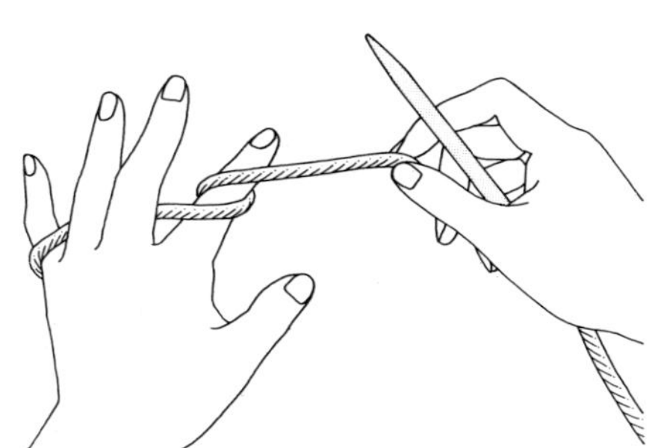

In the Continental method the stitches to be worked are also held in the left hand and the free needle in the right, but the yarn from the main ball is controlled by being wound around the fingers of the left hand. The LH forefinger feeds the yarn to the needles and should keep close to the needle points. Twist the RH needle point around the yarn from this finger to draw each new loop through the stitch on the needle.

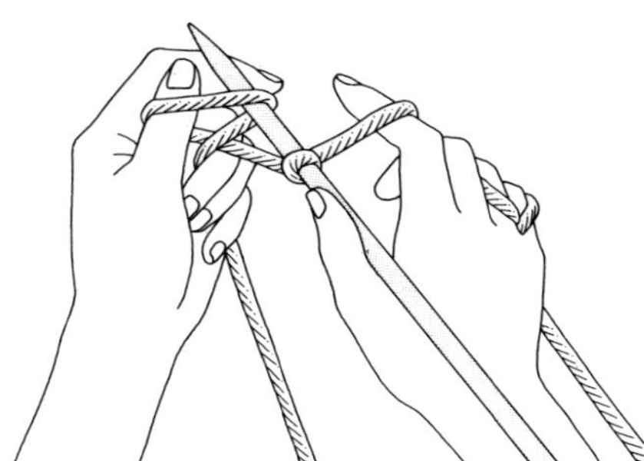

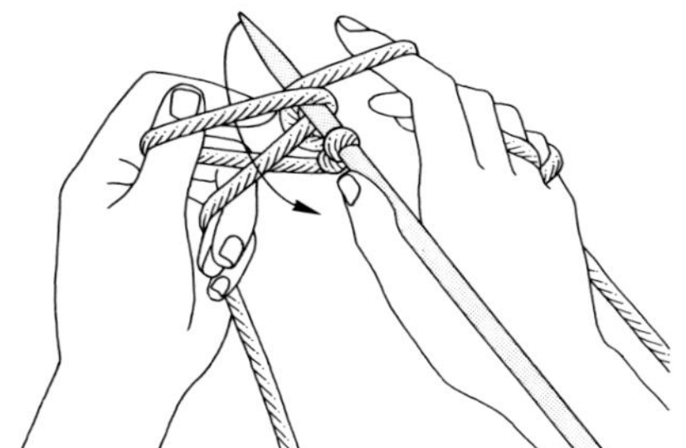

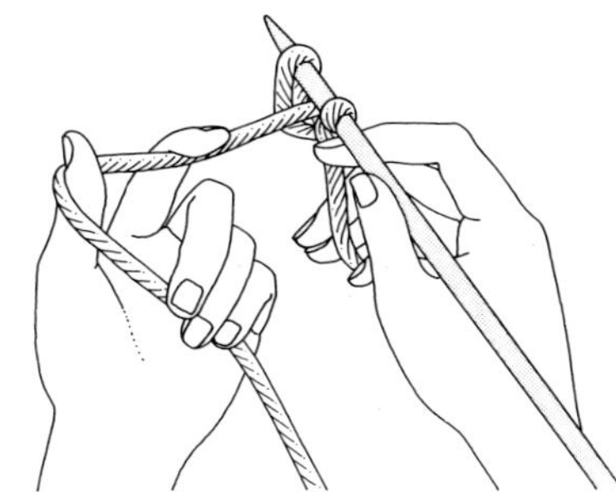

Thumb method
This produces a hard-wearing edge that is useful for items that need elasticity.

1 Make a loop in the yarn some distance from the end (about 1yd/1m yarn for 100 stitches) and place on the RH needle. The shorter end of yarn passes between the forefinger and thumb of your left hand, goes around the thumb and is then held across the palm by the other fingers (see diagram). Insert the needle into the loop on the thumb.

2 Wind the yarn from the main ball under and over the needle and draw it through the loop on your thumb to make a new stitch on the needle. Tighten.

3 Wind the yarn around your thumb again for the next stitch and make further loops in this way until you have the required number of stitches. When knitting the first row, use the yarn from the main ball and not the short end.

2 needle method for a firm edge
1 Make a loop on the LH needle. Holding the yarn in your right hand, take up the second needle and insert it into the slip loop from front to back. Wind the yarn under and over the point of the RH needle.
2 Draw a new loop through the slip stitch; transfer this new loop to the LH needle and withdraw the RH needle.
3 Insert the RH needle from front to back between the 2 loops on the LH needle. Wind the yarn under and over the point of the RH needle and draw a loop through. Transfer the new loop to the LH needle. Always inserting the RH needle between the last 2 loops on the LH needle, continue in the same way until you have the number of stitches that you want cast on.

2 needle method for a looser edge
1 Make a loop on the LH needle. Insert the RH needle into the loop from front to back and wind the yarn under and over the point of the RH needle.
2 Draw a new loop through the first stitch; transfer it to the LH needle.
3 Continue to insert the RH needle into the last loop on the LH needle, to wind the yarn around the RH needle and to transfer the new loop to the LH needle until you have the number of stitches that you want cast on.

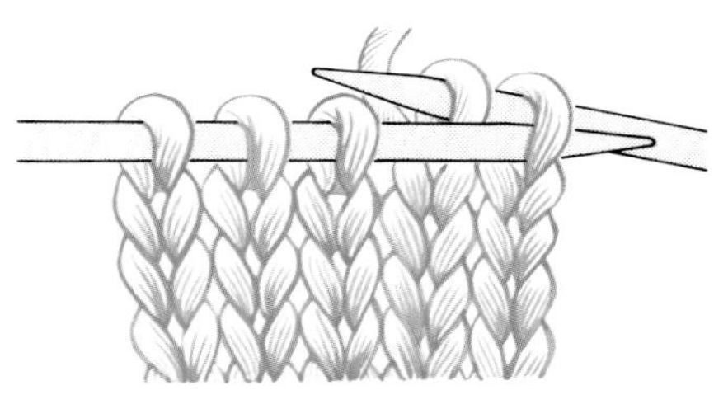

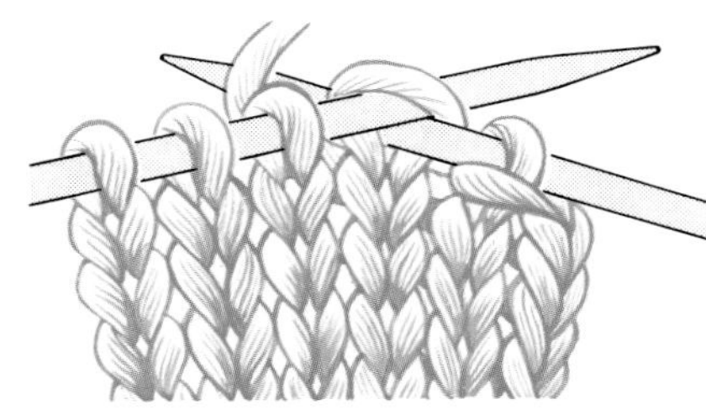

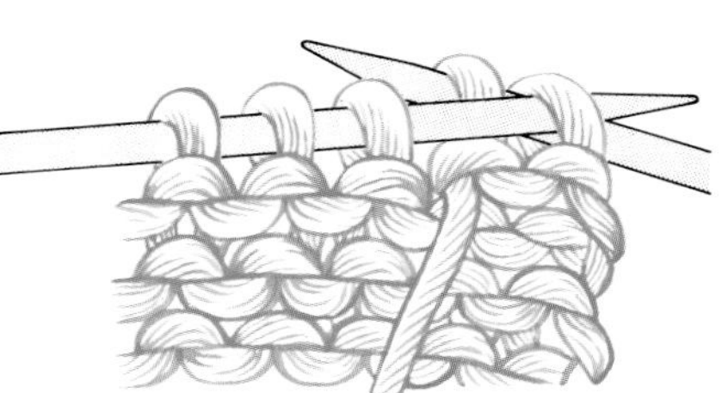

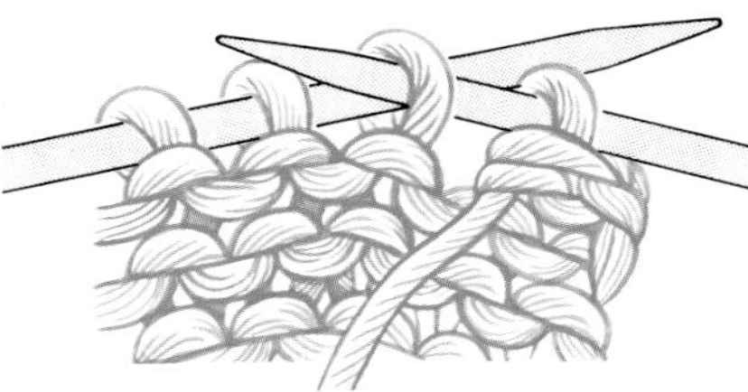

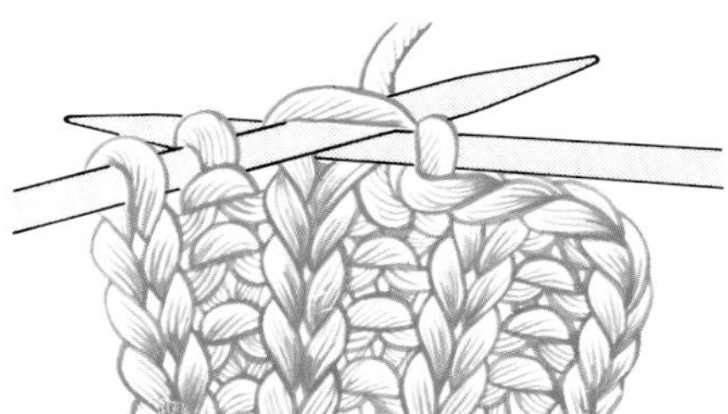

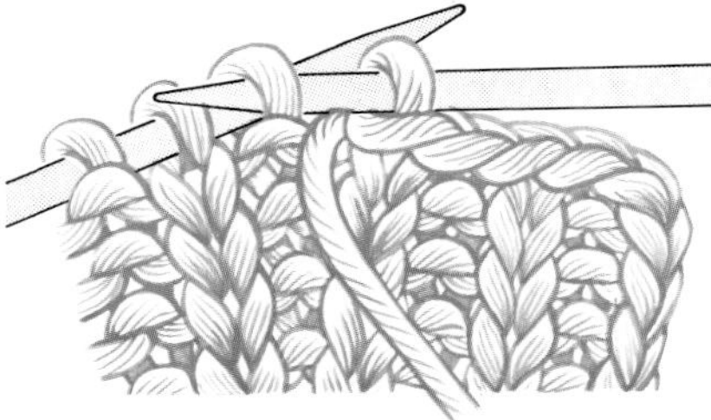

Binding off
1 With the yarn and needles in the usual working position, work the first 2 stitches so that they are transferred to the RH needle. Use the point of the LH needle to lift the first stitch worked over the second one and off the needle. This leaves 1 stitch on the RH needle.
2 Work the next stitch on the LH needle and repeat the process of lifting one stitch over another. Continue in this way until you have 1 stitch remaining on the RH needle. Secure this last stitch by breaking off the yarn about 4in (10cm) from the knitting, drawing this through the stitch on the needle and tightening. Darn in the end when finishing.

Binding off is usually done on a knit row, but the same principle applies when purling. When binding off ribwise, remember to take the yarn to the back of the work before knitting a stitch, and to bring it to the front before purling.

Basic stitches

Two simple stitches – knit and purl – are the basis of innumerable stitch patterns. These are smooth or textured depending on the combination of knit and purl stitches in a single row or in successive rows. Garter stitch, where you knit every single stitch, works on any number of stitches to a row; other patterns which combine different stitches within a row require a specific number – or multiple – of stitches so that the pattern repeats evenly across the row. A pattern may specify multiples of, say, '6 stitches plus 2'. You must then cast on 8, 14, 20 stitches or more, according to the width you require; in this case the 2 extra stitches will often go at either end of the row and be used for the seams.

Knitting stitches (K)

1 Hold needle with cast-on stitches in left hand and insert free RH needle from front to back into first stitch on LH needle. Keeping yarn at back of work, wind it under and then over RH needle point.

2 Draw new loop through stitch on LH needle.

3 The new stitch remains on RH needle and the one worked into falls from LH needle. Work into each stitch in same way until you have transferred them all to RH needle.

Garter stitch (g st)

No particular multiple of stitches is needed to make garter stitch; it works in rows containing any number of stitches. It consists of knitting (K) every stitch in every row and produces a textured, horizontally ridged effect.

Stockinette stitch (st st)

This works on any number of stitches. Knit and purl rows are worked alternately to produce a fabric that is universally popular for its smoothness. The RS of the fabric, with the familiar interlocking V-shapes, faces you when you are doing the knit rows; the WS when you are doing the purl. A slightly firmer fabric, known as Continental or twisted stockinette stitch, is made by knitting through back loops.

Reverse stockinette stitch (rev st st)

This is literally just the purl or 'wrong' side of stockinette stitch. Designers sometimes choose it for its densely looped texture, which resembles garter stitch but is more even. It is often used as a background for cable patterns.

Purling stitches (P)
1 Hold needle with cast-on stitches in left hand and insert free RH needle from back to front into first stitch on LH needle. Keeping yarn at front of work, wind it over and around RH needle point.
2 Draw new loop through stitch on LH needle.
3 The new stitch remains on RH needle and the one worked into falls from LH needle. Work into each stitch in same way until you have transferred them all to RH needle.

Knitting and purling 'tbl'
To give a stitch a twisted appearance and make it firmer, you can knit 'through back loop' (tbl). Insert RH needle into *back* of stitch on LH needle, then knit in usual way.

To purl through back loop, insert RH needle through *back* of stitch on LH needle and purl in usual way.

Single rib (K1, P1 rib)
This works on any number of stitches. Knit 1 stitch and purl 1 stitch alternately across the first row. Keep the yarn at the back of the work when you knit a stitch, bring it between the stitches to the front when you purl a stitch and take it to the back of the work for the next stitch. On the next and every subsequent row each stitch knitted in the previous row must be purled and each one purled must be knitted. Rib is a very elastic fabric ideal for the parts of a garment that need to grip, such as cuffs, waistbands and neckbands.

Double rib (K2, P2 rib)
To vary a ribbed pattern you simply choose a different number of stitches for the knit and purl 'ribs'. Double rib requires a multiple of 4 stitches plus 2 extra to make the pattern balance across a row. In the first row you knit 2 stitches and then purl 2 stitches alternately across the row. On the next and every subsequent row each stitch knitted in the previous row must be purled and each one purled must be knitted. The fabric formed is fairly elastic, but can be used on a close-fitting sweater as an all-over pattern.

Seed stitch
This simple variation of ribbing is sometimes called moss stitch. It works on any number of stitches. The first row is worked as in single rib. On subsequent rows each stitch knitted in the previous row must be knitted and each one purled must be purled again. A neat, all-over pattern is produced with a light texture. Larger multiples of stitches and rows can be treated in the same way to produce basketweave patterns. A variation is Irish moss stitch (p262).

Simple strips

Needles 212
Yarns 213
Casting on and binding off 214
Basic stitches 216

To practice basic stitches and get the feel of different yarns, it is a good idea to make something simple in strips or rectangles. One long strip makes a scarf; a number of rectangles made to a constant depth, stitched together in strips of patchwork and given a garter-stitch border, makes a cuddly afghan.

You will need
1 pair no. 5 needles
scarf: 1oz (25g) sports yarn; 4oz (100g) tweed; 4oz (200g) bouclé; 4oz (100g) mohair
afghan; 10oz (250g) sports yarn; 7oz (175g) tweed; 8oz (200g) bouclé; 7oz (175g) mohair; 16oz (450g) Aran-type yarn for border

These quantities of yarn will make a scarf 9 × 72in (23 × 182cm) and an afghan 44 × 56in (112 × 142cm). Choose your own combinations of stitches and colors, but use yarns that knit up to be approximately equivalent to the sports yarn in weight. Work separate blocks of garter stitch, stockinette stitch, double rib and seed stitch in the different types of yarn; cast on varying numbers of stitches to make strips of different widths, but work them to a constant depth of, say, 9in (23cm). Use oversewing (see p242) to join patches so that the finished items are reversible.
Scarf Work a knotted fringe (see p102), using four 12in (32cm) lengths of the different yarns for each knot.
Afghan First join patches into strips and then sew strips together. Add a 4in (10cm) border of garter stitch in Aran-type yarn to finish the edges, finishing corners as shown in the photographs.

Gauge

The gauge of a knitted fabric describes its elasticity and the tightness of its stitches. It is expressed in terms of the number of rows and of stitches that are worked over a given measurement. When you follow a pattern it is vital for you to have the same number of stitches and rows as the designer in order to produce an item that is the right size and shape. Remember that gauge is a personal thing. One individual may naturally knit far more tightly or loosely than another, while using identical yarn, needles and stitches. Even the designer of a garment – from whose knitting the gauge of the pattern will have been calculated – may not knit in an 'average' way, so that if you can't match this you may have to make some adjustment to get the right measurements in the gauge that is natural to you.

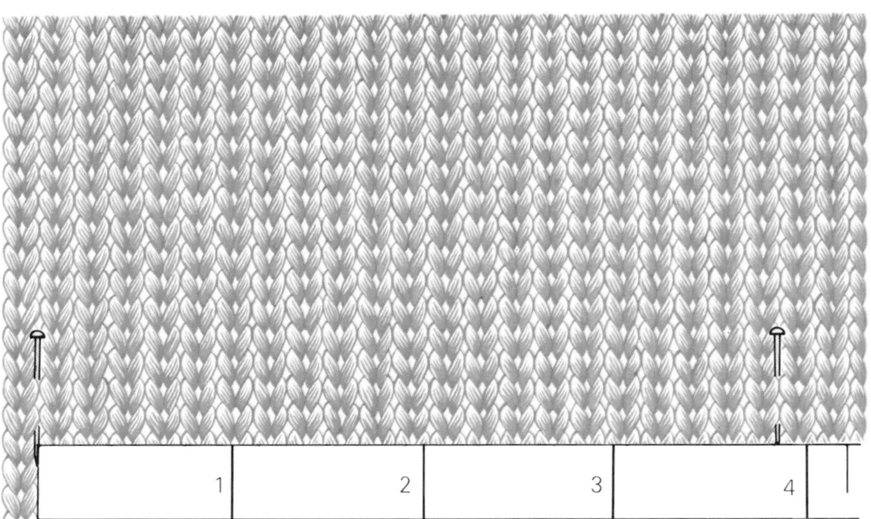

Checking gauge
Before beginning any piece of knitting you must make a gauge swatch using the yarn, needles and stitch pattern of your choice. Make the swatch at least 4in (10cm) square, lay it on a flat surface and pin it down. Stretch all-over ribbed fabrics slightly as you pin to give a true stitch count, since the fabric will open out over a body. Take a ruler, mark out 4in (10cm) across a row with pins, then count the stitches between these pins. Count the number of rows to 4in (10cm) in the same way. When designing your own garment, you can calculate how many stitches to cast on by multiplying the number of stitches to 1in or 1cm by the width measurement you want. Include fractions of stitches in your calculations. In the same way, multiplying the number of rows to 1in or 1cm by a vertical measurement will give the exact position for shaping.

Gauge symbols As a formula the gauge of the above swatch would read '21 sts and 26 rows to 4in (10cm) over st st'. This book uses a symbol (below) for the number of stitches and of rows to a constant measurement (knitting in symbol is always 4in/10cm square). Needle size is at the top; the upper figure on the symbol itself shows the number of rows. The stitch pattern over which gauge is calculated is below. The above swatch, using no. 5 needles, thus has this symbol:

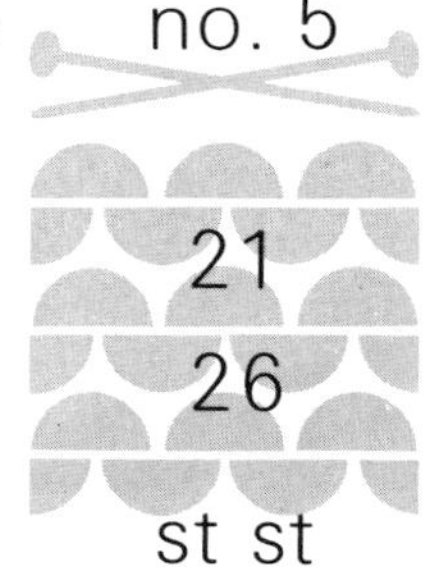

needle size

number of stitches

number of rows

stitch pattern

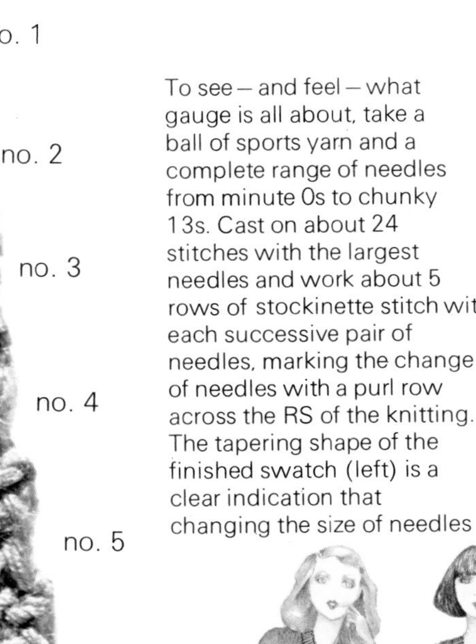

To see — and feel — what gauge is all about, take a ball of sports yarn and a complete range of needles from minute 0s to chunky 13s. Cast on about 24 stitches with the largest needles and work about 5 rows of stockinette stitch with each successive pair of needles, marking the change of needles with a purl row across the RS of the knitting. The tapering shape of the finished swatch (left) is a clear indication that changing the size of needles alters the gauge. Each time you change to one size smaller needle, you get approximately 1 stitch more across 2in (5cm).
At the top of the swatch minute, crowded stitches and a stiff fabric result from needles that are small in relation to the yarn. No. 5 needles in center of swatch work perfectly in conjunction with this sports yarn to produce neat, firm stitches in a soft, elastic fabric. In a square of knitting there are about one-third more rows than stitches. As the stitches become larger, their neat appearance is harder to control and the character of the stitch pattern becomes distorted. The soft, loose fabric produced at the base of the swatch on needles too large for the yarn will not keep its shape and is unsuitable for most garments; using a softer, thicker yarn, however, results in a warm fabric with an almost cellular quality.

Substituting yarns and stitch patterns

The ply and weight of yarns is not standardized; a pattern may call for 'sports yarn', but individual brands often vary in thickness and the gauge principles described opposite must be applied.
Be careful if you vary a classic stockinette-stitch garment by making it in a more textured pattern. Although you may use the same yarn and needles, different stitch patterns create their own gauges. Don't assume that because the original pattern tells you to cast on 28 stitches and work in stockinette stitch, you will get the same measurement if you work in garter stitch. Work a gauge swatch in the normal way to find out the number of stitches you need to cast on in the stitch pattern you have chosen for the width of fabric required.

Gauge in patterns

All measurements for a knitted garment are based on the designer's gauge. If you buy a pattern and want to make a correctly fitting garment, you must achieve the same gauge as the designer. Even if your gauge is only 1 stitch out over 4in (10cm), your garment may be as much as 2in (5cm) too baggy or too tight.
If your gauge doesn't match that of the designer, the remedy is fairly simple — but absolutely necessary. If you have too many stitches to 4in (10cm) your knitting is too tight and you should try needles one size larger; go on doing this until the gauge is correct. Too few stitches to the measurement means that your knitting is too loose; needles one size smaller might be the answer. In fact it does not matter if you have to try several changes of needle size as long as you end up with the right number of stitches, and of rows if possible, to the inch or centimeter.
If, after experimenting with different needle sizes, your gauge matches the required number of stitches in width, but not the number of rows in depth, choose the needles that give the correct gauge width. The depth of your knitting is more often assessed by measurement than by a specific number of rows.
Another way of achieving the correct gauge is to use a greater or smaller number of stitches. The disadvantage here when following a traditional pattern is that it can be confusing to have to remember that you are using a different number of stitches. More important, if the pattern requires particular multiples of stitches or involves a cable, it is likely to be incorrect unless you do your calculations very carefully.

Increasing and decreasing

One of the special characteristics of knitting is that you shape the fabric as you create it, by increasing or decreasing the number of stitches in a row. Doing this at the edge of a fabric alters the shape of the outline; doing it within a row distorts its flatness. There are various methods and knitting directions usually specify which is the most suitable to use in a particular situation, usually giving it in abbreviated form. The principles of increasing and decreasing are also the basis of lace patterns – see p274.

Simple increasing
The first two methods are classed as 'invisible' increasing since they do not leave a hole in the fabric; they are mainly used in the construction of garments. They are most easily worked in knit rows, although the same principle can be used when purling.

Increase 1 stitch (inc 1) The simplest way of increasing, making 2 stitches out of 1, can be worked anywhere in a row. It is a convenient way to shape side edges and gives a gathered effect when you increase into every stitch across a row. To make 2 stitches out of 1, knit or purl into the stitch as usual, but don't let the loop fall from the LH needle. Insert the RH needle into the back of this loop and knit or purl the same stitch again.

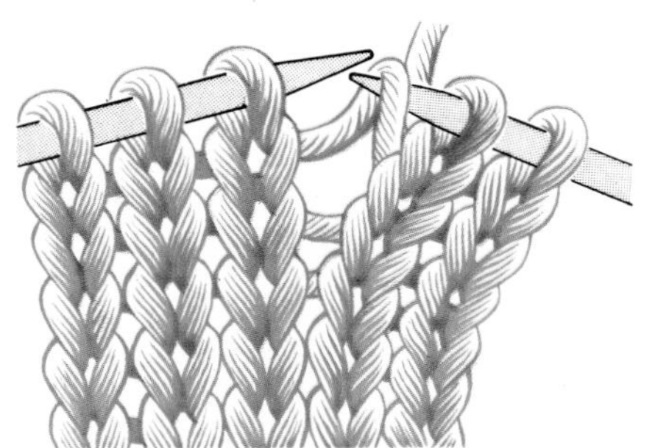

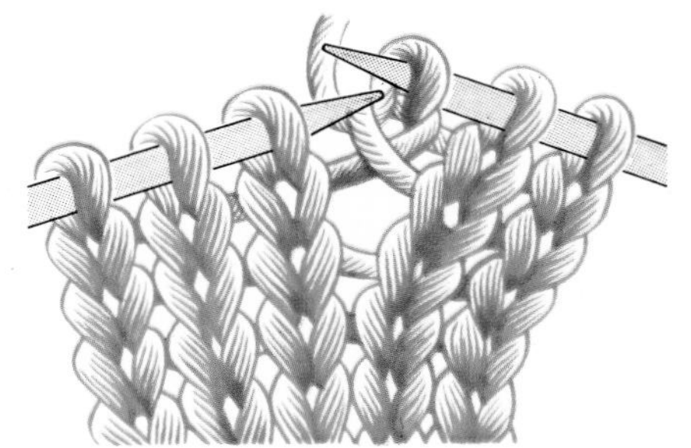

Make 1 stitch (M1) Increasing between stitches is often used for shaping tailored garments, being even more 'invisible' than the previous method, and is worked within the body of the knitting rather than at side edges. Use the RH needle to pick up the horizontal strand of yarn between the stitch just worked and the next stitch on the LH needle. Place the strand on the LH needle to form a loop. Knit into the back loop in the usual way so that the new stitch is twisted and does not leave a hole in the fabric. If the increase is on a purl row pick up the strand of yarn in the same way and purl into it from the back.

Decorative increasing
These three methods have many uses in knitting besides shaping. An eyelet hole can be a simple buttonhole; you can thread a drawstring cord through several eyelet holes worked in a row; making eyelet holes along the fold-back row of a knitted hem gives a scalloped edging (see p232). Work lace patterns by increasing stitches to form a decorative eyelet hole and decreasing within the same row to compensate for the made stitches. In lace knitting the yarn is generally taken around the needle in a particular way, depending on the sequence of knit or purl stitches that you are using.

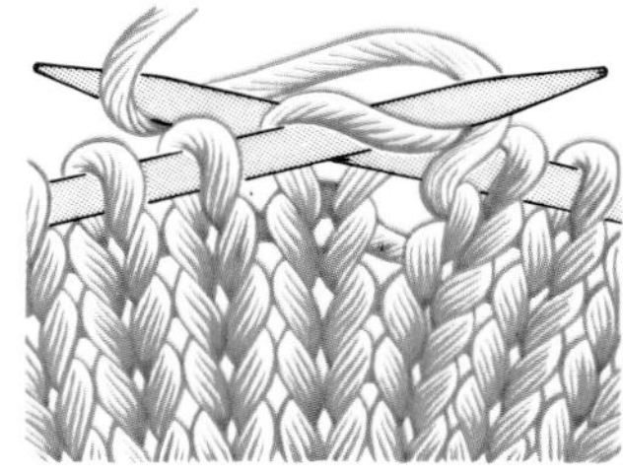

Yarn forward (yfwd) Increase a stitch between 2 knit stitches by bringing the yarn forward between the 2 needles to the front of the work and keeping it in that position while you knit the next stitch in the usual way.

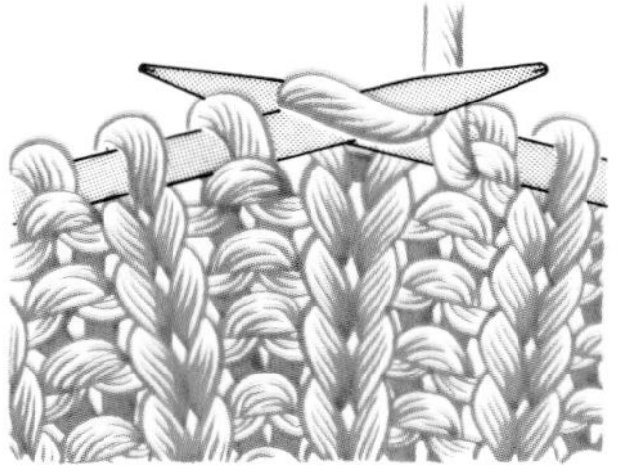

Yarn over needle (yo) If you want to make a stitch between a purl and a knit stitch, you will see that the yarn is already at the front of the work. Take it over the top of the RH needle to knit the next stitch in the usual way.

Yarn round needle (yrn) To make a stitch between 2 purl stitches, wind the yarn over the top of the RH needle and around between the needles to the front of the work again. The next stitch is purled as usual. The same method also applies to increasing between a knit and a purl stitch.

Simple decreasing

This is similar to simple increasing in that most decreases are fairly inconspicuous. You can choose a method that will make the decreased stitch slant across the fabric in a particular direction. You may want to emphasize this detail in such places as raglan armhole shaping. For instance, on the RS of stockinette stitch a K2 tog decrease appears to slant to the right. In the same way, slipped-stitch decreasing is useful where you want a stitch that definitely slants to the left.

Knit 2 together (K2 tog) Can be worked at either end of a row or at any given point. Simply insert the RH needle through 2 stitches instead of 1 and knit them both together in the usual way. The same procedure can be followed for purling 2 stitches together (P2 tog).

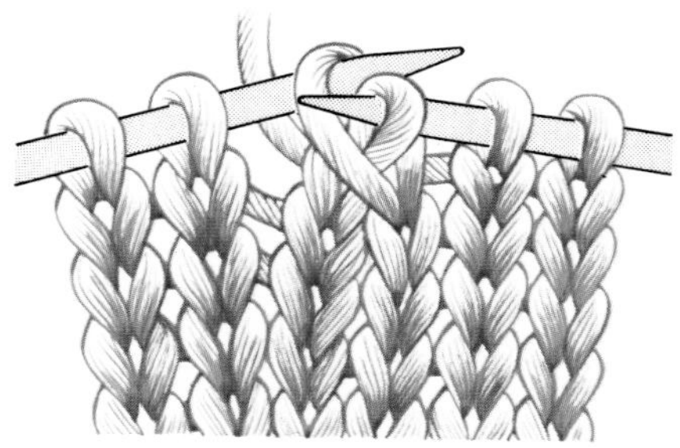

Slipped-stitch decreasing (sl 1, K1, psso) When you are ready to decrease, slip the next stitch from the LH needle onto the RH needle without knitting it, then knit the following stitch. Using the point of the LH needle, lift the slipped stitch over the knit stitch and off the RH needle.

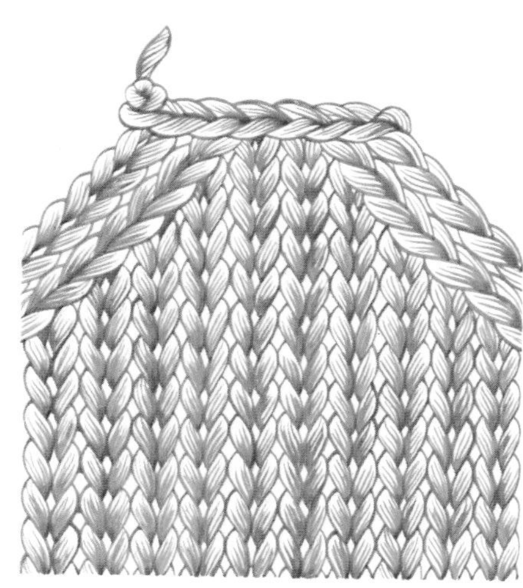

Paired decreases

There are a number of points on a garment where you may want to make a feature of decreasing – for example, on raglan shaping. When you are working paired decreases, remember that on the RS you want a decrease that slants to the left at the beginning of a row and one that slants to the right at the end of a row. This slanting effect is often emphasized by having a 2-stitch border outside the decreases at either side.
If you are working a stockinette-stitch fabric and decreasing on knit rows only, then you should use the slipped-stitch method at the beginning of the row and knit 2 stitches together at the end of the row. If the shaping entails decreasing on the purl rows as well as the knit rows, then purl 2 stitches together at the beginning of the row and purl 2 stitches together through back loops at the end of the row.

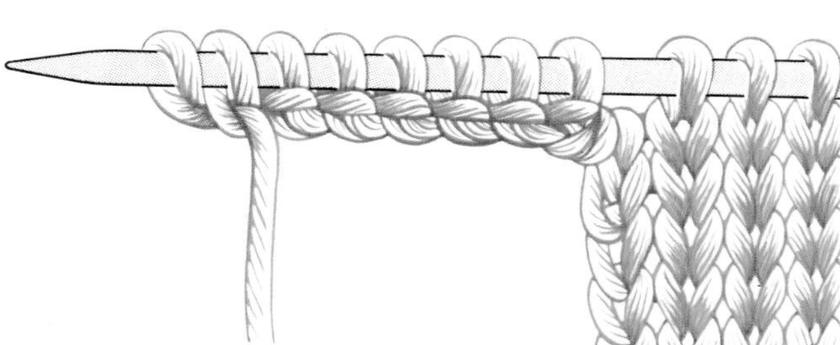

Multiple increasing

Where a large increase of stitches is required at the beginning or end of a row, as when knitting the sleeves in one with the back or front of a sweater, you should use a casting-on technique and make the increase at the beginning of a row. Using a 2-needle method, cast on the number of stitches required for the first sleeve at the beginning of the row. Work across these cast-on stitches and then to the end of the row. For the second sleeve reverse the work and cast on the required number of stitches again.

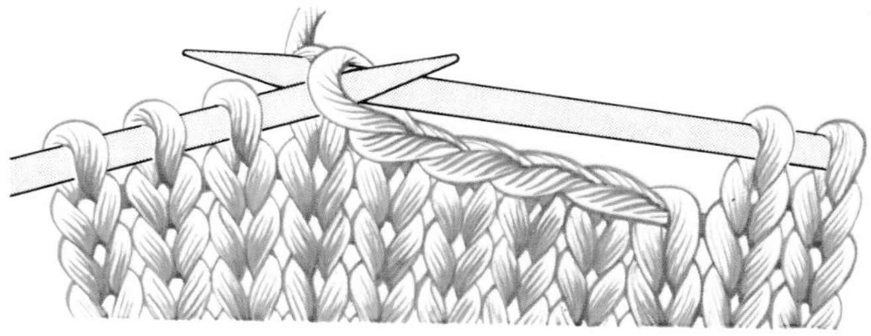

Multiple decreasing

Groups of bound-off stitches are worked at the beginning of a row at underarms, and in the center of a row for neck shaping. Where the bound-off group comes in the middle of a row, knit to that point. Knit the next 2 stitches and bind off the required number of stitches in the usual way. Note that the 1 stitch left on the RH needle next to the bound-off group is counted as one of the stitches worked to the end of the row. From this point on, the work is divided and the sections at either side of the bound-off group must be completed separately.

T-shaped sweaters

Basic stitches *216*
Gauge *220*
Increasing and decreasing *222*

There is no shaping in these T-shaped sweaters except the (optional) pocket of the woman's – fronts, backs, sleeves and collar are just basic rectangles. Create strong texture with stitch patterns, or simply use garter stitch and add interest with color or with embroidered edging stitches.

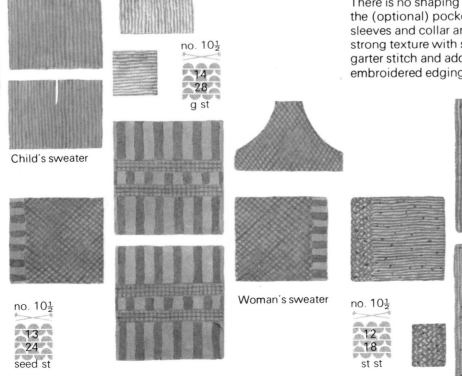

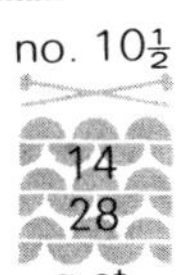
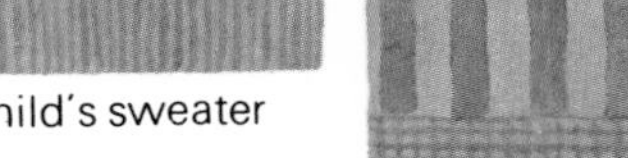

no. 10½
14
28
g st

Child's sweater

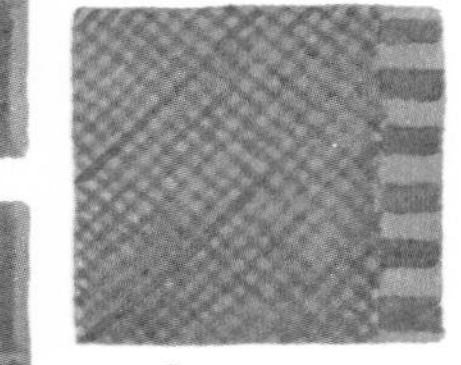
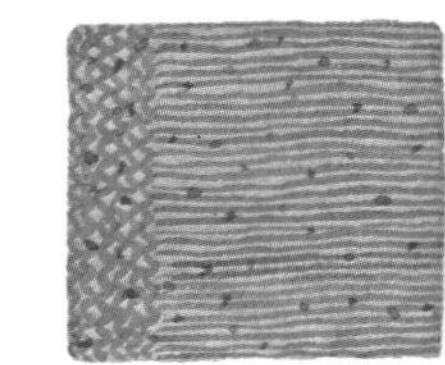
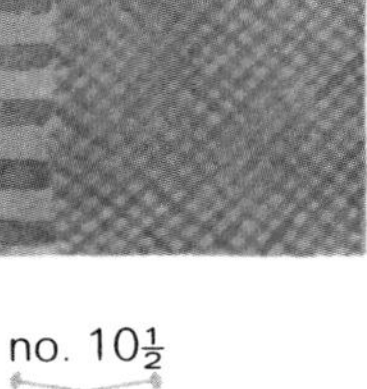
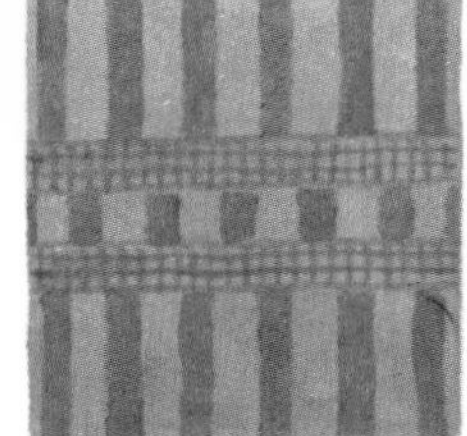

no. 10½
13
24
seed st

Woman's sweater

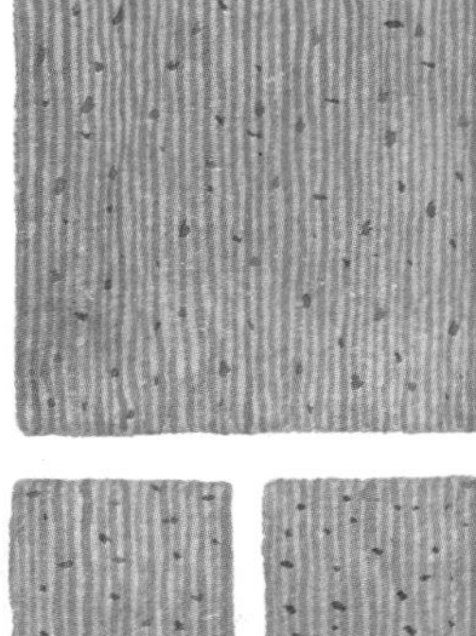
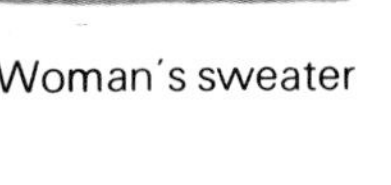
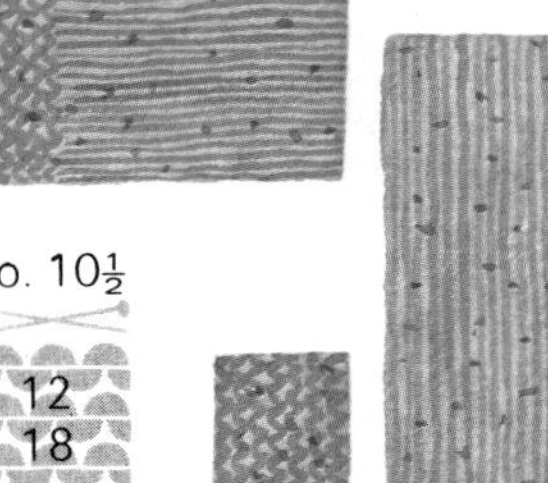
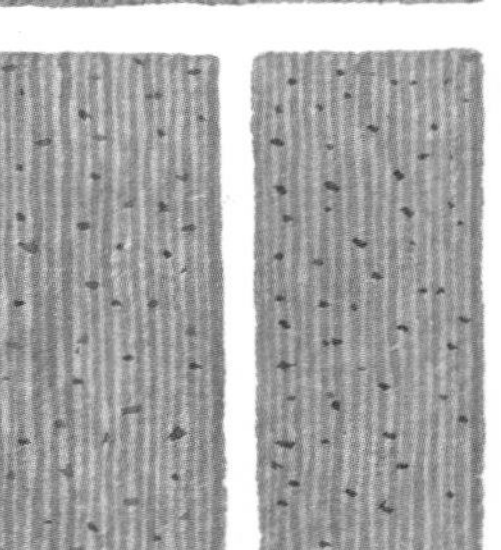
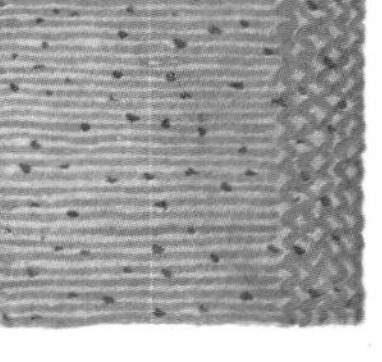
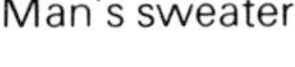

no. 10½
12
18
st st

Man's sweater

Pockets 236
Finishing 242
Design: squares and rectangles 284

Child's sweater
Size

chest	20	21½	23½	25½	27½	29½in
	(50	55	60	65	70	75cm)
length	11½	13	14½	16	17½	19in
	(29	33	37	41	45	49cm)
sleeve	6	7½	9	10½	12	13½in
	(15	19	23	27	31	35cm)

You will need
total of 13/15/18/21/25/29oz (350/400/500/600/700/800g) bulky yarn; 1 pair no. 10½ needles

Make this all in one color, or use a contrasting color for sleeves and collar. The garter-stitch ridges are vertical across the front and back and horizontal on the sleeves.

Back Cast on 41/46/52/57/63/68 sts for side edge. Work 11/12/13/14/15/16in (28/30/33/35/38/40cm) in g st. Bind off.

Front Work as for back, but halfway across make a slit for the neck opening by binding off 14/15/16/17/18/19 sts at beg of a row. K1 row, turn and cast on the same number of sts.

Sleeves Cast on 21/27/32/38/43/49 sts for sleeve seam. Work 8/9/10/11/12/13in (21/23/26/28/31/33cm) in g st. Bind off.

Collar Cast on 22/24/26/28/30/32 sts. Work 11/12/12½/13/13½/14½in (28/30/32/33/35/37cm) in g st. Bind off.

Finishing Do not press. Join shoulder seams for about one-third of total width from each side. Work blanket stitch (see p19) all around outer edges and across tops of sleeves. Mark center of sleeve top with a pin and position this on shoulder seam. With RS of work together, oversew sleeves to side edges. Join side and sleeve seams, leaving a slit at lower edge of side seams and reversing the seam for 1½in (4cm) at cuff edge. Turn back cuffs and trim with blanket stitch. Sew collar onto neck edge from top of one side of front opening all around to top of the other side. Finish outer edges of collar and sides of opening with blanket stitch.

Woman's sweater
Size
bust 32–35in (80–90cm); length 25½in (64cm); sleeve 18in (46cm)

You will need
34oz (950g) bulky yarn; 1 pair no. 10½ needles

A variety of textures gives a totally different appearance to a simple shape. Wide rib, seed and basketweave stitches are all basic patterns that work together very well. Since this rib is used for appearance rather than elasticity, you must block and press (p242) the front and back to achieve a rectangular shape.

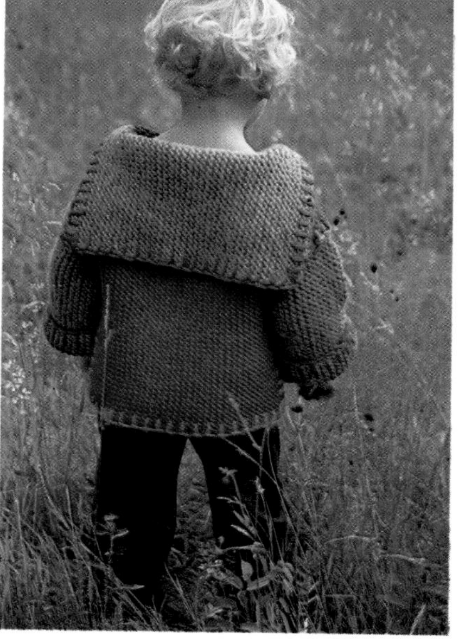

Back Cast on 72 sts.
1st row: (RS) K3, *P6, K6, rep from * to last 9 sts, P6, K3.
2nd row: P3, *K6, P6, rep from * to last 9 sts, K6, P3.
Rep these 2 rows of wide rib pat for 8½in (21·5cm), ending with a WS row. K2 rows. Commence basketweave pat.
Next row: *K3, P3, rep from * to end.
Rep last row 3 times more.
Next row: *P3, K3, rep from * to end.
Rep last row 3 times more, then first 4 rows again (12 rows in all). K2 rows. Work 3in (7cm) wide rib pat, beg and ending first row P3. K 2 rows, then work 12 more rows basketweave pat. K 2 rows. Work in wide rib pat, beg and ending first row with K3 until back measures 25in (64cm) from beg. Bind off.

Front Work as for back.

Sleeves Cast on 66 sts. Work 3in (8cm) wide rib pat. Cont in seed st until sleeve measures 18in (46cm) from beg. Bind off.

Pocket Cast on 40 sts. Work 4in (10cm) seed st. Dec 1 st at each end of next and every foll row until 16 sts rem.

Cont until work measures 9in (23cm). Bind off.

Finishing Block and press front and back to measurements required. Sew pocket in position as indicated on diagram. Join shoulder seams for about one-third of total width from each side. Sew sleeve tops in position along edge of wide rib pat on back and front. Join side and sleeve seams, reversing seam at cuff. Press seams. Turn cuff to RS.

Man's jacket
Size
chest 38–42in (95–105cm); length 27in (69cm); sleeve 18in (46cm)

You will need
42oz (1150g) bulky tweed yarn; 2oz (50g) sports yarn for edging; 1 pair no. 10½ needles; 25in (65cm) open-ended zipper

Yet another look for the basic T-shape. Make a sweater with front opening, add a zipper and you have a jacket. Basic stockinette stitch in tweed-textured yarn and an oversewn edging add to the casual appearance.

Back Cast on 67 sts and work 27in (69cm) in st st. Bind off.

Fronts Cast on 34 sts and work 27in (69cm) in st st. Bind off.

Sleeves Cast on 61 sts and work 4in (10cm) in g st. Cont in st st until sleeve measures 18in (46cm) from beg. Bind off.

Pockets Cast on 29 sts for side edges. Work 6in (15cm) in g st. Bind off.

Finishing Press each piece according to instructions with yarn. Join shoulder seams for about one-third of total width from side edges. Sew in zipper. Sew sleeve tops in position along side edges. Join side and sleeve seams. Using 3 strands of sports yarn, work large cross stitches (see p229) over sleeve-top seam. Stitch pockets in position leaving section open as shown in diagram. Using 3 strands of yarn, oversew lower, cuff, pocket-opening and neck edges. Press seams.

Following patterns

Apart from the knitting directions themselves, patterns usually contain basic information under a number of different headings so that you can see at a glance what size, gauge and materials they cover. Look at these sections when choosing a pattern to knit, and read through them before you actually begin, to check that you have everything you need and to give you an idea of the way the pattern is worked.

There are a number of different techniques that you may need to know while you are following a pattern, and that no individual instructions have space to tell you. These range from joining in a new ball of yarn to rectifying accidents like a dropped stitch, and you can find them on the opposite page.

Size

When you choose a design, remember that knitting creates an elastic fabric, so consider whether to make a garment clinging or loose-fitting to achieve the effect that you want and that suits you. Designers usually make an allowance in their calculations for 'ease' and this is included in the size quoted. Ease on a classic sweater worked in sports yarn would be about 2in (5cm); it would be correspondingly less on a clingy, fitting sweater and more on a bulky garment that was designed for wearing over other things. Scale drawings in a pattern, like the ones in this book, help you to see at a glance how many pieces you have to knit and what they should measure. Check the finished lengths of individual pieces and read the working directions to see if provision is made for you to make any alterations (see p234). A pattern may be given in one size only if the designer considers it the most suitable because it fits a range of sizes, or if it involves large multiples of stitches that make close grading of sizes impracticable. Where there is more than one size, instructions for larger sizes are usually given after the first one, e.g. 'cast on 40/44/48 sts', as in this book, or may be written in brackets, e.g. 'cast on 40 (44, 48) sts'. Read through the complete pattern and use a colored pen to underline or circle the figures relevant to the size you are making to avoid confusion.

Gauge

All patterns give you the recommended gauge that you need to achieve an item of the correct size. Whether you use the prescribed yarn or substitute an alternative, always work a swatch before you begin the pattern. See p220 for further details.

Materials

Choose yarn appropriate to the design. Consider whether the yarn needs to be hard-wearing or washable, as well as your own preference for natural or synthetic fibers. Most bought patterns are published by manufacturers to promote a specific yarn; if this is not available or you want to substitute an alternative, make sure in your swatch that the yarn you use knits up into a fabric of a suitable weight. Remember that choosing a different yarn may alter the quantity that you will need. Patterns also list the other major items for the design – from knitting needles to zippers.

Working directions

It is important to work the pattern pieces in the order in which they appear in the directions. Different pieces may have to be joined before you can continue knitting (e.g. shoulder seams sewn up before stitches for a neckband are picked up and worked). In some patterns specific directions, e.g. for a pattern repeat, may be given in full in the first section and referred to in more abbreviated form afterwards, or for the front of a garment you may be told to 'follow directions for back until armhole shaping is complete'. Asterisks, *, are often used to save repetition; in a pattern row an asterisk denotes that you should repeat the sequence of stitches from that point as instructed. A single or double asterisk at the beginning and end of a complete section of the pattern shows that a whole set of directions is later repeated.

Finishing

Pattern directions tell you the order in which pieces should be sewn together and how to make any final edgings and trimmings. This section sometimes gives hints on pressing; if you have substituted a different yarn, check with the label that these pressing instructions are appropriate. See p242 for full information on finishing.

Abbreviations

Knitting instructions are normally abbreviated to save space. In the list below a page number is given whenever appropriate to show where the technique is covered.

alt	alternate(ly)
approx	approximate(ly)
beg	begin(ning)
cont	continu(e/ing)
dec	decreas(e/ing) p222
foll	follow(ing)
g st	garter stitch p216
inc	increas(e/ing)
K	knit p216
K up	pick up and knit p240
K-wise	knitwise
LH	left-hand
M1	make 1 p222
no.	number
P	purl p216
pat	pattern
psso	pass slipped stitch over p222
p2sso	pass 2 slipped stitches over
P up	pick up and purl p240
P-wise	purlwise
rem	remain(ing)
rep	repeat
rev st st	reverse stockinette stitch p216
RH	right-hand
RS	right side
sl	slip
sl st	slip stitch
st(s)	stitch(es)
st st	stockinette stitch p216
tbl	through back loop(s) p216
tog	together
WS	wrong side
ybk	yarn back
yfwd	yarn forward p222
yo	yarn over needle p222
yrn	yarn round needle p222

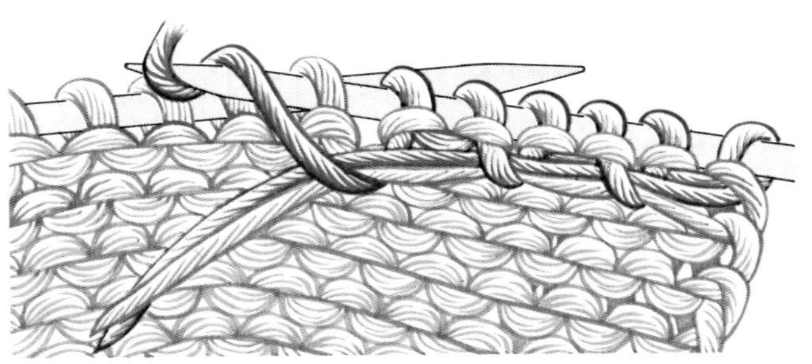

Joining a new ball of yarn Try to avoid doing this in the middle of a row. (It takes a length of yarn about 4 times the width of your knitting to complete a row.) Leave a 4in (10cm) end of yarn on the new ball and begin working with it at the start of a row. Cut off the old end to the same length and either weave in both ends of yarn as shown in the diagram or darn them in later with a darning needle.

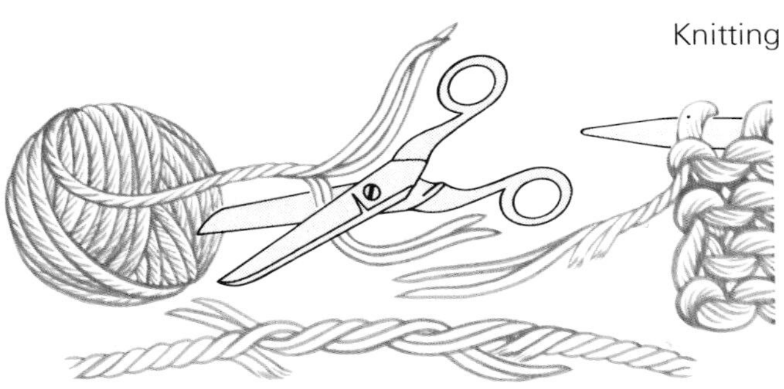

Splicing is an invisible method when joining yarn in the middle of a row is unavoidable. Take the end of the new ball of yarn and the end of the yarn in use and separate the plies for about 4in (10cm) on each. Cut away half the strands. Overlap the 2 ends and twist them together to produce a yarn that is the same thickness as the rest. Knit carefully with the twisted section and trim any odd ends when finishing.

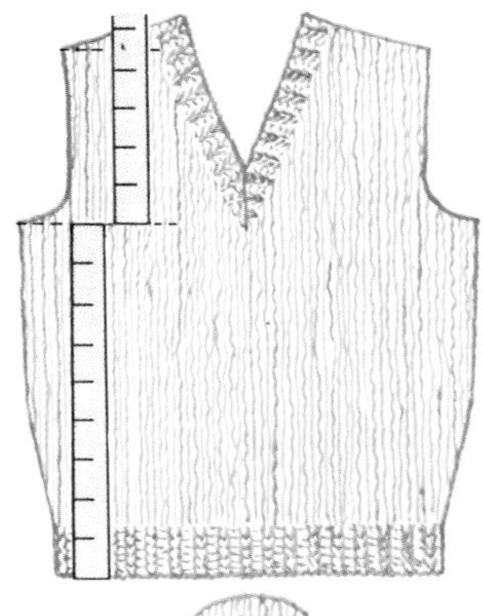

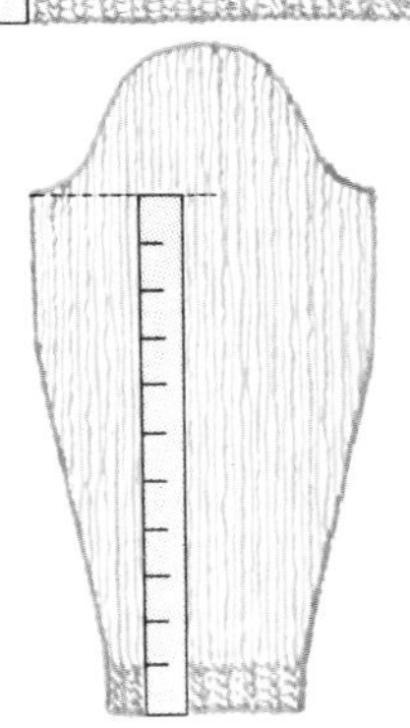

Measure knitting in progress on a flat surface using a rigid ruler. Since knitted fabric is elastic it is easy to distort it when measuring without taking these precautions. Never measure around the curve of an armhole or along the slanting edge of sleeve shaping; always measure the depth of knitting in a straight line following the vertical line of the stitches.

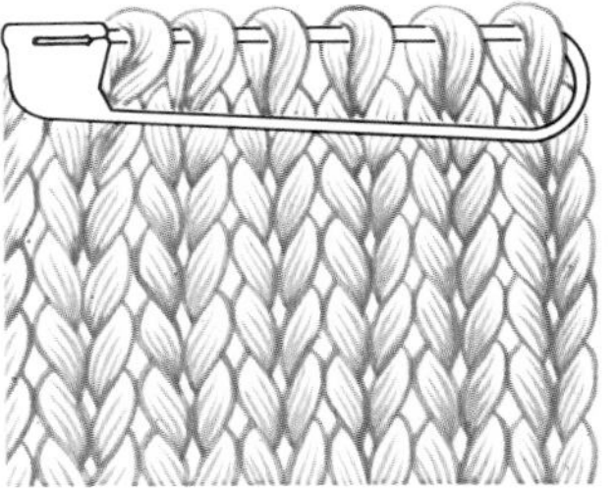

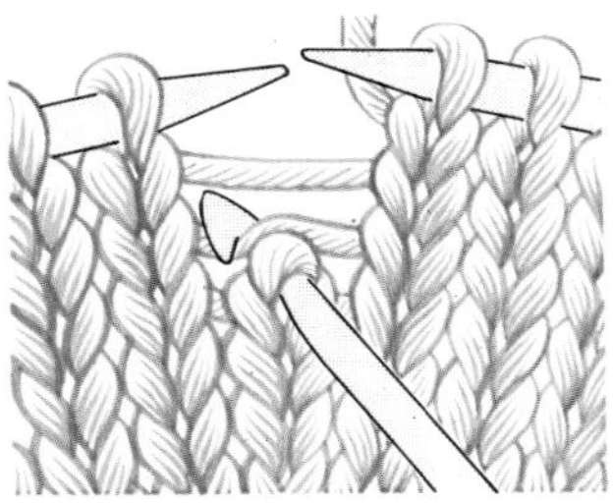

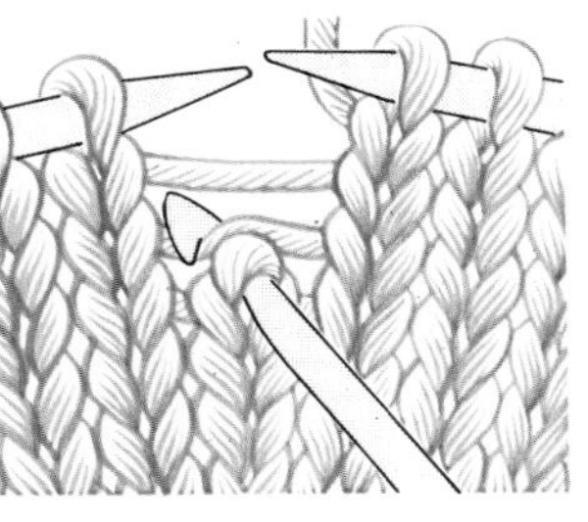

Holding stitches not in use On completion of sections of knitting – such as front, back and sleeves of a raglan sweater – where the stitches are not bound off but used for a neckband, a pattern will state 'leave rem sts on a holder'. Break off the yarn after the final row and simply slip all the stitches onto the holder; then fasten or secure the open end of the holder. Use a stitch holder to retain stitches at any position in a row while sections at one or either side of this are being worked – e.g. front and back neck shaping (p240) or pocket openings (p236).

An alternative to stitch holders is to run stitches onto a spare piece of thread. This is useful where a stitch holder is not available, or on intricate items like gloves where a stitch holder would be clumsy. Thread a darning needle with a length of spare yarn, preferably in a contrasting color, and run it through the stitches before slipping them off the needle. Knot the yarn loosely until you need to use the stitches.

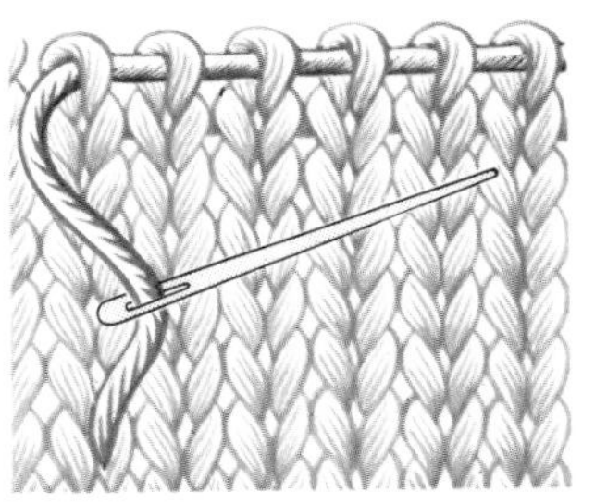

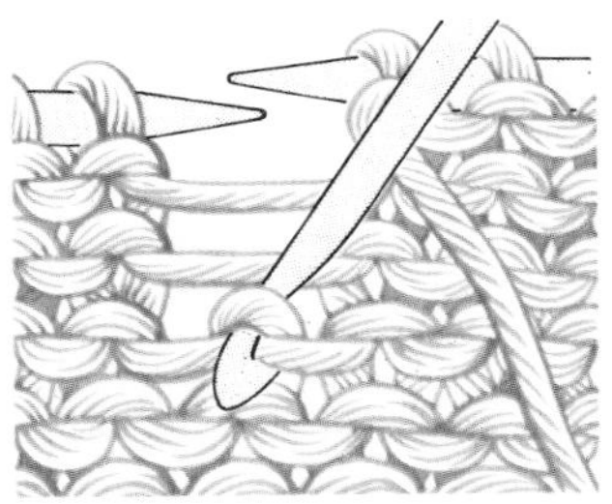

Picking up a dropped stitch In stockinette stitch where you are not constantly counting stitches it is easy to miss a dropped stitch and allow it to become a 'run'. On a knit row, insert a crochet hook from front to back into the dropped stitch. Push the hook under the horizontal thread above the dropped stitch and use the hook to draw this thread through the dropped stitch. Continue until the stitch is even with the last row worked and transfer it to the LH needle to be knitted as usual.

On a purl row, insert a crochet hook from back to front into the dropped stitch. Hook the horizontal thread above the dropped stitch and pull it through the dropped stitch. Slip the stitch onto a spare needle, remove the hook and re-insert it, from back to front again. Repeat until the dropped stitch is even with the last row worked, then transfer it to the LH needle to be purled as usual.

Duplicate stitching

This easy form of embroidery worked on a close-knit fabric such as stockinette gives the impression that the designs have been knitted in. Many people find it easier to duplicate-stitch a motif on a completed item than to handle more than one color yarn while in the process of knitting (as in Jacquard designs – see p270). Motifs can be as simple or as sophisticated as you choose, and can enliven an old sweater or personalize a child's garment. Duplicate stitching forms a double fabric and can therefore strengthen the points on a garment that get a lot of wear, such as the knees of a baby's overalls or the fingers and palms of gloves.

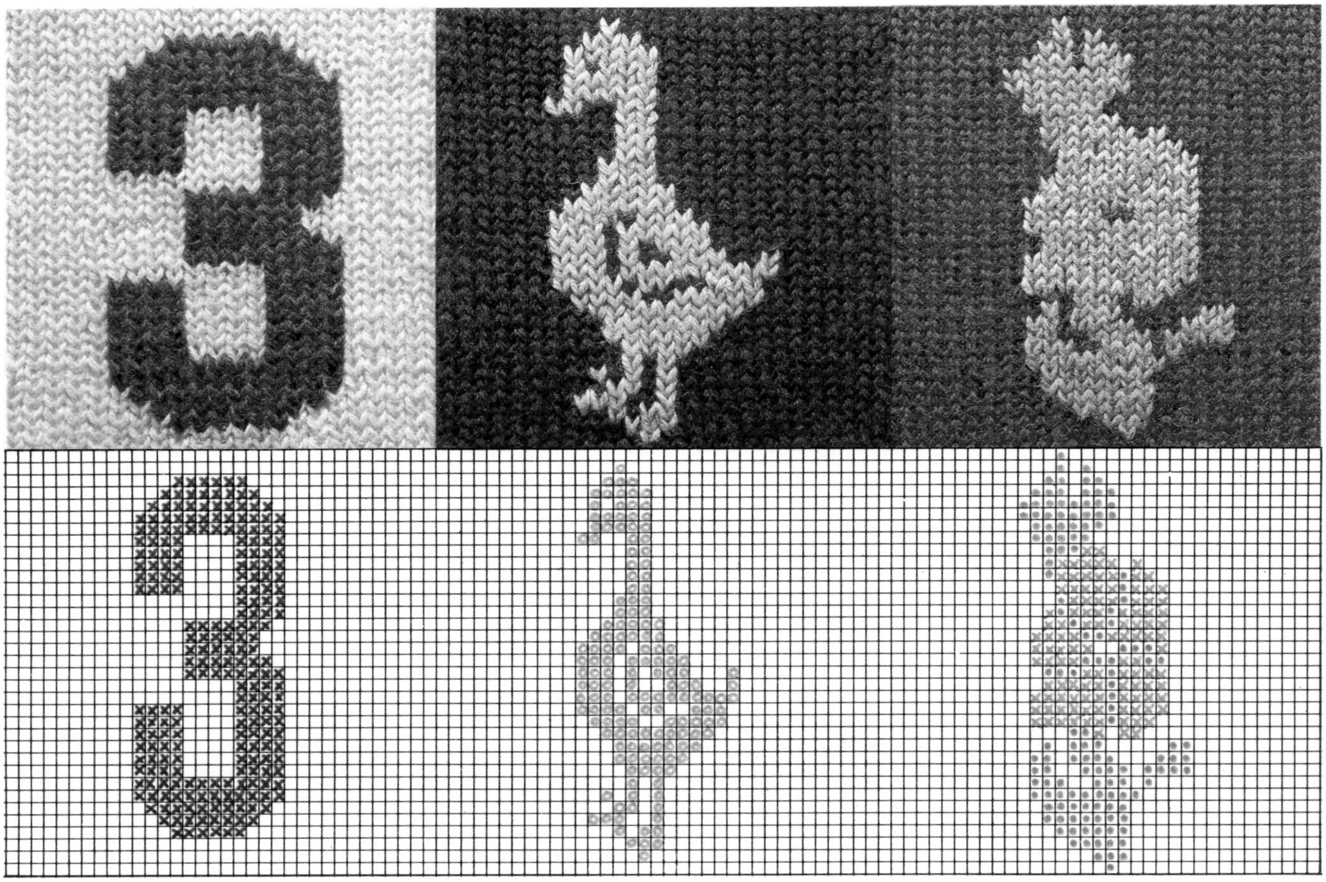

Thread a large darning needle with yarn of same ply as background. Begin at lower RH corner of motif and secure yarn at back of 1st stitch. Bring needle to front through base of 1st stitch, then insert it from right to left through same stitch 1 row above. Pull yarn through – gauge of stitches being formed must equal that of background; re-insert needle into base of 1st stitch and bring out to front again through base of next stitch to the left. For row above, insert needle into base of last stitch worked and then bring out to front through center of same stitch. Work 2nd and

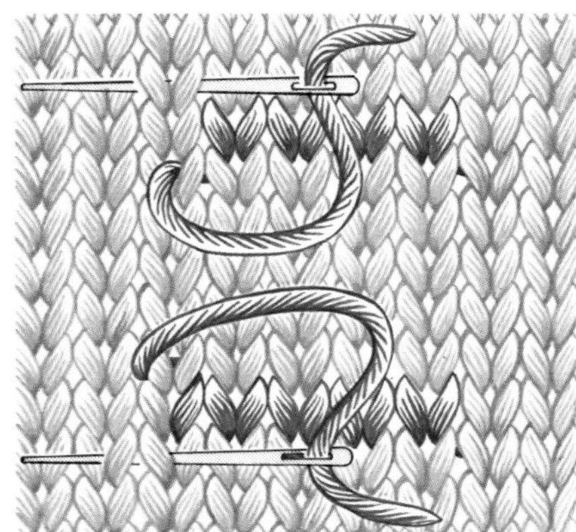

subsequent alternate rows by turning the motif upside down; the stitches look the same and once you get into the rhythm of working, following the design is easy. Don't let the plies of the yarn separate; twist them as you work. If you are adapting designs for duplicate stitch, remember to allow for the fact that knitted stitches are wider than they are deep; a motif that looks square on graph paper will turn out wider than its depth whether it is duplicate-stitched or knitted into a fabric.

Embroidery

Here are three ways of decorating a knitted fabric. They don't involve charts, although you must consider the position of a pattern or a motif before you begin working. Always use a large darning needle when embroidering on knitting; a sharp needle can split and damage the yarn. And don't try to embroider tiny chain stitches with a bulky yarn – always choose yarns of a weight appropriate to the knitted fabric. Watch that the plies of the yarn don't separate and become untwisted as you work.

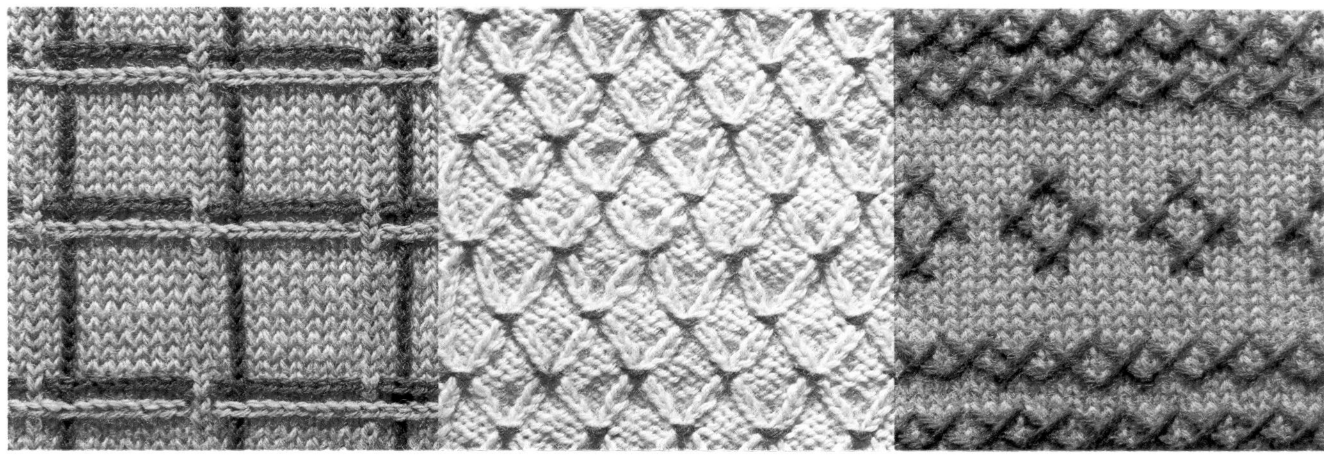

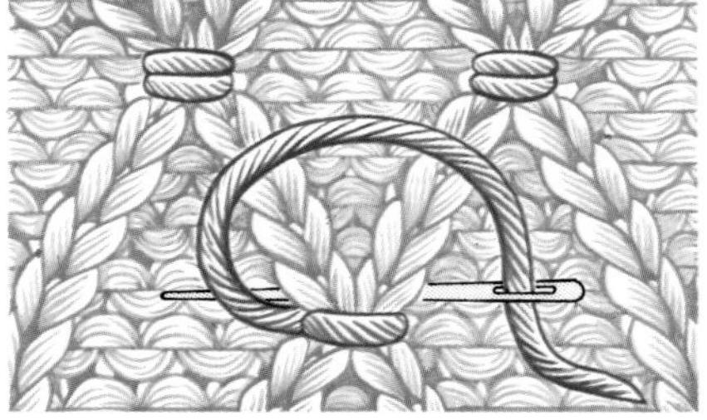

Chain stitch Embroider chain stitches on a plain or striped st st background to create a checked effect. Chain stitch is worked downward, so turn work upside down. Mark position for vertical chains allowing 1 st per row, depending on weight of fabric. Secure yarn at back of marked position and insert needle from back to front through center of 1st st. Work chain sts (see p170) referring to diagram above to see how chains are worked through centers of knitted sts. Remember to keep the embroidery relaxed so that the gauge is similar to that of the knitting. For horizontal chains turn work sideways and embroider into each st across a row.

Smocking This method of controlling fullness on cotton and linen fabrics (see p206) adapts well to knitting, where the back sts drawing the work together are embroidered onto a ribbed background. Wide ribs produce too bulky a fabric – 3 P sts and 1 K st make a good combination. Keep horizontal smocking sts evenly spaced by counting equal numbers of sts in the vertical ribs. Remember to cast on enough sts to give twice the required width, because the embroidery will pull the knitting in. Make sure you don't pull the embroidery yarn too tight on WS of work and so distort the fabric.

Cross stitch (see p170) can be worked over any number of knitted sts and rows, usually counting slightly more rows than sts – 2 sts and 3 rows or 3 sts and 4 rows. Insert needle between sts over which you are working to make sure that elasticity of knitting does not pull embroidery out of shape. Work a row of diagonal sts in one direction first, and complete the crosses by working diagonal sts back in the opposite direction; always make sure the top halves of the crosses lie in the same direction.

Children's dresses

no. 3

28
36
st st

Basic stitches 216
Gauge 220
Following patterns 226
Duplicate stitch 228

You can transform a basic dress pattern into an entirely individual garment by combining stripes of different colors with applied embroidery or duplicate-stitched motifs. If you prefer, you can use the same graph patterns to knit motifs into the dress rather than add them afterwards – see p270. Directions for the basic dress are given here; if you want to work in stripes calculate roughly what proportion of the dress each color will form when you buy your yarn.

Size

chest	18	20	21½in
	(45	50	55cm)
length	14	15½	17in
	(36	40	44cm)
sleeve	2in		
	(5cm)		

You will need

1 pair each no. 2 and no. 3 needles

5/6/7oz (125/150/175g) fingering yarn

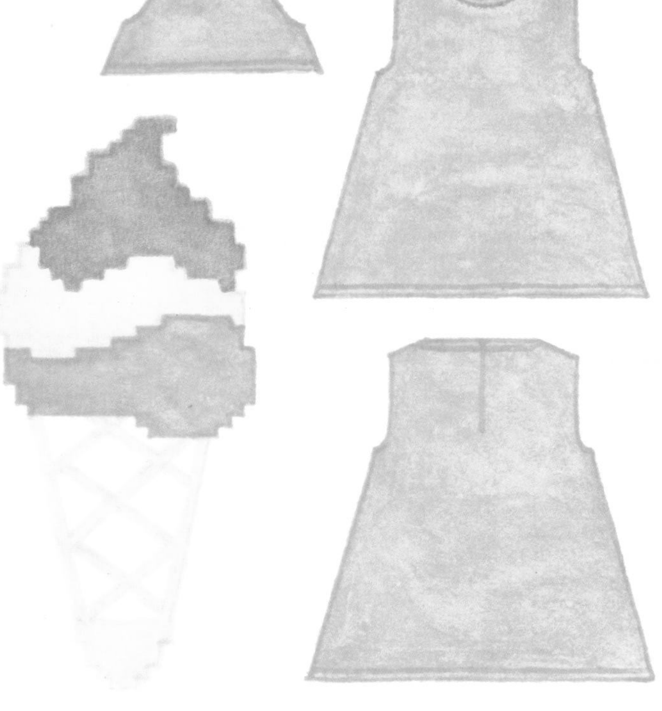

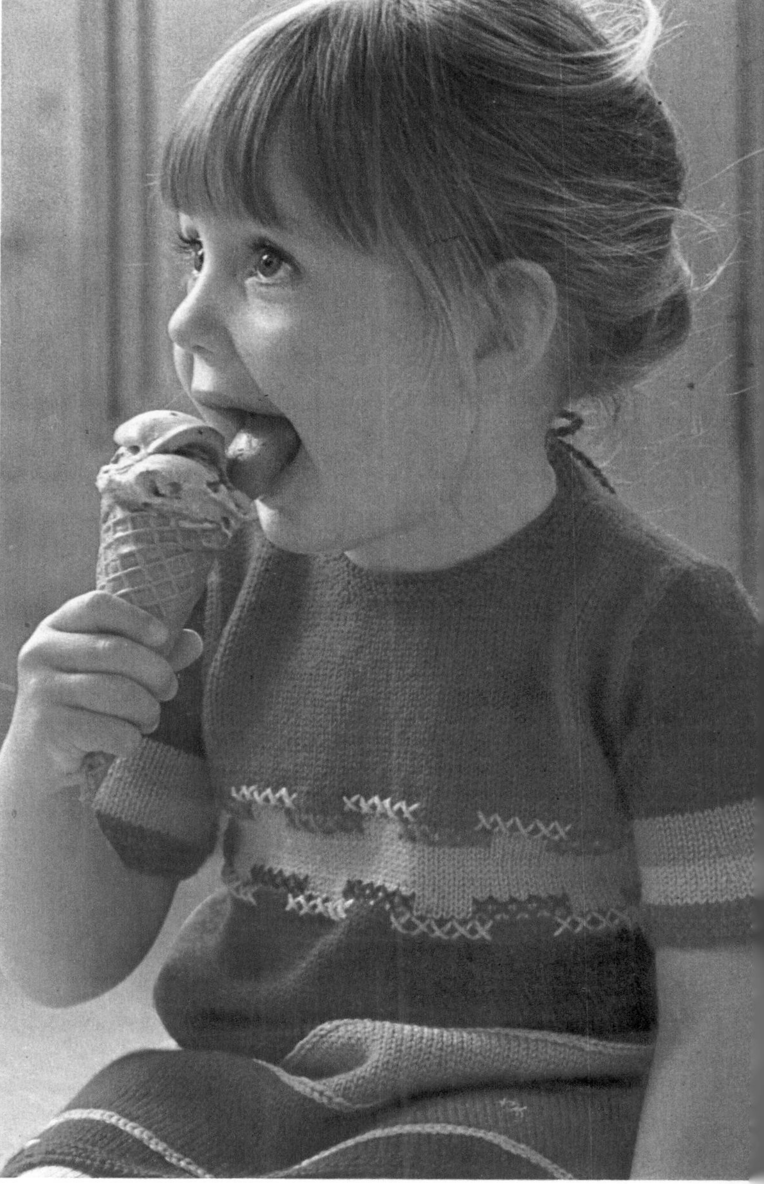

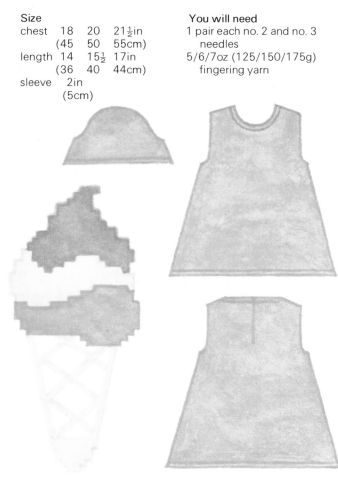

Back
With no. 3 needles cast on 102/110/118 sts and work 4 rows in g st. Cont in st st, dec 6 sts evenly by working 2 sts tog across every 12th/14th/16th row until 66/74/82 sts rem, then cont without shaping until work measures 9½/11/12in (25/28/31cm) from beg, ending with a P row.

Shape armholes Bind off 2 sts at beg of next 4 rows, then dec 1 st at each end of next and every alt row until 50/56/62 sts rem, ending with a P row.

Divide for opening Next row: K25/28/31, turn and cont on these sts until armhole measures 4¼/4½/4¾in (11/12/13cm), ending with a P row.

Shape shoulders Bind off 4/5/5 sts at beg of next and foll alt row, then 4/4/6 sts at beg of foll alt row. Leave rem 13/14/15 sts on holder.
Return to the other 25/28/31 sts and work to match.

Front
Work as for back until armhole shaping is completed, then cont without shaping until armholes measure 2¾/3⅛/3½in (7/8/9cm), ending with a P row.

Shape neck Next row: K20/22/24, turn and cont on these sts.
Bind off 2 sts at beg of next and foll alt row, then dec 1 st at neck edge on every alt row until 12/14/16 sts rem.
Cont without shaping until same length as back armhole, ending with a P row.
Shape shoulder to match back. Return to the other 30/34/38 sts; leave first 10/12/14 sts on holder for neck, rejoin yarn and cont to match first side.

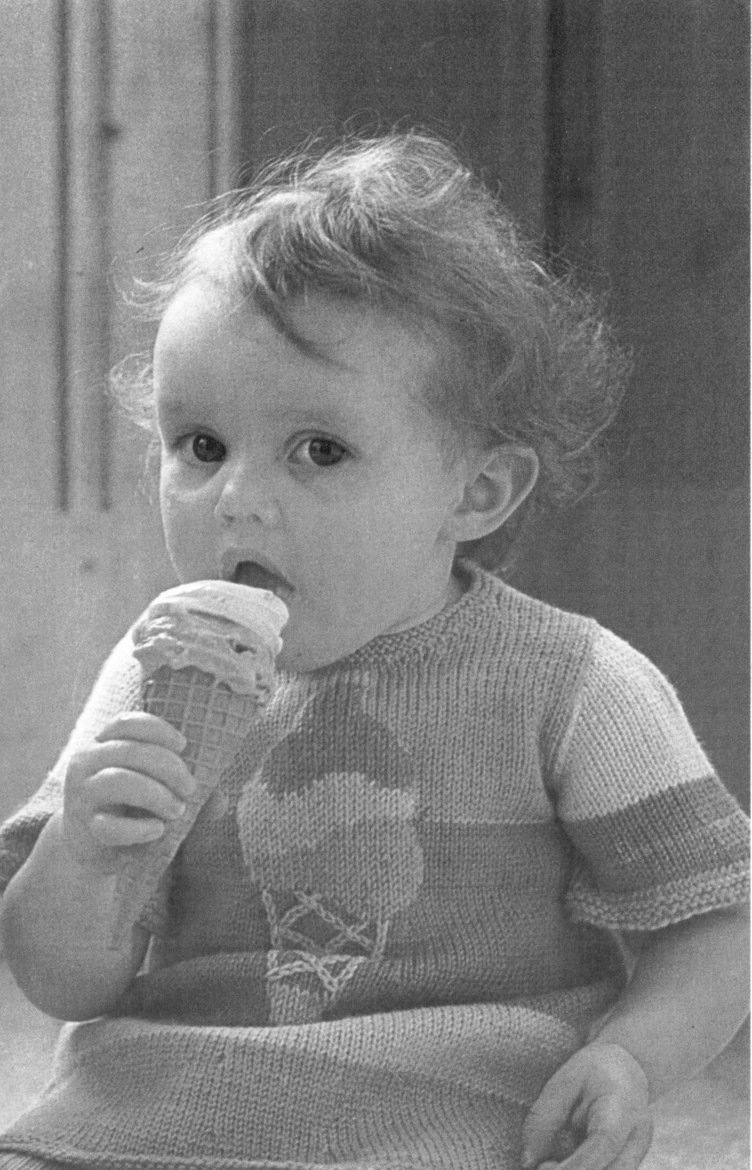

Sleeves

With no. 3 needles cast on 64/68/72 sts and work 4 rows in g st. Cont in st st, dec 4 sts evenly across 3rd row and every foll 6th row twice more (52/56/60 sts). P 1 row.

Shape top Bind off 2 sts at beg of next 4 rows. Dec 1 st at each end of next and every alt row until 28/30/32 sts rem, ending with a P row. Bind off 2 sts at beg of next 6 rows, then 3 sts at beg of next 2 rows. Bind off rem 10/12/14 sts.

Neckband

With no. 2 needles and RS facing, K up 66/72/78 sts around neck, including sts on holders. K4 rows. Bind off.

Back opening

With no. 2 needles and RS facing, K up 28/32/36 sts down left side of opening and 28/32/36 sts up right side. Bind off.

Finishing

Press work lightly with a warm iron over a damp cloth. Join shoulder seams. Sew in sleeves. Join side and sleeve seams. Make 2 twisted cords (see p102) and sew one to each side of back neck. Press seams. Work out designs like the ice-cream cone on our smaller dress on graph paper and then duplicate-stitch onto the garment (here the cone is in chain-stitch). The larger dress has chain-stitch and cross-stitch embroidery (see p170).

Adjusting patterns

When you have checked the sizes given against body measurements you may find that patterns need some adjustment. Alternatively, you may choose to incorporate a different neckline (p240), alternative stitch patterns (pp216, 234) or a more subtle variation such as a decorative hem. Whether the alterations are a matter of necessity or of choice, you should read through the whole pattern thoroughly as described on p226 and work out in advance how your modifications will change the directions and affect the amount of yarn you will need.

Substituting stitch patterns
Use a gauge swatch to see what happens if instead of stockinette you work a rib (making a clingy, elastic fabric) or a more deeply textured stitch (which can take extra yarn to work).

Sweater or cardigan length
Check finished length of sweater from shoulder to hem and add or subtract any difference in length from the main body of the sweater before reaching underarm shaping. If the pattern quotes an underarm length and is in a simple stitch such as stockinette, it is easy to adjust this length. With a complicated stitch pattern involving a large row repeat you may have to add or take away a whole pattern repeat.

Sleeve length
A sleeve seam is measured from underarm level to wrist along the straight line of stitches. Lengthen or shorten after completing the sleeve shaping; normally you work about 1½in (4cm) straight before shaping the sleeve cap, and this depth can be altered accordingly. See that the last row you work before binding off stitches for the underarm matches the pattern row on back and front at same point; the pattern should match up across the armhole and sleeve cap when the sleeve is in position.

Skirt length
Make only a small adjustment to a skirt length, i.e. add or subtract only a few inches; at this stage, don't try to make a short skirt into a long one or *vice versa* unless the pattern specifically allows for that. You can knit skirts upward or downward. With those that are made from the top downward and require continuous shaping you can stop at any length you like; otherwise you can alter the length in the straight section between the end of the shaping and the hem. The latter also applies to knitting upward from the hem: add or subtract length before you begin the shaping. Here you can't measure the skirt against you as you go to determine the finished length, so do your calculations first.

Fitting shoulders
A problem that can arise in a well-fitting classic garment with set-in sleeves is the width at the shoulders; it is easier to make them narrower than wider. To check this fit, look at pattern to calculate measurement across shoulders by working backward from number of stitches that remain after armhole shaping. Adjust by a combination of binding off more stitches at underarms and working extra decreases during armhole shaping.

E.g. if shoulders are 1½in (4cm) too wide in a garment with gauge of 30 sts to 4in (10cm), you need to lose 12 sts, 6 at either side. Bind off 3 extra sts at underarm and dec 3 extra sts during underarm shaping. You now have 6 fewer sts to dec at stepped shoulder shaping on either side: divide these evenly among the dec rows.

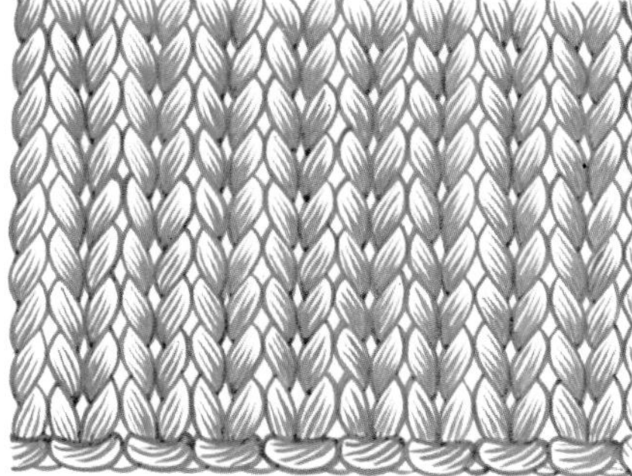

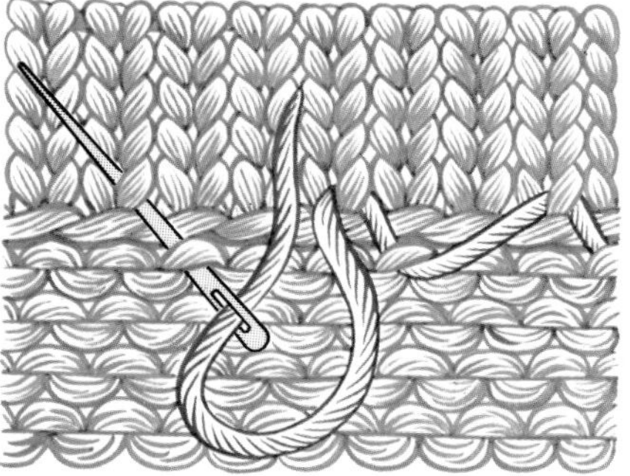

Turned-under hem

This hem is fairly elastic and so is suitable for the bottom edge of a sweater.

The hem is worked in stockinette stitch (which, being smooth, helps it to lie flat) irrespective of what stitch pattern the main fabric uses.

1 Cast on the required number of stitches using needles one size smaller than for main fabric.

2 Beginning with a K row, work an odd number of rows in stockinette, so ending with a K row.

3 Change to correct needle size. K each st in next row tbl, making a pronounced horizontal ridge on RS of fabric to mark the hemline.

4 Beginning with a K row again, continue in stockinette stitch or in garment pattern and work 1 row less than before, ending with a WS row. Complete garment according to pattern directions.

5 When assembling the finished garment, join side seams, then fold the knitting at the hemline so that the hem is on WS of work.

6 Use a slip-stitch seam (p242) to sew up hem; start by securing yarn at one seam.

7 Lightly use the needle to pick up 1 st from main fabric and pull yarn through.

8 Miss 1 st to the left, pick up next edge st on hem and pull yarn through.

9 Continue this way, picking up sts from main fabric and from hem alternately, until hem is complete.

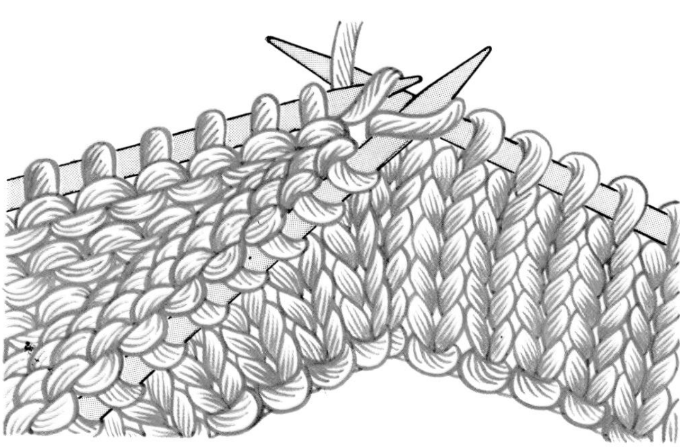

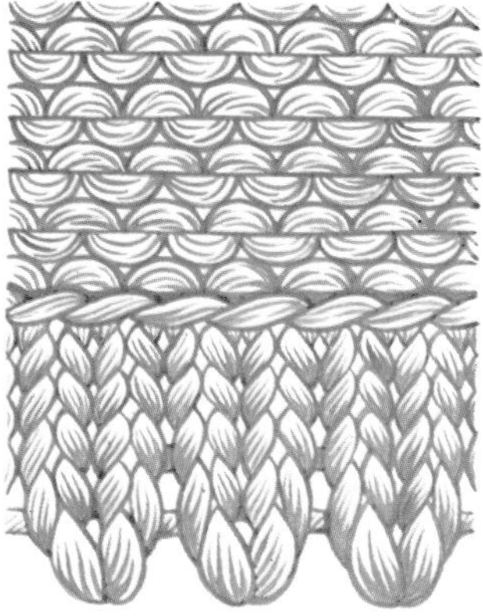

Knitted-in hem

This hem is slightly firmer than the turned-under hem above, and is useful for coats or jackets where elasticity is not important.

1 Work as given for turned-under hem from **1** to **4**.

2 Take a spare needle and pick up the loops from the cast-on sts – beginning at LH side and having the needle point lying in the same direction as the one holding the sts. The number of loops picked up should correspond with the number of sts you cast on.

3 Hold the needle with the loops from the cast-on sts behind the LH needle holding the sts.

4 Use the RH needle to work to end of row, knitting together 1 st from the LH needle and 1 st from the extra needle.

5 When assembling the garment, join side seams as usual, working through the double thickness of the hem.

Scalloped hem

This scalloped edge is formed when the foldline of the hem consists of a row of eyelet holes; it looks best in fairly fine yarns.

1 Cast on an odd number of sts using needles 1 size smaller than for main fabric.

2 Beginning with a K row, work an even number of rows in st st.

3 Change to correct needle size. Make the eyelet holes which form the foldline of the hem by knitting across the rows as follows: *K2 tog, yfwd, rep from * to last st, K1.

4 Beginning with a P row, continue in st st, working 1 more row than for the hem, so ending with a P row.

5 When assembling the garment, join side seams; then turn the hem to WS along the eyelet-hole row and slip-stitch in position as for turned-under hem.

Textured stitches

Pyramid pattern
Cast on a multiple of 15 sts plus 1 extra.
1st row (RS) K to end.
2nd row P4, *K8, P7, rep from * to last 12 sts, K8, P4.
3rd row K1, *K up 1, K2, sl 1, K1, psso, P6, K2 tog, K2, K up 1, K1, rep from * to end.
4th row P5, *K6, P9, rep from * to last 11 sts, K6, P5.
5th row K2, *K up 1, K2, sl 1, K1, psso, P4, K2 tog, K2, K up 1, K3, rep from * to last 14 sts, K up 1, K2, sl 1, K1, psso, P4, K2 tog, K2, K up 1, K2.
6th row P6, *K4, P11, rep from * to last 10 sts, K4, P6.
7th row K3, *K up 1, K2, sl 1, K1, psso, P2, K2 tog, K2, K up 1, K5, rep from * to last 13 sts, K up 1, K2, sl 1, K1, psso, P2, K2 tog, K2, K up 1, K3.
8th row P7, *K2, P13, rep from * to last 9 sts, K2, P7.
9th row K4, *K up 1, K2, sl 1, K1, psso, K2 tog, K2, K up 1, K7, rep from * to last 12 sts, K up 1, K2, sl 1, K1, psso, K2 tog, K2, K up 1, K4.
10th row P.
Pattern repeat is 10 rows.

Woven chevron stitch
Cast on a multiple of 5 sts plus 2 extra with needles at least 2 sizes larger than normal.
1st row (RS) K2, *yfwd, sl 3 P-wise, ybk, K2, rep from * to end.
2nd row P1, *ybk, sl 3, yfwd, P2, rep from * to last st, P1.
3rd row K1, yfwd, *sl 2, ybk, K2, yfwd, sl 1, rep from * to last st, ybk, K1.
4th row P1, ybk, *sl 1, yfwd, P2, ybk, sl 2, rep from * to last st, yfwd, P1.
5th row K1, *yfwd, sl 3, ybk, K2, rep from * to last st, K1.
6th row P2, *ybk, sl 3, yfwd, P2, rep from * to end.
7th row As 5th.
8th row As 4th.
9th row As 3rd.
10th row As 2nd.
Pattern repeat is 10 rows.

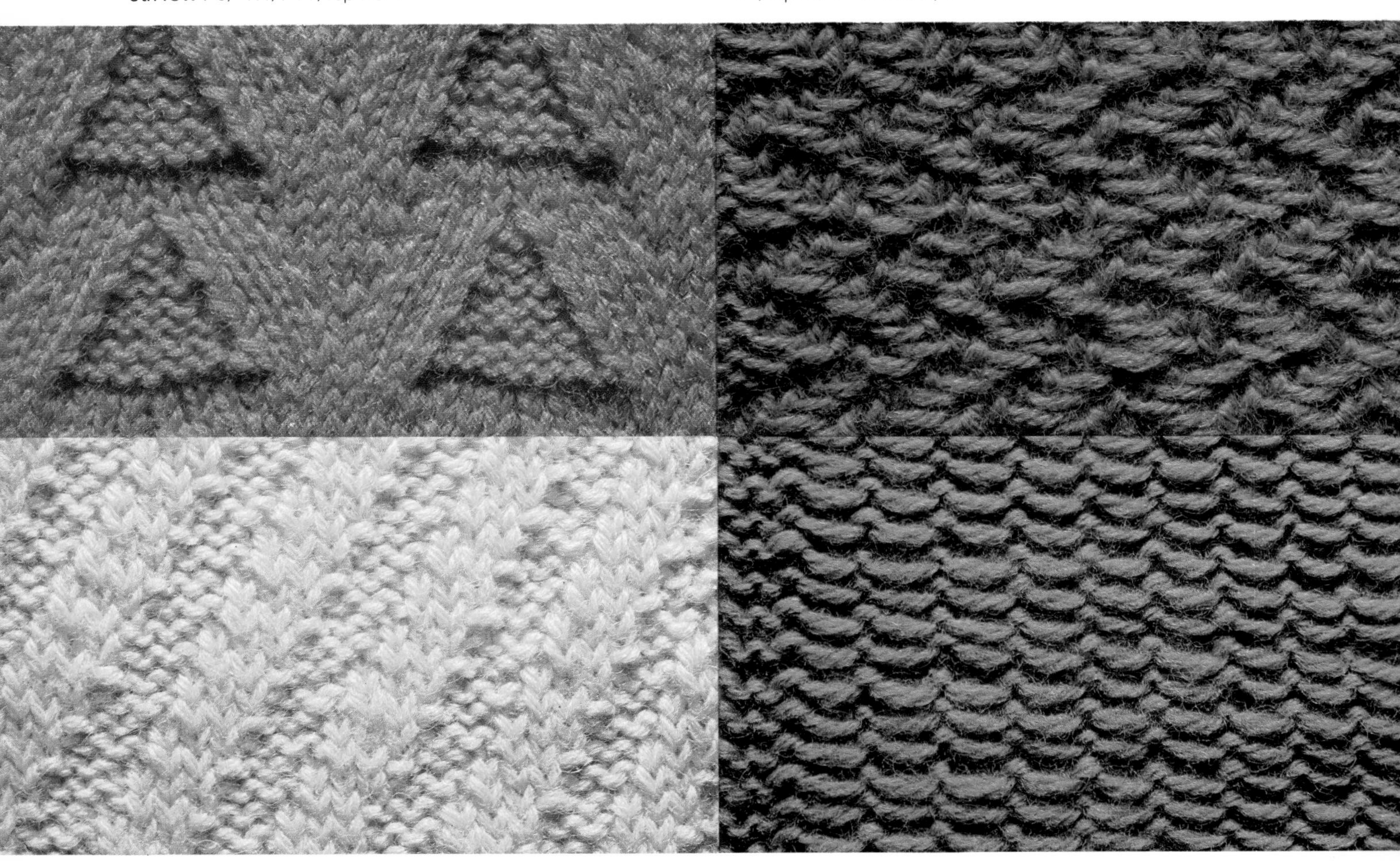

Steep diagonal rib
Cast on a multiple of 6 sts.
1st row (RS) *P3, K3, rep from * to end.
2nd and every alt row K all sts you purled in previous row and P all sts you knitted.
3rd row P2, *K3, P3, rep from * to last 4 sts, K3, P1.
5th row P1, *K3, P3, rep from * to last 5 sts, K3, P2.
7th row *K3, P3, rep from * to end.
9th row K2, *P3, K3, rep from * to last 4 sts, P3, K1.
11th row K1, *P3, K3, rep from * to last 5 sts, P3, K2.
Pattern repeat is 12 rows.

Woven bar stitch
Cast on a multiple of 3 sts plus 1 extra.
1st row (RS) K to end.
2nd row *K1, keeping yarn at back of work sl 2 P-wise, rep from * to last st, K1.
Pattern repeat is 2 rows.

Leaf pattern
Cast on a multiple of 24 sts plus 1 extra.
1st row (RS) K1, *K up 1, sl 1, K1, psso, K4, K2 tog, K3, K up 1, K1, K up 1, K3, sl 1, K1, psso, K4, K2 tog, K up 1, K1, rep from * to end.
2nd and every alt row P.
3rd row K1, *K up 1, K1, sl 1, K1, psso, K2, K2 tog, K4, K up 1, K1, K up 1, K4, sl 1, K1, psso, K2, K2 tog, K1, K up 1, K1, rep from * to end.
5th row K1, *K up 1, K2, sl 1, K1, psso, K2 tog, K5, K up 1, K1, K up 1, K5, sl 1, K1, psso, K2 tog, K2, K up 1, K1, rep from * to end.
7th row K1, *K up 1, K3, sl 1, K1, psso, K4, K2 tog, K up 1, K1, K up 1, sl 1, K1, psso, K4, K2 tog, K3, K up 1, K1, rep from * to end.
9th row K1, *K up 1, K4, sl 1, K1, psso, K2, K2 tog, K1, K up 1, K1, K up 1, K1, sl 1, K1, psso, K2, K2 tog, K4, K up 1, K1, rep from * to end.
11th row K1, *K up 1, K5, sl 1, K1, psso, K2 tog, K2, K up 1, K1, K up 1, K2, sl 1, K1, psso, K2 tog, K5, K up 1, K1, rep from * to end.
Pattern repeat is 12 rows.

Bobble rib
Cast on a multiple of 6 sts plus 2 extra edge sts.
1st row (RS) P2, *K1, P2, rep from * to end.
2nd row K2, *P1, K2, rep from * to end.
3rd row P2, *K1, P2, (P1, K1, P1, K1) all into next st – called K4 from 1, P2, rep from * to end.
4th row K2, *P4, K2, P1, K2, rep from * to end.
5th row P2, *K1, P2, P4, turn and K4, turn and P4, P2, rep from * to end.
6th row K2, *P4 tog, K2, P1, K2, rep from * to end. Rep 1st and 2nd rows once more.
9th row P2, *K4 from 1, P2, K1, P2, rep from * to end.
10th row K2, *P1, K2, P4, K2, rep from * to end.
11th row P2, *P4, turn and K4, turn and P4, P2, K1, P2, rep from * to end.
12th row K2, *P1, K2, P4 tog, K2, rep from * to end.
Pattern repeat is 12 rows.

Cane basket stitch
Cast on a multiple of 6 sts plus 2 extra edge sts.
1st row (WS) K2, *P4, K2, rep from * to end.
2nd row P2, *K4, P2, rep from * to end.
Rep these 2 rows once more.
5th row P3, *K2, P4, rep from * to last 5 sts, K2, P3.
6th row K3, *P2, K4, rep from * to last 5 sts, P2, K3.
Rep last 2 rows once more.
Pattern repeat is 8 rows.

Blackberry stitch
Cast on multiple of 4 sts.
1st row (RS) *(K1, yfwd to make 1 st, K1) all into next st, P3, rep from * to end.
2nd row *P3 tog, K3, rep from * to end.
3rd row *P3, (K1, yfwd to make 1 st, K1) all into next st, rep from * to end.
4th row *K3, P3 tog, rep from * to end.
Pattern repeat is 4 rows.

Pockets

Before adding pockets decide where they will go and check measurements carefully. Looking at the overall size of the garment, work out the depth of pocket you require; remember that the lower edge must not overlap a hem or ribbed waistband. Calculate the number of stitches for the pocket by multiplying required width by the number of stitches to 1 in or 1 cm in the gauge of the main fabric. For a professional look, take care with the sewing on. Patch pockets, knitted separately and sewn onto the finished garment, are the simplest to make. Inserted horizontal pockets consist of a separate knitted lining inset behind a horizontal slit in the main fabric. One or two inserted vertical pockets can be added to a jacket, or can be adapted into a 'kangaroo pouch', an elongated pocket with an opening at either side, for a sweater. The lining of vertical pockets always lies toward the center front of a garment, so check that there is enough room for it to lie flat within the front edge.

Sewn-on pocket

1 With same needles as used for main fabric, work pocket to the required depth. Allow ½–1in (2–3cm) for a ribbed top worked on smaller needles; or finish pocket top with a hem.

2 Position WS of pocket onto RS of garment, aligning lower edge of pocket with one row of the main fabric. Keep pocket and main fabric straight by using a fine double-pointed knitting needle to pick up alternate stitches along the main fabric. Catching 1 stitch from edge of pocket and 1 stitch from knitting needle alternately, slip-stitch around 3 sides.

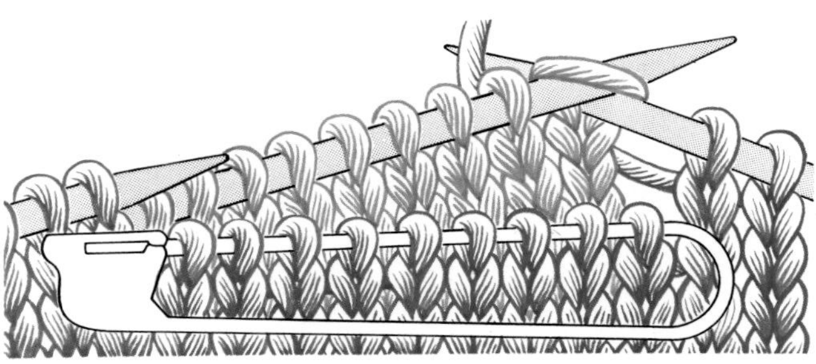

Inserted horizontal pocket

1 Using same size needles as for main fabric, work lining in st st ending with P row. Leave sts on a holder.

2 Work main garment fabric until deep enough to insert pocket, ending with WS row.

3 Work next row until you reach position for opening. Slip number of sts required for opening onto a holder; these correspond in number to the lining sts.

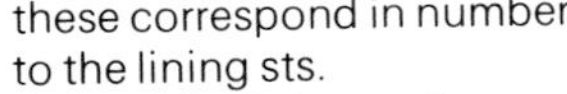

4 Transfer lining sts from holder to spare needle. Place RS of lining to WS of main fabric. Work across lining sts—incorporating them into main fabric—and to end of row.

5 Complete main fabric.

6 Neaten slit in main fabric; with RS facing, rejoin yarn to sts on holder. Work ½–1in (2–3cm) rib or garter st.

7 Complete pocket by stitching down 3 sides of lining on WS of work; secure side edges of pocket top by slip-stitching them down.

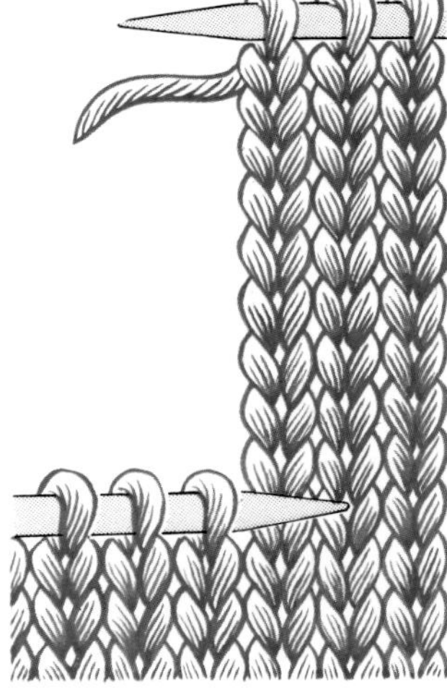

Inserted vertical pocket

1 To get the right depth calculate the exact number of rows necessary for the opening on main fabric. Work this number in lining using the same size needles and st st; bind off and leave on one side.

2 Work main fabric until you reach pocket position, ending with a WS row.

3 Work next row until you reach position for opening. Turn and work the number of rows for the side of the opening on this 1st section only, ending with a WS row. Break off yarn.

4 Rejoin yarn to rem sts and work same number of rows on this 2nd section, ending with WS row. Break off yarn.

5 With RS of work facing, rejoin yarn to 1st section and K across all the sts to close the opening. Complete fabric.

6 RH front of garment: pick up sts along 1 st section worked; LH front: along 2nd section worked. Using same needles as for garment waistband rib ½–1in (2–3cm) to finish opening.

7 Place RS of lining to WS of main fabric and join along other edge of opening.

8 Sew around other sides of lining; slip-stitch sides of rib to main fabric.

Buttonholes

Plan buttonholes before you begin knitting: take into consideration the style of your garment, the size of button and the width of any buttonhole band when you decide which type to work. The fineness or thickness of the yarn should dictate how you need to finish or strengthen buttonholes, or whether you can leave them as they are.

Vertical buttonhole
Make on pocket flaps or on a narrow buttonhole band.

1 Work to buttonhole position, ending at CF edge.

2 Work next row to position for opening; turn and, on 1st section only, work sufficient rows for depth of opening, ending with a WS row. Break off yarn.

3 With RS facing, rejoin yarn to 1st section and work same no. of rows on these sts; then K across all sts to close opening.

Simple eyelet buttonhole
This is the smallest, simplest buttonhole and is mainly used for children's clothes; it can be worked anywhere on a garment.

1 With RS of work facing, work to position of buttonhole.

2 Depending on stitch pattern being worked, put yarn forward, over or around the needle (see decorative increasing p222) to make a stitch, and decrease by knitting next 2 stitches together to compensate for the made stitch.

3 When finishing, overcast the small round hole to strengthen it, inserting needle between stitches as shown.

Horizontal buttonhole
Work this buttonhole on a separate buttonhole band and sew it to your coat or cardigan when finishing. If the band is in rib, bind off ribwise.

1 With RS of work facing, work to position of buttonhole – usually 3 or 4 sts from the edge. Bind off 3 or more sts according to size of button. Work to end of row.

2 On next row work to last st before the bound off sts. First increase by working into front and back of this st, then turn knitting and on RS cast on 1 st less than you bound off in the previous row – this prevents an unsightly loop at one end. Turn knitting to WS again and work to end of row.

Finishing and reinforcing buttonholes
Allthough buttonholes in a ribbed band can be left as they are, most buttonholes need to be finished off with buttonhole stitch or a ribbon facing; this not only gives a professional finish to a garment but strengthens and prevents wear. Work buttonhole stitch with matching sewing thread; working too few stitches can make a buttonhole smaller, but working too many stitches closely together can stretch and distort the buttonhole edges.

Buttonhole stitch

1 Use a darning needle threaded with the same yarn or with matching sewing thread.

2 Work buttonhole stitch (see p18) along both sides of horizontal and of vertical buttonholes. Finish both ends with 3 straight stitches.

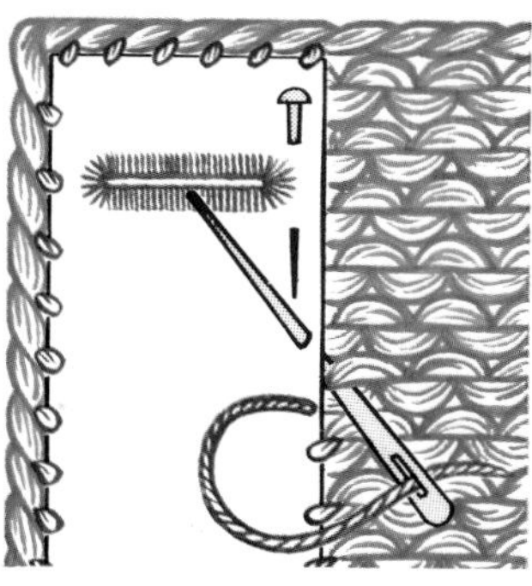

Ribbon facing
Choose a grosgrain ribbon wide enough to cover the buttonholes with ½in (1cm) left over at either side and allowing a ½in (1cm) overlap at each end of band. When measuring ribbon length, don't stretch the knitted fabric. Cut buttonhole and button-band facings together so that they match.

1 Fold under seams at either end of ribbon and pin in place on WS of knitting, easing in the knitted fabric and checking that buttonholes are correctly spaced.

2 Pin the ribbon at each side of every buttonhole to keep it firm.

3 Slip-stitch all 4 sides of ribbon to band, using an ordinary sewing needle and matching sewing thread.

4 Carefully cut through the buttonholes in the ribbon so that they are exactly the same size as the knitted ones.

5 Using sewing thread secure the knitted and ribbon buttonhole edges together with buttonhole stitch.

Basic sweaters

Changing necklines and sleeve styles makes all the difference to a simple sweater pattern – directions for the blue turtle neck are given here; see p240 for other variations. You could also substitute different stitches – but check gauge carefully first: heavy textures like blackberry stitch make a much tighter gauge and use more yarn than stockinette stitch.

You will need

- 1 pair each no. 3 and no. 4 needles
- 1 set of double-pointed no. 3 needles
- 10/11/12/15oz (250/275/300/375g) sports yarn

Size

chest	24	26	28	30in
	(61	66	71	76cm)
length	13	$14\frac{1}{2}$	16	$17\frac{3}{4}$in
	(33	37	41	45cm)
long	11	12	$13\frac{1}{4}$	$14\frac{1}{2}$in
sleeve	(28	31	34	37cm)

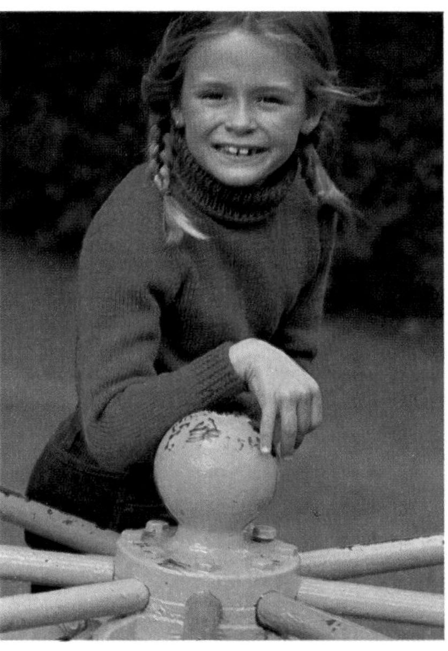

Back (all versions)
With no. 3 needles cast on 75/81/87/93 sts and beginning 1st row with K1, work in K1, P1 rib for 2in (5cm), ending with a WS row. Change to no. 4 needles and beg with a K row cont in st st until work measures 8/9/10/11½in (20/23/26/29cm) from beg, ending with a WS row.
Shape armholes Bind off 4 sts at beg of next 2 rows, then 2 sts at beg of next 2 rows. Dec 1 st at each end of next and foll 3/4/5/6 alt rows (55/59/63/67 sts). Cont without shaping until armholes measure 5/5½/6/6½in (13/14/15/16cm), ending with a WS row.
Shape shoulders Bind off 5/5/6/6 sts at beg of next 4 rows, then 5/6/5/6 sts at beg of next 2 rows. Leave rem 25/27/29/31 sts on holder.

Front (turtle neck)
Work as for back until armhole measures 3/3½/4/4½in (8/9/10/11cm), ending with a WS row.
Shape neck Next row: K23/24/25/26, turn and leave rem sts on spare needle. Bind off 2 sts at beg of next and foll alt row, then dec 1 st on every alt row until 15/16/17/18 sts rem. Cont without shaping until armhole measures the same as on back, ending at armhole edge.
Shape shoulder Bind off 5/5/6/6 sts at beg of next and foll alt row, then rem 5/6/5/6 sts.
Return to the sts on spare needle; sl first 9/11/13/15 sts onto holder, rejoin yarn and K to end. Cont to match first side.

Long sleeves
With no. 3 needles cast on 37/39/41/43 sts and work in rib as on back for 2in (5cm), ending with a WS row. Change to no. 4 needles and beg with a K row cont in st st, inc 1 at each end of every 7th row until there are 57/61/65/69 sts, then cont without shaping until sleeve measures 11/12/13/14½in (28/31/34/37cm), ending with a WS row.
Shape top Bind off 4 sts at beg of next 2 rows, then 2 sts at beg of next 2 rows. Dec 1 st at each end of next and foll 6/7/8/9 alt rows, ending with a WS row. Bind off 2 sts at beg of next 8/8/10/10 rows, then 3 sts at beg of next 2 rows. Bind off rem 9/11/9/11 sts. (For short sleeves see p240.)

Turtle neck
Join shoulder seams. With set of no. 3 needles and RS facing, K 25/27/29/31 sts, K up 20 sts down left front neck, K 9/11/13/15 front neck sts, then K up 20 sts up right front neck (74/78/82/86 sts). Cont in rounds of K1, P1 rib for 6in (15cm) or length required. Bind off very loosely ribwise. (For crew neck work 1½in (4cm) rib, then fold in half to inside and slip-stitch.)

Finishing
Press lightly with a warm iron over a damp cloth according to type of yarn. Join side and sleeve seams. Press seams lightly.

Neckbands

Neckbands, providing a finish to the neck edges of a sweater, are generally worked when the main pieces are complete. Although published patterns give you specific directions on how to work a specific style, they don't usually explain exactly how to pick up stitches (see below) or how to achieve the variations within neckband styles. These two pages look at the basic principles of the round neck, V-neck and square neck, and then give you specific directions for making the variations on the basic blue sweater pattern shown on p238.

Knitting up stitches from straight or curved edges
When you are shaping a garment at neckband or underarms the easiest method of working horizontal edges is not to bind stitches off but to keep them on a stitch holder until you need them. You then simply slip them onto the working needle and work your neckband. On horizontal or bound-off edges you normally need to pick up 1 loop for each stitch. The diagrams show picking up stitches on vertical and curved edges, where you need to count the number of rows on the main fabric to make sure that you pick up the correct number of stitches and that you do this evenly. On a vertical edge this number may correspond exactly to the number of stitches to be picked up, in which case you simply K up 1 stitch per row. Otherwise, mark main fabric with pins at regular intervals of, say, 2in (5cm); then K up an equal number of stitches between each pair of pins, on average 1 stitch for every 2 rows.

Method
1 Use 1 knitting needle and a new ball of yarn. With RS of work facing you (unless otherwise stated) insert needle from front to back under horizontal loop formed by bound-off stitch or, on a vertical edge, between stitches as shown in diagrams.
2 Leaving 4in (10cm) end of yarn to darn in later keep yarn at back of work and wind it under and over needle to form loop.
3 Draw this loop through to RS of fabric so that it stays on needle and forms a stitch.
4 K up required no. of sts in this way, picking up 1 loop for each st.

Square necks
This neckline needs very little shaping. It can be as deep as you require but should be 6–8in (15–20cm) wide, depending on size of garment. Finish with garter stitch or ribbing but make sure bound-off edge will slip over the head easily.

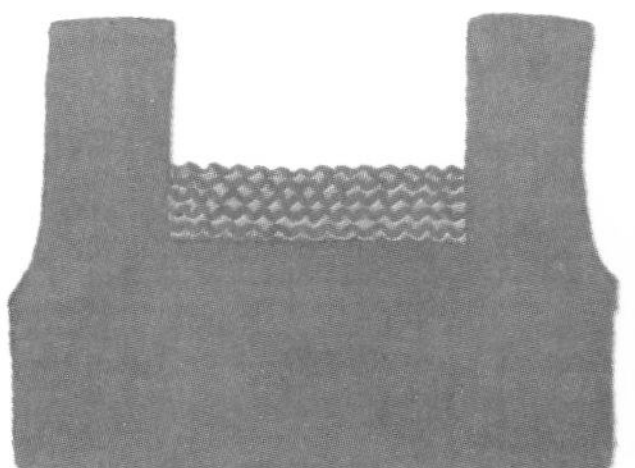

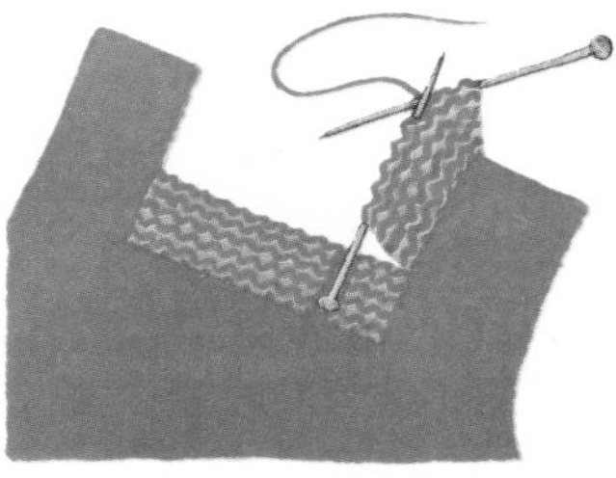

Garter stitch Decide how many sts you require for width of neckline. Cont working across each row in pat, but on these CF sts work in g st until horizontal part of neckband is required depth. Bind off neckband sts and complete garment on each side of neck separately. Using same needles as for main fabric, K up sts along sides of neck K sides to same depth of g st as on CF neckband; then bind off. Neatly slip-stitch row ends at CF in position. Finish back neckband separately. Join shoulder and neckband seams.

Ribbing Miter corners to make neckband lie flat. Leave center sts, preferably an odd no., on a holder and complete each side of neck separately. Either join both shoulder seams and pick up neckband sts with a set of 4 needles or join one seam and use a pair of needles. Use needles 2 sizes smaller than for main fabric. Pick up an odd no. of sts from sides and back of work so that total no. of sts in neckband is even. To miter corners mark each corner st with a loop of colored thread. On RS of work always K marked corner sts, whether you work in rows or rounds. Dec 1 st at either side of corner st on every row or round with dec sts slanting toward corners. Bind off ribwise, dec at corners as usual.

V-necks
V-neck shaping usually starts at same level as underarm shaping; divide work at CF and work each side of neck separately. For traditional neckband leave CF st on safety pin; for overlapped neckband K2 CF sts tog; then work to end of row.

Neck shaping Dec from center by working 2 sts tog every 3–4 rows, depending on gauge, so one side of V forms between CF and shoulder line. Return to sts at CF and complete 2nd side to match 1st, but be careful not to work armhole shaping at neck edge. For neatest band, rib with a set of 4 needles, joining both shoulder seams first. Alternatively, use 2 needles and leave one shoulder seam open. For either method use needles 2 sizes smaller than for main fabric. In the traditional V-neck style the CF st carries up through the neckband to form a vertical rib; dec at either side of this st to give effect of diagonal lines of rib converging on a central point. The same ribbed neckband can be overlapped at CF and requires no mitering. Join shoulder seams and pick up sts starting from the CF dec, using a set of 4 needles. Rib neckband to the required depth, working back and forth in rows and always turning your work at CF point. To finish, overlap neckband row ends at CF and neatly slip-stitch together.

Round necks
A turtle neck is simply a doubled-over extension of a crew neckband. Finish a round neck with either, worked in single or double rib to the depth you want. It should fit comfortably and the bound-off edge should not be too tight to slip over the head easily.
Neck shaping
Start shaping front neck about $1\frac{1}{2}$in (4cm) below shoulders. Bind-off, or leave on a holder, CF sts; then dec sts at either side until they meet the shoulder line, as described in pat. Often

back neck shaping is non-existent or is only about 1in (2cm) deep; again instructions usually specify. Use needles 2 sizes smaller than used for main garment. If you work neckband on 2 needles, leave one shoulder seam open and work in rows; with 4 needles join both shoulder seams and work in rounds (see p250).
Crew neck Pick up sts with RS of work facing. When you

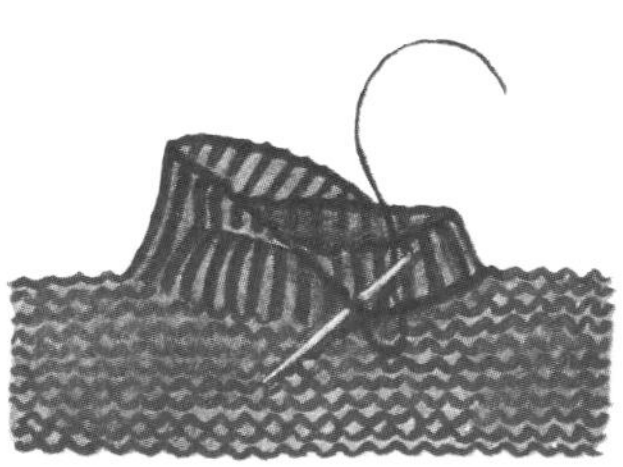

come to pick up any sts from a holder, take the free LH needle and slip them onto this from left to right before working them. Work to required depth and bind off very loosely but neatly ribwise.
Double crew neckband Rib twice required depth and bind-off loosely ribwise. Fold neckband in half to WS of garment and slip-stitch bound-off edge in position to

the original neckline.
Turtle neck For a good fit start the neckband with needles 2 sizes smaller than those used for main fabric and rib one-third of total length; change to needles only one size smaller than used for garment and rib another third; complete to required length with needles used for main fabric. Bind off loosely ribwise.

Basic sweater variations

Green sweater (square neck)
Front Work as for back (p238) until armhole measures $2/2\frac{1}{2}/3/3\frac{1}{2}$in (6/7/8/9cm), ending with a WS row.
Shape neck Next row: K15/16/17/18, turn and leave rem sts on spare needle. Cont without shaping until armhole measures the same as on back, ending at armhole edge.
Shape shoulder Bind off 5/5/6/6 sts at beg of next and foll alt row, then rem 5/6/5/6 sts. Return to the sts on spare needle; sl first

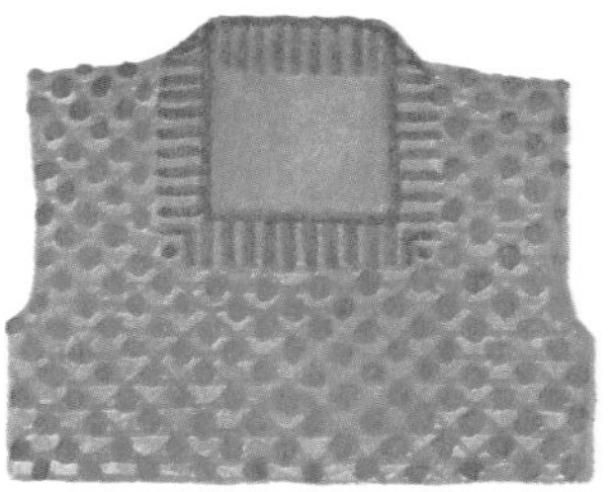

25/27/29/31 sts onto holder, rejoin yarn and K to end. Cont to match 1st side.
Neckband Join shoulder seams. With set of no. 3 needles and RS facing,

K25/27/29/31 back neck sts, K up 26 sts down left front neck, K front neck sts, K up 26 sts up right front neck (102/106/110/114 sts). Cont in rounds of K1, P1 rib, working P2 tog, K1, P2 tog at each front corner only on every round, for $\frac{1}{2}$in (1cm). Bind off ribwise, still dec.

Short sleeves
With no. 3 needles cast on 49/53/57/61 sts and work in rib as on back for 2in (5cm), ending with a WS row and inc 8 sts evenly across last row (57/61/65/69 sts). Change to no. 4 needles and beg with a K row cont in st st until work measures $4/4/4\frac{1}{2}/5$in (10/11/12/13cm) from beg, ending with a WS row. Shape cap as for long sleeve.

Red and yellow sweaters (V-necks)
Front Work as for back (p238) to armholes, ending with a WS row.
Shape armholes and divide for neck Next row: Bind off 4 sts, K33/36/39/42, turn and leave rem 38/41/44/47 sts on spare needle. Next row: P. Cont to dec at armhole edge to match back, at same time dec at neck edge on next and every foll 3rd row until 15/16/17/18 sts rem. Cont straight shaping until armhole measures same as on back ending at armhole edge.
Shape shoulder Bind off 5/5/6/6 sts at beg of next and foll alt row, then rem 5/6/5/6 sts. Return to the sts on spare needle. If working

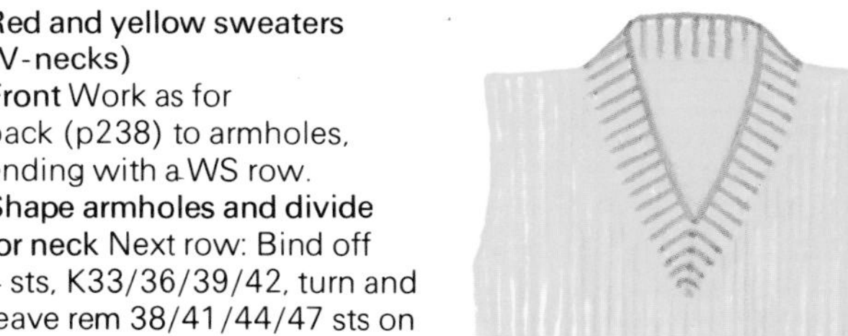

overlapped neckband, K2 tog, K to end; if working traditional neckband, sl 1st st onto safety pin, then K to end. Cont to match 1st side.
Traditional V-neckband Join shoulder seams. With set of no. 3 needles and RS facing, K25/27/29/31 back neck sts, K up 36/39/42/45 sts down left front neck, K center front st from pin, then K up

36/39/42/45 sts up right front neck (98/106/114/122 sts). Cont in rounds of K1, P1 rib, working P2 tog, K1, P2 tog at CF on every round, for 1in (2cm). Bind off ribwise, still dec.
Overlapped V-neckband Join shoulder seams. With set of no. 3 needles and RS facing, start at CF, K up 36/39/42/45 sts up right front neck, K25/27/29/31 back

neck sts, then K up 36/39/42/45 sts down left front neck (97/105/113/121 sts). Turn. Beg RS rows with P1, work in rows of K1, P1 rib for 1in (2cm). Bind off ribwise.
Armhole borders With no. 3 needles and RS facing, K up 75/83/91/99 sts around armhole. Beg WS rows with P1, work in K1, P1 rib for 1in (2cm). Bind off ribwise.

Finishing

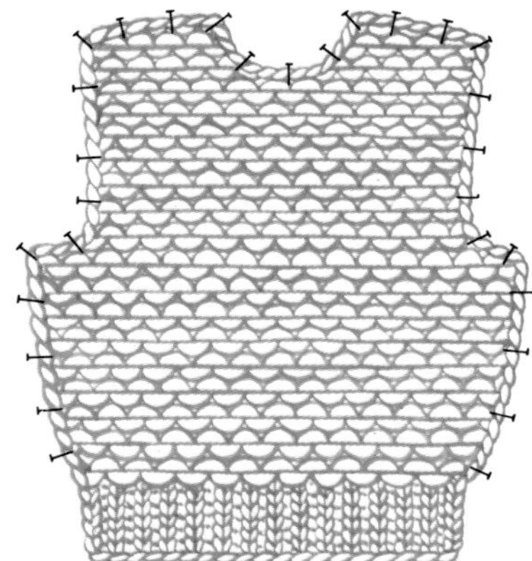

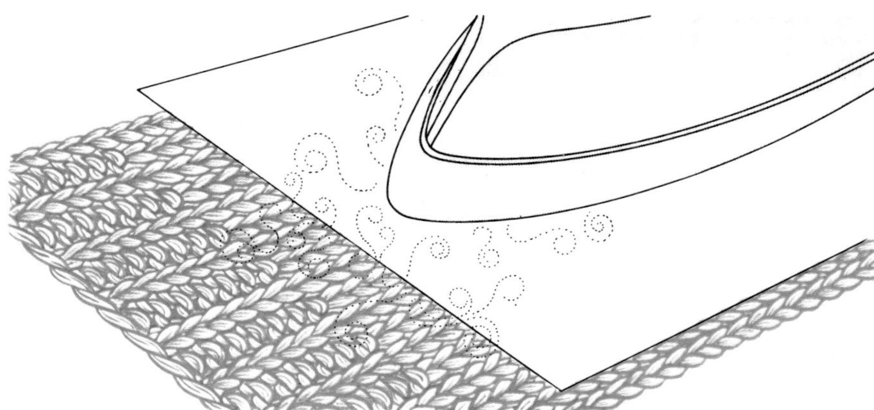

Blocking
By pinning down the sections of a knitted garment before pressing you can make sure that they are the correct shape and size.

1 Place each piece RS down on an ironing pad, which you can improvise with old folded blankets covered with a cotton sheet (an ironing board is too narrow to lay most knitting out flat).
2 See that stitches and rows run in straight lines and that the fabric is not pulled out of shape.
3 Pin knitting to pad with rustless tailor's pins; avoid stretching knitting, because pins can make the edge fluted.
4 With pins in position, check that measurements tally with those given in pattern.

Pressing
Many modern yarns require no pressing – so always check with directions on the label first. Heavy pressing destroys the quality of many textured yarns or stitch patterns – garter stitch, for example, needs no pressing. Ribbing loses its elasticity when pressed, so if you press a stockinette stitch sweater remember to leave any ribbed edges such as waistband and cuffs free.

1 Place a clean cotton cloth – damp or dry, depending on the pattern directions – over piece to be pressed.
2 Have iron at correct temperature for the type of fiber and lay it gently on top of cloth; don't move it around. Lift iron off again.
3 Repeat this action evenly, but not too heavily, over the whole area.

Seams
When seaming knitting use a darning needle. Work between knitted stitches and avoid splitting the yarn. You may have to use a matching finer yarn to sew items made from nubby or particularly bulky yarns.

Directions are given for right-handed people; if you are left-handed you may prefer to follow the directions in reverse.

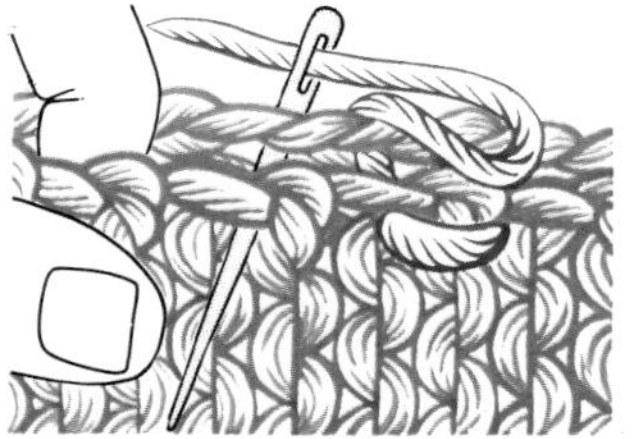

Back-stitch seams are most frequently used for side and sleeve seams of garments. Sew firmly but not too tightly, without stretching knitting.

1 With RS together, work along WS of fabric about 1 stitch in from the edge.
2 To secure the sewing yarn at the RH side, make 2 or 3 small running stitches one on top of the other.
3 With needle at back of work, move it 1 knitted stitch to the left; pull yarn through to front.
4 Move needle across front of work to the right, re-inserting it through to back at the point where you worked the last stitch.
5 Work in this way until the seam is complete.

Flat seams are ideal for joining ribbed sections as they avoid an extra-bulky ridge.

1 Place together the RS of both pieces with your forefinger separating them.
2 Secure sewing thread at RH side. Pass needle first through edge stitch on underside piece, then through corresponding stitch on the top piece and pull yarn through.
3 Work back through next stitch on the top piece to corresponding stitch on the underside piece.
4 Work backward and forward in this way until you complete the seam.

Invisible seams have the advantage of producing a soft edge which does not irritate. They are ideally suited, therefore, to baby clothes.

1 With RS of both sections facing you, secure yarn at lower edge of one piece.
2 Pick up 1 stitch from the other side as shown and pull yarn through.
3 Pass needle back to 1st side and pick up next stitch; pull yarn through.
4 Continue to pick up stitches from alternating sides in this way and pull each stitch up tightly so that it is invisible on RS of work.

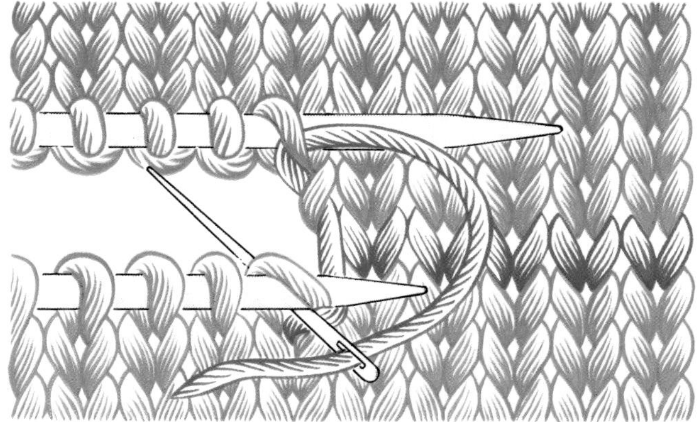

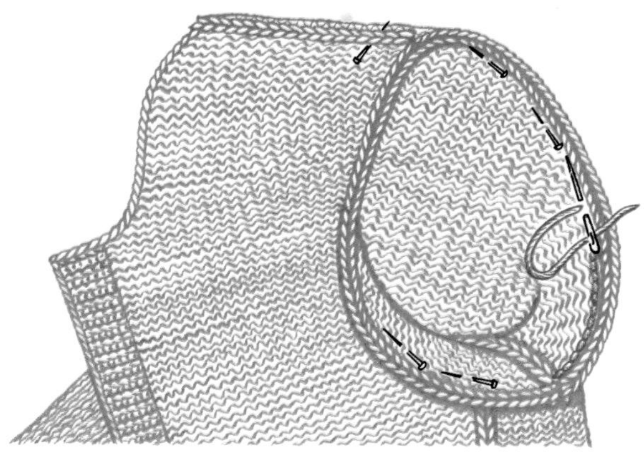

Grafting
This is a method of joining 2 sets of stitches invisibly without first binding them off. It is used on shoulders or the toe of a sock where a conventional seam would be too rigid.
1 Don't bind off the stitches of the 2 pieces to be joined. Leave them on 2 needles, one behind the other, with both points facing to the right and with WS of fabric together. Check that there is an equal number of stitches on both needles.
2 Break off yarn from 1 section leaving approximately 3 times the length of the edge to be woven. Thread yarn into a darning needle.
3 Insert darning needle K-wise through 1st stitch on back needle and pull yarn through; leave the stitch on the knitting needle. Repeat this action through the 1st stitch on the front needle, but slip this stitch off the knitting needle.
4 Insert darning needle P-wise through next stitch on the front needle and pull yarn through. Leave this stitch on the knitting needle. Repeat this action through next stitch on the back needle, but let this stitch slip off the knitting needle.
5 Follow these steps until you use up all the stitches from both needles.

Setting-in sleeves
First join the appropriate shoulder and side seams on the main section. Sew sleeve seam with RS together, then turn sleeve RS out.
1 Mark center top of the sleeve cap. With WS of main section facing you, position sleeve into armhole, starting under center top as shown in diagram.
2 Match and pin together center top of sleeve cap to shoulder seam, and bound-off stitches at underarms.
3 Using a back-stitch seam, sew directly onto the inner edge of the armhole, i.e. WS of the sleeve-cap shaping. Work in a smooth line around curve of armhole, gently easing in any fullness that occurs around sleeve-cap shaping.

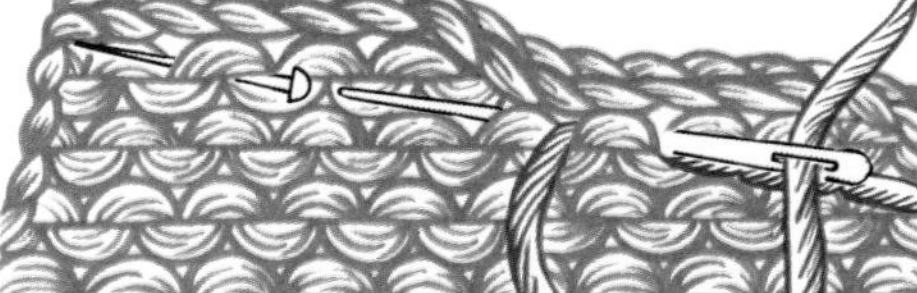

Shoulder seams
1 With RS of the 2 sections together, pin the shoulders, matching any stepped shaping.
2 Back-stitch across the shoulders, following a straight line. For extra strength on heavy outdoor garments, you can reinforce shoulder seams with tape.

Zippers
A zipper is a useful way of finishing back-neck or skirt openings, or, in the case of an open-ended zipper, of making a feature down the front of a jacket or cardigan.
1 Place edges of knitting even with inside edges of zipper teeth, taking care not to overlap the teeth.
2 Pin in position carefully to avoid stretching knitting.
3 Use thread that matches the yarn and an ordinary sewing needle. With RS of work facing you, sew in the zipper with a back-stitch seam, keeping as close as possible to edge of knitting.
4 For a closed zipper: work in a straight line down zipper from top to bottom. Make a few extra stitches across bottom end of zipper to anchor it and continue up the other side to complete.
For an open-ended zipper: keep the fastener closed while sewing so that both sides match and are not pulled out of shape. Work in a straight line from top to bottom.

Stripes

A combination of simple stitches and colorful yarns can produce a variety of regular, irregular, broken, unbroken, narrow and wide stripes – the possibilities are unlimited, and a beginner can quickly master the techniques involved. An easy way to make a sweater design individual is to work a plain pattern in stripes. Stripes don't alter the gauge unless you carry yarns across the back, so there is nothing complicated to calculate. Working in stripes is a good way to use up a quantity of left-over yarn, but do make sure your yarns match each other in thickness. To calculate yarn quantities, look at the rough proportions of one color to another in your fabric; for two colors in all-over stripes of equal depth you will need half the total yarn requirement in each of the two colors.

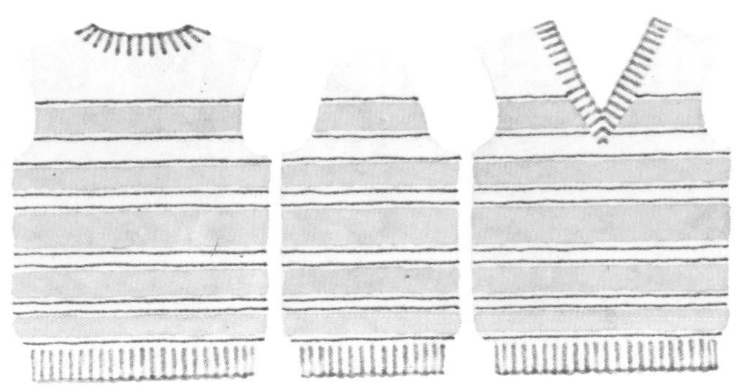

Matching stripes
To make stripes and other patterns match across armholes you should aim to do your initial armhole shaping at exactly the same point in your stripe sequence on both back or rront and sleeve. When sleeves are longer than main garment, calculate from the gauge how many rows you will work before you begin top shaping, and work backward from this to see which row in your stripe sequence to begin with. This technique also applies to large pattern repeats like cables of Aran motifs.

Knitting 2 rows per color in g st produces a single horizontal ridge in that color on RS of work. A random or controlled sequence of these narrow stripes is an attractive way to use up oddments of different-colored yarns; provided that these are of equal weight, sports yarn can be mixed with mohair or nubby yarns for a striped effect combining color with texture. You may choose to emphasize the 'reverse' side of the fabric with its more intricate pattern of broken stripes.

When striping st st, always change colors at the beginning of a K row; this gives an unbroken line of color on the smooth, K (i.e. RS) of the fabric. (You can, of course, choose to make a feature of the purled ridges and broken lines of the reverse side.) Patterns can consist of regular stripes, each with the same number of rows, or a more random effect where the number of rows in a stripe varies. But an even number of rows per stripe is essential to make the color change fall consistently on a K row.

Changing color

Horizontal stripes Here you will have no problem when joining in a new color; you simply introduce a ball of yarn at the beginning of a row as you would when changing balls (see p226). Don't break off the old color if you need it again within, say, 6 rows; carry it loosely up the side of the work and twist it once round the last color before you use it. As many colors as you need can be carried up the side – don't restrict yourself to just 2.

Vertical stripes You may need to change color several times across a row when knitting vertical stripes. With narrow stripes in 2 colors, twist each yarn as you start to use it with the last color to avoid making a hole. Carry the color not in use loosely across the back of the work – see p264 Vertical stripes more than, say, 5 sts wide require another method, since carrying yarn across the back here is wasteful, and it is difficult to control the gauge. Divide each color into small balls of yarn

before you begin work, and use a separate ball for each stripe. You must twist the yarns together when you change colors to prevent the stripes from separating; if you forget to twist the yarn on even one row, you will make a hole.

Looping yarns on K and P rows Each ball of yarn is at back of work on a K row or front on a P row, until you need it. K or P the last st in the 1st color, then loop

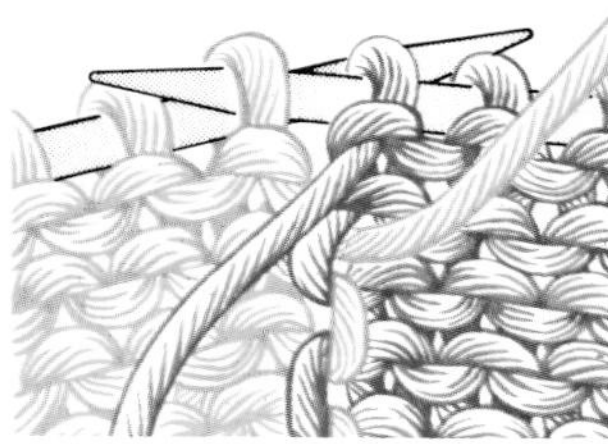

this end of yarn over the top of the 2nd color and put it down. Pick up the 2nd color under the 1st strand and loop it over this strand to work the next st.

Vertical patterns creating a sort of pajama-stripe effect are most effective in st st. This, 1, 2, 3-stitch repeat using 2 colors is a variation on this theme, but keep individual stripes no more than 5 sts wide. The WS shows the yarn not in use being carried across the stripes to form a fabric of double thickness. While this has the advantage of warmth, it uses extra yarn and tends to draw the fabric in; if you stripe an existing pattern in this way, try using needles one size larger to keep the gauge correct.

The technique of looping yarns when changing color (see above) is useful both for vertical stripes and for vertical panels of different color. Because the yarn is not carried across the stripes on the WS but is twisted together when you change color, wider vertical stripes create only a single-thickness fabric, which gives you no particular gauge problem. Remember to use a separate ball of yarn for each stripe. Changing color horizontally within the vertical stripes can produce a patchwork effect making an attractive all-over fabric similar to Jacquard (p270).

Crossed stitch
This design uses 2 colors, coded as A and B. Using A, cast on an odd no. of sts.
1st row (RS) Using A, K to end.
2nd row As 1st.
3rd row Using B, *K1, sl 1P-wise, rep from * to last st, K1.
4th row Using B, *K1, yfwd, sl 1 P-wise, ybk, rep from * to last st, K1.
5th–6th rows Using A, K to end.
7th row Using B, *sl 1 P-wise, K1, rep from * to last st, sl 1 P-wise.
8th row Using B, *sl 1 P-wise, ybk, K1, yfwd, rep from * to last st, sl 1 P-wise.
These 8 rows form the pat.

Ladder stitch
This design uses 2 colors, coded as A and B. Using A, cast on a multiple of 6 sts plus 5 extra.
1st row (RS) Using A, K2, *sl 1 P-wise, K5, rep from * to last 3 sts, sl 1 P-wise, K2.
2nd row Using A, P2, *sl 1 P-wise, P5, rep from * to last 3 sts, sl 1 P-wise, P2.
3rd row Using B, *K5, sl 1 P-wise, rep from * to last 5 sts, K5.
4th row Using B, *K5, yfwd, sl 1 P-wise, ybk, rep from * to last 5 sts, K5. These 4 rows form the pat.

Brick stitch
This design uses 2 colors, coded as A and B. Using A, cast on a multiple of 4 sts plus 1 extra.
1st row (RS) Using A, K to end.
2nd row As 1st.
3rd row Using B, sl 1 P-wise, *K3, sl 1 P-wise, rep from * to end.
4th row Using B, sl 1, *P3, sl 1, rep from * to end.
5th–6th rows As 1st.
7th row Using B K2, *sl 1 P-wise, K3, rep from * to last 3 sts, sl 1 P-wise, K2.
8th row Using B, P2, *sl 1, P3, rep from * to last 3 sts, sl 1, P2. These 8 rows form the pat.

Slip-stitch patterns
Tweed patterns like those on the opposite page are the result of combining 2-color horizontal stripes with slip stitches. They look colorful and intricate, but are quick and easy to knit. You can use more than 2 colors without difficulty, since with each color change you carry the yarn up the side of your work.

Chevron stripes
The undulating edge which is a feature of any chevron pattern forms when you alternately increase and then decrease stitches at intervals across each RS row. To make the chevron points deeper, work fewer stitches between the shaping positions; to make them shallower, work more stitches between these positions. If you do this, remember to adjust the multiple of stitches that you cast on accordingly. E.g. to make the narrow chevrons below deeper, cast on a multiple of, say, 12 sts instead of 14 and K4 instead of K5; to make them shallower cast on a multiple of, say, 16 sts and K6 instead of K5.

Diagonal stripes
When stripes are not more than 4 stitches wide you don't need to use separate balls of yarn for each color, since the yarn not in use strands across the back of the work (see p264 for further details of stranding). There is no need to loop yarns when you change colors as on narrow vertical stripes; the fact that the colors move across 1 stitch per row prevents holes from forming in the fabric. On the whole, diagonal stripes look best in the smooth fabric of stockinette stitch.

Narrow chevron stripes
This is a good way to use up remnants of yarn, working one garter-stitch ridge in each color. If you want to use that color again within about 6–8 rows, carry it up the side of the work; otherwise break it off and weave in the ends. The WS of the fabric is an attractive mass of broken stripes. Using any color, cast on a multiple of 14 sts plus 3 extra.
1st row (RS) K1, K2 tog, *K5, yfwd, K1, yfwd, K5, sl 1, K2 tog, psso, rep from * to last 14 sts, K5, yfwd, K1, yfwd, K5, sl 1, K1, psso, K1.
2nd row K1, P1, *K5, K1 tbl, K1, K1 tbl, K5, P1, rep from * to last st, K1. These 2 rows form the pat. Always change colors at the end of a 2nd pat row.

Narrow diagonal stripes
This design uses 2 colors, coded as A and B. Using A, cast on a multiple of 5 sts plus 3 extra.
1st row (RS) Using A, K3, *using B, K2, using A, K3, rep from * to end.
2nd row Using B, P1, *using A, P3, using B, P2, rep from * to last 2 sts, using A, P2.
3rd row Using A, K1, *using B, K2, using A, K3, rep from * to last 2 sts, using B, K2.
4th row Using A, P1, using B, P2, *using A, P3, using B, P2, rep from * to end.
Cont in this way, moving the stripes 1 st to the right on K rows and 1 st to the left on P rows.

Wider chevron stripes
If you work chevron stripes in stockinette, you can emphasize both the upward- and downward-pointing V-shapes by making decorative vertical lines of increasing and decreasing. Cast on a multiple of 13 sts plus 2 extra.
1st row (RS) *K2, M1, K4, sl 1 P-wise, K2 tog, psso, K4, M1, rep from * to last 2 sts, K2.
2nd row P to end.
These 2 rows form the pat. Rep them throughout, changing colors on a 1st row and carrying the yarns up the side of the work.

Chevron suit

Gauge 220
Following patterns 226
Finishing 242
Stripes 246

no. 2
38
38
chevron
pat

The pink tones of this sophisticated suit with a period flavor echo the chevron stripes on the previous page. A medium-weight cotton or synthetic yarn of the right gauge makes a firm fabric whose texture (see detail below) would look equally attractive in a single color. Choose your own combination of colors, and if you decide on stripes have one color dominating in the garter-stitch belt and edging. Making the stripes slightly deeper toward the bottom of the skirt gives a flattering effect.

Size

bust	$31\frac{1}{2}$	$33\frac{1}{2}$	$35\frac{1}{2}$in
	(80	85	90cm)
hips	$33\frac{1}{2}$	$35\frac{1}{2}$	$37\frac{1}{2}$in
	(85	90	95cm)
jacket length	26	26	$26\frac{1}{2}$in
	(66	66	67cm)
sleeve seam	18in		
	(46cm)		
skirt length	30in		
(adjustable)	(77cm)		

You will need
approx. 36/42/48oz (900/1050/1200g) medium-weight cotton yarn (about equal quantities of each of 3 colors for stripes)
1 pair each no. 0 and no. 2 needles
elastic to fit waist

Jacket back
With no. 0 needles cast on 135/154/154 sts. K 8 rows.
Change to no. 2 needles. Cont in pat.
1st row (RS): K2, *M1, K7, sl 1, K2 tog, psso, K7, M1, K2, rep from * to end.
2nd row: P to end.
Rep these 2 rows until work measures 19in (48cm), ending with a WS row.
Shape armholes Bind off 11 sts at beg of next 2 rows. Allowing for decs and incs in chevron pat, dec 1 st at each end of next and foll 7 alt rows (97/116/116 sts). Cont without shaping until armholes measure $7/7/7\frac{1}{2}$in (18/18/19cm), ending with a WS row.
Shape shoulders Bind off 7 sts at beg of next 6 rows, 5/9/9 sts at beg of next 2 rows and 5/10/10 sts at beg of foll 2 rows. Bind off rem 35/36/36 sts.

Left front
With no. 0 needles cast on 97/97/116 sts. Cont as given for back until work measures 10/10/8in (25/25/20cm) from beg ending with a RS row.
Shape front edge Keeping pat correct, dec 1 st at front edge on next and every foll 3rd row until work matches back to underarm, ending with a WS row.
Shape armhole Cont to dec at front edge, bind off 11 sts at beg of next row, then dec 1 st at armhole edge on foll 8 alt rows. Cont to dec at front edge only until 31/40/40 sts rem, then work without shaping until front matches back to shoulder, ending at armhole edge.
Shape shoulder Bind off 7 sts at beg of next and foll 2 alt rows, 5/9/9 sts at beg of foll alt row and 5/10/10 sts on foll alt row.

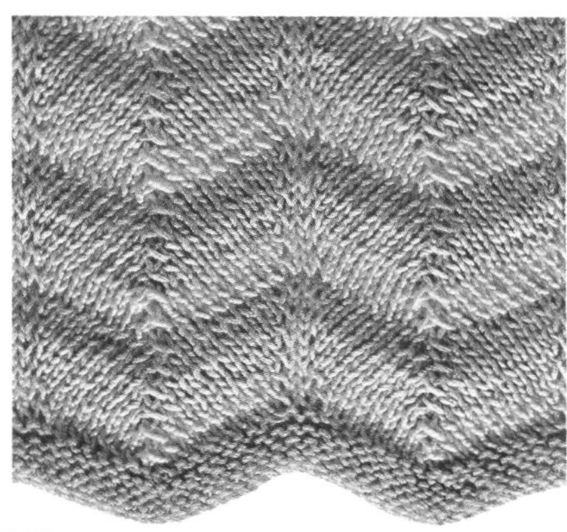

Right front
Work to match left front, reversing shaping.

Sleeves
With no. 0 needles cast on 116/116/135 sts. Cont as given for back until sleeve measures approx 18in (46cm), ending with same pat row as back.
Shape cap Bind off 11 sts at beg of next 2 rows. Dec 1 st at each end of next and every foll alt row until 38/38/63 sts rem, ending with a P row.
3rd size only Dec 1 st at each end of every row until 47 sts rem.
All sizes Bind off 4 sts at beg of next 2 rows and 4/4/5 sts at beg of next 4 rows. Bind off rem 14/14/19 sts.

Front band
With no. 0 needles cast on 11 sts. Work in g st until band is long enough to go up front edge, around neck and down other front. Bind off.

Belt
With no. 0 needles cast on 14 sts. Work about 60in (155cm) g st. Bind off.

Skirt back and front (alike)
With no. 2 needles cast on 154/154/173 sts for waist edge and work downward. Work 4in (10cm) pat as given for jacket back, ending with a WS row. Next row (inc): K2, *M1, K1, M1, K6, sl 1, K2 tog, psso, K6, M1, K1, M1, K2, rep from * to end (170/170/191 sts). Cont in pat, working extra sts into pat, until work measures 8in (20cm) from beg, ending with a WS row.
Next row (inc): K2, *M1, K1, M1, K7, sl 1, K2 tog, psso, K7, M1, K1, M1, K2, rep from * to end (186/186/209 sts). Work until skirt measures 13in (30cm) from beg, ending with a WS row.
Next row (inc): K2, *M1, K1, M1, K8, sl 1, K2 tog, psso, K8, M1, K1, M1, K2, rep from * to end (202/202/227 sts). Cont to inc in this way every 4in (10cm) until skirt measures approx 30in (77cm), or length required, ending with a WS row. Work 9 rows g st. Bind off loosely.

Finishing Press on WS, omitting front band and belt, according to type of yarn. Join shoulder, side and sleeve seams. Set in sleeves. Sew front band in position. Join skirt seams. Fold first 8 rows of pat to WS to form casing over elastic; slip-stitch in position. Press seams.

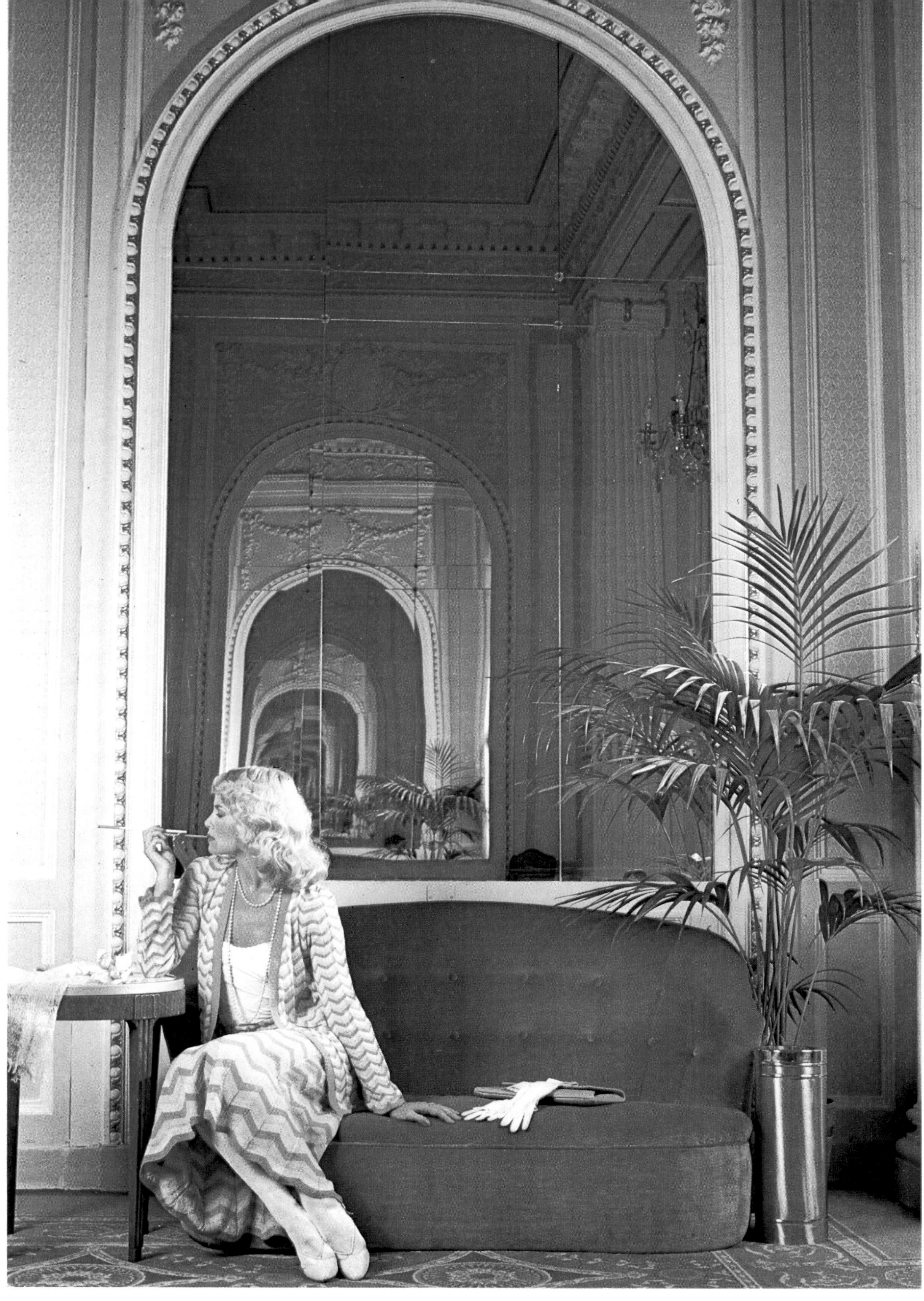

Knitting in rounds

This method of knitting is the traditional way of making socks, gloves, hats—even sweaters such as the fisherman's guernsey on p256—since it produces a seamless tubular fabric. You can use either a set of double-pointed needles or a circular needle; both have advantages and limitations, so you must decide which is the most practical for your purpose. Working in the round can also create flat medallion shapes useful for mats, pillows, shawls, the round base of a tubular duffel bag or the ends of a tube-shaped pillow.

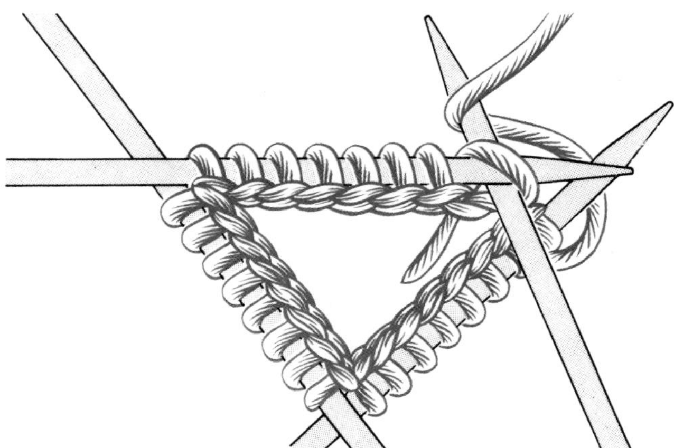

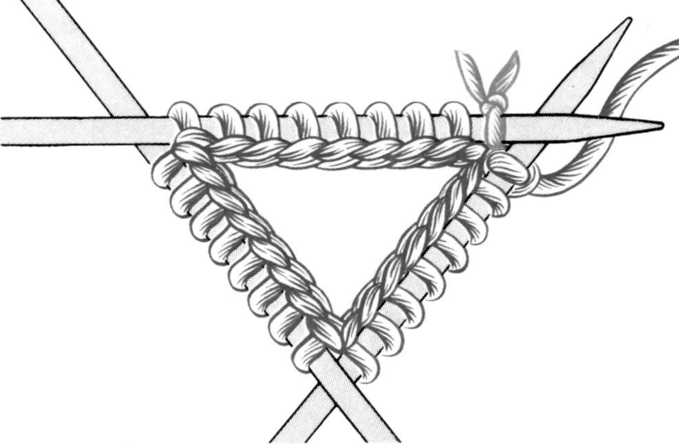

Sets of 4 needles
There are usually 4 double-pointed needles of uniform size in a set. They come in varying lengths, which you choose according to the total number of stitches in a round. You must use a set of needles in tubular knitting when working on relatively small items using less than, say, 80 sts, e.g. gloves or socks, and when beginning a flat medallion shape.

Casting on Either cast all the stitches required on to one needle and then divide them equally among 3 needles, or cast them on to each of the 3 needles separately; leave the 4th needle free for working with in both cases. Cast on (see p216), working the required number of stitches onto the 1st, 2nd and 3rd needles. Form the 3 needles into a triangle making sure the stitches are not twisted round the needles or between the needles and work with the 4th needle.

Working method Use the spare needle to work all the stitches on the 1st needle, then the 1st needle to work the stitches on the 2nd needle and so on.
Always pull the yarn tightly across to the 1st stitch of each needle to avoid making a loose stitch. One round is complete when you have worked the stitches on all 3 needles.

Marker loops It is helpful to slip a loop of yarn in a contrasting color from one needle to the next to mark the beginning of each new round.

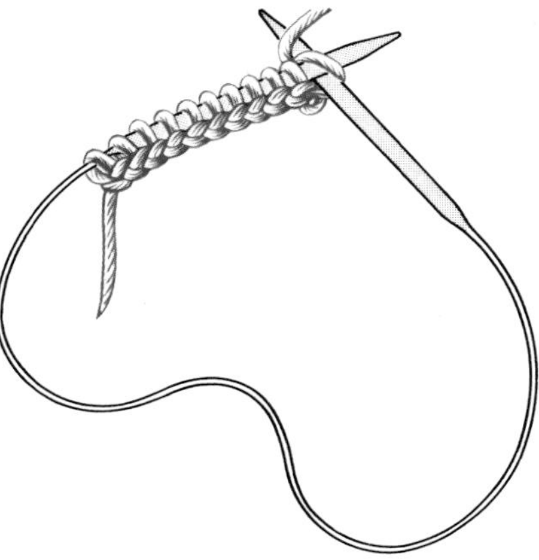

Circular needles
These comprise 2 small rigid shaped needle sections joined together by a flexible strip of nylon wire and are ideal for large-scale tubular knitting such as sweaters and pillow covers and for working larger medallions. Their advantage over sets of needles is that stitches don't stretch between needles; you can also work back and forth in rows with them—particularly useful to distribute the weight evenly when working with large numbers of stitches.

Casting on Use circular needles like an ordinary pair, with one section forming the stitches and the other holding the cast-on stitches. Make sure stitches are not twisted around the needles before joining into a round.

Working method Work each stitch in the normal way until you reach the beginning of the round. Use a marker loop as when working with 4 needles (see above) to indicate the beginning of each new round.

Length Circular needles come in the usual sizes but vary in length; the number of stitches and your gauge determine the length you use—the stitches should reach between needle tips without stretching the fabric.
The table shows the minimum number of stitches needed for different needle lengths; each length will hold at least 4 times the minimum number of stitches.

gauge (sts to 4in/ 10cm)	length of needle 16 (40	24 60	32 80	36 90	40in 100cm)
20	80	120	160	180	200
22	88	132	176	198	220
24	96	144	192	216	240
26	104	156	208	234	260
28	112	168	224	252	280
30	120	180	240	270	300
32	128	192	256	288	320
34	136	204	272	306	340
36	144	216	288	324	360

Tubular knitting

Stitch patterns When you work a tubular fabric the RS is always facing you; this has an unusual effect on the basic stitch patterns; the method of forming garter stitch and stockinette stitch in circular knitting is the reverse of that in flat knitting.

Garter stitch Knit 1 round and purl 1 round alternately.

Stockinette stitch Knit every round. The exterior of the tube has the familiar chain-stitch effect, while the interior looks ridged, like reverse stockinette.

Ribbing Knit each knitted stitch and purl each purled stitch in every round. Because the ends of the rounds are adjacent they must match up, so if you begin a round with one or more knitted stitches you must finish with the same number of purled stitches. Don't forget to bind off in rib, and to do so loosely enough for the head to pass through a neckband, for example.

Multiples of stitches

There is no need for the edge stitches that are normally allowed for seams. Use an exact multiple of the number of stitches in the pattern repeat.

Color patterns Tubular knitting is an ideal way of working multi-colored designs. You can easily see whether the pattern is forming correctly since the RS is always facing you. Be specially careful not to strand or weave yarn too tightly on the inside, however; in socks, for example, you must leave enough elasticity to insert the foot.

Stripes Carry the yarn loosely up the inside of tubular knitting, using the same method as given for stripes in flat knitting (see p244). Notice that you get a slightly staggered effect with stripes in rounds since the knitted rounds form a spiral; when you change color the first stitch in the new color is side by side with the last stitch in the old color – the detail above shows how the color change looks on a striped sock.

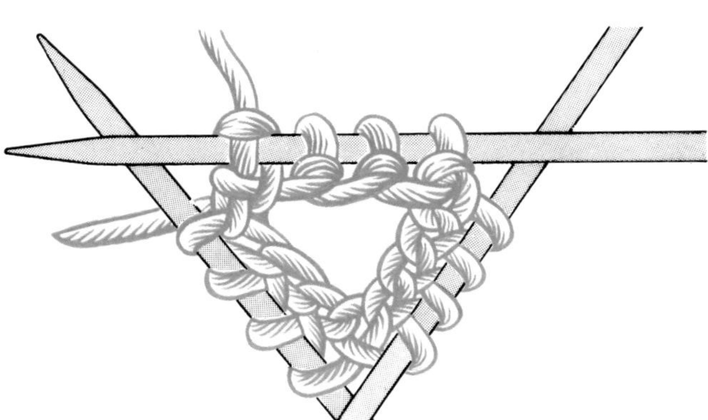

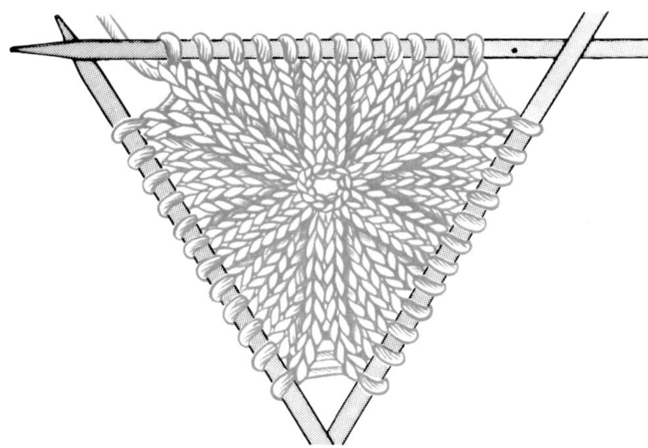

Flat medallion shapes

You can also knit flat medallion shapes in rounds. It is easiest to begin in the center with a small number of stitches and increase at intervals – either invisibly or making a decorative feature of the increasing. By working the increases at even intervals all around you make a flat circle; by increasing at either side of 3, 4, 5 or 6 radii of a circle you can make a triangle, square, pentagon or hexagon respectively.

Casting on Use the 2-needle method producing a looser edge (p216), i.e. working into each stitch. Being careful not to twist the stitches, join the 3 needles into a triangle and knit the first round through the back loops to keep the center flat.

Working method Begin small motifs with a set of 4 needles. You may have to begin using extra needles as your motif grows, or transfer to a circular needle when you have sufficient stitches to reach from one point to the other. But as long as your motif is relatively small it is easiest to manage only 4 needles as in the hexagon in the diagram – the number of sides in the shape makes no difference.

Working multi-sided shapes

Cast on 2 sts per side of shape – e.g. 6 sts for triangle, 8 sts for square, etc. Join into a triangle.

1st round K tbl.

2nd round (Inc 1, K1) to end.

3rd round K.

4th round (Inc 1 twice, K1), to end.

5th–6th rounds K.

7th round (Inc 1, K2, inc 1, K1) to end.

8th–9th rounds K.

10th round (Inc 1, K4, inc 1, K1) to end.

Cont working in this way, inc 1 st at either side of the K radius ribs and working 2 more sts between incs on successive 3rd rounds until the shape is the size you require. Bind off loosely after 2 K rounds.

Circles

Circles require a slightly different formula to flat-sided motifs with increases at regular intervals all around. Cast on 8 sts and work first 3 rounds as given for multi-sided shapes. Inc in every 3rd st on the next round and in every 4th, 5th, 6th st etc on successive 3rd rounds.

Hats

Gauge 220
Following patterns 226
Stripes 244
Knitting in rounds 250

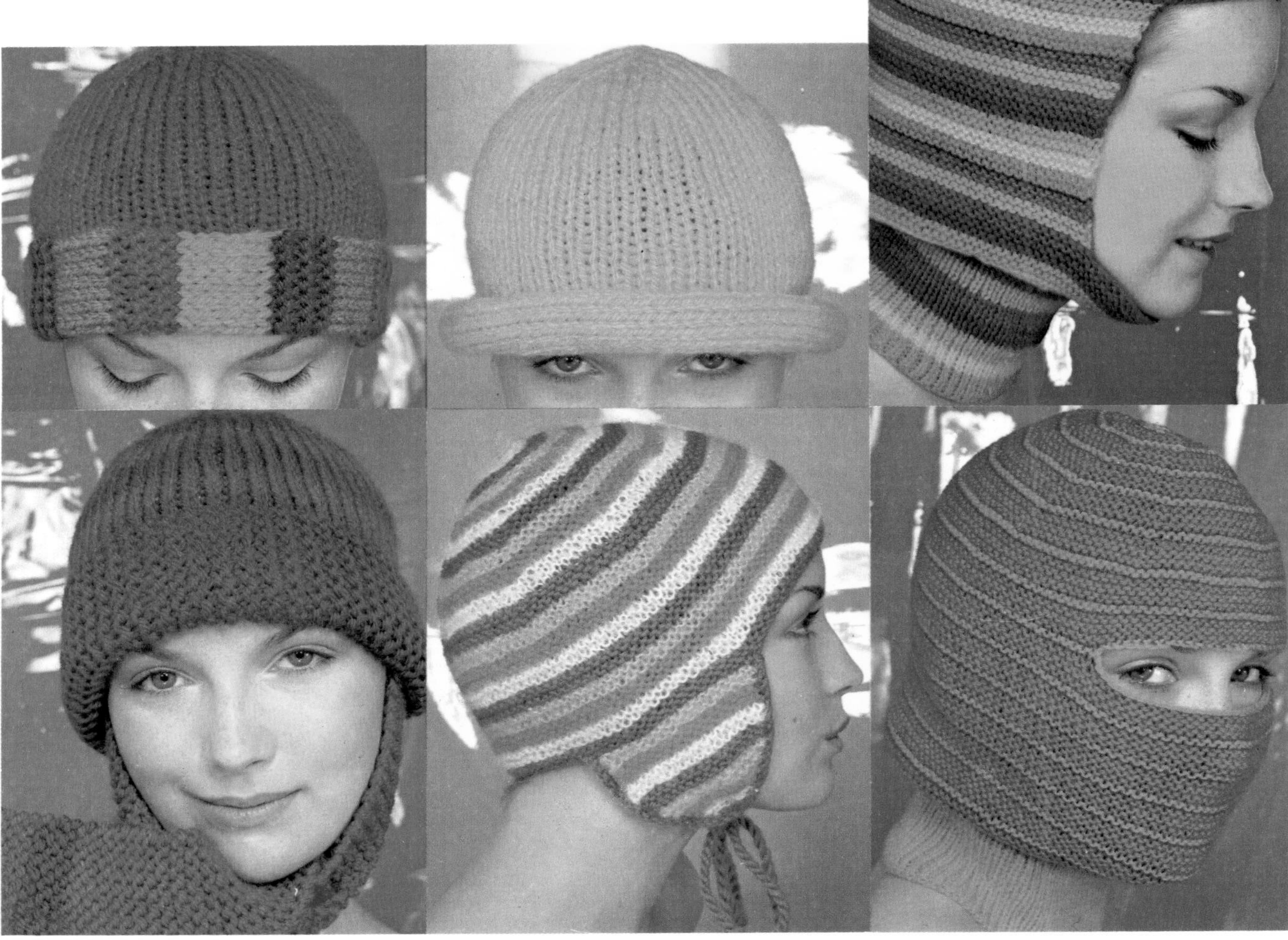

Hats are an obvious choice for knitting in rounds. You can use sets of needles for the hats in finer yarns, but needles thick enough for bulky yarns may only be available in pairs; although you can work the balaclava, helmet and hat with earflaps in rounds, use pairs of needles for the three hats in bulkier yarn. These patterns tell you how to stripe the hats, but you can obviously make the hats in a single color if you wish.

Yellow hat
You will need
about 4oz (100g) bulky yarn
1 pair no. 10 needles
Crown Cast on 57 sts. Work 5in (13cm) in st st ending with a P row.
Shape top Next row: (K5, K2 tog) to last st, K1.
Next row: P.
Next row: (K4, K2 tog) to last st, K1.
Next row: P.
Cont to dec in this way on every alt row until 17 sts rem, ending with a P row.
Next row: K2 tog to last st, K1. Break off yarn, thread through sts, draw up and tie off.
Edging Cast on 13 sts and work in st st for 19in (48cm) or length required. Bind off.
Finishing Join seam of crown. Join cast-on and bound-off ends of edging; sew edging to hat to turn up on RS.

Hat with ties
You will need
total of 6oz (50g) bulky yarn in 2 colours coded A–B
1 pair no. 10 needles
Crown As for yellow hat, but working throughout in 4-row stripes.
Edging With B cast on 13 sts and work in g st for 19in (48cm) or length required. Bind off.
Ties With A cast on 10 sts. Working in g st work 10 rows A, 6 rows B, then cont in A until work measures 18in (45cm) or length required. Bind off. Work 2nd tie in same way.
Finishing As for yellow hat. Sew tie ends at either side to cover ears.

Hat with striped edging
You will need
total of 4oz (100g) bulky yarn in 4 colors coded A–D
1 pair no. 10 needles
Crown Using A, work as yellow hat.
Edging With B cast on 13 sts. Work 6 rows st st in B, 6 rows g st in C, 6 rows st st in D, 6 rows g st in A. Rep these 24 rows 3 times more, or cont to length required. Bind off.
Finishing As for yellow hat.

Hat with earflaps
You will need
total of 2oz (50g) sports yarn in 4 colors coded A–D
set of no. 5 needles
Crown Cast on 16 sts; work 2 rounds in g st.
3rd round: (K into front and back of next st, K1) to end (24 sts).
4th round: P to end.
Join in B and work 2 rounds.
7th round: (K into front and back of next st, K2) to end (32 sts).
8th round: P to end.
Join in C and work 2 rounds.

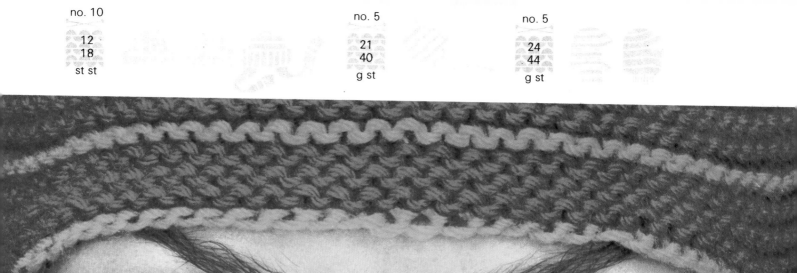

no. 10
12
18
st st

no. 5
21
40
g st

no. 5
24
44
g st

11th round: (K into front and back of next st, K3) to end (40 sts).
12th round: P to end.
Join in D and work 2 rounds.
15th round: (K into front and back of next st, K4) to end (48 sts).
16th round: P to end.
Cont working 4 rounds in each color as set, inc 8 sts in every 4th round until there are 104 sts, then cont without shaping until 71 rounds have been worked from beg (thus ending with a 3rd round of B).
Next round: Using B bind off 13 sts, P 18, bind off 42 sts, P18, bind off rem 13 sts.
Earflaps Using C, re-join yarn to one set of 18 sts. Work 16 rows in pat.
Cont in pat, dec 1 st at each end of next and every alt row until 4 sts rem, then K 1 row (ending with a 2nd row of B).
Break off yarn.
With RS facing and B, K up 15 sts down side of earflap, K the 4 sts, K up 15 sts up other side of earflap. Bind off K-wise.
Work 2nd earflap in same way.
Finishing Gather cast-on sts tightly. Using 4 strands of B, make 2 twisted cords (p102); sew one to each earflap.

Balaclava

You will need

total of 4oz (100g) sports yarn in 7 colors coded A–G
1 set each of no. 3 and no. 5 needles
With set of no. 3 needles and A cast on 112 sts and work in K1, P1 rib, 4 rounds each in A, B, C, D, E, F and G.
Cont in this sequence until work measures 4in (10cm) from beg, ending with the 4th round of a stripe. Change to no. 5 needles and still working in the same stripe sequence cont in g st (K1 round, P1 round) for 1in (3cm) ending with the 3rd round of a stripe.
Next round: P42, bind off 28 sts, P42.
Cont on last 42 sts in g st for 5in (12cm) ending with the 1st row of a stripe.
Break off yarn and leave sts. Return to the other 42 sts and work to match but do not break off yarn. With a separate length of the color you are working with cast on 28 sts.
Next round: P42, P the 28 sts, then P the other 42 sts. Cont without shaping for 1in (3cm), ending with a WS row.
Shape top Next round: (K12, K2 tog) to end. Work 3 rounds.
Next round: (K11, K2 tog) to end. Cont to dec in this way on every 4th round until there are 48 sts, then on every alt round until 16 sts rem, ending with a P round.
Break off yarn, thread through sts, draw up and tie off.

Helmet

You will need

total of 4oz (100g) sports yarn in 2 colors coded A–B
I set each of no. 3 and no. 5 needles
With set of no. 3 needles and A cast on 112 sts and work in K1, P1 rib for 4in (10cm). Change to no. 5 needles and cont in g st, working in stripes of 6 rounds B and 2 rounds A throughout.
Cont until work measures 5in (13cm) from beg of g st, ending with a P round.
Next round: K42, bind off 29, K to end.
Next round: P42, cast on 29, P to end.
Cont in g st until work measures 7in (18cm from beg of g st, ending with a P round.
Shape top As for balaclava.

Gloves and socks

no. 2

32
40
st st

Gauge 220
Following patterns 226
Duplicate stitch 228
Embroidery 229

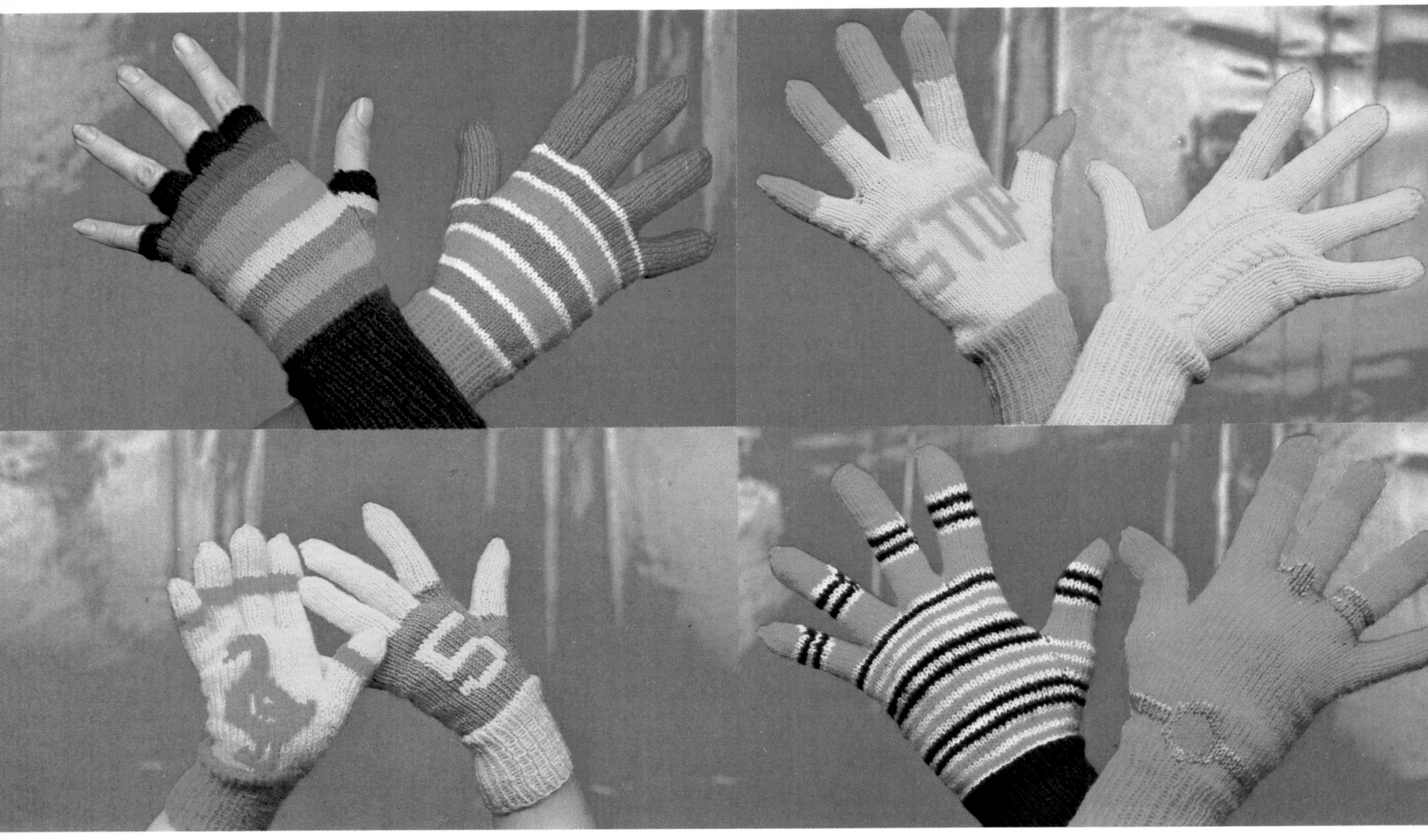

The basic patterns for gloves and socks given here can be varied by knitting them in stripes, or working sections in different colors. Use duplicate stitch or embroidery to make additional decoration.

Size (adjustable)

glove length	7	8½	10in
	(18	22	26cm)
(to fit 6–8yrs/10–12yrs/adult)			
sock leg	9½	12½	14in
	(24	30	36cm)
foot	6	7½	9in
	(15	19	23cm)

You will need
set of no. 2 double-pointed needles
gloves 2/2/3oz (50/50/75g) fingering yarn
socks 2/2/3oz (50/50/75g) fingering yarn

Right glove
Cast on 38/46/54 sts and work in rounds of K1, P1 rib for 2/2½/3in (6/7/8cm). Work 4 rounds in st st.
Shape thumb
1st round: K21/25/29, P1, M1, K1, M1, P1, K to end.
K 2 rounds.
Next round: K21/25/29, P1, M1, K3, M1, P1, K to end.
Cont to inc in this way on every 3rd round until there are 48/59/68 sts, then K 3 rounds.
Next round: K22/26/30, sl next 11/13/15 sts onto a thread, cast on 3, K to end (40/48/56 sts).
Cont without shaping for 1/1½/2in (3/4/5cm).
1st finger K17/20/23 sts and sl onto a thread, K12/14/16, turn and cast on 2, leave rem sts on another thread. Divide the 14/16/18 sts onto 3 needles and cont in rounds of st st for 2/2½/3in (5/6/7cm).
Shape top 1st round: K2 tog to end.
2nd round: K to end.
3rd round: K1/0/1. K2 tog to end. Break off yarn, thread through sts, draw up and tie off on inside.
2nd finger K4/5/6 sts from palm, cast on 2, K6/7/8 sts from back of hand, then K up 2 sts from base of 1st finger (14/16/18 sts). Cont as for 1st finger but making length 2/2½/3in (6/7/8cm).
3rd finger Work as for 2nd finger but making length as for 1st finger.
4th finger K the rem 8/10/12 sts, K up 2 sts from base of 3rd finger.
Cont on these 10/12/14 sts for 1½/2/2½ in (4/5/6cm), then finish as for 1st finger.
Thumb
Sl the 11/13/15 sts onto needles, K up 3 sts from cast-on sts at base of thumb, cont in rounds of st st for 1½/2/2½in (4/5/6cm), then finish as for 1st finger.

Left glove
As right glove, reversing all shaping, i.e. beg of thumb K14/18/22, P1, M1, K1, M1, P1, K to end.
1st finger K11/14/17 sts and sl onto a thread, K12/14/16, turn and cast on 2, leave rem sts on another thread.

Finishing Darn in all ends of yarn securely on WS of fabric.

Stripes 244
Rounds 250
Cables 258

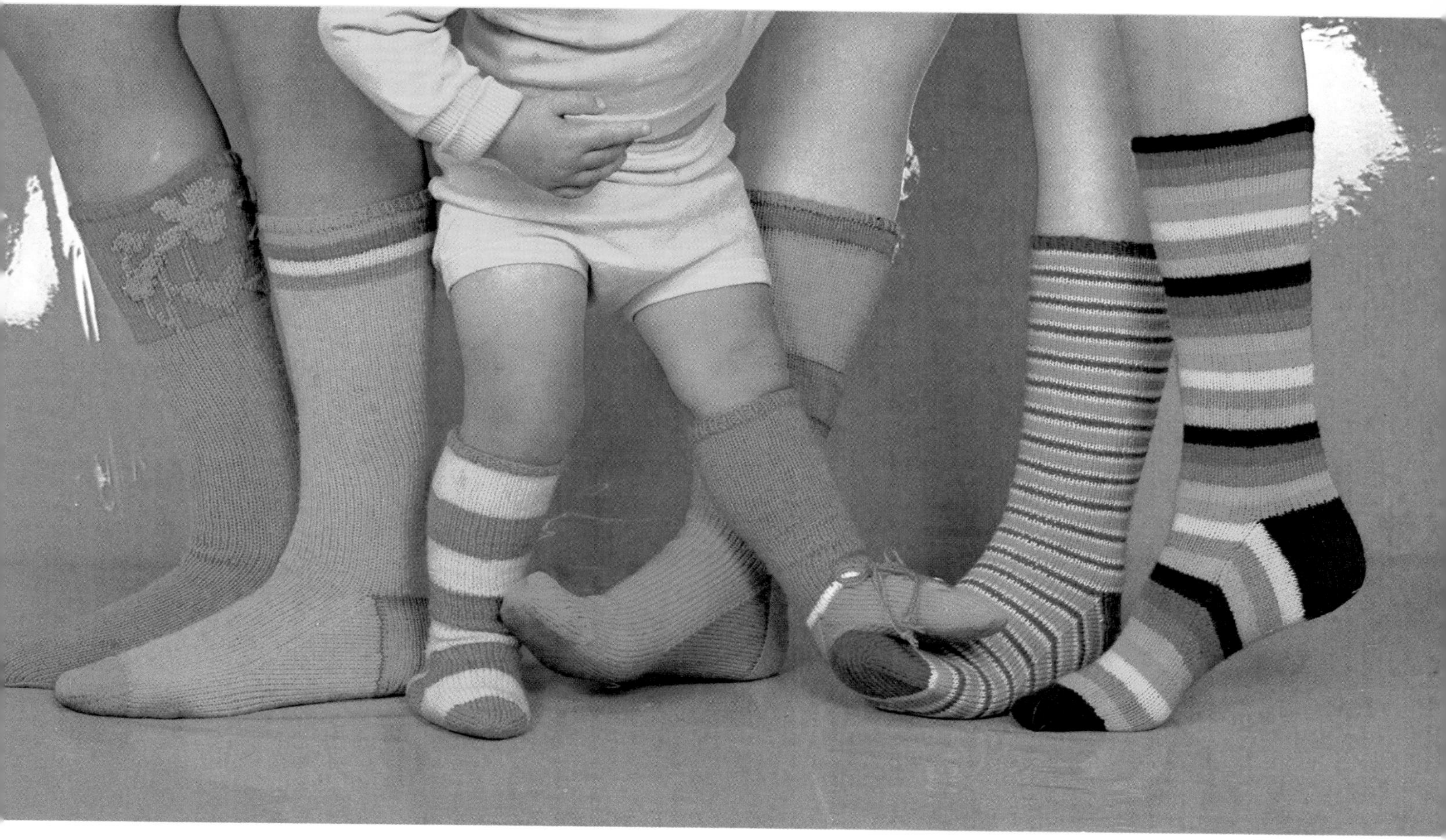

Socks
Cast on 52/62/72 sts and work 4 rounds in K1, P1 rib. Cont in rounds of st st until work measures 2/3/$3\frac{1}{2}$in (5/7/9cm) from beg.
Next round: K2 tog, K to last 3 sts, sl 1, K1, psso, K1.
Cont to dec in this way on every 4th round until 36/44/52 sts rem, then cont without shaping until work measures 7/9/11in (18/23/28cm) from beg, ending at the end of a round. Adjust length here if necessary.

Divide for heel
K8/10/12, turn and sl the last 9/11/13 sts of round onto the other end of this same needle. Divide the rem 19/23/27 sts onto 2 needles and leave for instep. Cont in st st on heel sts only for 2/$2\frac{1}{2}$/3in (6/7/8cm) ending with a P row.

Turn heel
K11/13/15, sl 1, K1, psso, turn.
Next row: P6, P2 tog, turn.
Next row: K7, sl 1, K1, psso, turn.
Next row: P8, P2 tog, turn.
Cont to work 1 more st on every row until all sts are worked, ending with a P row (11/13/15 sts).
Next row: K5/6/7. This completes heel.
Sl the instep sts back onto 1 needle.
With spare needle K6/7/8 heel sts, K up 18/21/24 sts along side of heel; with 2nd needle K the instep sts; with 3rd needle K up 18/21/24 sts along other side of heel, then K5/6/7 heel sts.
Next round: K to end.
Next round: On 1st needle K to last 3 sts, K2 tog, K1; on 2nd needle K to end; on 3rd needle K1, sl 1, K1, psso, K to end.
Rep the last 2 rounds until 38/46/54 sts rem, then cont without shaping until foot measures $3\frac{1}{2}$/5/6in (9/12/15cm) from where you picked up sts at heel, ending at the end of a round. Adjust length here if necessary.

Shape toe
Next round: On 1st needle K to last 3 sts, K2 tog, K1; on 2nd needle K1, sl 1, K1, psso, K to last 3 sts, K2 tog, K1; on 3rd needle K1, sl 1, K1, psso, K to end.
Next round: K to end.
Rep the last 2 rounds until 14/16/18 sts rem, then K the sts from 1st needle onto 3rd needle and graft together (see p243). Work 2nd sock to match 1st.

Finishing Darn in all ends of yarn on WS of fabric. For duplicate stitching or applied embroidery remember to use yarn of suitable weight.

no. 5

24
32
st st

Guernsey sweater

The classic fisherman's guernsey is worked in rounds to the underarms, and is divided to work the textured yokes separately. The sleeve stitches are picked up round the armhole and knitted toward the cuffs; underarm gussets give ease of movement. Oiled wool makes the most hard-wearing and authentic garment, but good sports yarn also gives a firm fabric.

Size

chest	31½	33½	35½	37½	39½	41½in
	(80	85	90	95	100	105cm)
length	24	25	25½	26½	27	28in
	(61	63	65	67	69	71cm)
sleeve	19	19	20	20	20½	21in
seam	(48	49	50	51	52	53cm)

You will need

23/24/25/26/27/27oz (625/650/675/700/725/750g) sports yarn

1 pair each no. 4 and no. 5 needles

no. 4 and no. 5 circular needles

sets of 4 each no. 4 and no. 5 double-pointed needles

Back and front (worked in one piece to armholes)

With no. 4 needles cast on 102/108/114/120/126/132 sts and work in g st for 4in (10cm) ending with a WS row. Break off yarn and leave sts for the present.

Work a second piece in the same way, but do not break off yarn.

With no. 4 circular needle K across both sets of sts and join into a round (204/216/228/240/252/264 sts).

Work 6 rounds in K2, P2 rib, then change to no. 5 circular needle and work in rounds of st st until work measures 15in (38cm) from beg.

Next round: *Inc 1, K1, inc 1, K101/107/113/119/125/131, rep from * once more.

Next round: K to end.

Next round: *Inc 1, K3, inc 1, K101/107/113/119/125/131, rep from * once more.

Cont to inc in this way for gussets on every alt round 6 times more, ending with an inc round (236/248/260/272/284/296 sts).

Next round: K17 and sl these sts onto holder, K101/107/113/119/125/131,

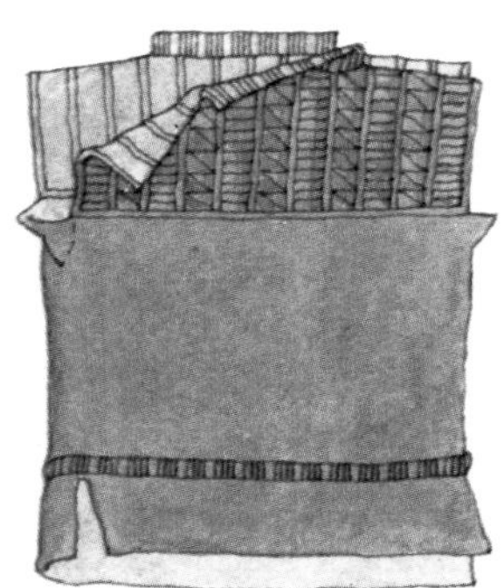

turn and cont on these sts for back, K 4 rows, dec 1 st in center of last row on 1st, 2nd, 3rd and 4th sizes, and inc 1 st in center of last row on 6th size (100/106/112/118/125/132 sts).

Cont in yoke pat thus:

1st row: P1, K1 tbl, P1, K4/5/6/4/5/6, P1, K1 tbl, P1, *K1, P8, K1 tbl, P1, K4/5/6/4/5/6, P1, K1 tbl, P1, rep from * to end.

2nd row: K1, P1 tbl, K1, P4/5/6/4/5/6, K1, P1 tbl, *K7, P2, K1, P1 tbl, K1, P4/5/6/4/5/6, K1, P1 tbl, rep from * to last st, K1.

3rd row: P1, K1 tbl, P6/7/8/6/7/8, K1 tbl, P1, *K3, P6, K1 tbl, P6/7/8/6/7/8, K1 tbl, P1, rep from * to end.
4th row: K1, P1 tbl, K6/7/8/6/7/8, P1 tbl, *K5, P4, K1, P1 tbl, K6/7/8/6/7/8, P1 tbl, rep from * to last st, K1.
5th row: P1, K1 tbl, P1, K4/5/6/4/5/6, P1, K1 tbl, P1, *K5, P4, K1 tbl, P1, K4/5/6/4/5/6, P1, K1 tbl, P1, rep from * to end.
6th row: K1, P1 tbl, K1, P4/5/6/4/5/6, K1, P1 tbl, *K3, P6, K1, P1 tbl, K1, P4/5/6/4/5/6, K1, P1 tbl, rep from * to last st, K1.
7th row: P1, K1 tbl, P6/7/8/6/7/8, K1 tbl, P1, *K7, P2, K1 tbl, P6/7/8/6/7/8, K1 tbl, P1, rep from * to end.
8th row: K1, P1 tbl, K6/7/8/6/7/8, P1 tbl, *K1, P8, K1, P1 tbl, K6/7/8/6/7/8, P1 tbl, rep from * to last st, K1.
Rep these 8 rows until work measures 24/25/25½/26½/27/28in (61/63/65/67/69/71cm) from beg, ending with a WS row.
Next row: Bind off 21/24/25/28/30/33, K to end.
Next row: Bind off 21/24/25/28/30/33, P to end, and inc 1 st at end of row on 5th size only (58/58/62/62/66/66 sts).
Change to no. 4 needles.
Next row: K2 tog, (P2, K2) to last 4 sts, P2, K2 tog.
Work 5 more rows in rib, dec 1 st at each end of every row.
Bind off in rib.
Return to the sts which were left, sl the next 17 sts onto holder, rejoin yarn to rem 101/107/113/119/125/131 sts and K to end.
Cont to match back.

Sleeves
Join shoulder seams.
With set of no. 5 needles K the 17 gusset sts, pick up and K84/90/96/102/108/114 sts around armhole.
Next round: Sl 1, K1, psso, K13, K2 tog, K to end.
Next round: K.
Next round: Sl 1, K1, psso, K11, K2 tog, K to end.
Next round: K.
Cont to dec in this way on every alt round in st st until 3 sts rem in gusset, then K 1 round.
Next round: Sl 1, K2 tog, psso, K to end (85/91/97/103/109/115 sts).
Cont in st st, dec 1 st at each side of seam st on next and every foll 6th round until 49/53/57/61/65/69 sts rem, then cont without shaping until sleeve seam measures 15½/16/16½/17/17½/18in (40/41/42/43/44/45cm), dec 1 st at end of last round (48/52/56/60/64/68 sts).
Change to no. 4 needles and cont in rounds of K2, P2 rib for 3in (8cm).
Bind off loosely in rib.

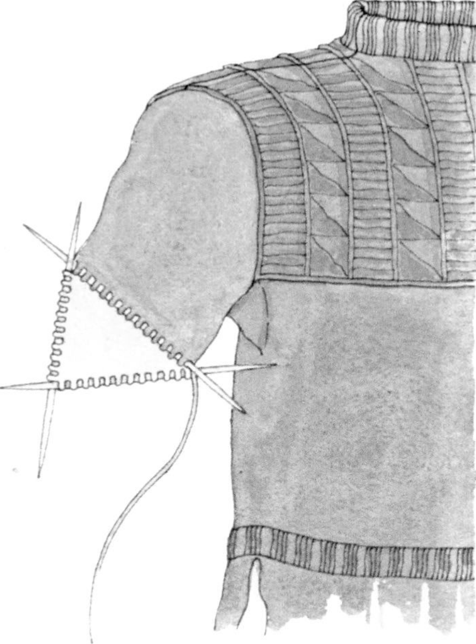

Cable stitches

Moving a group of stitches from one position in a row to another so that they become twisted to the front or the back of the fabric creates a rope-like effect called a cable. For this you need a short, double-pointed cable needle to hold the stitches that you are transferring until you are ready to work them. Cable needles come in different sizes, but if you don't have one the same size as your knitting needles, choose one that is thinner so that it won't stretch the stitches, thus spoiling their appearance.
Cables are usually most effective in stockinette stitch, and show up in sharp relief against a purl background. They can be worked singly in vertical panels or can be combined into an all-over design, each cable being separated by perhaps a single background stitch.
You can change the design of many basic cables, such as twists to right or to left, by working them over a greater number of stitches – 8, 10 or 12 instead of the usual 4 or 6 – to give a fatter, softer rope. Knitting additional rows between the twists is another variation, which elongates the design.
Once you have practiced the basic techniques, you can easily incorporate the panels shown here and on p260 into your own designs. Plan your design before

Cable twist to right or left
Each of these cables takes 6 sts and there are 4 background sts separating them.
1st row (RS) K6, P4, K6.
2nd row P6, K4, P6.
3rd–4th rows As 1st–2nd.
5th row Sl next 3 sts onto cable needle and hold at back of work, K3, then K the 3 sts from cable needle (called C6B), P4, sl next 3 sts onto cable needle and hold at front of work, K3, then K the 3 sts from cable needle (called C6F).
6th row As 2nd.
7th–8th rows As 1st–2nd.
Pattern repeat is 8 rows.

Braided cable
This cable takes 9 sts.
1st row (RS) K9.
2nd row P9.
3rd row Sl next 3 sts onto cable needle and hold at back of work, K3, then K the 3 sts from cable needle (called C6B), K3.
4th row P9.
5th–6th rows As 1st–2nd.
7th row K3, sl next 3 sts onto cable needle and hold at front of work, K3, then K the 3 sts from cable needle (called C6F).
8th row P9.
Pattern repeat is 8 rows.

Horseshoe cable
This cable takes 12 sts.
1st row (RS) K12.
2nd row P12.
3rd–4th rows As 1st–2nd.
5th row Sl next 3 sts onto cable needle and hold at back of work, K3, then K the 3 sts from cable needle (called C6B), sl next 3 sts onto cable needle and hold at front of work, K3, then K the 3 sts from cable needle (called C6F).
6th row P12.
7th–8th rows As 1st–2nd.
Pattern repeat is 8 rows.

beginning – see p286 for making a chart out of the shape. It is best to position a cable in the center of the back, front and sleeves, and to work outward on either side of this. Remember that armhole shaping interrupts a design so that for the back and front of a sweater it is simpler if your design doesn't exceed the number of stitches across the shoulders. A sleeve can feature just one large center cable which stretches from the cuff and is bound off in a straight line at the top; this avoids having any incomplete parts of the pattern around the armhole shaping.

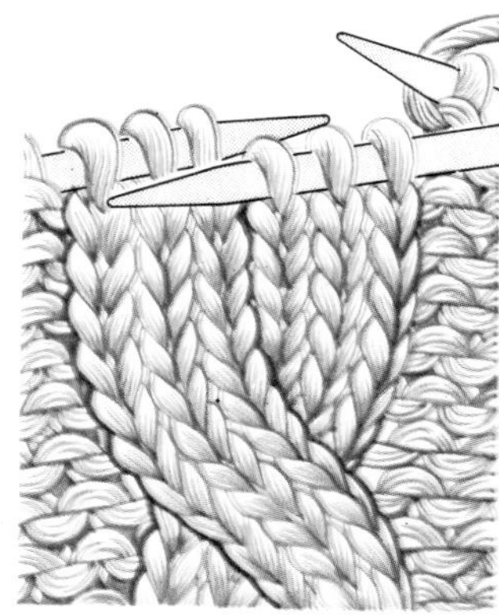

Cable twist from right to left (C6F): hold 3 sts at front.

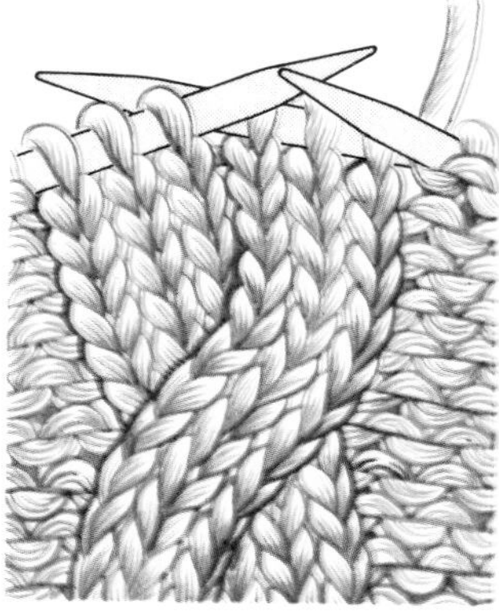

Cable twist from left to right (C6B): hold 3 sts at back.

Oxox cable
This cable takes 12 sts.
1st row (RS) K12.
2nd row P12.
3rd–4th rows As 1st–2nd.
5th row Sl next 3 sts onto cable needle and hold at back of work, K3, then K the 3 sts from cable needle (called C6B), sl next 3 sts onto cable needle and hold at front of work, K3, then K the 3 sts from cable needle (called C6F).
6th row P12.
7th–12th rows As 1st–6th.
13th–16th rows Rep 1st–2nd rows twice.
17th row C6F, C6B.
18th row P12.
19th–24th rows As 13th–18th.
Pattern repeat is 24 rows.

Ribbed cable
This cable takes 7 sts.
1st row (RS) K1 tbl, *P1, K1 tbl, rep from * twice more.
2nd row P1 tbl, *K1, P1 tbl, rep from * twice more.
3rd–6th rows Rep 1st–2nd rows twice.
7th row Sl next 4 sts onto cable needle and hold at front of work, K1 tbl, P1, K1 tbl, sl the 4th st from cable needle back onto LH needle and P1, then K1 tbl, P1, K1 tbl from cable needle.
8th row As 2nd.
9th–16th rows Rep 1st–2nd rows 4 times.
Pattern repeat is 16 rows.

Cabled braid
This pattern takes 10 sts.
1st row (RS) K10.
2nd row P10.
3rd row K2, *sl next 2 sts onto cable needle and hold at front of work, K2, then K2 from cable needle (called C4F), rep from * once more.
4th row P10.
5th row *Sl next 2 sts onto cable needle and hold at back of work, K2, then K2 from cable needle (called C4B), rep from * once more, K2.
6th row P10.
Repeat 3rd–6th rows for pattern.

Aran stitches

Intricate and densely textured designs involving cable, crossed and bobble stitches are typical of the patterns from islands off the western coast of Ireland.
Patterned panels are often worked against a purl background to give them definition. Individual panels may be outlined with a rope of twisted stitches or may be separated by blocks of moss stitch or of honeycomb or woven patterns.

If you work one of the patterns on this page as an all-over fabric, cast on an extra edge stitch at either side for seaming. Thick, homespun yarn known as *bainin*, meaning 'natural', is traditional for Aran knitting. Many spinners produce a yarn specially for Aran knitting, but any bulky, lightly twisted wool and large needles can create a similarly soft effect.

Honeycomb
Cast on a multiple of 8 sts (add 2 extra edge sts for an all-over fabric).
1st row (RS) K to end.
2nd row P to end.
3rd row K1, *sl 2 sts onto cable needle and hold at back of work, K2, then K2 from cable needle (called C4B), sl next 2 sts onto cable needle and hold at front of work, K2, then K2 from cable needle (called C4F), rep from * to last st, K1.
4th row P to end.
5th–6th rows As 1st–2nd.
7th row K1, *C4F, C4B, rep from * to last st, K1.
8th row P to end.
Pattern repeat is 8 rows.

Irish moss stitch
Cast on an even number of stitches.
1st row *P1, K1, rep from * to end.
2nd row *K1, P1, rep from * to end.
3rd row As 2nd.
4th row As 1st.
Pattern repeat is 4 rows. This fabric is reversible.

Woven lattice
Cast on a multiple of 6 sts (add 2 extra edge sts for an all-over fabric).
1st row (RS) K5, *P2, K4, rep from * to last 3 sts, P2, K1.
2nd row K3, *P4, K2, rep from * to last 5 sts, P4, K1.
3rd row K1, *sl next 2 sts onto cable needle and hold at front of work, K2, then K2 from cable needle (called C4F), P2, rep from * to last st, K1.
4th row As 2nd.
5th row K1, P2, *K2, sl next 2 sts onto cable needle and hold at back of work, K2, then P2 from cable needle (called C4R), rep from * to last 5 sts, K5.
6th row K1, *P4, K2, rep from * to last st, K1.
7th row K1, *P2, sl next 2 sts onto cable needle and hold at back of work, K2, then K2 from cable needle (called C4B), rep from * to last st, K1.
8th row As 6th.
9th row K5, *sl next 2 sts onto cable needle and hold at front of work, P2, then K2 from cable needle (called C4L), K2, rep from * to last 3 sts, P2, K1.
10th row As 2nd.
Repeat 3rd–10th rows for pattern.

Diamond and bobble
This panel requires 17 stitches.
1st row (RS) P6, K2, P1, K2, P6.
2nd row K6, P2, K1, P2, K6.
3rd row P5, sl next st onto cable needle and hold at back of work, K2, then P1 from cable needle (called Cr2R), P1, sl next 2 sts onto cable needle and hold at front of work, P1, then K2 from cable needle (called Cr2L), P5.
4th row K5, P2, K3, P2, K5.
5th row P4, Cr2R, P3, Cr2L, P4.
6th row K4, P2, K5, P2, K4.
7th row P4, K2, P2, (K1, yo, K1, yo, K1), all into next st, turn and P5, turn and K5, turn and P2 tog, P1, P2 tog, turn and sl 1, K2 tog, psso (called make bobble), P2, K2, P4.
8th row K4, P2, K2, P1 tbl, K2, P2, K4.
9th row P4, Cr2L, P3, Cr2R, P4.
10th row As 4th row.
11th row P5, Cr2L, P1, Cr2R, P5.
12th–16th rows As 2nd–6th.
17th row P3, Cr2R, P5, Cr2L, P3.
18th row K3, P2, K7, P2, K3.
19th row P2, Cr2R, P7, Cr2L, P2.
20th row K2, P2, K9, P2, K2.
21st row P2, Cr2L, P7, Cr2R, P2.
22nd row As 18th.
23rd row P3, Cr2L, P5, Cr2R, P3.
24th row As 16th.
25th–28th rows As 9th–12th.
Repeat 3rd–28th rows for pattern.

Aran diamond
This panel requires 14 sts.
1st row (RS) P5, K4, P5.
2nd and all even rows K all P sts of previous row and P all K sts.
3rd row P5, sl next 2 sts onto cable needle and hold at front of work, K2 sts from LH needle then K2 from cable needle (called C4F), P5.
5th row P4, sl next st onto cable needle and hold at back of work, K2 from LH needle then K1 from cable needle (called Cr2R), sl next 2 sts onto cable needle and hold at front of work, P1 from LH needle then K2 from cable needle (called Cr2L), P4.
7th row P3, Cr2R, P1, K1, Cr2L, P3.
9th row P2, Cr2R, (P1, K1) twice, Cr2L, P2.
11th row P1, Cr2R, (P1, K1) 3 times, Cr2L, P1.
13th row P1, Cr2L, (K1, P1) 3 times, Cr2R (but P1 instead of K1 from cable needle), P1.
15th row P2, Cr2L, (K1, P1) twice, Cr2R as 13th row, P2.
17th row P3, Cr2L, K1, P1, Cr2R as 13th row, P3.
19th row P4, Cr2L, Cr2R as 13th row, P4.
20th row As 2nd.
Repeat 3rd–20th rows for pattern.

Cable with bobbles
This panel requires 19 sts.
1st row P7, K2, (P1, K1, P1, K1, P1) all into the next st, turn, K5, turn, P5, sl 2nd, 3rd, 4th and 5th sts over the 1st st (called make bobble), K2, P7.
2nd row K7, P2, P1 tbl, P2, K7.
3rd row P6, sl next st onto cable needle and leave at back of work, K2, then P1 from cable needle (called C3B), K1 tbl, sl next 2 sts onto cable needle and leave at front of work, P1, then K2 from cable needle (called C3F), P6.
4th row K6, P2, K1, P1 tbl, K1, P2, K6.
5th row P5, C3B, P1, K1 tbl, P1, C3F, P5.
6th row K5, P2, (P1 tbl, K1) twice, P1 tbl, P2, K5.
7th row P4, C3B, (K1 tbl, P1) twice, K1 tbl, C3F, P4.
8th row K4, P2, (K1, P1 tbl) 3 times, K1, P2, K4.
9th row P3, C3B, (P1, K1 tbl) 3 times, P1, C3F, P3.
10th row K3, P2, (P1 tbl, K1) 4 times, P1 tbl, P2, K3.
11th row P2, C3B, (K1 tbl, P1) 4 times, K1 tbl, C3F, P2.
12th row K2, P2, (K1, P1 tbl) 5 times, K1, P2, K2.
Pattern repeat is 12 rows.

Aran sweater

no. 8

17
26
moss st

Basic stitches 216
Gauge 220
Increasing 222
Following patterns 226
Finishing 242
Aran knitting 260

These Aran panels are the same width throughout; change the number of stitches in the reverse stockinette-stitch background to obtain different size sweaters. The diagram shows the position of panels and the number of stitches to use for each section. To use different panels draw your garment shape to scale on graph paper and then plan where your panels will go.

Size

chest							
	27½	29	31	33	35	37	39in
	(70	75	80	85	90	95	100cm)
length							
	21½	22	23½	23½	24	25½	26in
	(55	56	60	61	62	66	67cm)

You will need

22/24/26/28/30/32/34oz (550/600/650/700/750/800/850g) Aran-type yarn: add 2 oz (50g) for polo neck
1 pair each nos. 5, 7 and 8 needles
1 cable needle

Irish moss st 10/10/12/12/14/14/16 sts
rev st st 1/2/2/3/3/4/4 sts
Aran diamond 14 sts
rev st st 1/2/2/3/3/4/4 sts
honeycomb 32 sts
rev st st 1/2/2/3/3/4/4 sts
Aran diamond 14 sts
rev st st 1/2/2/3/3/4/4 sts
Irish moss st 10/10/12/12/14/14/16 sts

Irish moss st
Aran diamond 14 sts
Aran diamond 14 sts
Irish moss st

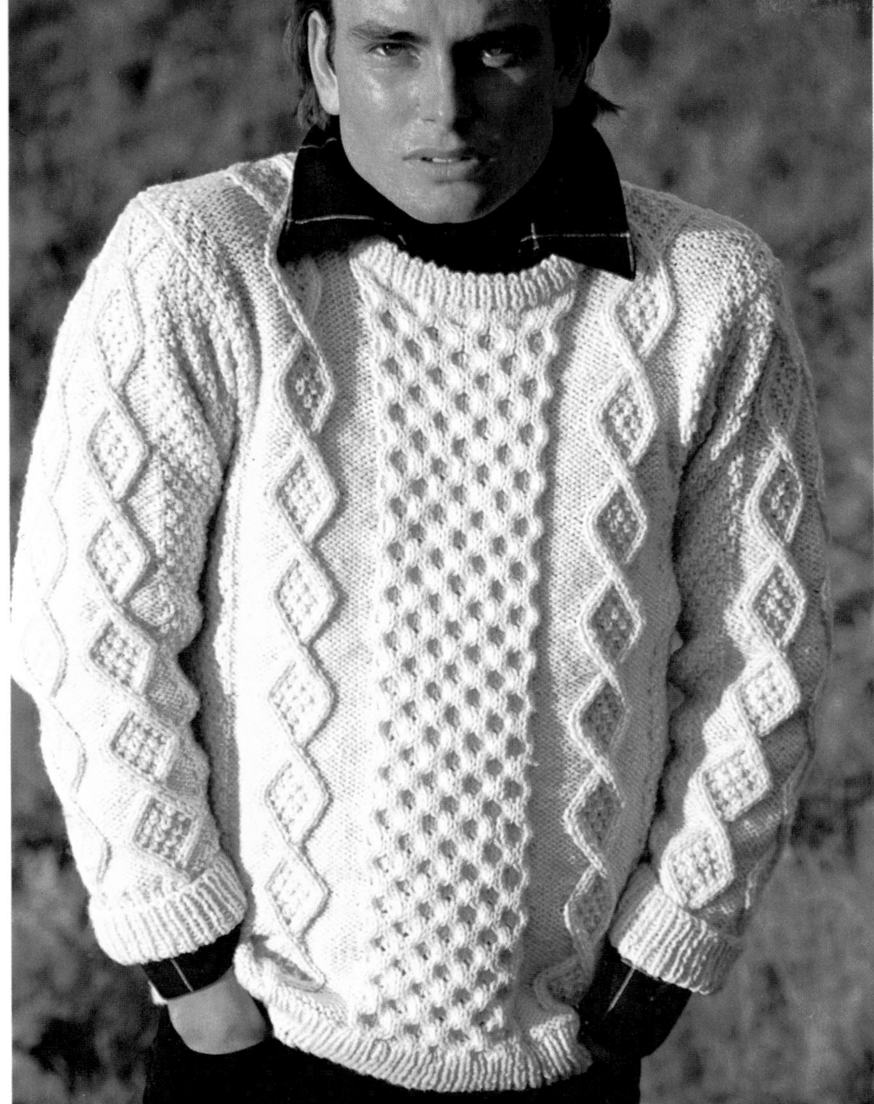

The panels in this sweater are Aran diamond on 14 sts, honeycomb on 32 sts and Irish moss st – see p260.

Back
With no. 7 needles cast on 79/83/87/91/95/99/103 sts.
Beg and ending 1st row (RS) with P1, work 9/9/11/11/11/13/13 rows K1, P1 rib.
Next row (inc): Rib 17/18/20/21/23/24/26, M1, rib 16/17/17/18/18/19/19, *M1, rib 7, rep from * once more, M1; rib 14/15/15/16/16/17/17, M1, rib to end (84/88/92/96/100/104/108 sts).
Change to no. 8 needles and cont in pat from diagram until work measures 15/15/16/16½/17/17½/18in (38/39/41/42/43/45/46cm) from beg, ending with a WS row.
Shape armholes Maintaining pat, bind off 6/7/7/8/8/9/9 sts at beg of next 2 rows (72/74/78/80/84/86/90 sts).
Cont without shaping until armholes measure 6½/6½/7½/7½/7½/8/8in (17/17/19/19/19/21/21cm), ending with a WS row.
Shape shoulders Bind off 7/7/8/8/8/8/9 sts at beg of next 4 rows and 6/6/5/6/7/7/7 sts at beg of foll 2 rows. Place rem 32/34/36/36/38/40/40 sts on a holder.

Front
Work as back until armholes measure 4/4/4¼/4¼/4¼/4½/4½in (10/10/11/11/11/12/12cm), ending with a WS row.
Shape neck Next row: Pat 28/28/30/31/32/33/35, turn and place rem sts on spare needle. Dec 1 st at neck edge on next 5 rows, then on every other row until 20/20/21/22/23/23/25 sts rem.
Cont without shaping until front measures same as back to shoulder, ending at armhole edge.
Shape shoulder Bind off 7/7/8/8/8/8/9 sts at side edge twice. Work 1 row. Bind off. Sl first 16/18/18/18/20/20/20 sts from spare needle onto holder, rejoin yarn and work other side to correspond.

Sleeves
With no. 5 needles cast on 41/41/45/45/45/49/49 sts. Rib 19/19/21/21/21/23/23 rows as on back.
Next row (inc): Rib 14/14/16/16/16/18/18, M1 (rib 6, M1) twice, rib to end (44/44/48/48/48/52/52 sts).
Change to no. 8 needles. Working 2 adjacent Aran diamond panels on center 28 sts as in diagram, work 8 rows in pat. Inc 1 st at each end of next and every foll 6th row until there are 68/68/76/76/76/82/82 sts. Cont without shaping until sleeve measures 18/18½/19/19/19/20½/20½in (46/47/49/49/49/53/53cm).
Shape top Bind off 7/7/8/8/8/9/9 sts at beg of next 6 rows. Bind off rem sts.

Neckband
Sew left shoulder seam. With RS of work facing and no. 5 needles, K across 32/34/36/36/38/40/40 back neck sts dec 1/3/3/3/5/5/5 sts evenly across row. K up 18/19/20/20/20/23/24 sts down LH side of neck, K across 16/18/18/18/20/20/20 front neck sts dec 1 st at center and K up 18/19/20/20/20/23/24 sts up RH side of neck.
Crew neck Rib 4 rows, P 1 row, rib 4 more rows. Bind off loosely ribwise.
Turtle neck Rib 10 rows. Change to no. 7 needles. Rib 20/20/22/22/24/24/26 rows. Change to no. 8 needles. Rib 3 more rows. Bind off loosely in rib.

Finishing
Join shoulder and neckband seams.
Join sleeve seams leaving 1⅛/1¼/1¼/1½/1½/1¾/1¾in (30/35/35/40/40/45/45mm) open at top edge. Set in sleeves.
Turn crew neckband to WS along P ridge and slip-stitch in position.

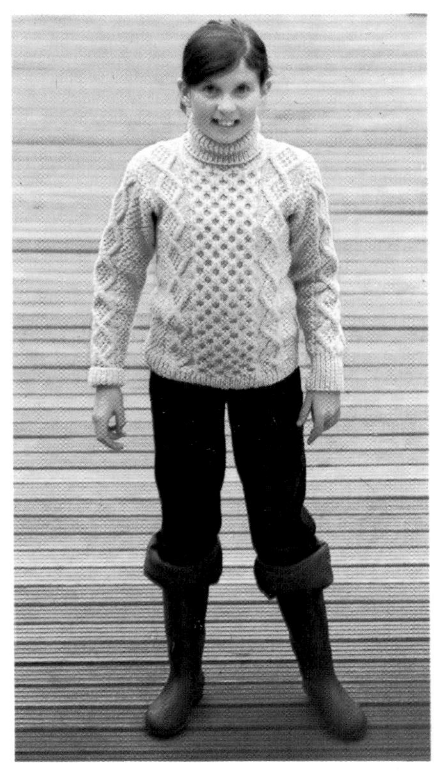

Traditional Fair Isle

Fair Isle patterns take their name from one of the Shetland Isles to the north of Scotland. Muted shades of color in lightly twisted Shetland wool are worked in bands of traditional motifs with natural backgrounds. Bands of pattern in different combinations of your colors one above another make a completely original fabric; it is simpler, though less striking, to highlight a plain garment with a band of Fair Isle above the waistband or cuffs, or at underarm level to give the appearance of a yoke. Shetland designs repeat to make an all-over fabric and are traditionally worked in natural shades. Try making the background fabric in blending stripes while keeping the pattern color constant throughout; this gives the impression of a banded Fair Isle but is less complicated to work.

Fair Isle techniques
Although the total design may contain many colors, true Fair Isle uses only 2 colors in a row, one forming the background and the 2nd the pattern. Working in this way is simple if you don't let the yarns tangle: try holding the yarn you are using in your right hand in the usual way and keep the color not in use clear of the knitting over the middle finger of your left hand.
Take 2nd ball of yarn across the back of the fabric until you need it again and, depending on the number of sts you bypass, carry or weave the yarn not in use (see right) to avoid long untidy strands of yarn which can catch and distort the fabric. Carry yarn over 5 sts or fewer, but weave over more than 5. Both carrying and weaving create a double-thickness fabric. Take care not to pull yarn too tight on WS and distort the gauge. If you feel this happening try using needles a size larger.

Repeat: 18 sts, 19 rows.

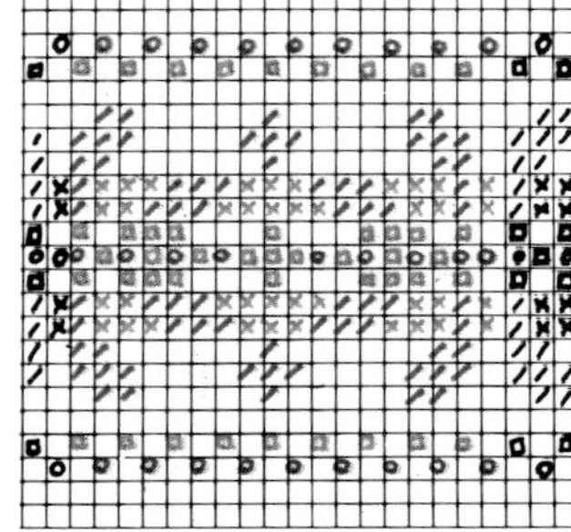

This pattern requires a multiple of 18 sts plus 1 extra edge st.
1st row (RS) K1 E, *1A, 1E, rep from * to end.
2nd row P1 A, *1C, 1A, rep from * to end.
3rd row Using A, K to end.
4th row P2A, *2B, 5A, 1B, 5A, 2B, 3A, rep from *, ending with 2A instead of 3A.
5th row K1A, *3B, 4A, 3B, 4A, 3B, 1A, rep from * to end.
6th row P1A, *2B, 6A, 1B, 6A, 2B, 1A, rep from * to end.
7th row K1D, *1B, (3D, 3B) twice, 3D, 1B, 1D, rep from * to end.
8th row P1D, *1B, 2D, 3B, 5D, 3B, 2D, 1B, 1D, rep from * to end.
9th row K1A, *1C, 1A, 3C, 3A, 1C, 3A, 3C, 1A, 1C, 1A, rep from * to end.
10th row P2E, *(1C, 1E) 3 times, 3C, (1E, 1C) 3 times, 3E, rep from *, ending with 2E.
11th–19th rows Work back from 9th to 1st row in that order.

Carrying yarn RS row: K required no. of sts with 1st color. Carry 2nd color across back of work; taking care not to pull loose strand of yarn too tight, K the necessary no. of sts with 2nd color. On a P row carry yarn across front of work. See carrying yarn on WS of first sample, below left.

Weaving yarn Keep both colors at back on a RS row and K first st in usual way. On 2nd and then every other st insert RH needle into the st as usual, then pass 2nd color in your left hand over top of RH needle; complete first st with color in your right hand. On a P row weave yarns in same way, carrying the colors across front of work and alternating position of yarns on the previous row.

Working from a chart
To save space and show how a design looks, Fair Isle patterns (like repeating Jacquard designs) are often given as charts. One square represents a stitch and a horizontal line of squares a row of knitting; work from right to left for the K rows and follow the line immediately above back from left to right for the P rows. When working in rounds, each round begins at the RH edge of the chart. Colored squares, or symbols, represent the different colors. In the graphs on these pages the pattern repeat itself is shown in color. Some patterns look best with an extra edge stitch worked at beginning or end of rows to complete the motif neatly. For this work the next stitch outside the actual pattern repeat. The same principle applies to patterns repeating vertically over a number of rows. For the first Fair Isle sample opposite you can see instructions in both graph form and conventional row-by-row pattern.

Repeat: 18 sts, 21 rows.

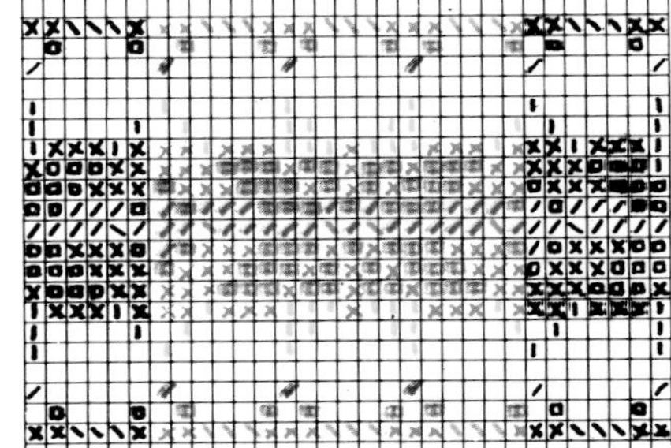

Repeat: 17 sts, 17 rows.

Repeat: 11 sts, 11 rows.

Baby bunting

no. 3
26
34
st st

Soft, light-weight Shetland yarn makes a baby bunting or a child's robe. An open-ended zipper enables you to open the bottom seam and adapt the bunting into a robe as the child grows and begins to walk. The basic instructions are given in stockinette stitch, into which you can work bands of the traditional Fair Isle motifs (use stripes, checks or small border designs to separate blocks of pattern) as on the baby bunting shown here, or the all-over designs on p265. Alternatively, create more abstract and original designs of your own like those on this child's robe. When planning your design remember to make patterns symmetrical across the front and to center them on the back. Work out a complicated design first on graph paper; draw in the motifs working from the center stitch outward.

Size

chest	$19\frac{1}{2}$	$21\frac{1}{2}$	$23\frac{1}{2}$in
	(50	55	60cm)
length	$23\frac{1}{2}$	$25\frac{1}{2}$	$27\frac{1}{2}$in
	(61	66	71cm)
sleeve seam	6	8	$9\frac{1}{2}$in
	(15	20	25cm)

You will need

1 pair each nos. 2 and 3 needles
about 5/6/7oz (125/150/175g) light-weight Shetland yarn
20/22/24in (50/55/60cm) open-ended zipper

Left front

With no. 2 needles cast on 36/39/42 sts. Work $2\frac{1}{2}$in (6cm) in g st. Change to no. 3 needles.
Next row: K to end.
Next row: K3, P to end.
Keeping 3 sts at CF edge in g st throughout, cont in st st until work measures 17/$18\frac{1}{2}$/20in (44/48/52cm) from beg, ending with a K row.
Shape sleeve K3, P to end, turn and cast on 39/52/65 sts (75/91/107 sts).
Working 10 sts at cuff edge in g st and maintaining CF border in g st, cont until work measures 22/$23\frac{1}{2}$/$25\frac{1}{2}$in (56/61/66cm) from beg, ending at cuff edge.
Shape front neck K62/77/92 sts, turn and leave rem 13/14/15 sts on a holder.
Dec 1 st at neck edge on next 5 rows (57/72/87 sts).
Shape shoulder Bind off 10 sts, K to end.
Next row: P2 tog, P to end.
Rep last 2 rows once more (35/50/65 sts).
Bind off 7/10/13 sts at beg of next and foll 4 alt rows.

Right front

Work as for left front reversing shaping.

Back

With no. 2 needles cast on 72/78/84 sts. Work $2\frac{1}{2}$in (6cm) in g st. Change to no. 3 needles. Beg with a K row, cont in st st until back is same length as fronts to underarm, ending with a P row.
Shape sleeves Cast on 39/52/65 sts at beg of next 2 rows (150/182/214 sts).
Keeping 10 sts in g st at each cuff, cont until back is same as fronts to shoulders, ending with a WS row.
Shape shoulders Bind off 10 sts at beg of next 4 rows and 7/10/13 sts at beg of foll 10 rows. Place rem 40/42/44 sts on a holder.

Hood

Join seams at shoulders and tops of sleeves. With no. 2 needles and RS of work facing, beg at top of right front and K across all sts on holders and also K up 18 sts from one side of front neck and 17 sts from the other (101/105/109 sts).
Maintaining 3 sts in g st at each end of needle, work 7 rows K1, P1 rib.
Next row: (RS) K26, (inc in next st, K3) 13/14/15 times, K23 (114/119/124 sts).
Change to no. 3 needles.
Cont in st st, keeping 10 sts in g st at each end, until hood measures 8/9/$10\frac{1}{2}$in (20/23/27cm) from beg.
Bind off.

Finishing

Press lightly with a warm iron over a damp cloth. Join seams at sides, underarms and top of hood. Join seam at lower edge and front of g st section for baby.
Sew zipper down front of robe or into opening of baby bunting. Press seams lightly.

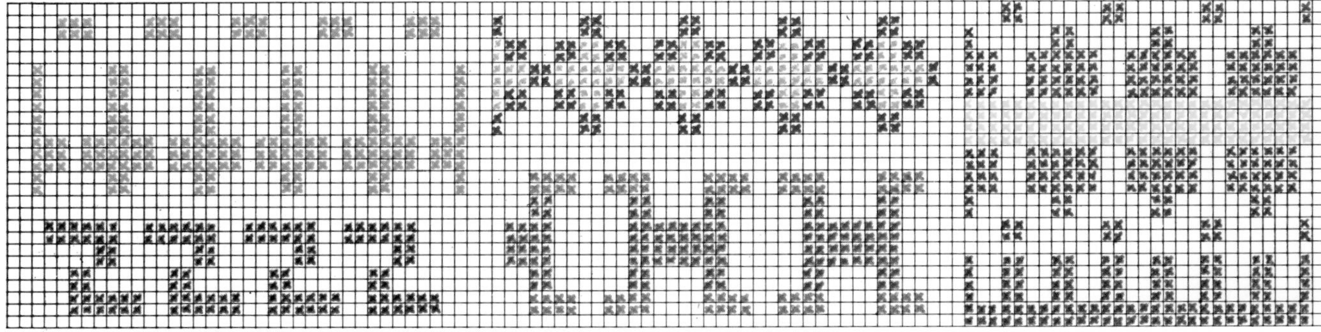

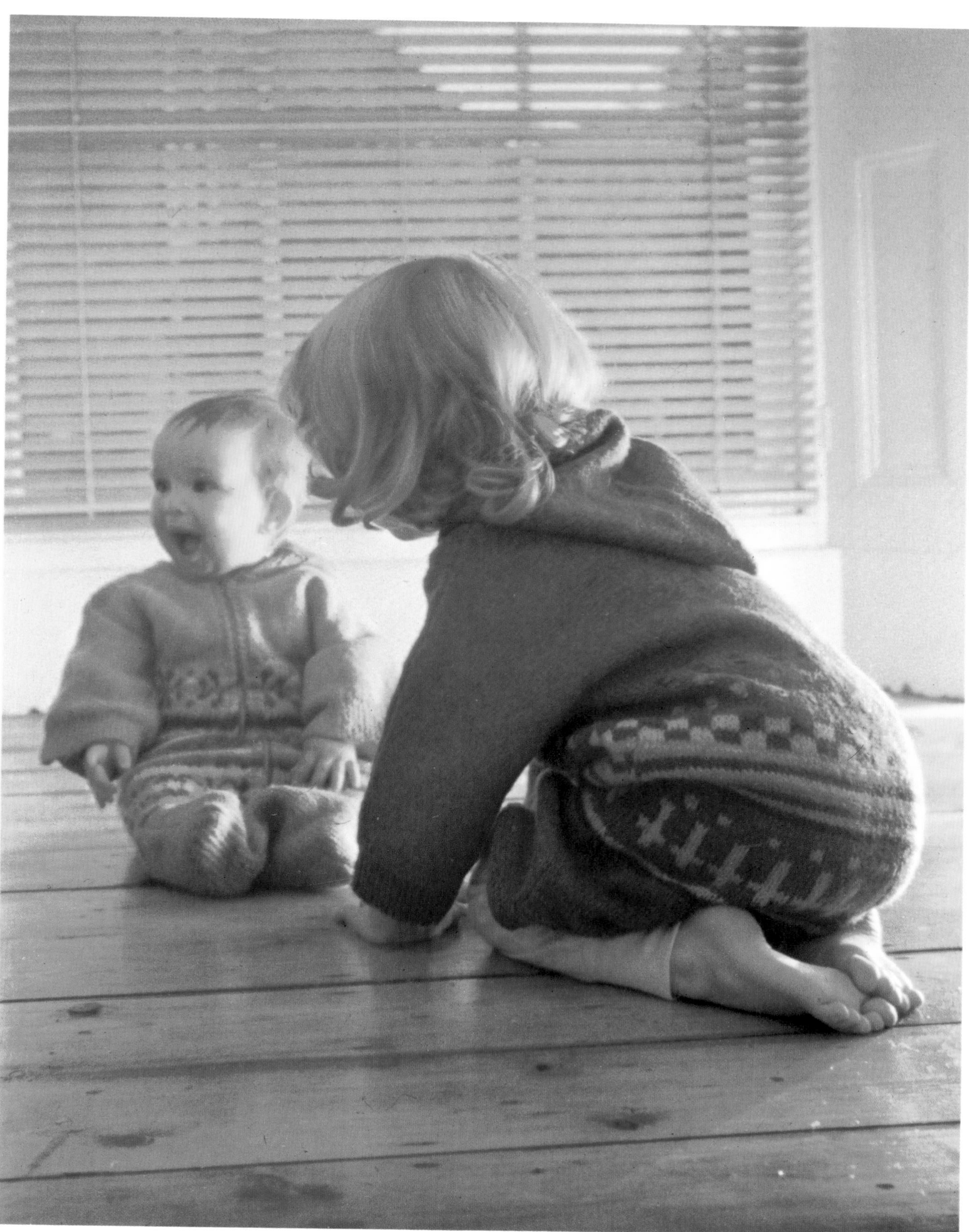

Mock Fair Isle

Traditional Fair Isle knitting has somewhat rigid rules: the choice of colors, the use of only two colors in any row, the relatively small number of stitches in a block of color. You can create designs which look equally complex without having to handle a number of different colors. The technique known as Mock Fair Isle is the use of a plain-colored yarn together with a second ball which is space-dyed or random-dyed either in a selection of different colors or in tones of one color. As you knit the random-dyed yarn produces striking multicolored effects: in charts like the Fair Isle ones on pp264–5 working all the pattern stitches in random-dyed yarn and the background in a plain color can produce color effects almost as rich as when you use four or five different colors in the traditional way. The contrast of random-dyed and plain yarn in blocks of more abstract pattern can make attractive all-over patterns or border designs as the samples and charts on these pages suggest. You still use two balls of yarn per row and weave or carry the yarn not in use on the WS of the work as in traditional Fair Isle knitting, but don't have to cope with following multicolored charts. Related to Fair Isle traditions but less formal are the snowflake or star motifs of Scandinavia (opposite). In these the color not in use is carried or woven on WS of work; where blocks of color are fairly isolated as in the RH sample you may find it easier to combine the Fair Isle techniques with the Jacquard method of using small separate balls of yarn where a color appears only in individual motifs in a pattern.

Repeat: 16 sts, 16 rows.

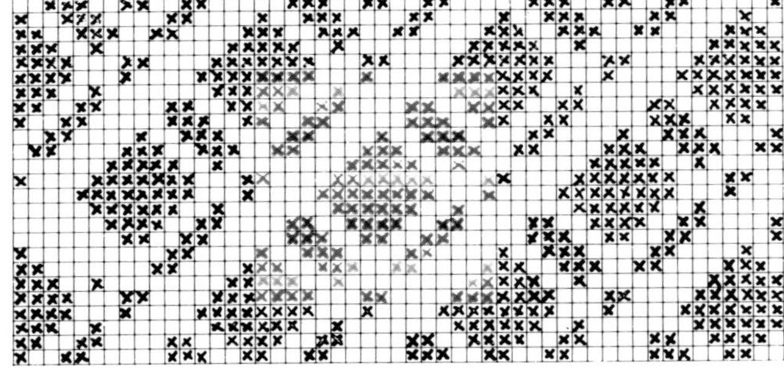

Repeat: 14 sts, 28 rows.

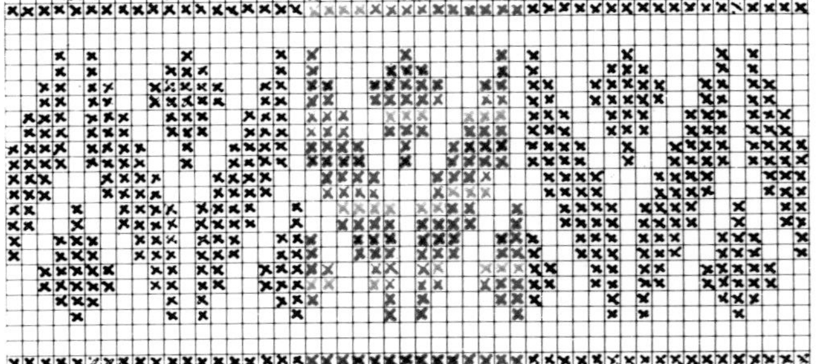

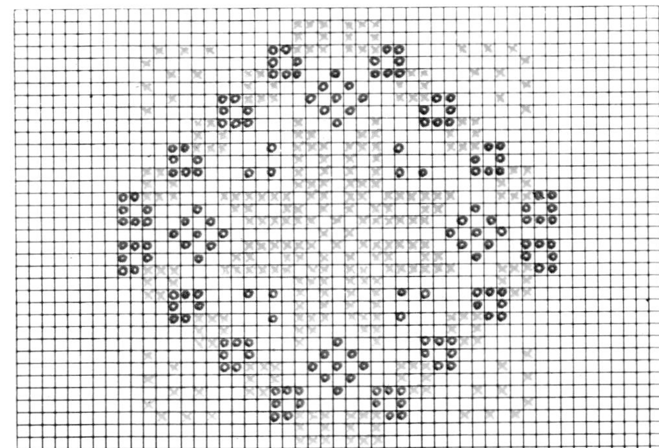

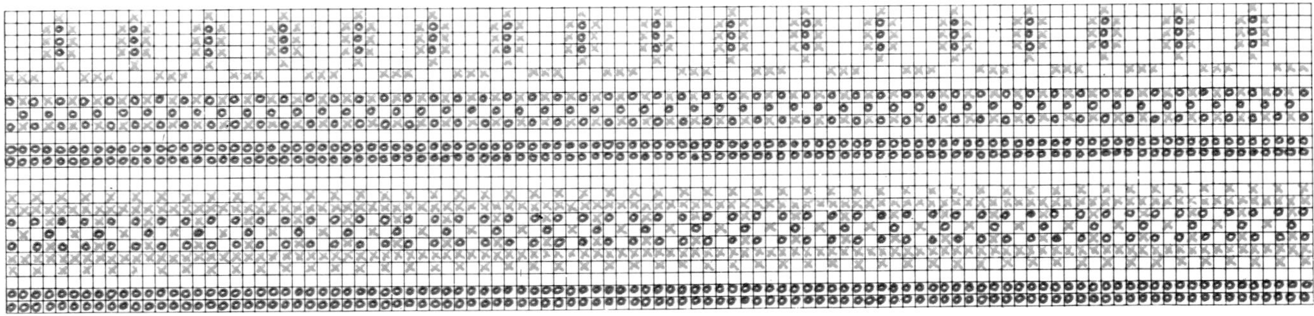

Jacquard designs

The term 'Jacquard' covers geometric-patterned fabrics, patchwork, border designs and individual motifs on a plain background. Sometimes Jacquard patterns are confused with Fair Isle knitting; like Fair Isle, you work most Jacquard designs from a chart (see p265 for details), but unlike Fair Isle you can use more than two colors in any one row. All-over geometric patterns can produce a striking patchwork effect and are an ideal way of using up scraps of yarn to make furnishings – pillow covers, bedspreads and rugs. Bold Jacquard borders are useful to emphasize an otherwise plain garment. Most multicolored designs look best in stockinette stitch, which focuses attention on the colors and design rather than on stitch texture.

Motifs (see p272) are another popular form of Jacquard knitting and an alternative to duplicate stitching. You knit in the motif as you make the main fabric rather than embroidering it on afterward. Quite often you can use a combination of the two techniques: knit in larger areas of color with the background fabric and duplicate stitch the small details or patches of color later.

Gauge in Jacquard
When working a small repeating Jacquard design like the gingham one below carry the yarns not in use loosely across the back of the work; if a color has to be carried over more than about 5 stitches, weave it in (see p265). When changing color be careful to pull the stitches equally tight. You may well find your gauge over a whole patterned section or over an individual motif becoming too tight: if this happens try using needles a size larger for Jacquard sections of an item. Check your gauge constantly until you are sure your size will be correct.

Pattern repeats
When planning an all-over Jacquard pattern it helps if the overall number of stitches you need for your fabric is divisible by the number of stitches in your pattern repeat. If not, when working a fairly bold pattern with a large multiple of stitches, make sure you center it; on front and back of a garment, for instance, a neckline which cuts into a bold pattern asymmetrically could look clumsy. In the graph patterns at the bottom of these pages the pattern repeat itself is shown in color and its all-over effect in black and white.

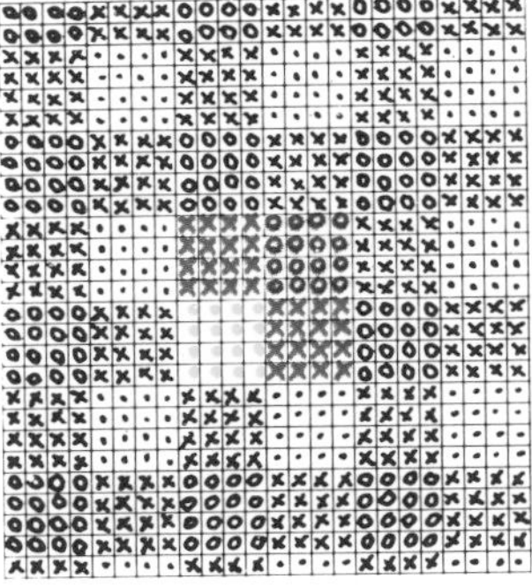

Gingham With blocks of only 4 stitches and only 2 colors per row you can easily carry yarn on WS of this pattern. Repeat: 8 sts, 8 rows.

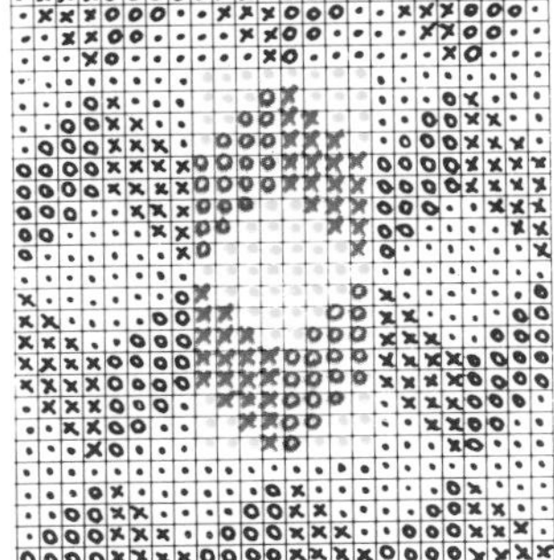

Boxes Carry the yarn on WS of this all-over pattern. When you work in 3 shades of a single color a 3-dimensional box-like effect is created. Repeat: 8 sts, 18 rows.

Keeping colors separate Taking more than one color any distance along a row can be complicated and difficult. The correct method of working multicolored patterns with relatively large blocks of color, such as the hexagonal pattern below, is to use small separate balls of yarn for each color. If you use a color more than once across a row each section of that color needs its own individual ball of yarn. This method forms a single-thickness fabric without any strands of yarn across the back. To avoid any holes in the fabric you must twist the yarns around each other when you change color, as you do with vertical stripes (p244).

Bobbins Instead of keeping many small balls of yarn at the back of your work, wind the separate colors onto bobbins before you begin; these hang on the WS and prevent the colors tangling. Use stiff cardboard and cut out bobbins about the size of the ones shown here. Wind the yarn around with the working end passing through the narrow opening.

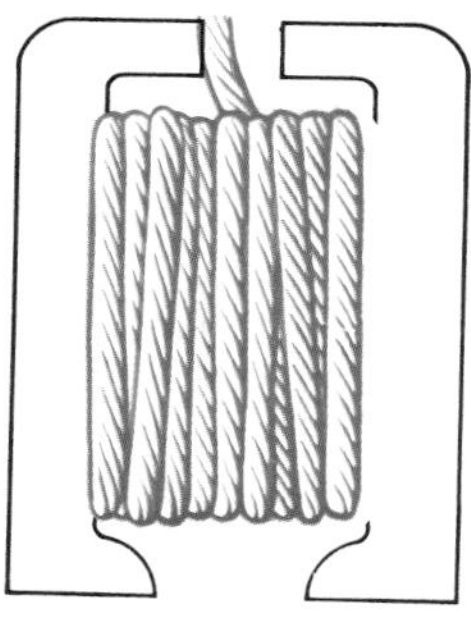

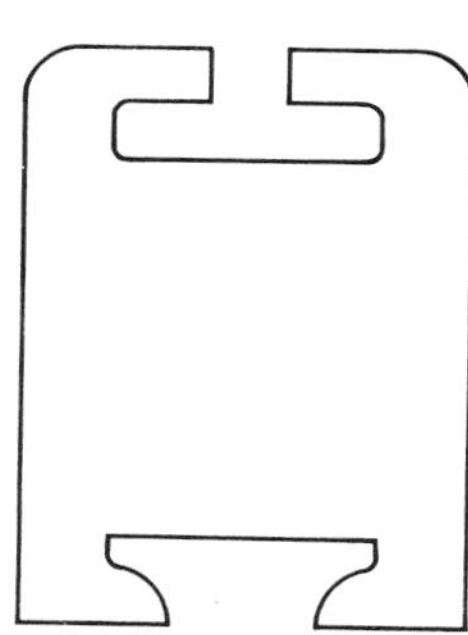

Patchwork
Use Jacquard techniques when working knitted-in patchwork as opposed to the type where you work separate patches and then stitch them together. Use separate balls or bobbins of yarn for patches of different color or texture, and twist the yarn together where color changes across a row to prevent holes from forming at vertical color divisions. You will need to do some planning ahead; in a complicated design you may even have to make a detailed stitch-by-stitch chart as described on p288 showing the shapes of individual patches.

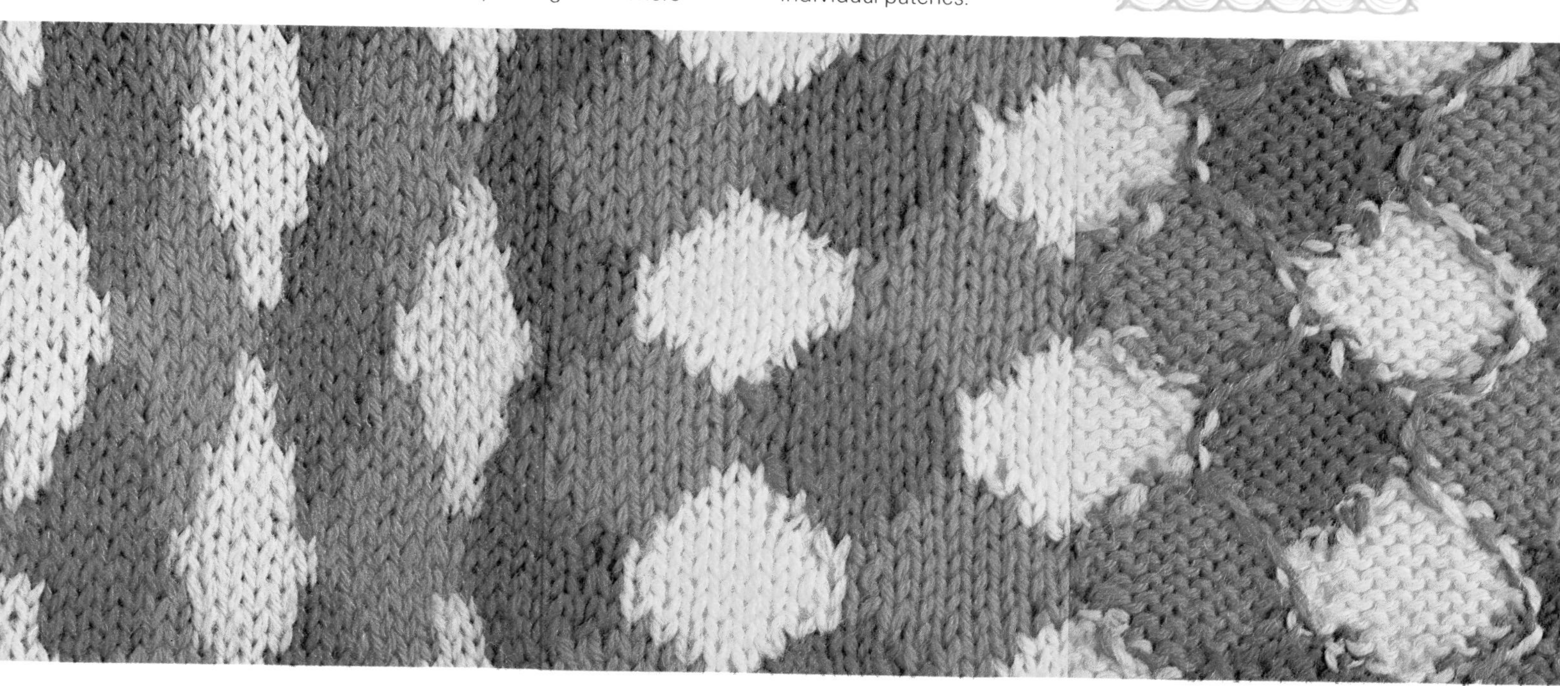

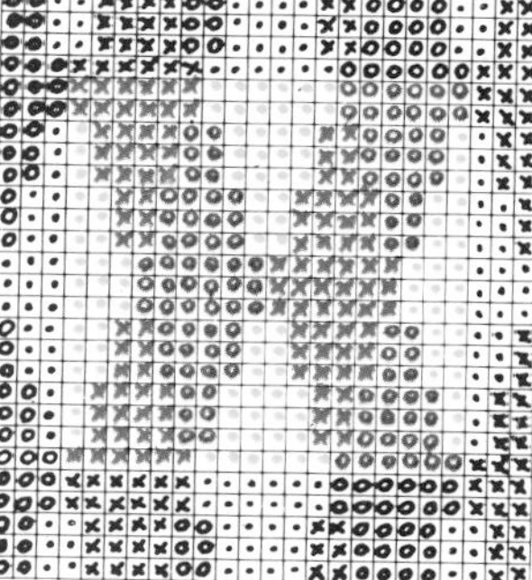

Diamonds A larger version of the diamond pattern would work best with separate balls or bobbins for each block of color; here, since each color recurs after only a few stitches, it is easier to weave in the yarn on the WS. Repeat: 18 sts, 18 rows.

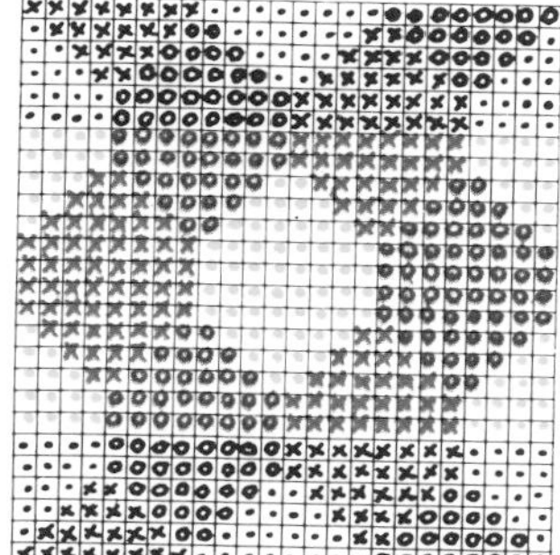

Hexagons Patches of this size or larger are best worked with separate colors on separate bobbins. Twist the yarns around one another where colors change in a row (see WS of sample). Repeat: 24 sts, 14 rows.

Jacquard-motif sweater

Gauge 220
T-shaped sweaters 224
Adjusting patterns 232

Here Jacquard motifs have been incorporated as a panel into the front of a T-shaped sweater. The first steps are to decide on the size and the design of your garment and to choose the yarn. Your gauge sample will then show you how many stitches and rows you have to play with in planning your design. Use graph paper to chart your own motifs (see working from a chart, p265) which you can combine into a panel like the one in this sweater – design borders to fill in any spaces between motifs; alternatively, work an individual motif on another part of the garment, such as center front.

You will need
total of about 30oz (750g) bulky yarn
1 pair needles (size according to gauge of yarn)

This garment is a simple T-shape made up of rectangles worked in stockinette stitch to the required size. Keep the basic shape quite simple and give the Jacquard panel full impact by using knitted-in hems (see p233) at the lower edge of back and front and on sleeves; leave a slash opening at the neck or finish a very shallow square neck with the same hemming technique.

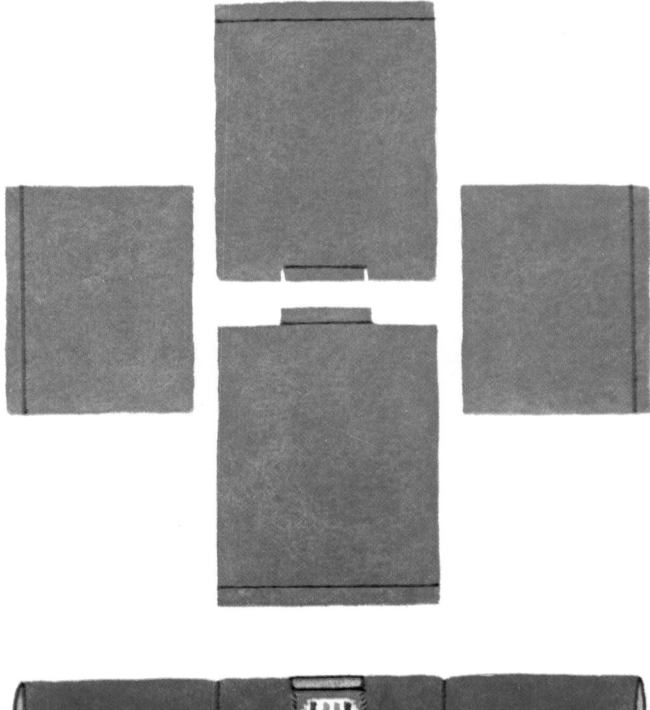

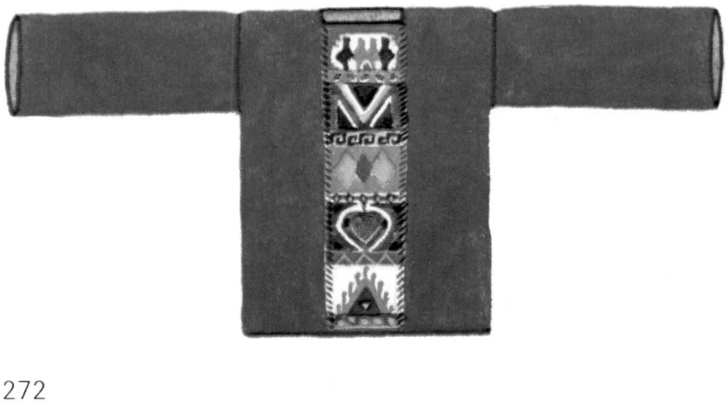

Finishing 242
Jacquard designs 270

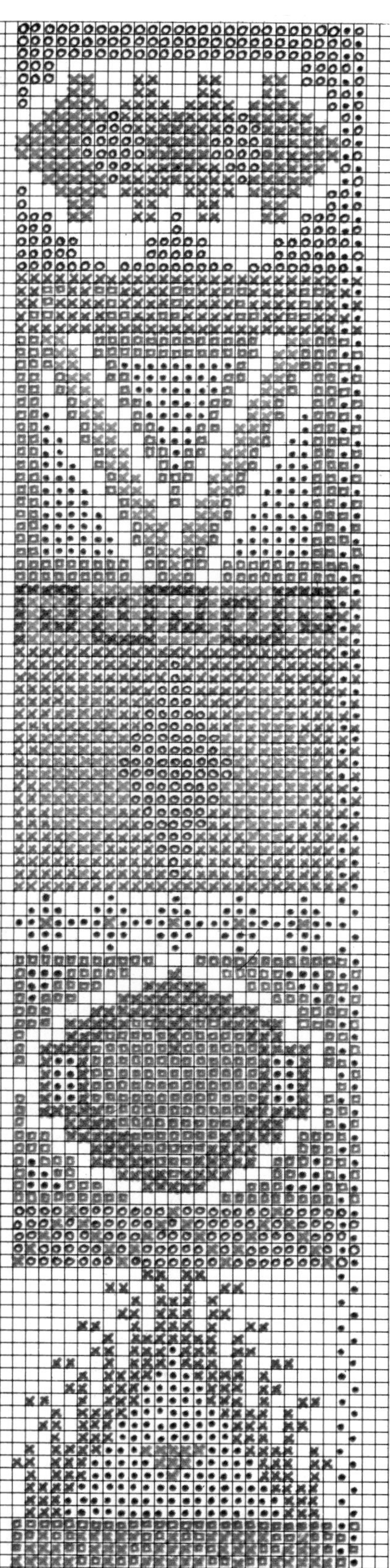

Lace knitting

Decorative increasing and decreasing (p222) shows that lace designs are arrangements of holes made by knitting two stitches together and making up for these decreases by bringing the yarn forward, over or around the needle. A simple rule is that each repeat of a lace pattern must have an equal balance of increases and decreases so that the number of stitches remains constant. Fine yarns usually need small needles, e.g. no. 00, but larger ones make a looser lacier fabric; experiment with sizes until the pattern no longer closes up. When making test samples for a design, start out with approximately three-quarters of the number of stitches you think you will need. Block and press the sample to the measurement you require, then revise your gauge – you need to stretch out a lace pattern slightly to see its effect clearly.

Arrow-tip (blue)
Cast on a multiple of 8 sts plus 1 extra.
1st row (RS) K1, *yfwd, sl 1, K1, psso, K3, K2 tog, yfwd, K1, rep from * to end.
2nd and all even rows P.
3rd row K2, *yfwd, sl 1, K1, psso, K1, K2 tog, yfwd, K3, rep from * to end, finishing with K2 instead of K3.
5th row P1, *K2, yfwd, sl 1, K2 tog, psso, yfwd, K2, P1, rep from * to end.
7th row P1, *sl 1, K1, psso, K1, (yfwd, K1) twice, K2 tog, P1, rep from * to end.
9th, 11th, 13th and 15th rows As 7th.
16th row As 2nd.
Pattern repeat is 16 rows.

Openwork (pink)
Cast on a multiple of 12 sts plus 2 extra.
1st row K1, *yfwd, K2 tog, rep from * to last st, K1.
2nd row P to end.
3rd row K to end.
4th row P to end.
5th row K1, *sl 1, K2 tog, psso, K4, yfwd, K1, yfwd, K4, rep from * to last st, K1.
6th row K1, *P3 tog, P4, yrn, P1, yrn, P4, rep from * to last st, K1.
7th row As 6th.
8th row As 5th.
9th row As 6th.
Pattern repeat is 9 rows. This fabric is reversible.

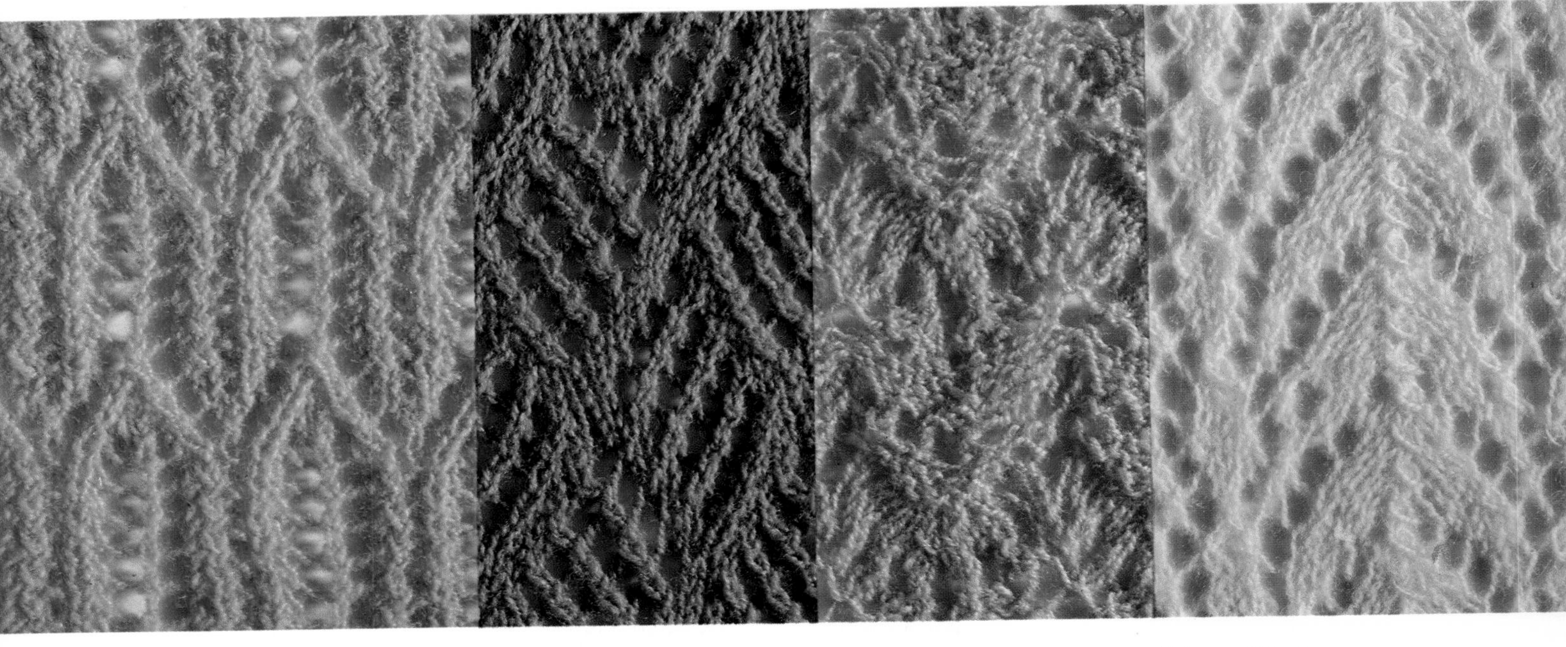

Diamond pattern (green)
Cast on a multiple of 10 sts plus 4 extra.
1st row (RS) K4, *yfwd, sl 1, K1, psso, K1, (K2 tog, yfwd) twice, K3, rep from * to end.
2nd and all even rows P to end.
3rd row *K3, (yfwd, sl 1, K1, psso) twice, K1, K2 tog, yfwd, rep from * to last 4 sts, K4.
5th row K2, * (yfwd, sl 1, K1, psso) 3 times, K4, rep from * to last 2 sts, yfwd, sl 1, K1, psso.
7th row K1, *(yfwd, sl 1, K1, psso) 4 times, K2, rep from * to last 3 sts, yfwd, sl 1, K1, psso, K1.
9th row As 5th.
11th row As 3rd.
13th row As 1st.
15th row K2 tog, yfwd, *K4, (K2 tog, yfwd) 3 times, rep from * to last 2 sts, K2.
17th row K1, K2 tog, yfwd, *K2, (K2 tog, yfwd) 4 times, rep from * to last st, K1.
19th row As 15th.
20th row P to end.
Pattern repeat is 20 rows.

Horseshoe lace (yellow)
Cast on a multiple of 16 sts plus 1 extra.
1st row (RS) Sl 1, K1, psso, *yfwd, K2, K2 tog, yfwd, K1, yfwd, sl 1, K2 tog, psso, yfwd, K1, yfwd, sl 1, K1, psso, K2, yfwd, sl 1, K2 tog, psso, rep from * ending with K2 tog instead of sl 1, K2 tog, psso.
2nd and all even rows P.
3rd row Sl 1, K1, psso, *K3, yfwd, K2 tog, yfwd, K3, yfwd, sl 1, K1, psso, yfwd, K3, sl 1, K2 tog, psso, rep from * ending with K2 tog instead of sl 1, K2 tog, psso.
5th row Sl 1, K1, psso, *(K2, yfwd) twice, K2 tog, K1, sl 1, K1, psso, (yfwd, K2) twice, sl 1, K2 tog, psso, rep from * ending with K2 tog, instead of sl 1, K2 tog, psso.
7th row Sl 1, K1, psso, *K1, yfwd, K3, yfwd, K2 tog, K1, sl 1, K1, psso, yfwd, K3, yfwd, K1, sl 1, K2 tog, psso, rep from * ending with K2 tog instead of sl 1, K2 tog, psso.
8th row P to end.
Pattern repeat is 8 rows.

Hard lines of casting on or seaming spoil the delicate effect of lace knitting, so use the 2-needle method that gives a looser edge (p214); use needles one size larger to bind off. Where appropriate graft cast-on and bound-off edges together (p243) so that the joining is invisible: cast on with a spare length of yarn, remove this before finishing and graft the loops of the first row to the loops of the last row on the needle.

Spider's web (yellow)
Cast on a multiple of 6 sts plus 3 extra.
1st row (RS) K2, K2 tog, *yfwd, K1, yfwd, K2 tog, yfwd, sl 1, K2 tog, psso, rep from * to last 5 sts, yfwd, K1, yfwd, K2 tog, K2.
2nd and all even rows P to end.
3rd row K1, K2 tog, *yfwd, K3, yfwd, K3 tog, rep from * to last 6 sts, yfwd, K3, yfwd, K2 tog, K1.
5th row K2, *yfwd, K2 tog, yfwd, sl 1, K2 tog, psso, yfwd, K1, rep from * to last st, K1.
7th row K3, *yfwd, K3 tog, yfwd, K3, rep from * to end.
8th row As 2nd.
Pattern repeat is 8 rows.

Cat's paw (green)
Cast on a multiple of 12 sts plus 1 extra.
1st row (RS) K5, *yfwd, sl 1, K2 tog, psso, yfwd, K9, rep from * to last 8 sts, yfwd, sl 1, K2 tog, psso, yfwd, K5.
2nd and all even rows P to end.
3rd row K3, *K2 tog, yfwd, K3, yfwd, sl 1, K1, psso, K5, rep from * to last 10 sts, K2 tog, yfwd, K3, yfwd, sl 1, K1, psso, K3.
5th row As 1st.
7th row K to end.
9th row K2 tog, *yfwd, K9, yfwd, sl 1, K2 tog, psso, rep from * to last 11 sts, yfwd, K9, yfwd, sl 1, K1, psso.
11th row K2, *yfwd, sl 1, K1, psso, K5, K2 tog, yfwd, K3, rep from * to last 11 sts, yfwd, sl 1, K1, psso, K5, K2 tog, yfwd, K2.
13th row As 9th.
15th row As 7th.
16th row As 2nd.
Pattern repeat is 16 rows.

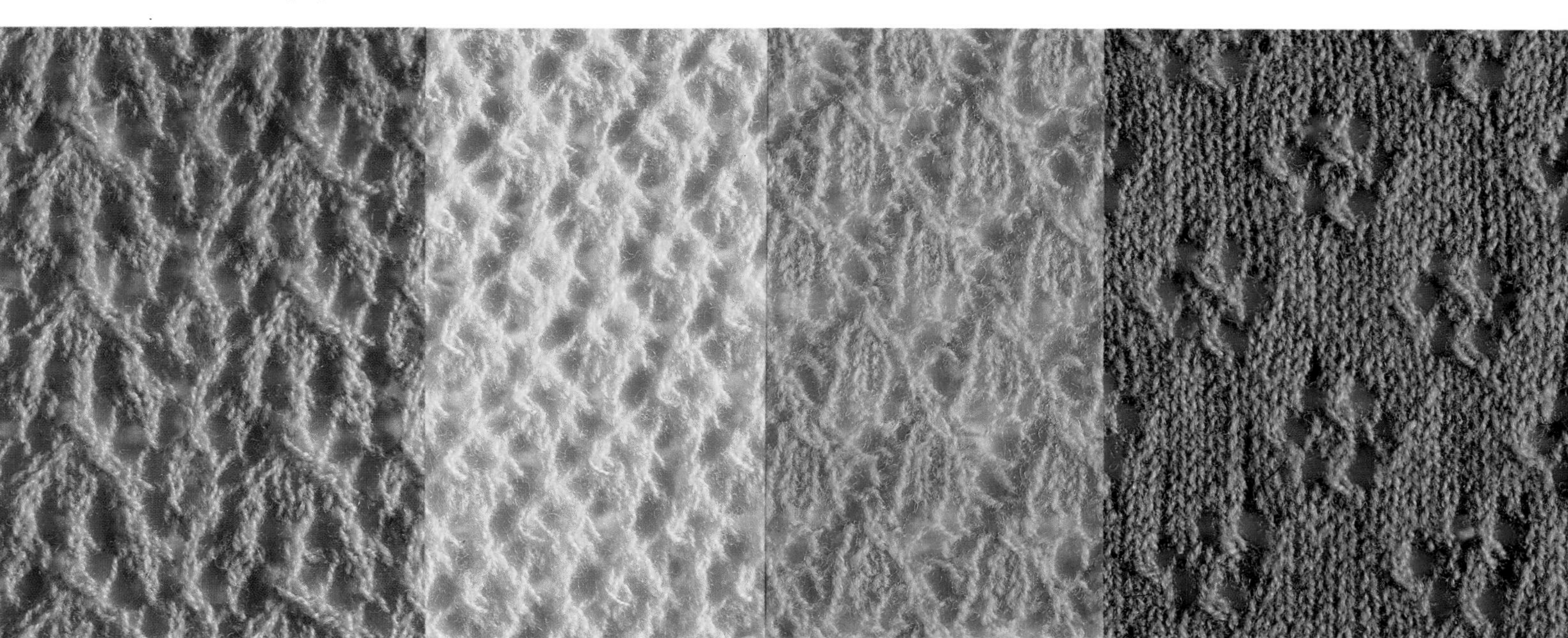

Rose-petal lace (pink)
Cast on a multiple of 10 sts plus 1 extra.
1st row (RS) K2 tog, *yfwd, K3, yfwd, K into front and back of next st, yfwd, K3, yfwd, sl 1, K2 tog, psso, rep from * ending with sl 1, K1, psso instead of sl 1, K2 tog, psso.
2nd and all even rows P to end.
3rd row Sl 1, K1, psso, *yfwd, sl 2 sts tog K-wise, K1, p2sso, yfwd, K2 tog, yfwd, sl 1, K1, psso, (yfwd, sl 2 tog, K1, p2sso) twice, rep from * ending with K2 tog instead of the 2nd sl 2 tog, K1, p2sso.
5th row K2, *K2 tog, yfwd, K3, yfwd, sl 1, K1, psso, K3, rep from * ending with K2 instead of K3.
7th row K1, *K2 tog, yfwd, K1 tbl, yfwd, sl 1, K2 tog, psso, yfwd, K1 tbl, yfwd, sl 1, K1, psso, K1, rep from * to end.
8th row As 2nd.
Pattern repeat is 8 rows. Note that the number of stitches varies from row to row, but the 6th and 8th rows contain the original cast-on number.

Bluebell (blue)
Cast on a multiple of 6 sts plus 3 extra.
1st row (RS) K3, *P2 tog, yrn, P1, K3, rep from * to end.
2nd row P3, *K3, P3, rep from * to end.
3rd row K3, *P1, yrn, P2 tog, K3, rep from * to end.
4th row As 2nd.
5th row K1, K2 tog, *(P1, yrn) twice, P1, sl 1, K2 tog, psso, rep from * ending with sl 1, K1, psso, K1 instead of sl 1, K2 tog, psso.
6th row K3, *P3, K3, rep from * to end.
7th row P1, yrn, P2 tog, *K3, P1, yrn, P2 tog, rep from * to end.
8th row As 6th.
9th row P2 tog, yrn, P1, *K3, P2 tog, yrn, P1, rep from * to end.
10th row As 6th.
11th row P2, yrn, P1, *sl 1, K2 tog, psso, (P1, yrn) twice, P1, rep from * to last 6 sts, sl 1, K2 tog, psso, P1, yrn, P2.
12th row As 2nd.
Pattern repeat is 12 rows.

Lace shawl

no. 5
25
36
g st

Casting on and binding off 214
Basic stitches 216
Gauge 220
Increasing and decreasing 222

Traditional Shetland lace shawls are sometimes so gossamer-fine they can pass through a wedding ring. This one in more substantial 2-ply lace-weight yarn is still delicate, though surprisingly warm. As the diagram shows it is worked in two parts and seamed together afterward. You need extra-long knitting needles to accommodate the large number of stitches that you pick up from the outer border around half the entire shawl, but you could use a circular needle here.

You will need
total of 7oz (175g) lace-weight Shetland yarn in 4 colors coded A–D: 3oz (75g) main color A, 2oz (50g) 1st contrast B, 1oz (25g) each C and D
1 pair long no. 5 needles

Size
about 39in (100cm) square

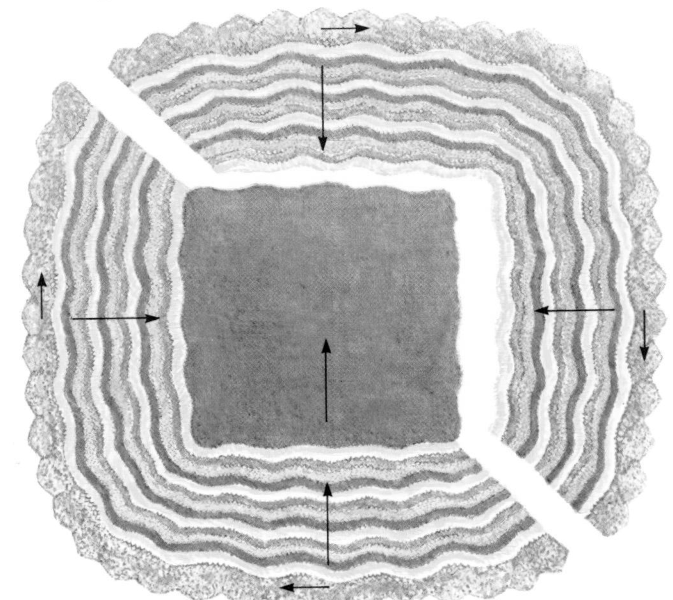

Following patterns 226
Finishing 242
Lace knitting 274

Outer border
Using no. 5 needles and B cast on 12 sts.
1st row: K12.
2nd row: K10, yfwd, K2 (13 sts).
3rd row: Yo, K2 tog, K11 (to make loop at beg of row).
4th row: K9, yfwd, K2 tog, yfwd, K2 (14 sts).
5th row: Yo, K2 tog, K to end.
6th row: K8, (yfwd, K2 tog) twice, yfwd, K2 (15 sts).
7th row: As 5th.
8th row: K7, (yfwd, K2 tog) 3 times, yfwd, K2 (16 sts).
9th row: As 5th.
10th row: K6, (yfwd, K2 tog) 4 times, yfwd, K2 (17 sts).
11th row: As 5th.
12th row: K5, (yfwd, K2 tog) 5 times, yfwd, K2 (18 sts).
13th row: As 5th.
14th row: K5, (K2 tog, yfwd) 5 times, K2 tog, K1 (17 sts).
15th row: As 5th.
16th row: K6, (K2 tog, yfwd) 4 times, K2 tog, K1 (16 sts).
17th row: As 5th.
18th row: K7, (K2 tog, yfwd) 3 times, K2 tog, K1 (15 sts).
19th row: As 5th.
20th row: K8, (K2 tog, yfwd) twice, K2 tog, K1 (14 sts).
21st row: As 5th.
22nd row: K9, K2 tog, yfwd, K2 tog, K1 (13 sts).
23rd row: As 5th.
24th row: K10, K2 tog, K1 (12 sts).
25th row: As 5th.
Rep the 2nd–25th rows 23 times more (577 rows in all).
Do not break off yarn, but K up 289 sts along the straight edge on border (i.e. 1 st for every 2 rows).

Inner border
Attach D and work as follows:
1st row: *K1, (K2 tog) 4 times, (yfwd, K1) 7 times, yfwd, (K2 tog) 4 times *, rep from * to * 11 times more, K1.
2nd–6th rows: K.
7th row: Attach A and work as for 1st row.
8th–12th rows: K.
13th row: Attach C and * K1, (K2 tog) 4 times, (yfwd, K1) 6 times, yfwd, (K3 tog) 3 times, (rep from * to * as in 1st row) 4 times, K1, (K3 tog) 3 times, (yfwd, K1) 6 times, yfwd, (K2 tog) twice *, rep from * to * once, K1.
This row begins the dec at the corners.
14th–18th rows: K.
19th row: Attach B and * K1, (K2 tog) 3 times, (yfwd, K1) 6 times, yfwd, K2 tog, (K3 tog) twice, (rep from * to * as in 1st row) 4 times, K1, (K3 tog) twice, K2 tog, (yfwd, K1) 6 times, yfwd, (K2 tog) 3 times *, rep from * to * once, K1.
20th–24th rows: K.
25th row: Attach D and *K1, (K2 tog) 3 times, (yfwd, K1) 5 times, yfwd, K2 tog, (K3 tog) twice, (rep from * to * as in 1st row) 4 times, K1, (K3 tog) twice, K2 tog, (yfwd, K1) 5 times, yfwd, (K2 tog) 3 times *, rep from * to * once, K1.
26th–30th rows: K.
31st row: Attach A and * K1, (K2 tog) 3 times, (yfwd, K1) 5 times, yfwd, (K2 tog) 3 times, (rep from * to * as in 1st row) 4 times, K1, (K2 tog) 3 times, (yfwd, K1) 5 times, yfwd, (K2 tog) 3 times *, rep from * to * once, K1.
32nd–36th rows: K.
37th row: Attach C and * K1, (K2 tog) 3 times, (yfwd, K1) 4 times, yfwd, (K2 tog) twice, K3 tog, (rep from * to * as in 1st row) 4 times, K1, K3 tog, (K2 tog) twice, (yfwd, K1) 4 times, yfwd, (K2 tog) 3 times *, rep from * to * once, K1.
38th–42nd rows: K.
43rd row: Attach B and * K1, (K2 tog) twice, K3 tog, (yfwd, K1) 4 times, yfwd, (K2 tog) twice, (rep from * to * as in 1st row) 4 times, K1, (K2 tog) twice, (yfwd, K1) 4 times, yfwd, K3 tog, (K2 tog) twice *, rep from * to * once, K1.
44th–48th rows: K.
49th row: Attach D and * K1, (K2 tog) 3 times, (yfwd, K1) 3 times, yfwd, K2 tog, K3 tog, (rep from * to * as in 1st row) 4 times, K1, K3 tog, K2 tog, (yfwd, K1) 3 times, yfwd, (K2 tog) 3 times *, rep from * to * once, K1.
50th–54th rows: K.
55th row: Attach A and * K1, (K2 tog) twice, (yfwd, K1) 3 times, yfwd, K3 tog, K2 tog, (rep from * to * as in 1st row) 4 times, K1, (K2 tog) twice, (yfwd, K1) 3 times, yfwd, K3 tog, K2 tog *, rep from * to * once, K1.
56th–60th rows: K.
61st row: Attach C and * K1, K2 tog, K3 tog, (yfwd, K1) twice, yfwd, (K2 tog) twice, (rep from * to * as in 1st row) 4 times, K1, (K2 tog) twice, (yfwd, K1) twice, yfwd, K3 tog, K2 tog*, rep from * to * once, K1.
62nd–66th rows: K.
67th row: Attach B and * K1, (K2 tog) twice, yfwd, K1, yfwd, (K2 tog) twice, (rep from * to * as in 1st row) 4 times, K1, (K2 tog) twice, yfwd, K1, yfwd, (K2 tog) twice *, rep from * to * once, K1.
68th–72nd rows: K.
73rd row: Attach D and * K1, (K2 tog) twice, yfwd, K3 tog, (rep from * to * as in 1st row) 4 times, K1, K3 tog, yfwd, (K2 tog) twice *, rep from * to * once, K1.
74th–78th rows: K.
79th row: Attach A and K1, (yfwd, K3 tog) twice, (yfwd, K2 tog to 6th pat—corner), (yfwd, K3 tog) twice, K1, (K3 tog) twice, (yfwd, K2 tog to last pat), (yfwd, K3 tog) twice, K1.
80th row: K.

Center (using A)
Next row: K to center of row, pick up 1 st from the next side, turn, K2 tog, K to end.
Rep this row until 1 st has been picked up on every row along side and center forms a square.
Bind off very loosely.

Work 2nd half of outer and inner border to correspond to first, ending with 80th row.
Bind off very loosely.

Finishing
Sew 2nd border to center square and sew up corners, keeping sts loose to allow for stretching. Dampen shawl, spread out and pin to correct size and leave to dry.

Beads

Beads and sequins are available in all shapes and sizes. You can either buy loose beads or use old ones — maybe from a broken necklace — as long as the hole in the center is large enough to take the thread or yarn being used. Small beads are better than large ones that might pull the fabric out of shape. Sequins also come in a variety of shapes and sizes, but remember that the hole for the yarn must be at the top of the sequin and not in the middle so that the sequin lies flat against the knitting instead of standing up. Use any type of thread or yarn that you think suitable; the size of hole is the only limitation, but the more you experiment with different beads and yarns the more rewarding the results. Beadwork is usually done against a background of stockinette stitch or garter stitch; openwork lace patterns (p274) provide another interesting backdrop since the beads emphasize the openness of the stitches by hanging in the spaces rather than lying flat against the fabric. You can use graph paper to plan an all-over design in the same way as working from a chart (p265). Stripes of beads or sequins look very effective and require little planning; the same applies to a random scattering of beads on a stockinette-stitch or chevron-patterned background.

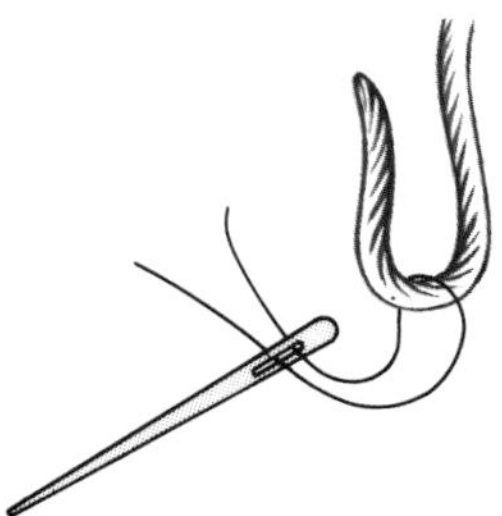

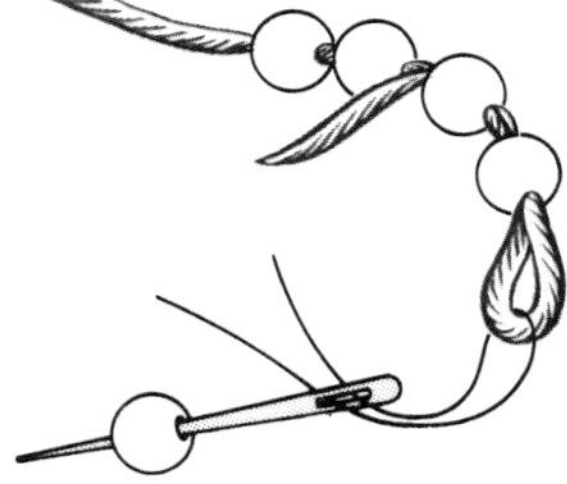

Threading beads
1 Before you begin, thread beads or sequins onto the ball of yarn you will be using; the easiest way is to cut a 10in (25cm) length of sewing thread and fold in half. Thread end through a sewing needle.

2 Pass about 6in (15cm) of the knitting yarn through the looped sewing thread. Thread the beads or sequins onto the needle, slide down the sewing thread over the doubled knitting yarn onto the ball of yarn.

Knitting in beads
1 On stockinette-stitch fabric add beads on RS rows. Knit until you reach the position for the next bead. Push 1 bead (or sequin) up the ball of yarn close to the back of the work. Insert the RH needle into the back of the next stitch on the LH needle.

2 Continue knitting tbl in the usual way, pushing the bead or sequin through to front of work at the same time as the loop of the stitch so that it lies flat against the fabric.

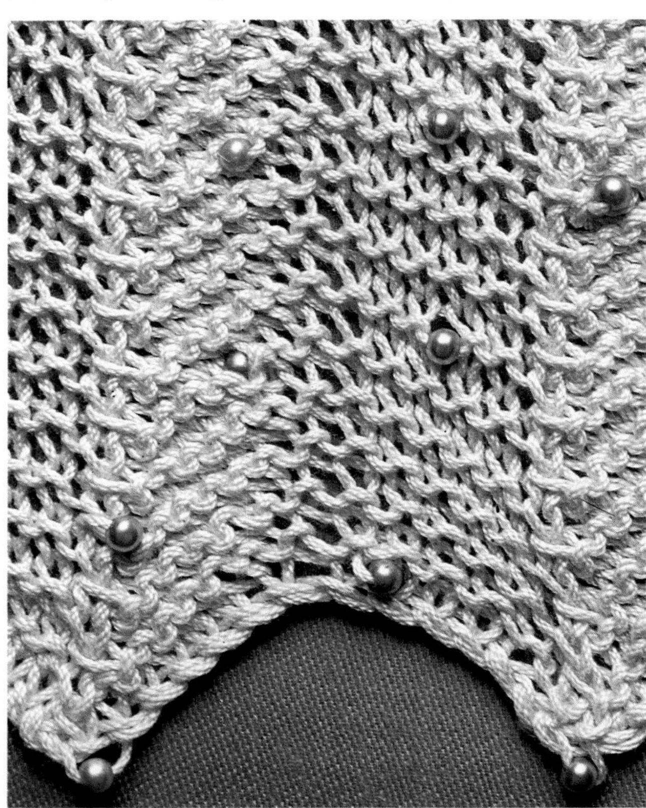

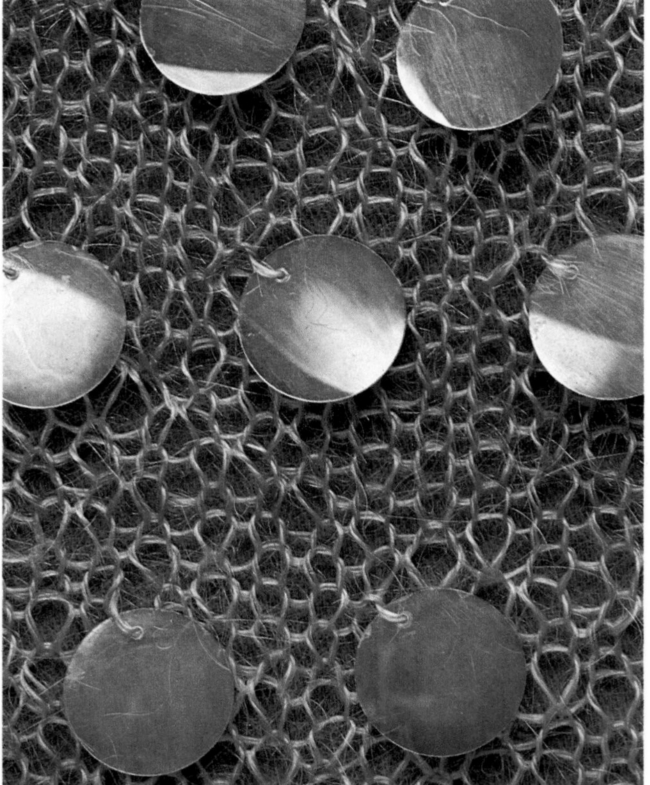

Loops

Looped knitting worked in a natural color closely resembles a woolly sheep's fleece and produces a fabric that is warm but can be reasonably light. It is ideal for outdoor wear such as jackets and coats, either as an attractive all-over fabric or for trimming on collar and cuffs, and is useful for some household items including pillows and cot or carriage covers. You can even knit a rug. The technique of winding the yarn around your thumb to create the loop takes some practice initially, but you can quickly become adept. You need not worry unduly about making the loops even, since the shaggy quality of the fabric is part of its character. Most yarns are suitable for this type of knitting; loop stitch shows the texture of the bouclé yarn used in the loopy coat on next page particularly well. It is best to avoid using yarn that is very thick, however, or you may make a fabric that is too heavy and that becomes distorted when worn. Remember that loops can be left as knitted or can be cut – an interesting texture would result from combining cut loops with uncut ones.

Cast on an odd number of stitches.

1st row (RS) K1, *K1 without letting st fall from LH needle, yfwd, wind yarn clockwise around left thumb to make loop approx 2in (5cm) long, ybk, K into back of same st – called L1, K1, rep from * to end.

2nd row K1, *K2 tog, K1, rep from * to end.

3rd row K2, *L1, K1, rep from * to last st, K1.

4th row K2, *K2 tog, K1, rep from * to last st, K1.

The extra stitch at each end of every loop row in this sample is useful when finishing – it avoids a bulky seam. Note that when you make a loop 2 stitches form on the RH needle out of the original one. You reduce these and secure the loop at the same time by knitting the 2 stitches together on the following WS rows. Remember when increasing or decreasing for shaping to count stitches on WS rows – the extra stitches you make while looping on RS rows can throw out your calculations. You can vary the length of loops by the number of times you wind the yarn around your thumb and the density of the loops by the number of times you work them into the background fabric. Here the loops are on alternate stitches on alternate rows.

Another variation of loop stitch is created by cutting loops with scissors after finishing knitting. You can make an all-over shaggy effect or simply work occasional rows of cut loops across a stockinette-stitch fabric for a fringed effect.

Loopy coat

Casting on and binding off 214
Gauge 220
Increasing and decreasing 222
Following patterns 226
Finishing 242
Loops 279

Long loops show up the unusual texture of this bouclé yarn to full advantage, at the same time making a really warm fabric. Once you have worked out your gauge with the yarn you have chosen, you can adapt the outline shown here to create something in the size you want – perhaps making a jacket instead of a long coat – or design your own garment (see p286). Instead of the loopy stitch you could work a textured pattern like one of the Aran ones on p260, or make an original combination of stripes and color patterns.

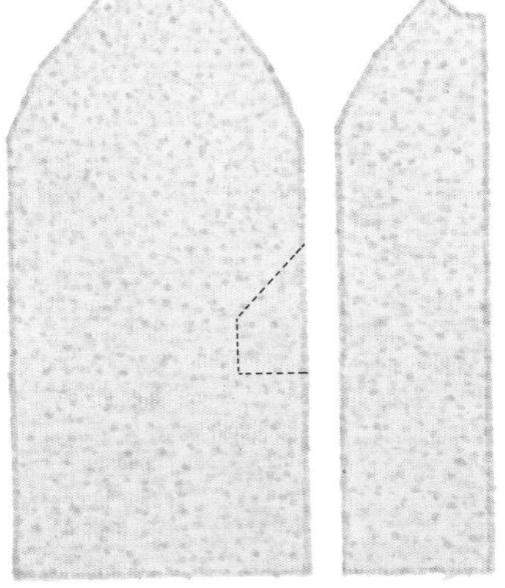

Size		
bust/hips	35in	(90cm)
length	47in	(120cm)
sleeve seam	$16\frac{1}{2}$in	(43cm)

You will need
80oz (2000g) bouclé yarn
1 pair no. 9 needles
lining material for pockets
matching sewing thread

Back
Cast on 57 sts. K1 row. Begin loop pat (see p279) and rep the 4 rows of pat throughout, maintaining pat through all shaping. Cont until back measures 38in (97cm) from beg, ending with a WS row.
Shape raglans Maintaining pat, cast off 3 sts at beg of next 2 rows. Dec 1 st at each end of next and every foll 4th row until 37 sts rem, then at each end of every foll alt row until 19 sts rem. Work 1 row. Bind off.

Left front
Cast on 29 sts. K 1 row. Cont in loop pat until front measures 38in (97cm) from beg, ending with a WS row.
Shape raglan Maintaining pat, bind off 3 sts at beg of next row. Work 1 row. Dec 1 st at beg (armhole edge) of next and every foll 4th row until 19 sts rem, then at beg of every foll alt row until 15 sts rem, ending at front edge.
Shape neck Bind off 5 sts at beg of next row. Cont to dec 1 st at armhole edge on alt rows as before, dec 1 st at neck edge at beg of foll 3 alt rows (4 sts). Dec 1 st at armhole edge twice more. Work 1 row. K2 tog. Fasten off.

Right front
Work to correspond to left front, reversing shaping.

Sleeves
Cast on 37 sts. K 1 row. Cont in loop pat, inc 1 st at each end of every 14th row until there are 47 sts. Cont without shaping until sleeve measures $16\frac{1}{2}$in (43cm) from beg, ending with a WS row.
Shape raglans Bind off 3 sts at beg of next 2 rows. Dec 1 st each end of next and every foll 4th row until 31 sts rem, then at each end of every foll alt row until 5 sts rem. Work 1 row. Bind off.

Finishing
Join raglan seams. Join side and sleeve seams, leaving a 6in (15cm) opening 10in (30cm) below underarm (for pocket linings) in side seam. Cut out and make pocket lining (see Pocket in side seam, p92) and overcast in position with sewing thread.

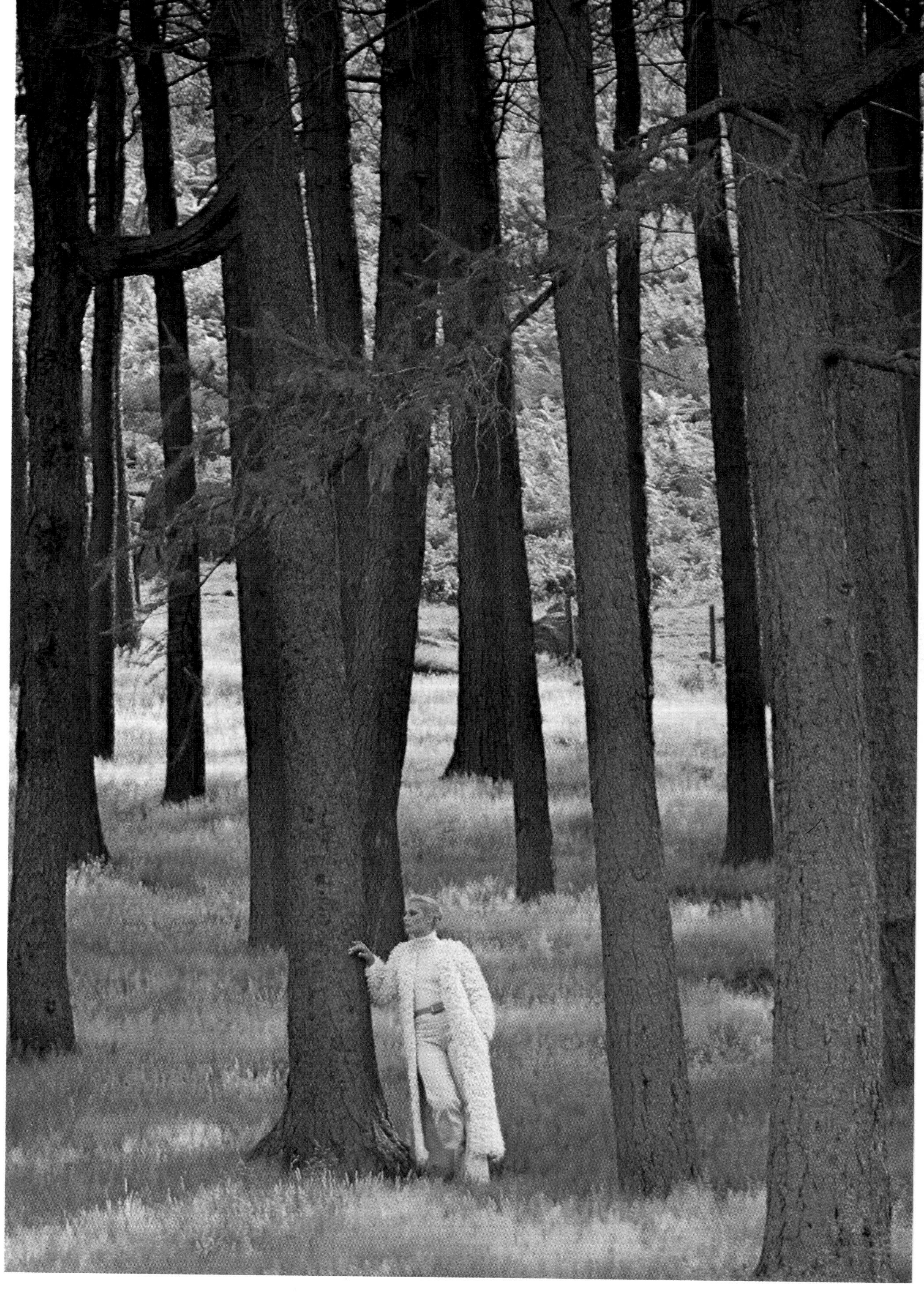

Remodeling clothes

Occasionally miscalculations happen and you knit something that is the wrong size. Forget your dress-making instincts about trimming the seams of an oversized garment to make it smaller: cutting knitting is an extremely difficult process which experts may do in some circumstances but which is not recommended even then. Apart from finding someone whom the garment fits, your best option is to open the seams, unravel the yarn and recycle it so that you can start again. This technique gives new life not only to disasters but also to garments which are slightly damaged or which have become unfashionable. However, yarn that you want to re-use does have to be in fairly good condition – if the knitting has matted it becomes very hard to unravel the stitches.

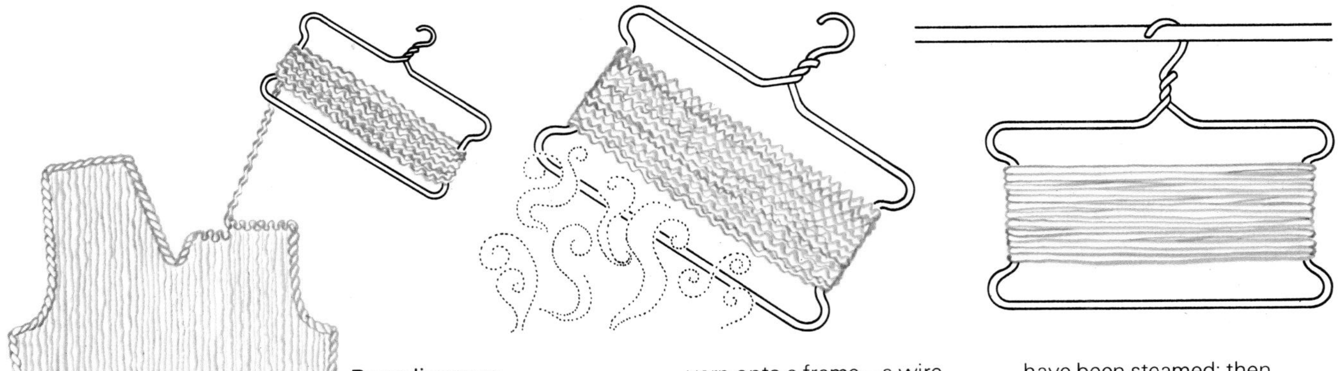

Recycling yarn

Yarn that has been knitted even for a short time and then unravelled has kinks that prevent it being re-knitted into a smooth fabric. Steam unravelled yarn to remove all the kinks. As you unravel the knitting wind the yarn onto a frame – a wire clothes hanger bent to shape is suitable. Don't wind too tightly or the steam will not penetrate thoroughly. Hold the skein of yarn in the steam from a boiling kettle or pan of water until all the folds of yarn have been steamed; then leave the yarn to dry completely away from direct heat before re-winding it loosely into balls for re-use.

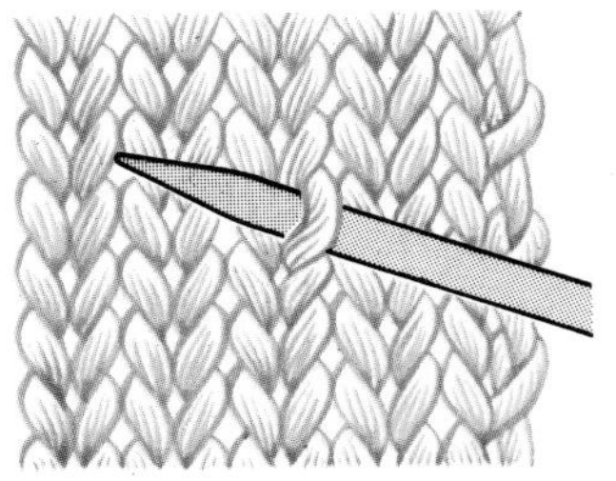

Lengthening and shortening

When altering knitting for a growing child, re-styling a favorite sweater, or repairing damaged knitting you may want to add or take away a section of the main fabric. You can easily alter a garment in garter stitch or stockinette stitch, but avoid complicated fabrics unless you are sure you can pick up the original number of stitches in their correct sequence.

Check the garment to find the best position for altering length: a sweater with sleeves and body too short needs extra length added above cuffs and waistband. Open sleeve and side seams to about 2in (5cm) above the adjustment point to allow you freedom to manipulate the needles when you re-knit. Note the exact number of rows below this adjustment point and in the cuffs and waistband; you need to add to or subtract from these to lengthen or shorten the garment. Don't cut the fabric, but divide it.

1 Insert a needle into the head of a stitch (1 or 2 sts in from RH edge).

2 Pull this stitch up tightly to form a long loop of yarn as you tighten the stitches across entire width of fabric.

3 Cut the loop and carefully pull fabric apart until you expose 2 sets of stitches. Gently unravel the cut end of yarn until the fabric is in 2 sections. Pick up the sts of the main section making sure you have the original number and each stitch lies in the correct direction. Unravel remaining yarn and steam it if you want to use it for re-knitting.

4 Attach yarn at beginning of a row and continue knitting in a downward direction adding or subtracting extra rows from the original number according to whether you want to lengthen or shorten the garment. In this way the cuffs or waistband are the last section of the garment you knit, but the stitches are non-directional and the new sections unnoticeable. Remember to bind off loosely.

Anticipating alterations

You may want to re-knit a fashion garment made in expensive yarn in a different style for a new season; with growing children you can predict having to make alterations on length as well as running repairs. If you envisage having to enlarge a garment don't forget to buy extra yarn of the same dye lot.
Seaming stitches are often difficult to detect in knitted fabric. If you anticipate taking a garment apart run a short length of fine thread in contrasting color under your stitches as you sew – this doesn't show on RS but indicates position of seam stitches for reopening.

Replacing worn ribbing

When a ribbed cuff or waistband gets worn it is best to replace all ribbed parts of the garment to make the repair look like part of a coordinated design rather than an emergency measure. Use yarn of the same weight as original garment; choose an entirely different color to avoid slight differences due to different dye lots or the combination of new yarn with a fabric that has discolored in use. Open side seams and sleeve seams to about 6in (15cm) above ribbing, and open one shoulder seam. Rip out the ribbing, pick up stitches (see opposite) and then re-knit ribbing, working to original length. This is also a way of changing a turtle neck to a crew neck or *vice versa* (see p240).

Altering sleeve length

Unless you can be sure of reversing sleeve shaping correctly as you work downward after ripping (see opposite) it is best not to try re-knitting long sleeves although you can add a few inches above the cuffs. When elbows or cuffs are irremediably worn, change long sleeves to short ones. Open the seam to a few inches above new length, rip fabric required distance, pick up stitches again and work a ribbed cuff or hem using recycled yarn or a contrasting color.

Using stripes

Re-knitting downward to lengthen or shorten can be conspicuous when dye lots vary or your gauge changes. Use stripes (p244) to disguise these problems – either working in a contrasting color or choosing a textured stitch (such as stripes of basket-weave against a stockinette-stitch background) that will make such discrepancies less noticeable. It is obviously easier to re-knit a comparatively shapeless garment than trying to reverse shaping points as you work downward. You can make a virtue of this by leaving side seams open at bottom of a long sweater, omitting ribbing and making it a tunic shape rather than a conventional fitted garment.

Removing sleeves

You can shorten worn set-in sleeves but you can also remove them completely and give a garment a new look. Unpick the sleeve seam and remove sleeve. Either use set of 4 needles to pick up sts around armhole or rip side seams of garment and use a pair of needles to work back and forth (see p240). Use yarn recycled from unravelled sleeve to finish off armband. An alternative method of finishing is to use binding.

Binding edges

Where a firm bulky fabric is wearing at the edges bind sleeve edges and pocket tops with soft leather; add patches to elbows and matching leather buttons to give a coordinated look. Binding is not, however, appropriate for ribbed cuffs which lose elasticity if bound. Binding with narrow strips of fabric or bias binding (see p25) is a good way of tidying up armhole edges which are not finished with knitted edgings and for disguising worn or uneven casting on and binding off. When the sleeves of a dress become too small for a growing child make a tunic by removing them and binding the edges.

Reinforcing knitting

Elbows and knees of knitted garments frequently show wear first. Strengthen the fabric by duplicate stitching over the worn area (see p228). You can either use the same yarn as the main fabric to make an invisible repair or make a decorative feature by working motifs.

Design: squares and rectangles

Probably the easiest way to create your own designs is to base them on squares and rectangles, which require no graduated shaping. Start off with a gauge swatch to establish what kind of fabric you want and to enable you to calculate size. Decide how your fabric needs to behave: a top like the silver and mohair one here could be strapless in a clinging K1, P1 rib, but needs support in less elastic fabrics like garter stitch. A garment featuring fullness, such as the gold top gathered into cuffs, needs to be worked in a fine, smooth texture that will drape well, rather than in a woolen yarn.

Experiment with yarn, pattern and texture until you have decided on a fabric, work out its gauge, then multiply the number of stitches to the inch by the width of your square or rectangle to find out how many stitches to cast on. Unless you are working a striped pattern with a definite row repeat it is easiest to calculate length by measurement rather than by the number of rows. As well as the simple tops shown here, squares and rectangles are, of course, the basis of the T-shaped sweaters on p224 and the sweater with the Jacquard motifs on p272. Designs based on these rectangular shapes can be in simple stitch

Neckbands *240*
Finishing *242*
Stripes *244*
Knitting in rounds *250*

patterns or can feature textured stitches or color patterns. You may need to take care over multiples of stitches with a bold pattern. If you choose a stitch pattern with a large repeat – say '15 sts plus 1' – and you calculate that you need 130 sts to give you the right width, add 5 sts plus 1 extra edge st to make the pattern work out symmetrically; if this gives you too much width, experiment with needles a size smaller to get the correct number of stitches to the right width measurement.

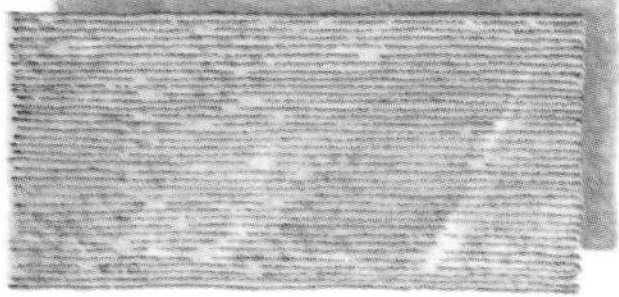

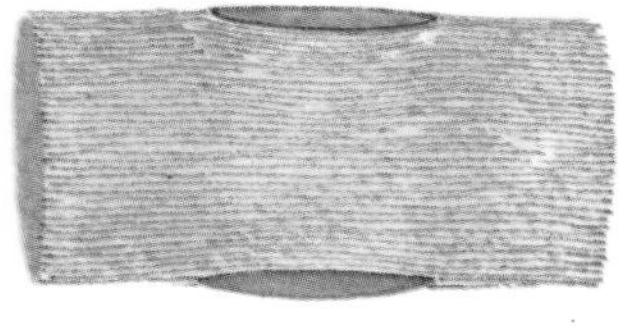

Gold top

1 Using a fine yarn with a fairly tight gauge to make a smooth fabric (e.g. 30 sts and 40 rows to 4in or 10cm), cast on sufficient sts to give depth from shoulder to top of waistband and work 2 rectangles each approx $13\frac{1}{2} \times 39$in (34×100cm).

2 Sew long edges tog into tube leaving slits for neck opening (see **5**) and waistband.

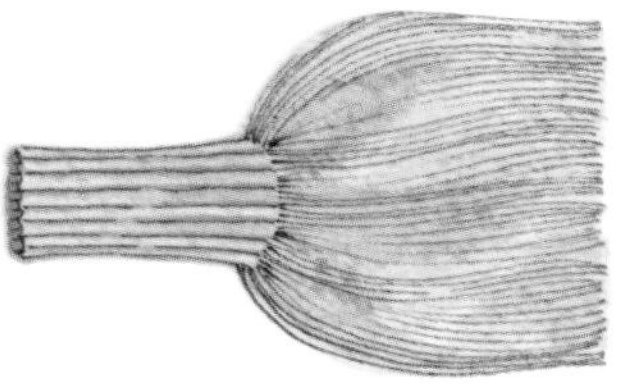

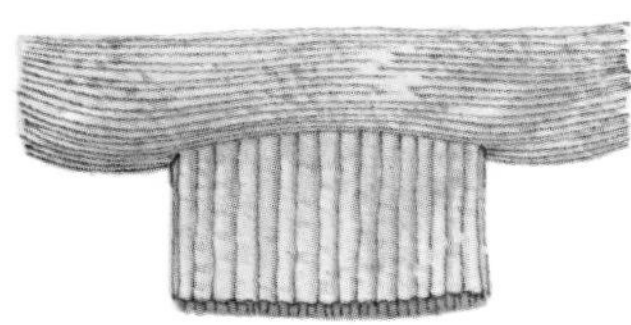

3 Using set of 4 needles and with RS facing, K up sts around sleeve edge, dec every alt st for 2 rows to reduce no. of sts to approx circumference of cuff (e.g. 6in/16cm). Work in K1, P1 rib for about $4\frac{1}{2}$in (12cm) or length required.

4 Using same set of 4 needles and with RS facing, K up sts around waistband and work K1, P1 rib for $7\frac{1}{2}$in (19cm) or length required.

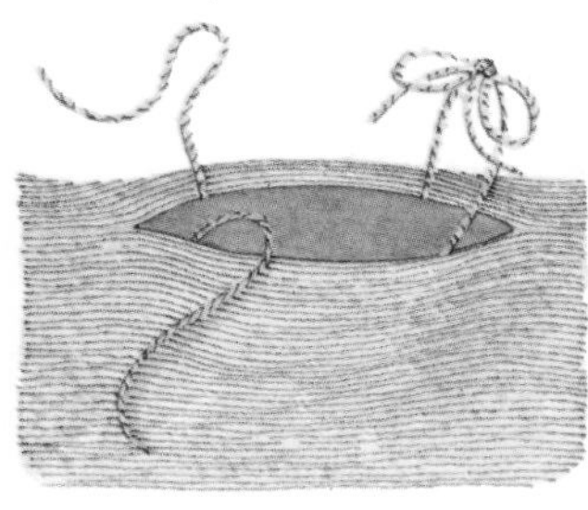

5 Attach 4 twisted cords (p102) about 6in (15cm) long to inner edges of neck opening for an off-the-shoulder look; or make neck slit narrower than shoulder width to cover shoulder.

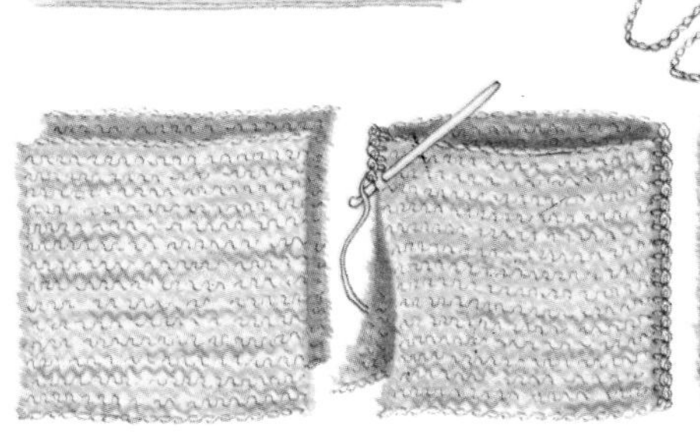

Silver and mohair top

1 Cast on sufficient sts to make a rectangle half the total width required – e.g. cast on 16in (41cm) for 32in (82cm) bust. Work in chosen st pat (here stripes of g st) for about 10in (25cm) or required depth. Bind off very loosely. Work 2nd piece to correspond

2 Seam sides into a tube, you can join pieces with single crochet (see p302) in same yarn as bound-off stripe.

3 Make twisted cords (p102) for straps to tie on shoulders. Alternatively, knit narrow straps.

Design: shapes

Design in knitting involves not only establishing the basic shapes of the component parts of the garment or item you are making but also deciding exactly how and where to do the increases and decreases that will achieve the necessary shape. Remember that increases and decreases worked at the ends of rows, i.e. around the edges of a fabric, create a flat shape; for example, this is the method for making armhole curves and sleeve-top shaping as well as the segments of the pumpkin on p294. Increases and decreases placed within the fabric – i.e. worked in the middle of a row – distort its flatness and create a flared or concave effect – as in the slightly flared shape of the child's sleeve (p230) or the knitted tomatoes and onions (p294).

Here are three different systems of designing shapes. The paper pattern method is the simplest but can be somewhat hit-or-miss if you are trying to make anything more accurate than a fairly loose-fitting garment. The graph system used by professional designers is on the whole too complicated for the beginner to design classic fashion garments, though it can be useful for simpler forms like some of those on pp294–7. The most satisfactory method for relatively inexperienced knitters is to take the paper pattern outline as the basis for the rough shape and then use the gauge grid system to give a stitch-by-stitch breakdown of shaping and pattern. This method is suitable for working out color as well as shape – see picture knitting on p288.

Yarn and stitch patterns
Whichever method you choose, keep yarn and stitch pattern simple for your first attempts at design. Only when the shape is successful can you afford to experiment with textured stitches and yarns. It is easier at first to work out gauge and to see what you are doing – as well as to rectify mistakes – in a stockinette-stitch fabric worked in 4-ply or knitting worsted yarn.

Gauge is vital to your design whichever method you choose. Start with the usual 4in (10cm) sample (p220) with the yarn and needles of your choice to establish how many stitches per inch you will need. If you decide on the gauge grid method of design this sample gives you the basis to work from.

Matching When what you are making comprises 2 (or more) sections that must correspond to each other – 2 cardigan fronts, 2 sleeves, or the individual segments of a 3-dimensional shape such as a sphere – make sure that subsequent sections correspond exactly to the first. Either note down the number of stitches and rows and the positions of shaping or constantly compare the pieces of knitting, counting stitches and rows to make sure they are identical.
You can get different results if you compare the pieces of knitting only with the pattern and not with each other, since the elasticity of the fabric can give slightly different results each time.

Ribbing Since ribbing is so elastic it is difficult to stretch it flat to make it correspond to a paper outline. When you want ribbed cuffs or waistbands ignore these while you do preliminary calculations for the main stockinette-stitch fabric. These give you the number of stitches to cast on; you can work these stitches in ribbing if you want to before changing to stockinette stitch for the remainder of the fabric.

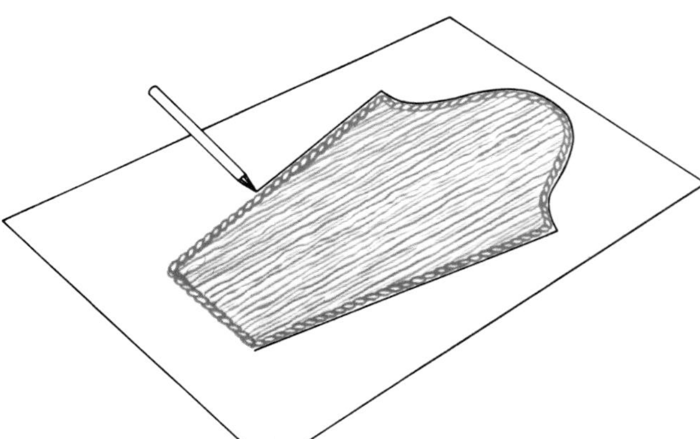

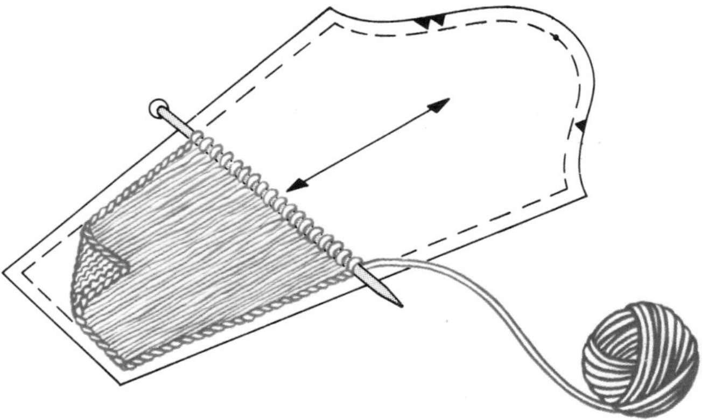

Paper patterns
One fairly basic method of design involves working from a paper pattern. As a basis you could use the parts of a garment that you have taken to pieces and drawn around to make a template, or a paper dressmaking pattern (excluding seam allowances) provided this doesn't have complicated shaping such as darts. Either way, keep the component parts as simple as possible. Work out from your gauge sample how many stitches to cast on to achieve the width of your pattern piece and then begin knitting; check your work constantly against the paper template or pattern to make sure they correspond exactly, increasing and decreasing when it looks necessary. This is not a very accurate method since your knitting is not as flat as the paper, but you should try to be as careful as possible.
A more accurate way to knit a shape corresponding to a paper pattern uses the gauge grid method (opposite), starting with the outline of the shape you want, then working out the number of stitches you'll need to make it from the gauge sample, and referring to the paper pattern as a check.

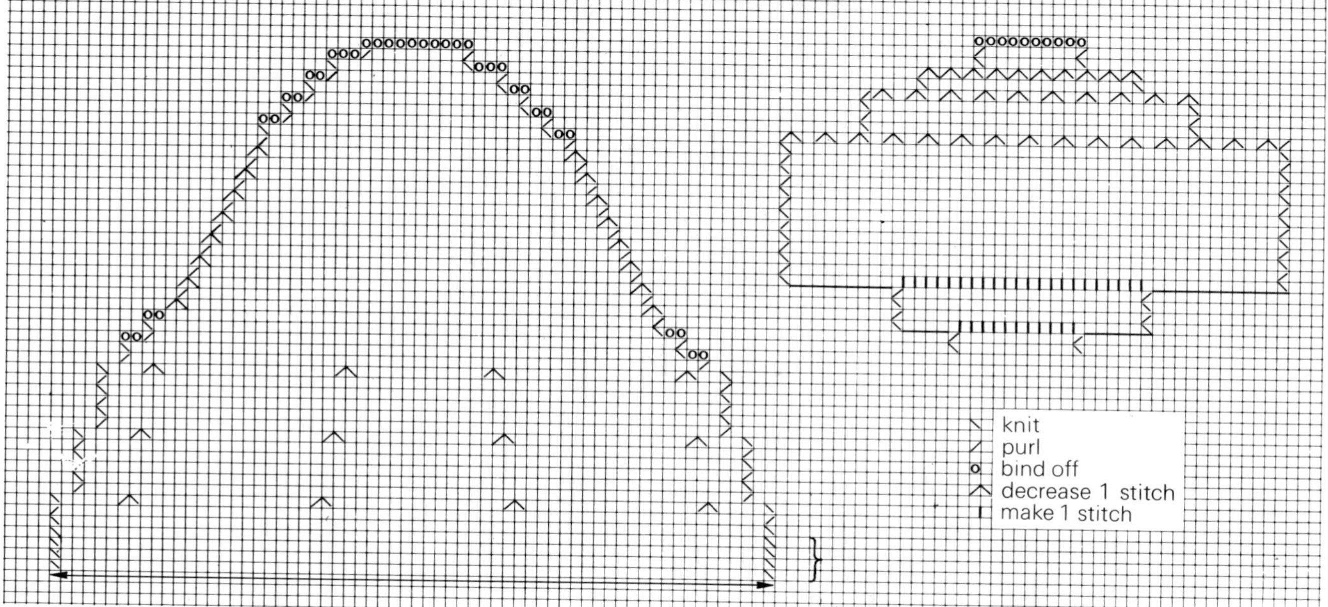

Graph paper method

Professional knitting designers work out their designs mathematically and then use graph paper to chart them out as a visual check and as a basis for their written instructions. Each square represents a stitch and symbols are used to indicate K and P rows, binding off, increases and decreases. Begin following a graph at the bottom RH edge and work back along the rows of squares from left to right and right to left alternately. Decreases within the knitting or at the edge give a stepped effect to the graph outline. Where shaping takes place at the edge of the fabric only (as in the top of the sleeve of the child's dress on p230) you see graduated shaping on the graph roughly resembling the curve of the actual knitting; where shaping takes place within the fabric as in the 'tomato' from p294 this has to be indicated in a stylized way that doesn't represent the curving effect created in the fabric itself.
Although designers' patterns worked with this method are easy enough to follow once you understand the symbols, it takes a good deal of knitting experience to be able to work out your own. You need to know just how to decrease to curve an armhole and make a set-in sleeve fit exactly, for example. Always bear in mind that you are dealing on squared paper with stitches that are not in fact square so that your calculations can't be done directly – the depth of a pattern on the graph paper is about one-third as long again as it is on the actual knitted fabric.

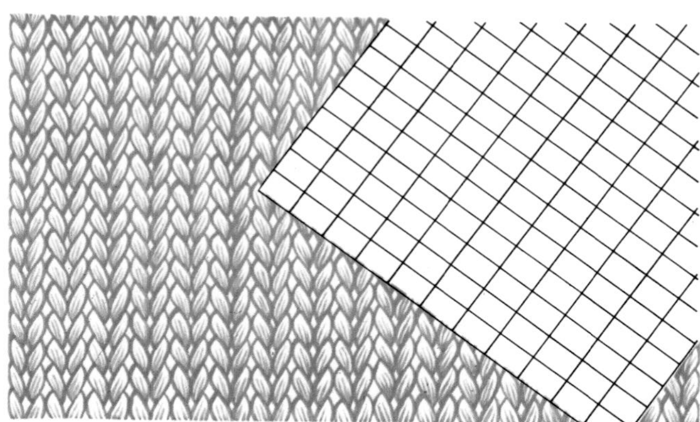

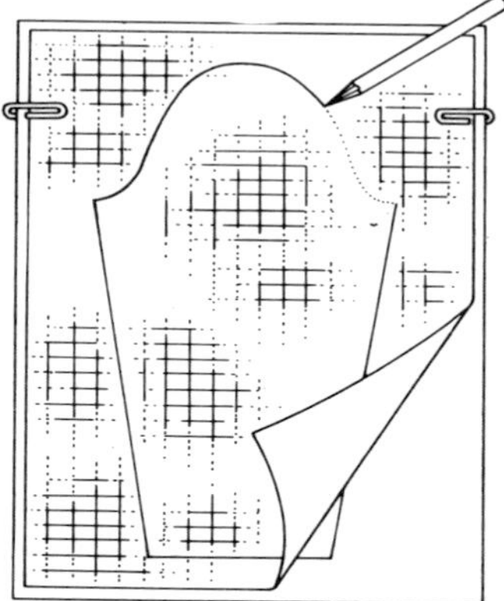

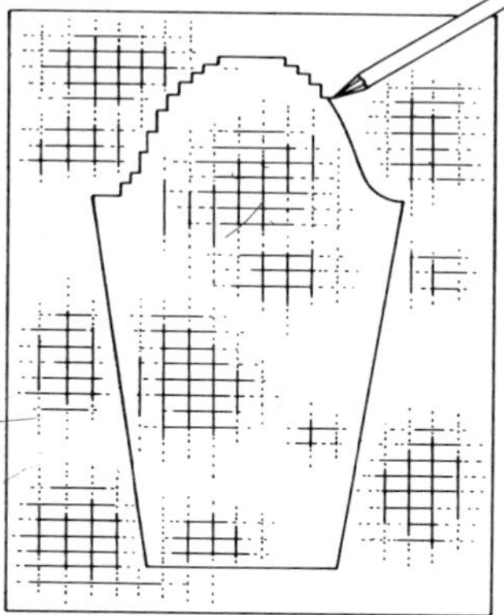

Gauge grid

If you want an accurate picture of what will happen to the outline you have drawn or copied when it is made up of knitted stitches, the best way of finding out is to draw a grid of squares which correspond more or less exactly to your chosen gauge. This shows more clearly that stitches are almost always shallower than their width. Take your gauge sample and measure it. Rule up on tracing paper in ink a large grid showing the same number of squares to 4in (10cm) across as you have stitches and the same number of squares vertically as you have rows. You should now be able to see from the grid not only how many squares, i.e. stitches, you need to cast on to make a given width in inches, but also how frequently you would have to place your increases or decreases to create the desired shape.

1 Measure the gauge of your knitting sample – in this example the gauge is 20 sts and 30 rows to 4in (10cm).

2 Draw a grid on tracing paper to correspond to your gauge sample with 5 squares to the inch across and $7\frac{1}{2}$ squares down.

3 Draw the full-size outline of the shape you want to make and clip it under the gauge grid. (You can use a piece of knitting as a template, a paper pattern or your own sketched outline.)

4 Go over your outline with a colored pencil changing the rough curve of your sketch into a stepped line corresponding to the squares on your gauge grid, to show where the actual stitches of your knitting need to be.

Picture sweater

Casting on and binding off 214
Basic stitches 216
Gauge 220

Unless you use the simplest T-shapes, it is a good idea to work a picture on a ready-made pattern rather than trying to cope with designing a shape as well as a scene. A classic crew neck with set-in sleeves like this one worked in 3-ply yarn is ideal – the fineness of the yarn gives plenty of scope for detail. Use yarns of approximately equal gauge for the different parts of your design; remember that you needn't be confined to color contrasts alone but can introduce texture as well – here the clouds are shades of angora; chenille has been used for the tree, sheep and some foliage; the water is a yarn spun with a Lurex thread. The back of this sweater is in plain sky-blue; blocks of color corresponding to the front are introduced in the sleeves, and interest is focused in the front. It is very effective to carry a detail like the tree on the left shoulder across from the front to the sleeve top, but precise matching of shapes on two parts of a garment can be tricky. The solution may be to duplicate-stitch details on after the garment has been finished (see p228); this is also the best method for working small details like the sheep's legs, the flowers or the distant trees.

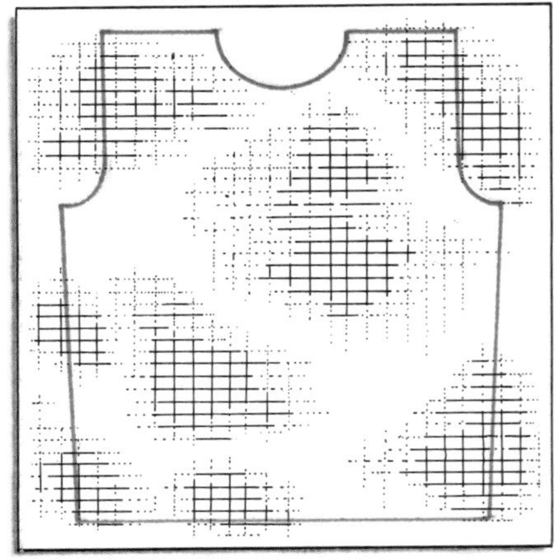

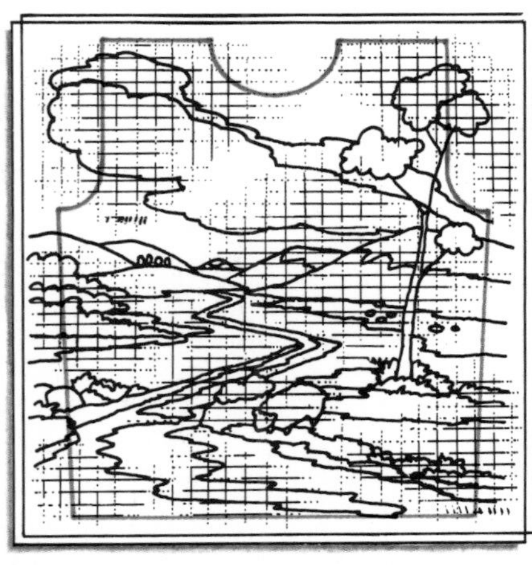

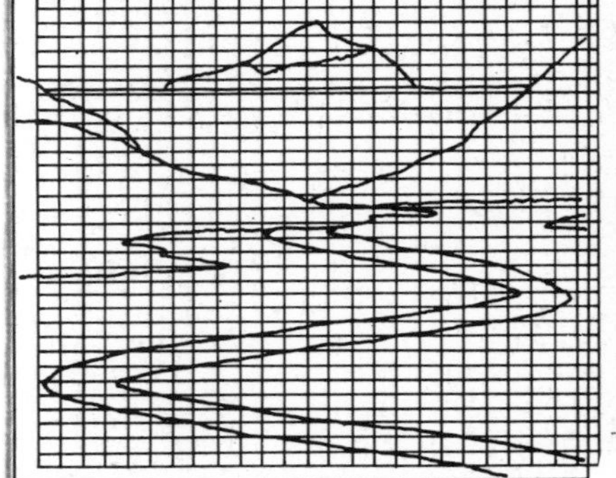

Picture knitting
Once you have made a rough sketch or color drawing of your picture you need to translate this into grid form to know which stitch to knit in which color. Use a fairly fine yarn and stockinette stitch as its smooth fabric shows color most clearly. Start with the gauge sample and chart out the number of stitches and rows you have available for your design. You can do this on ordinary squared graph paper, but remember that this distorts the image since stitches are shallower than their width. You will get by far the most accurate representation of your design in graph form by using the gauge-grid method as explained on p286 and using this for color as well as to show the outline. These diagrams show the gauge-grid technique.

1 Draw up your gauge grid on tracing paper using ink.

2 On your gauge grid chart out the shape of your fabric so that you can see how large an area you have for your picture.

3 Sketch your picture roughly corresponding to the area outlined on your gauge grid. Try to keep lines bold and simple; think in terms of blocks of color rather than intricate detail at this point. If you are working from an illustration, trace off the outlines onto a separate sheet of paper first.

4 Lay your gauge grid with its outline shape over the sketch and hold it in place with paperclips.

5 Translate the rough outlines of the sketch into stepped lines following the outlines of the stitches in the grid. Block in the different areas of color. If you find you have a large number of isolated stitches, color these in with the background as it is easier to work fairly large areas of color at a time.

6 Work from the colored chart as usual, beginning at bottom RH corner with a K row, working 2nd row in P from left to right, etc. Refer to Jacquard techniques (p270) for information on multicolored knitting, including using separate balls of yarn. Don't forget to twist yarns around each other (p244) when changing color in the middle of a row to prevent holes forming in the fabric. Remember too that it is easier to duplicate-stitch small details when main fabric has been completed.

3-D knitting

The techniques on these pages have greatest impact in a knitted rug like the one on p292, where they create a deep, three-dimensional texture. They can add individuality to the most basic garment too – ridges above the hem of a jacket or skirt, or on sleeves; bobbles decorating a hat, on part of a garment such as sleeves or yoke, or studded at random all over a fabric; flaps can be positioned over functional or imitation pockets, or can just be an unusual decorative feature. They look best against the smooth fabric of stockinette stitch. You can work in a color contrasting with the background or, for example, in mohair to contrast with a plain yarn. Flaps and ridges can feature stitches whose texture contrasts with the background. Bobbles can be worked to show either the knit or the purl side. French knitting is a somewhat different technique worked with a bobbin or 'knitting nancy' instead of with needles, and produces a cord composed of rounds of four knitted stitches.

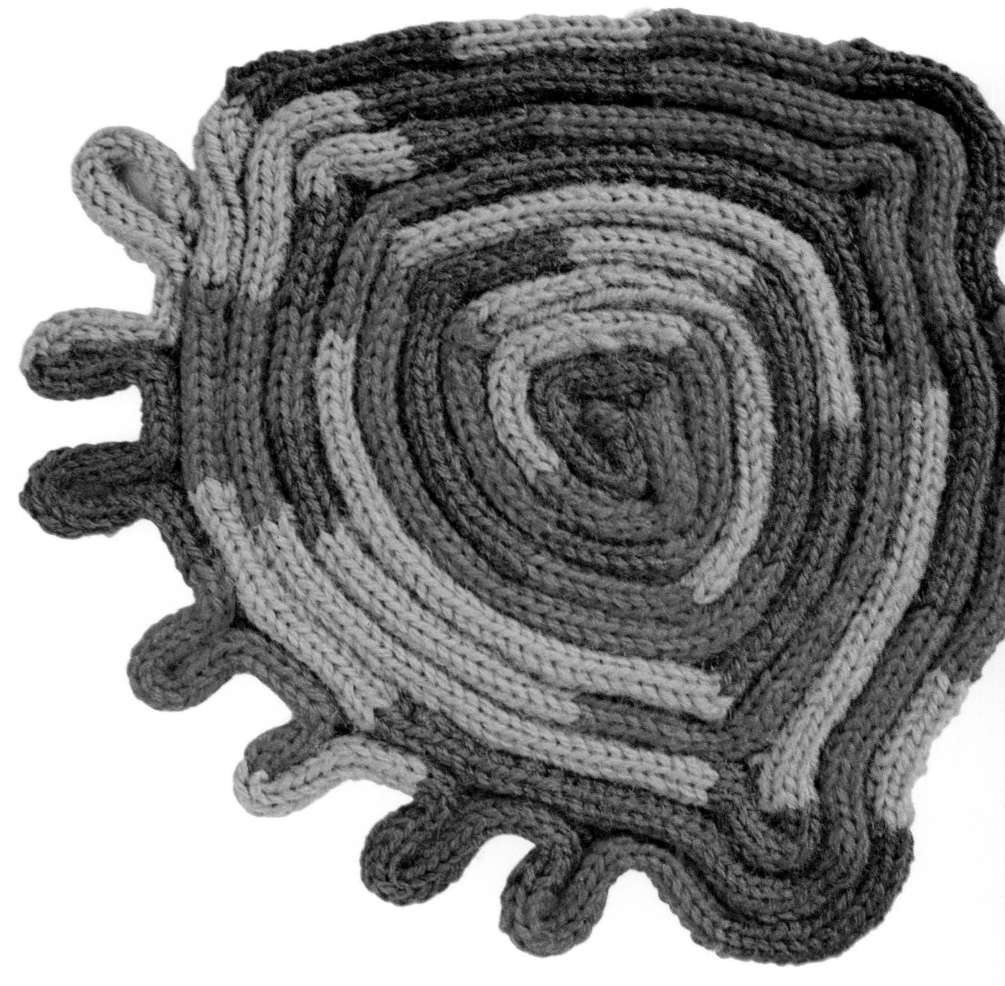

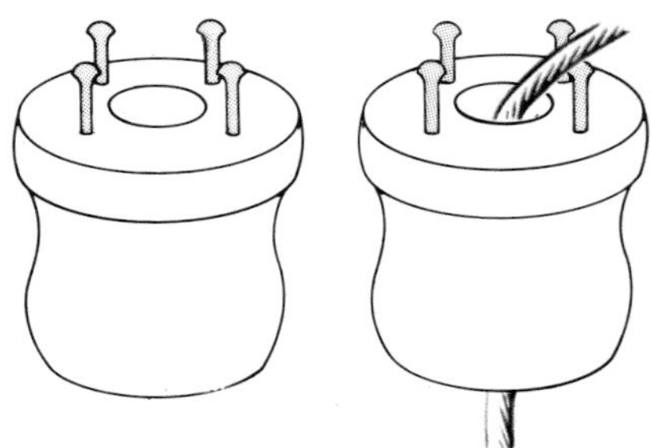

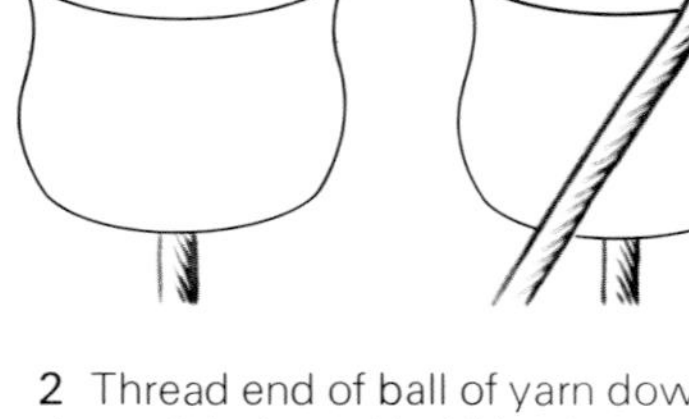

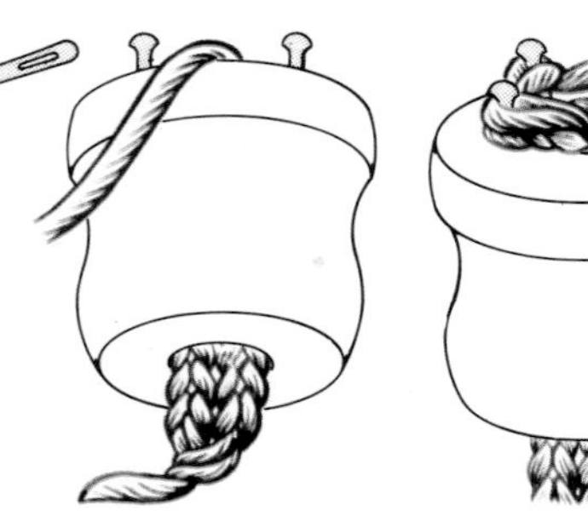

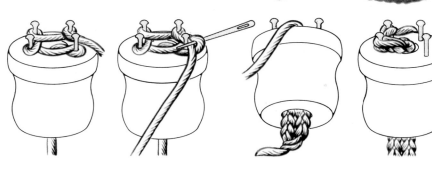

French knitting
By working in rounds of 4 stitches using a bobbin you can make a knitted rope that could act as belt, choker, bag handle or tie fastenings for a jacket. You can stitch it as a neat edging round a piece of knitting. Or you can coil it into rounds and stitch it to make mats, bags or just abstract shapes.

1 Use a block or cylinder of wood with a hole up to $\frac{3}{8}$in (1cm) diameter through it – traditionally people use empty wooden cotton reels. Hammer 4 small nails at equal intervals around the center hole.

2 Thread end of ball of yarn down through hole and hold in place with left hand while working.

3 Wind yarn around each nail in the direction shown.

4 Working in clockwise direction, bring yarn around outer edge of each nail in turn. Use a blunt-ended yarn needle or a bodkin to pull the bottom loop up over the top loop and over the nail. Continue working in rounds in this way.

5 Gradually cord will appear through bottom of hole as you work; draw it down gently with tail of yarn. To change color or attach new ball, knot new yarn in and make sure ends pass through to inside of cord.

6 To bind off pass each loop over next nail in clockwise direction. When 1 loop remains, break off yarn 4in (10cm) from work, pass end through last loop and draw up firmly.

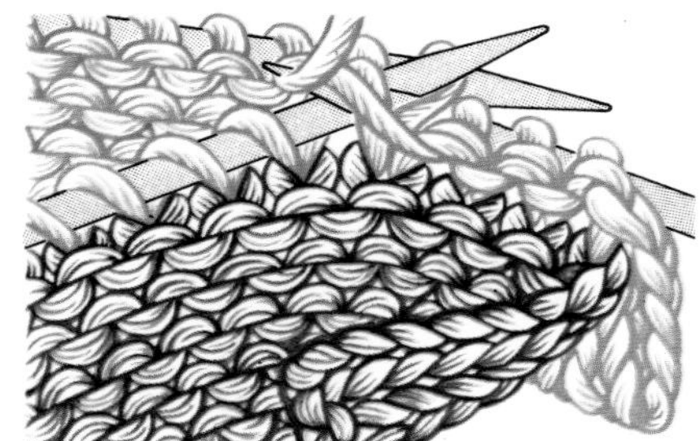

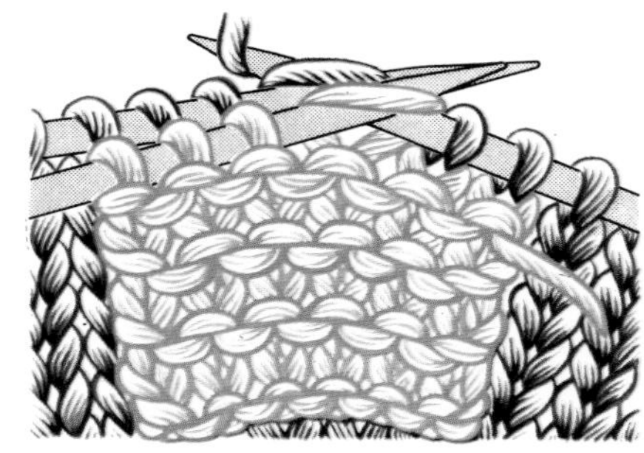

Bobbles
You can work bobbles anywhere on the surface of a fabric and vary their size by increasing the number of stitches worked from 3 upward. Work bobbles in K row of st st fabric using same yarn as background fabric or contrasting color. In this sample from bottom to top 1st 3 rows of bobbles are made with 5 sts, next 2 rows with 3 sts and top row with 7 sts. Instructions here are for bobbles with 5 sts. K to position of bobble. *Make 5 sts out of next st on LH needle thus: (K into front and back of next st) twice, then K again into front, (turn and K5, turn and P5) twice, use LH needle to lift 2nd, 3rd, 4th then 5th st over 1st st on LH needle and off needle. Cont in K to position of next bobble and rep from * as required.

Ridges
Vary the depth of a ridge by working a greater or smaller number of rows – but always work at least 5 rows before the joining row. Work a ridge in basic color or in a contrast, in the same stitch pattern as background or a different textured one; rev st st against a st st background all in one color could be attractive. Here instructions are for contrast ridge, all in st st, with a background color coded A and contrast B. Work in A in st st to position of ridge ending with a P row. Don't break off A. Using B work an odd no. of rows in st st ending with a K row. With WS facing and using a smaller spare needle, pick up loops of 1st row of B starting at LH edge. Hold spare needle in front of and parallel with LH needle and using B, P tog 1 st from LH needle with 1 st from spare needle to end of row. (This folds rows of B P-sides tog into ridge.) Break off B. Cont working in A to position of next ridge.

Flaps
A stitch like garter stitch or seed stitch that doesn't cause a fabric to curl up is best for flaps. Before beginning on main fabric work as many separate flaps as you want, making squares, triangles or rectangles; don't bind off when you reach the required depth, ending with a WS row, but break off yarn and slide all flaps onto one spare needle. In st st work background fabric until you reach position for flap on a K row. With RS of both flap and main fabric facing, hold spare needle with flap in front of LH needle and K tog 1 st from each needle until you have worked all flap sts. K to end of row or position of next flap. Darn in ends of flaps when finishing.

Landscape rug

Children love playing on this knitted 'garden' with its lawns, rocks, vegetable patches and ponds. Use a garden, park, landscape or sea shore for your own inspiration. Bring in as much color and texture as you can and experiment with the yarn you plan to use to make stitch samples using the techniques described in this book. A rug for the floor is more durable in Turkey rug wool than in ordinary knitting yarn; a burlap backing helps give strength. You could use the same techniques in a wall-hanging, afghan, or even a pillow, and here softer bulky knitting yarns would be suitable. Rug yarns have the advantage of offering graduated shades of color which can look more natural than the less subtle colors available in any single range of knitting yarn. This rug was knitted in one piece, but you may find it easier to work individual patches in the main areas and join them together afterward.

This rug measures 1 × $1\frac{1}{2}$yd (1 × 1·5m). After making initial sketches the knitter made a detailed plan of the design to actual size on brown paper, then experimented with stitch textures and effects in the rug yarn. In order to work the rug in one piece, a pair of extra-long needles was made from two 22in (55cm) lengths of $\frac{1}{2}$in (1cm) dowelling sharpened to a smooth point at one end. The rug was cast on at one narrow edge and the knitting was divided about one-third of the way along, half the stitches being left on a spare length of thread. One side of the garden was completed first, then the stitches on the thread were picked up and the path and the second side of the garden worked on these. The two sections were joined along the side of the path when finishing. Although a good deal of the texture and the color effects were created by the stitch patterns themselves, some items were worked separately (see below).

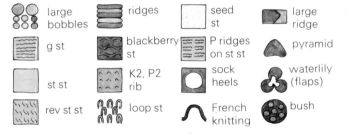

large bobbles
ridges
seed st
large ridge
g st
blackberry st
P ridges on st st
pyramid
st st
K2, P2 rib
sock heels
waterlily (flaps)
rev st st
loop st
French knitting
bush

Whether you work a rug in one piece or in smaller patches, you need to do the same initial planning. Work out details of the individual sections in terms of shape, color and stitch pattern. (See p286 to work out how to achieve a precise shape in your knitting.) At the planning stage decide how much of your design to knit in and how much to add later – either by sewing on items knitted separately or by applying embroidery. Use basic textured stitches – garter, seed, rib and reverse stockinette stitch. Use loop stitches, too, either as an all-over fabric or scattered about over other stitch patterns – see the individual loops worked over K2, P2 rib. Create more pronounced texture with ridges, bobbles and lumps (worked from part of the sock heel pattern on p254). Note that loops and bobbles can be worked in the same color as the background or in a contrasting one. Refer to Jacquard (p270) for the techniques to use when knitting patchwork. Most of the different areas of color in a design like this are large enough to be worked with separate balls of color, but you may choose to carry or weave the different-colored yarns used recurrently for loops or bobbles (see p264).

As well as some of the flowers which were embroidered onto the knitted rug, a few features were worked separately and attached afterward.

Round bushes Work g st squares, run a thread around the edges, gather up to form ball and fasten off.

Pointed bushes Work a wedge shape by decreasing sharply at one edge and gradually at the other until the knitting tapers to a point. Form into a cone shape and seam sides together.

Fence French knitting (see p290) caught down into loops at regular intervals.

Waterlily leaves Small pieces of g st are shaped into circles by first increasing and then decreasing at ends of rows.

Pyramids are made by working decreases at both edges of a piece of knitting as well as at 2 shaping points within the fabric itself; the result is a 3-sided figure tapering to a point at the top. Seam side edges together.

Toys

Basic stitches 216
Increasing and decreasing 222
Duplicate stitching 228
Embroidery 229

Cuddly animals and vegetables show the versatility of knitted shapes; they make amusing toys and some have more practical uses. Spheres like the pumpkin are made from shaped flat segments joined together – stuffed with foam this could be a pillow or a child's seat. The cucumber – which is long enough to use as a protector against drafts – and the zucchini are simple tubes; in the same way you could knit a snake, caterpillar (adding embroidered decoration) – or even a string of sausages. Different color and detail turns the small ball shape into a tomato or an onion. You can adapt the oval which is the basis of the eggplant to make a variety of animals, including the rat on this page, by adding appropriate legs, ears and features. Work the cabbage shape in a suitable color and assemble it slightly differently to make a rose.

Charts for knitting these shapes are on pp296–7 and if you study the way in which these shapes are achieved you should be able to develop your own ideas. You may even like to try to work some of the simpler shapes in the toys section, pp112–23. When creating your own designs look carefully at details like stalks and leaves, and choose stitch patterns that give the appropriate texture – seed stitch for the corn cob, loop stitch for fur or feathers. Look at the way the more complicated shapes like the owl and the hedgehog are built up. To some extent you can mold the stuffing to shape and then stitch it – see how the shape of the cat's body is sculptured out of a circle. The owl and hedgehog are worked in knitting worsted and the cat in mohair; all other items use lighter-weight 4-ply yarn which permits you to work fairly minute details.

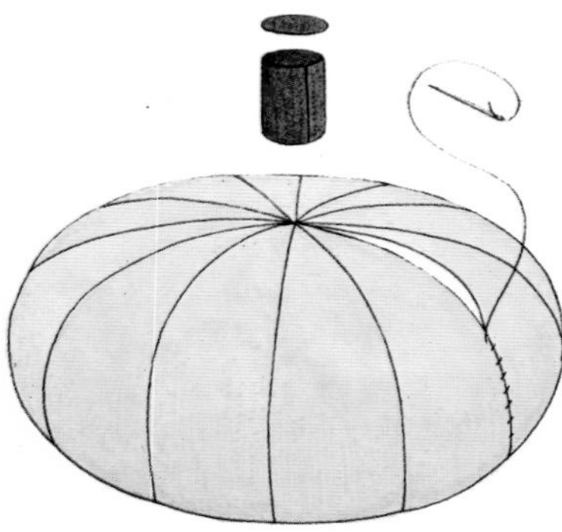

Pumpkin
yellow, st st: 12 main sections (1)
green, st st: stalk (2, 3)

Work 12 main sections in st st from chart on the next page. Sew sections tog, enclosing stuffing. Seam side edges of stalk and sew in top. Stuff stalk and attach to top of pumpkin.

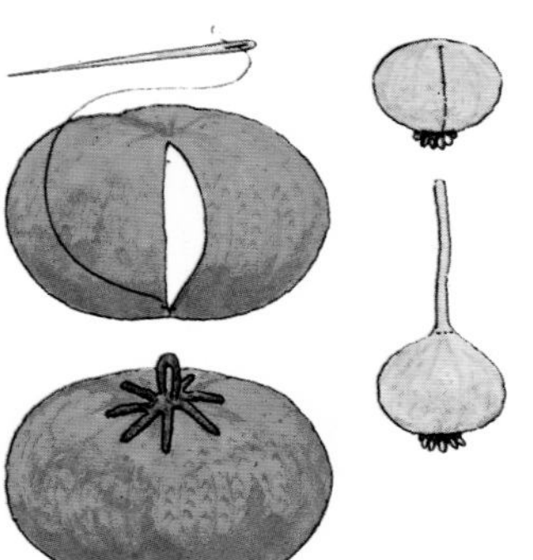

Tomato/onion
Using appropriate color, work 2 main sections in st st from chart on p287. Seam sides tog, gathering up top and bottom after stuffing.
Tomato: using green, duplicate-stitch 'spider' shape for flower and stalk.
Onion: attach a few strands of knotted fringe to base for roots. Attach onions tog with length of French knitting.

Textured stitches 234
Loops 279
Design: shaping 286
3-D knitting 290

Cucumber
green, rib: 1 main section
yellow, g st: flower

Cast on 67 sts and work 25in (65cm) K3, P1 rib. Next row: *K3 tog, P1, rep from * to last 3 sts, K3 tog (33 sts). Work 6in (15cm) K1, P1 rib. Next row: *K2 tog, rep from * to last st, K1 (17 sts). K2 rows. Bind off. Seam long edges and short end tog. Stuff, run thread around cast-on edge and gather up. Flower: cast on 12 sts, work 2 rows g st, bind off. Work 2 more pieces in same way. Attach 3 petals to gathered end.

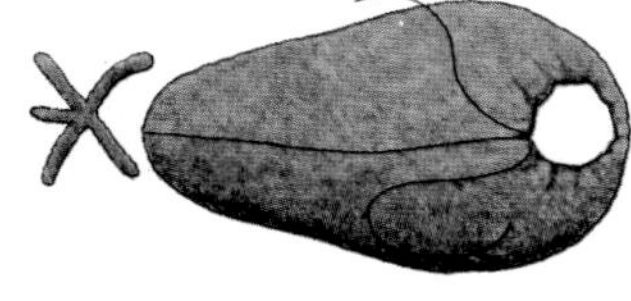

Eggplant
purple, st st: 2 main sections (4)
green, g st: leaves
green, French knitting: 1in (3cm) stalk

Work 2 main sections in st st from chart. Seam tog all around, gathering up cast-on edge and fastening off after inserting stuffing. Make 2 leaves: cast on 25 sts, work 2 rows g st, bind off. Form into cross and attach at same time as French-knitting stalk.

make 1 st
K2 tog
inc evenly across row
dec evenly across row

Begin all charts at bottom RH corner; work 1st row from right to left, 2nd row back from left to right, etc. Arrows at LH edge of chart indicate half chart only is given: work 2nd half of section to correspond to 1st, reversing all shaping. See individual instructions for number of pieces, color and stitch pattern.

Needle size depends on gauge, but as a rough guide use no. 2 needles for all 4-ply items.
Owl: no. 4 for sections 13–15; no. 2 for 16–20.
Hedgehog: no. 4 for sections 21–22; no. 5 for section 23.
Cat: no. 5 for sections 27–28; no. 3 for 29–32.

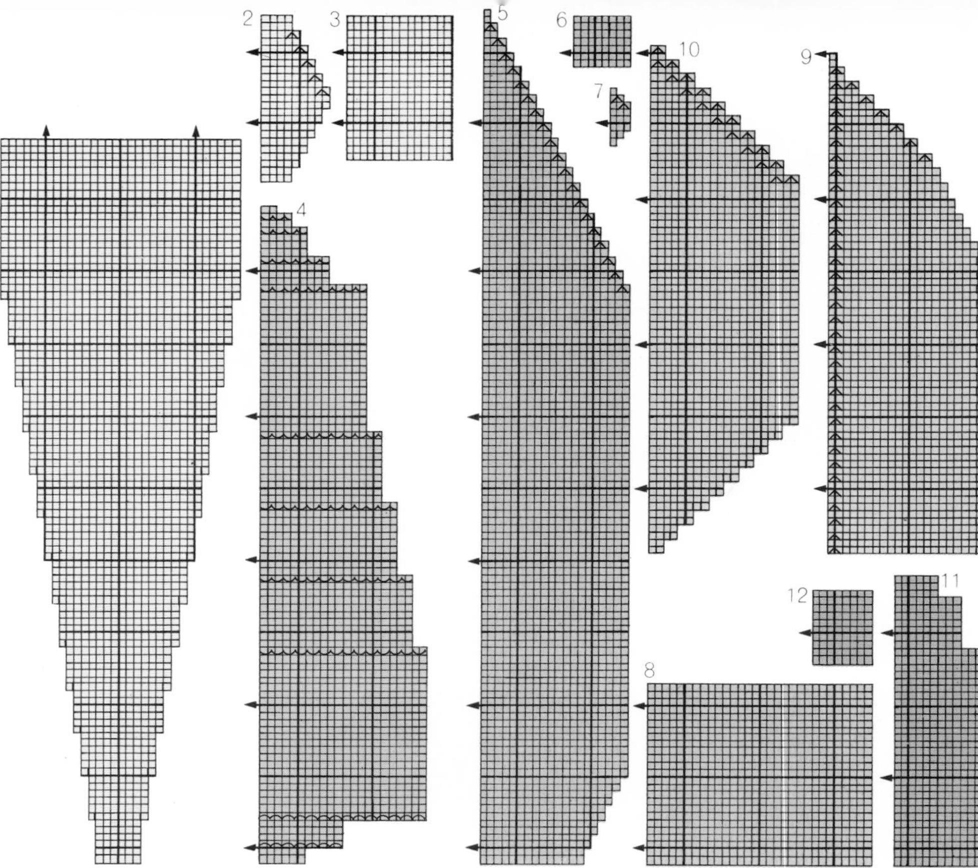

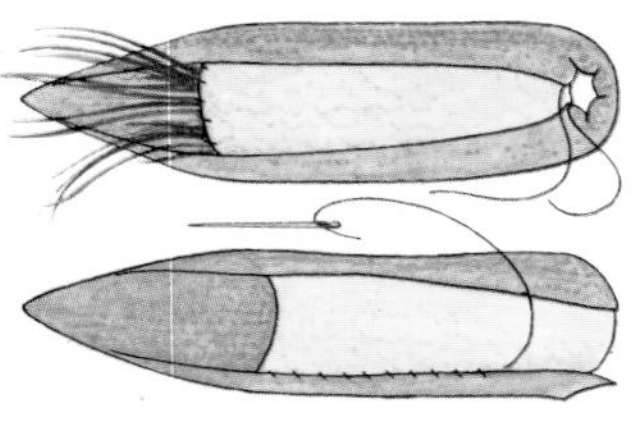

Corn cob
green, st st: leaf (5), stalk and base (6, 7)
yellow, Irish moss st: corn cob (8)

Work leaf and stalk in st st from charts; work 'corn' in Irish moss st. Make cylinder shape by wrapping green leaf section around yellow, seaming lengthwise. Tuck in yellow section at top and stitch to green. Add a few strands of knotted fringe for 'silk'. Stalk (6): stitch short sides tog to form cylinder and sew in base (7). Stuff cob and stalk, gather base of cob into stalk and seam.

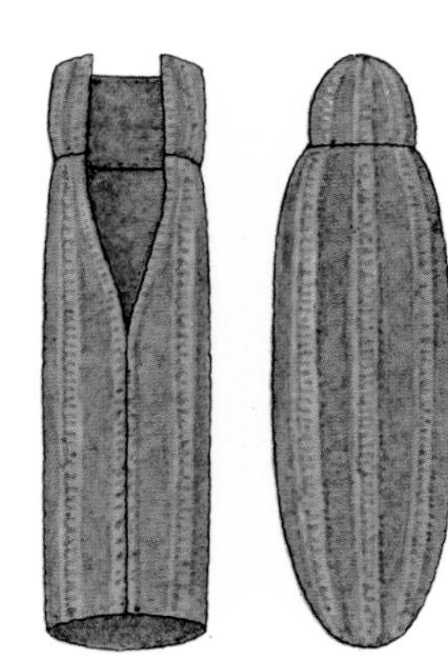

Zucchini
green, rib: main section (11), top (12)

Work 30 rows main section (11) in K3, P1 rib. Dec row: (K1, K2 tog, P1) to end. Work 6 rows K2, P1 rib. Dec row: (K1, P1) to end. Work 2 rows K1, P1 rib. Work top section in K2, P1 rib. Gather cast-on edge to fit top and seam. Sew long edges tog to form cylinder, closing top. Stuff, run thread around open end, gather up and fasten off.

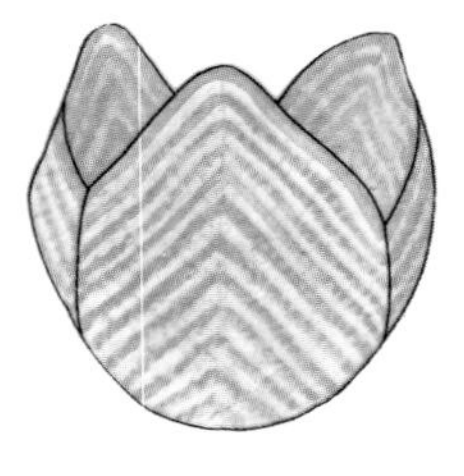

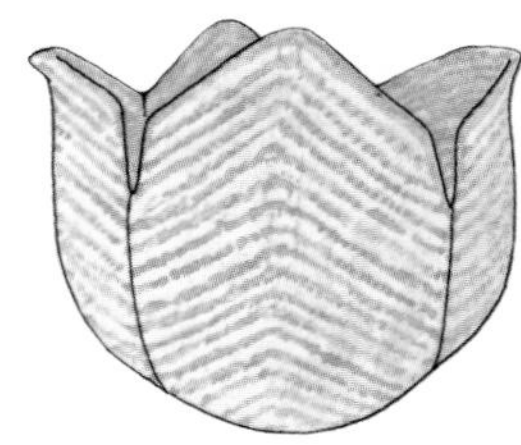

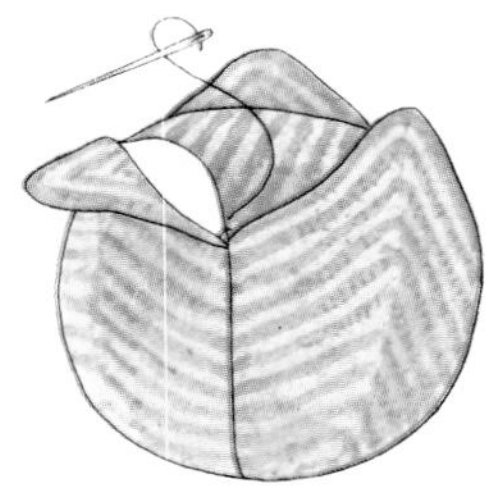

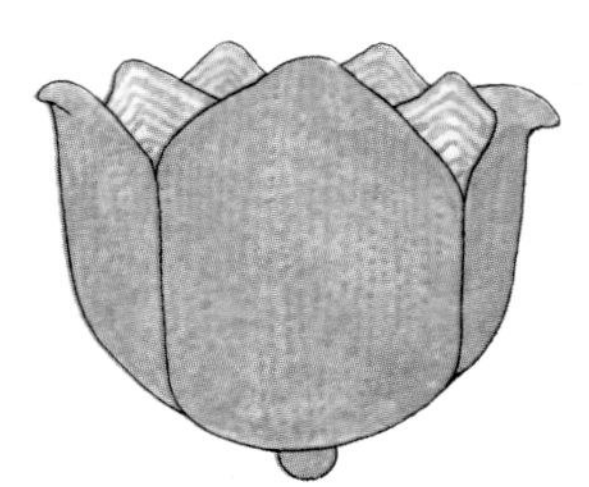

Cabbage
striped st st: heart, 3 inner leaves (9)
striped g st: 3 middle leaves (9)
green st st: 4 outer leaves (10)
stalk: as corn cob

Heart: cast on 32 sts and work 44 rows in striped st st. Work leaves as indicated above from charts. Work stalk as for corn cob. Seam 3 inner leaves tog along increase edges to make cup shape. Insert heart, overlapping with leaves, stitch invisibly level with widest point of leaves, leaving an opening for stuffing. Stuff and complete seam. Seam tog 3 middle leaves in same way, then 4 outer leaves. Place tog with leaves overlapping and blind-stitch at intervals to keep in place. Add stalk as for corn cob.

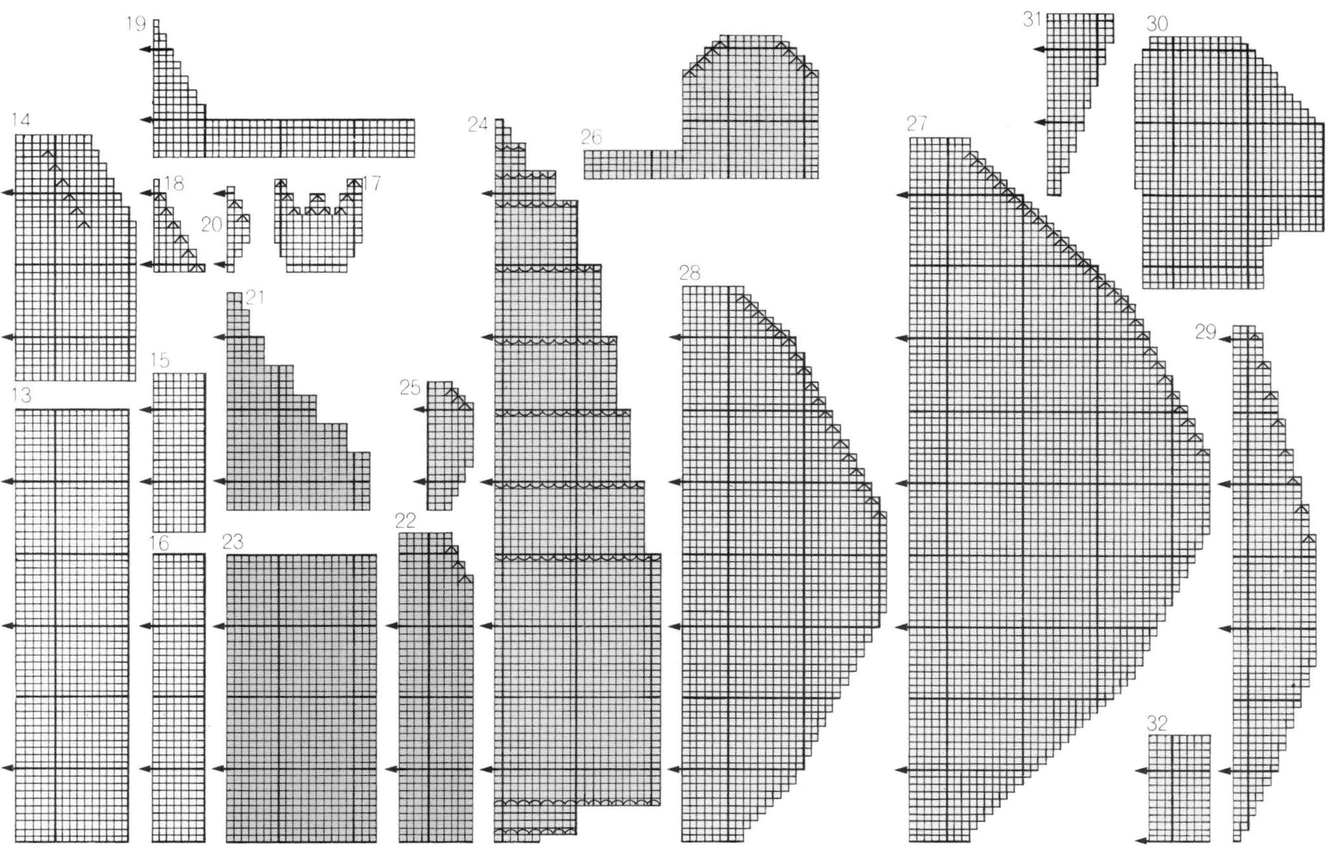

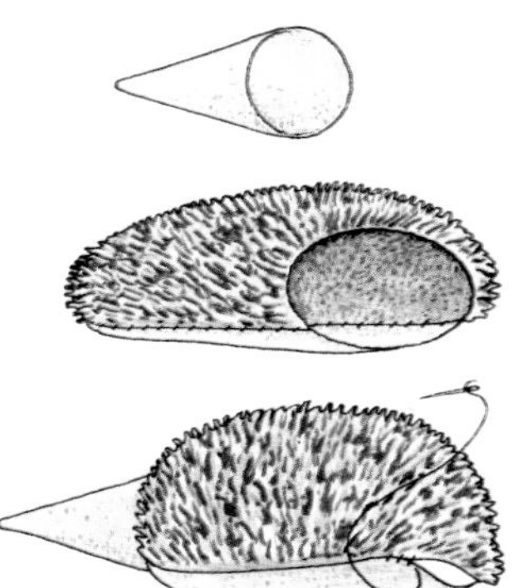

Hedgehog
fawn, st st: head (21), base (22)
tweed and dark brown (1 strand each used tog), loop st: back (23)

Work head and base in fawn st st from chart; work back section in loop stitch. Seam head to make cone shape. Sew back and base tog into tube shape. Sew base of head to body. Stuff from open end, then seam. Attach button eyes and embroider nose.

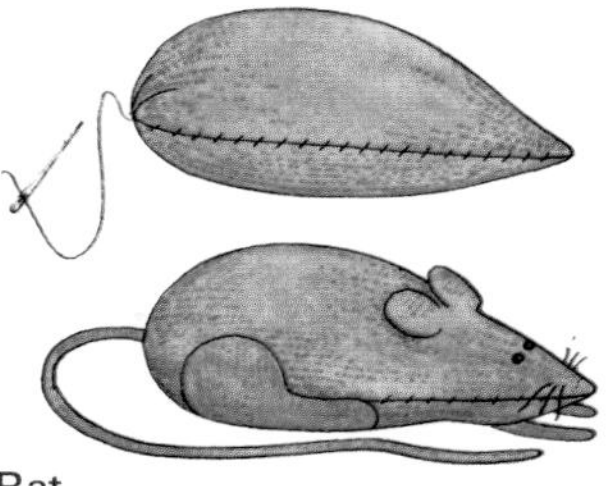

Rat
gray, st st: 2 body sections (24), 2 ears (25), 2 hind legs (26)
gray, French knitting: tail, 2 × 2in (5cm) front legs

Work 2 body sections, 2 ears and 2 hind legs from charts. Sew body sections tog, leaving cast-on edges open for stuffing. Stuff, run thread through cast-on edges, gather up and fasten. Attach tail. Sew on hind legs as shown, stuffing slightly. Sew on front legs. Attach ears and tiny buttons or beads for eyes. Run lengths of black mohair through muzzle for whiskers.

Owl
tweed, st st: body front (13), head front (14)
brown, loop st: back (13), 2 wings (15), head back (14)
brown, st st: base (16), 2 feet (17)
brown, rev st st: face (18, 19)
yellow, st st: beak (20)

Work sections as shown on charts. Seam long edges of 2 back sections and front to make tube. Join 2 head pieces and attach to top of body tube. Sew in base, leaving slit for stuffing. Stuff. Sew feet to base. Sew on top face section, curving long sides around to make 'eyebrow' shape, and bottom face section; sew on wings. Attach beak and button eyes. Work duplicate stitch in brown to join top of beak and point of top face section.

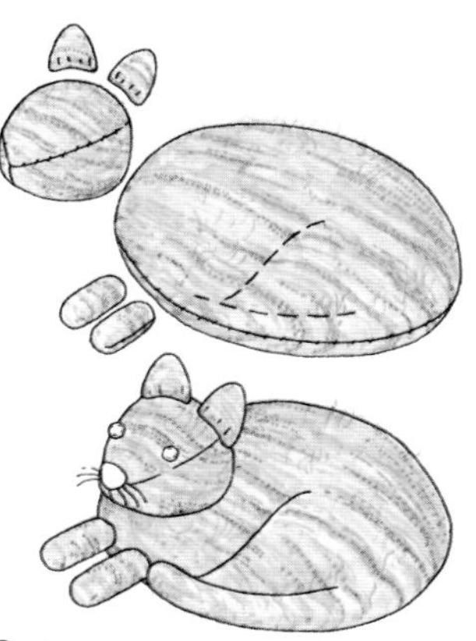

Cat
random-dyed mohair, g st: (no. 5 needles) top (27), base (28); (no. 3 needles) head gusset (29), 2 side face pieces (30), 2 ears (31), 2 front paws (32)

Work sections as shown on charts. Sew top to base and stuff. Sew side seams of paws, run thread through cast-on sts to close up, and fasten off. Stuff paws and sew in position on body. Mold stuffing into shape of cat's tail and hind leg and work back stitch through all layers to make shape of seated cat. Make head: join side face pieces below chin and insert gusset from nose to back of head. Stuff head and sew to body. Gather base of ears slightly and attach. Sew on glass button eyes. Pass a few strands of thread through muzzle for whiskers. Embroider or duplicate-stitch nose.

Crochet

Crochet invites comparison with knitting since both crafts consist of building up a fabric from loops of yarn; in this respect crochet shares the same advantages of being a money-saving and satisfying pastime. The fact that in crochet you manipulate a single basic loop at a time, however, means that in some ways you have greater control over your fabric, and many people find crochet more physically relaxing than knitting. The fabrics you can create with formal crochet patterns range from the finest laces through filet nets and open patterns to firm, substantial fabrics; besides these there are the sculptural forms of Irish crochet and many different types of cord and fringing.

Experiment with crochet in any yarn that is available – from parcel string and garden raffia to soft rope. Without following a pattern and with the simplest basic stitches you can make household items, bags, mats and even garments with exciting textured effects. Don't ignore the possibilities of combining crochet with other materials like leather or woven fabrics, either in its simplest form as seaming or in more elaborate insertions and edgings.

Basic information

Yarns and hooks

The following recommendations give a rough indication of what hook to use with what yarn to make an 'average' fabric texture. Bear in mind that you can make a vast variety of crochet fabrics from the basic stitches, ranging from stiff, almost rigid textures to supple and loose ones. Be prepared to break the rules and use a hook smaller or larger than the ones suggested here; above all, experiment until you get the look and feel you want.

Very fine yarns Use with steel hooks from no. 5 to no. 14 to make extremely delicate lacy crochet with a traditional look – like the finer edgings on p336.

Fine yarns need steel hooks from no. 00 to no. 4.

Light-weight yarns include a wide variety of cottons with different textures as well as wool and wool mixtures equivalent to 4-ply weight. Aluminum hooks between sizes B and E are most appropriate and give a wide variety of effects.

Medium-weight yarns include knitting worsted and heavy cottons; hooks from sizes E to G are used for an average fabric, but experiment until you find the hook you want.

Heavy yarns range from bulky yarn, thick cotton and string to parcel twine and even fine jute rope; choose a hook from size G upward.

very fine fine light-weight medium-weight heavy

Hooks

Hooks for use with wool and thicker cotton yarns are usually made of aluminum; hooks for finer yarns are of steel. Since they only have to hold the working loop, hooks are made to a standard length. In the ISR (international standard range) hooks listed below, thickness is gauged by the measurement of their diameter in millimeters – the larger the number, the larger the hook size.

American	Metric
Aluminum hooks	
–	7·50
K	7·00
J	–
I	6·00
H	5·50
H	5·00
G	4·50
F	4·00
E	3·50
D	–
C	3·00
B	2·50
Steel hooks	
1	2·00
4	1·75
7	1·50
10	1·00
12	0·75
14	0·60

Measuring gauge

Gauge in crochet, as in knitting (see p220), is the number of stitches and rows you obtain over a given measurement with a specfic hook and yarn. When following a pattern which gives a recommended gauge practice with various hooks until you get the same gauge, otherwise the design will be unsuccessful. Before beginning any crochet work, make a sample using the appropriate stitch and yarn and with the recommended hook. Mark out an area at least 2in (5cm) square with pins. Count the stitches and rows between these, and include fractions of either in your calculations. When your gauge doesn't coincide with the designer's, change to a hook one size smaller to obtain more stitches or one size larger to obtain fewer stitches. Getting the number of rows right is important since many crochet stitches are deeper than they are wide; when counting rows rather than measuring to achieve depth, pattern shaping can become distorted if gauge is wrong.

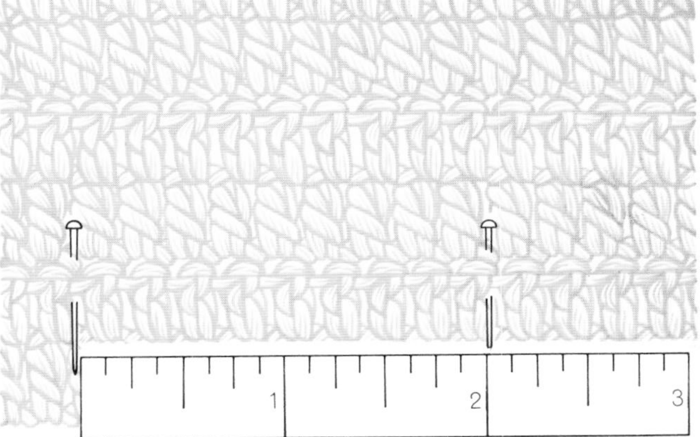

Gauge symbol Crochet hook size is at the top and stitch pat used below the symbol. Upper figure on symbol itself refers to no. of sts (or groups of sts) and lower figure to no. of rows – both over a 4in (10cm) square unless otherwise stated. Thus in this symbol you should have 30 sts and 37 rows in a 4in (10cm) square of single crochet worked with a no. 1 hook.

no. 1	hook size
30	no. of sts
37	no. of rows
SC	stitch pat

Abbreviations

alt	alternate(ly)	gr	group	RS	right side
approx	approximately	hdc	half double	sc	single crochet
beg	begin(ning)	inc	increase	sp(s)	space(s)
ch	chain	LH	left-hand	sl st	slip stitch
cont	continu(e/ing)	no.	number	t ch	turning chain
dc	double crochet	pat	pattern	tog	together
dec	decrease	rem	remain(ing)	tr	treble
dtr	double treble	rep	repeat	WS	wrong side
		RH	right-hand	yo	yarn over

Joining in a new ball of yarn

Always try to do this at the beginning of a row; undo the stitches if you are in the middle of a row and run out of yarn. Ripping out crochet stitches is easy because each is separate and you have only one working loop to pick up.
The technique of joining in a new ball is similar to the one used for changing colors in horizontal stripes (see p328). Introduce the new yarn to complete the last stitch of the previous row, then use the new yarn to work the turning chain of the new row. If the yarn is not too thick, work over the ends of both old and new balls for a few stitches to anchor them as described on p328; there is no need to darn them in if you use this method. Very thick yarns are too bulky to enclose both ends; work over one end of yarn as usual and darn the other end in down the edge of the work when it is complete.

Blocking and pressing

Whether or not you need to do this depends on the type of yarn you are using. Cotton, often used for crochet, needs careful pressing under a damp cloth with a warm iron. Often traditional openwork designs such as filet benefit if you block them out, cover with a damp cloth and leave them until the cloth is dry. For other information on blocking and pressing, see p243.

Finishing

Seams As with knitting you need to take great care when sewing together your completed work. Sew the pattern pieces together as you do in knitting (see p242) using a back stitch or an overcast seam as appropriate. You can also crochet the pieces together with a single crochet seam; this method gives a very firm edge and is often worked as a decorative feature on the right side of the work (see p340).
Picking up stitches You may need to do this to finish a neckband or border. Follow the instructions on p334 for working an edging directly onto a crochet fabric.

Slip loop and chains

To begin any piece of crochet, make a slip loop with your yarn and place it on the hook; this is a working loop and never counts as a stitch.
Most fabrics require a length of chain stitches as a foundation for the first row of crochet; chains are the most simple form of drawing one stitch through another, which is the basis of all crochet.
There is always one loop on the hook when you complete a stitch and you finish off at the end of your work by breaking off about 4in (10cm) of yarn; draw this through the loop on the hook and pull the cut end up firmly.

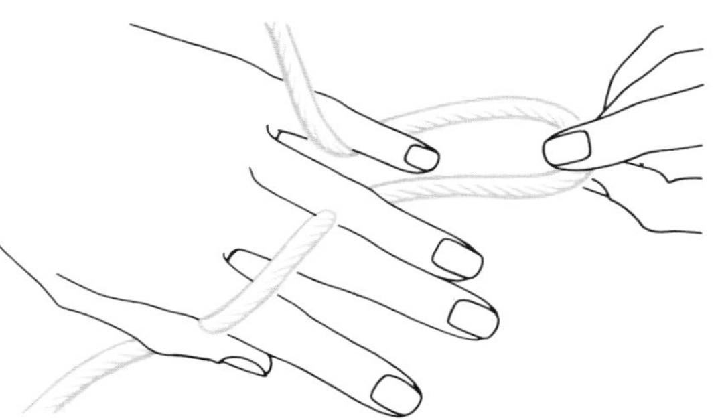

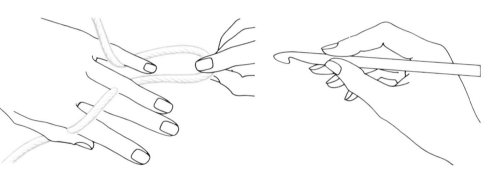

Holding the hook and controlling the yarn

You must hold the hook and control the yarn in the correct way both for ease of work and to keep the gauge even. If you are right-handed loop the end of a ball of yarn over the forefinger and 2nd finger of your left hand, then under the 3rd finger; finally wind it once around your little finger. Hold the hook in your right hand between your thumb and forefinger, exactly as you grip a pen, with the hooked end lightly resting against the tip of your 2nd finger. Left-handed people can reverse the positions shown here; use a mirror to reverse these diagrams if you like.

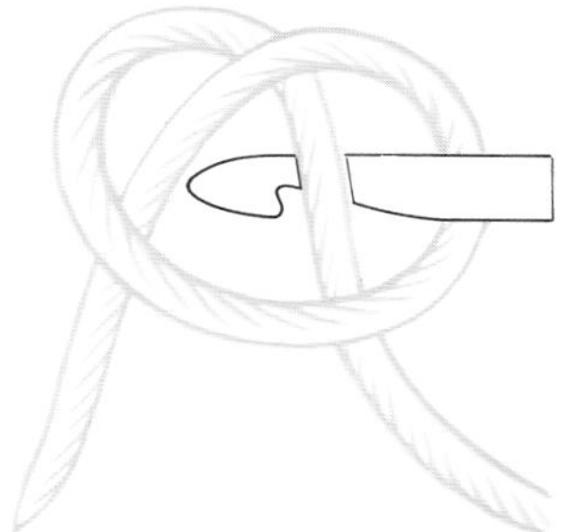

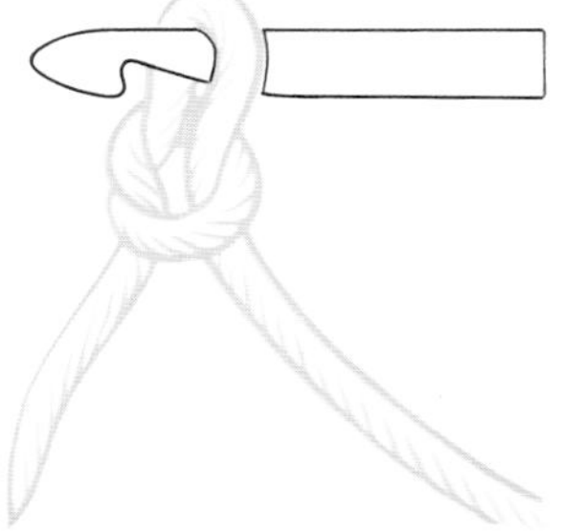

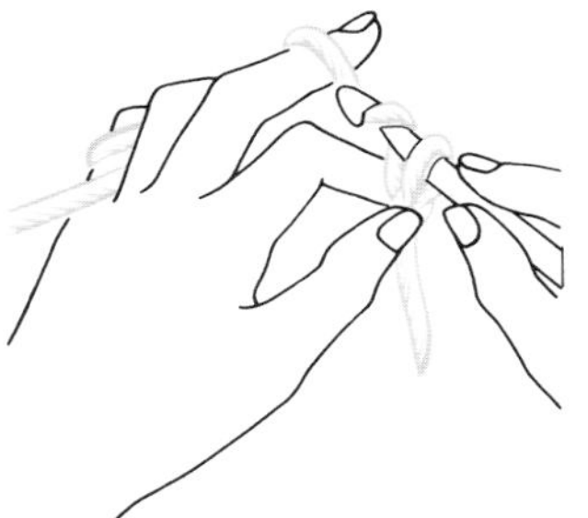

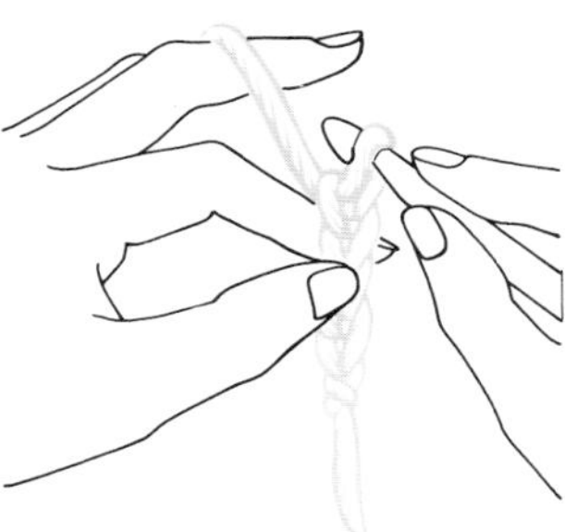

Making chains (ch)

1 Begin with a slip loop on the hook: make a loop about 4in (10cm) from the end of your yarn. Insert hook behind the vertical strand as shown, then pull the ends of yarn to tighten the loop.
2 Hold the hook with the slip loop in your right hand and control the yarn with your left hand as shown. Bringing the hook toward you, take it under and then over the top of the yarn in your left hand, so catching it in the curve of the hook—this is called 'yarn over' (yo).
3 Holding the knot of the slip loop firmly between thumb and forefinger of your left hand, draw the yarn from back to front through the slip loop, so completing 1 chain. Notice that 1 working loop remains on the hook.
4 Repeat the motions in **2** and **3** until you have the length of chain you need, always holding the stitch just made and not restricting the way the yarn runs through your left hand.

Basic stitches

The stitches which are the basis of most crochet patterns range in size from single crochet, which is the smallest, to double treble which is very deep. At the start of a new row you must work a number of chains to bring the hook up to the height of the stitches in that row so that you can work the first patterned stitch without distorting it. These extra chains are 'turning chains' and the number you need varies according to the stitch you are working. Remember that the turning chain always forms the first stitch of a new row; you work the first patterned stitch into the second stitch in the row below.

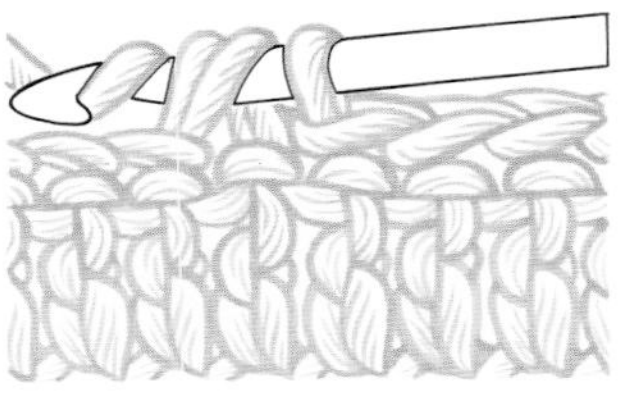

Slip stitch (sl st)
This stitch is so shallow that it seldom forms an entire fabric; it does have three specific uses. It is a way of getting from one point in a row to another when shaping a garment, such as at the underarms; when you work in rounds you can use a slip stitch to link the last stitch of the round to the first; and you can join one motif to another by slip-stitching at certain points.

1 To work a slip stitch, insert the hook in the usual way into the next chain or stitch.
2 Wind the yarn around the hook from the back as in diagram.
3 Draw the yarn through the chain or stitch and loop on the hook; a single loop remains on the hook and 1 sl st is complete.
4 If you are working across a row, complete the required number of slip stitches; begin the pattern by slip-stitching into the next stitch and making the necessary number of turning chains to count as the 1st stitch, then work to the end of the row in pattern.

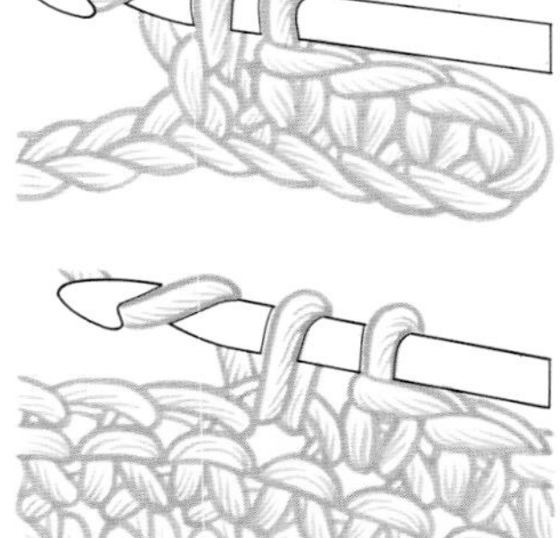

Single crochet (sc)
(1 turning chain)
Make the required number of chains plus 1 extra.
1 To work the 1st row, insert the hook from front to back into the 3rd chain from the hook; wind the yarn around the hook from the back as in diagram and draw a loop through the chain, so making 2 loops on the hook.
2 Wind the yarn around the hook again and draw it through both loops on the hook; a single loop remains on the hook and 1sc is complete.
3 Repeat **1** and **2** into each chain until you reach the end. Still holding the hook in your right hand, turn the work from right to left so that the last stitch of this row becomes the 1st stitch of the next row.
4 To work the 2nd and subsequent rows, make 1 turning chain to count as the 1st sc; work 1 stitch into each stitch in the previous row by inserting the hook under the 2 horizontal loops at the top of the stitch.

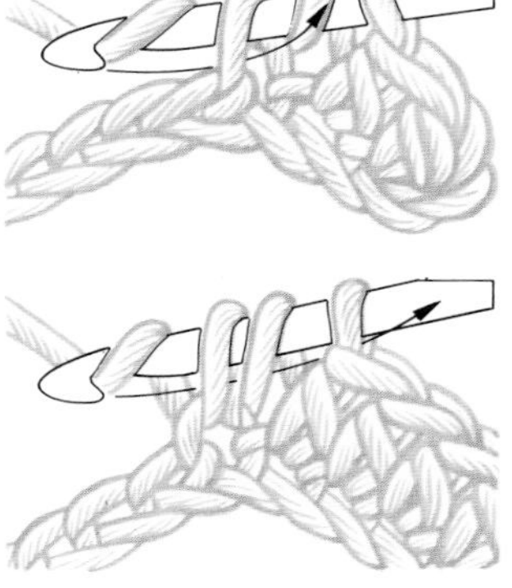

Half double crochet (hdc)
(2 turning chains)
Make the required number of chains plus 1 extra.
1 To work the 1st row, wind the yarn completely around the hook as in diagram; insert the hook into the 3rd chain from the hook and draw a loop through the chain, so making 3 loops on the hook.
2 Wind the yarn around the hook again and draw it through all 3 loops; a single loop remains on the hook and 1hdc is complete.
3 Repeat **1** and **2** into each chain until you reach the end. Turn the work so that the last stitch of this row becomes the 1st stitch of the next row.
4 To work the 2nd and subsequent rows, make 2 turning chains to count as the 1st hdc; insert the hook under the 2 horizontal loops at the top of each stitch in the previous row.

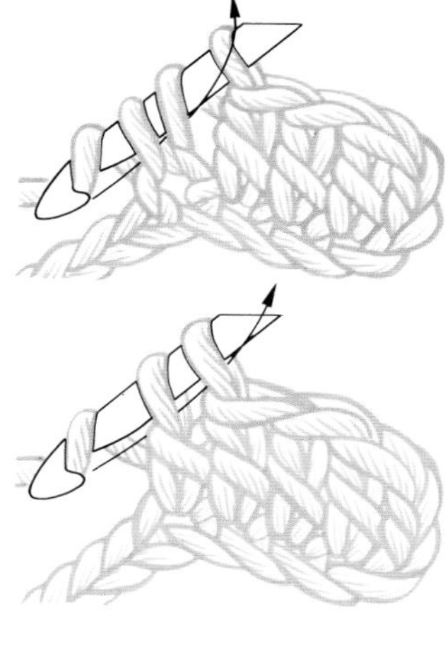

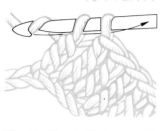

Double crochet (dc)
(3 turning chains)
Make the required number of chains plus 2 extra.
1 To work the 1st row, wind the yarn around the hook; insert the hook into the 4th chain from the hook and draw a loop through, so making 3 loops on the hook.
2 Wind the yarn around the hook and draw it through the 1st 2 loops on the hook, so leaving 2 loops on the hook.
3 Wind the yarn around the hook again and draw it through the remaining 2 loops; a single loop remains on the hook and 1dc is complete.
4 Follow **3** and **4** of single crochet, working 3 turning chains at the beginning of each new row.

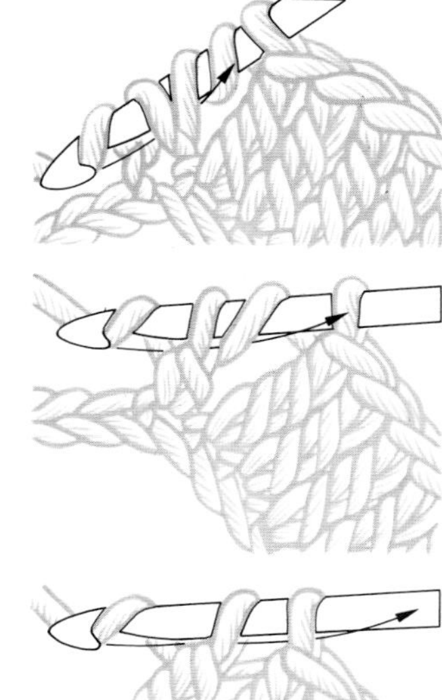

Treble (tr)
(4 turning chains)
Make the required number of chains plus 3 extra.
1 Yarn twice around hook; insert hook into 5th chain from hook and draw a loop through so making 4 loops on hook.
2 Wind yarn around hook and draw it through 1st 2 loops leaving 3 loops on the hook.
3 Repeat **2** so that there are 2 loops on the hook.
4 Wind yarn around hook and draw it through remaining 2 loops; a single loop remains on hook and 1 tr is complete.
5 Follow **3** and **4** of single crochet, working 4 turning chains for each new row.

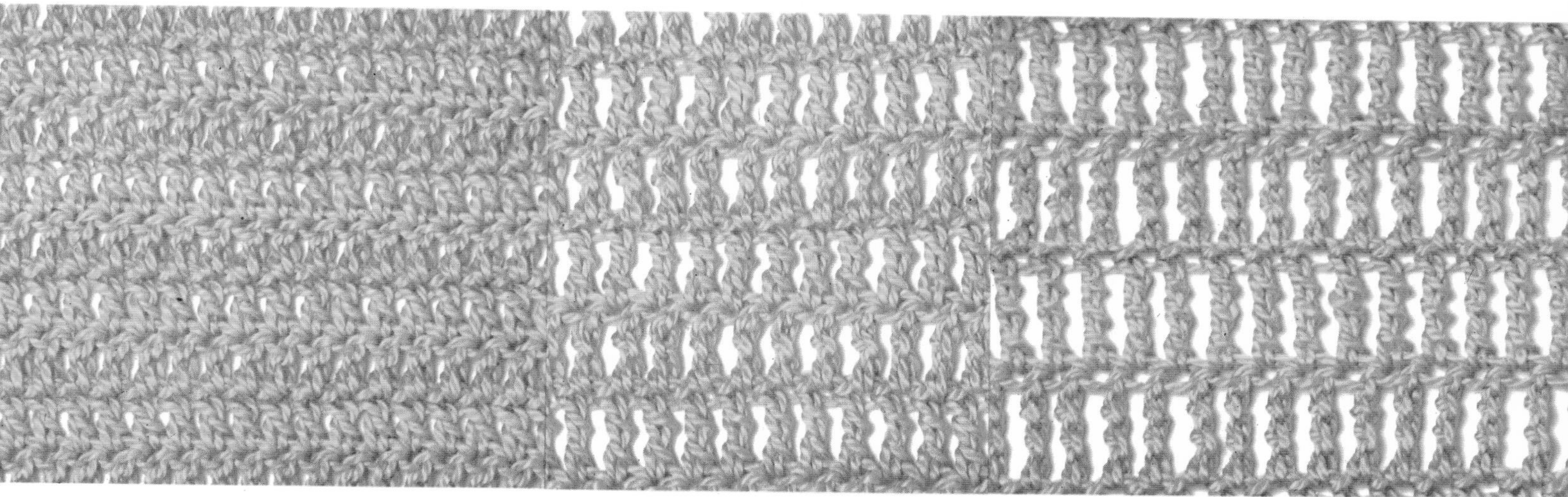

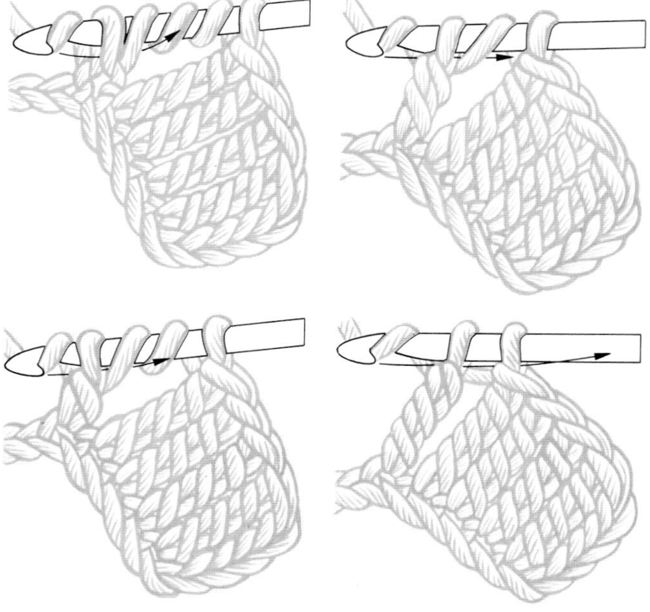

Double treble (dtr)
(5 turning chains)
Make the required number of chains plus 4 extra.
1 To work the 1st row, wind the yarn 3 times around the hook; insert it into the 6th chain from the hook and draw a loop through, so making 5 loops on the hook.
2 Wind the yarn around the hook and draw it through the 1st 2 loops on the hook, leaving 4 loops on the hook.
3 Work **2** twice more so that there are 2 loops on the hook.
4 Wind the yarn around the hook again and draw it through the remaining 2 loops; a single loop remains on the hook and 1dtr is complete.
5 Repeat **1–4** into each chain until you reach the end. Still holding the hook in your right hand, turn the work from right to left so that the last stitch of this row becomes the 1st stitch of the next row.
6 To work the 2nd and subsequent rows, make 5 turning chains to count as the 1st dtr; work 1 stitch into each stitch in the previous row by inserting the hook under the 2 horizontal loops at the top of the stitch.

Increasing and decreasing

There are different methods of shaping in crochet which depend on what stitch pattern you are using, the position of the shaping in the row and the number of stitches affected. Increasing and decreasing need careful planning since the depth of most crochet stitches can give a shaped edge an ugly stepped appearance; working increases or decreases after the turning chains at the beginning of a row and before the last stitch of the row looks neater and makes seaming easier.

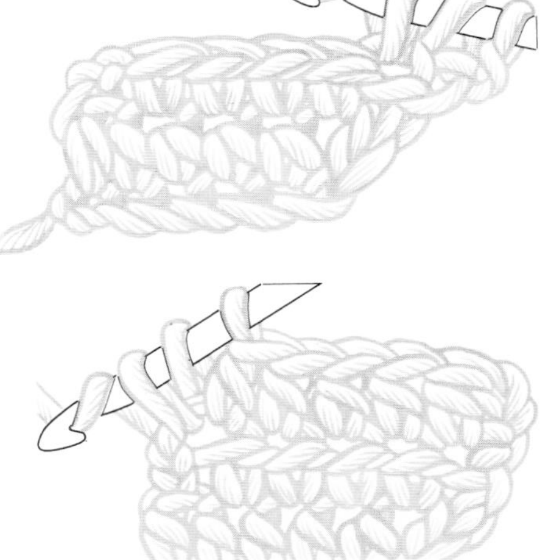

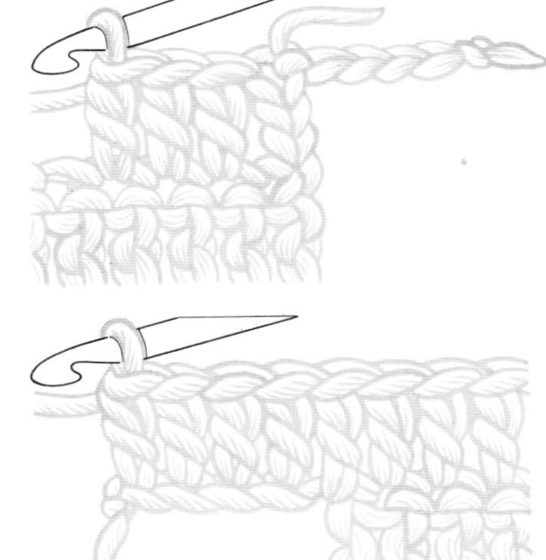

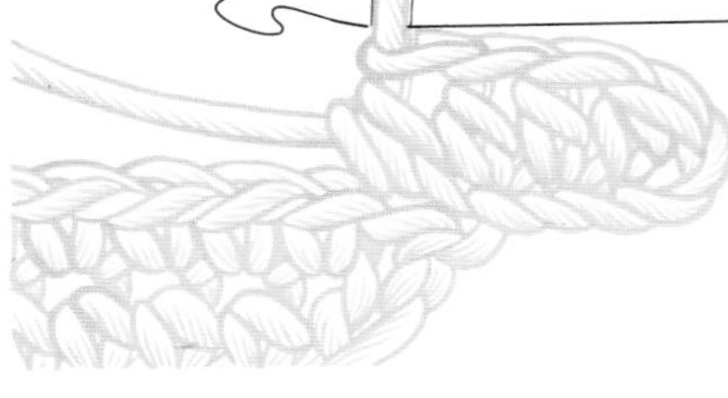

Increasing 1 stitch at each end of row
1 At the beginning of the row make 2 stitches out of 1 by working the necessary number of turning chains for the stitch pattern you are using; don't skip the 1st stitch as you normally do, but work another stitch into this one.
2 Work across the row in pattern until 2 stitches remain.
3 Increase another stitch by working 2 stitches into the next stitch.
4 Work the last stitch into the turning chain of the previous row as usual.

Increasing several stitches at the beginning of a row
1 Using the working loop on the hook, work chain stitches equivalent to 1 less than the extra stitches required plus the correct number of turning chains; e.g. if you are working in half double and need to increase 4 stitches at the beginning of a row you must work 3+2=5 chains.
2 Begin the next row by working into the extra chains; in this case work 1 hdc into each of the next 2 chains.
3 Continue working across the row in hdc, noting that the position of the turning chain is now at the beginning of the increased stitches.

Increase several stitches at the end of a row
1 Make provision for the extra stitches before you start the increase row: take another ball of the yarn you are using and make a separate length of chain containing the exact number of stitches you want to increase.
2 Join the length of chain with a slip stitch to the top of the 1st stitch at the beginning of the last row you worked; break off the yarn and fasten off.
3 Return to the main fabric and pattern to the end of the row, then work 1 stitch into each of the separate chains.

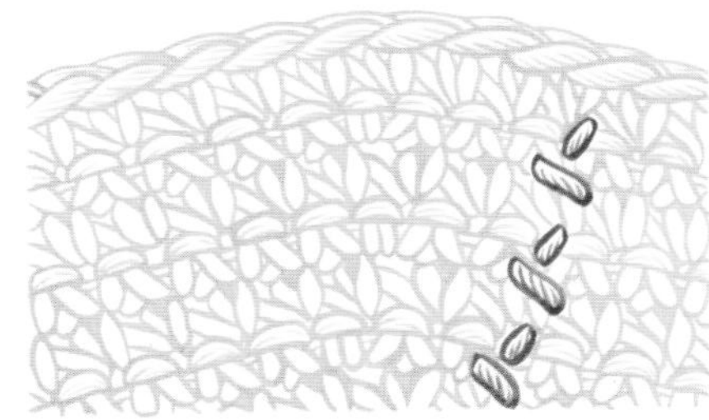

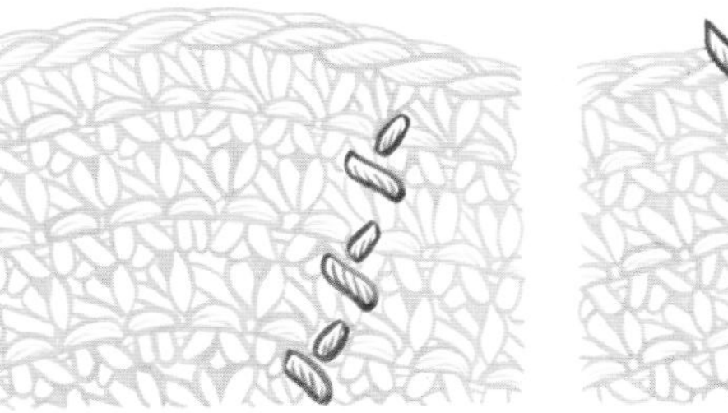

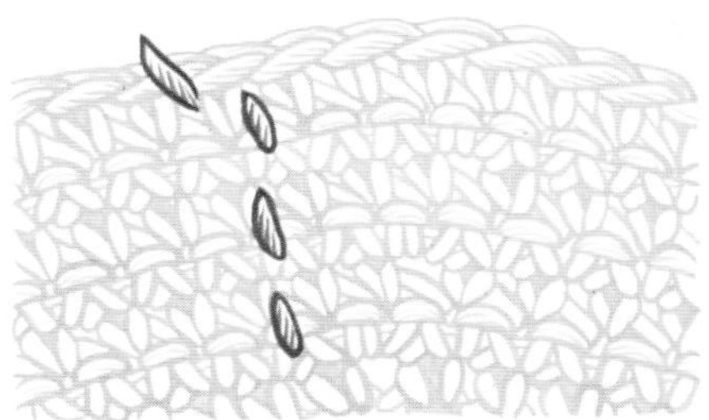

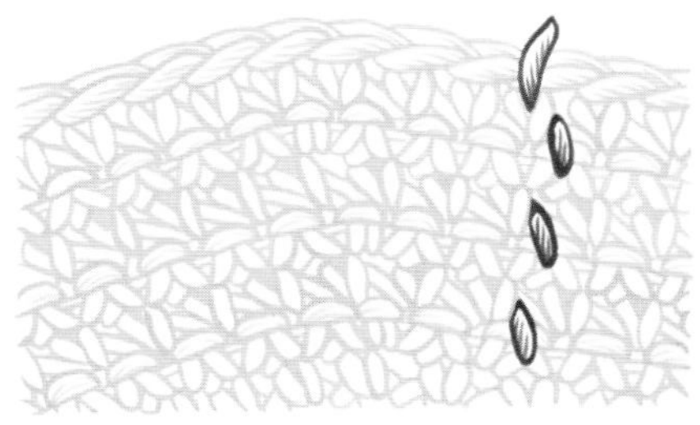

Increasing 1 stitch in the middle of a row
Work twice into any stitch on the previous row. Always work subsequent increases on RS rows. Tie a length of contrasting yarn to carry up the fabric to mark position for increases. Work twice into the stitch before the marker on 1st row, 2 stitches before marker on next row, then 3 stitches and so on to give a pronounced line of increasing which slants to the right. Work increases after the marker in the same way for a line that slants to the left. Keep increases in a straight line by increasing into the stitch before the marker on 1st increase row, then 2 stitches before marker on 2 subsequent increase rows, 3 stitches before on following 2 increase rows, and so on.

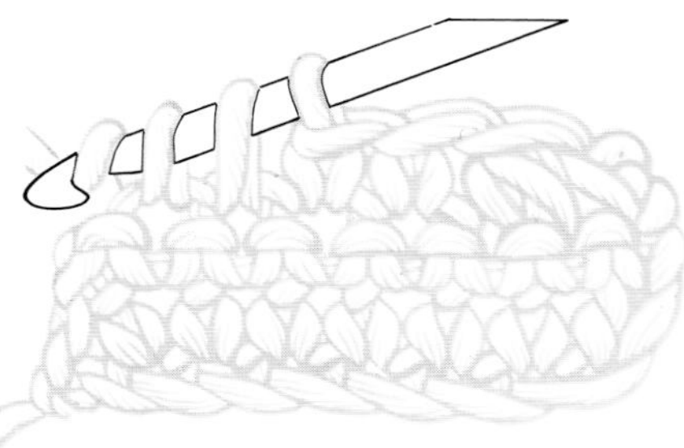

Decreasing 1sc at each end of a row

1 Decreasing within a 1-stitch border gives the neatest finish; make 1 turning chain to count as the 1st stitch.
2 Insert the hook into each of the next 2 stitches and draw a loop through, so making 3 loops on the hook.
3 Wind the yarn around the hook and draw through all 3 loops, so making 1 stitch out of the previous 2.
4 Pattern across the row until 2sc and the turning chains of the previous row remain; work the last 2sc together and then work the last stitch into the chains.

Decreasing 1 hdc at each end of a row

1 Make 2 turning chains to count as the 1st stitch.
2 Wind the yarn around the hook, insert the hook into the next stitch and draw a loop through.
3 Insert the hook into the following stitch and draw a loop through, so making 4 loops on the hook.
4 Wind the yarn around the hook and draw through all 4 loops, so making 1 stitch out of the previous 2.

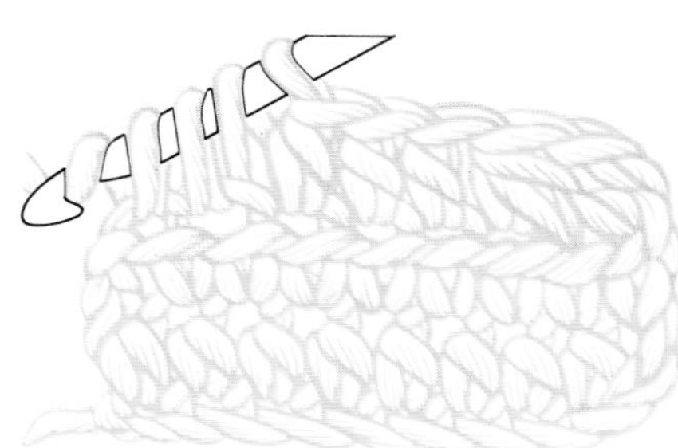

5 Follow **4** under single crochet, but remember to work in half doubles.

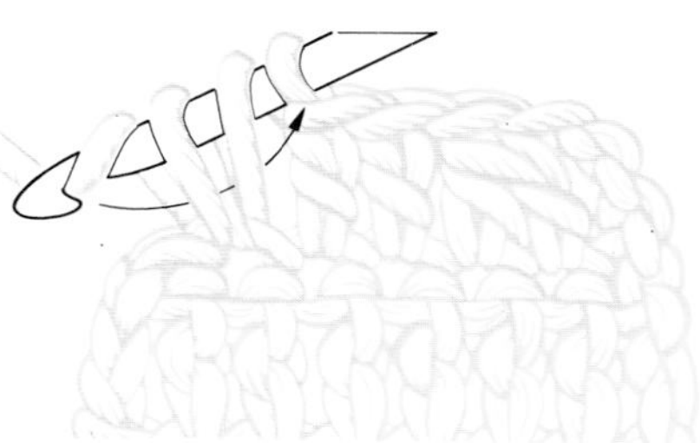

Decreasing 1dc at each end of row

1 Make 3 turning chains to count as the 1st stitch.
2 Wind the yarn around the hook, insert the hook into the next stitch and draw a loop through.

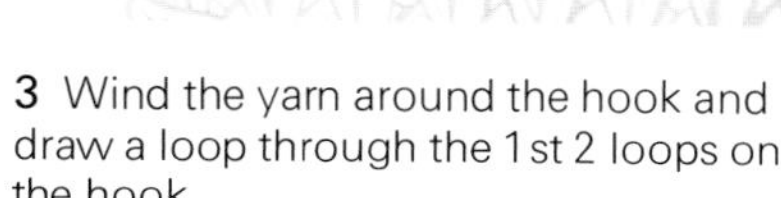

3 Wind the yarn around the hook and draw a loop through the 1st 2 loops on the hook.
4 Repeat **2** and **3** into the following stitch, so making 3 loops on the hook.
5 Wind the yarn around the hook and draw through all 3 loops so making 1 stitch out of the previous 2.
6 Follow **4** of single crochet, but remember to work in doubles.

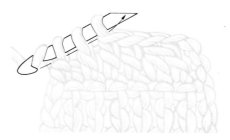

Decreasing 1 stitch in the middle of a row

1 According to the pattern you are working, work 2 stitches together in the same way as at the end of a row.
2 On subsequent rows, working the previous decreased stitch together with the next stitch gives a line of decreases that slants to the left; working the previous decreased stitch together with the one coming before it makes the line of decreases slant to the right.
3 Working the previous decreased stitch alternately with the stitch before it and the stitch after it keeps the decreases in a straight line.

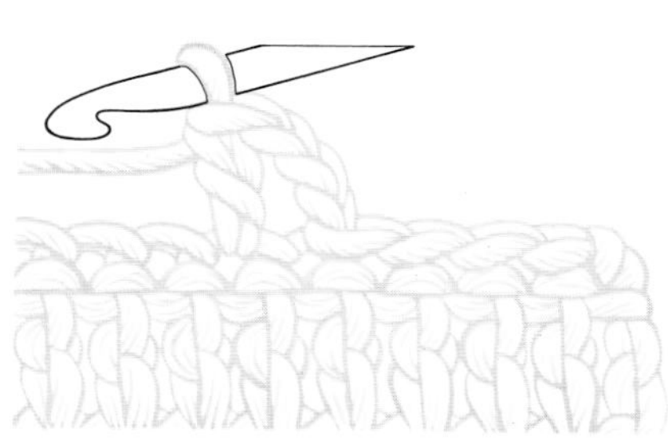

Decreasing several stitches at the beginning of a row

1 Slip-stitch into each of the stitches that you need to decrease, then begin a new row by slip-stitching into the next stitch.
2 Work the required number of turning chains to count as the 1st stitch and work in pattern to the end of the row.

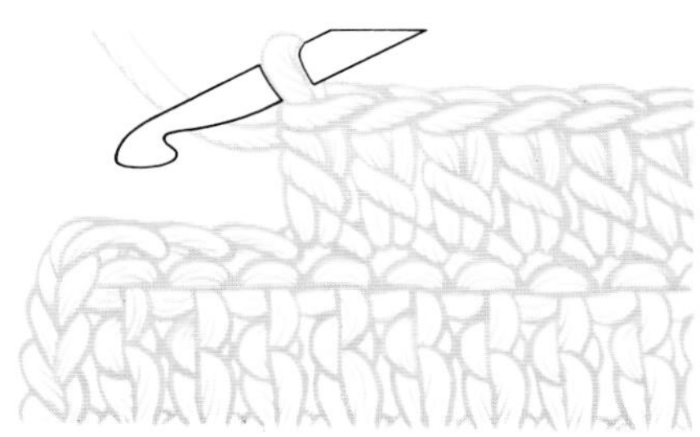

Decreasing several stitches at the end of a row

1 Pattern across the row until the number of stitches to be decreased remains unworked; the turning chain of the previous row counts as 1 of these stitches.
2 Leave the stitches unworked and simply turn your work ready to start the next row.

Beach outfit

Basic information 302
Basic stitches 304
Increasing and decreasing 306
Edgings and trimmings 334

The simplicity of the fabric textures and the geometric shaping in this beach outfit make it easy for beginners to work. The tiny bag and pouch are ideal first projects in single crochet; the bikini top, also in single crochet but involving some shaping, can become the yoke of a dress – see p338. The triangular scarf and the cover-up overleaf are worked in doubles and are similar to filet techniques, since the crochet stitches here don't make a solid fabric but are interspersed with regular chain spaces to form a mesh. Finishing touches such as the single-crochet edging, tassels and ties look professional and help to disguise any unevenness in the edges of your fabric. Detailed instructions are given here, but once you have learned the basic stitches and the techniques of increasing and decreasing, you should be able to work out similar designs for yourself.

Size
bust 32in (82cm), hips 34in (87cm) (adjustable)

You will need
6oz (150g) medium-weight cotton yarn
no.1 crochet hook

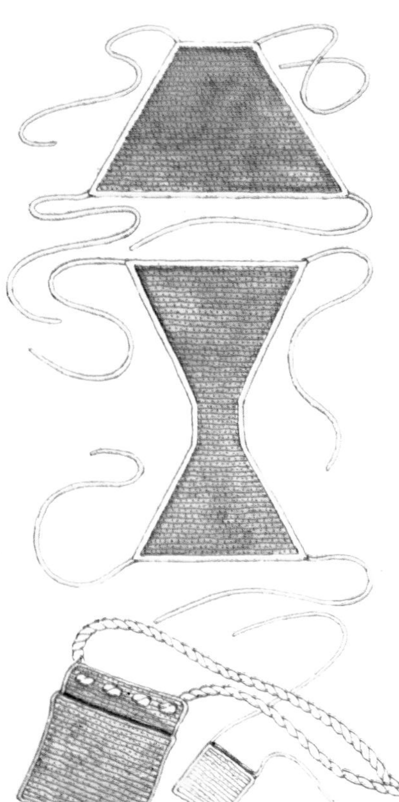

Bikini
You can adjust the size of both top and bottom. To alter the depth of bikini bottom, begin with a larger number of stitches, decrease as here until 10 sts rem, then continue to increase so that front depth is equal to back. Alter the depth of the top in same way.

Bottom Beg at back. Make 72ch.
1st row: 1sc into 3rd ch from hook, 1sc into each ch to end. Turn. (70sc.)
Cont working every row in sc, decreasing 1st at beg of every row until 10 sts rem. (Work measures 7½in/19cm.) Cont without shaping until bikini measures 8½in (22cm) from beg.
Shape front Inc 1 st at beg of next and every row until there are 58 sts and bikini measures 15in (38cm) from beg, working 4sc into last st to form corner.
Edging Turn and work a row of sc evenly down side edge to corner, 4sc into corner, sc across back to next corner, 4sc into corner and work up 2nd side in sc working corner as before. Fasten off. Join 1st contrast color at center of side edge and work in sc all around including front, working 2sc into each corner st. Fasten off.
Using 2nd contrast color make a 2nd row in same way, inc at corners as before and making a tie at each corner as it is reached by working 100ch after the 1st sc worked into the 2nd corner st, sl st back along ch, ending with 2nd sc into same corner st.

Top Using main color make 127ch.
1st row: 1sc into 2nd ch from hook. 1sc into each ch to end. Turn.
Cont working in sc throughout, dec 1 st at beg of every row until 43 sts rem (9in/23cm), working 4sc into last st to form corner.
Edging Work 1 row sc evenly around edge to opposite corner, working 4sc into each corner st, including the last corner. Fasten off. Using 1st contrast, work 1 row sc all around edge including top, working 2sc into each of 3 corner sts at each corner. Using 2nd contrast color, work another row of sc all around making a tie at each corner as given for bikini bottom, but working 170ch instead of 100ch.

Pocket (work in one piece)
Make 37ch.
1st row: 1sc into 3rd ch from hook, 1sc into each st to end. Turn.
2nd row: 1ch (= 1st sc), *1sc into next sc, rep from * to end, working last sc into t ch. Turn. (35sc.)
3rd row (eyelet hole row): 1ch, 1sc into next sc,* 2ch, skip 2sc, 1sc into each of next 2sc, rep from * 7 times more, 1sc into t ch. Turn
4th row: Work 1 sc into each

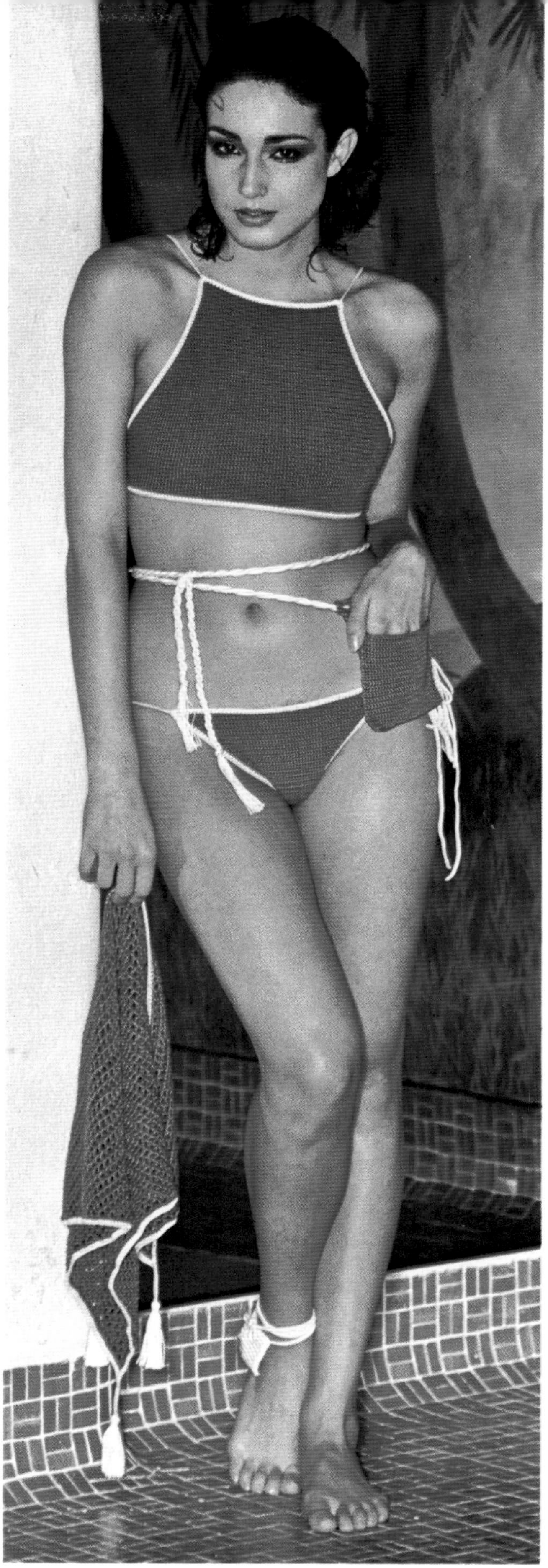

sc and 1sc into each ch to end. Turn.
Cont working in sc until pocket measures 10in (26cm) from beg. Fold 4in (11cm) over to front, leaving eyelet holes at top. Work in sc down one side of pocket, joining front and back tog, across bottom of pocket and up other side joining 2 sides tog in same way and working 4sc into each corner. Fasten off.
Using 12 strands of each contrast color make a twisted cord (see p102) about 7in (18cm) long. Slot rope through eyelet holes. Tie a knot at each end leaving about 3in (8cm) free for tassel.

Mini bag (work in one piece)
Make 16ch.
1st row: 1sc into 3rd ch from hook, 1sc into each sc to end. Turn.
2nd row: 1sc (= 1st sc) *1sc into next sc, rep from * to end, 1 sc into t ch. Turn. Rep 2nd row 34 times more, working 150ch on last sc, turn and sl st back along chain for tie.
Fold work in half to form bag.
Next row: 1sc into each row end to corner joining 2 sides together, 4sc into corner st, 1sc into each sc along bottom, 4sc into corner st, 1sc into each row end up other side, joining 2 sides tog as before. Make another tie as before on last st. Fasten off.

Basic information 300
Basic stitches 302
Increasing and decreasing 304
Edgings and trimmings 334

Cover-up
You will need
about 26oz (650g) dishcloth cotton
size K crochet hook

Make 83ch.
1st row: 1dc into 3rd ch from hook, *1ch, skip 1 st, 1dc into next st, rep from * to end. Turn.
2nd row: 3ch (= 1dc and 1ch), *1dc into next ch sp, skip 1dc, rep from * ending with 1dc into t ch. Turn.
The last row forms the pat.
Cont in pat until work measures 24in (62cm) from beg, ending with a WS row.
Yoke Cont working along side edge, work 1ch, *2sc into next sp, rep from * to end. Turn. Cont working rows in sc until yoke measures 2in (5cm).
Next row: Work in sc making a tie 11in (28cm) from each side by working 22ch, turn and sl st back to beg. Fasten off.
Front Work as for back.
Sleeves With RS of back facing, join yarn to 15th sp from yoke, 2ch, cont working in pat as given for back to edge of yoke, work in pat across yoke sts, working dc into every other sc row at edge and cont in pat to 15th sp on front. Turn. (37 sps.)
Cont in pat decreasing 1sp at beg of every foll 3rd row, until 31 sps rem. Cont without shaping until sleeve measures 13in (34cm) from yoke, ending with a WS row.
Next row: Work 1sc into each sp to end. Cont working 1sc in each sc until cuff measures 2in (5cm). Fasten off.

Finishing
Join side and sleeve seams. With RS of work facing, rejoin yarn to bottom edge at seam. Work 2sc into each ch

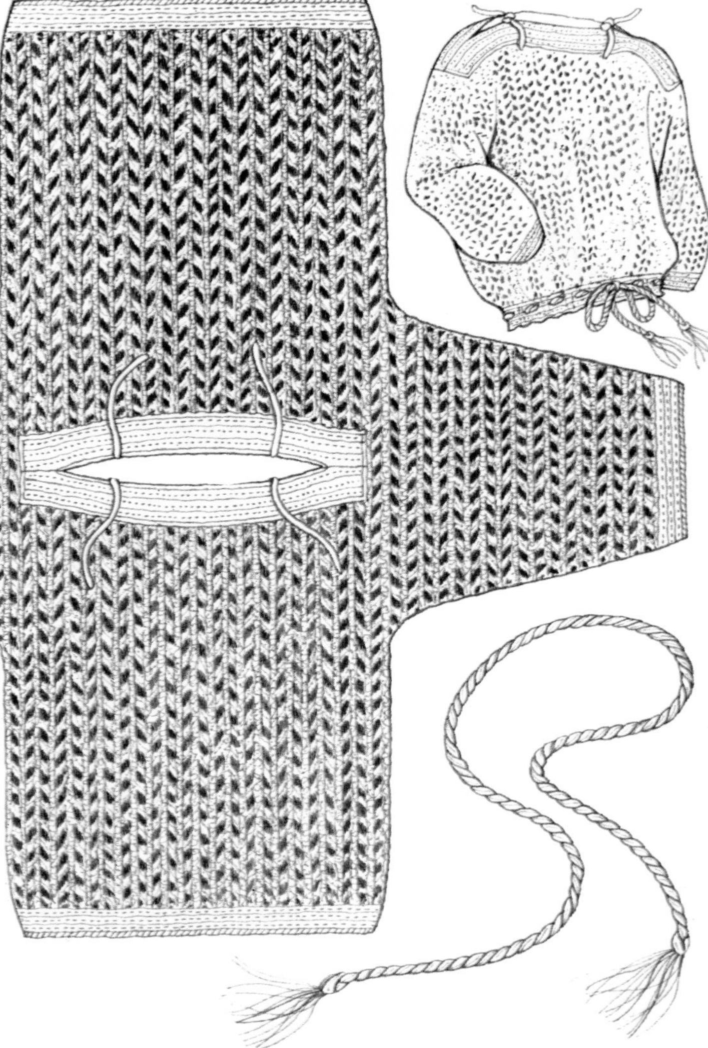

sp all around. Work 4 rounds sc, working into each sc all around.
Next round: make eyelet holes in band being made by working (2sc, 2ch, skip 2 sts) all around.
Work 3 more rounds sc, working 2sc into each 2ch sp on eyelet round. Fasten off. Make a twisted cord (see p102) with 12 strands of cotton about $2\frac{1}{2}$yd (240cm) long, weave through holes in bottom band and knot at each end, leaving a tassel about 3in (8cm) long. Trim ends.

Scarf
You will need
total of about 5oz (125g) medium-weight cotton in 3 colors (4oz/100g main color, few yards each of 2 contrast colors)
no.1 crochet hook

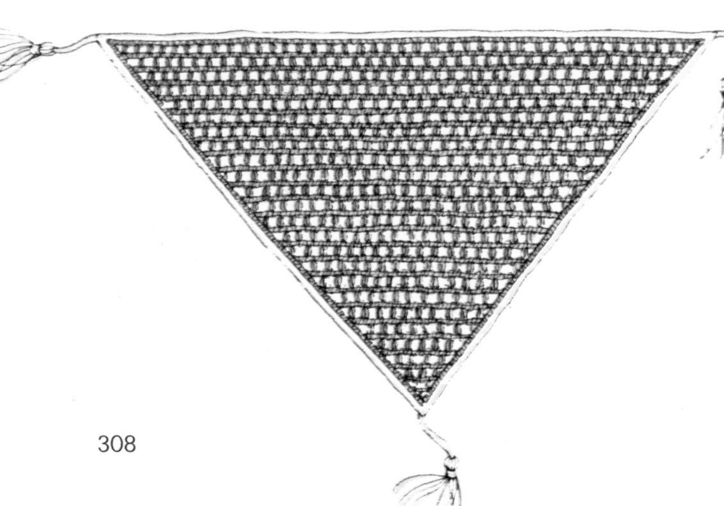

Begin at bottom corner. Using main color, make 4ch. Join with a sl st to 1st ch to form a ring.
1st row: 4ch, 1dc into ring, 1ch, 1dc into ring. Turn.
2nd row: 4ch, 1dc into 1ch sp, 1ch, 1dc into same sp, 1ch, 1dc into next sp, 1ch, 1dc into same sp. Turn. (4sps.)
3rd row: 4ch (= 1dc and 1ch), (1dc into 1st sp, 1ch) twice, 1dc into each ch sp to last sp, 1dc into last sp, 1ch, 1dc into same sp. Turn. (6sps.) Cont working in open trellis pattern and inc one sp at each end of every row in this way until there are 106 sps.

Edging Using main color, work 1sc all around shawl, working 2sc into each sp along top edge, 3dc into each sp along side edges and 5sc in each corner sp. Fasten off.
Next row: Using 1st contrast, work 1sc into each sc around edge, working 2sc into each of 3 corner sts. Fasten off.
Make 3 small tassels about 3in (7cm) long (see p103).
Next row: Using 2nd contrast color, work 1sc into each sc all around edge as before, working a tie at each corner by making 10ch at the corner, attaching the tassel by working 1sl into the tip and sl st back along 10ch.

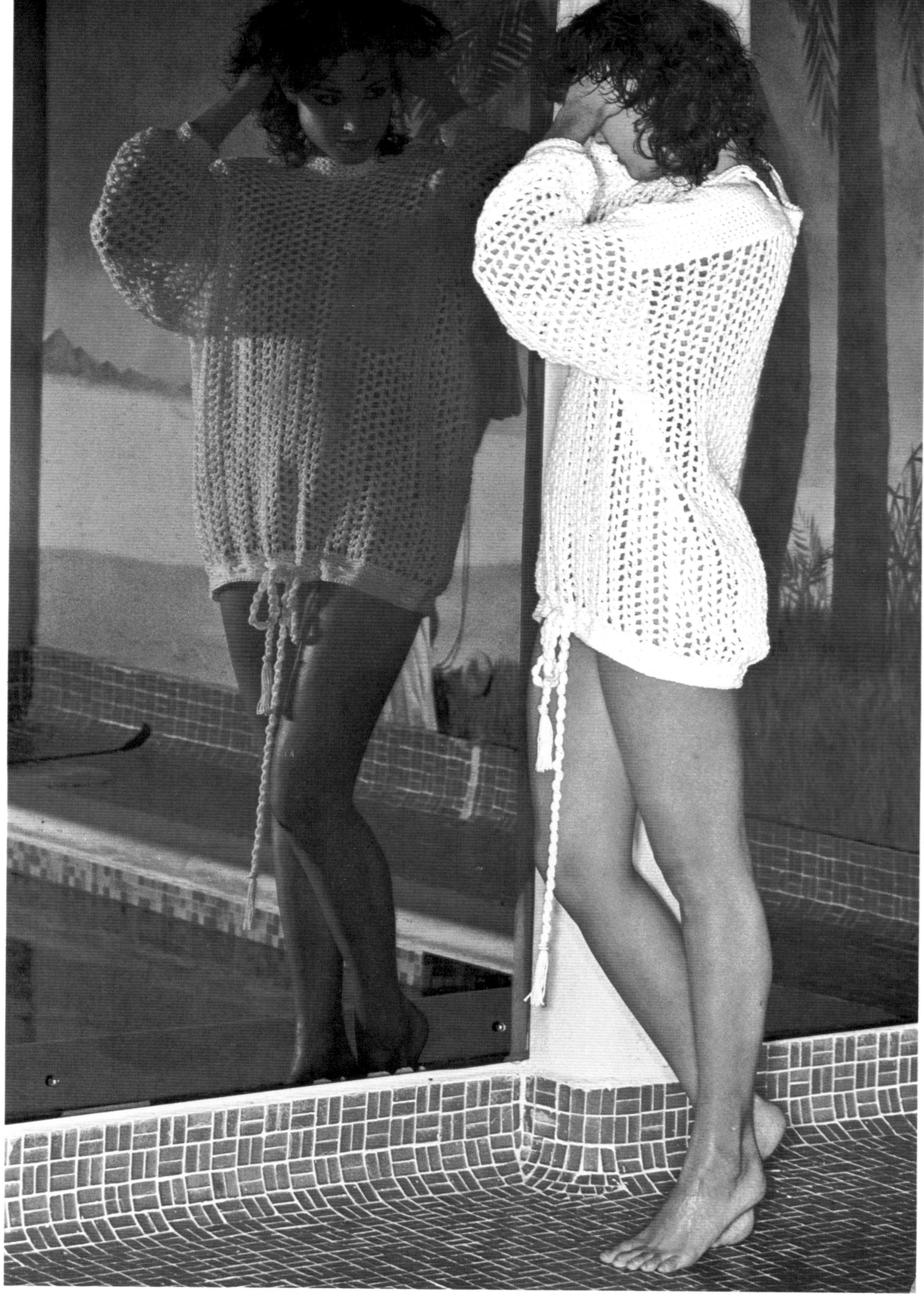

Stitch variations

Picot mesh
Chain arches often form openwork mesh designs in crochet; here is one where the arch is decorated with a picot. Make a multiple of 4+1 chains and 5 turning chains.
1st row (RS) 1sc into 10th ch from hook, 3ch, 1sc into same ch, *5ch, skip 3ch, (1sc, 3ch, 1sc – called 1 picot) into next ch, rep from * to last 4ch, 5ch, skip 3ch, 1sc into last ch. Turn.
2nd row 5ch, 1 picot into 3rd of 1st 5ch loop, *5ch, 1 picot into 3rd of next loop, rep from * to last loop, 5ch, 1 picot into 6th of 1st 9ch, 2ch, skip 2ch, 1dc into next ch. Turn.
3rd row 6ch, *1 picot into 3rd ch of next 5ch loop, 5ch, rep from * to last loop, 1 picot into last loop, 5ch, 1sc into 3rd of 1st 5ch. Turn.
4th row As 2nd, ending 5ch, 1 picot into 4th ch of last 6ch loop, 2ch, 1dc into 1st ch. Turn.
Repeat 3rd-4th rows for pattern.

Spaced shell
A number of stitches (usually 3, 5, 7 or more doubles) worked into the same place form a simple shell pattern; shallower stitches at either side act as anchors making the stitches within the shell fan out. Here shells form one above another in a regular repeating pattern.
Make a multiple of 6+1 chains.
1st row (RS) 5dc into 4th ch from hook, *skip 2ch, 1sc into next ch, skip 2ch, 5dc into next ch, rep from * to last 3ch, skip 2ch, 1sc into last ch. Turn.
2nd row 3ch (= 1st dc), *2ch, 1sc into 3rd of 5dc, 2ch, 1dc into next sc, rep from * to last shell, 2ch, 1sc into 3rd of 5dc, 2ch, 1dc into 3rd of 3ch. Turn.
3rd row 1ch (= 1st sc), *5dc into next sc, 1sc into next dc, rep from * ending with last sc into 3rd of 3ch. Turn.
4th row As 2nd, working last sc into 3rd of 3ch. Turn.
Repeat 3rd-4th rows for pattern.

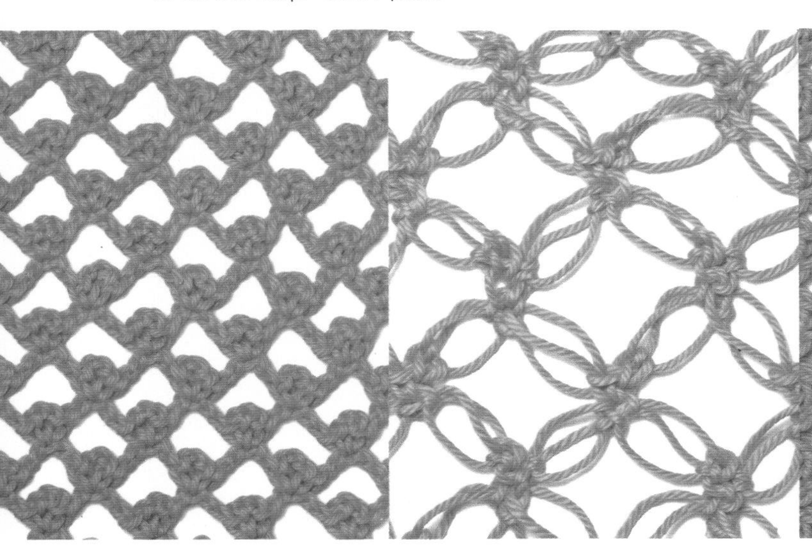

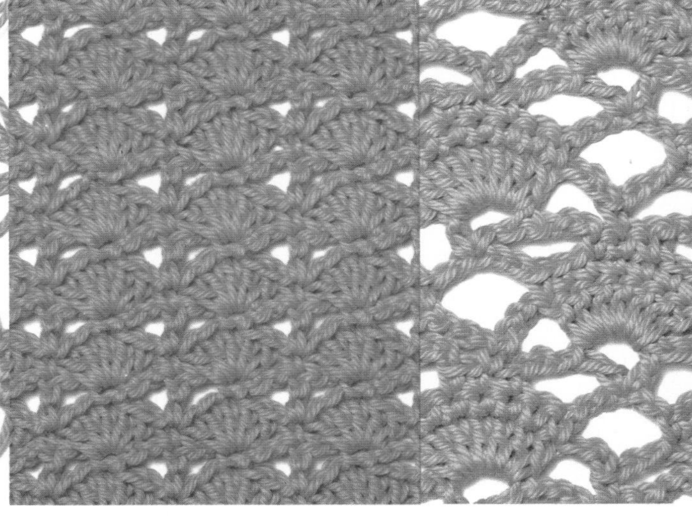

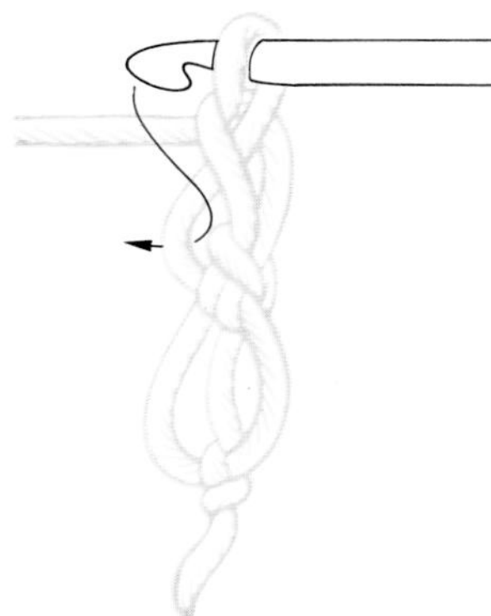

Solomon's knot
This delicate openwork fabric is ideal for scarves and shawls. The fabric forms quickly by the unusual method of extended stitches and crochet knots.
Begin with a slip loop on the hook and work 1ch.
1st row *Extend the loop on the hook for ½in (1cm), yo and draw a loop through, insert hook into back of loop just made (see diagram), yo and draw a loop through, yo and draw through both loops on hook – 1 knot complete, rep from * for required length, making an even number of knots. Turn.
2nd row Skip knot on hook and next 3 knots, 1sc into center of next knot, *make 2 knots, skip next knot on 1st row, 1sc in next knot, rep from * working last sc into 1st ch of 1st row. Turn.
3rd row Make 3 knots, 1sc into next unjoined knot on last row, *make 2 knots, 1sc into next unjoined knot on last row, rep from * to end. Turn.
Repeat 3rd row throughout to form pattern.

Openwork spaced shell
This is a less formal arrangement of shells alternating against a background of chain arches to make a very delicate pattern.
Make a multiple of 10+1 chains and 5 turning chains.
1st row (RS) 1dc into 6th ch from hook, *3ch, skip 3ch, 1sc into each of next 3ch, 3ch, skip 3ch, (1dc, 3ch, 1dc) into next ch, rep from * ending with (1dc, 2ch, 1dc) into last ch. Turn.
2nd row 3ch (=1st dc), 3dc into 1st 2ch sp, *3ch, 1sc into 2nd of 3sc, 3ch, 7dc into next 3ch sp between dc, rep from * ending with 4dc into sp between turning ch and 1st dc. Turn.
3rd row 1ch (= 1st sc), 1sc into each of next 3dc, *5ch, 1sc into each of next 7dc, rep from * to last shell, 5ch, 1sc into each of next 3dc, 1sc into 3rd of 3ch. Turn.
4th row 1ch, 1sc into next sc, *3ch, (1dc, 3ch, 1dc) into 3rd of 5ch, 3ch, skip 2sc, 1sc into each of next 3sc, rep from * ending with skip 2sc, 1sc into next sc, 1sc into 1st ch. Turn.
5th row 1ch, *3ch, 7dc into 3ch sp between dc, 3ch, 1sc into 2nd of 3sc, rep from * ending with last sc into 1st ch. Turn.
6th row 3ch, *1sc into each of next 7dc, 5ch, rep from * to last shell, 1sc into each of next 7dc, 2ch, 1sc into 1st ch. Turn.
7th row 5ch, 1dc into 1st sc (edge st), *3ch, skip 2sc, 1sc into each of next 3sc, 3ch, (1dc, 3ch, 1dc) into 3rd of 5ch, rep from * ending with (1dc, 2ch, 1dc) into 1st ch. Turn.
Repeat 2nd-7th rows for pattern.

Crochet seed stitch

A combination of half doubles and slip stitches produces a heavy textured fabric similar to the knitted seed stitch. You can achieve other Aran effects entirely in crochet. Make an uneven number of chains.

1st row (RS) 1sl st into 3rd ch from hook, *1hdc into next ch, 1sl st into next ch, rep from * to end. Turn.

2nd row 2ch (= 1st hdc), skip 1st sl st, *1sl st into next hdc, 1hdc into next sl st, rep from * to last st, 1sl st into 2nd of 1st 2ch. Turn.

Repeat 2nd row throughout for pattern.

Crochet rib

Crochet rib looks like knitting but lacks knitting's elasticity. Work it from side edge to side edge; don't fasten off when the ribbing is wide enough, but turn the work sideways so that the ribs are vertical. Work first row of main fabric into row ends of the ribbing. Make a length of chains to the depth of ribbing you want.

1st row (RS) 1sc into 3rd ch from hook, 1sc into each ch to end. Turn.

2nd row 1ch (= 1st sc), skip 1st sc, *work 1sc into horizontal loop under chain loop of next sc (see diagram), rep from * ending with last sc into turning ch. Turn.

Repeat 2nd row throughout for pattern.

Long bobble rib

Working the initial stages of a number of stitches into the same place and then joining them all to form one stitch creates a bobble of yarn on one side of the fabric. This fabric is heavily textured: you can obtain different effects by varying the number of rows between bobbles or their spacing within the row. Make a multiple of 4+1 chains and 1 turning chain.

1st row (RS) 1sc into 3rd ch from hook, 1sc into each ch to end. Turn.

2nd row 1ch (= 1st sc), 1sc into next sc, *(yo, insert hook into next sc and draw up a loop, yo and draw through 1st 2 loops on hook) 5 times into same sc, yo and draw through all 6 loops on hook – called 1 bobble, 1sc into each of next 3sc, rep from * to last 3sc, 1 bobble into next sc, 1sc into next sc, 1sc into 2nd of 2ch. Turn.

3rd row 1ch, 1sc into each st to end. Turn.

4th row 1ch, *1sc into each of next 3sc, 1 bobble into next sc, rep from * to last 4 sts, 1sc into each of next 3sc, 1sc into 1st ch. Turn.

5th row As 3rd.

6th row As 2nd, ending with 1sc into 1st ch.

Repeat 3rd-6th rows for pattern.

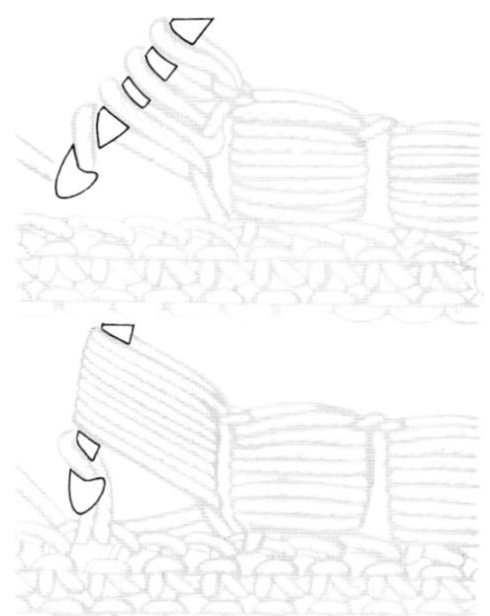

Pineapple stitch

Make a multiple of 3+2 chains and 1 turning chain.

1st row (RS) 1sc in 3rd ch, 1sc into each ch to end. Turn.

2nd row 1ch (= 1st sc), 1sc into 1st sc (edge st), 1ch and extend this to ½in (1cm), (yo, insert hook into vertical loop of sc, yo and draw a loop through extending it to ½in (1cm) 4 times into same place, skip 2sc, insert hook from front to back into next sc, yo and draw a loop through sc and all 9 loops on hook – called 1 cluster, *2ch, extend last ch to ½in (1cm), (yo, insert hook into vertical loop at side of last cluster, yo and draw loop through extending it up to ½in/1cm) 4 times into same place, skip 2sc, insert hook into next sc and complete cluster as before, rep from * ending with 1ch, 1dc into 2nd of 1st 2ch. Turn.

3rd row 3ch (= 1st dc), 3dc into each cluster to end, inserting hook under top 2 loops of each cluster, ending with 1dc into 1st ch. Turn.

4th row 1ch, 1sc in dc (edge st), work clusters as 2nd row, but skip 2dc instead of 2sc. End 1dc in 3rd of 3ch. Turn.

Rep 3rd-4th rows for pattern.

Circles

Crochet in rounds can produce two different types of result — a flat disk or a tubular fabric. The first is the basis of mats of all types and of circular pillow covers; your increasing has to be carefully spaced so that the fabric lies flat, although you can curve your shape intentionally to make a hat, for example. Tubular fabric has the advantage of being seamless, but as in knitting the RS is always facing you as you work so that the appearance of the crochet stitches is not the same as in flat, back-and-forth crochet. The two types can be combined as in the bags shown here to make a round flat-bottomed shape. Vary stitch patterns or use chain spaces to give interesting textures.

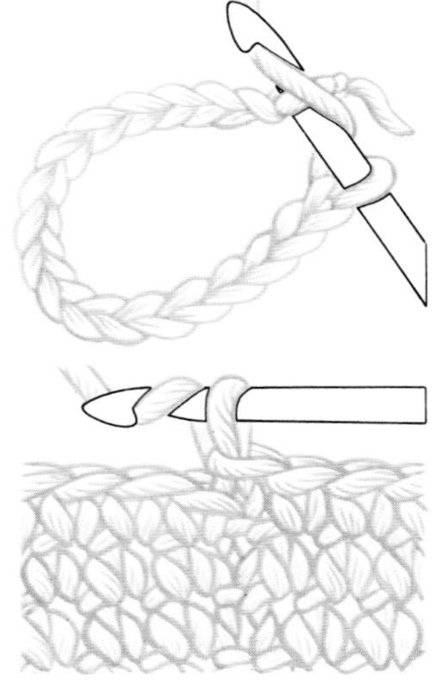

Tubular fabric
Work the precise number of chains you need to make your tube the right circumference and join them into a circle with a slip stitch, making sure that the work is not twisted. Work the necessary number of turning ch to give you the right depth for your stitch pattern, skip 1ch and work 1 st into each ch to end. Join with a sl st to top of turning ch. On pattern rounds the RS always faces you; this is convenient if you are working a motif or multicolored pattern, but can play tricks with conventional patterns worked flat in rows. If you want your tubular fabric to match one worked in rows as a flat fabric, you can turn work at the end of each round so that the last stitch of the previous round becomes the first stitch of the next round, and then work as above.

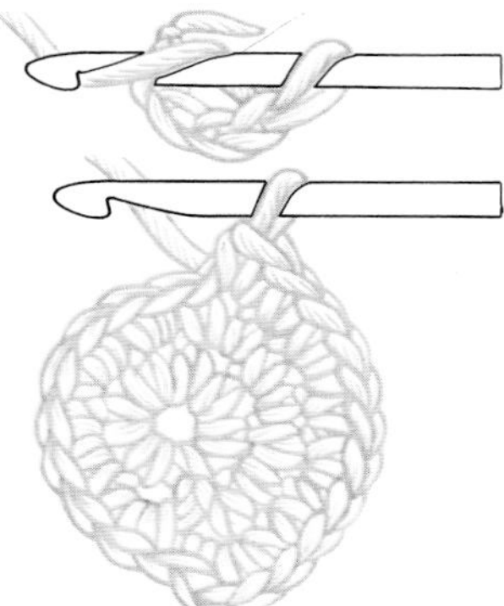

Flat disks
Make a few chains and join into a ring with a slip stitch. Making the necessary turning chains for your stitch pattern, work twice as many stitches as you have chains into the ring for the 1st round, and on subsequent rounds increase the same number of stitches evenly throughout the round.
Make 4ch. Join with a sl st into 1st ch to form ring.
1st round Work 8 sts into center of ring. Join with a sl st to top of turning ch.
2nd round Work turning ch into 1st st and once more into st at base of turning ch and then twice into every st to end (16sts). Join with a sl st to top of turning ch.
3rd round Work turning ch and 1 more st into same place (work once in next st, twice in next st) to end of round (24sts).
4th round Work turning ch and 1 more st into same place (work once into each of next 2 sts, twice into next st) to end of round (32sts).
Cont to inc 8 sts at regular intervals on foll rounds until motif is size you require.
Watch your work carefully: if circle buckles at edges you may be increasing too frequently; in that case work 1 or 2 rounds without increasing before continuing with increase rounds.

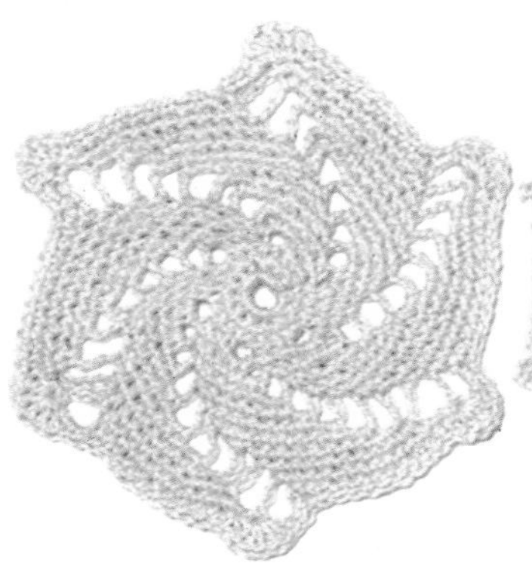

Spiral motif
Make 6ch. Join with a sl st into 1st ch to form a ring.
1st round 1ch, 12sc into ring. Don't join this or subsequent rounds (12sc).
2nd round 2sc into each sc all around (24sc).
3rd round *1sc into each of next 3sc, 3ch, skip 1sc, rep from * 5 times more.
4th round *1sc into each of next 3sc, 2sc into 3ch sp, 3ch, rep from *5 times more.
5th round *Skip 1sc, 1sc into each of next 4sc, 2sc into 3ch sp, 4ch, rep from *5 times more.
6th round *Skip 1sc, 1sc into each of next 5sc, 2sc into 4ch sp, 4ch, rep from *5 times more.
7th round *Skip 1sc, 1sc into each rem sc of group, 2sc into ch loop, 5ch, rep from * 5 times more.
Rep 7th round 5 times more, working 1 more sc in every round between each 5ch sp.
13th round Skip 1 sc, sl st into next sc, 1ch (= next sc), 1sc into each of next 10sc, 5dc into next sc, 2sc into ch loop, * skip 1sc, 1sc into each of next 11sc, 5dc into next sc, 2sc into ch loop, rep from * 4 times more. Join with a sl st to 1st ch. Fasten off.
Increase size of motif by repeating 7th round, changing number of chains between each group and adding 1 extra chain for every 6 rounds you work. Note that in last round there is 1 more sc in each group for every extra repeat of 7th round.

Wheel motif
Make 6ch. Join with a sl st into 1st ch to form a ring.
1st round 3ch, 15dc into ring. Join with a sl st to 3rd of 1st 3ch (16 sts).
2nd round 8ch, * skip 1dc, 1dc into next dc, 4ch, rep from * to end. Join with a sl st to 4th of 1st 8ch (84ch sp).
3rd round Sl st into 1st 4ch sp, 3ch (= 1dc), 7dc into same ch, *8dc into next 4ch sp, rep from * to end. Join with a sl st to 3rd of 1st ch.
4th round (work tbl) 3ch, 1dc into each of next 7dc, *1ch, 1dc into each of next 8dc, rep from * to end, ending 1ch, sl st to 3rd of 1st 3ch.
5th round (work tbl) 3ch, 1dc in each of next 7dc, *4ch, 1sc in 4th chain from hook (picot), 1ch, 1dc into each of next 8dc, rep from * to end ending with picot, 1ch. Join with a sl st to 3rd of 1st 3ch.
6th round (work tbl) 3ch, 1dc in each of next 7dc, *1ch, picot, 2ch, 1dc into each of next 8dc, rep from * to end, finishing with picot, 2ch. Join with a sl st to 2nd of 1st 2ch. Fasten off.

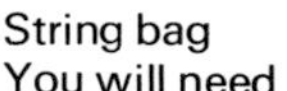

String bag
You will need
about 12oz (300g) heavy cotton
size F crochet hook

Work a flat disk (see opposite) varying your increasing by working 2ch at even intervals in one round, then working 3 sts into the ch sp on following rounds. When disk is about 6in (15cm) in diameter, cont to work without decreasing so that fabric turns upward to form sides of bag. Vary stitch pattern, e.g. work bands of several rounds of 2dc, 1ch and of 1dc, 2ch. When sides measure 13in (35cm) or desired length, fasten off.
Cord: Make 3ch + turning ch; work in sc on these sts for 35in (90cm) or desired length.

Round pillows
Using knitting worsted yarn and a medium crochet hook, work flat disks about 12in (30cm) in diameter; vary your stitches and work stripes of different colors. Work 2-sided pillows or back with matching fabric; slip-stitch 2 sides of pillow together around a pillow form.

Jute mat
This mat is the disk formula worked on a larger scale, in soft jute rope with a jumbo-size Q hook (about $\frac{1}{2}$in/15mm diameter). You may find yourself limited to using finer yarns because of the smallness of the hooks generally available. If you want to work with very thick twine or soft rope consider making your own hook: sharpen a length of dowel or smooth stick to a rounded point at one end and use a sharp knife to whittle the hook shape, using a smaller bought hook as a guide.

Tablemats
Using the basic formula opposite, work disks of heavy cotton or parcel string to the diameter you want. Vary stitch patterns and use chain spaces and picots to give pattern and texture.

Striped bag
You will need
about 12oz (300g) medium-weight cotton
size E crochet hook

Work a flat disk (see opposite) about 8in (20cm) in diameter. Cont to work without decreasing so that fabric turns upward to form sides of bag, varying stitch patterns and colors, until sides measure about 12in (30cm) or desired length.
Drawstring round: work 2ch sp at even intervals on round.
Next round: work into all sts and all ch. Cont for 1 or 2 more rounds.
Cord: make 4ch + turning ch and work in sc on these sts for 1yd (90cm) or desired length.

Square motifs

Motifs, especially the 'granny square', are usually a far easier form of crochet for learners to try than the more complicated instructions for a garment. Initially you may have problems with gauge which is difficult to control because of the depth and the openness of crochet stitches. Crocheting motifs means that you can afford to relax about gauge and become familiar with the techniques. Things you can make with squares include bedspreads, rugs, bags, shawls and garments (see p318); trial squares need not be wasted, but can be joined together to make mats or a small rug.

Motifs are a form of crochet in the round. You don't turn the work at the end of each row as you do when working back and forth, but the last stitch of each round is joined to the first.

You begin a square in exactly the same way as when working a circle (see p312), by making a few stitches into a ring; to keep the motif flat and develop the square shape you must increase in some form at 4 equal radii of the circle to make corners. On subsequent rounds you increase the number of stitches or of chain spaces; in this way you can adapt the basic formula to include as many rounds as you like until the motif is the required size. Remember, especially when tackling a large item like a bedspread, that the larger your motifs the less work you will have sewing them together.

If you want a patchwork effect, or have scraps of yarn to use up, working a quantity of square motifs is the answer. Use yarns equal in weight, however; e.g. if you want to mix a mohair with a knitting worsted, make sure that both give equal gauge.

Joining squares The most inconspicuous method of joining the squares together is to overcast the edges on the WS using an ordinary sewing needle and matching thread. You can make a feature of the joining by crocheting the motifs together on the RS. See p334 for information on joining knitted or crochet fabrics with crochet.

Granny square

In this traditional square, blocks of 3 doubles with chain spaces between them form the design and you increase by working 2 blocks of doubles into the corner spaces. Monochrome squares in cotton yarn can look quite elegant; alternatively work each round in a different color – a good way to use up scraps of yarn as long as you make sure all are of equal weight.

Make 6ch. Join with a sl st into 1st ch to form a ring.

1st round 3ch (= 1st dc), 2dc into ring, 3ch, *3dc, 3ch, rep from * twice more. Join with a sl st to 3rd of 3ch.

2nd round Sl st into 1st 3ch sp, (3ch, 2dc, 3ch, 3dc) into sp, *1ch, (3dc, 3ch, 3dc) into next 3ch sp, rep from) * twice more, 1ch. Join with a sl st to 3rd of 3ch.

3rd round Sl st into 1st 3ch sp, (3ch, 2dc, 3ch, 3dc) into this sp, *1ch, 3dc into next 1ch sp, 1ch, (3dc, 3ch, 3dc) into next 3ch sp, rep from * ending with 1ch, 3dc into next 1ch sp, 1ch. Join with a sl st to 3rd of 3ch.

4th round Sl st into 1st 3ch sp, (3ch, 2dc, 3ch, 3dc) into this sp, *(1ch, 3dc into next 1ch sp) twice, 1ch, (3dc, 3ch, 3dc) into corner 3ch sp, rep from * – ending last rep (1ch, 3dc into next 1ch sp) twice, 1ch. Join with a sl st to 3rd of 3ch.

5th round Sl st into 1st 3ch sp, (3ch, 2dc, 3ch, 3dc) into this sp, *(1ch, 3dc into next 1ch sp) 3 times, 1ch, (3dc, 3ch, 3dc) into corner 3ch sp, rep from * ending last rep (1ch, 3dc into next 1ch sp) 3 times, 1ch. Join with a sl st to 3rd of 1st 3ch. Cont working rounds in this way, with 1 more group of doubles between each corner until square is required size.

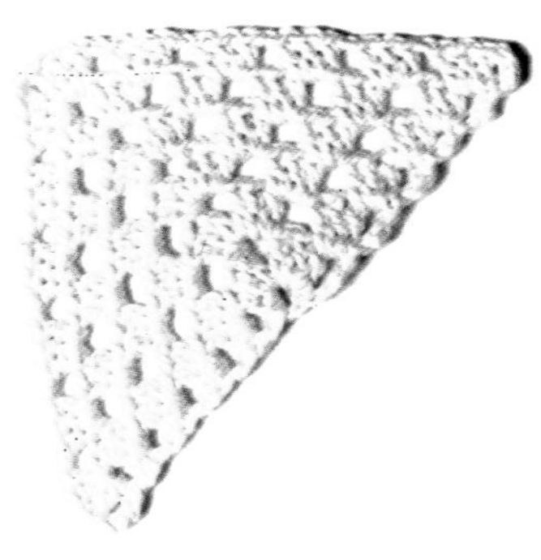

To make a triangular half of the granny square, work in rows so that RS is always facing as when you work in rounds. Break off yarn at the end of each row and rejoin it to the 1st stitch of the previous row. Make 5ch. Join with a sl st into 1st ch to form ring.
1st row 4ch (= 1st dc and 1ch sp), (3dc, 2ch, 3dc) into ring to form corner, 1ch, 1dc into ring. Fasten off.
2nd row Join yarn to 3rd of 1st 4ch with a sl st, 4ch, 3dc into 1st ch sp of previous row, 1ch, (3dc, 2ch, 3dc) into next 2ch corner sp, 1ch, 3dc into last 1ch sp, 1ch, 1dc into last dc of previous row. Fasten off.
3rd row Join yarn to 3rd of 1st 4ch of previous row, 4ch, 3dc into 1st ch sp of previous row, 1ch, 3dc into next 1ch sp, 1ch, (3dc, 2ch, 3dc) into next 2ch corner sp, (1ch, 3dc into next 1ch sp) twice, 1ch, 1dc into last dc of previous row. Fasten off.
4th row Join yarn to 3rd of 1st 4ch of previous row, 4ch, 3dc into 1st ch sp of previous row, 1ch, (3dc into next 1ch sp, 1ch) twice, (3dc, 2ch, 3dc) into next 2ch corner sp, (1ch, 3dc into next 1ch sp) 3 times, 1ch, 1dc into last dc of previous row. Fasten off.
Cont in this way, working 1 more group of doubles between each corner, until triangle is required size.

Make 8ch. Join with a sl st in into 1st ch to form a ring.
1st round 3ch, (yo, insert hook into ring, yo, draw 1 loop through, yo, draw 2 loops through) twice, yo, draw 3 loops through (=½ cluster), 5ch, (yo, insert hook into ring, yo, draw 1 loop through, yo, draw 2 loops through) 3 times, yo, draw 4 loops through (=1 cluster), 2ch, * 1 cluster, 5ch, 1 cluster, 2ch, rep from * twice more. Sl st to 3rd of 3ch.
2nd round Sl st into 1st 5ch sp, 3ch, ½ cluster into next 5ch sp, 2ch, 1 cluster into same sp, 2ch, 3dc into next 2ch sp, 2ch, *(1 cluster, 2ch, 1 cluster) into next 5ch sp, 2ch, 3dc into next 2ch sp, 2ch, rep from * to end. Join with a sl st to 3rd of 3ch.
3rd round Sl st into next st, 3ch, *(1 cluster, 2ch, 1 cluster) into next 2ch sp (corner made), 2ch, 2dc into next 2ch sp, 1dc into each of next 3dc, 2dc into next 2ch sp, 2ch, rep from * to end. Join with sl st to 3rd of 3ch.
Cont working dc into dc of last row, clusters at corners and 2dc into 2ch sp at side of each corner. until required size.

Make 8ch. Join with a sl st into 1st ch to form a ring.
1st round 3ch, 15dc into ring. Join with a sl st to 3rd of 3ch.
2nd round 5ch (= 1st dc and 2ch), *1dc into next dc, 2ch, rep from * to end. Join with a sl st to 3rd of 1st 5ch. (16dc.)
3rd round 3ch, 2dc into 1st 2ch sp, 1ch, *(3dc, 1ch) into next 2ch sp, rep from * to end. Join with a sl st to 3rd of 3ch.
4th round *(3ch, 1sc into next 1ch sp) 3 times, 6ch, 1sc into next sp (corner), rep from * to end. Join with a sl st to 1st of 3ch.
5th round 3ch, 2dc into 1st 3ch sp, 3dc into each of next 2 3ch sp, *(5dc, 2ch, 5dc) into corner sp, 3dc into each of next 3ch sp, rep from * twice more, (5dc, 2ch, 5dc) into last corner sp. Join with a sl st to 3rd of 3ch.
6th round 3ch, 1dc into each dc all round and (1dc, 1tr, 1dc) into each 2ch sp at corner. Join with a sl st to 3rd of 3ch. Fasten off.

Make 10ch. Join with a sl st into 1st ch to form a ring.
1st round 10ch, *4tr into ring, 7ch, rep from * twice more, 3tr into ring. Join with a sl st to 3rd of 1st 10ch. Sl st into each of next 3ch. Turn work.
2nd round *1sc into each of next 10 sts, skip next st, rep from * to end. Join with a sl st to 1st sc.
3rd round 10ch, 2tr into 1st sc, 1tr into each of next 8sc, 2tr into next sc, 7ch, (2tr into next sc, 1tr into each of next 8sc, 2tr into next sc, 7ch) twice, 2tr into next sc, 1tr into each of next 9sc. Join with a sl st to 3rd of 1st 10ch. Sl st over 3ch, turn work.
4th round *1sc into each of next 18sc, skip 1sc, rep from * to end. Join with a sl st to 1st sc.
5th round 3ch, * 6tr into corner st, 1tr into each st to next corner, rep from * to end. Join with a sl st to 3rd of 3ch. Fasten off.

Make 12ch. Join with a sl st into 1st ch to form a ring.
1st round 5ch, *1tr into ring, 1ch, rep from * 14 times more. Sl st to 4th of 1st 5ch.
2nd round 4ch, 3dc into 1st ch sp, drop loop from hook, insert hook into top of 1st 4ch and through dropped loop, draw loop through, 2ch, *4dc into next 1ch sp, drop loop from hook, insert hook into top of 1st of 4dc and through dropped loop, draw loop through, 2ch, rep from * 14 times more. Join with a sl st to 4th of 4ch.
3rd round Sl into 1st 2ch sp, 3ch (= 1st dc), (3dc, 2ch, 4dc) into same sp, *(3ch, 1sc into next 2ch sp) 3 times, 3ch, (4dc, 2ch, 4dc) into next 2ch sp, rep from * twice more, (3ch, 1sc into next 2ch sp) 3 times. Join with a sl st to 3rd of 3ch.
4th round Sl st into 1st 2ch corner sp, 3ch, (3dc, 2ch, 3dc) into same sp, *(4dc into next 1ch sp) 3 times, 4dc, 2ch, 4dc into next corner sp, rep from * twice more, (4dc into next 1ch sp) 3 times. Join with a sl st to 3rd of 3ch. Fasten off.

A bedspread in silky, medium-weight cotton yarn looks and feels luxurious and will last for years. An item of this size may seem an ambitious project but the individual squares are relaxing to work on, and only at the finishing stage when you are sewing or crocheting them together do you have anything bulky to handle. Some planning is necessary before you begin: consider the design of the motifs themselves and how to arrange them – perhaps combining fairly plain squares with more ornate ones. After joining the squares together, finish the edges as here with two or three rows of single or double crochet, and add fringe if you like.

Size
1 square measures 7in (18cm); total size 90×70in (235×180cm)

You will need
about $5\frac{1}{2}$lb (2500g) medium-weight cotton
size E crochet hook

Square (make 130)
Make 8ch. Join with a sl st to form a ring.
1st round: 3ch (=1dc), 15dc into ring. Join with a sl st to 3rd of 1st 3ch. (16 sts.)
2nd round: 5ch, *1dc into next dc, 2ch, rep from * to end. Join with a sl st to 3rd of 1st 5ch.
3rd round: 4ch, *3dc into next sp, 1ch, rep from * to last sp, 2dc into next sp. Join with a sl st to 3rd of 1st 4ch.
4th round: *(1sc into 1ch sp, 3ch), 3 times, 1sc into 1ch sp, 6ch, rep from * 3 times more. Join with a sl st to 1st sc.
5th round: 4ch, *(3dc into 3ch sp, 1ch) 3 times, (5dc, 2ch, 5dc) into 6ch sp, 1ch, rep from *twice more, (3dc into 3ch sp, 1ch) 3 times, (5dc, 2ch, 4dc) into 6ch sp. Join with a sl st to 3rd of 1st 4ch.
6th round: *(1sc into 1ch sp, 3ch) 4 times, 1sc into 4th of 5dc, 6ch, 1sc into 2nd of next 5dc, 3ch, rep from * 3 times more. Join with a sl st to 1st sc.
7th round: 4ch, (3dc into 3ch sp, 1ch) 4 times, *(5dc, 2ch, 5dc) into 6ch sp, 1 ch, (3dc into 3ch sp, 1ch) 5 times, rep from * twice more, (5dc, 2ch, 5dc) into 6ch sp, 1ch, 2dc into 3ch sp. Join with a sl st to 3rd of 1st 4ch.
8th round: (1sc into 1ch sp, 3ch) 5 times, *1sc into 4th of 5dc, 6ch, 1sc into 2nd of next 5dc, 3ch, (1sc into 1ch sp, 3ch) 6 times, rep from * twice more, 1sc into 4th of 5dc, 6ch, 1sc into 2nd of next 5dc, 3ch, 1sc into 1ch sp, 3ch. Join with a sl st to 1st sc.
9th round: 3ch, (3dc into 3ch sp) 5 times, *(5dc, 2ch, 5dc) into 6ch sp, (3dc into 3ch sp) 7 times, rep from * twice more, (5dc, 2ch, 5dc) into 6ch sp, 3dc into 3ch sp, 2dc into next 3ch sp, sl st to 3rd of 1st 3ch.
10th round: 3ch, 1dc into each dc all around and (1dc, 1tr, 1dc) into 2ch sp at each corner, end with sl st into 3rd of 1st 3ch. Fasten off.

Finishing
Join squares into 13 strips of 10, then join the strips. With RS facing, work a round of dc all round, working (2dc, 1tr, 2dc) into the tr at each corner. Turn.
Next round: With WS facing, work in hdc all around, working 5hdc into the tr at each corner. Fasten off. Block work with a warm iron over a damp cloth.

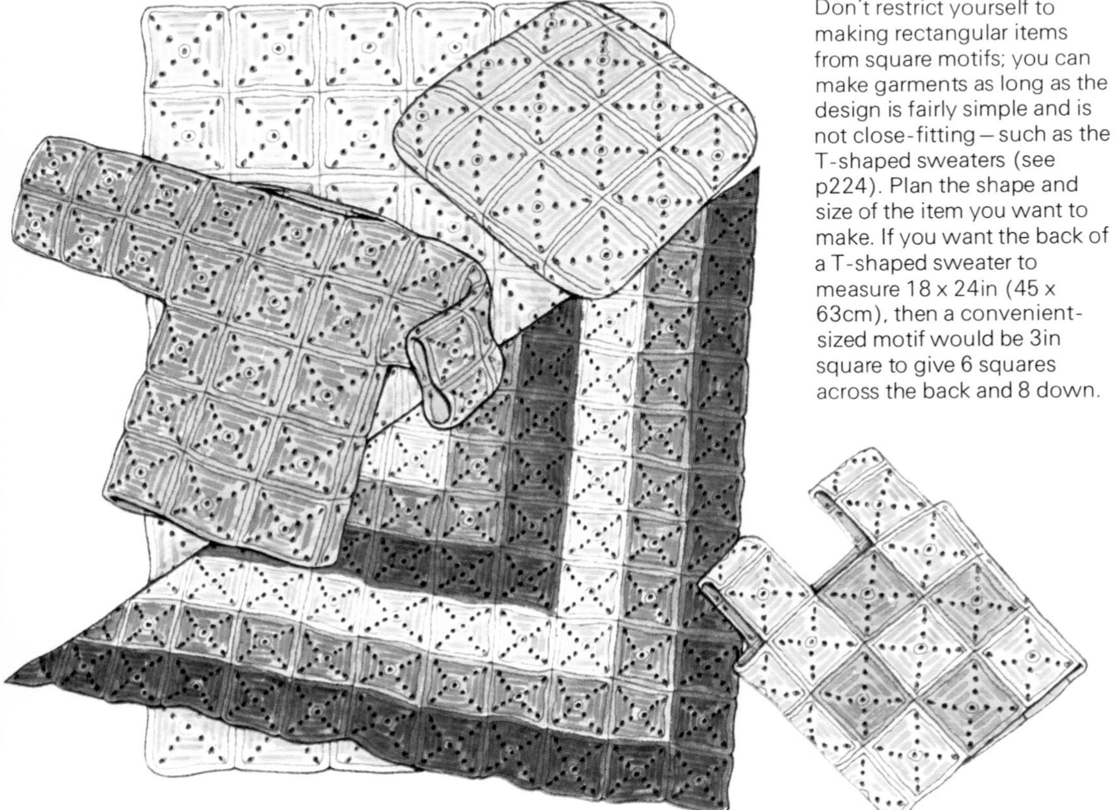

Designing with squares
Don't restrict yourself to making rectangular items from square motifs; you can make garments as long as the design is fairly simple and is not close-fitting – such as the T-shaped sweaters (see p224). Plan the shape and size of the item you want to make. If you want the back of a T-shaped sweater to measure 18 x 24in (45 x 63cm), then a convenient-sized motif would be 3in square to give 6 squares across the back and 8 down.

Work the square using your yarn and an appropriate hook size (see p300) so that the fabric is neither too stiff nor too loose and open. Measure the finished square and assess your gauge. If the square is too large or too small then you may need to work 1 round less or 1 round more; if this makes too drastic a difference, change the hook to 1 size smaller to reduce size or 1 size larger to increase it.
You may like to neaten out the edges of something made from square motifs by working a couple of rows of single crochet or doubles, as in the bedspread here.
Triangles Shaping with square designs is done mainly by omitting complete squares at appropriate places such as armholes and necks. A triangle is a useful shape, both as a means of shaping in a more complicated pattern and to fill in the indented edges of squares used at an angle to make a straight line.

Shawl

Basic information 300
Basic stitches 302

Angora or mohair mixtures give a soft, cuddly look to crochet designs, particularly those that are webby and open rather than densely textured. A fringed shawl is an ideal way to use square motifs and triangular fill-ins. Although this shawl appears to be made up of a number of motifs joined together, in fact it is worked in one piece, beginning at the bottom corner and gradually increasing at each side to make the triangular shape. You could vary the size of the shawl by working fewer or more of the pattern repeats in the 8th–12th rows.

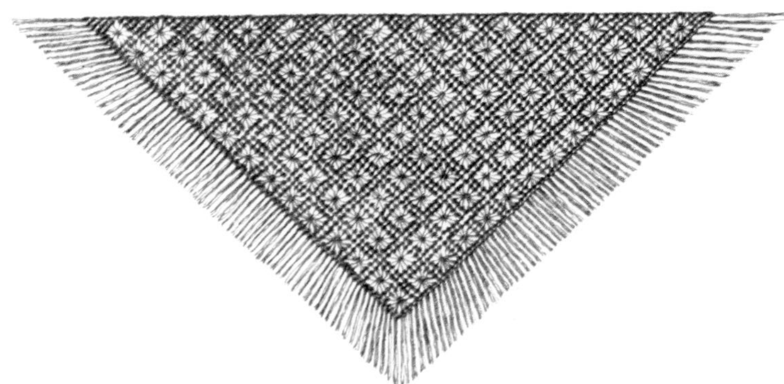

You will need
about 10oz (250g) yarn of knitting worsted weight
size H crochet hook

Size
long edge: 74in (190cm)
depth: 37in (95cm)
(1 motif measures 5in/13cm)

Beg at bottom point. Make 5ch.
1st row: 1dc into 5th ch from hook. Turn (loop made).
2nd row: 5ch, 3dc into loop, 2ch, 1dc into 3rd of 1st 5ch. Turn.
3rd row: 5ch, 3dc into 2ch sp, 9ch, 3dc into next sp, 2ch, 1dc into 3rd of 1st 5ch. Turn.
4th row: 5ch, 3dc into 2ch sp, 5ch, 1sc into 9ch loop, 5ch, 3dc into last sp, 2ch, 1dc into 3rd of 1st 5ch. Turn.
5th row: 5ch, 3dc into 2ch sp, 5ch, 1sc into 5ch loop, 1sc into next sc, 1sc into 5ch loop, 5ch, 3dc into last sp, 2ch, 1dc into 3rd of 1st 5ch. Turn.
6th row: 5ch, 3dc into 2ch sp, 5ch, 1sc into 5ch loop, 1sc into each of next 3sc, 1sc into 5ch loop, 5ch, 3dc into last sp, 2ch, 1dc into 3rd of 1st 5ch. Turn.
7th row: 5ch, 3dc into 2ch sp, 1ch, 3dc into 5ch loop, 5ch, skip 1sc, 1sc into each of next 3sc, 5ch, 3dc into 5ch loop, 1ch, 3dc into last sp, 2ch, 1dc into 3rd of 1st 5ch. Turn.
8th row: 5ch, 3dc into 2ch sp; * motif: 9ch, 3dc in 1ch sp, 1ch, 3dc in 5ch loop, 5ch, skip 1sc, 1sc in next sc, 5ch, 3dc in 5ch loop, 1ch, 3dc in 1ch sp *, 9ch, 3dc in last sp, 2ch, 1dc in 3rd of 1st 5ch. Turn.
9th row: 5ch, 3dc in 2ch sp; * motif: 5ch, 1sc in 9ch loop, 5ch, 3dc in 1ch sp, 1ch, 3dc in 5ch loop, 1ch, 3dc in next

5ch loop, 1ch, 3dc in 1ch sp *, 5ch, 1sc in 9ch loop, 5ch, 3dc in last sp, 2ch, 1dc in 3rd of 1st 5ch. Turn.
10th row: 5ch, 3dc in 2ch sp; * motif: 5ch, 1sc in 5ch loop, 1sc in next sc, 1sc in 5ch loop, 5ch, (3dc in 1ch sp, 1ch) twice, 3dc in 1ch sp *, 5ch, 1sc in 5ch loop, 1sc in sc, 1sc in 5ch loop, 5ch, 3dc in last sp, 2ch, 1dc in 3rd of 1st 5ch. Turn.
11th row: 5ch, 3dc in 2ch sp; * motif: 5ch, 1sc in 5ch loop, 1sc in each of next 3sc, 1sc in 5ch loop, 5ch, 3dc in 1ch sp, 1ch, 3dc in 1ch sp *, 5ch, 1sc in 5ch loop, 1sc in each of next 3sc, 1sc in 5ch loop, 5ch, 3dc in last sp, 2ch, 1dc in 3rd of 1st 5ch. Turn.
12th row: 5ch, 3dc in 2ch sp; * motif: 1ch, 3dc in 5ch loop, 5ch, skip 1sc, 1sc in each of next 3sc, 5ch, 3dc in 5ch loop, 1ch, 3dc in 1ch sp *; 1ch, 3dc in 5ch loop, 5ch, skip 1sc, 1sc in each of next 3sc, 5ch, 3dc in 5ch loop, 1ch, 3dc in last sp, 2ch, 1dc in 3rd of 1st 5ch. Turn.
The 8th-12th rows form the pat. Rep them 12 times more, noting that the motif instructions worked from * to * are worked one extra time in every row on each pat rep, so that on the 72nd row you will work the pat rep 13 times in all.
73rd row: As 8th, but working 1ch instead of 9ch.
74th row: 5ch, 3dc in 2ch sp, *1ch, (3dc in 1ch sp, 1ch) twice, 3dc in 5ch loop, 1ch, 3dc in next 5ch loop, 1ch, 3dc in 1ch sp, rep from *, ending with 3dc into last sp, 2ch, 1dc in 3rd of 1st 5ch.
75th row: 1ch, 1sc into each dc to end.
Fasten off.

Fringe
Cut yarn into 15in (40cm) lengths. Using 3 strands together each time, knot into every space along two shorter sides. Trim fringe.

Filet

This form of crochet consists of a mesh background made up of individual doubles separated by chain – hence the name 'filet', meaning net. Chain spaces filled in with doubles become blocks, and you can create a variety of designs and motifs by arranging blocks on the mesh background. Filet is also the simplest form of lacy crochet and has long been used on household items, particularly as edgings and insertions for delicate linens (see examples on p324). You can apply the same techniques very successfully to garments; a rope-like heavy cotton and thick hook can quickly form a plain mesh cover-up for the beach similar to the one on p308, while more delicate patterns, perhaps featuring an intricate motif, are ideal for evening tops or shawls. Panels of filet crochet are often incorporated with dressmaking, for example as the yoke of a fabric dress.

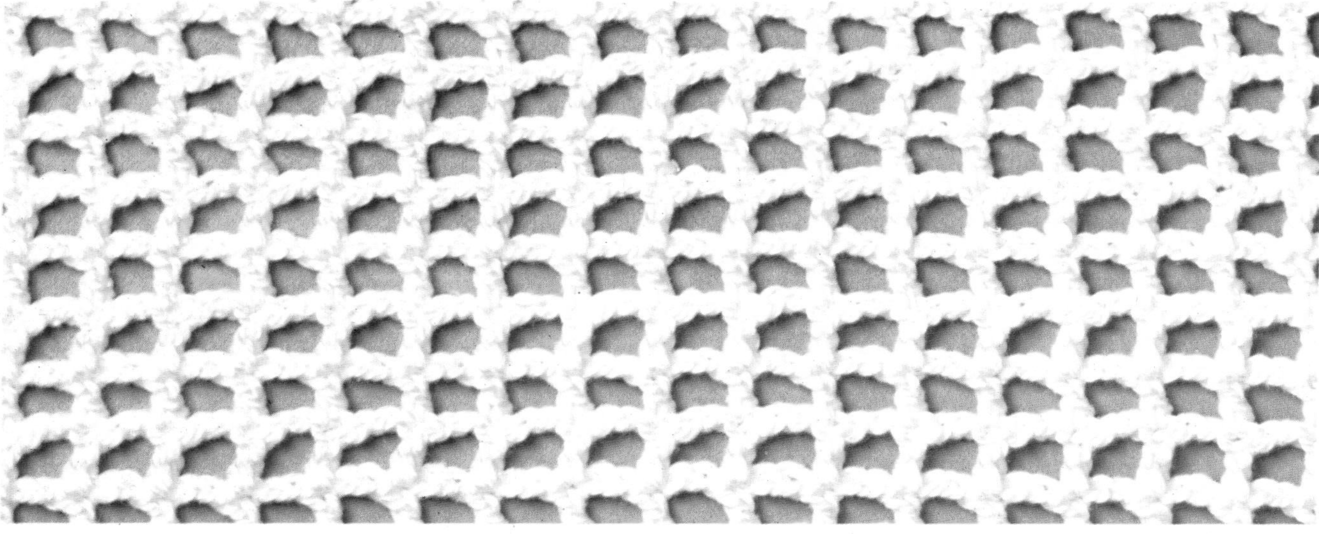

Basic mesh background
Usually a filet background consists of doubles separated by 2 chains, although the number of chains can vary according to the density of mesh required.

Make a multiple of 3+1 chains and 4 extra chains.
1st row (RS) 1dc into 8th ch from hook (7 skipped chains form a 2ch sp – 2ch along the lower edge, next 3ch = 1dc and last 2ch form sp on row being worked), *2ch, skip 2ch, 1dc into next ch, rep from * to end. Turn.
2nd row 5ch (= 1st dc and 2ch sp), skip 1st dc and sp, 1dc into next dc, *2ch, skip sp, 1dc into next dc, rep from * ending with last dc into 5th of 1st 7ch. Turn.
Repeat 2nd row throughout for pattern. Note that you work subsequent last doubles into 3rd of 1st 5ch.

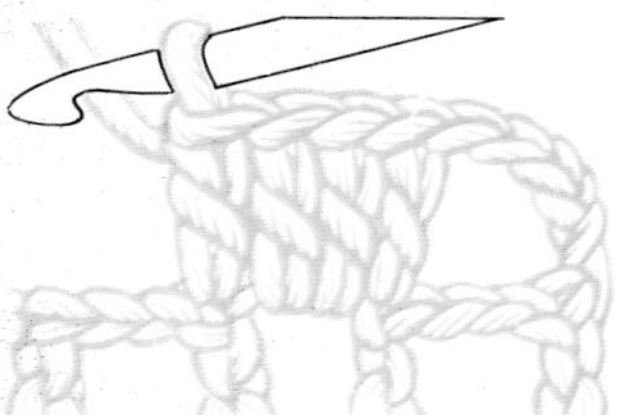

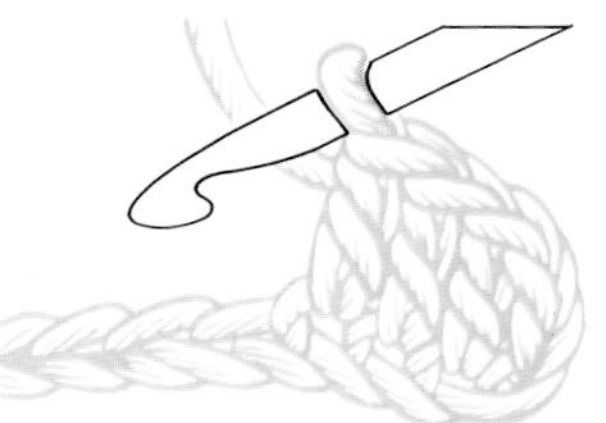

Incorporating blocks and spaces into background
You use the filet mesh as a background for patterns consisting of blocks and spaces; spaces are as they appear in the background (i.e. 2ch separating 2 single doubles) and blocks are spaces filled in with doubles which correspond in number to the chains in the space. Practice these simple rules for blocks and spaces and you can apply them to any mesh.

To work a block over a space make 1dc into corresponding dc of the previous row, 2dc into the next 2ch sp and 1dc into the next dc so that the block consists of 4dc.
To work a block over a block work 1dc into each of the 4dc of the block in the previous row.
To work a space over a block work 1dc into 1st dc of the block, 2ch, skip 2dc, 1dc into last dc of block.

To begin 1st row with a space make 7 extra chain (1st 2ch = sp along lower edge, next 3ch = last dc, and final 2ch = sp along top edge). Begin 1st row by working 1dc into 8th ch from hook.
To begin subsequent rows with a space make 5 chain (1st 3ch = 1st dc and next 2ch = 2ch sp), then work 1dc into next dc (if working over a space) or into last of 4dc (if working over a block).

To begin 1st row with a block make 3 extra chain (= 1st dc), work next dc into 4th ch from hook and complete block by working 1dc into each of next 2ch.
To begin subsequent rows with a block make 3 chain (= 1dc), then work 1dc into each of next 3dc (if working over a block) or 2dc into 2ch sp and 1dc into next dc (if working over a space).

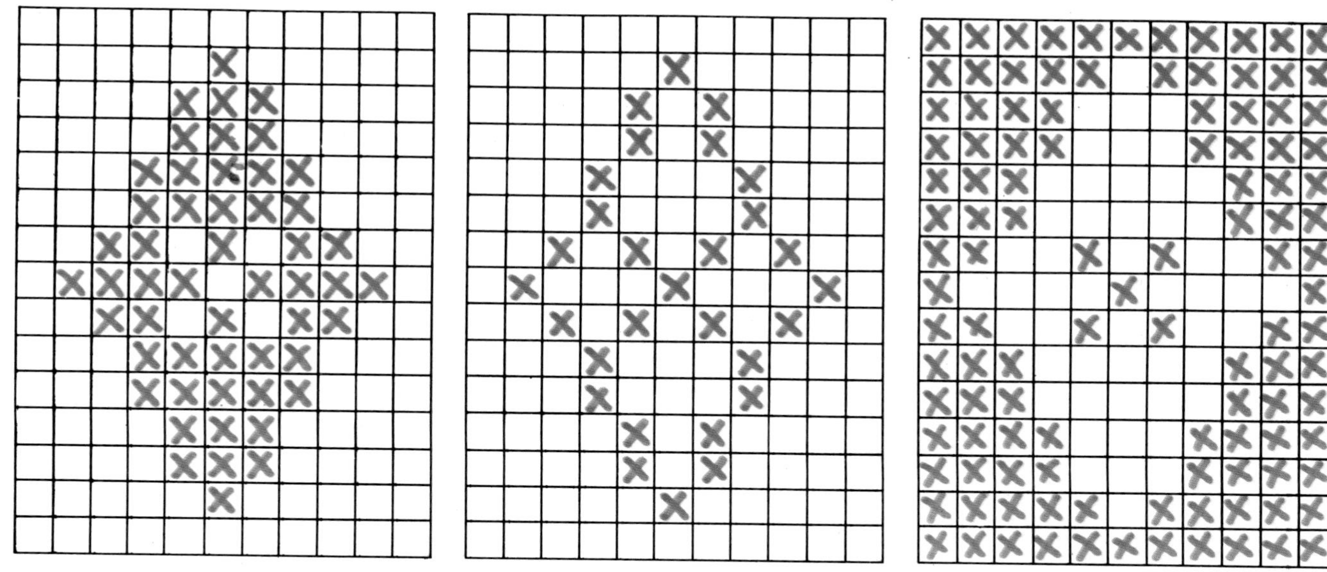

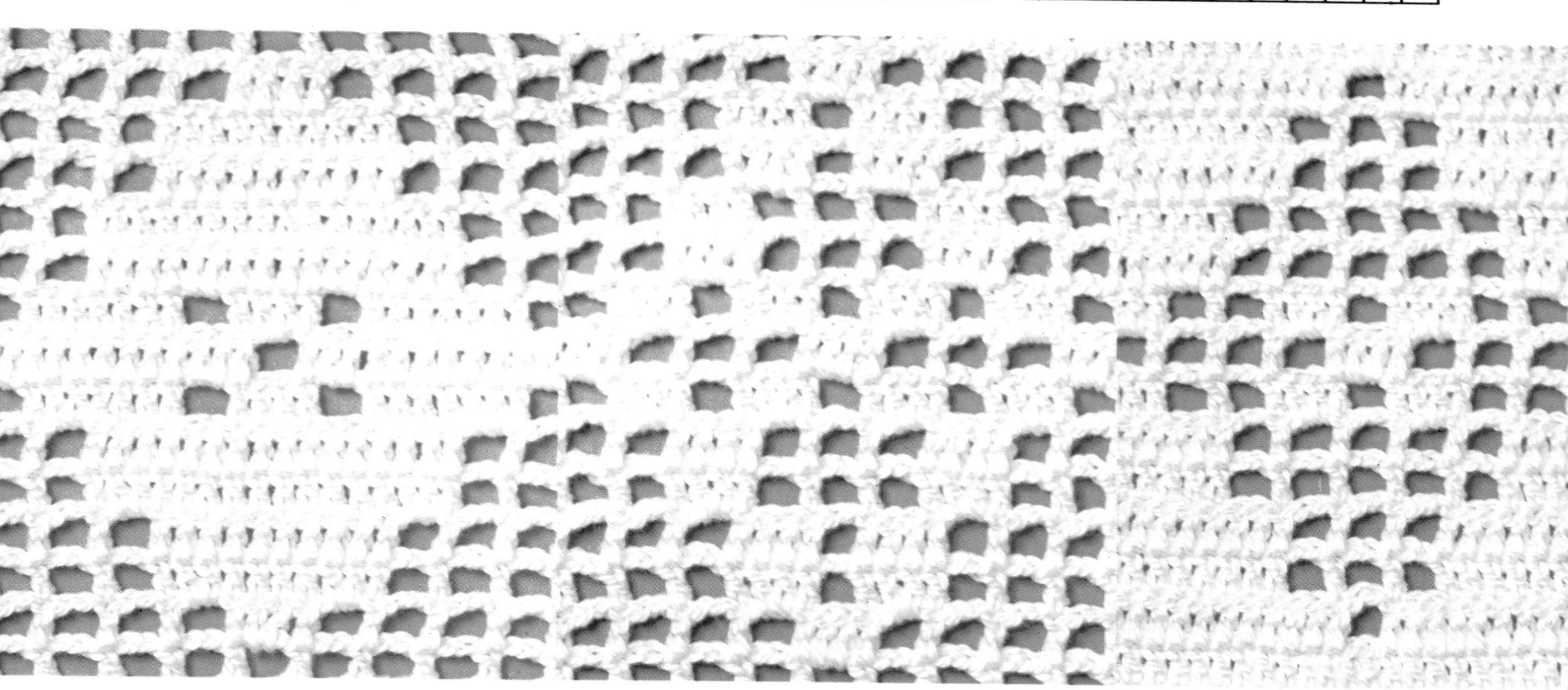

Designing for filet mesh
Once you understand the techniques of working blocks and spaces onto a filet mesh and of increasing and decreasing (see p324) so that you can shape your fabric and keep a pattern consistent, you will be able to plan your own designs.
Any type of pattern which can reduce to black and white and so be interpreted in terms of spaces and filled blocks is suitable. You can use motifs designed for embroidery or Jacquard knitting as long as you remember that the scale and proportion of your design may come out differently. The larger your grid of crochet mesh and the smaller your area, the fewer details you will be able to represent; for this reason geometric designs are often the most successful. With a large area like a filet curtain you could create quite an elaborate stylized design. Use rich, dark colors for items which will contrast with a light background, for instance for curtains against a window.
You need a chart, similar to the ones used in Fair Isle knitting (see p265) to give a visual impression of your design – row-by-row instructions are long and laborious to read. To get a clear idea of how your design will work, draw up a grid according to the gauge of your background mesh.
Transfer the design to the grid and lightly color in all the spaces that become blocks; keep your coloring faint so that the lines of the grid show through. An alternative is to use squared graph paper to plan your design and a symbol such as X to denote the blocks.

Apart from the block and space designs worked within the mesh, much filet crochet—especially borders for household linens—has patterned jagged edges. (An example is the edging at the bottom of the opposite page.) These edges are formed by increasing and decreasing blocks and spaces, and the principles are the same when you shape garments made in filet work.

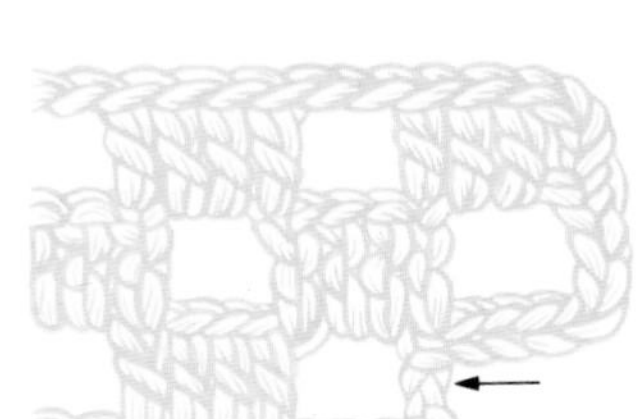

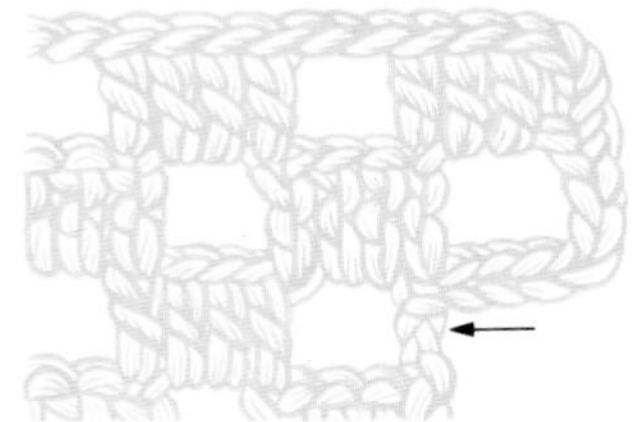

To increase a space at the beginning of a row make 7ch (as when beginning 1st row with a space), then work 1dc into 1st dc of the row; this is the edge stitch that you normally skip.

To increase a space at the end of a row plan for increase at beg of the row before (see arrow). Make 7ch, skip 1st ch, sl st into each of next 3ch; 3 rem ch equal 1st dc of row. Inc at end of foll row by working 2ch, skip next 2 sl sts, 1dc into last sl st.

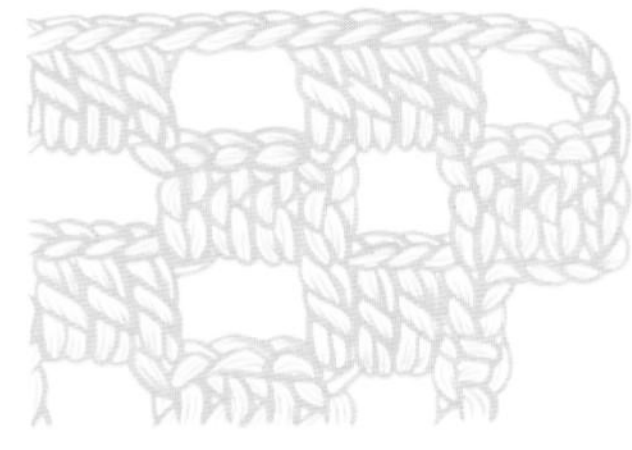

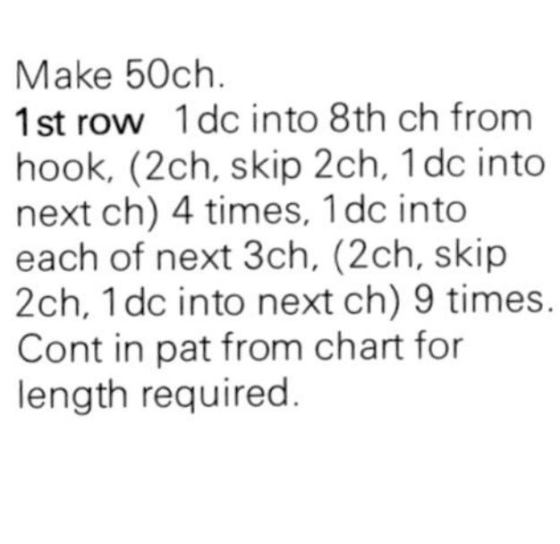

To increase a block at the beginning of a row make 5ch, work 1dc into 4th ch from hook, 1dc into next ch and 1dc into last dc of previous row.

To increase a block at the end of a row work in the same way as when increasing a space at the end of a row by making provision at beg of row before; when you reach position for increase on foll row work 1dc into each of the 3 sl sts at the beg of the previous row.

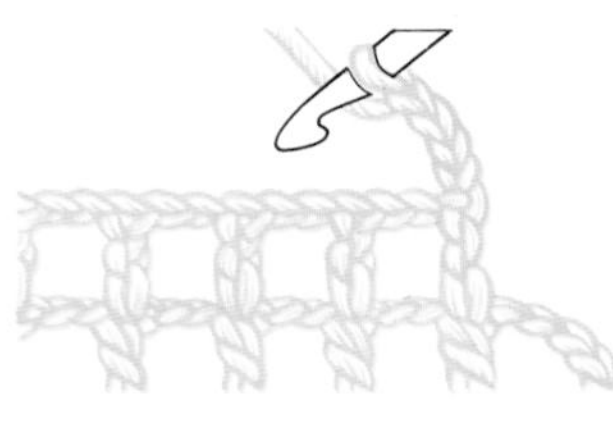

To decrease a block or space at the beginning of a row skip 1st block or space by slip-stitching into each of 1st 3 stitches, and into next dc work 3ch (=1st dc) or 5ch (=1st dc and 2ch sp); then continue in pattern.

To decrease a block or space at the end of a row pattern to the last block or space, then turn your work and simply omit the last stitches.

Make 38ch.
1st row 1dc into 8th ch from hook, (2ch, skip 2ch, 1dc into next ch) 3 times, 1dc into each of next 3ch, (2ch, skip 2ch, 1dc into next ch) 6 times. Cont in pat from chart for length required.

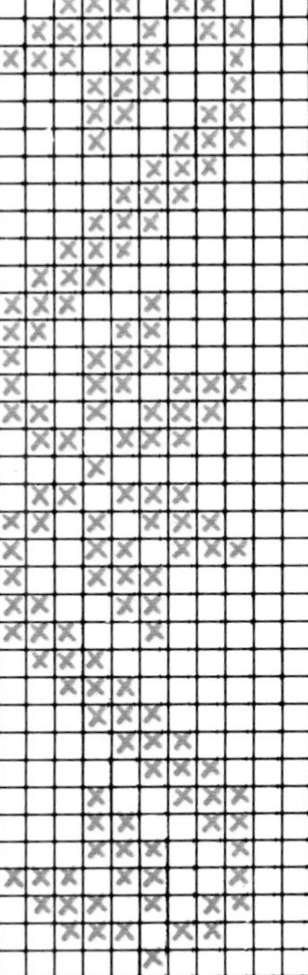

Make 50ch.
1st row 1dc into 8th ch from hook, (2ch, skip 2ch, 1dc into next ch) 4 times, 1dc into each of next 3ch, (2ch, skip 2ch, 1dc into next ch) 9 times. Cont in pat from chart for length required.

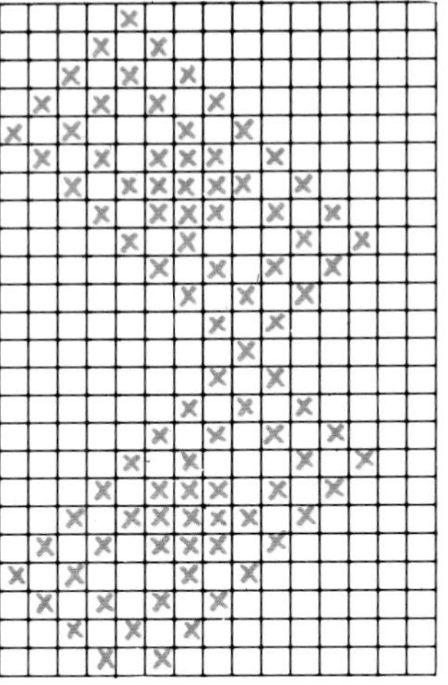

Make 50ch.
1st row 1dc into 8th ch from hook, 1dc into each of next 3ch, (2ch, skip 2ch, 1dc into next ch) 7 times, 1dc into each of next 3ch, (2ch, skip 2ch, 1dc into next ch) 5 times. Cont in pat from chart, repeating 8 rows as required.

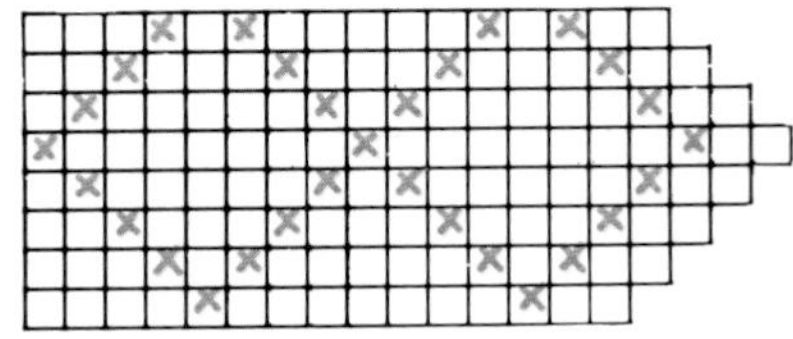

Café curtain

Basic information 300
Filet 322

A filet café curtain designed to fit a particular window or door and worked in a rich color gives privacy and casts a pleasant light in a room. Work two or three rows of doubles at the top of the filet pattern to give a firm edge for hanging. Use split curtain rings so that you can slide them easily between the crochet stitches to hang the curtain; you can also remove them easily for washing. If you are designing a filet curtain of a different size, use the quantity of yarn shown here as a rough guide to the amount you will need.

You will need (for a curtain $18\frac{1}{2}$ x 30in/48 x 75cm):
about 6oz (150g) medium-weight cotton yarn
size B crochet hook
brass curtain rod and split brass rings

Gauge
1 block or 1 space=$\frac{1}{2}$in (1cm)

Make 147ch.
1st row: 1 dc in 4th ch from hook, 1dc in each of next 2ch, *(2ch, skip 2ch, 1dc in each of next 4ch) twice, (2ch, skip 2ch, 1dc in next ch) twice, 1dc in each of next 6ch, (2ch, skip 2ch, 1dc in next ch) 3 times, 1dc in each of next 3ch, (2ch, skip 2ch, 1dc in next ch) 4 times, 1dc in each of next 3ch, * (2ch, skip 2ch, 1dc in each of next 4ch) twice, (2ch, skip 2ch, 1dc in next ch) 3 times, 1dc in each of next 6ch, (2ch, skip 2ch, 1dc in next ch) twice, 1dc in each of next 6ch, rep from * to *

Cont in pat from chart until work measures 30in (75cm) from beg, or length required.
Next row: 3ch, 1dc in each dc and 2dc in each sp to end.
Next row: 3ch, 1dc in each dc to end.
Repeat the last row once.
Fasten off.

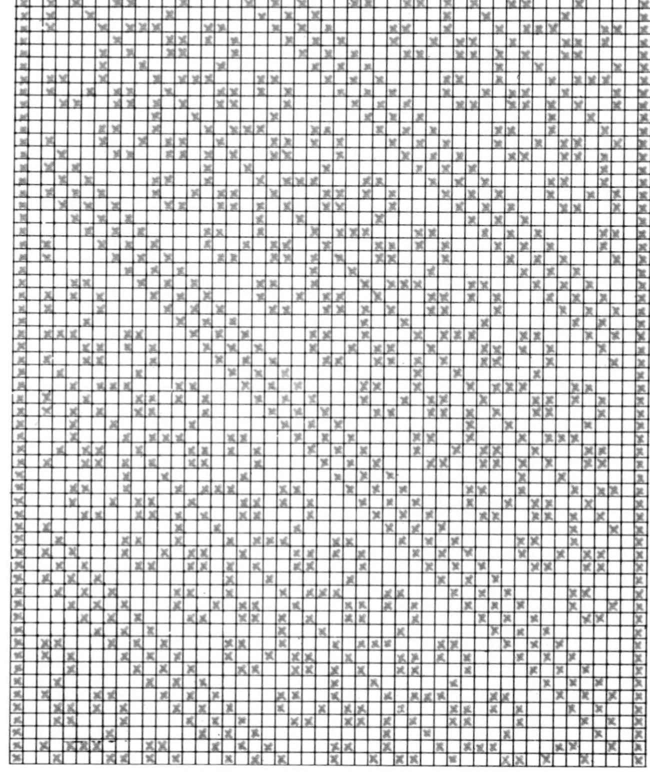

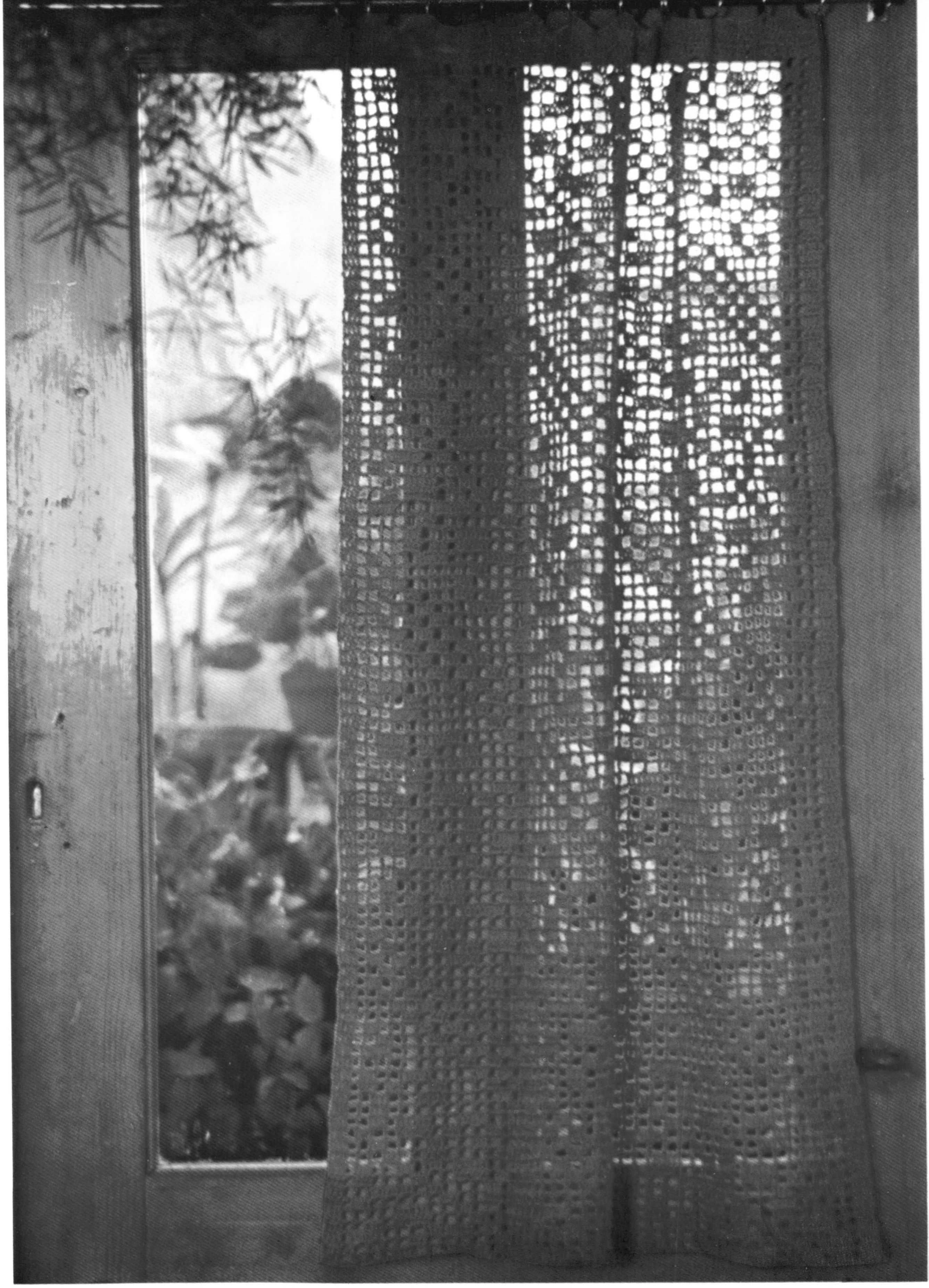

Color effects

Simple horizontal or vertical stripes can be both attractive and an economical way of using up scraps of yarn of similar weight: the techniques involved are useful for other types of crochet work where different colors are combined to form the basis of Jacquard and patchwork designs. The more intricate striped patterns at the foot of these pages are used in the pillows on p330.

Horizontal stripes

Work an even number of rows in each stripe if you want to carry a color not in use up the side of the work until you need it again. (An uneven number of rows means a color may be at the wrong edge when you need it; if so, break off the yarn and start again.)

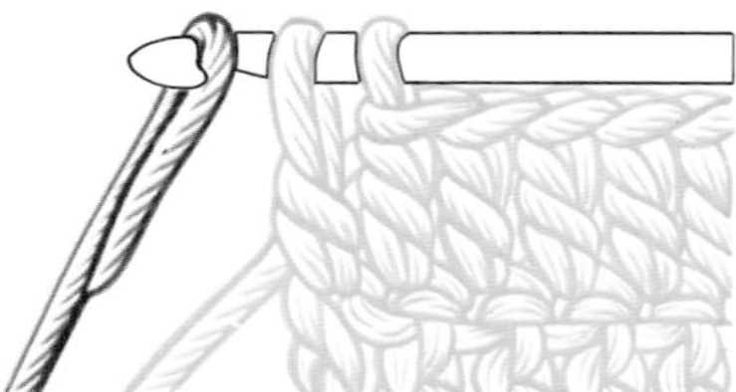

Introducing a new color at the beginning of a row
Work the last stitch of the previous row in the old color until 2 loops are left on the hook, then draw the new color through the 2 loops to complete the stitch. Turn and continue working with the new color.

Narrow vertical stripes

You need to change colors several times within the same row; if the stripes are narrow (e.g. a maximum of 4 or 5 stitches in each) then you can carry the yarn across the fabric, picking up the new color each time you need it.
It is best not to use too many colors within a row; a limit of 3 colors per row means that you can work over the colors not in use so that they are completely hidden within the fabric and the back of your work is not strung with strands of yarn which may snag.

Carrying yarn across work
Simply lay the color not in use along the chain edge of the previous row. Work the next stitch as usual over the yarn and it automatically becomes enclosed in the center of that stitch.
When you need to change color within a row, work the last stitch in the old color until 2 loops remain on the hook, pick up the new color behind the old yarn and draw a loop in the new color through the 2 loops on the hook. Continue working with the new color, enclosing the old one as before.

Wide vertical stripes

Carrying yarn across the back of wide stripes is both wasteful and tends to distort the fabric by pulling it too tightly. Before you begin work divide the yarn into small separate balls; each time you start a new stripe within a row use a different ball of yarn.
To avoid making a hole each time you change color, you need to twist the yarns in the same way as when knitting wide vertical stripes (see p244). Bring in the new color to complete the last stitch in the old color, having first twisted the yarns. If you don't introduce the new color correctly the edge of the stripe will be out of line.

Chevron Many crochet patterns are suitable for striping; chevron patterns look very effective in ever-changing colors of varying widths. No matter how complicated the fabric looks, the color techniques are the same as for horizontal stripes. A close fabric like single crochet shows the chevron to its best advantage; remember too that the top and lower edges of the fabric have a jagged edge.

Broken stripes This colorful fabric with an intricate tweed effect looks more complicated to work than it really is. Each row is worked in a single color, but because the stitch formation is irregular and each stitch encroaches on the row above, it looks as if individual rows are two-colored.

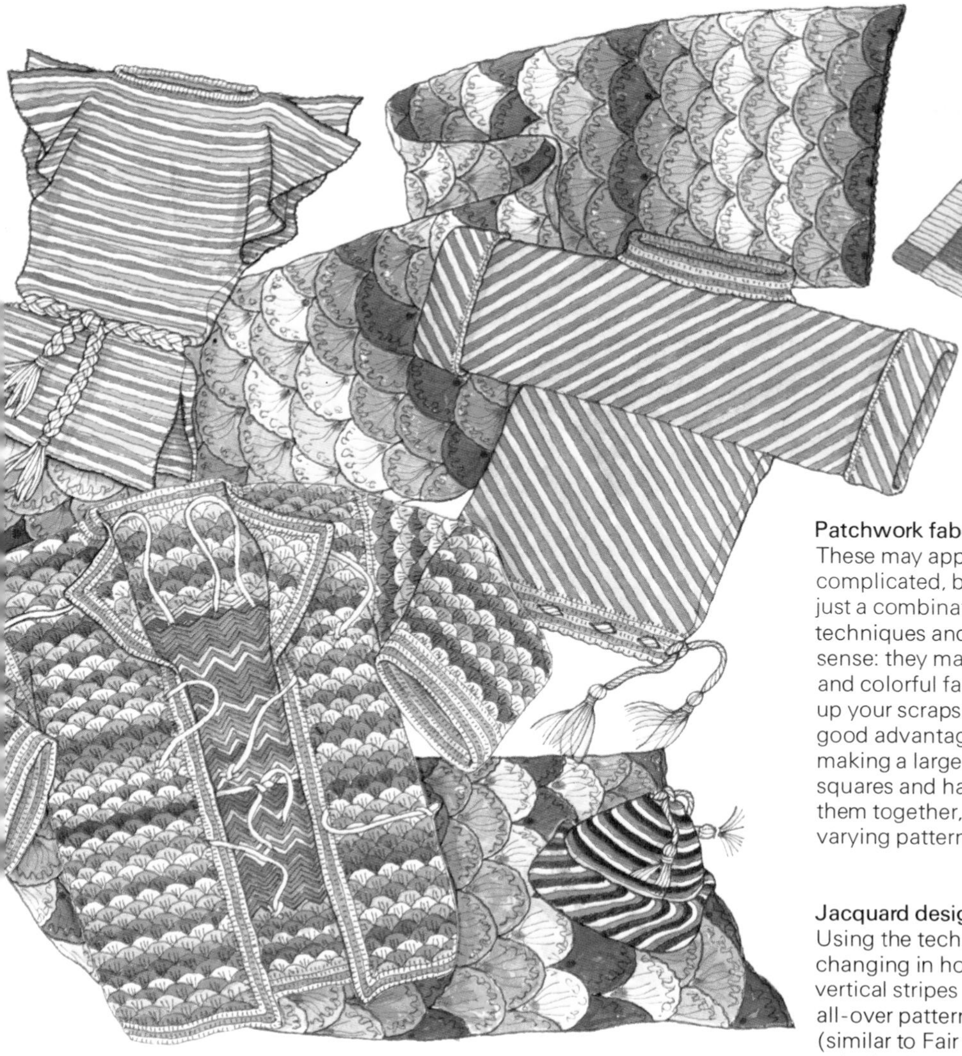

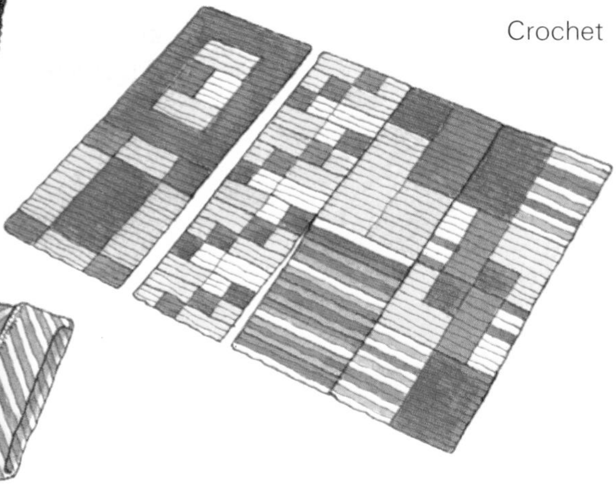

Patchwork fabrics

These may appear to be complicated, but are really just a combination of striping techniques and a good color sense: they make an unusual and colorful fabric and use up your scraps of yarn to good advantage. Instead of making a large number of squares and having to sew them together, work strips of varying patterns. Keep the same number of stitches in each strip, work to the length required, then sew the long edges of the strips together. Using this method you can quickly make a pillow cover or start a blanket and add to it gradually. Once you decide on the number of stitches in a strip, then you can plan the designs you want to include on graph paper.

Jacquard designs

Using the techniques of color changing in horizontal and vertical stripes you can work all-over patterned fabrics (similar to Fair Isle knitting) or individual motifs on a plain background. For an all-over design you can work across the colors not in use, but single motifs may require separate balls of yarn for each color. Avoid intricate designs with a lot of detail: geometric patterns such as squares and diamonds are a good choice for this type of work. Using a shallow stitch such as single or half double crochet for the fabric helps the motif to stand out clearly.

The easiest way to work a Jacquard design is from a chart in the same way as when knitting (see p265): since crochet stitches have more depth, however, it is even more important to draw up a grid for the stitch and row gauge and block in your design so that you have an idea of the finished scale.

Shells Although this design appears to have 2 different colors within a pattern row, each row is worked in just a single color: simply following a shell pattern and applying horizontal striping techniques achieves the effect of very irregular lines of color like overlapping scallop shells.

Pillows

Basic information 300
Basic stitches 302
Color effects 328

size E	size E	size E	size E
20	4 shells	30	20
15	6 shells	18	15
hdc	pat	chevron pat	pat

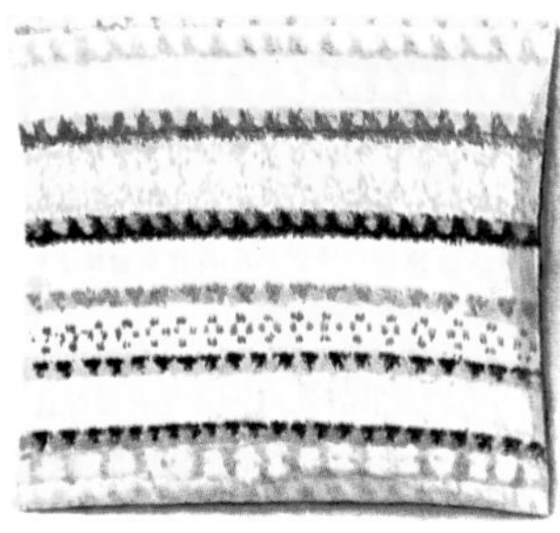

Broken stripe pillow
You will need
total of 6oz (150g) fingering yarn in 4 colors coded A-D (1oz/25g each A, B; 2oz/50g each C, D)
size E crochet hook
pillow form approx 14in (35cm) square

Using A make 73ch.
1st row: 1hdc into 3rd ch from hook, *skip 1ch, 2hdc into next ch, rep from * to end, joining in B in last hdc. Turn.
2nd row: Using B, 2ch (=1st hdc), *2hdc between gr of 2hdc, rep from * ending with 1hdc into turning ch, joining in C. Turn.
3rd row: Using C, 2ch, 1hdc into same place, *2hdc between gr of hdc, rep from * to end. Don't turn.
4th row: Return to beg of 3rd row, join in B, 2ch, work as 2nd row, changing to C on last hdc. Turn.
5th row: As 3rd, joining in D at end of row. Turn.
6th row: Using D, as 2nd. Turn.
Cont in this way noting that you don't have to break off a color every time you use it. Without turning work, return to color required, draw yarn through 1st st of previous row and cont in pat with this color. When introducing new color turn work and begin at RH side as usual.
7th–12th rows: Work as 1st–6th in stripe pat C D A D A B.
Rep these 12 rows until work measures 14in (35cm).
Fasten off. Make 2nd piece in same way.

Finishing
Press lightly. Slip-st 3 sides tog, insert pillow form and overcast open edges neatly.

Shell pillow
You will need
total of 6oz (150g) fingering yarn (1oz/25g each of 6 colors).
size E crochet hook
pillow form approx 14in (35cm) square

Using A make 88ch.
1st row: 2dc into 4th ch from hook, *skip 2ch, 1sc into next ch,skip 2ch, 5dc into next ch, rep from * to last 6ch, skip 2ch, 1sc into next ch, skip 2ch, 3dc into next ch, joining in 2nd color on last dc. Don't break off A. Turn.
2nd row: Using B, 1ch (=1st sc), *5dc into next sc, 1sc into 3rd of 5dc, rep from * working last sc into turning ch. Break off B. Don't turn.
3rd row: Return to beg of 2nd row, draw A through 1st st, 3ch, 2dc into same place, *1sc into 3rd of 5dc, 5dc into next sc, rep from * ending with 3dc into turning ch and joining in C on last dc. Turn.
4th row: Using C, as 2nd.
Cont in stripes (see below) until work measures 14in (35cm). Fasten off. Work 2nd piece to match.
This fabric is reversible, so a new color can be joined at either end. Work a sequence such as A B A C A C D C D E D E F E F B. When working a single row break off yarn and introduce new color at same edge. When repeating a color on an alternate row don't break off yarn or turn work; return to this yarn and begin the row at same edge, drawing yarn through 1st st of previous row. You thus avoid rejoining the yarn every time you use it.

Finishing
As for broken stripe pillow.

Chevron pillow
You will need
total of 6oz (150g) fingering yarn in 4 colors coded A–D (1oz/25g each A, B; 2oz/50g each C, D)
size E crochet hook
pillow form approx 14 x 18in (35 x 45cm)

Using A make 180ch. Join with a sl st into 1st ch to form a ring.
1st round: 1ch (=1st sc), 2sc into same place, *1sc into each of next 3ch, work 3sc tog over next 3ch, 1sc into each of next 3ch, 3sc into next ch, rep from * to last 9ch, 1sc into each of next 3ch, work 3sc tog over next 3ch, 1sc into each of next 3ch. Join with a sl st into 1st ch.
2nd round: Using B sl st into next sc, 1ch, 2sc into same place, *working into back loop only of each sc throughout, work 1sc into each of next 3sc, work 3sc tog over next 3sc, 1sc into each of next 3sc, 3sc into next sc, rep from * to last 9sc, 1sc into each of next 3sc, work 3sc tog over next 3sc, 1sc into each of next 3sc. Join with a sl st into 1st ch. Rep 2nd round throughout, working in color sequence A B C D until work measures 18in (45cm). Fasten off.

Finishing
Fold tube flat, matching chevrons at either end. Overcast one end, insert pillow form and overcast open edges tog neatly.

Multicolored pillow
You will need
total of about 7oz (175g) fingering yarn in 7 colors
size E crochet hook
pillow form approx 14in (35cm) square

Make 70ch.
1st row: 1hdc into 3rd ch from hook, 1hdc into each ch to end (69sts). Cont in hdc, working pat motifs from chart in varying color sequence, until work measures 28in (70cm) from beg. When working in 2 colors, carry yarn along the top of the row and work over it.
Fasten off.

Finishing
Fold in half, sew side seams and complete as for broken stripe pillow.

Irish crochet

Irish crochet techniques developed in imitation of lace-making. Traditionally worked in fine white cotton thread, designs are inspired by natural shapes like flowers and leaves and are often three-dimensional. The heavier form of Irish crochet, often worked in slightly thicker thread, resembles Guipure lace and the effect of relief is created by working the stitches over a padding—perhaps of several strands of yarn, or of fine wire. The finer type of Irish crochet is called 'bébé' after its traditional use in trimming layettes.

Motifs may be joined in a number of ways. You can work an irregular filling of chains and picots after pinning motifs in position on paper. A simpler way is to crochet a background and then to apply motifs afterward: filet mesh (see p322) shown opposite is one suitable background; picot mesh (p310) is even more typical. You could also apply motifs to a dress fabric. The bébé sample on this page suggests another way of making an all-over fabric: work motifs as the center of a square and use as you would any square motifs (see p316).

White motif
Make 4ch and join into a ring with a sl st.
1st round: 1ch, 7sc into ring. sl st to 1 ch.
2nd round: 4ch, *1dc into next sc, 1ch, rep from * 6 times more, sl st to 3rd of 4ch.
3rd round: 1ch, *1sc into 1ch sp, 1sc into dc, rep from * 6 times more, 1sc into 1ch sp, sl st to 1ch.
4th round: 5ch, *1dc into next sc, 2ch, rep from * 14 times more, sl st to 3rd of 5ch.
5th round: 3ch, 2dc into 2ch sp, *1dc into dc, 2dc into 2ch sp, rep from * 14 times more, sl st to 3rd of 3ch. (48dc).
6th round: *6ch, skip 5dc, 1sc into next dc, rep from * 7 times more, working last sc into sl st at end of 5th round.
7th round: Into each loop work 1sc, 1hdc, 5dc, 1hdc, 1sc, sl st to 1st sc.
8th round: *7ch, 1sc into back of next sc on 6th round, rep from * to end.
9th round: Into each 7ch loop work 1sc, 1hdc, 3dc, 1tr, 3dc, 1hdc, 1sc, sl st to 1st sc.
10th round: *8ch, 1sc into back of next sc on 8th round, rep from * to end.
11th round: Into each 8ch loop work 1sc, 1hdc, 3dc, 3tr, 3dc, 1hdc, 1sc, sl st to 1st sc.
12th round: *9ch, 1sc into back of next sc on 10th round, rep from * to end.
13th round: Sl st into 1st loop, 7ch, 1sc into same loop, (7ch, 1sc) twice into each of next 7 loops, 7ch, sl st to beg of round.
14th round: Sl st into next loop, *7ch, 1sc into next loop, rep from * to end, ending with 7ch, sl st to beg of round.
15th round: As 14th round but working 9ch instead of 7ch.
16th round: Sl st into loop, 9ch, 1sc into next loop, *(9ch, 1sc) twice into next loop, (9ch, 1sc into next loop) 3 times, rep from * twice more, (9ch, 1sc) twice into next loop, 9ch, 1sc into next loop, 9ch, sl st to beg of round.
17th round: Sl st to center of loop, 5ch, 1sc into next loop, *(5ch, 1sc) twice into next loop, (5ch, 1sc into next loop) 4 times, rep from * twice more, (5ch, 1sc) twice into next loop, (5ch, 1sc into next loop) twice, 5ch, sl st to beg of round.
18th round: * 5sc in 5ch loop, 1sc in sc, rep from * around.

Whirligig
Make 100ch (or length required).
1sc into 3rd ch from hook, 1sc into each ch to end. Fasten off. Twist work anticlockwise into 7 loops (or as required) using a needle threaded with the same yarn to catch down each loop as you go.

Small leaf
Make 8ch.
1st round: 1sc into 3rd ch from hook, 1sc into each of next 4ch, 3sc into last ch, turn work and cont along other side of the ch, work 1sc into each of next 5ch, then 3sc into turning ch, sl st to 1st sc, turn.
2nd round: 1ch, 1sc into next sc, 3sc into next sc (point), 1sc into each sc along side of work, 3sc into point at other end, 1sc into each sc along side, sl st to 1st ch, turn.
3rd round: 1ch, 1sc into each sc along side, 3sc into point, 1sc into each sc along other side, 3sc into point, 1sc into each sc to beg of round, sl st to 1st ch, turn.
4th round: Sl st around point and over next 3sc, 1ch, 1sc into each sc to point, 3sc into point, 1sc into each sc to last 3sc before point, turn.
5th round: 1ch, 1sc into each sc to point, 3sc into point, 1sc into each sc to beg of last round.
Fasten off.

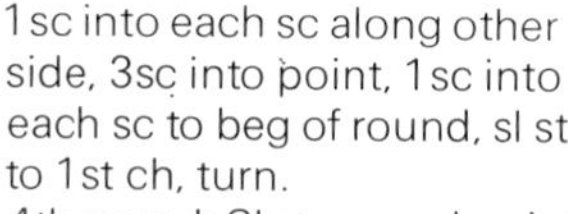

Large leaf
Make 12ch.
1st round: 1sc into 3rd ch from hook, 1sc into each of next 8ch, 3sc into last ch, turn and cont along other side of chain, 1sc into each sc to end, 3sc into turning ch, sl st to last sc. Turn.
2nd–3rd rounds: As for small leaf.
4th–5th rounds: Cont working in rounds in the same way.
6th round: Sl st around point and over next 5sc, 1ch, 1sc into each sc to point, 3sc into point, 1sc into each sc to last 5sc before point, turn.
7th–8th rounds: Work 5th round of small leaf twice.
Fasten off.

Small flower
Wind yarn 6 times around little finger or around a pencil, insert hook into the ring and fasten with a sl st.
1st round: 1ch, 19sc into ring, sl st to 1st ch.
2nd round: *5ch, skip 3sc, 1sc into next sc, rep from * 4 times more, working last sc into sl st at end of 1st round.
3rd round: Into each 5ch loop work 1sc, 5dc, 1sc.
Fasten off.

Shamrock
Make 12ch.
1st round: 1sc into 12th ch from hook, (11ch, 1sc into same ch as before) twice.
2nd round: Into each loop work 20sc, then join with a sl st to beg of 1st loop.
3rd round: Skip 1sc, 1sc into each of next 18sc, (skip 2sc, 1 sc into each of next 18sc) twice, skip last sc, join with a sl st to 1st sc.
Stalk Make 10ch, turn and work 1sc into each ch back to 1st petal. Fasten off.

Large flower
Wind yarn 4 times around finger, insert hook and fasten with a sl st.
1st round: 1ch, 23sc into ring, sl st to 1st ch.
2nd round: *3ch, 1sc into next sc, rep from * to end.
3rd round: *10ch, skip 3sc on 1st round, then keeping hook behind the loops of 2nd round, work 1sc into back of next sc on 1st round, rep from *5 times more.
4th round: Into each 10ch loop work 1sc, 1hdc, 12dc, 1hdc, 1sc. Fasten off.

Edgings, insertions and trimmings

You can use crochet both practically and decoratively to join the different parts of a garment or article together as well as to finish off edges neatly. You can work the crochet trimming separately and sew it on afterward or you can work it directly onto the items to be joined. Don't restrict yourself to knitted or crocheted fabrics — the techniques shown on the opposite page suggest ways of working directly onto woven fabrics of different weights as well as non-woven materials like leather, suede or vinyl. When choosing yarn for an edging or insertion take into consideration both the kind of fabric you are using and the function of what you are making — for instance, whether strength or elasticity is important. In traditional household linens the weight of fabric and crochet yarn tends to be matched fairly closely. In garments some contrast in weight and type of yarn can be attractive — it is usually more effective to decorate a heavier main fabric with a lighter-weight yarn for the trimming, or finish a textured main fabric with a smooth yarn. Experiment with different yarns and stitches to find out what kind of effect you can achieve, and to work out how close together your stitches should be if you are working directly into the main fabric. When choosing yarn for edging and seaming a relatively soft fabric like some leathers and very loose-weave wools, beware of using an edging yarn that is too harsh and may cut and tear the main fabric whenever any strain is put on it.

Decorative edgings often have a scalloped or jagged outer edge, while insertions tend to have two straight parallel edges so that they can be placed along the grain of two separate sections of fabric. Often used on sheets, pillowcases, tablecloths, curtains and other household items, fine insertions worked in cotton are also attractive when incorporated into garments. You need to plan a design with some care, however, to make sure that the insertion follows the straight grain of the fabric. You can use insertions across a yoke, up the front of a bodice, or parallel with a hem in a dirndl skirt, for example — but you may find they distort when used in curving fabrics or at an angle to warp and weft threads. See p336 for several examples of delicate cotton insertions and one edging, all of which you attach separately; you can use the filet work examples on p324 in a similar way. On pp338 and 340 you can see how crochet combines with different fabrics to create a variety of effects.

Two crochet trimmings that are useful are a crochet fringe, which you could work around a shawl in fairly fine yarn, and the double chain cord, which works well as a tie fastening on something you have edged with single crochet.

Beginning an edging This sample shows how to begin a single crochet edging worked on a crochet fabric, although the principle is substantially the same for other fabrics. With RS of work facing, insert hook into RH edge st from front to back, loop yarn around the hook leaving a short end free and draw through to RS; holding both ends together at back of work, insert hook into next st, put both ends of yarn around hook and draw through making a double st which will be counted as one on the next row. Complete sc in usual way using working strand only. Cont across edge working 1sc into each st to end. To turn a right-angle corner work 3sc into the corner st. Darn in the ends of yarn when finishing. Depending on the thickness of yarn in your main fabric, you may have to work into every alternate stitch across the edge, or may have to make 1ch between the crochet stitches to space them out sufficiently.

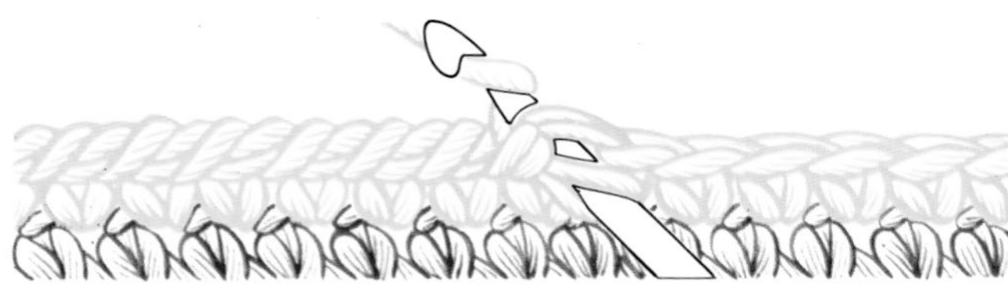

Crab stitch
This substantial rope-like edging is a simple variation of an ordinary single-crochet edging. With RS facing, work a row of sc along the edge of the fabric but do not turn. Work the next row of sc into the stitches of the 1st row — but working back from the LH edge to the right. Fasten off.

Picot edging
Picots occur incorporated in a number of stitch patterns and are a delicate edging when applied to a different fabric as well as being a good way of finishing off a fabric made entirely in crochet. This pattern needs a multiple of 3 sts, but you can vary this. With RS facing, 1sc into each of 1st 3 sts, *4ch, remove hook from loop, insert into 1st of 4ch, pick up last of 4ch and draw through loop on hook to form picot, 1sc into each of next 3 sts, rep from * to end of row.

Knitting and crochet
The ends of rows in both knitted and crocheted fabrics are often uneven, especially when shaping is taking place; a crochet edging conceals this and when worked in the same yarn can make a neat edge. Working in a fine firm-spun yarn around a fabric made of a more bulky woolen type of yarn provides textural contrast while keeping the edges of the main fabric from stretching. Always insert the hook between the stitches or rows – never split the yarn; the frequency with which you make your stitches will depend on the gauge of the item you are working on.

Loose-weave fabrics
Provided your hook and yarn are not so thick that they distort the woven fabric too badly, you can just insert your crochet hook between the warp and weft threads of a loose-weave fabric. If you work over a finished edge you don't need to prepare the fabric, but you should first finish a raw edge with machined zigzag stitching or by overcasting with sewing thread. Don't insert your crochet hook so near to the edge that it will cause fraying.

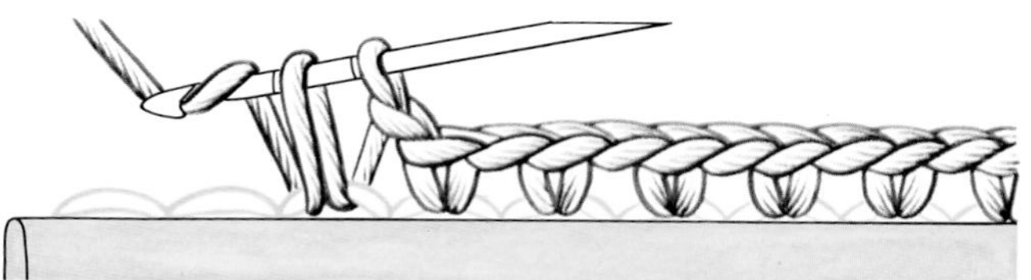

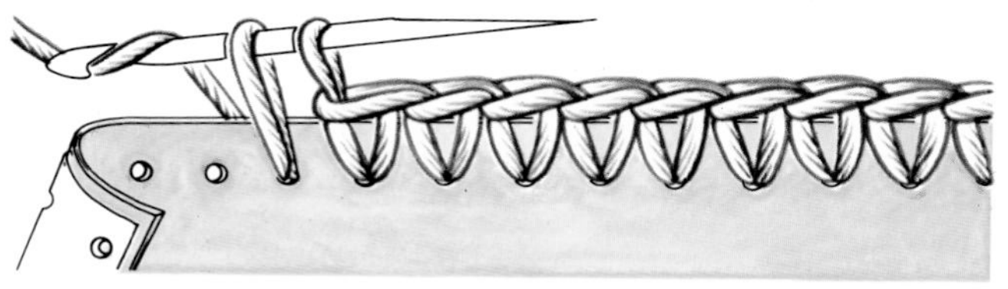

Fine fabrics
It is easiest to work your crochet strip separately and then to sew it on. Finish off the edges of your fabric by hemming neatly in the usual way, then apply your crochet edging or insertion by overcasting invisibly with matching sewing thread. This method has the advantage that you can remove the crochet and re-use it later. A traditional technique for fine bed- and table-linen involves working a row of small back stitches along the foldline of the hemmed fabric, and then inserting the hook into these stitches to work the edging.

Leather and vinyl
Use a leather punch to make a regularly spaced row of holes between $\frac{1}{4}$ and $\frac{1}{2}$in (5 and 10mm) from the edge of the fabric. The size of hole will depend on the thickness of the yarn and hook you are using. Make sure your crochet hook is small enough to carry the loop of yarn easily through the hole. For vinyl, and for leather which is thin or which will need to take some strain, back the material with bonded interfacing, using an adhesive suitable for fabric, before you punch the holes.

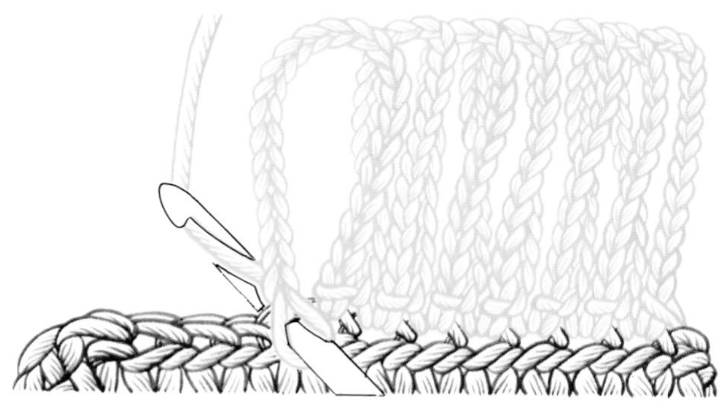

Crochet fringe
You can work this fringe either as an edging with a border to be attached separately, or directly onto an existing fabric, omitting the border.
Make a ch the required length.
1st row 1hdc into 3rd ch from hook, *1hdc into next st, rep from * to end. Turn.
2nd row 2ch (=1hdc), *1hdc into next st, rep from * to end. Turn.
3rd row 1ch, skip 1st st, *insert hook into next st, yo and draw through a loop, yo and draw through both loops on hook, make 24ch, insert hook into same st, yo and draw through both loops on hook, rep from * to end. Fasten off.

To work fringe directly onto a fabric draw a loop through 1st st at edge of fabric (see beginning an edging, opposite) and work 3rd row as above from *. Depth of fringe can be varied by increasing or decreasing the number of chains in each loop.

Double chain cord
This is a useful alternative to a twisted cord for making a drawstring or tie fastenings.
Make 2ch.
Insert hook under LH vertical loop of 1st ch and work 1sc.
Cont inserting hook under LH vertical loop of previous st and working 1sc until chain is required length.

Make a multiple of 6 chains + 4.
1st row 1 dc into 6th ch from hook, *1ch, skip 1ch, 1dc into next ch, rep from * to end. Turn.
2nd row 4ch (=1st dc and 1ch), 1dc into next dc, *1ch, 1dc into next dc, rep from * to end, working last dc into 4th of 5ch. Turn.
3rd row 1sc into 1st dc (edge st), *7ch, skip next 2dc, 1sc into next dc, rep from * to end, working last dc into 3rd of 4ch. Turn.
4th row 1ch, *8sc into 7ch loop, 1sl st into sc, rep from * to end. Turn.
5th row 4ch, * skip 2sc, 1sc into next sc, 1ch, skip 2sc, 1sc into next sc, 1ch, 1dc into sl st, 1ch, rep from * to end, working last dc into sl st and omitting 1ch. Turn.
6th row 4ch, *(1dc into next sc, 1ch) twice, 1dc into next dc, 1ch, rep from * ending with 1dc into turning ch and omitting 1 ch. Turn.
7th row Sl st into 1ch, *3ch, sl st into next 1ch, rep from * to end. Fasten off.

Make 11ch.
1st row 1sc into 3rd ch from hook, 1sc into next ch, 7ch, 1tr into last ch. Turn.
2nd row 1ch (=1st sc), 1sc into each of next 2ch, 6ch, skip 1sc, 1sc into next sc, 1sc into turning ch. Turn.
3rd row 13ch, skip 1st 2sc and 6ch, 1sc into each of next 2sc, 1sc into turning ch. Turn.
4th row 1ch, 1sc into next sc, 6ch, skip next sc and 5ch, 1sc into each of next 3ch. Turn.
5th row 1ch, 1sc into each of next 2sc, 7ch, 1tr into turning ch.
Repeat 2nd–5th rows for pattern. When you have the length you want, work a row of sc along each edge making sure that the work lies flat.
Fasten off.

Make a multiple of 12 chains + 2.
1st row 1sc into 3rd ch from hook, 1sc into each ch to end. Turn.
2nd row 1ch (=1st sc), 1sc into next sc, *1ch, skip 4sc, keeping last loop of each dc on hook, work 2dc into next sc, yo and draw through all 3 loops on hook – called 2dc gr, (2ch, 2dc gr) 3 times into same sc, 1ch, skip 4sc, 1sc into each of next 3sc, rep from * to end, ending with 2sc. Turn.
3rd row 6ch, 1tr into edge st, * 1ch, 1dc into 2ch sp, 2ch, 1sc into next 2ch sp, 2ch, 1dc into next 2ch sp, 1ch, (1tr, 2ch, 1tr) into 2nd of 3sc, rep from * to end. Turn.
4th row 1ch, *2sc into 2ch sp, 1sc into tr, 1sc into 1ch sp, 1sc into dc, 2sc into each of next 2 2ch sps, 1sc into dc, 1sc into 1 ch sp, 1sc into tr, rep from * to end, 1sc into 4th of 1st 6ch.
Break off yarn, turn work around and rejoin yarn to beg of starting ch; work along the other side of the chain in the same way as the 1st side.

Make 20ch.
1st row 1dc into 5th ch from hook, 3ch, skip 6ch, 1dc into next ch, (1ch, 1dc) 4 times into same ch, 3ch, skip 6ch, 1dc into each of last 2ch. Turn.
2nd row 3ch (=1st dc), 1dc into next dc, 1ch, 1sc into 3ch sp, (3ch, 1sc into next 1ch sp) 4 times, 3ch, 1sc into 3ch sp, 1ch, 1dc into next dc, 1dc into turning ch. Turn.
3rd row 5ch, 1dtr into next dc, 5ch, (1dc, 2ch, 1dc) into center 3ch sp, 5ch, 1dtr into next dc, 1dtr into turning ch. Turn.
4th row 3ch, 1dc into next dtr, 5ch, (1dc, 2ch, 1dc) into 2ch sp, 5ch, 1dc into dtr, 1dc into turning ch. Turn.
5th row 3ch, 1dc into dc, 3ch, 1dc into 2ch sp, (1ch, 1dc into same 2ch sp) 4 times, 3ch, 1dc into dc, 1dc into turning ch. Turn. Repeat 2nd–5th rows for pattern.

Make 10ch.
1st row 7dc into 10th ch from hook. Turn.
2nd row 5ch, skip edge st and next dc, 1dc into next dc, (2ch, skip 1dc, 1dc into next dc) twice, 4ch, 7dc into 9ch loop. Turn.
3rd row 5ch, skip edge st and next dc, 1dc into next dc, (2ch, skip 1dc, 1dc into next dc) twice, 4ch, 7dc into 4ch loop. Turn.
Repeat 3rd row for pattern.
Last row Do not turn at end of previous row; * make 7ch, 1 sc into 5ch loop at beg of next row, rep from * along one side of work, then work in the same way along the other side.

Make 21ch.
1st row 1dc into 4th ch from hook, *2ch, skip 2ch, 1sc into next ch, 2ch, skip 2ch, 1dc into next ch *, 5ch, skip 3ch, 1dc into next ch, rep from * to *, 1dc into last ch. Turn.
2nd row 3ch, 1dc into next dc, 5ch, 1dc into next dc, 2ch, 1sc into 5ch loop, 2ch, 1dc into next dc, 5ch, 1dc into next dc, 1dc into turning ch. Turn.
3rd row 3ch, 1dc into next dc, *2ch, 1sc into 5ch loop, 2ch, 1dc into next dc *, 5ch, 1dc into next dc, rep from * to *, 1dc into turning ch. Turn.
Repeat 2nd–3rd rows for pattern.

Make 13ch.
1st row 1dc into 6th ch from hook, 1ch, skip 2ch, 2dc into next ch, 2ch, 2dc into next ch, 1ch, skip 2ch, 1dc into last ch. Turn.
2nd row 5ch, 1dc into 1ch sp, 1ch, (2dc, 2ch, 2dc) into 2ch sp, 1ch, 1dc into 1ch sp. Turn.
Repeat 2nd row twice more.
5th row As 2nd row but don't turn; 3ch, then keeping the last loop of each on hook work 3tr into 5ch loop at side of work, yo and draw through all 4 loops on hook – called 1tr cluster, (3ch, 1tr cluster) 3 times into same loop, 3ch, 1sc into next 5ch loop at side of work. Turn.
6th row *(1sc, 1hdc, 1dc, 1hdc, 1sc) into 3ch loop, rep from * 4 times more, 3ch, 1dc into 1ch sp, 1ch, (2dc, 2ch, 2dc) into 2ch sp, 1ch, 1dc into 1ch sp. Turn.
7th–10th rows Repeat 2nd row 4 times.
Repeat 5th–10th rows for pattern, ending with a 6th row.

Bikini dresses

Beach outfit 306
Filet 322
Irish crochet 332
Edgings, insertions and trimmings 334

Here are a number of suggestions for combining crochet with light-weight fabric to make dresses for summer or night wear. The two dresses photographed are simple tubes of fabric elasticized to fit under the bust and with a crochet bodice or bra top attached. The skirt of this type of dress can be as long and as full as you like, and can incorporate tiers or ruffles; see p30 for the variations on the dirndl skirt.

Both dresses shown here are backless; the crochet bodice sections are attached only to the front of the skirt, and enough elasticity remains for you to put it on and take it off easily. When designing a dress with a bodice back as well as a front you would have to make an opening either in one underarm seam or at center back and provide for a fastening.

You may like to decorate the hem of the dress with a crochet edging, or to separate tiers with insertions. Another form of decoration would be to work a number of Irish crochet motifs and apply a scattering of them to a filet bodice and the fabric skirt.

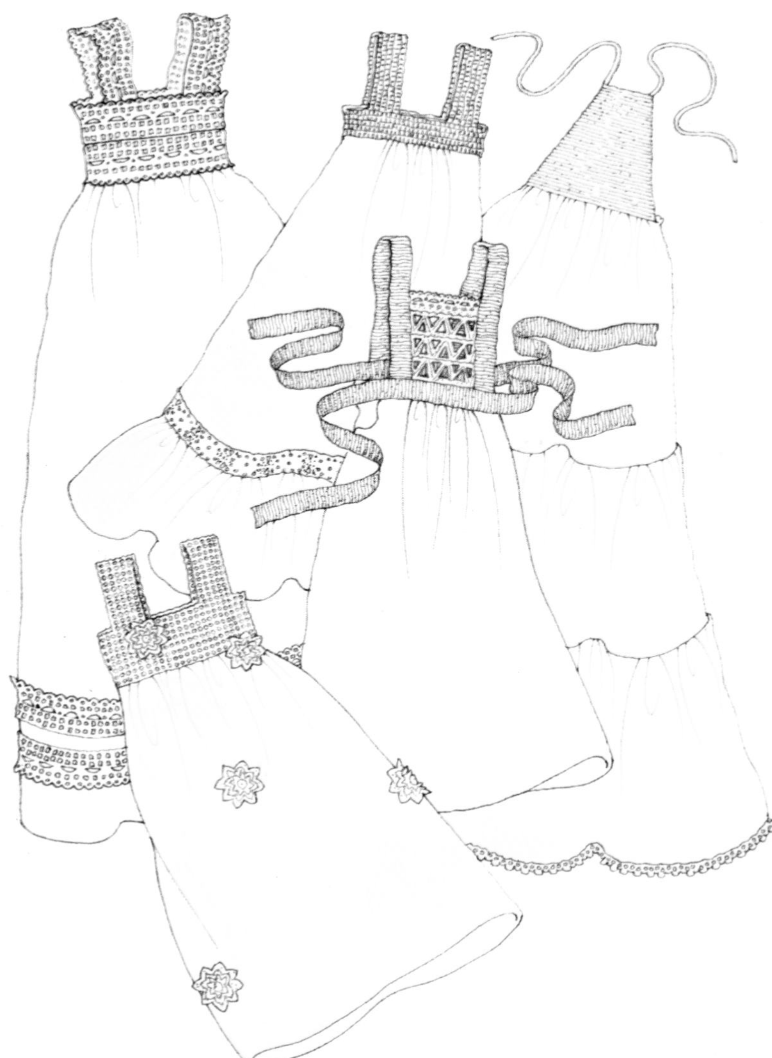

You will need
pink dress: 3oz (75g) medium-weight cotton yarn; no. 2 crochet hook; $1\frac{1}{4}$yd (1·10m) light-weight fabric 54in (140cm) wide
beige dress: 4oz (100g) medium-weight cotton yarn; no.1 crochet hook; $1\frac{3}{4}$yd (1·50m) light-weight fabric, 36in (90cm) wide
matching sewing thread
elastic to fit under-bust measurement

Bikini triangles
Make 6ch. Join with a sl st into 1st ch to form a ring.
1st round: 1ch (=1st sc), 9sc into ring. Join with a sl st into 1st ch.
2nd round: 1ch, 2sc into same place, 2sc into each sc to end. Join with a sl st into 1st ch. 21sc.
3rd round: 3ch (= 1st dc), 2dc into same place, 1dc into each of next 6sc, *3dc into next sc, 1dc into each of next 6sc, rep from * to end. Join with a sl st into 3rd of 3ch.
4th round: 3ch, 2dc into same place, 1dc into each of next 8dc, *3dc into next dc, 1dc into each of next 8dc, rep from * to end. Join with a sl st into 3rd of 3ch.
5th round: 3ch, 2dc into same place, 1dc into each of next 10dc, *3dc into next dc, 1dc into each of next 10dc, rep from * to end. Join with a sl st into 3rd of 3ch.
6th round: 3ch, 4dc into same place, 1dc into each of next 12dc, *5dc into next dc, 1dc into each of next 12dc, rep from * to end. Join with a sl st into 3rd of 3ch.
7th round: 3ch, 6dc into same place, 1dc into each of next 16dc, *7dc into next dc, 1dc into each of next 16dc, rep from * to end. Join with a sl st into 3rd of 3ch.
8th round: 3ch, 6dc into same place, 1dc into each of next 22dc, *7dc into next dc, 1dc into each of next 22dc, rep from * to end. Join with a sl st into 3rd of 3ch.
Last round: 3ch, 1dc into same place, 1dc into each of next 28dc, 4dc into next dc, make a length of chains about 22in (55cm) long, sl st back into each ch, 3dc into same dc as previous 4, 1dc into each of next 28dc, 2dc into next dc. Fasten off.
Work 2nd triangle to match.

Pink edging
Make 8ch.
1st row: 4dc into 4th ch from hook, 3ch, skip 3ch, 1dc into last ch. Turn.
2nd row: 6ch (= 1st dc and 3ch), 4dc into 1st dc of next group. Turn.
3rd row: 3ch, 4dc into 1st dc of group in previous row, 3ch, 1dc into 3rd of 6ch. Turn.
Repeat 2nd and 3rd rows for required length.

Beige dress
Work bikini top from instructions on p306, but omit ties at lower corners.

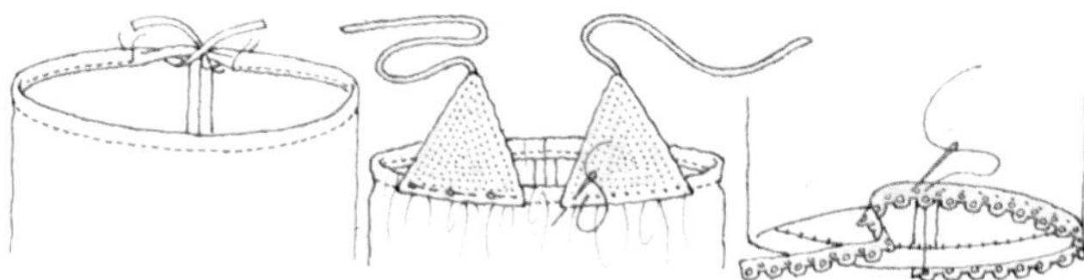

Finishing
Sew side seam or seams of skirt fabric. Press. Turn top edge under $\frac{1}{4}$in (5mm) then $\frac{5}{8}$in (15mm) and stitch to form casing (leave narrow opening to insert elastic). Thread elastic through casing and stitch ends together. Close opening. Adjust fullness evenly. With single seam at back, or a seam at either side, pin crochet bodice or bikini triangles in position. Stitch invisibly in place over gathers with matching sewing thread. Hem neatly at lower edge and attach crochet edging if you wish.

Tunic and bag

Use crochet edgings to link two different textures into a coordinated outfit. Firmly twisted cotton with a silky sheen contrasts well with a soft bulky yarn which is loosely spun, as well as with supple suede or leather. Instructions here give fairly detailed information for making the tunic and bag, but you can use them as guidelines to develop your own ideas. You could make the tunic from an entire crochet fabric or from a warm, loose-weave woolen cloth, and you can obviously adapt the shape of the garment or use a ready-made pattern if you prefer. The exact size and shape of the bag you make should depend on the shape of the leather pieces you have available, so be prepared to adapt the formula given here. For example, you could make a four-sided bag with a square motif as its base if this is less wasteful of material. When you have cut out the rectangular pieces for the bag you will have small odd-shaped scraps of leather left over—use these to make tiny pouches or purses joined with crochet edgings in the same way.

Tunic
You will need
about 40oz (1000g) bulky yarn
about 3oz (75g) medium-weight crochet cotton
size B crochet hook

1 Work T-shaped sweater sections: 2 rectangles 28x20in (70x50cm) for front and back and 2 sleeves 18 x 15½in (45 x 40cm) in garter stitch.
2 With RS of front facing work 1 row sc up RH side, across top edge and down LH side. Use cotton double throughout. Work 2nd row of sc into 1st row. Work back to match. Work 2 rows sc across each sleeve top in same way.
3 Whip-stitch crochet edges of front and back tog at shoulders for about 7in (18cm) on either side, sewing evenly into each sc. Place center of top of sleeve to shoulder seam and whip-stitch crochet edges tog. Place underarm and sleeve edges tog; use knitting yarn to join sleeve seams. Use crochet cotton for side seams and leave lower side edges open for about 8in (20cm).
4 Finish lower corners: draw 6 strands of cotton about 10in (25cm) long through each corner sc. Knot, divide into 3 groups, braid strands for about half their length, then knot again.

Bag

You will need

soft leather or suede
3oz (75g) medium-weight crochet cotton
size B crochet hook

1 Cut 5 4 x 15in (11 x 39cm) rectangles of leather. With leather punch make small holes $\frac{1}{4}$in (5mm) apart and $\frac{1}{4}$in (5mm) in from edge.

2 Work 1sc in each hole all around, and 3sc in each corner hole. Next round: work 1sc into each sc all around, working 2sc into each corner sc. Fasten off. Work rem 4 pieces of leather in same way.

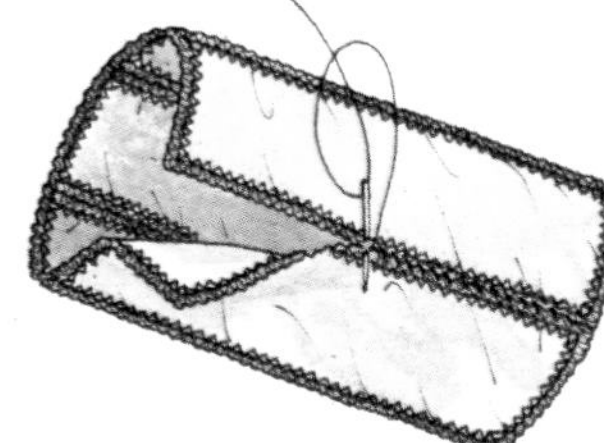

3 Sew long edges tog on WS to make tube shape. Work 1 round sc around bottom edge.

4 Base: Make 4ch. Join with a sl st into 1st ch to form a ring.
1st round: 1ch (=1st sc), 4sc in ring. Join with sl st to 1st ch.
2nd round: 1ch, 1sc into same place, 2sc into each st to end. Join with a sl st into 1st ch.
3rd round: 1ch, 1sc into same place, 1sc into next st, *2sc into next st, 1sc into next st, rep from * to end. Join with a sl st into 1st ch.
4th round: 1ch, 1sc into same place, 1sc into each of next 2 sts, *2sc into next st, 1sc into each of next 2 sts, rep from * to end. Join with a sl st into 1st ch. Cont to inc regularly at these 5 radii of circle until you have approx same no. of sts around base as bottom edge of leather tube. Fasten off.

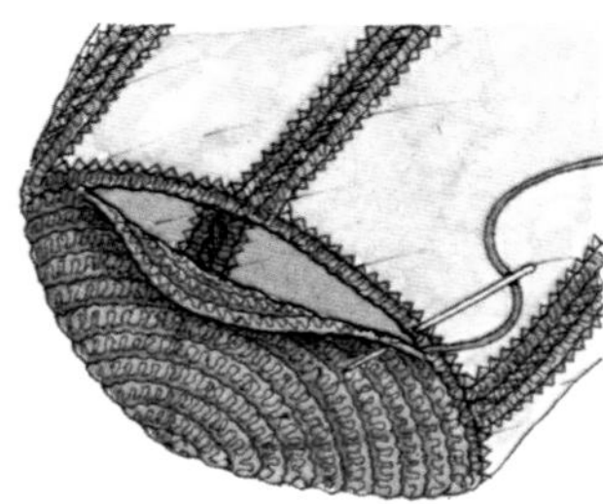

5 Slip-stitch bag sides to base.

6 Finish top with eyelets.
1st round: 1ch, 1sc in each st to end. Join with sl st to 1st ch.
2nd round (make eyelets): 1ch, 1sc into each of next 2sc, *3ch, skip 3sc, 1sc into each of next 3sc, rep from * to end. Join with a sl st into 1st ch.
3rd round: 1sc into each sc and 3sc into each 3ch sp to end. Join with sl st to 1st ch.
4th round: as 1st. Fasten off.

7 With 6 strands of yarn make 2 twisted cords 60in (150cm) long (p102); draw through eyelet holes and knot ends tog.

Glossary

You will find many of the terms defined here explained more fully in the text; see index for reference.

Aran
Island to north-west of Ireland whose characteristic knitting patterns incorporating cables and twisted stitches and worked in natural yarns have given its name to a type of sweater.

Arrowhead
Stitched triangle worked by hand at top of pleat, jacket vent or at top of pocket seams for decoration and for added strength.

Balance points
Marks and notches made on each separate pattern piece indicating the positions of applied pieces and where seams should be matched.

Basting
Large stitches made by hand or machine to hold fabrics temporarily in place before final sewing. Also known as tacking.

Bias
Any line of fabric at an angle to the straight grain. A 'true' bias is formed diagonally when the selvedge is folded at a right angle across the fabric parallel to the weft and the bias runs at 45° to the grain.

Block
To flatten or straighten some kinds of embroidery and knitted fabrics after working. Item is pinned to correct shape and steamed lightly with iron over damp cloth; allow fabric to dry before removing pins and handling.

Bodkin
A long blunt-ended needle with a large eye, used for threading tape, elastic, cord, etc, through a casing and pulling rouleaux through to the RS.

Cable
Knitting pattern where groups of stitches are twisted around each other in various combinations to create a vertical rope-like effect along the knitted fabric.

Canvas
Stiffened ground fabric woven from cotton or linen thread as single or double mesh in a range of widths. Its coarseness is measured as the number of threads per inch or per centimeter. Used for needlepoint and rugmaking.

Carbon paper, dressmaker's
A marking paper, available in black, white and various colors, used in dressmaking and tailoring to transfer construction lines and markings from pattern to WS of fabric, and in embroidery to transfer the outlines of the designs to be worked.

Casing
A hem or tuck made on a garment for threading ribbon, cord or elastic through, e.g. at waistband or cuffs. Alternatively, a channel made at the top of a curtain for a rod or at the bottom edge of a shade for a slat.

Damp stretching
The technique used to straighten out needlepoint which has become distorted during working. Before making up it should be dampened, stretched to shape, pinned onto a wooden board and left to dry.

Domett
Plain woven fabric with cotton warp and woolen weft. Used as interlining.

Duplicate stitching
A decorative or strengthening form of embroidery on knitting, usually stockinette stitch, where the embroidery yarn follows exactly the shape of each knitted stitch, giving the appearance of a motif that is knitted into the fabric.

Ease, tolerance
The amount added to body measurements in cutting a paper pattern to allow for movement and comfort in the finished garment.

Evenweave
A descriptive term for fabric which has the same number of evenly woven threads in the warp and weft, counted over a set measurement.

Eyelet
A hole formed in ground fabric (woven, knitted or crochet), and finished with buttonhole stitch, oversewing, or in metal by means of a purchased kit. May be decorative as in embroidery (e.g. cutwork, broderie anglaise) or functional, e.g. a buttonhole, or may carry lacing or a drawstring.

Feed dog
The serrated part of the sewing machine bed, directly under the presser foot, which moves back and forth pushing the fabric forward as it is being stitched.

Filet
A net-like crochet mesh whose spaces may be filled in with blocks of stitches making an all-over decorative fabric.

Glover's needle
Short, stout needle with sharp, three-cornered point used in hand-sewing leather.

Grading seams
Trimming all seam allowances to different widths where several seams meet, e.g. at shirt underarm, or where several layers of fabric are sewn together. Layering in this way removes bulk so that the seam lies flat.

Grafting
A method of sewing two sets of knitted stitches invisibly together without first casting them off, e.g. at the toe of a sock or at shoulder seams, by following the contour of the knitted yarn through the stitches to be joined.

Grain
The lengthwise or crosswise direction of the threads used in woven fabrics – i.e. the warp or weft.

Gusset
A small piece of fabric, usually diamond-shaped, set into a slash or seam to add ease to a garment, e.g. at underarms.

Hoop
A pair of wooden, metal or plastic rings one of which fits closely within the other. Fabric to be embroidered is held taut between the rings, which are available in various sizes and may have an adjustable screw allowing fabric of different thicknesses to be inserted.

Iron-on interfacing
Commercially bonded fabric treated on the underside with a fine coating of adhesive which melts as the interfacing is pressed into place with a warm iron.

Jacquard
Technique of weaving or knitting a fabric in two or more colors, either creating an all-over pattern repeat, or incorporating individual motifs in the background.

Miter
1 The diagonal line formed at 45° to the sides when fabric is joined or two hems meet at a square corner. Used on jacket vents, curtains and household linens.
2 The vertical line formed in the center of a knitted V-neckband where two lines of ribbing converge.

Mount
1 To add a second layer of fabric to a garment or section of a garment, often cut with the main fabric, for strength or to make a sheer fabric opaque.
2 To hold a ground fabric to be embroidered taut in a frame for ease of working.

Nap
Soft, downy raised surface given to fabric by a finishing process – e.g. flannelette and brushed denim. If the nap is raised or shaded it may lie in one direction – see under **pile**.

Picot
One of a series of small ornamental loops usually forming an edging on knitting, crochet or embroidery, and an integral part of cutwork and lacemaking.

Pile
Raised surface on fabric made in the weaving process from short fibers which may be left as loops or cut and brushed in one direction. Pile should lie in the same direction on a finished item, and extra fabric may be required to achieve this.

Raglan
A type of sleeve in which the cap forms part of the shoulder; from the armhole it gradually diminishes upward to a point where it meets the neckline or neckband.

Rouleau
Narrow strip of fabric cut on the bias and stitched into a roll, often around a core of piping cord for strength and firmness. Used for ties, buttonhole loops, and fastenings, and also attached for a decorative finish, like piping.

Sacking needle
Heavy-gauge needle with sharp three-cornered point and eye large enough to take string, used for sewing through burlap, rugs, carpets and upholstery.

Scalloping
A shell-shaped decorative edging used on fabric hems and borders. Can be finished with facing or, on single fabric, by close machine zigzag or by hand-sewn buttonhole stitch.

Seam ripper
Small hand tool with sharp hook-shaped blade for cutting through machine stitching to undo a seam.

Selvedges
The lengthwise edges of woven fabric parallel to the warp which are finished and therefore do not fray. On printed fabrics the design may not extend onto selvedges. Where a wider unprinted selvedge is left on some furnishing fabrics it is necessary to remove only the firmly woven outer edge, leaving the remainder to form the seam allowance.

Shirring
Three or more parallel rows of hand or machine stitching, gathered to control fabric fullness – used as a fashion detail. Also worked with fine elastic thread to gather a complete bodice or waistband which allows for body movement.

Slash
A straight line cut into the fabric of a garment for ease or access. May permit insertion of a gusset for ease of movement, or be faced as an opening, e.g. above the cuff in a sleeve.

Smocking
The technique of controlling fabric fullness, often at yoke of cuffs, by gathering with running stitches into regular soft pleats and securing with decorative overstitching.

Smocking transfer
Commercial iron-on transfer dots marked on tissue paper at regular intervals of $\frac{1}{4}$–$\frac{1}{2}$in (6–10mm). Dots indicate exact position for running stitches used to gather fabric prior to smocking.

Spearpoint needle
A machine needle with sharp three-cornered point used to stitch suede and leather, obtainable in various sizes.

Steam press
Use controlled steam iron, or hot dry iron with damp cloth, to flatten seams, to shrink and to remove creases by forcing steam through fabric. Do not slide the iron across the fabric, but use up-and-down movements.

Stitch holder
A device resembling a safety pin used in knitting for holding stitches that are temporarily not being worked, e.g. at the center of a neckline while the neck and shoulders are being formed.

Stranding
When using 2 colors in a row of knitting, e.g. a Fair Isle pattern, the yarn not in use is carried across not more than 5 stitches along the WS of work behind the stitches being knitted.

Tapestry needles
Large needles made in different sizes with long, oval eyes for thick yarn and with rounded points to avoid piercing threads of ground fabric – e.g. canvas and loose-weave fabrics.

Template
Cut-out shape, often geometric such as hexagon or diamond, used as a pattern for regular repeating designs or for a single motif or pattern shape. May be used as a guide for position of embroidery stitching, or as an outline for cutting fabric for patchwork, appliqué, etc.

Tracing wheel
A hand tool for transferring simple outlines or pattern markings to fabric – used with dressmaker's carbon paper. As it is pushed along the pattern markings, the teeth around the wheel transfer them through the carbon paper to the WS of the fabric.

Underlay
An additional piece of fabric placed underneath the main fabric for reinforcement at points of strain, e.g. under buttonholes, pockets and pleats.

Yoke
Upper section of a garment, e.g. section of dress between shoulders and above bust, usually made from double fabric for strength. Often cut on different grain from main garment, or in contrasting fabric. Variety of shapes may be functional or decorative.

Credits

Illustrators

10 Sally Launder
12–13 Grahame Corbett
14–15 Elsa Willson
16–17 Coral Mula
18–19 Elsa Willson
20–21 Coral Mula
23 Grahame Corbett
24 Terry Evans
25 Elsa Willson
26–7 Elsa Willson
28–9 Sally Launder
30–31 Lynne Riding
32–3 Sally Launder
34–35 Terry Evans
36–7 Elsa Willson
38–9 Elsa Willson
40–41 Elsa Willson
42–3 Elsa Willson
44–5 Elsa Willson
46 Lynne Riding (t); Marion Appleton (c)
47 Lynne Riding (tl); Marion Appleton (tr, c)
48 Grahame Corbett (t); Terry Evans (c, br); Lynne Riding (bl)
50 Grahame Corbett (tc); Terry Evans (b)
51 Terry Evans
52 Grahame Corbett (tr); Terry Evans (c, b)
53 Lynne Riding
54 Terry Evans (t, br); Lynne Riding (bl)
55 Terry Evans
56–7 Richard Phipps
58–9 Richard Phipps
60–61 Coral Mula
62–3 Richard Phipps
64–5 Terry Evans
66–7 Terry Evans
68 Sally Launder
69 Terry Evans
72–3 Coral Mula
74–5 Elsa Willson
76–7 Elsa Willson
78–9 Grahame Corbett
80–81 Grahame Corbett
82 Grahame Corbett (cr); Terry Evans (cl, b)
83 Terry Evans
84 Lynne Riding (t); Terry Evans (c, b)
86–7 Terry Evans
88 Marion Appleton
90–91 Marion Appleton
92–3 Coral Mula
96 Grahame Corbett
97 Terry Evans
98–9 Elsa Willson
100–101 Terry Evans
102–3 Coral Mula
104–5 Nigel Osborne
106–7 Lynne Riding
108 Grahame Corbett
109 Terry Evans
110 Grahame Corbett (tr); Terry Evans (c)
115 Marion Appleton
117 Paul Higginson
119 Paul Higginson
121 Terry Evans
122 Terry Evans
123 Paul Higginson
126–7 Coral Mula
128–9 Coral Mula
130–31 Marion Appleton
132–3 Grahame Corbett
134–5 Grahame Corbett
138–9 Grahame Corbett
140–41 Coral Mula
144–5 Coral Mula
146–7 Marion Appleton
149 Marion Appleton
150–51 Coral Mula
152–3 Coral Mula
156–7 Elsa Willson
158–9 Elsa Willson
160–61 Elsa Willson
163 Richard Phipps
164 Richard Phipps
166–7 Grahame Corbett
168–9 Grahame Corbett
170–71 Elsa Willson
174–5 Elsa Willson
176–7 Elsa Willson
178–9 Anne Quinn
180–81 Richard Phipps
182 Marion Appleton
183 Marion Appleton (r); Terry Evans (bl)
184 Terry Evans
186–7 Richard Phipps
188–9 Grahame Corbett
191 Coral Mula
192–3 Coral Mula
194 Coral Mula
196–7 Coral Mula
198–9 Coral Mula
202–3 Marion Appleton
204–5 Marion Appleton
206–7 Elsa Willson
208–9 Elsa Willson
212 Marion Appleton
213 Coral Mula
214–15 Coral Mula
216–17 Coral Mula
220 Coral Mula
221 Lynne Riding
222–3 Coral Mula
224 Terry Evans
227 Coral Mula
228 Terry Evans (t); Grahame Corbett (c); Coral Mula (b)
229 Terry Evans (t); Coral Mula (c)
230–31 Richard Phipps
232 Terry Evans
233 Coral Mula
236–7 Coral Mula
238 Terry Evans
240 Coral Mula (t); Terry Evans (c)
241 Terry Evans
242–3 Coral Mula
244 Terry Evans
245 Coral Mula
246 Terry Evans
248 Richard Phipps
250–51 Coral Mula
256–7 Terry Evans
259 Coral Mula
262 Richard Phipps
264 Grahame Corbett
265 Coral Mula (t); Grahame Corbett (b)
266 Richard Phipps (t); Grahame Corbett (b)
268–9 Grahame Corbett
270 Grahame Corbett
271 Coral Mula (t); Grahame Corbett (b)
272 Terry Evans
273 Grahame Corbett
276 Richard Phipps
278–9 Coral Mula
280 Richard Phipps
282 Coral Mula
283 Lynne Riding
285 Terry Evans
286–7 Coral Mula
288 Grahame Corbett
290–91 Coral Mula
292 Richard Phipps
294–5 Richard Phipps
296 Paul Higginson (t); Richard Phipps (b)
297 Paul Higginson (t); Richard Phipps (b)
300 Coral Mula (c); Paul Higginson
301 Coral Mula

Practical contributors

Dressmaking
Fabrics:
Epatra Fabrics Ltd 23 (poncho)
Exquisite Fabrics Ltd 51, 55(l), 70(r)
Hoechst UK Ltd and John Heathcoat & Co Ltd 54(l)
Moygashel 55(r), 71(r)
Tootal Fabrics Ltd 30–31 (dresses, skirt), 70(l), 82(l), 85(r)

Designers:
Sheila Brull 35, 108
Janet Kirkwood (all patterns)

Finishing:
Beryl Miller
Lindsay Vernon

Master pattern sheet:
Ian Kirkwood

Toys
Design and finishing:
Ilse Gray

Home sewing
Fabrics:
Bayer Fibres Ltd and F. C. Moore 124–5 (curtains)
Tulley's Ltd 142–3 (slipcovers)

Design and finishing:
Eleanor Hobbs 124–5 (tablecloth), 136 (window shades and lampshades)
Jane Iles 137 (appliqué)
Anne Lloyd 124–5 (pillows)
Tulley's Ltd 142–3 (slipcovers)
Lindsay Vernon 124–5 (lampshade)
Ryagarn yarns 124–5 (rug)

Embroidery
Suppliers:
Pingouin Tapis 165
Viyella 175

Dressmaking patterns:
Janet Kirkwood

Finishing:
Deborah Barclay
Sue Honey
Beryl Miller

Designers:
Philippa Bergson 191 (far right), 195 and 200–201 (curtains)
Carolyn Cannon 172–7
Marcia Greenberg 199 and 200–201 (bedspread)
Jane Iles 184–5
Bonnie Phipps 181, 188
Margaret Rivers 164, 186

Embroiderers:
Deborah Barclay 172–3 (blouse and jacket), 175, 176
Philippa Bergson 191 (far right)
Carolyn Cannon 173 (skirt and shawl), 174, 177
Heather Clarke 162
Valerie Davies 168
Marcia Greenberg 199 and 200–201 (bedspread)
Eleanor Hobbs 208–9
Margaret Humphrey 168
Caroline Hurry 163 (pin), 181
Jane Iles 184–5, 190, 191 (l), 195 and 200–201 (curtains), 205
Bonnie Phipps 189
Margaret Rivers 165, 187

Knitting
Spinners and yarns:
Jamieson & Smith Ltd 266, 278
Lister & Co Ltd 218 (Lavanda DK, Poodle 2, Fashion Tweed, Tahiti Mohair, Aran), 262 (Aran)
Patons & Baldwins Ltd 292 (Turkey Rug Wool)
Phildar 248 (Camargue, Perlé), 282 (Gevaudan)
Pingouin 224 and 238 (Madame), 252 (Mohair, Iceberg), 254 (Mademoiselle)
3 Suisses 272 (Suizasport)
H. G. Twilley Ltd 284 (Goldfingering)
Wendy (Carter & Parker Ltd) 256

Design and knitting:
Mary Ann Barnett 294–7
Jill Bennett 266
Sandy Black 288 and 292
Jean Litchfield
Margaret Maino

Crochet
Spinners and yarns:
Emu Wools Ltd 340 (Fiord)
J. Henry Smith Ltd 306–7, 308–9 and 338 (Dorina)
James Templeton & Sons Ltd 330 (Shetland Fleece)
3 Suisses 320 (Barbara)
H. G. Twilley Ltd 310–11 (Stalite), 326 and 340 (Crysette)

Design and crochet:
Jean Litchfield
Edy Lyngaas 306, 308, 340
Margaret Maino
Celia Thompson 310–11 (bags)

b bottom
c center
l left
r right
t top

302–3 Coral Mula
304–5 Coral Mula
306 Terry Evans
308 Terry Evans
310–11 Coral Mula
312 Coral Mula
318 Terry Evans
320 Terry Evans
322 Terry Evans
323 Grahame Corbett
324 Coral Mula (l); Grahame Corbett (r)
326 Grahame Corbett
328 Coral Mula
329 Terry Evans
330 Richard Phipps (t); Grahame Corbett (b)
334–5 Coral Mula
338–9 Terry Evans
340–41 Terry Evans

Photographers

Front cover Mike Goss
1 Roger Phillips
2–3 Roger Phillips
4–5 Roger Phillips
6–7 Roger Phillips
8–9 Sandra Lousada
22 John Carter
23 George Wright (t); John Carter (b)
30 Steve Campbell
31 John Carter
34–5 John Carter
35 Sandra Lousada
43 George Wright
49 John Carter
50 John Carter
51 John Carter
53 Michael Boys
54–5 John Bishop
70–71 John Bishop
82 Monty Coles
83 George Wright
84 Steve Campbell
85 Steve Campbell
86 Monty Coles
87 George Wright
96–7 Steve Campbell
108–9 Bill Carter
111 Bill Carter
112–13 Spike Powell
114–15 Mike Goss
116 Mike Goss
117 Mike Goss
118 Mike Goss
120–21 Sandra Lousada
124–5 Roger Phillips
131 Roger Phillips
133 Roger Phillips
134 Roger Phillips
135 Roger Phillips
136–7 Roger Phillips
142–3 Roger Phillips
145 Roger Phillips
146 Roger Phillips
148 Roger Phillips
152 Roger Phillips
154–5 Mike Goss
162 Mike Goss
163 Mike Goss
165 Roger Phillips
168 Alan Randall
172–3 Alan Randall
174 Mike Goss
175 Alan Randall
176 Alan Randall
177 Mike Goss
181 Alan Randall
184 Mike Goss
185 John Carter
187 Alan Randall
189 Alan Randall
190 Mike Goss
191 Mike Goss
195 Spike Powell
199 Spike Powell
200–201 Spike Powell
205 John Carter
208 Steve Campbell
209 Steve Campbell
210–11 Adam Woolfitt
216–17 Pamla Toler
218 George Wright (t); Adam Woolfitt (b)
219 Adam Woolfitt
220–21 Pamla Toler
224 John Carter
225 John Carter
228 Pamla Toler
229 Pamla Toler
230–31 Sandra Lousada
234–5 Pamla Toler
238 Steve Campbell
239 Steve Campbell
244–5 Pamla Toler
246–7 Pamla Toler
248 Pamla Toler
249 John Bishop
252 Murray Irving
253 Murray Irving
254 Murray Irving
255 Murray Irving (t); Bill Carter (b)
256 Adam Woolfitt
257 Adam Woolfitt
258–9 Pamla Toler
260–61 Pamla Toler
262 John Carter
263 John Carter (t); Steve Campbell (b)
264–5 Pamla Toler
267 Bill Carter
268 Pamla Toler
269 Mike Goss
270–71 Pamla Toler
272–3 Murray Irving
274–5 Pamla Toler
276 John Carter
277 John Carter
278 Pamla Toler
279 Pamla Toler
280 John Carter
281 John Carter
284–5 John Bishop
289 John Carter
290 Pamla Toler
291 Pamla Toler
293 Bill Carter
294 Ian Yeomans
295 Ian Yeomans
298–9 Alan Randall
300 Mike Goss
302–3 Mike Goss
306–7 John Carter
309 John Carter
310–11 Mike Goss
312 Mike Goss
313 Mike Goss
315 Sandra Lousada
316 John Carter
317 John Carter
318–19 Mike Goss
321 Mike Goss
322 Alan Randall
323 Alan Randall
324–5 Mike Goss
327 Spike Powell
328 Mike Goss
329 Spike Powell
330–31 Spike Powell
332 Mike Goss
333 Mike Goss
337 Mike Goss
338 Alan Randall
339 Alan Randall
340 John Carter
341 John Carter

Suppliers

Anello & Davide Ltd 70–71, 209
Austin Reed Ltd 96–7, 224, 225, 262
Barkers of Kensington 136–7
Robert Blake Antiques 195, 200–201
Blyth Bygones 195, 200–201
British Crafts Centre 124–5, 133, 142–3
Browns for Living 8–9, 315
Burberrys Ltd 43
The Button Queen: Front cover
Patricia Calderhead 2–3, 4–5, 6–7
Casa Pupo Ltd 124–5, 152
The Craftsmen Potters Shop 165
Crockford's Club 84, 85, 284–5
Cubestore Ltd 136–7
The Danish House 148
Dartington Glass Ltd 124–5
Design Aspect 124–5
Dickins & Jones Ltd 8–9, 30, 43, 54–5, 267
Alfred Dunhill Ltd 284–5
Elliott and Sons Ltd 249
Emeline Jewellery 22
Fenwick of Bond Street 45, 53, 54–5, 70–71, 205, 224, 280, 281
J. Floris Ltd 189
R. D. Franks Ltd 8–9
James Galt & Co Ltd 96–7, 108–9, 112–13, 136–7
Go Downtown Ltd t/a Joy International 219
Greenfield Milletts Ltd 172–3
Husqvarna Ltd 8–9
Hyde Park Hotel 249
Joseph 280, 281
Kickers (London) Ltd 238, 239
Kids in Gear 238, 239
Kobi Clothing Ltd 172–3, 340
Laura Ashley 276, 277
Liberty & Co Ltd 8–9
Made In Heaven 51, 272–3
Mothercare 224, 225
The Needlewoman Shop: Front cover, 1, 2–3, 4–5, 6–7, 181
The New Neal Street Shop 148, 195, 200–201, 298–9
Pant House Ltd 218, 289
Paris House Ltd: Front cover
Peter Robinson 54–5, 111, 172–3, 205, 249, 284–5
The Reject Shop Ltd 124–5
St Katherine Haven Ltd 263(b)
Sacha Shoes 49
Simpson (Piccadilly) Ltd 96–7, 219
Sylvia's Jewellery Ltd 284–5
Taylor's 1, 2–3, 4–5, 6–7
Tigermoth Ltd 238, 239, 255, 263(b)
Top Shop 23(t), 218(t)
Trade Unlimited 112–13
Wallers Clothing Stores 284–5
Wallis Fashion Group 54–5, 284–5
James Ward (Southwold) 199
Workshop Wales 322

Index

G

H

I

J

K

L

M

S

T

Metric conversion: length

1in=25·4mm exactly, but to calculate most lengths a factor of 2·5 gives you a sufficiently accurate measurement. Figures are often rounded up or down to the nearest whole number for convenience and for consistency. When working from this book choose one system or the other and follow it to avoid discrepancies.
This table gives an easy-to-read equivalent for measurements in yards, feet and inches and in centimeters and millimeters up to 1 meter.

Imperial	Metric	
$\frac{1}{16}$in	2mm	
$\frac{1}{8}$in	3mm	
$\frac{1}{4}$in	5–6mm	
$\frac{3}{8}$in	10mm	1cm
$\frac{1}{2}$in	12mm	1·2cm
$\frac{5}{8}$in	15mm	1·5cm
$\frac{3}{4}$in	20mm	2cm
$\frac{7}{8}$in	22mm	2·2cm
1in	25mm	2·5cm
1$\frac{1}{8}$in	30mm	3cm
1$\frac{1}{2}$in		4cm
2in		5cm
2$\frac{1}{4}$in		6cm
2$\frac{3}{4}$in		7cm
3in		7·5cm
3$\frac{1}{8}$in		8cm
3$\frac{1}{2}$in		9cm
4in		10cm
4$\frac{1}{4}$in		11cm
4$\frac{3}{4}$in		12cm
5in		13cm
5$\frac{1}{2}$in		14cm
6in		15cm
6$\frac{1}{4}$in		16cm

Imperial		Metric	
6$\frac{3}{4}$in		17cm	
7in		18cm	
7$\frac{1}{2}$in		19cm	
7$\frac{7}{8}$in		20cm	
8in		20·5cm	
8$\frac{1}{4}$in		21cm	
8$\frac{5}{8}$in		22cm	
9in		23cm	
9$\frac{1}{2}$in		24cm	
9$\frac{3}{4}$in		25cm	
10in		25·5cm	
10$\frac{1}{4}$in		26cm	
10$\frac{1}{2}$in		27cm	
11in		28cm	
11$\frac{3}{8}$in		29cm	
11$\frac{3}{4}$in		30cm	
12in	1ft	30·5cm	
18in	$\frac{1}{2}$yd	45·5cm	
19$\frac{3}{4}$in		50cm	0·5m
27in	$\frac{3}{4}$yd	68·5cm	
35$\frac{1}{2}$in		90cm	
36in	1yd	91·5cm	
39$\frac{1}{2}$in		100cm	1m

Abbreviations

alt	alternate(ly)
approx	approximate(ly)
beg	begin(ning)
CB	center back
CF	center front
ch	chain
cm	centimeter
cont	continu(e/ing)
dc	double crochet
dec	decreas(e/ing)
DK	double knitting
dtr	double treble
foll	follow(ing)
ft	foot
g	gramme
g st	garter stitch
htr	half treble
in	inch
inc	increas(e/ing)
K	knit
K up	pick up and knit
K-wise	knitwise
LH	left-hand
m	meter
M1	make one
mm	millimeter
no.	number
oz	ounce
P	purl
pat	pattern
psso	pass slip stitch over
p2sso	pass 2 slip stitches over
P up	pick up and purl
P-wise	purlwise
rem	remain(ing)
rep	repeat
rev st st	reverse stockinette stitch
RH	right-hand
RS	right side
sl	slip
sl st	slip stitch
sp(s)	space(s)
sq	square
st(s)	stitch(es)
st st	stockinette stitch
t ch	turning chain
tbl	through back loop(s)
tog	together
tr	treble
tr tr	triple treble
WS	wrong side
ybk	yarn back
yd	yard
yfwd	yarn forward
yo	yarn over needle
yrh	yarn round hook
yrn	yarn round needle